BLAIR
UNBOUND

ALSO BY ANTHONY SELDON

Churchill's Indian Summer (1981)

By Word of Mouth (with Joanna Seldon, 1983)

Contemporary History (ed., 1987)

Ruling Performance (with Peter Hennessy, 1987)

Political Parties Since 1945 (ed., 1988)

The Thatcher Effect (ed. with Dennis Kavanagh, 1989)

Politics UK (joint author, 1991)

The Conservative Century (ed., 1994)

The Major Effect (ed. with Dennis Kavanagh, 1994)

The Heath Government 1970–1974 (ed. with Stuart Ball, 1996)

The Contemporary History Handbook (ed. with Brian Brivati, 1996)

The Ideas That Shaped Post-war Britain (ed. with David Marquand, 1996)

How Tory Governments Fall (ed., 1996)

Major: A Political Life (1997)

10 Downing Street: An Illustrated History (1999)

The Powers Behind the Prime Minister (with Dennis Kavanagh, 1999)

Britain Under Thatcher (with Daniel Collings, 2000)

The Foreign Office: An Illustrated History (2000)

The Blair Effect 1997–2001 (ed., 2001)

A New Conservative Century? (with Peter Snowdon, 2001)

Public and Private Education: The Divide Must End (2001)

Partnership not Paternalism (2002)

Brave New City (2002)

New Labour, Old Labour (ed. with Kevin Hickson, 2004)

Blair (2004)

The Conservative Party: An Illustrated History
(with Peter Snowdon, 2004)

The Blair Effect 2001–05 (ed. with Dennis Kavanagh, 2005)

BLAIR
UNBOUND

Anthony Seldon

with

Peter Snowdon *and* Daniel Collings

**SIMON &
SCHUSTER**

London · New York · Sydney · Toronto

A CBS COMPANY

First published in Great Britain by Simon & Schuster in 2007
An imprint of Simon & Schuster UK Ltd
A CBS COMPANY

PICTURE CREDITS
1, 5, 7, 9, 10 © Rex
2, 8, 20, 23 © PA Photos
3, 16, 17, 18, 24 © Nick Danziger/ nbpictures
4, 11, 12, 13, 14, 15, 19, 21, 22 © Getty Images
6 © Corbis
25 © AP Images

3 5 7 9 10 8 6 4 2

Simon & Schuster UK Ltd
Africa House
64–78 Kingsway
London WC2B 6AH

Simon & Schuster Australia
Sydney

www.simonsays.co.uk

A CIP catalogue for this book is available
from the British Library.

Hardback ISBN: 978-1-84737-078-5
Trade Paperback ISBN: 978-1-84737-215-4

Typeset in Caslon by M Rules
Printed and bound in Great Britain by
Mackays of Chatham Ltd

This book is dedicated to the
memory and example of my father,
Arthur Seldon (1916–2005),
described in his obituary in *The Economist*
as 'The architect of Thatcherism and Blairism'.

Contents

Introduction

From the Making of Tony Blair to *Blair Unbound*

This is the second volume of a two-part biography. The first volume, entitled simply *Blair*, was published in 2004, and concentrated on Tony Blair's life up to his second term in office. My aim in that book was to explain how an initially unambitious man, who displayed little interest in politics or public life at school, university or in his early legal career, rose to become one of the most successful Labour leaders in modern British politics. Almost all other Prime Ministers, including Margaret Thatcher, John Major, and latterly Gordon Brown, displayed from their earliest years not only an acute interest in politics but also a burning ambition to rise through the ranks. Not Tony Blair. The structure of the first book was designed to help explain this essential conundrum: it consisted of forty chapters, twenty devoted to the people and twenty to the events that emboldened, inspired and moulded this unformed and callow young man into the person he became by 2001. The argument was that, under their influence, Tony Blair forged himself into a superbly effective, election-winning force. He excelled at presentation and at politics, but he had yet to mature as a policy-maker, or to work out what he wanted to do with power. His own policy preferences remained incomplete and naive, consisting of a mish-mash of Christianity, social democracy and the vogue-ish and ultimately insubstantial 'third way'. *Blair* was a story of electoral success but disappointment on policy.

All the individuals who had helped shape him on his rise to power played key parts, but none more so than his mother, who died when he was just twenty-two years old, and who helped give him his boundless self-confidence and his life-long anchor in religious faith. Another woman, his wife Cherie, was the other dominant force in his life, firing his zeal for the Labour Party, grounding him in the stability of family life and encouraging him to live out his faith. He loved her deeply and would not have become, nor remained, Prime Minister for so long without her. The dominant non-family figures who made possible his rise, and that of New Labour, were the 'quartet', Gordon Brown, Alastair Campbell, Peter Mandelson and lifelong friend Anji Hunter. In the early 1990s they had been bound together by a mutual love, a deep commitment and a shared sense of purpose: the determination to see Labour sweep John Major's Conservatives from power. Subsequently, this tight-knit group split up with spectacular consequences. The first blow to their unity came in 1994, when Brown felt betrayed by Blair over his succession as Labour leader following the death of John Smith in May that year. Brown could scarcely believe that a man he considered his junior and inferior had leapfrogged over him to lead the party. Consolation came from the understanding Brown believed he had reached with Blair at the Granita restaurant at the end of May: that he would effectively be running domestic policy in a joint premiership and that Blair would stand down for him mid-way through the second term.

As Leader of the Opposition from 1994 to 1997, Blair boldly weaned the party off its attachment to the symbolically significant 'Clause Four', but caution overcame him in the latter two years as he became fixated on a Labour victory at the General Election. Nothing was more illuminating about him at this time than his first appointment on winning the leadership election in July 1994. It was not a policy chief, nor a figure with deep experience in either the party or government, but a head of media relations, Alastair Campbell. Blair was so desperate to have him onside that he pursued him personally to the South of France to persuade him. Blair also leaned heavily on another brilliant media guru, Peter Mandelson, who like Campbell was far more versed in presentation than policy. The 1997 manifesto was unsurprisingly light on detailed commitments. Substance, Blair insisted, would flow once Labour was safely in power. As with most other of his predecessors in Number 10, however, he found devising policy on the wing took second place to the business of running the nation. His first term showed that Labour was 'safe' to run the country, but he was strong on windy aspiration and rhetoric, and low on personal domestic policy achievements. Hubris came to the fore. He had transformed the Labour Party: surely transforming the country, and creating a 'new' Britain, would not be too difficult? Only towards the end of the first term did Blair wake up to reality: time was being squandered, and changing Britain was a more serious and difficult proposition than he had imagined. His personal record was all the more disappointing when measured against the advantages – a large majority, a united party and a strong economy – few incoming Prime Ministers have ever enjoyed.

By contrast, Gordon Brown's domestic record in the first term was impressive. Credit for Labour's governing credibility during it, moreover, owed much to his successful stewardship of the economy. Unlike Blair, Brown had thought deeply about what he wanted to achieve once in office. Beginning with the granting of independence to the Bank of England in his first days as Chancellor, a string of policy achievements flowed from his fertile mind and that of his close-knit team. Blair might have been in the top job, but in the first term Brown was the more creative and effective figure, as *Blair* reveals. He was the deeper thinker and strategist, a politician of extraordinary brilliance whose obsession with the succession had not yet damaged his performance and stature.

During the years 2001–07, the period covered by *Blair Unbound*, a different story emerges. If my earlier book was about the making of Tony Blair as a politician, this second volume tells the story of the emergence of Tony Blair as a leader, increasingly taking his own decisions and developing his own distinctive policy agenda. September 11th was a crucial milestone in Blair's political journey; he emerged a tougher and clearer leader in its wake. In this transition, he had to divest himself of many of those earlier supporters who had helped him on the way up, in favour of relying on steadier and more thoughtful figures like US and Northern Ireland specialist, Jonathan Powell; Sally Morgan, who after 2001 took over some of the female support role from the departed Anji Hunter; and David Hill, who succeeded Campbell as media chief in 2003. He also brought on Andrew Adonis, who more than any other person helped formulate his domestic policy agenda. Among the 'quartet', becoming his own man meant having to cut himself away from Campbell and Mandelson. By 2001, if not before, both had outlived their usefulness. They were obsessively focused on the short term, inflaming Blair's image in the media, sometimes damaging his relations with colleagues (with Mandelson more to blame) and detracting from his standing in the country at large because of their identification with spin. Blair was wholly to blame for his reliance on them. Campbell at least knew his time was up, and had been striving for a long time to leave, but Blair resisted. Only in the summer of 2003 did Blair finally consent to his departure. But his closest male friend stayed in touch, and played a crucial role behind the scenes in Blair's final years as Prime Minister. With Philip Gould, who equally bridged both camps, Campbell helped bring about a smooth transition to Brown, which had often looked a far from likely outcome.

What of Brown? By the second term it was time for Blair to face up to him if he was to succeed in developing his personal agenda, something Brown was keen to thwart. Twice he thought hard about replacing him at the Treasury, in 2001 and 2005: twice he pulled back. The second term saw bloody battles and the degeneration of their relationship. Only in the third term, however, did he push Brown to the brink, and finally prevail over him. Blair's final months also displayed a new element of assertiveness against another figure with whom he failed to be sufficiently firm in his premiership, President Bush. Blair's defence was always that if he had pushed Bush harder, he would have lost his voice, and that the concessions he extracted were very significant, though insufficiently recognised in Britain.

Blair took some bold steps in his first term, above all the Good Friday Agreement in 1998 and Kosovo in 1999. But the bulk of his policy decisions did not come until after 2001, with the long-drawn-out evolution of his 'choice and diversity' agenda on public service reform, on Europe, after he abandoned the Euro in favour of a liberalising and activist policy agenda, and with his advocacy of greater urgency to combat climate change and poverty in Africa. Most controversial of all, of course, was his decision to join the United States in military action against Iraq in March 2003, which has been widely condemned across the political spectrum at home and abroad. Rather than merely join in the chorus of denunciation, *Blair Unbound* seeks instead to understand the decisions through the eyes of Blair, and what was politically possible and desirable for him at the time. What decisions did he take and why? What else could he have done? And what were the consequences of his decisions as best one can judge them in 2007? The picture that emerges is of a man standing up for what he believed to be right, in the face of enduring unpopularity, but falling short in his anticipation of what would befall Iraq after the invasion.

While Blair became a more impressive figure in 2001–07, Brown failed to build on the momentum of the first term. Many of Brown's creative ideas had been enacted by 2001. He itched to initiate more – but as Prime Minister, not Chancellor. He was right to defeat Blair on the Euro in 2003, as he had been in 1997, and to see off aspects of policy on foundation hospitals. But some of his resistance to Blair's public service reform agenda was motivated by personal animosity, and a desire to store up ideas to announce himself once he became Prime Minister, as shown by his adopting Blair's policies almost wholesale after he succeeded, and by announcing ideas, such as citizens' juries in September 2007, which the Treasury had previously blocked. On Iraq he provided neither leadership nor alternative strategy, which is surprising given that it was the most serious issue any British government had faced in fifty years. Such passivity might have been acceptable for a mere Chancellor of the Exchequer – but for a man who expected very soon to become Prime Minister?

In the third term, Blair's superiority over Brown became more marked. He needed Brown to help him win the 2005 General Election, but with victory in the bag, Blair cut loose. Brown then let himself be captured by those in the party who wanted Blair out, and his failure to distance himself from those who were trying to undermine Blair compromised his own standing. On some domestic policy decisions, he absented himself, as on the EU Budget in 2005, while on others, including pensions and giving more autonomy to schools, he found himself on the wrong side of the argument. While Blair's qualities of calm, resolution and compassion grew over the ten years, Brown's did not mature in step. His anger and resentment that Blair had not stood down earlier was fully understandable, but the evasiveness and petulance it induced in him was surprising in a future Prime Minister, even for one who felt provoked to the extreme. His immense qualities, and his deep love for Blair, which was mutual, was masked, and was only periodically displayed during these difficult years for him, until they blossomed again at the end. If this book gives a less positive portrait of Brown during 2001–07, than in volume one, then it is not because it set out to be unsympathetic to him: it reflects the reality. When he did work with Blair, notably on Africa and debt relief, they achieved much. Officials regularly commented that when both principals worked in harmony, the combination had exceptional force, rivalling that of any two front-rank politicians in the last hundred years.

This book is a study of Tony Blair's final years in office, and of Downing Street at large. It does not seek to cover all aspects of policy: for readers who want to know more about policy, I refer them to the three volumes I have edited on his government, and most recently *Blair's Britain* (Cambridge University Press) which covers the whole period, 1997–2007. There is no stand-alone conclusion summing up Blair at the end of the book. Instead, conclusions can be read at the end of each of the thematic sections at the end of the book. Dividing up the biography into themed sub-sections has given a misleading impression that Blair dealt with each issue separately, whereas in fact each day saw several crowd in on him at once. To have made the book strictly chronological would have sacrificed coherence for the reader. Biographies, like all history books, are artificial reconstructions of the reality.

Blair's was a paradoxical premiership. He was a 'late developer' as Prime Minister. The picture of him in *Blair* is thus less favourable than in this book. Peter Riddell similarly gave a less positive view of him in his important book *The Unfulfilled Prime Minister*, published first in 2005. Most successful Prime Ministers, including H. H. Asquith, Stanley Baldwin, Clement Attlee and Margaret Thatcher, achieve early on, and fade towards the end. Political capital and authority is strongest at the outset, followed by decay. Blair too suffered from increasingly difficult circumstances by the end of his premiership, yet he did more than many Prime Ministers to buck this trend, notching up achievements at home and abroad, including Northern Ireland, to the very end. He succeeded where few Prime Ministers ever have: leaving at the moment, more or less, of his own choosing, and handing over a united party to his chosen successor, weaning him on to his own agenda, with a good chance of victory at the following election. His youth – he was the youngest Prime Minister to take office since Lord Liverpool in 1812 – his tardiness in developing his own agenda, and his over-long reliance on spent advisers, made Blair's premiership the mirror image of the norm. In the first volume, Blair took Labour into the centre ground of British politics; in this volume, he managed to keep it there while also driving forward reform, albeit achieving far, far less than he would have done had he begun earlier. 'My final two years have probably been my most productive,' Blair admitted just after stepping down. He began his life with a whimper, and went out with something of a bang, though with far less impressive a sound than could have been the case. This is the theme of *Blair Unbound*.

BLAIR
UNBOUND

I

9/11

A little before 11 A.M. on the 11th of September 2001, as Tony Blair was being checked into the Grand Hotel on Brighton's seafront, Mohammed Atta, ringleader of the 9/11 conspiracy, boarded a flight from Portland, Maine to Boston's Logan Airport. The standard screening process identified Atta as requiring special security measures. Airport authorities ensured that he boarded the same plane as his luggage, but no further steps were taken.[1] In Brighton, the threat of global terrorism was far from Blair's mind. Re-elected just three months before in the June 2001 General Election, his speech to the annual Trades Union Congress (TUC) provided the first post-summer platform for him to stamp his new agenda on the country. His plans to introduce private providers in key public services were deeply unpopular with the unions. The GMB union had taken out a series of advertisements asking if you could 'trust' Blair not to privatise the NHS. The Prime Minister was infuriated and ready to give John Edmonds, the GMB General Secretary, a 'real hammering'.[2] The press had seized avidly on the prospect of a show-down.[3] The atmosphere on the south coast that crisp Tuesday morning was far from holiday humour.

Blair has always liked shirts with long sleeves and cuffs. Before a big speech he often tugs at the cuffs, or fiddles with his tie or his hair, mentally rehearsing for what lies ahead: 'It's how he psyches himself up,' recalled one aide.[4] He knew that he was in for a rough ride on the conference floor. But the Prime Minister had a trick up his sleeve. The government's thinking towards the single European currency, or euro, remained a hotbed of speculation, with every pronouncement emanating from Number 10 pounced on by the press and dissected in molecular detail. By sprinkling the speech with some provocatively positive comments about the euro, Blair hoped to capture the media's imagination, divert it from talk of divisions and set his own agenda.[5] The speech had to be pitched just right, but it wasn't quite ready. His adrenalin was pumping. With a little over an hour to go, Blair was still tinkering with his text. And tugging at his cuffs.

The Prime Minister's party was based in the Grand Hotel's prestigious Fitzherbert Suite, facing Brighton's pebbly beach. The suite is on two levels, a small internal staircase separating the bedroom upstairs from the main room below. Blair's office had been set up in the bedroom, while the rest of his party, including his senior aides, the Downing Street typists (known as the 'Garden Room Girls') and his Special Branch detectives, busied themselves downstairs. A television flickered idly in the background. Blair's latest handwritten comments were collected from the bedroom before freshly typed scripts made their way to him back up the stairs. As Blair's aides kept half an eye on the television's conference coverage, the screen cut away suddenly from the familiar figure of Adam Boulton, Sky News' political editor, to images from the other side of the Atlantic.[6] At 8:46 A.M. Eastern Standard Time (EST), 1:46 P.M. British Summer Time (BST), an aeroplane had, in what look like an accident, collided with the North Tower of the World Trade Center in New York City. Live and rather grainy pictures of smoke billowing from the iconic edifice were being beamed around the world. The party downstairs converged around the screen, shocked but not unduly disturbed. The ticking clock to the conference speech remained resolutely at the front of their minds.

Anji Hunter, Blair's close aide, teenage friend and confidante, headed up the stairs to the Prime Minister's bedroom-cum-office with the latest typed draft of his speech. Handing over the text, she passed on news of an accident in Manhattan. Alastair Campbell, Blair's Director of Communications, also joined him, along with political secretary Robert Hill. 'Oh my God,' Blair said, almost absent-mindedly. He turned to Campbell: 'I'll have to refer to it at the beginning of my speech, won't I, Ali?'[7] They discussed briefly how he might do this, and Blair asked for some time alone to finish working on the speech.[8]

While he mused on his last-minute changes, 4,454 miles away President George W. Bush was just arriving at the Emma E. Booker Elementary

School in Sarasota, Florida. The White House was trying to promote Bush's education reform agenda and had arranged for the President to read to the children with TV cameras rolling. Just before Bush walked into the classroom, Karl Rove, his senior adviser and chief strategist, took the President aside. Rove told him that a small, twin-engine plane had hit the World Trade Center.[9] 'This is pilot error,' Bush responded. Turning to Andy Card, his Chief of Staff, he said, 'The guy must have had a heart attack.'[10] At 8:55 A.M., US time, Bush spoke briefly with National Security Advisor Condoleezza Rice. She relayed that the plane involved was actually a commercial aircraft: 'That's all we know right now, Mr President.'[11] A concerned President walked into the classroom where the schoolchildren were patiently waiting. What to think? He did not know exactly.

In Brighton, Blair continued writing down to the wire alone in the bedroom. His advisers were now glued to the story unfolding on the TV downstairs. Sky News was still talking about a tragic accident, and speculating on what might be happening inside the North Tower. Then, at 9:03 A.M. EST, 2:03 P.M. in Brighton, a second plane – United Airlines Flight 175 – flew into the South Tower of the World Trade Center. 'We all saw it live,' recalled Godric Smith, one of Blair's official spokesmen. 'What was that?' someone asked. 'The first one or . . .'. 'It's terrorism,' stated a Special Branch detective bluntly.[12] Robert Hill, sensing what was unfolding, immediately climbed the stairs to tell the Prime Minister.[13] 'At first he was slightly brusque with me as he wondered why he was being interrupted,' Hill recalled, 'but when I explained what had happened he said very quickly, "I must speak to Alastair." He wanted both Alastair and Anji to join him in the room. Always when it's something new and important, he wants the key people around him.'[14]

Hunter came up almost immediately. Campbell followed shortly afterwards and turned on the upstairs TV so that the Prime Minister could see the awful images for himself. Blair, making short work of a banana, discussed with his closest advisers what to do.[15] How should he respond? What exactly was happening? Could he still deliver his speech? The atmosphere in the suite was suddenly electric: none present can recall the exact sequence of events. At some stage Blair descended the stairs into the main suite and put in a call to Number 10, asking to be kept up to date with the latest developments – no one at Downing Street knew any more than the party in Brighton did about exactly what was going on.[16] Jeremy Heywood, Blair's Principal Private Secretary at Number 10, recalled that the Prime Minister raised an additional concern: 'You'd better make sure no planes are coming to Downing Street,' he instructed.[17] That same thought was dawning on the others in that building. Their powerlessness to do anything about it was not the least of their mounting concerns.

While Blair's detectives conferred about any immediate risk to the Prime Minister, he tried to establish the facts from New York and assess the risks to London, still unsure what to do or say to the gathering TUC delegates, and aware that with all this last-minute distraction he had not got the speech exactly right in his mind. With her eye on the clock, Anji Hunter became anxious about Blair getting to the conference hall in time.[18] Others were now asking whether it was appropriate to go ahead with the speech. The enormity of what was happening had still not fully sunk in. At around 2:30 P.M. Blair left the suite for the conference hall. He would have to say something, even if it was only to state he was shelving the speech.

Blair told Hunter to stay in the hotel room and keep in touch by phone. Meanwhile he, Campbell and his Special Branch detail headed to the Conference Centre. For security reasons the police insisted he was driven the short distance. Five minutes after they left, Hunter called Campbell on his mobile. 'This is really serious,' she said. 'He can't possibly go ahead with his speech.' Campbell agreed: 'Yes, I'm getting this too.'[19] 'The scale of the horror and the damage was increasing all the time. It was perfectly obvious he couldn't do the speech,' Campbell wrote in his diary.[20]

Bush learned about the second plane at 9:05 A.M., 2:05 P.M. BST. He was sitting in front of the children, about to listen to them reading a book called *The Pet Goat*, when Andy Card whispered in his ear: 'A second plane hit the second tower, Mr President. America is under attack.'[21] For a moment, Bush froze. The TV cameras captured a distant look of confusion and disbelief. Bush then remained with the children for another five to seven minutes. Later criticised for not leaving the classroom immediately, most popularly by Michael Moore in his film *Fahrenheit 9/11*, Bush explained that his instinct was to project calm rather than add to the nervous excitement.[22]

At 9:15 A.M. Bush retreated to a holding room. He spoke again with Rice, and for the first time with Vice-President Dick Cheney. Bush knew that the American people needed to hear from him. While his staff prepared for an immediate return to Washington DC, Bush crafted a brief statement in consultation with his senior advisers.[23] At 9:30 A.M. he appeared live on American television. The statement was not a success.

Echoing his father's famous words, 'This will not stand' – delivered after Iraq invaded Kuwait in August 1990 – Bush Junior declared: 'terrorism against our nation will not stand.' But he appeared shaken, his language uncomfortably informal. He would chase down, he declared, 'those folks who committed this act'.[24] 'I'll tell you this,' Bush later said in self-defence, 'we didn't sit around massaging the words. I got up there and just spoke.'[25]

Blair too had to pluck words from the air. At 2:45 P.M., British time, just before he was due to appear on the platform at the Conference Centre, he spoke over the phone to Jonathan Powell, his Chief of Staff, as well as to Richard Wilson, Cabinet Secretary and Britain's most senior civil servant. 'You've got to come back,' they insisted. 'Something very serious is going on in the States. You can't go on to the platform and pretend this isn't happening.'[26] Blair needed no convincing. Powell realised that he had decided to call off the speech even before he picked up the phone.[27] 'How are the Americans reacting?' Blair asked. Neither Powell nor Wilson could tell him anything about what was going on at the heart of the US administration.[28]

Blair's staff began to sort out the logistics: how could they most speedily and safely get him back to London? John Monks, TUC General Secretary, readily supported the decision to pull the speech, while Blair and Campbell honed the outline of a brief impromptu statement.[29] While they were doing so, at 2:59 P.M. British time, the South Tower of the World Trade Center collapsed, forcing clouds of debris and smoke hundreds of feet across Manhattan. Minutes later, visibly shaken, and beginning to comprehend the enormity of what was unfolding before his eyes, Blair stood before the TUC. This was not the speech for which he had been preparing. 'There have been the most terrible, shocking events in the United States of America in the last hours,' he told them. 'I am afraid we can only imagine the terror and carnage there and the many, many innocent people who have lost their lives. This mass terrorism is the new evil in our world today.'[30] The delegates broke into spontaneous applause as Blair rushed from the podium. Unlike Bush, Blair had captured the public mood perfectly. Those who were with him noted his calm and resolve. They saw a man in command of himself.

As Blair was speaking, Special Branch's concerns for his safety were heightened. One aide recalled 'a sense of danger everywhere. The detectives were very calm but there was a look in their eyes that suggested that everything was not all right.'[31] They resolved to take Blair straight back to the hotel while Special Branch assessed the position more clearly. Once there, Blair again picked up the phone to ask Jonathan Powell to arrange a series of conference calls with Foreign Secretary Jack Straw, Defence Secretary Geoff Hoon and Home Secretary David Blunkett.[32] He didn't stop for long in the hotel. He wanted to get back to London as soon as possible and take control from the centre. Special Branch insisted that he travel by train. Their fear was that the terrorists might have got hold of a helicopter, and argued that if they went back by car, the PM's convoy would be much more visible from the air than if they secreted themselves in a train.[33] After a 'mad dash' to Brighton station, Blair's party managed to catch the waiting 3:49 P.M. Connex service to London Victoria.[34]

Just as Blair wanted to get back to London, so too did Bush seek to return to his own capital. At 9:35 A.M. EST the presidential motorcade headed for Sarasota Bradenton International Airport. Four minutes later, the third hijacked plane, American Airlines Flight 77, was flown into the west side of the Pentagon. The explosion was heard all around Washington DC. By around 9:45 A.M., as the White House was being evacuated, Bush arrived at Sarasota Airport. The Twin Towers were not the only target. Where else might the terrorists strike? The President was witnessing the most serious attack on American soil in the modern era, and no one could tell him whether the assaults were ending, or merely beginning. The President's lead Secret Service agent decided it was too dangerous for him to return to Washington. Cheney called Bush, already on Air Force One preparing to take off from the runway, and insisted that he keep away from the capital at all costs. The President agreed and so, at 9:54 A.M., his plane took off from Florida with no fixed destination: 'The objective was to get up in the air – as fast and as high as possible – and then decide where to go.'[35]

While Bush took to the skies, the situation in Washington was developing into an ever-heightened state of emergency. It was known that a number of planes remained unaccounted for. The evacuation of all but a small core of senior staff from the White House was already in full swing. Staff were told at first to leave in orderly file, but then Secret Service agents screamed at them to run as fast as they could. Some were told to remove ID badges to make them less obvious targets for possible snipers outside the White House gates.[36]

At 9:36 A.M., Secret Service agents had burst into Cheney's West Wing office. They ordered the Vice-President down into the tunnel beneath the White House immediately, and from there into the East Wing bunker.[37] Once Cheney, together with his wife, Rice and several officials, were locked securely behind the bunker's secure vault doors, the Secret Service set up outside with body armour, shotguns and MP5 machine guns.[38] Cheney worked hard to keep in contact with Bush throughout, and ensure the President remained in charge. Shortly after 10 A.M. Bush, at Cheney's request, authorised the military to shoot down any civilian airliners that might be considered a threat. But communication between Air Force One and the bunker was patchy. The phone calls between America's two most senior leaders kept cutting out.[39] To many, Cheney, the most senior official in Washington, became the pivotal figure, while the President, somewhere in the skies over America, was the more shadowy presence.

Senior staff not in the bunker remained at their desks in the White House Situation Room. They had no special protection and the vulnerable old building, even with modern strengthening, would have been reduced to rubble by an incoming plane. Rumours of just such a threat continued. At 10:02 A.M. came the news that United Flight 93 was heading towards Washington and not responding to air traffic control. The staffers held a discussion about whether they should evacuate the White House, but resolved that they should stay at their posts. Each wrote their name on a list, which was then e-mailed out of the building: it would be easier this way, it was calculated, for rescuers to identify their bodies.[40] In the event United 93, precise destination unclear, never made it to the capital. The plane crashed into the Pennsylvania countryside after passengers attempted to storm the cockpit.

The British Embassy lies on rising ground in north-west Washington, three miles from the White House. Ambassador Sir Christopher Meyer sat in front of the television with his wife and senior staff, transfixed by the images of the World Trade Center. The first thoughts in the Embassy were practical and logistical. Former Prime Minister John Major was staying as a guest before attending a business meeting. Meyer's wife Catherine tried to persuade Major to remain with them, but he headed downtown regardless.[41] The Embassy staff worried about dignitaries expected to arrive soon: 'John Prescott was due to fly in that day and the Duke of York was already in mid-air,' recalled one Embassy official. 'I remember that the Ambassador wasn't immediately convinced that the visits in train needed to be cancelled. Realising the sheer scale of what was happening took us all time.'[42]

The attack on the Pentagon shook those in the Embassy. 'The exploding aircraft was clearly audible,' Meyer recalled. 'The smell of blazing kerosene drifted on the light breeze.'[43] What they were witnessing now began to hit home. 'There were all kinds of rumours,' said one Embassy official, 'including threats to the security of the Embassy because the Vice-President's residence was just next door, and that could very easily have been at risk.'[44]

Anxious for the safety of his staff, Meyer ordered everyone home except a core team. This 'council of war' set to work immediately, seeking to establish exactly what was happening and to what degree British citizens were caught up in the attacks.[45] It was quickly apparent that there would be significant British casualties, not only in Manhattan but also among the many British personnel working in the Pentagon. Meyer put in a call to Rice. 'Condi sounded very cool and collected. There would, she said, be no knee-jerk reaction from the United States.'[46] Meyer suggested that Blair would appreciate a conversation with Bush as soon as possible and Rice promised to set one up.

In London, as further news of the attacks came through, there was a vacuum at the heart of government. Most Number 10 officials heard the news when they returned from lunch some time after 2 P.M. Jonathan Powell's primary concern was to find out exactly what was happening in the United States. He was also worried that the terrorists might try to strike on British soil, particularly at Canary Wharf. He considered Number 10 too difficult a target.[47] Others were less calm. 'No one seemed to be in charge or giving orders,' recalled one number 10 official.[48] 'People can easily underestimate the fear that we felt,' said another. 'When we heard that the White House may have been a target we knew that Number 10 could be a target too. There was a stronger fear in the building than most people later realised.'[49] And if the terrorists had targeted it correctly a plane could have hit Downing Street. 'There was no one to phone, no defensive system, no contingency plan.'[50]

Richard Wilson was being driven back to Whitehall after lunch at the Gran Paradiso when he heard news of the second plane hitting the World Trade Center. 'I was in Parliament Square. I can recall vividly the precise location' – a sentiment shared by many on hearing the news that day. Almost immediately he received a call from Heywood, at Number 10. 'Do we have anything that suggests an attack on Number 10 is imminent?' Heywood asked. 'Should we be evacuating?' 'If you evacuate,' countered Wilson, 'where will you evacuate to?' 'I'm not sure.' Heywood replied. 'Well,' said Wilson, the consummate mandarin, 'I guess it's quite a good rule not to evacuate until one knows where one is planning to go to.'[51] In the event, evacuation never became a serious option.[52]

Wilson's plan was to convene the newly established 'Civil Contingencies Unit', whose task is to deal with such emergencies. But he learned that the unit was up in Yorkshire on a 'bonding' exercise. Meanwhile, the key members of the Defence and Overseas Policy Secretariat, the Whitehall body responsible for co-ordinating foreign and defence policy, had recently left for Herefordshire by coach for their own team exercise. Worse, Blair's newly appointed senior foreign policy adviser, David Manning, was caught in New York returning from a visit to see Rice and could not be contacted.[53] From his plane over Manhattan, Manning, uniquely among the top aides on either side of the Atlantic, had a bird's-eye view of the mayhem unfolding in south Manhattan. He saw smoke billowing from the World Trade Center below, but had no idea what was going on.[54] With the British state's top personnel so scattered, if London was to have been a target, the terrorists could not possibly have chosen a better day.

Beyond assembling the best personnel available, Wilson's immediate responsibility was an assessment of the threat to London: were sensitive targets in immediate danger from hijacked planes? He spoke to the Secret Intelligence Service (SIS) and to MI5, but the dearth of information and intelligence made the position all the more worrying. In addition to Number 10, Wilson's concerns included Buckingham Palace, the Houses of Parliament and the safety of London more generally. He called the key figures in the Royal Household and in Parliament to check that they knew what was at stake and to ensure they were taking the most appropriate action available to them. In conjunction with the Palace, it was arranged for Prince Andrew's plane to turn around and return home.[55]

City Airport, close to Canary Wharf, was swiftly closed down. Wilson also contacted the Ministries of Defence and Transport and requested protection for London's airspace. 'We're on the job,' he was told.[56] Defence Secretary Hoon scrambled two fighter jets to enforce a 'no-fly' zone over the capital.[57] The coach heading to Herefordshire was recalled to return to London immediately in time for an emergency meeting set for 4:30 P.M.[58]

The 3:49 P.M. from Brighton was a scheduled train service, but the Prime Minister's party were in their own secure part of the train 'with Special Branch either side.'[59] Facilities were, however, minimal: there was no refreshment trolley, no internet access and even a VIP tea urn provided courtesy of the train company packed up on the Prime Minister.[60] Blair spent some of the fifty-minute journey making phone calls. He was in regular touch with Jonathan Powell, who had himself been working the

phones trying to find out more about what was going on, and he spoke
to Blunkett and Hoon. 'What about London?' was his first question to
them. The ministers recounted steps actioned so far and he seemed
satisfied. His mind moved to the global stage and he called Straw to hear
his thinking on what it might mean internationally.[61] 'We agreed on what
was by now blindingly obvious, that this was an event which would
shape the century,' recalled Straw. 'We also spoke about recalling
Parliament, convening Cabinet, and handling the press. The
practicalities were very much on our minds.' Mobile phone reception
between London and Brighton is dreadful and Blair lost his Foreign
Secretary as he entered a tunnel.[62]

On the train, those around the Prime Minister were all too conscious
of their dearth of hard information: the truth was they knew no more
than the media about what was happening in America. Blair repeatedly
asked Powell to keep him updated, while Hill fed through snatches of
news from his personal radio – as and when reception allowed.[63]

The mood on the train was 'quite shocked, very sober and reflective',
recalled one aide '"What is this thing?" I remember Tony saying.'[64] 'The
enormity of what had happened had sunk in,' recalled another in his
group, 'and the Prime Minister was very sombre and began to think
through some of the consequences.'[65] Blair was deep in thought. 'During
a lot of that journey he had that far-away look in his eyes. He was
thinking about what he would say to the public. He knew he'd have to
say something soon to quell the anxiety and the sense of panic. He knew
he needed to assert authority and calm.'[66] He wanted to get on television
and assure the nation that 'the institutions of the British state have not
collapsed. It's still there, in control.'[67]

But Blair's thoughts were also travelling more widely. Although there
was no hard information yet as to who was behind the attacks: 'it was
pretty clear even at that stage that it was Muslim fundamentalism,'
recalled Godric Smith. 'I remember in particular discussing with the PM
on the train the importance of avoiding a Muslim backlash.'[68] Blair
talked a lot to Hunter, by his side throughout the journey.[69] 'TB asked
for a pad,' Campbell recorded in his diary, 'and started to write down
some of the issues we would have to address when we got back. He said
the big fear was terrorists capable of this getting in league with rogue
states that would help them.'[70] But his most immediate worry at this
stage was the Americans. 'Where's Bush?' one aide recalled him asking.
No one knew. 'What worried him most was the uncertainty about where
the President was and what exactly was happening.'[71]

*

The truth about Bush, had they known it, would have offered little reassurance. While Blair's train sped towards London, the President remained airborne and distracted. At 10:32 A.M. (3:32 P.M. UK time) Cheney called Bush. The White House had just received word of a direct threat to Air Force One. An anonymous caller had used the plane's secret codename 'Angel'. Was it an inside job? Had the terrorists penetrated the American state? There was little anyone could do. Andy Card was told that it would take somewhere between forty and ninety minutes before a USAF fighter escort could reach the President's plane to protect it.[72] 'Bush told an aide that Air Force One "is next". He was in an angry mood. "We're going to find out who did this," he said to Cheney, "and we're going to kick their asses."'[73]

At 10:41 A.M. Cheney called again. He stressed the continuing threat to Washington and urged Bush not to return. Rice backed him up. Bush agreed. A few minutes later his plane banked and plotted a new course for Barksdale Air Force base in Louisiana. It was relatively close and would allow the President access to more sophisticated communications systems. He was increasingly anxious to speak again to the American people and work immediately began on a fresh statement. Only later did it emerge that the threat to Air Force One was a hoax. The caller had not even used the 'Angel' designation. The message had become garbled in the machinery of government. The jitteriness and uncertain response of the American state at this time of highest anxiety was not inspiring confidence.

As Bush landed at Barksdale at 4:45 P.M. British time, Blair's train was pulling into Victoria station. The Prime Minister's party was met by police escort and whisked straight to Downing Street, arriving just before 5 P.M.[74] Powell was at the door waiting for him. 'We've got Scarlett and everybody else here,' he told the Prime Minister.[75] Tom Kelly, an official spokesman, recalled seeing Blair walk into the building: 'You'd have expected him to have his head down but his head was up. You'd have expected him to be looking intimidated but he looked like a man who not only understood the significance of what happened, but had in some way anticipated what had happened and knew precisely what he meant to say and do.'[76]

Blair headed down the corridor to his small office adjoining the Cabinet Room, known as the 'den'. Waiting for him were Britain's top intelligence officials: John Scarlett, Chairman of the Joint Intelligence Committee (JIC), and Stephen Lander, Director of MI5 (but also covering for MI6, whose director Richard Dearlove was away), as well as

Powell and Wilson. Campbell and Anji Hunter entered with him. Blair looked at the faces around the room: 'This is grim,' he told the assembled company.[77]

Blair set the tone with his opening question: 'Who's done this?' he demanded, looking straight at the 'spooks' (as the intelligence community are known) sprawled on the sofas. 'Well,' replied Lander, 'there are two possibilities. The most likely is Osama bin Laden's organisation, though it could have been a Middle Eastern Islamist group because it was a suicide attack.'[78] Scarlett thought at this stage there was an 'outside chance' that a far-right militia group could be responsible, as happened with Timothy McVeigh's deadly bomb attack in Oklahoma in April 1995, but he was 'almost certain' that Bin Laden was responsible – he was really the only one with the capability to mount it.[79] Both Blair and Campbell pushed them on why they were so sure there were no rogue governments directly involved in the plot. 'Because Bin Laden was able to do it himself, and that suited his purposes better,' came the response.[80]

Lander reminded Blair about earlier al-Qaeda attacks on the US embassies in Kenya and Tanzania in 1998, and the attack on the *USS Cole* while it was moored in Aden harbour in 2000. He spoke also about Afghanistan. 'Did I know about this?' Blair asked. There was an awkward silence. The spooks coughed a little. Although Blair clearly felt all this talk of al-Qaeda and Bin Laden, and still more the Taliban and Afghanistan, was unfamiliar ground, earlier JIC reports had alluded to the issues, albeit not in a way that had aroused any particular or immediate concern to the UK. 'Well,' Lander answered, 'if you'd read the JIC material fully you would have come across some of this stuff.' 'Fair enough,' Blair replied.[81]

To some of Blair's aides, the suggestion of Bin Laden's involvement came as a real surprise: 'We thought honestly that al-Qaeda was a bit of an American obsession,' confessed one.[82] But to those who had been fully digesting the voluminous intelligence reports, the attacks fitted the profile only too well. Lander's rebuttal to Blair was based, at least in part, on a JIC report from 16 July 2001, warning that al-Qaeda, operating from their bases in Afghanistan, were in 'the final stages' of preparing an attack on the West, with UK interests 'at risk, including from collateral damage in attacks on US targets'.[83]

Peter Ricketts, chair of the JIC until the week before 9/11, pointed out that, 'while we were aware of the threat from al-Qaeda certainly, we had no sense of the scale of the attack of 9/11. Our assessment was that they'd continue to mount a threat on US targets abroad, but we had no idea that they were planning something in the US.'[84] According to Ricketts, Blair was an 'avid reader of intelligence', who read with great interest the JIC summary reports selected for him by his staff. The references to Afghanistan, which had not been fully picked up, were pretty thin pickings: 'Although we knew quite a lot about al-Qaeda, we knew that the PM might well not have been aware of the extent of al-Qaeda's links with the Taliban.'[85] Al-Qaeda has its origins in the late 1980s and the final period of resistance to the Soviet occupation of Afghanistan: 'They were seriously on our radar screen from the early 1990s,' recalled a senior intelligence official.[86] It was known that al-Qaeda had been behind the unsuccessful attack on the World Trade Center in February 1993, when a bomb was detonated in an underground car park. The device caused extensive local damage and killed six people, but the leader, Ramzi Yousef, escaped to plan an assassination attempt on Pope John Paul II on 12 January 1995 as part of the 'Bojinka plot'. This was to be followed the same month by an effort to blow up eleven passenger airlines simultaneously over the Pacific Ocean and crash a further twelve planes into prominent US buildings.[87]

Blair's mind was focused on the Taliban and on Afghanistan. His instructions to the group in the den were clear. 'Tomorrow morning,' he said, his gaze fixed on Lander and Scarlett, 'I want a meeting on Afghanistan.'[88] Sensing the way his boss's mind was moving, Powell wanted to do his own homework, so he sent out for a book on the Taliban by leading Pakistani journalist Ahmed Rashid, which he later read intently at his desk just by the door to Blair's office, allowing others to take over directing the Number 10 machine.[89] With Manning still out of contact in the US, Powell deemed he needed more help in Number 10 and phoned John Sawers, who had served as Blair's Foreign Affairs Private Secretary before Manning, and summoned him away from his preparations to take over as Ambassador in Cairo.[90]

Wilson now briefed Blair on the measures being developed to mitigate any threat to the UK. Before he returned to the building, Wilson had chaired a meeting of officials and Cabinet ministers in Cabinet Office Briefing Room 'A', or 'COBRA', which lay deep under the Cabinet Office and is activated at times of emergency. As Wilson told them of their progress to date, Blair turned to Lander. 'Are we at risk?' 'I don't think so, not at present,' his intelligence chief replied.[91] Blair was reassured by what he heard, but no one knew for sure. 'We had no intelligence of a specific threat to London and couldn't recall intelligence of a heightened threat from al-Qaeda,' said a top Blair aide.[92] 'We took the view that al-Qaeda were anti-American,' said one senior intelligence officer, 'precipitated by dislike of the US and what they were doing in Israel, rather than seeing al-Qaeda as a direct threat to us.'[93] For all that, Bin Laden's organisation had in fact been involved in an abortive attack on British soil less than a year earlier. One British-born man, Moinal Abedin, was later convicted for amassing bomb-making materials.[94] To those present in the den, it was clear that Blair was far more interested in the global picture: 'What are the Americans doing? What is Bush doing?' he demanded.[95] And how would they deal with Bin Laden? 'If I were Bush I would demand the Taliban deliver him up,' Blair mused.[96] 'TB's immediate concern, apart from the obvious logistical steps we had to take,' Campbell recorded in his diary, 'was that Bush would be put under enormous pressure to do something irresponsible.'[97]

At 5:30 P.M. Blair and his den companions went down the steps to COBRA where the Prime Minister chaired a formal meeting. The room was packed and included not only Blair's inner core of advisers, but also Brown, Straw, Blunkett, Hoon, Byers and Milburn and their officials. The mood was sombre but calm. 'I remember feeling just an incredible sense of relief that we were with the very best people we could possibly be with,' said one Number 10 aide.[98] Blair swiftly approved the package of domestic protection measures that had already been worked out.[99] 'Our biggest concern at COBRA,' remembered Geoff Hoon, 'was whether something similar could happen in Britain imminently.'[100] London's airspace had already been closed and special security imposed around the Stock Exchange and Canary Wharf.[101] Office workers in the latter had already voted with their feet and decided to evacuate the building: the pictures of the collapsing Twin Towers, and those jumping from the flaming building, had been enough. The military rules of engagement – for enforcing the ban on London's airspace – were discussed and 'there was talk of moving some of the planes based at RAF Leuchars in Scotland to London in the event of a hijack'.[102] Blair seemed mildly irritated when Wilson sought to clarify whether the Prime Minister or Michael Boyce, the Chief of the Defence Staff, should make the final decision to shoot down a plane suspected of hostile intent. It all seemed overly bureaucratic to Blair. They agreed that formally it would be Boyce who issued the order to fire, but only after the PM had authorised the action.[103]

The Prime Minister worked his way crisply round the room so ministers and officials could give their reports,' recalled one Number 10 aide. 'The meeting was in effect an up-to-date "data dump" of everything that seemed necessary and relevant to the position we were in.'[104] Gordon Brown gave what Metropolitan Police Commissioner John Stevens considered an 'impressive and concise' account of the economic situation.[105] Health Secretary Alan Milburn spoke about the health preparations being made for any attack, while Geoff Hoon discussed preparations for military defence. Hoon was 'gung-ho', Blunkett recorded in his diary. '"We are ready," he said to Tony, "to put our Air Force and our facilities at the disposal of the intelligence services." I said, "I think we need a moment's pause on this." I could tell they were getting carried away.'[106] Stevens highlighted reports that 'up to 2,000 Britons might have been killed' in the attacks so far.[107] Straw intervened to urge caution on this figure. Everyone wanted to be sure the number was absolutely right.[108] 'We had done our own back-of-the-envelope calculation,' said one of Blair's aides, 'and we felt that it might be as high as 200.'[109] The final British death toll was in fact 67.

Blair's focus shifted quickly on to the Americans. Acknowledging that he had not yet managed to make contact with the President, Blair seemed frustrated. 'I'm supporting the US in a disaster for which they were not prepared,' he observed.[110] The COBRA meeting broke up before 6 P.M., with Blair having a public statement to make. 'We knew he had to speak before the six o'clock news, that was the crucial time,' recalled Tom Kelly. 'The key was reassurance and an explanation of what would be done in response. He had to show that he was in control. The worst thing, we agreed, would have been to show that you were panicked, that you were hiding and that you had no resolve.'[111] Blair's resulting statement was an expression of the widespread horror at the attacks: 'It is hard even to contemplate the utter carnage and terror which has engulfed so many innocent people . . . for those that carried out these attacks, there are no adequate words of condemnation. Their barbarism will stand as their shame for all eternity.' But Blair also presented a down-to-earth practical list of measures that were being taken to step up security in Britain, especially at airports. The statement ended with a very precise proclamation of solidarity with the US: 'This is not a battle between the United States of America and terrorism, but between the free and democratic world and terrorism. We, therefore, here in Britain stand shoulder to shoulder with our American friends in this hour of tragedy, and we, like them, will not rest until this evil is driven from our world.'[112]

These were Blair's own words, which he had been turning over in his mind for the last three hours. Blair had written out the first draft on an A4 pad. Kelly recalled: 'It was difficult, as the Prime Minister had not been able to speak to George Bush and therefore we felt our knowledge was patchy. But Blair reached a quite conscious decision to use the phrase "stand shoulder to shoulder". He wanted the Americans to know that they were not on their own.'[113]

While Blair was at COBRA, Bush made a second statement of his own. At 12:36 P.M. US time, 5:36 P.M. London time, the President appeared in front of the cameras once again, this time from Barksdale Air Force base. In contrast to Blair's delivery, Bush spoke haltingly and tripped over his words. He offered just 219 of them, and took no questions from reporters.[114] America was not reassured. Nine minutes before the President spoke, the borders with Canada and Mexico were closed. The financial markets were shut and even Disney World locked its doors. At 1:30 P.M., Air Force One taxied down the runway at Barksdale and headed for Offutt Air Force base in Nebraska. Bush was growing increasingly frustrated at being forced to hop from one airport to the next. 'I want to go back home ASAP,' he told Andy Card. 'I don't want whoever did this holding me outside of Washington.'[115] But the Secret Service insisted the situation still remained too uncertain. Card agreed with them and Bush reluctantly acquiesced. At least the Offutt base had facilities for the President to hold a National Security Council meeting over video link.

As Air Force One cruised towards rural Nebraska, in Downing Street Blair's frustration was growing. He was increasingly anxious to speak with the President, rather than second-guessing his thoughts: 'We were certainly worried that the President might retaliate quickly and do some sandblasting in the Middle East by firing off a few missiles,' recalls one of Blair's inner circle.[116] Might there be war in the Persian Gulf by morning?

Blair was growing more certain of what he wanted to say to Bush: 'That he should deliver an ultimatum to the Taliban to hand over Bin Laden and his people and then hit them if it didn't happen.'[117] Blair's staff had been calling the White House repeatedly, but with little joy. Why had Blair, who had already established himself as Bush's closest overseas ally, not been able to speak to him? The leaders do not call each other's mobile phones direct. Calls are routed through the switchboards at the White House and Number 10. One senior Bush administration official based in the White House Situation Room that day remembered calls coming in from around the world. 'Sure, they were coming in, but we were simply not in "making calls mode". It was a stressed environment. The President often wasn't available, the Vice-President and Condi Rice were downstairs in the bunker, and we had virtually no communication with them. We had our hands full in those early hours. We just weren't ready to start making calls.'[118] A senior State Department official went further: 'While the Prime Minister and those around him were actually thinking ahead in the hours after the attacks, I'm not certain that the senior-most American officials were doing much more than reacting. It was almost as if Washington, inadvertently, had out-sourced its thinking.'[119]

Blair wanted to hold urgent conversations with fellow world leaders. Number 10 fixed calls with French President Jacques Chirac, Prime Minister Lionel Jospin, and German Chancellor Gerhard Schröder: the last wanted to hold a special G8 meeting, but the other two were not convinced.[120] He also spoke with Russian leader Vladimir Putin. 'They all reflected the sense of shock,' noted Jonathan Powell, 'the feeling from all four was very much what they said in public, "We are all Americans now."'[121] Blair claimed to have been gratified in particular by his conversation with Putin: 'It was straight from the heart. He was outraged by it. He supported America.'[122] It was not all altruism. Through his backing the West in their war on terror, Putin hoped he could gain their support, or at least acquiescence, in what he saw as his own fight against terrorism in Chechnya.

Blair spent some time that evening learning more about al-Qaeda as papers from the JIC started to flow in.[123] As the evening wore on Blair became thoughtful. Huddled in the den with Hunter, Campbell and Powell, 'he was in one of those moods when he was not articulating very much'.[124] 'At this stage the action was almost totally going on inside the PM's room,' recalled one Number 10 aide.[125] With the immediate strain of the day passing, and the media statements, the formal chairing and decision-taking over, he became, for a while, 'very emotional', although not tearful. It was part of Hunter's role to manage his normally very even emotions.[126] Sitting there closeted with him, alongside the others, in that closest and most trusted group, Blair's anxiety was obvious: 'We just don't know what's going to happen,' he confided.[127] Unaware of the advice the President had been receiving that Washington was not safe for him, Blair was troubled that Bush's priority appeared to be keeping out of danger, rather than returning to the centre to take command, which was always his own instinctive reaction. 'It's odd,' Blair mused, 'and it's not right.'[128]

At 3:30 P.M. EST, Bush convened an NSC meeting via secure video link from his bunker at Offutt Air Force base to the White House. His absence from the centre had gone on long enough: 'At the State

Department, our attitude was that it was ridiculous that the President of the United States should be missing in action,' recalled former Assistant Secretary Elizabeth Jones.[129] The President was equally frustrated. 'The last item on the agenda was supposed to be where the President should be,' recalled US counter-terrorism czar Richard Clarke. 'Instead, we began there. "I'm coming back to the White House as soon as the plane is refuelled," the President ordered. "No discussion."'[130] Bush reviewed actions already taken and heard from George Tenet, Director of the CIA, that the agency was virtually certain that Bin Laden was behind the attacks. 'Get your ears up,' Bush replied. 'The primary mission of this administration is to find them and catch them.'[131] Meanwhile at home, it was agreed that the administration would do all it could to promote a return to normality as soon as possible. The Secret Service again tried one last time to prevent Bush returning to Washington. Bush overruled them.[132]

Not until 6:34 P.M., 11:34 P.M. UK time, did Bush eventually land at Andrews Air Force base just outside Washington, almost ten hours since the first plane had struck the Twin Towers. By this time, most of Blair's aides had left Downing Street for the night. Having established that the West's major powers were on-side, that the realm was as secure as it could be, and that the President was still incommunicado, there was nothing more that Blair could do. 'A lot of us in Number 10 spoke with our families that night,' recalled one close aide. 'We were all worried. I remember leaving Number 10 late that night and going out into the street. It was an extraordinary feeling, after all that we'd been through that day, just to go out into the street and call a cab. There was a really eerie atmosphere. We just didn't know whether there would be a war coming that night.'[133]

   Blair himself remained deep in thought long after his aides had left the building and all was quiet. 'He knew straight away that it would be the defining issue for Bush, and thus probably for him too for the coming years,' said John Sawers.[134] 'What Blair saw most clearly,' continued Sawers, 'was the need for the inevitable response to 9/11 to be targeted against those responsible'.[135] Iraq, which had been in his sights since 1998, crossed his mind, but the focus for now would be Afghanistan. Iraq would have to be dealt with separately. In one day, Blair had found his calling on the world stage. His sense of purpose in domestic policy would take longer to evolve.

2

Finding His Theme

January–September 2001

'I didn't get the first term right,' Tony Blair confided to one of his closest aides in late 2000.[1] The months leading up to 9/11 were to be crucial in the formation of Tony Blair's remaining domestic policy. As the 2001 General Election drew near, he began to focus on the strategy, build the team, and develop the stronger Number 10 he needed for his second term. It would probably be his last – he wasn't sure. Reform of the public services – education, health, transport and criminal justice – and taking Britain into the Euro, were to be his core themes. Yet little of this thinking found its way into the election manifesto in 2001. It was safe. As the election approached, he had worried that anything too radical could jeopardise the result, and run up against the all too familiar opposition from elements of the Labour movement. During the campaign, Blair deliberately ramped up the temperature, yet it was only after victory was in the bag that he began the detailed planning with his new Number 10 team. Over the summer, and in the early days of September, his thinking and programmes for action began to emerge. The green shoots of a personal domestic agenda were at last beginning to appear.

The Struggle to Engage: Early 2001

In 2000, Tony Blair spent Christmas and New Year at Chequers. Typically he would work right up to Christmas, stopping on 22 or 23

December. Aides at Number 10, anxious to do their Christmas shopping, would breathe a sigh of relief when Blair finally called it a day. Some senior aides would hear from him again on Christmas Eve. Ostensibly he wanted to say 'Happy Christmas', but in fact he wanted to continue mulling over politics. The Blair family would normally spend three or four days at Chequers and then on Boxing Day or 27 December, they would go somewhere warm, accompanied by the ever-present Special Branch detectives and 'Garden Room Girls'. Over this particular New Year, he went with Cherie and the children to Mauritius. During these short breaks, he never switched off completely, as he did for at least the first week of his summer holidays, and he would return to Downing Street armed with a long hand-written note setting out his thinking. When he returned to Number 10 in early January 2001, his scribblings were immediately typed up by the Garden Room Girls, beavering away in the rooms immediately beneath the Cabinet Room and his own 'den'.[2] This New Year memo took careful stock of the impending election year. The coming months would be crucial. Although he knew that difficult choices lay ahead, he looked back with some satisfaction to what had been achieved since the May 1997 election victory that had brought him to power: the focus then had been on proving that Labour could be trusted to govern again.[3] No one now asked that question.

There were significant achievements in the first term: constitutional change had proved relatively straightforward; the government had provided economic stability, and introduced the minimum wage and a whole raft of welfare reforms. Much of the credit for the economic achievements, as Blair knew all too well, was due to Gordon Brown. In the autumn of 2000, the talk in Number 10 was that the first term had been about 'laying the foundations', and that the second term would be about 'delivery'. And he would be at the heart of it.

But what exactly did Blair want to deliver? His hand-written notes towards the end of the first term, mostly penned at weekends, show a growing dissatisfaction with the Home Office and the Department of Health, where he was frustrated by the lack of tangible progress, and with Number 10's limited ability to exert influence across Whitehall.[4] 'Not getting the machinery right became a huge issue for Tony Blair,' said one special adviser. He had become so focused on winning elections and making symbolic change that he had not focused on substantive policy. David Miliband, then head of the Policy Unit in Downing Street, did not help Blair oversee a distinctive policy platform. Derek Scott, his economics adviser, did not keep Brown awake at night. His key supporters, above all Alastair Campbell, Peter Mandelson and Anji Hunter, were not 'policy people'.[5] From at least late 2000, Blair knew he needed a fresh approach. And people who did policy.

What had impressed him? The first-term work of the Department for Education and Employment (DfEE) stood out, where Secretary of State David Blunkett had worked closely with Michael Barber, a former professor of education, in creating a system to improve literacy and numeracy in primary schools. He was inclined to importing both Barber, and his 'delivery' model, into the heart of Downing Street. It would give him the teeth he had lacked. Number 10, not the Treasury, would drive the new domestic reform programme.[6] He never accepted that there had been any kind of binding 'deal' in the summer of 1994; it was 'a myth' for Brown and his allies to suggest that an agreement had been reached at the Granita dinner that gave Brown effective say over vast swathes of economic and welfare policy.[7] Nevertheless, this was exactly what tended to happen in the first term. After his second election victory, he was determined that things would be different.

In the first term, conflict between the Treasury and Number 10 had been containable: Jeremy Heywood, Principal Private Secretary to the Prime Minister since 1999, said: 'There were some issues that the Treasury didn't really care about, and there were other issues that Number 10 didn't really care about. So that was easy. There were a few issues on which we had a difference of view, and David Miliband and I would sit down with Ed Balls [Gordon Brown's senior adviser] and Treasury officials and we would try to narrow or iron out differences rather than have them exposed to other departments. It was a system that worked fairly well.'[8] But it was also an unsustainable *modus operandi*, not least because of a strange mirror image: 'Blair started off being safe and became radical,' observed a close aide. 'As the General Election approached, Brown became less radical at the very same moment as Blair increased his radicalism.'[9]

A stronger Number 10, capable of standing up to the Treasury, was then a prerequisite for a successful second term. But what of his policy agenda? Education would be the number-one priority. 'Education was much easier in the first term than it later became,' said one senior official. 'The Prime Minister gave us the resources, stood back and let us get on with it. Morale in the department was very high, particularly on improving primary education.'[10] Blair wanted the second term to be about secondary schools. Transforming the comprehensive school, a by-word for failure for much of the middle class, would be key. Yet in the first term, the DfEE had abolished the quasi-independent 'Grant Maintained' schools, a decision Blair later regretted. It was the arrival of Andrew Adonis – an Oxford don turned *Financial Times* journalist – as Blair's education adviser in 1998 that led to a change of gear. Adonis started working with Blunkett's advisers on reforms to promote greater diversity and quality in secondary education, which led to the publication of 'Excellence in Cities' in 1999 and the drive for far more specialist secondary schools. A schools green paper published shortly before the 2001 election heralded a more fundamental drive to abolish the 'bog-standard comprehensive' – a phrase briefed by Campbell on the day of the launch.[11] The phrase caught the attention: only in time did the radicalism of the green paper – in particular the creation of new 'academies' as 'independent' state schools managed by the voluntary and private sectors – come to be realised.

Health would be a second area of particular Blairite interest in the second term. He had set up a committee under Adair Turner, former Director General of the CBI, to probe into the NHS, but he realised that it would need much greater investment and reform. His promise to boost health spending to the EU average when he appeared on BBC Television's *Breakfast With Frost* in January 2000, was an indication of what he wanted to achieve. It was a clear signal that he, not Brown, would be calling the shots. Transport was another department that began to worry him by end of the first term. For all Prescott's pride in his achievement there, Blair was far from convinced. Here again, however, he had little clear idea how to make progress.

Crime was the final area where Blair wanted to make a mark. According to Sally Morgan, then Political Secretary at Number 10, 'Tony always knew what he wanted to do on crime. He had the background. He did not need to rely on others for ideas, as he did in health and education.'[12] 'Towards the end of the first term', another aide recalled, 'the Prime Minister became increasingly frustrated that crime always rose and the Home Office said there was little more that could be done about it. He liked Jack Straw, the Home Secretary, but we could sense his frustration with Jack, and still more with the fatalistic view of the system that the Home Office had.'[13] One of Blair's responses was to bring in John Birt, until recently Director-General of the BBC, whom he had known since the early 1980s, to produce a 'private' report on crime, much to the irritation of Straw and the Home Office. A 'fierce exchange' with Cabinet Secretary Richard Wilson had been necessary before Birt established his territory and could build up a small team in Downing Street to undertake a root-and-branch analysis of the pattern of offending, and the success of the criminal justice system overall in countering crime.[14] Birt's approach – analysing from first principles upwards – chimed with Blair's barrister-trained mind. 'He found Birt's way of working very compelling. He liked the way that John was willing to get right down into the data and understand the evidence, and come up with a real sense that you could do things in a totally different way,' Heywood recalled.[15] But as Blair became more interested in crime, he rubbed up against his old mentor Derry Irvine, the Lord Chancellor. 'In the first term he increasingly had to say "no" to Derry. It became ever clear that he could no longer work well with Derry, but he always pulled back because he found it so hard to have a direct clash with him.'[16]

The General Election was approaching, and Blair's second-term agenda was still inchoate in his mind. He had impulses and ideas only: he was still miles away from sorting it out. Why after nearly four years, had he and his Policy Unit not done more to prepare for the all-important second term? According to Geoff Mulgan, the other key figure alongside Miliband in the first-term Policy Unit, 'more was done to win the second term than to plan for it – partly because Blair still lacked a serious capacity for strategy and planning'.[17] Brown's conservatism was blamed by some in Number 10. As the General Election approached, the Chancellor displayed a 'fanatic' determination to win a second victory, thinking of his own succession which he was confident would occur just a few years later.

But is it right to blame Brown? Blair merits far more responsibility than Brown for caution in the 2001 election. 'Blair was simply not engaged in dragging the agenda forward in a consistent way in the first term,' said one insider.[18] Those in Number 10 who favoured consolidation were able to gain the upper hand. Blair's biggest commitment to thinking about policy remained the nebulous 'third way', to which he gave great attention domestically and internationally, in league with President Bill Clinton. Yet hopes of translating these ideas into a practical set of policies were fading by 1999. Blair did not seem at times to comprehend the void. 'He was very concerned that the 2001 election should give him a personal mandate for radical reform, but he was uncertain exactly what the radical reform should be,' one aide recalled. It took him time to realise that attending 'third-way' jamborees, or announcing policy initiatives in speeches, did not automatically translate into hard policy.[19]

Blair's fluid state of mind is revealed in a fifteen-page confidential memo sent to his senior aides in Number 10 on 21 April 2001. He opens by examining his core beliefs, and the continuing relevance of New

Labour. But he does not state precisely its purpose, nor how his core beliefs might translate into policy. The paper states very clearly that he wants to be re-elected on his 'own clear personal mandate'. What does it say of his agenda? He wants to break away both from Thatcherism and 'old-style social democracy', and to work in a 'post-Thatcherite political system' (without spelling out exactly what that means). Abroad, he wants Britain to play a major 'positive' role in Europe, but offers no set goals or timetable for his policy on the Euro. He wants to concentrate on social services and to introduce 'radical' reforms. But he does not say how. He talks about the importance of 'community', harking back to the very impulses that first caught his imagination about politics when he was an undergraduate at Oxford University from 1972 to 1975.[20] But he retains a student fuzziness. The fifteen pages amount to little more than chapter headings. The substance, he says, will come in his speeches during the election campaign.[21]

Some in the Labour Party were pressing for a radical manifesto. They believed that the 1997 manifesto had been too cautious and lacking in detail. They may have accepted the need for 'safety first' back then, but now they demanded more. Stephen Byers articulated such hopes in a speech in early April: 'The election provides us with a once-in-a-generation opportunity to change our country fundamentally. We need to ensure the manifesto is modernising and radical. It is a golden opportunity.'[22]

The search for a 'big idea', or even a series of smaller ideas, to shape Labour's second-term agenda intensified as the election approached. It is indeed surprising that with so many intellectually brilliant advisers at the centre, and in the departments, more was not achieved. Requests were sent out to 'ministers, think-tanks and anyone else with a fertile idea that this time Mr Blair seeks a sweeping programme of far-reaching reform to put to voters'.[23] Think-tanks, however, were to provide just one significant idea that was incorporated into the manifesto, the 'child trust fund', and its ownership was quarrelled over by the Fabians, the Social Market Foundation (SMF) and the Institute for Public Policy Research (IPPR).[24] The feisty Ed Richards, who had been brought into Whitehall after running corporate strategy for the BBC, was charged with working up ideas for the manifesto, which included a strong push on social mobility and opportunity. Yet many of these ideas were smothered by both Blair's and Brown's preference for caution. Senior aides, including Mulgan, saw the writing on the wall and expressly warned Blair that caution now could leave the government short on policy half-way through the second term.[25]

The Campaign: May–June 2001

The assumption, in the media and in the country at large, was that the election would be held on 3 May, on the same day as the local elections. But this date, long written into the diary at Labour Party headquarters at Millbank, had not taken account of the outbreak of the 'foot and mouth' farm animal epidemic. The first sign of a problem came on 21 February with confirmation that pigs from an abattoir in Essex had the disease. The realisation followed that the disease had spread throughout the country. Other countries swiftly imposed bans on British beef exports and thousands of farmers watched helplessly as their cattle became worthless. Nick Brown, Gordon Brown's long-standing ally, was in charge as Minister for Agriculture, Fisheries & Food (MAFF). For four weeks he battled to gain control, fiercely asserting his right to handle the dispute. But in the second half of March, Blair's patience snapped. On 23 March, he summoned Wilson. 'I want you to take control of this crisis,' he told him. 'Get a group of officials together because this is disastrous.'[26] Wilson promptly convened a meeting of relevant Whitehall departments. David King, the government's Chief Scientific Adviser, now assumed a central role: his evidence-based approach to combating the epidemic combined with the logistical expertise of the armed forces proved crucial to the government establishing control.[27] King's advice also made an impact on the thinking about election timing.

With Wilson's help Blair took personal charge of the crisis, utilising COBRA, as he had done during the fuel crisis in late 2000. A clash with the Treasury was not far away. 'It thought that it should have no role in foot and mouth,' said one Number 10 official, 'but any half-decent finance ministry would have been challenging MAFF's thinking, putting forward alternative solutions, not ducking for cover.'[28] Number 10 told the Treasury how much they would need to get over the initial crisis and got on with it. They infuriated Brown by 'simply ignoring him'.[29] At COBRA meetings there would often be an empty chair for the Treasury. Brown resented Blair claiming the initiative: 'At some point, Cabinet government will have to be re-imposed,' Brown told Campbell, and 'TB will have to extricate himself from being in charge of this'.[30] Campbell baulked at this: 'MAFF have been hopeless,' he told Brown. 'The idea TB should not be taking this over is absurd.'[31]

Learning from the fuel crisis, when he had been criticised for being insufficiently visible, Blair made a point of visiting disaster-ridden areas across Britain and listening to those affected. With his own credibility now at stake, he could not be seen to fail. For six weeks, from late March to early May, the crisis consumed him. 'He was constantly frustrated by his inability to solve it: every time he thought he had got the problem cracked, it went wrong again,' said an official.[32] Blair's approach came at a price. As he admitted on 20 April, he lacked the energy to write his introduction to the election manifesto: 'All he could think about, with foot and mouth going round in his head, was sheep!'[33]

The crisis sparked divisions within Number 10 about the timing of the election. Most wanted to stick with 3 May, even after the crisis had broken out. A delay might jeopardise Labour's lead in the polls, giving the impression of a government not in control. Crunch time was the week beginning Monday, 19 March. An hour-long meeting with Brown at the Treasury on 21 March was inconclusive. The Chancellor was in two minds, and the mood was tense. Labour Party figures in Number 10 favoured 3 May, as did Prescott, Straw and Blunkett.[34] By contrast, Anji Hunter and Sally Morgan fought strongly for a delay.[35] Heywood and the other officials working in the crisis were concerned too that the earlier date might distract Blair's focus at a crucial time.[36] Mounting concerns that the US economy was wobbling, and might have an unsettling effect on the British economy with knock-ons to the electorate, added to the tension.[37]

Blair's dilemma burst into the open when European Commission President Romano Prodi asked at an EU summit in Stockholm on Friday 23 March how long he had to decide on the timing. 'Ten days,' Blair replied: words picked up by an ITN microphone.[38] On the plane home from Sweden, he asked his foreign policy advisers for their personal opinions. Stephen Wall (Europe) was in favour of sticking to May. John Sawers (rest of the world) commented that, as an ordinary voter, he thought a month's delay would be judicious and appreciated by the electorate.[39] On the Saturday Blair had a long phone conversation with Blunkett, whose diary records: '[Blair's] instincts are to postpone both the local elections and the General Election until 7 June, but he would not make up his mind for a couple of days. It was a really hard decision.'[40] Lance Price, Labour's Director of Communications, recorded in his own diary that Blair had become 'very twitchy' about what to do.

Mandelson, an advocate of delaying until June, now began to recognise reality: 'The umbilical cord between us and 3 May has snapped,' he declared on Sunday 25 March.[41] The next day 'Jack Straw was still urging 3 May', Campbell noted in his diary, but 'TB was pretty convinced we had to go for June as a way of taking out some heat'.[42]

Campbell, who had already given the *Sun* an exclusive on the election date, was furious at the delay. At the morning meeting at Number 10 early the following week, when the postponement decision was formally taken, he was visibly angry, banging his fist and shouting at the head of communications of MAFF, the department he blamed for the delay. As he walked out of the meeting, he muttered, 'Bloody stupid day, bloody stupid decision.'[43] Blair was uncomfortable that Campbell's views were opposed to Hunter's: he was never happy when his closest colleagues – Campbell, Mandelson and Hunter – were at odds with each other.[44] On 2 April, Blair announced that the local elections would be rescheduled to 7 June, sending a clear, if implicit message, that the General Election would also be held on that day. Blair was adamant, however, that he would not under any circumstances delay the election until the autumn. 'Even if the lead is down to 6 per cent in June, I'm still going in June,' he told colleagues in private.[45] Blair had been under intense, and conflicting, pressure from the press over the delay. Yet after the decision was taken, Price recorded, 'The media generally supported [the delay] with everyone, except the *Mirror*, suddenly discovering they were in favour all along.'[46]

What finally convinced him to delay? Election timing is one of a Prime Minister's most lonely decisions. The polls showed 44 per cent were strongly against a May election. But public opinion was not the decisive reason. Brown saw the risks of both May and June, but left the final decision to Blair: he then let it be known that he thought Blair had got it wrong once he announced the delay.[47] The foot and mouth crisis was the key factor: Blair could not imagine canvassing while the epidemic still raged across large parts of rural Britain. The government had first to master the crisis, and David King told him its peak would be passed by 7 June. 'I would say that this was the first time in British history that science had been used to predict the date of a general election,' King said.[48] There remained the risk, however, that the crisis might still be raging, and the decision would then have been savaged. Delay was a brave decision by Blair, and it showed that he had a better feel for the national mood than many of his colleagues.

Blair formally opened the campaign on Tuesday 8 May, at St Saviour's and St Olave's, an inner-city 'beacon' school in Bermondsey, south London, announcing finally that the General Election would be held on 7 June. A school was deliberately chosen to highlight Blair's education priority, but the choice backfired. 'I stand before you today with a sense of humility and hope,' Blair told the bemused audience of schoolgirls. 'Four years ago you gave us, New Labour, a majority larger than I or anyone else believed you would.' Blunkett recorded in his diary: 'So there we are, sitting in the front row, and Tony comes in with a live broadcast, filming not just his speech, but of course, the reaction of the audience. No wonder the young people present were bewildered, because the speech itself had to address the adult audience across the country. But for the teenagers, all of this was a bit too much – as the press the following morning demonstrated with photographs of bewildered looks on young faces, the nudging and the closed eyes.'[49]

Closed eyes and stifled yawns also greeted Labour's manifesto, *Ambitions for Britain*, launched by Blair in Birmingham on 16 May. 'It is a manifesto with a big ambition for Britain – a mission for the reform of public services,' he said, promising a future Labour government would recruit 10,000 more teachers, 20,000 more nurses, 10,000 more doctors and 6,000 extra police. But for all the promises of it being 'radical', it failed to ignite much interest. Hugo Young, the doyen of left-of-centre commentators, summed it up when he described the manifesto as 'exceedingly boring. There's not a trace of glamour about it.'[50] The party responded defensively that the comprehensive spending review (CSR) of 2000 had settled the spending commitments for the three years 2001–04, and 'left us with the problem of having little genuinely new to say'.[51]

The four-week campaign contrasted with the vivid and often exuberant excitement of 1997. William Hague led a beleaguered Tory Party struggling to overcome internal divisions and poor organisation, fixated upon its campaign to 'Save the Pound'.[52] Blair compared it to getting into a boxing ring and finding there was no opponent.[53] Bob Shrum, the US Democrat Party consultant, observing the election at Millbank, told one Labour aide that it was 'like machine-gunning a corpse'.[54] But Blair felt uneasy during the first week of campaigning, when Campbell recorded that he was 'lacking in confidence, tired-looking, still a bit nervy and it was draining having to pump him up the whole time'.[55] Poor relations with Brown were also chipping away at his morale. 'Tony Blair was almost impatient to get the campaign over with. He didn't relish it. He found it quite unpleasant, and hated the politics and the campaign. Gordon decided what the politics were, and he let Gordon run it from the centre and he ran the campaign on the road.'[56] On 23 May, with two weeks to polling day, Price recorded: 'Blair seems strongly disengaged from the campaign. His mind seems to be elsewhere.'[57] Another aide recalled, 'Frankly, the campaign was awful and Gordon was a real bully. It annoyed Gordon that even though he was running it at the centre the media would always want to follow Tony on to the road.'[58] Mandelson was one of many in Blair's camp aggrieved by Brown running the campaign. Brown in turn resented Mandelson's efforts to influence strategy. He exploded in front of Campbell at party headquarters: he 'went on a great tirade, said we were letting [Mandelson] destroy the campaign, undermine him, be ill-disciplined, on and on he went'.[59] Brown wanted to fight a narrow and negative campaign to 'destroy the Tories in the first week',[60] while emphasising the strength of the economy and improvement in living standards; Blair wanted it to be broader and was desperate to win a personal mandate.[61] Relations between both individuals, and their camps, became progressively more poisonous as the campaign wore on. 'The problem with Gordon during the campaign was he didn't want to share decisions or the limelight with anyone,' said one neutral observer.[62] The froideur, desperately downplayed by both sides, was obvious for all to see. Robert Harris, the novelist, wrote: 'The Brown body language during the campaign whenever Blair was speaking (yawning, consulting his watch, discovering hitherto unsuspected fluff on his jacket) was as obvious as semaphore.'[63]

Anxieties that he had crafted an overly cautious manifesto now began to strike home. 'Blair's big worry was that we would win big, but he would not actually have a mandate for big change,' recalled a close confidant.[64] He decided to make his personal contribution in six keynote speeches, a strategy envisaged in his confidential memo of 21 April. He wanted to use the speeches to fill in the detail absent from the manifesto. But did he succeed? The first such speech came at Trimdon Labour Club, at the heart of his own constituency of Sedgefield, in County Durham. An assault on Thatcherism was his theme. 'More than once I took flak inside the party for saying not everything Mrs Thatcher did was wrong.' But he attacked her now for her 'four great failings': economic recession, under-investment in public services, a belief in selfish individuals and a 'destructive' rejection of Europe. 'I stand as New Labour,' he told his audience, pledging to lead a 'modern, liberal, social democrat party', occupying the centre ground between 'crypto-Thatcherites' and 'old-style Socialists'.[65] It was necessary electioneering, but it did not mean much.

In Birmingham on 16 May to make his second speech he pushed for a greater role for the private and voluntary sectors in delivering public services and provoked an argument not only with Brown but also with the unions. He deliberately sought to convey the impression that the manifesto was more radical in its role for the private sector – anathema to old Labour – than in fact it was. From now on, the election was dominated by the very kind of row Brown had sought to avoid. The news headlines that night led on another story, however – Blair being accosted outside a hospital by Sharon Storer, a member of the public whose partner was undergoing treatment for cancer. As she harangued Blair for the inadequate treatment she believed her partner was receiving, Blair could only stand by, apparently lost for words.[66] The incident made a mark, not only on the public: 'It was very significant in heightening his conviction that the health service was changing too slowly,' said Simon Stevens, who joined Number 10 after the election as Blair's key adviser on health.[67]

The most significant of Blair's speeches during the campaign came at Gravesend in Kent on 21 May, when he articulated his core themes for public services in the second and third terms: 'high standards' nationwide, 'devolution of decision-making' and 'flexibility'. His fourth and seminal principle, 'diversity and choice', was added only after the General Election. Blair had relied heavily on his speechwriting team of Alastair Campbell, Peter Hyman and the Policy Unit for drafting his other speeches during the campaign. This was a speech he wrote himself. 'He was very proud of it. It reflected the way his thinking had been developed.'[68] Four days later, he spoke in Edinburgh about Europe. Brown was even more unhappy about this speech than Gravesend. 'Gordon very concerned about TB's speech tomorrow on Europe,' recorded Lance Price. 'Asked AC if he could see it but AC said it didn't yet exist . . . Gordon didn't believe it.'[69] Labour's polls showed working-class Labour voters were hostile to the Euro, and there were fears that Hague might make capital out of playing the Eurosceptic card. Blair pressed ahead regardless. He doubted Hague's ability to inflict much damage, and he was damned if he was going to let Brown stop him.[70] He spoke to aides in a macho way about how his second term would see decisive action on the EU. No one in Blair's team knew in advance exactly what he would say on the day, nor did he, and in the end caution again won out. On the Euro he said it would be in Britain's interest to join the single currency, without saying when or why. This was not new. The speech nonetheless was seen by some as the beginning of a two-year campaign for a referendum on joining the Euro. A *Guardian* leader said that the speech 'started the process . . . which could lead either to Mr Blair's own apotheosis or nemesis'.[71]

Despite encouraging opinion polls and confidence in Party HQ that the overall strategy was proving to be effective, Blair became progressively disheartened as the campaign wore on. As a result, he decided to change tack, 'going into lots of community centres and making it much of a more micro-campaign while we left Gordon to go it alone running the macro-campaign from London'.[72] He let slip to two interviewers that he was 'not happy' being Prime Minister.[73] Blair's fifth main speech, in Newport, Shropshire on 30 May, was on a subject close to his heart, law and order. He stressed the three 'R's', 'rights, responsibilities and reform', and signalled that law and order was going to become a major theme. But everyone knew this. Blair rounded off on 5 June with his final speech in Yardley, in the West Midlands, two days before polling day. This was a plea against voter apathy, a growing worry during the campaign. Blair painted the election as an opportunity for Britain to put the 'Saatchi' years behind it.

On the evening before polling day, he went to his home, Myrobella, in the village of Trimdon in his constituency. His pollster and confidant Philip Gould told him that evening that the worst-case scenario was a majority of 75 and the best 200. Everything would hinge on the turnout.[74] Blair held discussions on Thursday morning principally about the post-election reshuffle, with Campbell, Powell, Hunter and Morgan. During the day, he toured the constituency, going to the polling stations and voting booths, meeting voters and chatting to party workers. When he returned home in the afternoon he continued to work on the Cabinet. By early evening his mood was described as 'anxious and concerned. He was waiting desperately to hear the results, and was forever asking us "have you heard anything, is there any news, is there any indication?"'[75] 'We were reasonably confident but really unsure about the size of the majority,' recalled one aide.[76] But he was more assured as he left for his own count at Newton Aycliffe Leisure Centre after news from Millbank that exit polls were indicating another triple-figure majority. He still refused to relax: 'It's not over until it's over,' he insisted.[77] One aide described how they all felt. 'There was a real sense of anti-climax. Above everything, we were all just incredibly tired.' The atmosphere at his count and at the Trimdon Labour Club lacked the euphoria of 1997. He hugged Cherie several times, as he did his children Euan and Nicky and Katherine and forgetting the cameras, he held his father Leo close to him, and stroked his hair quite unselfconsciously. It was a rare personal moment.[78]

The party were driven to Teesside Airport where they were flown south on a jet loaned by the Chairman of British Midland. 'Tony was very downbeat and sober. We had to wait an incredibly long time on the tarmac for the press corps to arrive. It was all very different from the private jet that flew us south in 1997.'[79] During the flight Blair had 'that far-away look in his eyes. It looks as though he's listening to you but his mind is not there. He was thinking ahead to the reshuffle, thinking about the next steps.'[80] The plane landed at Stansted, from where they were driven to Labour's party in Millbank. He arrived shortly after 5:30 A.M., tried to be cheerful but gave the impression that he could not wait to get away.[81] Observers noticed that he and Brown could barely bring themselves to shake hands, let alone exchange a sentence in public.[82] The mood at the party was different from the excitement at the Royal Festival Hall in 1997. 'We were tired and emotional,' one aide working on the campaign recalled, 'but it felt better than 1997.' The historic achievement of winning a full second term with an almost unchanged majority was still sinking in.[83]

By the time he was driven back to Number 10, he had only time for a short rest in the flat before being driven to Buckingham Palace to meet the Queen. On his return, on the steps of Downing Street, he delivered a deliberately solemn message: 'It is a mandate for reform and for investment in the future and it is also very clearly an instruction to deliver.' Of his preceding four years in office, he gave a prosaic assessment. 'I believe in the last four years we've laid foundations. I believe our victory in this election shows that the people understand that we've laid foundations, but now is the time to build upon them.' In contrast to the windy rhetoric of 1997, he wanted to set a businesslike tone for his second and probably final term in office: 'I've learned, I hope, from the mistakes, as well the good things. But above all I've learned of the importance of establishing the clear priorities of government. Of setting them out clearly for people, then focusing on them relentlessly whatever events may come and go.'[84] He turned his back on the cameras, and, stepping in through Number 10's black door, walked down the corridor between the lines of assembled Downing Street staff for the 'clapping in' ritual before settling down to business.

'At the Peak of His Power': Reshuffle and Remoulding

'You are now at the peak of your power. You may never be as strong again as you are now,' said Richard Wilson when he greeted Blair moments later.[85] Wilson remembers his words chiming with Blair's mood, and the Prime Minister giving him a look that suggested he understood. Together, they settled down to finalise his plans. The most significant decision of Blair's reshuffle entailed no change. It was to retain Brown at the Treasury. Shortly before the election, Blair was told that in the view of several civil servants, serving and retired, he would be making a mistake to retain Brown at the Treasury for a second term.[86] Several in his den argued for a change, believing Blair could not continue to function as Prime Minister properly if Brown remained *in situ*.[87] Powell, long-time foe of Brown, saw the attraction of removing him, though he did not think it politically possible.[88] Sally Morgan thought similarly, as did Mandelson, a vehement voice from the wings.[89] Campbell had become thoroughly disillusioned with Brown's antics at Millbank during the campaign when he 'wound up Alastair very badly'. One aide said, 'Alastair began to think that Tony would get on much better with Gordon out of the way!'[90] Anji Hunter was less sure, aware of Blair's deep inner conflicts over him. There were 'endless discussions about moving Gordon, which went on and on and on and on', recalled one senior source.[91] Blair 'blew hot and cold', particularly in the previous three months when his irritation was at its highest. But he would keep on coming back to the point that 'if we move him against his wishes, he will go on to the backbenches and it will be very difficult'.[92] He worried that Brown would lead a rebellion. But according to Robert Peston, author of *Brown's Britain*, 'This was probably the last occasion when Blair could have ousted Brown and not destroyed himself in the process.'[93]

Brown did not hear of these discussions until some months later and was reportedly shocked when he heard the news.[94] The so-called pro-Blair (and anti-Brown) 'ultras' in Number 10, whose numbers were to swell by the 2005 General Election, were disappointed that when it came to the crunch, Blair felt unable to act. Eighteen months later, Blair told a senior Whitehall official, 'I really can move him. I'm not frightened of moving him.'[95] But there was always something residing deep inside Blair – love, fear, compassion – that held him back. Another plan discussed in the den was to switch Brown to the Foreign Office, to be legitimised by the argument that he needed to gain foreign experience to prepare him for the premiership. Again caution won through. The prospect of Brown blocking him on foreign policy for the next four years, as he had on domestic policy in the previous four, was less of a factor than indications that Brown would not buy it. Thought switched to retaining Brown as Chancellor but moving the post of Chief Secretary within the orbit of Downing Street. This plan too, which would be raised again before 2005, was aborted.

So if Brown was to stay, another 'big beast' had to move. Blair's sights fixed on Robin Cook, who had not been the successful or loyal Foreign Secretary he had imagined.[96] Sacking him was his most brutal move: he was ever a reluctant executioner. So why did it happen? 'Blair saw the danger of allowing him to stay in the one job for too long, acquiring more authority and more independence. He had that in spades in the Treasury, and didn't want it in the Foreign Office in the second term as well,' said one senior official.[97] Blair had stood by Cook when he had had his first-term marital difficulties and set up home with his former secretary, Gaynor Regan. Having backed him then, he felt he could move against Cook with impunity now, knowing he never enjoyed widespread support in Cabinet or among the Parliamentary Labour Party (PLP). Secrecy was key. One senior official put it brutally. 'He went because Blair did not trust him, including not trusting him to keep quiet if he told him in advance.'[98] Blair did not even tell Wilson, giving the Cabinet Secretary the impression that he had decided to move Cook only the day before.[99] But as one aide said, 'We'd planned to move him all along. Robin received a lot of assurances that he wasn't going to move, but these did not come from us. He was not part of our plans for the Foreign Office.'[100] Another said, 'we had to move someone at the top to make room for new blood lower down.'[101] It later emerged that Lord Levy, the Labour fund-raiser, had told Cook that he was not to be moved. Cook accepted this, believing that it had come from Blair himself.[102] The fears were that if Cook learned of his intention, it would result in campaigning for him to stay. Cabinet and indeed most in Number 10 were thus not informed: not even Prescott knew for certain whether Cook would be moved.[103]

The news came as a complete surprise to Cook. 'My first warning that something was wrong was the way that Anji Hunter treated me when I arrived at Number 10,' Cook wrote in his diary. 'Anji is a prime exponent of the touchy-feely school of expression, and this morning she was keeping to her own private space.' He was shown in to see Blair. 'Perhaps because of exhaustion he wasted no time in getting down to business. "I want you to move. I know this is not fair. You have not done anything wrong, but I need to make changes."'[104] In his diary, Cook implies that he took it all quite philosophically. In fact, he was deeply distressed. A disconsolate Cook went back to his room in the Foreign Office and was seen to be sitting with his head in his hands, a brandy by his side, repeating to himself, 'What shall I do, what shall I do? Tony has sacked me.' Officials learned that Blair had offered him the Leadership of the House. 'What should I do?' he asked them. A conversation followed with Gaynor so he could talk it over with her.[105] To others in the Foreign Office he said, 'Tony's lost his mind, he doesn't know what he's doing. You've got to save him. He's acting totally irrationally.'[106] Later that day, a torn Cook agreed to move to his new post.

Blair settled on Jack Straw as the most suitable successor, appointing him partly *faute de mieux* and partly because he trusted him. 'Although Jack and TB did not see eye to eye on many Home Office issues,' said one Number 10 insider, 'Jack was fundamentally loyal. They'd have their arguments in private, but then Jack would stick to the script and decisions in public, something Robin hadn't done.'[107] Straw's inexperience in foreign policy would have an added bonus for Blair. It would take him time to get up to speed. Straw had been expecting to take over from Prescott at the Department for Environment, Transport and the Regions (DETR), and had already been to the ministry to meet the staff. He was 'flabbergasted' when he was told the news that he was about to be appointed Foreign Secretary. Blair in fact had decided on his appointment for some time. 'After he offered me the job, we talked about the world picture and then about Europe, and he asked me what my attitude to the Euro would be (I was known as a bit of a Eurosceptic): I said, "My mind was open, but if we entered, we must do so on the right terms."'[108] Given the priority Blair wanted to give to British entry in the second term, it was hardly a big sell.

Blair had another surprise for Wilson that Friday. 'You're not going to be pleased with me over this,' he told the Cabinet Secretary, 'but I've decided that John Prescott should be moved into the Cabinet Office.'[109] 'This came as a considerable shock to Wilson and civil servants because they had done a huge amount of work on the role of the Cabinet Office which Blair had signed up to in detail,' remarked a senior official. 'There was no "John Prescott" slot in it.'[110] Worse for the mandarins, Prescott was already in the waiting room. Wilson couldn't quite understand what Blair was doing. He thought he was exhausted certainly, and although he didn't normally find him a rebellious man, he found him in a 'rebellious mood' on that day.[111] Number 10 had not judged Prescott to be a success at DETR, and moving him into the Cabinet Office was designed to play to his strengths, as a chair of Cabinet committees and an enforcer of the Prime Minister's will, without giving him further departmental responsibilities. Prescott learned only that night that his beloved DETR was to be split up: 'Bloody mad idea,' he said.[112]

Straw's move created a vacancy at the Home Office. Blunkett's work at Education recommended him for a bigger post. 'The PM wanted someone who shared his instincts in relation to security, law and order, criminal justice, immigration and asylum,' Blunkett said. '"Follow your instincts and I'll back you," he told me.' Blair felt he had found a kindred spirit. 'Remember there is a disjunction about how MPs feel in Parliament and how our supporters feel in the community. Don't worry about the flak you'll get from the liberal left: they don't experience the things that we're talking about.' Blair wanted him to learn from Michael Howard's uncompromising period as Home Secretary from 1993 to 1997. Blair respected what he had tried to do in that post, in contrast to his one-time mentor Roy Jenkins, who had told him that 'the Home Secretary could not make any impact on reducing crime'.[113]

Blair knew that it was imperative to get not only Blairites but also high talents into the core 'delivery' departments. Education was going to be as important as they got. Blunkett had lobbied hard for Estelle Morris, his Minister of State. The expectation was that his job would be given to Blairite Stephen Byers but in the middle of the election campaign, the *Sun* ran a story that it would be Morris, 'So that was who we assumed in the Department would get the job, because Alastair Campbell or one of his aides had leaked it,' said a senior Education official wryly.[114] Blair admired Morris's skills as a communicator, her commitment when a schools minister, and her excellent relations with teachers (she had been one herself). He was always keen also to promote women to senior positions. Byers instead was given Transport – another frontline department. At Health, Alan Milburn, another arch-Blairite, was retained as Secretary of State. The reshuffle saw former 'Kinnock-ites' rewarded: Charles Clarke became Party Chairman, with a seat in Cabinet, Patricia Hewitt was promoted to Cabinet as Trade and Industry Secretary, while John Reid remained at Northern Ireland. Margaret Beckett had her wish granted for a bigger department, and became Secretary of State for the new Department for Environment, Food and Rural Affairs (DEFRA), a reward for her loyalty in the first term.

Blair went to bed early on the Friday night and spent all Saturday and Sunday seeing more lowly ministers, determined to get all the junior appointments right. He was very clear in the instructions that he gave to all his new appointees: any verbal instructions were shortly followed by letters amplifying what he wanted them to do. By the end of the weekend, Blair was satisfied. He had soulmates in key positions (Milburn, Blunkett, Byers and Morris), supported by Hilary Armstrong, promoted to Cabinet as Chief Whip, along with Tessa Jowell, the Secretary of State for Culture, Media and Sport (DCMS). He regretted there was no place for Mandelson, but after two resignations, there was no way back. The question now was, would his new team be strong enough to see the job through?

Blair's brave new second-term vision also required him to put the right structures in place. 'Is this it? Is this all I've inherited from John Major?' he had said back in 1997. 'We are the fourth largest economy in the world and a major role in Europe, and I don't even have a proper department to serve me.'[115] Not till 2000, prompted by Powell and Heywood, did he realise he needed much stronger support at the heart of Downing Street. Too much attention had gone into managing the media and communications at Number 10, and insufficient to overseeing policy, delivery and politics.

To Andrew Turnbull, who succeeded Wilson as Cabinet Secretary in 2002, it took Blair most of the first term to realise that he needed much better support. 'He did not have a Strategy Unit, he did not have a strong personnel function, nor did he have an IT function and nor did he have a performance management capability. He realised all this needed to change if he was going to lead the government effectively.'[116] The solution, Blair proposed, would be to turn the Cabinet Office effectively into a Prime Minister's Department by incorporating Number 10 within it, supplemented by other functions raided from across Whitehall.[117] This grand design did not initially go down well with the civil service. To Wilson, the Cabinet Office's very purpose was to support collective government and the Cabinet as a whole, not just the Prime Minister. Such a move, he said, was a huge constitutional change and a very decisive step towards the Prime Minister becoming presidential, which he thought unwise politically and administratively.[118] The controversial and disputed proposal included Wilson becoming the Prime Minister's overall Permanent Secretary, running Number 10 and the Cabinet Office combined, with all key figures, including Powell, Campbell, Hunter and Heywood working for him as the supremo running the Prime Minister's Department.[119] The prospect of overwhelming power was dangled tantalisingly before Wilson. He rejected it out of hand.[120]

Blair changed tack. Talking with Wilson in the Number 10 flat in late April, he said, 'My Cabinet Ministers have a Permanent Secretary, why shouldn't I have a Permanent Secretary here in Number 10? Why shouldn't my Principal Private Secretary become a Permanent Secretary?' Wilson responded that to do so would be to over-grade the post, and that he wasn't certain that there would be anybody good willing to do the job, 'because Permanent Secretaries want to run large departments, not just a couple of hundred people in Downing Street.'[121] Blair also pressed Wilson on strengthening his foreign policy support in Number 10. It had become evident to Blair and others during the Good Friday Agreement talks in 1998, and the Kosovo crisis in 1999, that he needed more of a foreign policy infrastructure in Number 10. John Sawers, then his Foreign Affairs Private Secretary, discussed with Powell the idea of blending the foreign policy elements in Number 10 and Cabinet Office and creating two high-powered figures, one covering

Europe and the other all non-Europe foreign policy areas. Wilson conceded, but insisted that these figures should have a 'dual nationality'; they should belong to both the Cabinet Office and to Number 10. Blair agreed.[122] For the European job, Blair asked Stephen Wall, who had been running the European Secretariat in the Cabinet Office since 2000, but who had little appetite to return to Number 10.[123] For the foreign job, David Manning, Sawers's donnish successor at Number 10, was selected. Blair at last had the firepower on foreign and European policy that he wanted. In Wall he had the man considered to be the 'greatest expert on the EU in Whitehall' and in Manning, an official of very high intelligence and subtlety. The innovation proved a success.

Instead of the nuclear option of a Prime Minister's Department, Blair settled for the halfway house of a strengthened Number 10, with a closer link to a still separate Cabinet Office. Number 10 was reshaped under three separate commands. A 'Policy Directorate' was formed merging together the Policy Unit and the Private Office to take charge of the Prime Minister's day-to-day work and short-term policy advice. This was headed overall by Heywood, with Andrew Adonis as the special adviser acting as 'Head of Policy'. The new directorate was the brain child of Heywood, who wanted to create machinery to fit in with Blair's preferred method of working, which was to have just one 'expert' advising him on each subject, as well as creating a more dynamic engine capable of driving forward Blair's agenda throughout Whitehall.[124] The development aroused concern within Number 10 and across the Labour Party. Not only was the directorate to be overseen managerially by the career civil servant, Heywood, but his deputy, Adonis, was regarded (rightly) as more social democrat than Labour.

A Communications and Strategy Unit was set up under Campbell's direction, separating it from the Press Office, to be run by two career civil servants, Godric Smith and Tom Kelly. Removing Campbell from day-to-day media handling, and reducing the perception of 'spin', lay behind its change. A Government Relations Division, the third of the 'commands', was set up to oversee relations between Number 10, the Labour Party and outside bodies including business. The changes created a different atmosphere. 'Number 10 was much smaller and more compact in the first term,' said Robert Hill, the new Number 10 Political Secretary. 'We all knew each other, and had a shared political history. Access to the PM was simple. In the second term, Number 10 became very different. It was a much more formal and less personal place.'[125] A more professional office, though, was exactly what Blair needed.

Government relations was to be run by Anji Hunter, who had initially decided that she was going to be leaving after the election, and told Blair as much in early 2001.[126] Blair was unhappy. Gazing ahead at a second term without her by his side, he resolved to make her change her mind. 'Tony likes Anji because he likes people who have made it work for him in the past,' said a close aide. 'She made him feel secure.'[127] Blair enticed her on the road during the campaign with the prospect of this bigger job and salary. They agreed, in utter confidence, that she would accept this new post, but also to keep the news strictly to themselves. One senior Number 10 official, who thought he knew everything about the reshuffle, was stunned to be told by an exhausted Blair on the Friday that she was staying.[128] Blair told Cherie about it in the den that Friday afternoon. Her relations with Hunter had never been good, but soured considerably after May 1997. One insider, sympathetic to both parties, put it, 'You have to describe Cherie's and Anji's relationship as a total disaster.'[129] Cherie, as a highly qualified person in her own right, had wanted to play a role in Number 10, akin to that of her friend Hillary Clinton in the United States. Such a role, however, did not materialise and Cherie resented seeing Hunter, who she could never forget had known her husband longer than she had, spending so much more time with him. 'Most women would have found it very hard to have their husband so close to somebody else,' said one insider. 'Wherever he was, Anji was always turning up. She took that as saying Anji was more important to him than she was.'[130] When Cherie was told by her husband that Anji was staying on, she emerged from the den with a face described as 'frozen'.[131] His meeting with Cherie in the den in the afternoon lasted up to an hour and a half. It was clear to all around that she was furious. One official said, 'What was so bizarre was that we had six major government changes to process that afternoon, but our time was taken, not on the new people and briefings, but on sorting out the rumpus that followed his announcement that Anji was staying on.'[132]

None of the three commands proved an enduring success. Campbell left Number 10 in the summer of 2003, though it had become clear long before that he was unable to play the more strategic and detached role he and Blair wanted. Hunter quickly regretted her decision to stay and left in the autumn. Sally Morgan, who had not welcomed the increase in power to Hunter and who officially left Number 10 at the election, came back to an enhanced role in November – although she was never entirely cut off, and continued to attend the Monday morning meetings even after she left, and talked regularly on the phone to Blair. The Policy Directorate never worked fully as intended. It worked well as long as Heywood was there, but it needed someone of his intellectual and personal authority to hold it together. Blair, nevertheless, had substantially sculpted the Number 10 team he wanted. In Heywood, Manning and Wall he had three of the most high-powered brains and operators in Whitehall. He remained very close to Campbell and Hunter even after they left, while on a day-to-day basis Morgan rapidly came to fulfil the 'female' role that Blair needed. 'Tony Blair likes women,' said one observer: 'He's more likely to open to them about his feelings and also to admit when he's down. Alastair is the one man who he'll be confessional to when he is really down. He's a kind of "honorary girl" in that sense.'[133] Powell was never quite on the same personal friendship terms with Blair, although he became more central to Blair as the second term wore on, and other figures fell away. Mandelson remained a constant figure who Blair consulted by telephone, particularly on his weekend 'round of chats'. Adonis rapidly proved himself indispensable. As he himself declared, 'I know almost telepathically what he will think on any big issue. We are both Christian Democrats as much as social democrats, with a keen sense of the futility of the old left–right British party system to reflect modern progressive society and politics, and I was always willing him on to be himself.'[134] Blair would say of Adonis, 'He thinks fundamentally the same as me. He reaches the same conclusion before I do. He's brilliant.'[135]

If the second term was not to be like the first, Blair needed a new organisational weapon. The Delivery Unit, set up after the election in the Cabinet Office, was to be that weapon operating across Whitehall. Impressed by Michael Barber's record working with Blunkett at Education since 1997, Blair decided to import his unit and its methodology wholesale into his own empire, concentrating not only on education but also on a core list of delivery priorities – health, crime, drugs, asylum and road congestion. Much of its effectiveness derived from the knowledge within Whitehall that it carried the Prime Minister's imprimatur. Barber worked from early June to the end of July deciding on the Delivery Unit's agenda, and then until October getting departments to work out the plans on how they would achieve their objectives. A letter was sent to permanent secretaries across Whitehall asking them to submit final 'delivery plans' by the end of October while he bombarded them with a string of sayings, irritating to some, such as, 'if everything is under control, you're not going fast enough'.[136] The finite time in the second term was forensically carved up to ensure none was wasted. Barber correctly understood how much of the first term had been squandered as he recalled in his book, *Instruction to Deliver*: 'At one of my first meetings with him in my new role, he agreed he wanted reform to be "more radical, more urgent and more comprehensive".'[137] Another catch-phrase deployed was 'A week is a long time in politics, but four years is a very short time'.[138] The unit organised 'stock-takes' that took place in Number 10 usually on Tuesday mornings, so the four key second-term departments – Home Office, Education, Health, Transport – would come in every two to three months. It asked penetrating questions of both the Secretary of State and the senior officials, and in this way, priorities were identified and progress very closely monitored.

The Treasury did not like the sound of Blair increasing Number 10's firepower one bit. Would the Treasury's sway in Whitehall be reduced? Ed Balls argued the Delivery Unit cut across the Treasury's own 'Public Service Agreement' (PSA) targets, and worried that it would lobby for prime ministerial priorities against the Treasury.[139] An immediate wedge between Number 10 and the Treasury after the election was only averted by tough negotiations with Treasury officials bringing into line the Unit's priorities with PSA targets.[140] Not all Number 10–Treasury disagreements in the second term were to be so readily dispatched.

While Blair's focus was chiefly on creating the Number 10 he needed, Wilson's was to produce the most radical restructuring of Whitehall for twenty years.[141] At the heart of the plan had been dismembering the DETR and setting up the new Department for Environment, Food and Rural Affairs (DeFRA), as well as creating the Department of Work and Pensions (DWP) and the Department for Education and Skills (DfES), while the Home Office, which Wilson thought overloaded (he had previously been its Permanent Secretary), lost several of its functions to allow more focus on crime and justice. It was not to be the last stab at perfecting the Home Office. Wilson, concerned by Blair's tendency to centralise, did not have a high regard for his management skills. 'Your problem is that neither you nor anyone in Number 10 has ever managed anything,' he told a shocked Blair. 'I've managed the Labour Party,' he replied, indignantly. 'You never managed them, you led them. There's a big difference,' the Cabinet Secretary retorted.[142] Wilson explained that overseeing the delivery of a complex public service was very different from barking out instructions to party officials, or standing up at party conference and announcing a major change of policy. 'Blair wasn't the least interested in management,' said one of his Cabinet ministers, who had ceased to serve beyond the first term. He had the 'Blair garden look', where his eyes glazed over and he looked out at the Number 10 garden whenever the word 'management' was used.[143] 'His experience as a barrister didn't prepare him for managing people, or institutions,' said a former Treasury mandarin. 'Worse for him and the government,' he continued, 'Gordon Brown had no more idea. Gordon hadn't the faintest clue how to get himself out of a paper bag.'[144]

Blair was deadly serious about ensuring that his second-term ran to plan. The changes in Downing Street amounted to the biggest upgrading of the Prime Minister's resources in the history of the office. Even Number 12 Downing Street was commandeered from the Whip's Office to house some of the newly appointed units. But were the people and the new structure – utterly different from what he had available to him during 1997–2001 – finally going to be sufficient to allow him to make the mark on Britain he wanted for his premiership?

Finding His Stride: June to September

'If we back off from this, we might as well pack our bags and walk out of this building now.'[145] Blair was talking about introducing the private sector into public services at Number 10's Monday morning meeting on 25 June, two weeks after the General Election. Blair saw winning the argument as 'another Clause IV battle'. The meeting concluded with Blair commissioning Heywood and Adonis to work out concrete plans.[146] Peter Hyman recollects Blair telling his close advisers at this time, reflecting back on the first term, 'We did the symbolic and easy things, like the minimum wage. Now we are on to the really hard stuff.'[147] Said one of Blair's aides in 2007, 'It was only at the beginning of the second term that he really identified what it was he wanted to do.'[148] Blair himself would say, 'There's an irony that everyone said we hit the ground running in 1997, but we'd been slow in 2001.'[149] In Blair's mind the exact reverse was the case. 'We did the eye-catching stuff in 1997 based on pre-worked out plans, but in terms of actually doing the real work, that's only beginning now.'[150]

The Queen's Speech delivered on 20 June should have been a grand unveiling of an exciting, vibrant programme. Instead it revealed the paucity of thinking before the election and in the manifesto. In the debate that followed, Blair promised 'the most fundamental reform of public services for many years'.[151] Odd then that only two of the twenty bills announced in the speech – on education and welfare – visualised extending the role of the private sector in public services. Beneath the bold rhetoric, caution remained. One exception was law and order, where a raft of proposals to reform the criminal justice system, including jury trial, was included. But there could be no disguising it: it was a tepid

Queen's Speech. 'The country stands at Blair's feet,' Hugo Young wrote. 'There is no rival power. We're about to witness a regime that stands alone, unencumbered by any obstacle – but also unable to avail itself of the alibis or absolutions that might excuse its failure.'[152] He had just won an enormous and unprecedented second term majority, the Opposition was weak, the economy strong, his command of the party unquestioned. He knew he could do much better.

Blair was determined to step up the drive before the summer. Much of the hard work he knew would be done out in the Whitehall departments, in particular by his four 'big hitters' in the key departments: Blunkett, Milburn, Byers and Morris. So in July he invited all four to dinner in the flat at Number 10 where he told them, 'You guys are going to stay in these departments for the rest of this Parliament. You've got that assurance because I want you to be there. No, you're not going to get reshuffled, because you've got to focus on what you're going to achieve at the end of the four years.'[153] Another recalled, 'I think Tony at that point certainly saw us all doing the full term.'[154] They all seemed to share the same outlook. Blair admired Blunkett the most personally, not the least for achieving so much despite his blindness. He was close to both Milburn and Byers politically and personally. 'He felt comfortable talking to us both, whether about football or whatever, or just blowing off steam,' said Byers.[155] Morris was never close, personally or politically, but he admired the way that she had moved from teaching to becoming a senior minister. Together, these four were his stars, and on their prowess and capabilities would rest not only the success of his domestic policy in the second term, but more widely his whole premiership.

Blair sounded the battle cry at the Royal Free Hospital in north London on 15 July, in his most important speech between the election and the conference season. In a deliberate challenge to his critics in the unions and on the left of the party, he said he would not back down from his 'crusade' to reform public services, including an expanded role for the private sector, regardless of the opposition. He labelled it a 'great progressive cause. It is reform or bust.' To plan ahead for the autumn, Blair wanted to bring his team together before they all went away. An 'away day' at Chequers was thus convened on 25 July. The meeting was far from conclusive. Campbell opened the presentations, pointing to 'ten policy and communications questions' which needed urgent attention.[156] Adonis followed on the direction of policy, warning presciently that 'a lot of the big questions were still being ducked' and that only the foundations had been laid.[157] Heywood highlighted the

major spending issues ahead, while Barber explained how the Delivery
Unit would operate. In the discussion that followed, there was a growing
sense that, as Campbell recorded, there was 'not a strong enough forward
narrative' on investment and reform.[158] 'No decisions on precise
measures, but reiteration of the need for proper "audit" of public
services and policies to match, including more choice, use of
private/voluntary sectors, etc.,' was the less than euphoric record of one
present.[159] Robert Hill recalls Blair saying that 'he had started off
believing in 1997 that "standards not structures" were important
(particularly in education), but he had begun to believe that in fact the
very opposite was the case'.[160] Blair was in bullish form, dismissing
anyone who urged caution on reform: 'When someone suggested
"preference" might be an easier sell to the unions and the party, he
replied simply: "Choice is choice."'[161] At one point in the discussions
Blair added: 'It's going to be hell for a large part of the time we're doing
this . . . I don't see any point in being Prime Minister unless we take
risks.'[162]

Contemporary records reveal Blair's evolving thinking after the
election. In mid-June, he had written to Number 10's new health
specialist Simon Stevens to say 'I need a note now' on how to increase
the role of the private sector in health. On 3 July, he took part in a no-
holds-barred talk about using incentives to kick-start the modernisation
of the NHS, and said he was attracted to the use of incentives to increase
the quality of health care and to see the customer driving progress
throughout the NHS.[163] He had come to realise that it had been a
mistake after 1997 to dismantle some of the Conservatives' reforms
which devolved power away from government, notably GP fund-holders
and 'grant-maintained' schools. But Blair was still a long way from
deciding how he wanted to move ahead.

By the end of July, Blair was described as 'exhausted, absolutely
knackered. As July went on, we just had to wait for him to get to the
holiday.'[164] Before going away he wrote to key figures in the Policy
Directorate asking for holiday reading, including literature on how to
increase consumer choice across all of health care.[165] That August he
spent much time at Chequers, and was away from 3 August with the
family in Mexico and later in Cornwall. His staff at Number 10 anxiously
watched the weather reports, praying for good weather. 'You realised that
the weather must be good if he didn't phone,' said Morgan.[166] He liked
to read political biography: the bookshelves at Chequers are lined with
biographies which he has read, mostly on holiday. He did not enjoy
novels. In the latter part of the holiday, he worked on his hand-written

notes, which focused on the reform agenda, with a recurring theme tying increases in spending to reform and modernisation.[167]

By late August, it became clear that insufficient progress on his policy agenda was being made. Heywood, Barber and Adonis realised separately that unless the reform agenda for the second term was constructed imminently, 'we could wave goodbye to the second term as a reform period'.[168] One aide told Blair: 'You've only got two years of really serious legislative and political authority in a cycle before you have to start planning for the following General Election.'[169] Blair was not the only one to feel that the three months since the election had not been best used. 'We realised that we risked losing the second term. It was a colossal task to do it all in the limited time we had.'[170] Blair himself was fretting that the politics were not working out. The case for reform, he worried, was not being well enough made to the party, and the agenda could be derailed in the autumn before it had even fully coalesced. One solution he seized upon was asking Morgan to come back full-time into Number 10 to manage the 'politics'.[171]

With so much still up in the air, and the conference season fast approaching, Blair was impatient to settle on the way ahead. Another 'away day' was convened at Chequers on Thursday 6 September, with the same cast as for 25 July but with Charles Clarke in his new capacity as Party Chairman. The focus was on Blair's own paper written in August on 'The Second Term Mission'. He defined the mission as 'harnessing US economic dynamism and enterprise with European solidarity, while avoiding the inequity of the American system and the sclerosis of the present European social model'. The day started with discussion of a paper written by Mulgan on 'choice': by this time, 'choice and diversity' was emerging as the fourth key principle – alongside decentralisation, flexibility and uniform high standards which he had first outlined in his Gravesend speech. Adonis then set out a catalogue of specific policies to take forward this new agenda: he also stressed to Blair that time was short, and he had to decide many practical reform issues by Christmas 'if the second term is really to be about reform'.[172]

By early September the planning had moved on, but not by enough. 'Implicitly and explicitly in those Chequers meetings in July and September, we were thinking about where the Prime Minister was going in the conference season and beyond,' said Barber.[173] The chapter headings had been identified, but still not the detail nor the timetable. Blair nevertheless was in fighting mood as he contemplated his major speech to the TUC's annual conference in Brighton on 11 September. Union leaders had been planning their response. John Edmonds, leader of the GMB, had already pledged to cut £1,000,000 from future Labour contributions. Hewitt, the Trade and Industry Secretary, had been greeted with a stony silence when she had spoken to the conference. Edmonds had told the BBC on the morning of Blair's speech that it was his last chance to 'step back from the brink' of conflict with the unions over any increased private involvement in the public sector. Dave Prentice of UNISON was threatening strikes throughout the NHS. The talk was of a new generation of union leader taking over from those who had fallen in so readily with Blair from 1994 to 2001. To deflect the storm, the media that morning had been briefed that Blair was going to make a strong pro-Euro message, reiterating his enthusiasm to join the single currency if 'the economic conditions were met'. This was feeble: no hard thinking had yet taken place in Number 10 on the Euro in the second term. It was playing at policy.

Blair arrived in Brighton by train that morning, and was driven by police escort to the Grand Hotel to put the finishing touches to his speech. He took the lift to the Fitzherbert Suite on the seventh floor and laid out his papers in the bedroom area up the short flight of stairs. He pondered on his defiant if still inchoate message. As he mused on his words, thinking to himself they should have been much further forward on policy than this now that the conference season had begun, he tugged nervously at his cuffs.

3

Riding Two Horses

September 2001–May 2002

September 11th changed everything. In the immediate term, it delayed Blair's battle with the unions over public service reform. It altered the way that he saw the world, and led directly to the war in Afghanistan and, eventually, to the war in Iraq. Both wars took Blair's attention away from what he had identified as his crucial task, shaping and entrenching his domestic agenda in the vital first two years of the new government. 'Just getting meetings into his diary for domestic policy was a great struggle after 9/11,' one Number 10 aide recalled. 'He was very distracted by the international scene.'[1] This period from September 2001 to May 2002 saw Blair riding two horses: forging a radical agenda at home and making some of the most serious decisions over war taken by any Prime Minister since 1945. He had already taken Britain into wars and worked on domestic reform, but never on this scale. He was walking into virgin territory.

Bonding With Bush: 12 September–20 September 2001

Shortly after Blair awoke on 12 September, he was briefed on the night's events. No further terrorist activity in the US. No retaliation by the Bush administration. London not attacked. While Britain slept, Bush had spoken again to the American people, at 8:30 P.M. on Tuesday evening, EST, 1:30 A.M. Wednesday UK time. Back in the Oval Office, the

President was surer of himself. One line from his speech stood out: 'We will make no distinction between the terrorists who committed these acts and those who harbour them.' Blair realised at once that Bush was broadening out American military ambitions.

Blair's relationship with the American President was less than seven months old. The two had first met at Camp David on 23 February, 2001 just over a month after Bush's inauguration. Given Blair's very close relationship with the previous incumbent, Bill Clinton, how would the Bush camp react to the British Prime Minister? Well before Bush's election, British Ambassador Sir Christopher Meyer had worked diligently to cultivate his closest advisers. 'Our most significant bilateral relationship has always been with Britain,' he was told by the new National Security Advisor Condoleezza Rice. 'We must ensure it gets off to a good start.'[2] 'The President was mildly amused by the suggestion that Blair's relationship with Clinton might come into play,' recalled Karl Rove, 'that people would see him as that small-minded. Both men came at the relationship with a clear understanding of the special relationship and both approached it with no pre-conditions.'[3] At their shared press conference at the conclusion of their first Camp David meeting Bush seemed unable to name anything concrete they had in common except Colgate toothpaste, but behind the scenes a bond had been forged. Blair slipped easily into the informal atmosphere that Bush likes. They showed 'great honesty and straightforwardness with each other', recalled Rice; neither was 'overly cautious about how one was perceiving the other'.[4] The British verdict on the visit was positive: 'TB clearly felt yesterday went well,' Campbell noted in his diary. Bush and Blair 'had a couple of fairly long conversations alone and [Blair] said he found him clear and straightforward'.[5] In July Bush stayed the night at Chequers en route to the Genoa G8 and, through his public reference to the 'special relationship', signalled his growing closeness to Blair. The two stayed in regular touch over the summer. 'On the eve of 9/11,' recalled one senior British diplomat, 'the relationship between the President and Prime Minister was warmer than anyone would have imagined from before the 2000 presidential election.'[6]

No one had anticipated how quickly the new relationship would be tested. In the aftermath of 9/11, it yielded dividends. On September 12, Blair's day began with an 8 A.M. COBRA meeting. The latest domestic security measures were discussed, but Blair's principal concern was still 'the Americans, and how we should handle them'.[7] He remained fearful that Bush would lash out at Iraq, without establishing any real link to the recent attacks. He believed that the US needed time to reflect over who was responsible and target any response accordingly.[8] Speaking with Bush remained paramount to Blair, but he knew that to score maximum credit, and offer something Bush's advisors might not, he needed to be in command of his ground. Blair understood that, to influence world events, he had to impress his views upon the President. Hence his frustration that others might establish themselves in Bush's mind before he got to him. The British secret state had not been idle since the attacks. Lights had burned long into the night at the headquarters of MI6 at Vauxhall Cross and in the JIC offices housed in a secure area on the second floor of the Cabinet Office in Whitehall. Blair now pored over the fruit of these labours: detailed intelligence briefings on al-Qaeda, the Taliban and Afghanistan. For all their tough work 'he still didn't feel it inside himself, he just wasn't sure of his ground', recalled Wilson.[9] A briefing, planned for forty-five minutes but in the end lasting two hours, was thus convened mid-morning in the Cabinet Room. Whitehall's best brains from the intelligence services, the FCO and Ministry of Defence (MoD), drilled the Prime Minister. He was shown satellite and aerial photographs of Afghanistan. 'He listened and then fired sharp questions at those briefing him. He locked away the information as soon as he was sure of it. He was terrific.'[10] Blair's mind was clear. 'We'll just have to do something about Afghanistan, won't we?' he said at the end.[11] 'I felt that nobody else saw it politically as quickly as Tony Blair,' said one intelligence chief. 'The fact that here we had a basket-case of a regime, supporting a terrorist conspiracy, started with Tony Blair. He was the one who saw it.'[12] Campbell noted in his diary, 'TB was sure we would need to do a lot more than just take out OBL [Osama bin Laden].'[13]

The meeting over, Blair was now ready for his all-important phone call with the President, which came through at 12.30 P.M., 7.30 A.M. Washington time. Blair was relieved: he was the first foreign leader Bush called. The official listening in on the conversation recalls that 'Blair had woven everything that he had picked up that morning into his advice to Bush and the way to handle him. Indeed, he had mastered it to the point that he could spiel out information on al-Qaeda as if he was one of the world's great experts.'[14] All traces of his previous day's frustration and irritation at Bush's 'disappearance' had evaporated. He began by expressing outrage at what had happened and relief that the President was safe, and moved on to the US response. Declaring (despite himself) that he had 'no concerns' that the US might act precipitously or disproportionately, he still made the perils of such a course abundantly clear. Bush was calm: 'I know what I've got to do,' he told Blair. 'I'm not a good mourner. I'm a weeper. I'll weep with the country but then act, but I don't just want to hit cruise missiles into the sand.'[15] They agreed to move swiftly to build support in NATO and the UN, capitalising on the outpouring of sympathy across the globe. Blair was strongly multilateralist, and sounded him out on holding a special G8 to forge a united front against terrorism; Bush, tellingly, did not seem keen. Blair raised the importance of distinguishing between 'rapid' (i.e., knee-jerk) and 'effective' action, the latter requiring proper preparation and planning. Bush reminded Blair that he had pledged to make no distinction between the terrorists and those who harboured them, and stressed it would be a long haul, a 'mission for a presidency'.[16] With these words, Bush heralded the war on terrorism.

Blair promised to send Bush a follow-up note collating his thoughts.[17] Blair sat down with his fountain pen and drafted some closely argued paragraphs. When typed, his words became a five-side memorandum, sent to the White House via secure fax for Bush's personal perusal. The style was typical Blair: bullet points and staccato sentences, as opposed to the polished, fluent (if anodyne) prose preferred by officials. Blair's memos were 'depressingly well written,' recalled Dan Fried, the NSC's European Director: 'You'd look at them and say "Goddammit! How does he do it?"' 'His memo is a lot better than yours,' Bush would tease his staff, 'that's why I listen to him.'[18]

But did Bush listen? Blair's core argument was that Bush should prepare for a measured response, bolstered by international support, focusing expressly on hitting al-Qaeda. They had 'to prove to the bar of public opinion who is responsible', Blair insisted; and argued even then that a 'dossier' of information should be released, proving beyond doubt Bin Laden's complicity.[19] Blair argued that the Taliban regime in Afghanistan sheltering al-Qaeda be given an ultimatum: hand over Bin Laden and his senior associates, shut down terrorist training camps and let in international inspectors, or face attack. 'Blair saw it as a two-step process,' said one aide, 'and if the Taliban refused to hand over Bin Laden, Blair was ready to deal with them militarily.'[20] To prepare for that eventuality, improved relations with Afghanistan's neighbours – particularly Pakistan and Iran – would be essential; Blair's military advisers had told him that without their support, an attack on the land-locked Afghanistan would be impossible. Critically, Blair argued that restarting the Middle East peace process (MEPP) should be a priority, to build Arab support for the war on terrorism. Finally, Blair's note stressed that the cancer was not confined to Afghanistan, nor indeed al-Qaeda. They would have to act against all who financed, supported or sponsored terrorism, wherever they were in the world.[21]

Blair's mood that afternoon lifted now that he had said his piece.[22] Bush's advisers began to detect evidence of a 'deeper emotional bond' between the two men: 'Blair understood quicker than anybody else how profound this was and how serious,' said Fried.[23] Bush relayed to his staff that he told Blair 'that above all he wanted military action that would hurt the terrorists, not just make Americans feel better. He understood the need for planning and preparation but his patience had limits. "I want to get moving," he said.'[24] Within scarcely twenty-four hours of the attacks, Blair had sketched out his positions: pursue the terrorists to Afghanistan and beyond; conduct a wide-ranging campaign against terrorism; build an international coalition to advance this end; give unequivocal backing and support to the United States as the best way of exerting British influence on the world stage; and ensure material progress was made in the MEPP. These themes would come to dominate the last six and a half years of his premiership.

Blair spent the rest of 12 September taking stock and phoning other world leaders. The heads of MI5, MI6 and GCHQ, he decided, should be flown over to the US by the RAF to meet their counterparts the very next day. They returned overnight on 13/14 September, bringing with them a sorely missed David Manning as well as the stranded John Major.[25] The media was full of lurid stores about the atrocities that the new style of terrorist could inflict on Britain. Blair arranged with Robin Cook, in his new capacity as Leader of the Commons, for an emergency recall of Parliament that Friday, 14 September, and he worked on his opening statement with Campbell. He did not intend to pull his punches. 'Both Hilary Armstrong [Chief Whip] and Robert Hill [Political Secretary] warned him that the PLP may be a bit dodgy on this,' Campbell recorded. 'TB said, "Are they mad? Do we just let these people get away with killing thousands of people?"'[26] During the recall debate Blair told a rapt House of Commons that actions over the coming months might change the present world order. Nations harbouring or assisting terrorists would have to choose between them or the West. The risk of nuclear, biological or chemical (NBC) attacks from terrorist groups, he said, justified extending war to the 'rogue states' who protected them. Mindful of the concerns among some MPs and in the country at large, he praised US restraint to date. 'They did not lash out. They did not strike first and think afterwards.' The need for concerted international action on extradition was emphasised, and the proscription of terrorist groups and their funding. Foreign Secretary Straw turned up the rhetorical temperature: 'To turn the other cheek,' he said, 'would not appease the terrorists, but would lead to a still greater danger.' He drew comparisons with the disastrous attempts to appease Europe's rising dictators during the 1930s. Bar a few discordant voices, the Commons was united behind the Prime Minister.[27]

A second phone call to Bush was made that Friday. Blair's enduring worry, noted Campbell, 'was that GWB would turn inwards'.[28] The President thanked Blair for his memo, which 'mirrored' his own views. Blair pressed the need to win over world opinion by presenting clear evidence linking the 9/11 attacks to al-Qaeda, whose complicity was clearly confirmed by the intelligence. The immediate focus should be on al-Qaeda bases in Afghanistan, though he believed they would have to pursue the terrorists far beyond the shores of that country. Bush again agreed, and spoke of an analogy of a series of circles emanating from a pebble dropped into water: 'We focus on the first circle,' Bush said, 'then expand to the next circle.' Iraq was not explicitly mentioned as the 'second circle'.[29] Bush's cool attitude towards building global support disturbed Blair, noted Campbell. 'TB was quite troubled afterwards, said we had to think of a way of getting him to the US for a face-to-face meeting. He said he needed to see him in a room, and look in his eyes.'[30] Blair instructed Manning to keep on Rice's tail to ensure the Americans 'did nothing too rash'.[31]

The weekend of 15/16 September gave Blair time to take stock. He continued to worry about unilateral, ill-considered US retaliation. After Chirac, who did not impress Washington, Blair was the longest-serving leader of all the West's major powers. His standing on the world stage had been further bolstered by his words during the week, which had come over, in contrast to Bush, as assured and statesmanlike. He wanted to use his leverage to persuade Bush to focus on Bin Laden and Afghanistan, rather than Iraq.

The possibility of going after Iraq first was in fact being discussed by the administration, unknown to him, that very weekend. Donald Rumsfeld, Secretary of Defense, suggested here was 'an opportunity' to attack Iraq, a view advocated vociferously by his deputy, Paul Wolfowitz. Most of Bush's advisers begged to differ. After exhaustive debate at Camp David that Saturday, Bush's inner circle were united against an attack on Iraq, with the exception of Rumsfeld, who abstained.[32] A thousand miles to the south Air Chief Marshal Jock Stirrup, the senior British military adviser seconded to CENTCOM, the US military HQ in Tampa, Florida, made it clear to General Tommy Franks, who would become the US Commander for the war in Afghanistan, that 'we are completely alongside you for al-Qaeda and Afghanistan, but we have no appetite for Iraq'. 'Iraq is completely off our radar screen,' he was told.[33]

How much influence did Blair have in shaping American thinking? 'There was not much of a role for Blair in helping to shape the American response to the attacks of 9/11, to be honest,' said a senior Bush administration official. 'By the end of that first weekend at Camp David, we knew what we were going to do.'[34] Where Blair's advice mattered was on the margins: Bush phoned Putin early on at Blair's suggestion, and he also phoned Ariel Sharon in Israel, again following Blair's prompting, about restarting the MEPP. But to the administration this was left-field. British intelligence helped out: 'With Britain's colonial heritage, it had huge insights into Pakistan and India that were very helpful to us with the Taliban. It made a big difference,' said Richard Armitage, Colin Powell's deputy at the State Department.[35] Where Blair's advocacy may have counted was in pushing the administration towards an international coalition. Rumsfeld and Cheney questioned the need for a wide military coalition, which they feared would tie their hands.[36] 'For a few days after 9/11 it wasn't clear that Washington was going to admit of any close friendships or co-operative efforts, even that of our closest partner,' said a State Department official.[37] But Colin Powell saw the opportunity to use Blair's support to broaden the military alliance. 'Blair was saying to us, don't rush. Make it a global coalition. It helped Powell win the argument,' said Armitage.[38] Bush observed carefully Blair's unfailing public support. Like his father, he valued loyalty, and Blair had been unquestionably loyal. Perhaps he could be useful.

Over the weekend of 15/16 September, the White House passed on an invitation from Bush for Blair to visit Washington that coming Thursday. The President was to deliver an address to a joint session of Congress and wanted Blair to attend as honoured guest.[39] Here was Blair's opportunity to meet with Bush 'face-to-face'. Not everyone in Number 10 was thrilled at this prospect. Campbell worried that the trip 'would play into the whole poodle thing' and felt that they should only accept if Blair also could speak.[40] But the suggestion that Bush would share the limelight in front of his own Congress just a few days after his country had been attacked was never a realistic, or indeed reasonable, proposition. Campbell called Meyer. 'Chris, does he have to do it? Couldn't he slip away before the speech?' 'It won't go down at all well if he says no,' Meyer warned, 'it's a moment in history.'[41] The 'poodle problem' continued to weigh on Campbell's mind, but Blair agreed to make the trip.

Before he left London, Blair took the temperature of fellow world leaders. On Sunday 16 September he had lunch with Italy's Silvio Berlusconi. 'He was reasonably supportive on the idea of military action "provided not too many people die",' Campbell recorded in his diary.

'TB said there was no such thing as a painless war.'[42] With Bush sounding increasingly like a trigger-happy cowboy (the US wanted Bin Laden 'dead or alive' he proclaimed on 17 September), the need for Blair to act as Bush's explainer was all too obvious. Much of the Monday and Tuesday, he spent on the phone, including a call to President Jiang Zemin of China, as well as discussing preparations for the British contribution to military action. On Wednesday, 19 September, Blair flew with Manning to Berlin, where he had dinner with Schröder in the new Chancellery building. The German Chancellor told them he was sympathetic to action in Afghanistan, but with limited military forces at his disposal, and the anti-war Green party in his ruling coalition, he had to restrict his contribution to political, not military, support (though German troops did later serve as peacekeepers). Later that Wednesday evening, Blair flew to Paris and spent the night at the British Embassy, bought from Napoleon's sister in 1814 by the Duke of Wellington.

Thursday 20 September was to be one of the longest and most emotional days in Blair's premiership. It began with breakfast at the Elysée with Chirac who had just flown back from meeting Bush in Washington. Blair was 'struck by Chirac's determination to stick with Bush' he told one official, 'provided – and Blair himself believed this essential – that the response is tough but targeted and moderate Arabs are kept on side'.[43] At 10:30 A.M. Blair's flight left Charles de Gaulle airport, en route to New York. Half an hour into the flight, Blair placed a call to President Mohamed Khatami of Iran whose support would be very helpful for a war in Afghanistan. This was the first time a British Prime Minister had spoken to the leader of Iran since the Shah's overthrow in 1979. Past differences were laid aside in their new common interest: Iran too disliked the Taliban regime because it had flooded its borders with refugees. In their fifteen-minute conversation, Blair thanked him for his support and stressed his emerging theme – that this was not a struggle between Islam and the West, but between civilisation and terror. Blair was proud of his breakthrough and later surprised Bush with this news.[44] After the call, four military and MI6 personnel, all authorities on al-Qaeda, were called up to join Blair in the screened-off first-class cabin at the front of the plane, and briefed him on their current knowledge of Bin Laden's likely whereabouts and strategies for his capture.[45] Blair was keen to court the US militarily as well as diplomatically: this was one of several lengthy sessions he held with British military planners to ensure he was fully inside the latest thinking in this area.[46]

The plane touched down at New York's JFK airport in the early afternoon, local time. The roads into the city were gridlocked, as they had often been since the attacks. The service at Manhattan's St Thomas's Church in memory of the British victims, the prime purpose of the New York stopover, had to be delayed. During the service Blair read a passage from Thornton Wilder's *The Bridge of San Luis Rey*, which described love as 'the only survival, the only meaning'. Meyer relayed a message from the Queen, ending with the line, 'Grief is the price we pay for love', words that are now carved into the stonework of the church.[47] Blair also spoke some of his own words: 'Nine days on, there is still shock and disbelief. There is anger, there is fear, but there is also, throughout the world, a profound sense of solidarity, there is courage, there is a surging of the human spirit.'[48] In the congregation were the families of the British dead, as well as Kofi Annan and Bill Clinton. Blair was very visibly moved – he usually masters his emotion in public – but the harrowing meetings he had with relatives were almost too much for him. Already behind schedule, he lingered – offering crumbs of comfort to those who were grieving.[49]

Further delays back to JFK meant Blair's party touched down badly behind schedule at Andrews Air Force base at 4:45 P.M. A convoy of black Lincoln limousines carried them on the short journey to Washington. Arriving at the White House too late for their planned meeting, Blair and his aides were ushered straight into the Blue Room for drinks.[50] Bush took Blair to one side, and they spoke by the window, looking out onto the South Lawn in the evening light. Blair looked into his eyes: but it was far from the face-to-face meeting he envisaged. Bush reassured Blair that 'the job in hand is al-Qaeda and the Taliban. Iraq we keep for another day.'[51] Blair did not take this to mean Iraq would necessarily be invaded 'another day', but merely that the administration's initial focus was firmly on Afghanistan. Blair stressed the need for a measured response.[52] It was 'funny', Jonathan Powell noted later, that 'Thatcher had gone to see Bush Senior to say, "This is no time to wobble" while TB was visiting Bush junior – "This *is* a time to wobble"', referring to when she went with his brother Charles, her foreign policy private secretary, to gird Bush's father to be resolute after Saddam invaded Kuwait in 1990.[53] Bush shared with Blair what he would tell the Joint Session of Congress later that evening, including the ringing phrase: 'Either you are with us or you are with the terrorists.' Blair was pleased to be given the preview. Not that he was being asked for comments: the American press corps had already been told what the President would say.[54]

An early dinner followed. Over scallops, veal and salad the Americans filled in the details of their joint CIA–military attack plans, information-giving rather than an invitation to debate strategy and tactics. Bush dilated on the 'full force of the US military with bombers coming from all directions'.[55] After the ultimatum he would go for the Taliban: 'The country was run by a bunch of nuts and we had to get a new government in there.'[56] The British party were struck by the sang-froid Bush displayed throughout, just hours away from delivering the most important speech of his life. Meyer felt himself getting nervous on the President's behalf.[57] Bush was determined to make Blair feel special and honoured, so he invited him up to the private White House residence after dinner. In the lift on the way up, Blair asked him directly if he felt apprehensive about the speech. Bush's reply was: 'Well, actually I'm not that nervous about it because I know what I want to say, and I know what I am saying is right.'[58] Blair travelled in the President's car – another special honour – down Pennsylvania Avenue to Capitol Hill. As guest of honour for Bush's speech, Blair took his seat in the 'heroes' gallery next to the First Lady, Laura Bush. Traditionally, during presidential addresses to Congress, these seats are occupied by 'all-American heroes': those who 'inspire others to greatness and embody the American dream'. Today, the British Prime Minister assumed the mantle. In a speech punctuated by thirty-one standing ovations, Bush singled out Blair: 'I'm so honoured the British Prime Minister has crossed the ocean to show his unity with America.' And then, in his Texan drawl, 'Thank you for comin', friend.' The Congressmen and Senators sprang to their feet as Blair, clearly moved and a little uncomfortable, acknowledged their applause.

Why had Blair been invited to Washington? It was clearly not to be briefed by him, or to seek his approval. But the symbolism was important. 'The symbol of the Prime Minister of Great Britain coming here for a matter of hours in order to be at the speech was huge,' recalled Karl Rove, Bush's long-time confidant and chief strategist. 'I'm not sure that the ordinary Brit understands how absolutely powerful that was for the American people.'[59] The Bush administration also wanted to bind Blair into their project. They believed that they would have Blair's support wherever the war on terrorism would lead. In the months that followed he gave them little reason for doubting it.

Preparing the World for War: September–October

Blair was a man possessed. While the US worked rapidly to finalise its attack plans on Afghanistan, the extent of international support had still to be finalised. This Blair saw as his role: 'He believed that every country would have to take a stand,' recalled Manning.[60] In the eight weeks after 9/11, he undertook thirty-one flights covering 40,000 miles and held fifty-four meetings with foreign leaders.[61] 'He found extraordinary long-distance energy for a man who normally had the stamina of a sprinter,' said one official.[62] In this marathon he was helped by the wide network of contacts he had built up since taking office: 'He was incredibly good at getting to know foreign leaders and making a positive impression on them.'[63] At a time when many were dazed and cautious, Blair 'developed a new certainty about his own role, which was really quite remarkable', recalled Wilson. 'He gave out a sense of having truly found himself.'[64] Sally Morgan was struck by the change that came over him: 'It was as if a rod had been inserted into his spine.'[65] What exactly was Blair so sure about? That terrorism, backed up by the threat of WMD, was the major threat the West faced; that a tough military response was the way to deal with it; that he himself possessed unique persuasive powers to bringing the international community behind US plans and that he was engaged in a clear-cut moral struggle in which the forces of good were pitted against evil.

His very certainty disinclined him from consulting beyond a circle of trusted aides and colleagues – principally Powell, Manning, Campbell, Morgan, Straw and Wilson, and the intelligence chiefs Scarlett, Richards, Lander and Dearlove. They met regularly. 'I must have been to Number 10 every day for the first three weeks after 9/11,' recalled Lander.[66] Blair asked Anji Hunter, due to leave imminently for a post at BP, to stay on and help him with his meetings with world leaders. Above all it was her emotional support he wanted on his epic journey. 'It was an incredible time to be at Number 10,' Hunter felt. 'There was a real sense of history about what we were doing.'[67] Cabinet met rarely: on 13 September and then again on 26 September. It was clear, as Campbell noted in his diary following the first session, that 'TB was very much in charge'.[68]

Just three weeks after 9/11, Blair was back in Brighton speaking on the second day of the Labour party conference. This time, nothing intervened to prevent the speech, though he delivered a very different text from the one he had been planning over the summer. More than any other conference speech except his last, it was the fruit of his own words and thinking: 'We often had differences over what the key conference theme was going to be,' said Morgan. 'Not this time. This speech will write itself. I know what I have to say,' he announced.[69] Lawrence Freedman, who contributed to Blair's defence speeches, felt it was 'pure milk of Blair. He articulated the basis for the war on terror, which Bush wasn't very good at. Blair articulated the vision. It was old-fashioned

Labour internationalism with attitude.'[70] Blair himself rated it as one of the speeches of which he was most proud.[71]

The speech presented Blair's personal credo, a vision of a better, more moral world. It was a call to arms. 'We were with you at the first,' he reminded the American people. 'We will stay with you to the last.' Al-Qaeda, not Islam, he stressed, was the enemy: 'There is no compromise possible with such people, no meeting of minds . . . Just a choice: defeat it or be defeated by it . . . I say to the Taliban: surrender the terrorists or surrender power.' This section of the speech caused some consternation in Washington when briefed in advance to the White House. Blair left no doubt that military action would follow should the ultimatum be ignored: 'They felt it was too forward, too clear re: what we intended to hit, with reference to camps and military installations.'[72] But at the centre of the speech stood Blair's ethical concerns. Nations had a 'moral duty' not to stand aside in global conflicts. Intervention would have stopped the slaughter, he said, in Rwanda, where one million had been killed in 1994, and told delegates he was glad that he had acted to limit ethnic cleansing in Kosovo in 1999. Afghanistan had over four million refugees, ousted by the Taliban, needing food and shelter, and action was a moral imperative. Here was an attempt to develop the central theme of Blair's Chicago speech of April 1999 – the doctrine of the international community – providing a justification for enlightened intervention in the affairs of other sovereign nation states. 'He liked to think that the Chicago speech had been important in anticipating the catastrophe of 9/11. He would say that it was prescient,' said one aide.[73] Blair widened out his vision to those subjects closest to him. He made particular play of wanting to help Africa: 'The state of Africa is a scar on the conscience of the world. But if the world as a community focused on it, we could heal it. And if we don't, it will become deeper and angrier.' The need for progress in the MEPP was also targeted. He pledged to tackle the 'slums of Gaza', by easing the Israeli–Palestinian conflict. 'The starving, the wretched, the dispossessed, the ignorant, they are our causes too,' he said with deep feeling. Global warming was a further wrong to be addressed. Blair was talking from his heart. His conclusion referred directly to an idea Jonathan Powell had advanced, that the post-Cold War, post-9/11 world would offer new dangers, but also new opportunities: 'This is a moment to seize. The kaleidoscope had been shaken. The pieces are in flux. Soon they will settle again. Before they do, let us re-order the world around us.'[74]

Blair's speech earned him much praise: 'shows bulldog spirit', roared the *New York Post*[75]; 'the most statesmanlike and mature he has delivered in seven years', beamed the *Independent*.[76] But soon the cynics surfaced, with the word 'hubris' on their lips: 'Missionary Tony will cleanse the planet of disease, poverty and conflict. The sun will never set on a Holy British Empire. The tough and tender third way will rule from Kinshasa to Kabul,' wrote Andrew Rawnsley in the *Observer*.[77] Blair had no ear for such criticism. He was confident of what he was saying, and glad he had a chance to articulate the three themes – Africa, peace in the Middle East and climate change – which were to be a leitmotif of his remaining years in power.

When the applause, and sneers, died away, Blair returned to immediate military and diplomatic concerns. 'From that period on, he just started to work ferociously,' Morgan recalled.[78] British planning for Afghanistan had begun shortly after his return from his visit to Washington in September: 'When he returned, we geared up for the offensive,' said the then Chief of Defence Staff, Michael Boyce. 'The submarine effort (with Tomahawk missiles) was our contribution in the initial stage. I had to switch some of our subs from the Atlantic to south of Pakistan. We moved pretty quickly – within two or three weeks.' Blair received briefings on military options and accepted the military's recommendations, and he was 'bullish' about what needed to be done. Air base rights close to Afghanistan as a launch pad for troops and planes had to be obtained. 'We were able to persuade Pakistan to allow us to base some of our support planes there, and the US persuaded Uzbekistan.'[79] Blair turned his attention also to the public case against al-Qaeda and the Taliban. On 4 October, he published – as he had advocated to Bush on 12 September – a document entitled 'Responsibility for the Terrorist Atrocities in the United States'. Prepared by Scarlett and the JIC, it laid out evidence that al-Qaeda had carried out the 9/11 attacks, that they were helped by the Taliban regime in Afghanistan, and that British targets were under threat from terrorists.[80] Blair never succeeded in generating American enthusiasm for the dossier, but he remained convinced that the public deserved to have the facts brought before them. Blair sought to build support also for tough domestic anti-terrorist measures that were being frantically drafted in Whitehall. Fears of nuclear or chemical attacks by al-Qaeda on mainland Britain were high. 'Previously we had made all our precautions against an attack from the Provisional IRA. Now we had to switch to thinking about what al-Qaeda might do,' said a senior official.

A major upgrade of security took place at Number 10. Shortly after 9/11 Blair's staff had been gripped by an anthrax scare. Wilson recalled: 'I was told that the people who opened the mail for the Cabinet Office had encountered a package with white powder in it. They were understandably distressed, so I went to see them. "I am so sorry about all this, it's going to be all right," I said. "I'm sure it's not anthrax." But of course by doing this I'd exposed myself to the powder. I was admonished by the security people and told never, ever to do that again.'[81] One senior aide recalled: 'We were all given briefings about what to do and were told about the secret "alternative" Number 10.'[82] 'It took a long time before we could hear a plane and not ask "is that coming at us?"' recalled another Downing Street aide.[83]

Blair became intensely frustrated by his inability to do more to protect British citizens at large: 'We told him that there was a list of about ninety terrorism suspects who could be dangerous,' recalled one intelligence officer, 'and a list of twelve to twenty who could pose a serious threat. We debated whether we could bring them in but there were no legal grounds. The Prime Minister was totally paranoid that he had this list but legally could do nothing about it. He found it intolerable. And so we decided that we had to rush through legislation to take them into custody.'[84] The resulting Anti-Terrorism Bill, unveiled by Blunkett on 15 October, met with outcry from civil liberties groups. It was Blair's first taste of how responding to the post-9/11 world would drive him headlong into conflict with the liberal left.

Blair was itching to win support beyond the shores of the British Isles. He already agreed with Bush that he should go to see Putin 'to try and secure bases and then to Pakistan to try and get a proper fix on Musharraf'.[85] A visit to India was added after a personal intervention from Prime Minister Vajpayee, who insisted that Blair could not visit Pakistan without coming to India.[86] In the evening of Thursday, 4 October, Blair arrived in Russia and met with Putin. The two leaders had enjoyed a strong relationship ever since the Russian leader hosted Blair and Cherie in St Petersburg in March 2000, before he was formally elected President. Blair had already encouraged the Bush administration to treat the Russians as serious partners.[87] 'Blair was the first world leader to seize on Putin as a senior figure,' said one Number 10 aide, 'and the first to realise later he was no good.'[88]

Blair was driven straight to the Kremlin for talks. Putin asked him and Manning to have supper with him in his *dacha*, a thirty-minute drive from Red Square by high-speed motorcade. Halfway through the meal they broke off for a three-way telephone conversation with Bush. To Blair's surprise, Putin then took him for a midnight walk in the woods, part of the quaint Russian ritual, according to British Ambassador, Roderick Lyne.[89] An exhausted Blair arrived back at the ambassador's residence at about 2 A.M., where Powell and Campbell were waiting up, eager to hear what had happened. They heard that an effusive Putin had pledged not only to support the action in Afghanistan but to share his intelligence, and to offer former Soviet bases in Central Asia.[90] With Putin, however, there were always ulterior motives, but they could not have hoped for more.

The next leg of Blair's journey was physically the most dangerous: Islamabad, the Pakistani capital, to see President Pervez Musharraf. Blair had ignored advice from his security staff to avoid the visit, enraging a normally phlegmatic Cherie. 'Do you want to be a martyr or what?' she exploded at Campbell.[91] Blair spent part of the plane journey deep in thought. One aide recalled that Hunter and Blair would often sit in the cockpit, right up with the pilot. 'He seemed to like it there. I remember them looking down at the "Stans" [Uzbekistan, Kurdistan] as we crossed over. It seemed to be interminable as we came south from Russia down to Pakistan. "Look at it," Hunter said to him. "Isn't it extraordinary, inhospitable, rugged."'[92] A great spirit of closeness was forged between Blair's team – Powell, Manning, Hunter, Scarlett and Dearlove – during the trip. Dearlove emerged as the key newcomer with whom Blair bonded: one present described him as 'a fantastically comforting presence for the Prime Minister and the rest of us'.[93]

The old RAF VC-10, then on one of its last outings, made a very steep dive into the capital to avert the risk of missile attack. Blair became maudlin and, unusually for one normally so philosophical about personal danger, began to talk about death.[94] Safely on the ground, on 5 October, he met with Musharraf. Blair had prepared for the meeting with the help of Charles Guthrie, recently retired as Chief of the Defence Staff, who had known the Pakistani general since his time as a student at London's Royal College of Defence studies. At Blair's request Guthrie had flown out to visit Musharraf shortly after 9/11, to 'talk through with him the advantages and disadvantages of the courses of action he could follow'.[95] Blair now followed up where Guthrie had left off. 'We had everyone out of the room and just talked, the two of us,' Blair explained.[96] He was both surprised and delighted when the Pakistani leader agreed to abandon support for the Taliban, and to work actively to round up al-Qaeda members in his country. A triumph for Blair's diplomacy? Not entirely. Just two days after 9/11, Colin Powell had sent Musharraf a list of similar demands, requiring the Pakistani leader to re-orientate his pro-Taliban policy fundamentally. After Powell followed up with a tough phone call that same day, Musharraf agreed to comply.[97] Blair's visit, over two weeks later, served more to flesh out the details and pull the Pakistani leader further into the pro-US camp. After the stop-off in

Delhi, Blair headed home, drained but pleased by his reception in the three capitals.[98] Over the past month Blair had helped the UK forge a genuinely broad international coalition in support of action against Afghanistan, which would come to number some 68 nations. At lunchtime the next day, Sunday, 7 October, he received a call in his car from Bush. The first air attacks in Afghanistan, he was told, would begin that evening. A moment of 'the utmost gravity' had been reached, a sombre and tense Blair told the press. 'None of the leaders involved in the action wants war. None of our nations want it. We are peaceful people. But we know that sometimes to safeguard peace, we have to fight.'[99]

The Afghanistan Campaign: October—November

Just before 5:20 P.M. BST, the Afghanistan war opened with a barrage of cruise missiles, including some launched from the Royal Navy's nuclear submarines *Triumph* and *Trafalgar*, and repeated bombing runs from US Stealth bombers and B-52s.[100] The first ground incursion was made by American Special Forces, with a limited number of British Special Forces in support.[101] As Defence Secretary Hoon put it, 'We always accepted that this was the Americans' show.'[102] Blair chaired a small War Cabinet of seven throughout the war. 'We had daily meetings for a month. We'd be up half the night getting papers and information ready for it and he'd come down straight from the flat in shirt-sleeves. He was very impressive. Very clear. Very determined,'[103] recalled one attender. Blair was content to delegate operational military responsibility to Hoon and Boyce, working with his American counterpart, General Richard Myers.[104] His paramount concerns were trying to ensure the war was conducted speedily with minimal British loss of life, while maintaining domestic support and keeping the international coalition together.

None of these concerns could be taken as given. During October, media images of innocent Afghan victims, of refugees and anti-war riots in Pakistan supplanted the pictures of the collapsing Twin Towers. The simple moral verities of the early days after the attacks had clouded. Concerns were growing too about the government's anti-terrorism legislation. Was it too restrictive? On 30 October, polls showed a twelve-point drop in support for the war from 74 per cent to 62 per cent. Blair responded with a highly charged speech to the Welsh Assembly in Cardiff that same day: 'It is important that we never forget why we are doing this,' he declared. 'Never forget how we felt watching the planes fly into the Trade [Center] towers; never forget those answerphone messages; never forget how we felt imagining how mothers told children they were about to die . . . September 11 is no less appalling today than it was on September 11.'[105]

Reservations were also beginning to emerge in Whitehall about American war aims. Blair himself had spoken in public about widening the war on terrorism, but crucially only on the basis of evidence of terrorist complicity in 9/11. On 8 October, however, just one day into the conflict, Bush issued a statement saying the war in Afghanistan was merely the 'first phase' of a general war against terrorists. The 'sense being communicated by the US', Campbell wrote later, was 'that they were constantly trying to link Iraq into the equation. TB was keen to pull it back.'[106] The influence of Cheney and Rumsfeld and the 'neocons', such as Wolfowitz and the former Reagan aide, Richard Perle, began to be raised in London. These hawks were unilateralists who were as passionate about rooting out terrorism, as those of a similar mind had been in rooting out communism in an earlier generation. 'People like Wolfowitz and Perle were talking this incredible crap in the latter part of 2001,' said a senior FCO mandarin. 'They were already pushing for going straight on and doing Iraq.'[107] John Kerr, Permanent Secretary at the FCO, asserted that the legality of the Afghanistan war lay squarely in the undisputed right of self-defence. The carefully drafted British war aims had specified that the British quarrel was with al-Qaeda and its Taliban protectors, not with the Afghan people.[108] Disquiet began to grow in the FCO and elsewhere at how far British support for unbridled American power would extend.

Blair wanted to reassure Muslim opinion that the struggle was not with Islam but only with terrorists. On 10 October, armed with a copy of the Koran, which he was said to have studied in depth, he began a two-day visit to Oman and Egypt. His aim was to discuss with moderate Arab leaders how, in his own words, to 'capture some of the ground from the extremists who said they were talking on behalf of Islam, when no sensible Islamic scholar or cleric could possibly support such an interpretation of Islam permitting something such as the attack in New York'.[109] The tour began with a brief stopover in Geneva, to see the veteran President of the United Arab Emirates, Sheikh Zayed. 'They were completely on our side: they realised it was bad for them and they were keen to clearly disassociate themselves from what had happened,' recalled one present.[110] In Oman, Blair delivered a blunt message for consumption worldwide: 'No country will be attacked unless there is evidence'; aides emphasised that there was no evidence linking Iraq to the 9/11 attacks.[111] Blair became increasingly aware that an invasion of Iraq would shatter moderate Arab opinion. While dining with the Sultan of Oman, Blair received a call from Palestinian leader, Yasser Arafat, about kick-starting the MEPP.[112] The next day he headed to Cairo to see President Mubarak, who then spoke of 'our intensified international effort to combat terrorism following the despicable terrorist attacks against the United States', before he returned to London late on 12 October.[113] Blair's brief tour was punctuated by frequent interviews on Arab television stations, and was accompanied by a 'blizzard' of articles penned in Downing Street for Middle Eastern newspapers.[114] The importance of the tour, said Manning, was 'the cumulative effect of the Prime Minister meeting a number of Arab leaders. We were not looking for any particular change in policy. What we wanted to do was to make sure that the Arabs were ready to condemn the acts of terror, and they all did.'[115]

Blair had foreseen progress on the MEPP, leading to Israel living peacefully alongside a democratic, sovereign, Palestinian state, as a moral necessity, and the key to combating militant Islam. 'It was always core to him, even in opposition,' recalled a long serving aide. 'It was religious and moral. He has always been a friend of Israel, but equally he felt that the Palestinian situation was unfair.'[116] According to Sawers, 'He saw Israel/Palestine through the prism of Northern Ireland. He had a belief in his own powers of persuasion and bringing people together to establish a common end.'[117] He did not believe that the Israeli–Palestinian conflict 'was the cause of what al-Qaeda were doing, but it was an injustice that was making things worse'.[118] The post-9/11 world gave him a chance for real progress. What he had not anticipated was the uncompromising attitude of the Bush administration. Even before Bush was elected, Rice warned Meyer that he 'had no intention of becoming the Arab–Israeli "desk officer" like Clinton'.[119] Once in power, the administration seemed content to 'let it fester for a while, let the Israelis have their head', admitted Lawrence Wilkerson, later Colin Powell's Chief of Staff.[120] By distancing himself, some British diplomats believed that Bush failed to appreciate how close Clinton had come in his last few months to resolving the problem.[121] 'The Arab–Israeli issue was the most difficult, protracted issue between us and the Americans over the whole ten-year period of Blair's premiership,' said a senior FCO official.[122] Ken Adelman, who served on Rumsfeld's Defense Policy Board, encapsulated the thinking of his fellow travellers: 'I always thought that Blair's pleas for progress on the Middle East were a lot of "BS". It was nice listening to Blair talking about it. It was the kind of stuff you'd expect from a European leader. So you kept on saying, "Yeah, OK, OK, we have all the intention in the world," but the fact is the players weren't there, the timing wasn't there, the substance wasn't there. Tony Blair would respond, "Yes, but you have to create all those." It just wasn't going to happen.'[123]

Blair set off on 30 October for another foray into the Middle East on one of the least happy trips of his premiership. He began in Damascus, where a promising meeting with the youthful new Syrian leader Bashar al-Assad gave way to a disastrous joint press conference. Assad embarrassed Blair by defending terrorism against Israel and attacking the war in Afghanistan. 'It could have been worse,' Blair later joked with Campbell. 'He could have taken out a gun and shot me.'[124] Things did not improve in Riyadh or in Amman: neither Crown Prince Abdullah of Saudi Arabia nor King Abdullah of Jordan were prepared in public to endorse the bombing of Afghanistan. On the morning of 1 November Blair, in search of better luck, flew to Israel to see Ariel Sharon, elected Prime Minister earlier that year. Blair hoped for a sympathetic response on the peace process, but instead Israel adamantly declined to withdraw its troops from disputed territories to help restart peace talks. According to Campbell 'they really just wanted to whack the Palestinians the whole time.'[125] A helicopter journey to Gaza to meet Arafat proved no more encouraging.[126] 'By all accounts,' declared Simon Jenkins, 'his voyage to the Middle East was brave, miserable and fruitless.'[127] The visit to Gaza, though, made a deep impression on him: 'It brought home to him the scale of the deprivation and squalor the Palestinians lived in,' said Sawers, 'and the huge political task of trying to turn that around in the territories.'[128]

Criticism of Blair for his self-appointed role as peace-broker and America's fixer now began to be heard in the capitals of the EU. With the support of Chirac and Schröder, Blair had secured EU backing for the action in Afghanistan. But now he blundered. The French President was due to meet Bush on 6 November, the day before Blair was due to visit Washington himself, so he proposed that he and Chirac meet on 4 November to co-ordinate their message over dinner at Number 10. As Schröder had just returned from important talks with Putin in Moscow, Blair wanted him added to the party.[129] He had long seen the benefits of trilateralism, working in league with France and Germany. And if it couldn't work at a time of crisis like this, when could it? But he did not cater for intra-EU jealousies. First, Berlusconi found out about the meeting and invited himself.[130] Complaints from others forced Blair to widen his cosy guest-list to eight. To recover lost ground Blair proposed a European-wide response to terrorism and to explore ways to reinvigorate the peace process. But concerns over American military intentions dominated their conversation. Chirac delivered a Jeremiah-like warning of civilian casualties – 'a mosque will be bombed during Ramadan' – and the risk of a humanitarian catastrophe, which heightened the tension and foreboding.[131] Blair suggested he would represent their concerns when he saw Bush three days later. This proposal did not slide down as easily as the fine Number 10 wine. His very role as 'envoy' of the EU to America was in question. Blair did not hold the EU presidency and nor was Britain the temporary chair of the UN Security Council. None was angrier at his presumption than Romano Prodi, the EU Commission President, a man for whom Blair's disdain was obvious.[132]

By early November Blair was growing anxious over the course of the Afghanistan campaign. Fought largely by Afghan resistance groups, under the umbrella of the Northern Alliance, it was essentially a surrogate war, 'all about Special Forces, intelligence and suitcases of money'.[133] 'There was some impatience from across the road [i.e., Number 10],' recalled Boyce. 'He asked us why we were not delivering faster and where Bin Laden was.'[134] In early November Blair's frustration boiled over in a 'testy' note to Hoon: 'Shouldn't it have been sorted out by now?'[135] While seasoned hands worried that too swift an advance on Kabul could lead to a bloodbath, Blair had no such qualms: 'His judgement was that we were in a war, and the task in a war is to take the capital.'[136]

On 7 November, against a backdrop of falling public support for the war, Blair headed to Washington. This fleeting six-hour visit was his most difficult trip to the US to date. Bob Woodward captured the essence of their meeting: 'Bush wanted to unburden, talk things through with a peer, another head of state. He wanted some eyeball time with his chief ally. He and Blair were in this together . . . The situation was not as happy as they had portrayed it publicly. Afghanistan was bogged down.'[137] Blair briefed Bush about the concerns of EU leaders, and the need to maintain the international coalition. The President was less convinced. But it was when Blair insisted that a settlement of the Arab–Israeli conflict was the lynchpin of winning Muslim hearts and minds that Bush began to realise that he and Blair had real differences. Colin Powell had already been pressing the President for permission to deliver a keynote speech on the MEPP, but to no avail.[138] Bush was not to be moved by his persuasive and charming 'friend' who had 'crossed the ocean' a second time to see him. Al-Qaeda would be defeated 'peace or no peace in the Middle East', Bush declared at their joint press conference.[139] Blair was worried: the war was not going well, and he and Bush were in different places.

To the surprise of many, progress then came swiftly in Afghanistan. Two days after Blair's return from the US, the strategic town of Mazar-i-Sharif fell, followed on 13 November by Kabul itself, bringing the Taliban's rule to an end. The relief in Downing Street was palpable. Almost immediately, fresh problems emerged in the American relationship. London and Washington disagreed fundamentally over how to handle Afghanistan now that the Taliban had been deposed. 'CENTCOM was absolutely focused on getting Bin Laden and destroying al-Qaeda. They saw almost anything else as a distraction,' recalls Stirrup.[140] 'They pounded Tora Bora, and hunted for al-Qaeda high and low. It wasn't a safe place to be if you were a tall man with a beard,' recalled one intelligence figure.[141] Osama bin Laden and many senior al-Qaeda fighters escaped. Blair believed strongly that the coalition must now provide troops for peacekeeping and reconstruction: 'He felt it was very important to send a signal of continued involvement after Kabul had fallen,' recalled Manning.[142] Washington took a very different view. 'Our desire was to do whatever minimal amount was necessary to avoid being seen as an occupying power,' explained one senior Pentagon official, 'and avoid contributing to a dependency by doing everything for them.'[143] 'US forces will not stay,' Bush told an NSC meeting on November 13. 'We don't do police work.'[144] The Americans were 'immensely allergic to the notion of either "nation-building" or "peacekeeping"', Meyer recalled. 'We had to come up with another phrase so we weren't mentioning those hideous terms.'[145] The solution lay in a new force, the NATO International Security Assistance Force (ISAF), set up at the behest of the UK with Washington's grudging acquiescence.[146] Although seventeen nations contributed, Britain's 1,800 troops made up the lion's share. The US did not offer any troops, but faced intense pressure to agree to rescue ISAF, should the NATO force get into difficulties. Rumsfeld resented this extra US commitment, which he considered hopelessly unrealistic, and blocked the deal. 'That led to difficult discussions between the President and the Prime Minister,' recalled Hoon, 'in which the Prime Minister prevailed, eventually.'[147] But only after the Americans succeeded in limiting their proposed role. In the end, noted Rumsfeld, 'we did not have a written commitment to drop everything else we may have been doing anywhere in the world to solve an ISAF problem. I wanted to make sure that whatever the US agreed to do, we would be ready and able to do. It took some time and I'm sure people would have preferred that we signed a blank cheque, but we didn't. I wouldn't and I was right not to.'[148] ISAF could now begin its work, but tensions between the NATO force and the US military would continue for years to come.

Blair signalled his commitment to nation-building in Afghanistan by flying with Cherie to Bagram just before midnight on 7 January 2002 in a secret and risky mission. Fears of a missile attack from Taliban units still at large meant that they travelled in an RAF Hercules plane specially equipped to counter ground-to-air missiles.[149] Once on the ground, Blair met Hamid Karzai, the interim leader, and pledged his support: 'Britain would stay with them for the long term.'[150] But to many in Washington, Afghanistan was now history. The victory, according to the British Embassy in Washington, strengthened those in the administration who believed in the essential benevolence and omnipotence of American power.[151] While their attention now swung eastwards, to Iraq, Blair's shifted back to the domestic front.

Health First: September 2001–April 2002

'[The year] 2002 could well be your watershed – akin to 1946 for Attlee, 1969 for Wilson and 1984 for Thatcher – determining whether the government's early successes turn into historic achievements, or a slow process of disintegration,' wrote Adonis to Blair on 7 January 2002. 'Your seminal issues are international security, Europe and the public services.'[152] Blair's Christmas and New Year notes reflect a similar priority, and his frustration that more work had not yet been done to shape his agenda on public services.[153] The bones of Blair's second-term agenda had emerged piecemeal in the six months following the General Election, and focused on health, law and order, schools, university finance, House of Lords reform and the Euro.[154] 'Security' was an extra priority bequeathed by 9/11. Powell, Heywood, Adonis and Barber repeatedly drummed into Blair that he had two years to make his mark before planning would have to start for the next election. He realised that if his policies did not achieve real traction, and soon, his second term would go the way of the first. 'The next six months until the summer of 2002 will be crucial,' wrote Hyman, the Blairite speechwriter in Number 10, adding to the urgency. By July 2002 'it will be clear whether the second term will be more radical than the first'.[155] He offered Blair clear objectives over the following months: a 'successful exit from the war' and using his 'enhanced reputation abroad' to press forward with his goals on the 'Middle East, Africa and environment'; 'real momentum on public services and convince people that radical reform is on its way', 'win the tax-and-spend argument' by 'greater public willingness to pay' and, finally, 'crank up the temperature on Europe' as a precursor to preparing the case for entry to the single currency.

Health saw the first evidence of second-term reformism. Eventually Blair would announce the most thorough reforms to the NHS since its inception in 1948: any Labour Prime Minister would be bound to run up against huge resistance in attempting such a task. Before 2001, Blair had paid little attention to it, until his dramatic announcement on BBC Television's *Breakfast With Frost* on 16 January 2000 that he would bring expenditure on Britain's seriously underfunded NHS up to the EU average of 8 per cent of GDP. Blair believed that a very significant increase in government spending, from just 5.7 per cent of GDP, was a precondition for solving the NHS's problems.[156] By the autumn of 2001, however, he realised money alone was no panacea. "Tony was irritated that waiting times weren't falling quickly enough, and we still hadn't cracked the problem of how to modernise the NHS or introduce more choice and responsiveness. He wanted the NHS to be like the private sector where patients could choose, and he couldn't understand why that couldn't happen,' said a minister.[157] Radical reform, he concluded, was vital if the health service was to function properly. The traditional top-down NHS model, in his eyes, was totally flawed. Blair wanted to make it much more patient- and less producer-driven. He decided to use his party conference speech in Brighton to take up the cudgels against the unions and those in the PLP resisting reform, reproducing almost verbatim the text he would have delivered to the TUC on 11 September. 'Without reform, more money and pay won't succeed,' he stated unequivocally, before attacking head-on those who were resisting change. 'There are too many old demarcations, especially between nurses, doctors and consultants; too little use of the potential of new technology; too much bureaucracy; too many out-dated practices . . . It's not reform that is the enemy of public services. It is the status quo.' Then he stated: 'Part of any reform package had to be 'partnership with the private or voluntary sector'.[158] He had travelled a very long way in a year.

Opponents of Blair's ideas were not restricted to the unions and the left: Gordon Brown and the Treasury were distinctly unhappy. Brown did not welcome Blair venturing on to his own territory: he considered health spending to be a no-go area for Number 10. In the weeks leading up to the pre-Budget report (PBR) on 27 November, the NHS became a running sore in Whitehall. Brown had commissioned the respected banker Derek Wanless in March 2001 to look at NHS funding, and as a result, he recognised that Labour would have to increase tax revenue. Blair was insistent that any increase in money had to be tied to new thinking. 'It is becoming clear that the NHS is not producing much extra performance to show for all the increase in money that is going in from the Treasury,' a Number 10 aide noted in mid-November.[159] Several officials in the Treasury agreed. Brown and Balls did not. To them Blair's agenda smacked of privatisation by the back door and an assault on the traditional NHS model. Notes flew between Number 10 and the Treasury, with Blair, now back from his foreign tours and distractions in October, clearly more focused. At a 9 A.M. Monday meeting in the den, Blair worried that 'departments were slowing and slacking a bit whereas now, with so much media focus on the international, it was the time really to be driving forward'.[160] On the day Brown delivered the PBR, he cautioned Milburn that some of his proposals had serious implications for the public sector and risked undermining NHS morale.[161] Brown was ignored. 'We just went ahead with it,' said one Number 10 aide.[162] According to Campbell, Milburn was 'livid . . . that GB was trying to use his position to take over NHS policy, and he wasn't having any of it'.[163] It did not augur well for the future.

What were the new ideas and who was pushing them? In Number 10, the key figures were Blair himself and his tenacious health adviser Simon Stevens, while in the Department of Health it was Milburn, special advisers Paul Corrigan and Darren Murphy, and Minister of Health John Hutton. Putting power, and effectively money, in the hands of NHS patients, by giving them a choice over which NHS-approved provider to use, lay at the heart of the emerging policy. Patients would continue to get free healthcare; but in future, Blair believed, they should be able to choose which hospital or which doctor they wanted to treat them. On 1 August, before his holiday in Mexico, Blair had asked for detailed proposals on how to increase consumer choice across healthcare.[164] By mid-October he was writing that, of all the options open to him for reforming health, he was most interested in choice of different patient providers, choice of hospital for surgery and choice of provider for maternity care. On 25 October, a discussion was held at Number 10. Incentives and a diversity of supply of services emerged as the means towards shifting the NHS culture in the direction of 'patient-centred care'.[165] Brown did not agree and worried about the impact of any changes on public spending. 'Gordon seems to believe incentives don't really affect health professionals,' said Stevens. 'By contrast, Tony operates on the opposite assumption, that doctors are quite transactional and financially orientated.'[166] The drive on choice bore fruit in mid-2002 when patients waiting more than six months for heart operations were given the choice to go to another hospital. The detail was worked out by Barber and Stevens. 'Our aim in the first months of 2002 was to ensure that hospitals were given an incentive to hurry up and get the patients dealt with more quickly; hitherto they had had no incentive,' recalled Corrigan.[167]

Milburn and his team led in developing an even more radical policy, 'foundation hospitals', which became the flagship health reform of the second term, even though other less high-profile reforms were changing health more profoundly. Number 10 was impressed by Milburn from early in the second term. 'I became convinced that the idea of being able to run a huge organisation like the NHS, employing close to 1.5 million people from an office in Whitehall, was frankly a joke,' he said. 'We had to find different ways of managing it.'[168] The genesis of foundation hospitals can be found in the NHS White Paper of 2000, written by Milburn and Stevens, which proposed autonomy for 'green' (i.e., successful) hospitals. At the end of September 2001, data was published for the first time on hospitals awarded either three, two or one stars, according to their performance. Chief Executives of 'three-star' hospitals were invited to meetings in October and November and asked, 'Would you like more autonomy?'[169] But the most fundamental autonomy was ownership: all hospitals were nominally owned by the Secretary of State. Could that be changed? On 6 November, Milburn had come back from Spain where he had seen the largely independent Alcorcon Hospital which was a so-called 'Fundacion Hospital'. The idea, and name, was born. The Tory proposal to give independence to local hospitals was an additional impetus. 'Let's pre-empt them,' it was suggested.[170] Milburn had been very excited when the department turned up an article Nye Bevan, folk hero of the Labour left and founder of the NHS, had written in the *New Municipal Journal*, in which he wondered whether he had been right not to have given hospitals to local authorities. This discovery was used to undermine a core argument from the left which was that Bevan's original model of the centrally owned, top-down model of the NHS was set in stone. By April, Milburn and Corrigan were confident they had the model clear in their minds, and it was made public in a speech Milburn gave on 22 May in London.[171] The Treasury were to fight foundation hospitals with a vengeance – and success.

Differences over the PBR were to re-emerge in the run-up to the Budget in April 2002. At a meeting in the Cabinet Room on 18 January,

Blair said, 'I am prepared to see tax rise a little as a proportion of GDP, provided we are tough on reform, and target the extra spending on health and education.'[172] Number 10 and the Treasury had a succession of meetings in February, March and April to hammer out an agreement on the reform proposals that would need to accompany the increased money.[173] On 7 March, Heywood sent a note to Brown and Balls setting Number 10's expectations on how the extra money would be spent as well as its thinking on patient choice.[174] In the Budget on 17 April, Brown announced a huge injection of public money for the NHS over the following five years, with an average 7.5 per cent rise annually. Much of this increase was to be paid for by a 1p increase in National Insurance contributions. Brown did mention in the Budget the prospect of giving greater management autonomy to hospitals that proved their competence, but he explicitly did not refer to 'foundation hospitals'.[175] The next day the 'Delivering the NHS Plan' White Paper was published, described by Stevens as 'the most important of all the NHS papers on health'.[176] Brown was not so convinced. That morning he complained to Blair, somewhat perversely, that 'there was not enough reform in Milburn's follow-through statement'.[177] Its authors' response was that they were handicapped by the Treasury not telling them until only three to four weeks before the Budget exactly how much extra money there would be. The new money proved vital to driving through the whole raft of NHS reforms. 'We couldn't have made the kind of progress on reform we did during the spending famine after 1997,' said Corrigan. 'The money was the key to everything.'[178] Blair's domestic policy train was at last moving forward, but the battle was far from won. 'Reform was every bit as important as money,' Campbell recorded Blair saying to Cabinet on the day after the budget. 'If we can't feel confident about these arguments we don't deserve to be in business.'[179]

Law and Order: February–May 2002

One of Blair's deepest political instincts, and one of his earliest, was his sense that Labour had been historically wrong to side too heavily – or appear to side – with the perpetrators of crime rather than its victims. His work as a barrister during the late 1970s and early 1980s, and his conversations with activists and supporters in his Sedgefield constituency from 1983, had helped convince him that it was the working class who suffered most from crime. He had grown increasingly disenchanted with the Home Office in his first term, with its mentality of 'You don't understand crime, Prime Minister: if unemployment increases, it's simple, crime will increase.'[180] 'It absolutely infuriated him,' said one close aide.[181] Commissioning Birt to produce his analysis of crime sprang from Blair's desire to seek advice from outside the traditional Whitehall mindset. 'He became so involved after 2001,' said a member of the Policy Directorate, 'because he thought the traditional criminal justice system we inherited was not working.'[182] On the morning after the 2001 General Election, Blair declared outside Number 10, 'There is no issue that touches our citizens more deeply than crime and law and order on our streets.'[183] As he was so in line with his new Home Secretary, he was more than content to let Blunkett steer through the tough post-9/11 anti-terrorist legislation in the autumn of 2001. Not until the first few months of 2002 did Blair return to law and order as an area of primary personal attention. The catalyst was the sudden upsurge in street crime in January and February 2002. On 17 March Blair and Blunkett launched the 'Street Crime Initiative' aimed at reducing muggings, mobile phone theft and other forms of street crimes in those areas where 80 per cent of such crime was occurring. 'Only after we had seen the provisional crime data for the first couple of months of 2002 did it become clear just how serious street crime was,' said Huw Evans, Blunkett's special adviser.[184] Blair was frustrated: 'fluffy partnerships between agencies' would not be enough to match the 'scale of the immediate problem'.[185] When Barber said that it would take six weeks to work up proposals with the Home Office, Blair demanded more urgent action.[186] Blunkett agreed. Blair viewed his struggle with crime akin to fighting a war. He decided to swing COBRA into action to pull together departments and front-line agencies, including the police, the magistrates' courts and the probation service. This was the first time that COBRA had been used to bring about an immediate change in domestic policy, rather than resolving a crisis. 'Blair had been very impressed by the "can-do" culture and sheer professional competence of the armed forces during foot and mouth,' said Heywood. 'When faced with a compelling policy emergency he would ask himself: "Why can't the rest of the civil service be like our armed forces?"'[187]

'We need a tough response now ... We must get cracking,' Blair commented before the first COBRA meeting on Wednesday 20 March.[188] When it assembled, he challenged those present: 'Are we giving the police enough support?' and 'Where's the synergy between what you are doing, what the police and what the courts are doing?'[189] John Stevens, Commissioner of the Metropolitan Police, was impressed: 'He was strong. He didn't shy away from things. He thought more arrests needed to be made on the street, and if that meant prison numbers going up, then so be it.'[190] In the following weeks, Blair and Blunkett were presented every Friday with figures from each of the ten targeted police forces. Chief constables from poor-performing areas were invited to attend COBRA meetings to explain their lack of progress.[191] Barber also recalled that 'various absurdities of the criminal justice system came to light', on which Blair wanted 'instant action'.[192] Momentum from the 'Safer Streets' campaign and the approach adopted by the Delivery Unit and the Home Office began to pay dividends. On 24 April, Blair was able to tell the House of Commons that he was 'confident that by the end of September we will have brought this problem under control'.[193] By that August, the Street Crime Initiative had secured a 14 per cent drop in robberies and snatched thefts across the ten police forces across the country.[194] Two lessons Blair learned from this experience were: not to trust the Home Office, and that the whole criminal justice system was in need of fundamental change.[195]

Very early on, Blair identified illegal drugs as a core driver of crime – Birt pointed to this conclusion. He also saw drugs lying behind much of the homelessness in Britain's cities. Motivated in part by his Christianity and concern for the downtrodden, he set up a Rough Sleepers' Unit in April 1999, appointing the feisty and combative Louise Casey, formerly of Shelter, to be its head. 'They had talked about exclusion stuff in Opposition but it took them ages to set up the Rough Sleepers' Unit,' Casey said. 'What I liked about the Prime Minister was the fact he seemed to care, and he wasn't just concerned about meeting government targets. You could have bundled all the sleepless people into warehouses, frankly, but it was the quality of the support that mattered to him.'[196] Blair went out on to the streets with Casey in early December 2001 to talk to rough sleepers behind the Savoy Hotel in London. He asked them why they were there and they replied, 'It is not our fault.' 'So what are you going to do about it?' he said. 'Are you going to co-operate with the people who are trying to help you?'[197] It seemed as if Blair was taking personal responsibility for those who were rejected by society. It was a side of his character the public rarely saw.

If rough sleepers showed the soft side of Blair, asylum and immigration showed the other. 'In terms of time,' one Number 10 aide believed, 'it became his number-one domestic priority from the summer of 2001.'[198] Blair wrote in an internal memo that asylum had become 'the toughest immediate issue' with 'the capacity to explode at any moment'.[199] Numbers began to take off in the summer of 2001, as repeated attempts by refugees to escape to Britain from the Sangatte camp across the

English Channel in Calais received widespread media coverage. Gould's research had repeatedly warned Blair that asylum and illegal immigration were major issues for voters. A tough line during the 2001 election would have played well with the *Daily Mail*, but as some in Number 10 repeatedly reminded Blair, they needed to avoid upsetting Labour voters with an illiberal response.[200] The election over, Blair worked on asylum closely with Blunkett, who was responsible in the first half of 2002 for the closing of the Sangatte camp, aided by good relations with Nicolas Sarkozy – then the French Interior Minister.[201] Blair felt increasingly frustrated by the existing asylum regime, which he considered perverse and dysfunctional. His political antennae told him that the public did not understand or respect the asylum system, and felt it was being too readily exploited.[202] From early 2002, he demanded asylum figures every week. The more involved Blair became, the less impressed he was by Blunkett's strategy of accommodation centres, which he thought would have taken years to put in place. In February the 'Nationality, Immigration and Asylum' White Paper proposed a raft of measures to bring the situation back under control. But Number 10 was not happy. 'We wasted six months on Blunkett's strategy, which the Treasury was rightly opposed to and which never had any chances of succeeding.'[203]

'Blair felt very passionately that establishing and then effectively implementing firm but fair rules on asylum was something which the British people expected the government to get right,' said Heywood.[204] A failure to do this would also bolster political parties with racist undertones. Blair's response emerged only after 'hours and hours of brain-storming in Number 10 about how to get applications down and put the system on a proper footing'.[205] He concluded that an urgent forensic examination of the whole system of asylum claiming was required, and he eventually opted for a rules-based system, which he ensured was tightly applied. Blair made considerable use of Barber and the Delivery Unit, which continued to grind away at getting asylum numbers down, as Blair became heavily distracted by the approaching drum-beat of the Iraq war. Many Labour MPs were restless in the first half of 2002 and thought that Blair and Blunkett were being too heavy-handed. But the Cabinet was supportive, 'with the exception of Gordon', recalled one close aide, 'who never wanted to spend any money on asylum or crime, because he hated Blunkett and wouldn't give over the cash'.[206] For a while, relations with the Treasury and party became unpleasant as they accused the Prime Minister and Home Secretary of pandering to the right-wing press. Yet as Huw Evans said, 'David and Tony could foresee the 2005 General Election and how it was going to be fought. Winning this battle on asylum they saw as not only central to New Labour's reputation for competence, but also showing they understood the concerns of middle- and working-class Britain.'[207] The February White Paper was strengthened heavily in September before it became the Asylum Act later that autumn. After November 2002 the rate of increase in asylum applications began to slow. When Michael Howard played the asylum card in the 2005 election, its effect had been largely neutered.

Royals and Reshuffles: April–June 2002

On 30 March, Queen Elizabeth, the Queen Mother, died at the Royal Lodge at Windsor, aged 101. 'The Queen Mother's been a symbol of Britain's decency and courage,' said Blair from Chequers. 'Her sense of duty and her remarkable zest for life made her loved and admired by people of all ages and backgrounds, revered within our borders and far beyond. She was part of the fabric of our nation and we're all immensely proud of her.'[208] The words may have been mundane compared to his 'people's Princess' speech when Diana died, but they were sincere and deeply felt nevertheless. 'TB spoke to the Queen around 7,' Campbell noted in his diary, 'and told me afterwards she was "very sad but dignified".'[209] Parliament was recalled on 3 April. Blair said, 'There's nothing false or complicated about the public response to her death. It's the simplest equation. She loved her country and the country loved her.'[210] Some 2,200 people crammed into Westminster Abbey for her funeral on 5 April: the arrangements, codenamed 'Tower Bridge', had been in place for many years.

What hadn't been foreseen was an unsightly spat that took place between Number 10 and the media. On 11 April, two days after the funeral, Peter Oborne claimed in the *Spectator* that Clare Sumner, a Number 10 official, had spoken to Lt-Gen. Sir Michael Willcocks, known as 'Black Rod' (the House of Lords official in charge of ceremonial events in the Palace of Westminster), to enhance the Prime Minister's role at the laying-in of state. The suggestion was that Blair should be the person to meet the coffin as it arrived at Westminster Hall. Oborne wrote under the headline 'How Tony Blair tried to muscle in on the mourning', 'The events surrounding the Queen Mother's death have come as a blow to New Labour. This is because the government asserts for itself a much grander and wider role in national life than previous administrations . . . New Labour feels that the British monarchy occupies an area of public space that rightly belongs to itself.'[211] Campbell saw red. He met with Sumner and Simon Virley, another of Blair's private secretaries, to establish what had happened. Whatever may or may not have been said, and Sumner's words may have been open to misconstruction, Number 10 maintained there was no attempt, least of all sanctioned by Blair himself, to upstage the Royal Family, or to act in an inappropriate way at such a sensitive time. 'All we were trying to do in the phone call to Black Rod was establish what the Prime Minister, who was going to be returning specially from his holiday, was being asked to do and what exact role was expected of him. We knew we had no control whatsoever over the arrangements and would never have tried to interfere with what the Palace wanted or expected,'[212] said a senior Number 10 official. How should Number 10 react? 'Ignore it,' said some, as objecting would only give publicity to a story in a weekly magazine 'which only 20,000 people read'. But those who said Oborne's piece was potentially damaging won the day.[213] The story was spiralling, with flames fanned by the *Mail on Sunday*, now Blair and Cherie's chief critic in the national press. On 18 April Campbell went public and demanded that the *Spectator* and *Mail on Sunday* issue an apology. They refused and on 24 April Campbell referred the matter to the Press Complaints Commission (PCC). The row did not, however, die away. When Campbell withdrew his complaint on 11 June followed by a long published dossier from Number 10 outlining its version of events, all hell broke loose, and the papers stood by their story speculating that, had a case proceeded, the PCC would have ruled against the Prime Minister on the basis of Black Rod's evidence. The full truth may never be ascertained, though it is evident that Sumner was under no instructions from Blair to give him an elevated role in the funeral arrangements.

To the embarrassment of several in Number 10, including Campbell, Blair was a firm monarchist. He looked forward to his audiences with the Queen, enjoyed them and greatly admired her. 'He never talks about his conversations, he's really proper about it,' said one aide.[214] Even in the privacy of his small circle in the den, no one ever heard him make a single disparaging comment about the Royal Family, above all not the Queen. 'It's just a no-go area with him. He is totally deferential to the Royal Family and, particularly at moments of great sadness, he wanted to do exactly what they wanted him to do,' said one aide.[215] The impression was nevertheless left of an over-mighty and venal Number 10 trying to lord it over the Royal Family. Tension between Downing Street and the media ratcheted to a new level. Blair and Number 10 were left simmering.

Another unwelcome distraction for Blair that spring focused on Stephen Byers at Transport. Blair had remained unswerving in his determination to keep the four key 'delivery' ministers – Blunkett, Byers, Milburn and Morris – firing together. He had already held three dinners in Downing Street, as much to assist in developing an *esprit de corps* as to talk through policy.[216] The hard graft was done at a new 'public services group' consisting of the four ministers, plus Blair and Brown, which had first met on 31 January 2002.[217] But the group, with the exception of Milburn and Blunkett (mostly), were not performing as Blair hoped. His despondency was palpable at a Cabinet 'away-day' at Chequers on Friday 8 March. There was an 'aimless and unfocused discussion, full of platitudes in a lengthy *tour de table*', recorded one present. It was obvious to his ministers that Blair was not happy. 'TB clearly bored,' noted one.[218] On 11 March, he held a dinner at Number 10 flat with close allies, including Mandelson and Gould, to discuss what had gone wrong since the election. Blair insisted it was media-spun perception, not reality. The others were not so sure. 'Lack of clarity on the agenda,' said Mandelson. Campbell agreed. Gould asked him point-blank whether he 'enjoyed dealing with foreign policy more than domestic?' The answer seemed obvious to many of them. They can't be separated, was Blair's reply. He agreed he would try to doctor a 'better media strategy'. But it wasn't deficient presentation that was the problem: it was deficient domestic policy.[219] Campbell and Mandelson were the very last people Blair needed to be listening to. They had helped get Blair where he was. They would get him no further. Not until he started listening to a different breed of adviser would he begin to make progress.

The second term was not going as expected. The Mittal party funding episode, when Blair wrote a letter to the Romanian Prime Minister Adrian Nastase in support of Lakshmi Mittal's company LNM taking over the Romanian steel company (after he had donated £125,000 to the Labour party at the 2001 election), provoked weeks of bad media stories. Jo Moore, from Byers' press office, had famously described 9/11 as 'a good day to bury bad news', which showed New Labour's spin policy at its most raw. Other problems were mounting on Byers, with criticism from survivors of the Paddington rail crash, over Railtrack going into administration, his ten-year rail strategy being 'ridiculed', and concerns over his management skills at Transport. 'He simply ran out of lives,' said one Number 10 aide. 'He was incredibly calm and pretty tough, but his support in the PLP was declining and some were gunning for him.'[220] Blair knew that 'Byers was pretty shot', confiding in

Campbell on 9 May that it was 'monstrous the way Steve had been treated internally, but ultimately ministers have to be responsible for their departments, and he would have to go pretty soon'.[221] On Monday 27 May, Byers remained in Number 10 after a morning meeting with Blair to tell him that he was thinking that it was time for him to go. 'I think I've become a liability,' Byers said.[222] Blair told him to come back and see him later in the day. 'He hates losing people, he really does.'[223] When Byers returned, Blair said, 'I want you to announce your resignation from Number 10 Downing Street,' adding, 'I want you to do that because it's a public demonstration that you're going with my support.'[224] Into his place came Alistair Darling who, although a senior Brownite, was viewed by Blair as having the required qualities of steadiness and leadership to get the department back on its feet. But some felt Byers had been singled out to take the blame for the general malaise in domestic policy.

Blair had tried to 'ride two horses' since 11 September, but had often fallen between them. The war in Afghanistan had been concluded, though Bin Laden and senior al-Qaeda operatives had eluded capture, and the future stability of the country was very far from certain. His domestic agenda had been only partly formed and his control of the domestic scene was coming under increasing fire. He was not happy about the way his second term had begun, and was showing rare signs of despondency. At this vulnerable point, a new foreign distraction came on to his horizon.

4

The Road to Baghdad

January–September 2002

The Iraq war was the single defining issue of the Blair premiership, and the most controversial. Why did he commit Britain to fighting, and when? Whose advice did he rely on most in Number 10 and beyond? Why did he commit to support Bush, and on what conditions? Were those conditions, including involving the UN to try to pre-empt war, and pursuit of the MEPP, dictated by his beliefs or expediency? Did he raise the risks of the campaign or what might happen afterwards? New evidence on both sides of the Atlantic confirms some existing impressions, and changes others.

Iraq on the Radar Screen: Early 2002

'As we gather tonight, our nation is at war . . .' At around 2:30 A.M. London time on Wednesday, 30 January 2002 as Tony Blair slept in Downing Street, President George W. Bush stood in Congress delivering the most controversial State of the Union address of his presidency. Bush opened by recalling the horrors of 9/11 and reviewing the military success in Afghanistan. 'What we have found in Afghanistan confirms that, far from ending there, our war against terror is only beginning.' Threats still remain, he insisted, before singling out North Korea, Iran and Iraq: 'States like these, and their terrorist allies, constitute an axis of evil, arming to threaten the peace of the world.'[1]

Echoing Reagan's description of the Soviet Union as an 'evil empire', Bush was sending a clear signal that his administration was now broadening its sights in the war on terror. The speech disturbed many in Bush's own administration and sent shockwaves around the world. 'At the State Department we were horrified,' recalled Assistant Secretary Elizabeth Jones. 'I had to deal right away with calls from governments all over Europe saying, "What are you talking about? What is this?"'[2] While the phrasing and the timing of Bush's public pronouncement caught Number 10 on the hop, its intent would have come as no surprise. The British Embassy in Washington had sent a warning that the administration had already turned their attention to Iraq: there was 'strong pressure to do something, but no clear plan yet'.[3] But the American fixation with Iraq was hardly something confined to the secret world of ambassadorial telegrams. Ever since 9/11, media speculation over US plans to strike at Saddam Hussein had mushroomed. Had the time come to remove this long-term irritant in US foreign policy?

A growing body of opinion in Washington felt that Bush senior and Bill Clinton had been too soft on Iraq. In 1991, in response to Iraq's invasion of Kuwait in 1990, a coalition of thirty-four countries mobilised in the Gulf to repel Saddam's armed forces. The armies had, however, stopped short of 'regime change' – chasing the retreating Iraqi forces over the border to Baghdad and toppling Saddam Hussein. UN resolutions followed, limiting Saddam's military capability and requiring full and verifiable disarmament of weapons of mass destruction (WMD). Over the years that followed Saddam played cat and mouse with the UN, persistently failing to comply. In October 1998, Congress passed the 'Iraq Liberation Act' declaring that the US would support efforts to remove Saddam Hussein's regime from power. That December, Madeleine Albright, Clinton's Secretary of State, explained that the policy of containing Saddam had changed to 'containment plus regime change'.[4] Later that December, with Blair's ready backing, Clinton authorised 'Operation Desert Fox', four days of bombing (using US and UK forces) aimed at suspected WMD sites and related infrastructure. This was the limit of direct military action under Clinton. 'Containment plus regime change' never foresaw a US invasion to overthrow Saddam. At most it visualised working with Iraqi opposition groups 'to do what we can to make the opposition a more effective voice for the aspirations of the Iraqi people'.[5]

During the 2000 presidential election campaign, Bush surrounded himself with a group of pro-military foreign policy advisers, many of whom went straight into high-ranking positions in the new administration.[6] They included Vice-President Dick Cheney, Defense Secretary Donald Rumsfeld, his deputy Paul Wolfowitz, Secretary of State Colin Powell, his deputy Richard Armitage and National Security Advisor Condoleezza Rice. The 'Vulcans', as they were called, were drawn together by their core conviction that 'American power and ideals are, on the whole, a force for good in the world'.[7] From this assumption, they helped Bush to foster a 'revolution' in American thinking about its world role.[8] Two theses were central: American security demanded that it act unilaterally, shedding traditional constraints imposed by allies or international bodies; and American power should be used pre-emptively to seek out its enemies before they could attack the US. The neoconservatives, or neocons, comprised an important subset within the Vulcans, believing that America's mission was actively to spread democracy throughout the world, rather than simply containing tyrants like Saddam Hussein. Many of the neocons had ties to the 'Project for the New American Century', a conservative organisation which in January 1998 had organised a letter to President Clinton advocating urgent regime change in Iraq. The signatories included Rumsfeld, Wolfowitz and several other future Bush appointees, but not Colin Powell. Although he had no love of Saddam, Powell did not share the widespread Vulcan obsession with Iraq.

For all the hostility to Iraq, there is no evidence before 9/11 that the Bush administration was planning an invasion. 'At Camp David in February 2001 it was quite striking that there was no sense of a US mission on Iraq,' recalled Sawers. 'To the contrary, Iraq was seen as a problem that had to be managed.'[9] When Blair visited Washington on 20 September, Bush reassured Blair that he had no imminent designs on Iraq. 'I don't think that 9/11 had a qualitative effect on the President to do something about Iraq – not right away,' insisted Rice. 'He deliberately set Iraq aside because we were about to go to war in Afghanistan. Everybody understood that.'[10] In London, however, they were not so sure: '9/11 made America's decision to go to war with Iraq inevitable,' insisted one senior official. 'The timing was the only question.'[11] Saddam smartly reappeared on Bush's radar screen just eight days after Kabul fell. Unbeknownst to Blair, on 21 November 2001, Bush secretly asked Rumsfeld to update invasion plans for Iraq.[12] 'It wasn't exactly a big secret that Iraq was already being discussed,' said Jones, 'but none of us in the State Department thought it was real. There had been a lot of push-back by the CIA briefers saying "it's not Iraq; it's Afghanistan". We thought it would be so easy to push back on the Iraq stuff. It was nonsense.'[13] Elsewhere in the administration a very different view was taking hold. By the time of 2002 State of the Union address, the neocons had captured the citadel.

As Blair pondered how to respond to the growing US belligerence, he consulted his inner circle rather than the FCO. 'The fact is that Tony Blair was his own Foreign Secretary. There was no clear slot for Jack Straw, who hit rock bottom in early January 2002,' recalled one official.[14] After some effective diplomacy in India and Pakistan that spring, Straw's confidence returned, but he never became as central to Blair or as trusted as those in Number 10. Blair preferred to turn to his den, where his key advisers on foreign policy had now crystallised: Powell, Manning, Campbell and Morgan, in descending order of importance. Their absolute loyalty led some to the conclusion they were all of one mind, but they were no more united than Bush's advisers. Blair appreciated the difference in perspective. 'Tony Blair knew there were conflicting views and he agonised a great deal,' insisted Manning. 'There were long discussions with the Prime Minister and sometimes profound disagreements. But he wouldn't hold that against you. He liked to have a sounding board, but when it came to the crunch he would make up his own mind.'[15]

Powell was the strongest advocate for 'hugging America close'. He had been plucked from the British Embassy in Washington as Blair's Chief of Staff in January 1995. On Iraq it was Powell's clear judgement that Britain would best be able to sway American policy by working closely with the White House and trying to influence it from the inside. His enthusiasm and support for Blair rippled outwards. 'Jonathan instinctively supported Tony Blair and he helped create a culture that Number 10 should support and back his instincts. That really affected the whole thinking in the building,' said one official.[16] Manning was naturally more cautious than Powell, and had reservations about aspects of the Iraq strategy, though once he had made his case, he loyally supported Blair. 'Powell encouraged Tony in his instincts on Iraq, Manning held on to the coat tails,' said a senior diplomat.[17] Manning's particular contribution was to ensure that Blair understood and digested each new step as they came along, 'to check whether he was tying himself to a machine that was taking him in the right direction'.[18] 'David was always saying to the Prime Minister, "You don't have to do this, you don't have to go to war." He was trying to hold the Prime Minister back from giving the negotiating game away too soon,' said one FCO official.[19] Campbell and Morgan differed in that both were Labour Party tribalists, not foreign policy professionals, nor natural Atlanticists. 'They would argue throughout for Blair keeping a distance from Bush,' one official said. '"He's Republican and we're on the left," was their mantra, mixed with a bit of "He's an American, and you, Tony, are a European."'[20] Campbell, who enthusiastically supported Blair's first-term wars, came round to the inevitability of war, and when spirits flagged bolstered them by saying public opinion favoured dealing with Saddam.[21] His ebullience and big personality carried them all along through difficult times. He remained apprehensive over relations with Bush: 'Have we become a pawn in a right-wing American conspiracy?' he later mused.[22] For Campbell and Morgan, as good Labourites, the moral case against Saddam weighed heaviest. Morgan remained the most dove-ish of the four, pressed hard for the UN route, and was never sold on the prospect of war.[23] Outside the den these top four advisers kept their views to themselves: when Cabinet ministers and others joined them at meetings, they let Blair do the talking.[24]

For all Blair's reliance on his team, the decisions at each step of the Iraq story were absolutely his own. His burning inner conviction impressed, or troubled, those around him. One sceptical senior figure characterised it thus: 'I can persuade Parliament, I can persuade my Cabinet, I can persuade my civil servants this is the right way to go – we're *going* to do it and I won't listen beyond a certain amount to the gainsayers.'[25] Lt-General Sir Rob Fry was an admirer: 'He had this fixity of purpose and moral conviction which was extraordinary.'[26] But of what exactly was he convinced? His Iraq decisions were the most important of his premiership. His motivation needs to be probed. Many impugned his motives, and thought them ill-conceived or insincere. But were they?

Blair's thinking about Iraq by early 2002 comprised four separate strands of thought. The dangers of WMD proliferation, especially if allied to terrorism, concerned him. He had not come to the premiership with a background in foreign policy, but early on in Number 10 had been influenced, among many others, by the thinking of diplomat Robert Cooper, that the greatest threat to international security in the twenty-first century would come from WMD proliferation combining with international terrorism.[27] Blair 'soon felt in his bones the risk of terrorists getting together with states who possessed WMD', recalled one close aide.[28] Six months into office, Blair told Liberal Democrat leader Paddy Ashdown that he had been reading the intelligence reports on Saddam's WMD: 'I have now seen some of the stuff on this. It really is pretty scary. He is close to some appalling weapons of mass destruction . . . We cannot let him get away with it.'[29] Dirty bombs, where conventional explosive is used to disperse radioactive matter, were a particular fear of Blair's, owing to the ease of construction and the difficulties of detection.[30] 'Tony

Blair believed very strongly that if we did not deal with the weapons now, we would have to deal with them in ten years' time when proliferation would have made the problem intractable, and international checks and systems would be overwhelmed,' said Manning.[31] Straw concurred: 'Blair was on to the issue of WMD long before 9/11: he has greater facility for seeing beyond the horizon than anyone else I've met in politics.'[32] Intelligence about A. Q. Khan (the Pakistani nuclear scientist who shared secret technology with Libya, Iran and North Korea) particularly unnerved him. 'He didn't want al-Qaeda getting their hands on the technology. He had been hearing things long before 9/11. He began to see the grains of it all coming together. I'm not sure that any of us saw the full threat clearly until 9/11,' said one close aide.[33] For Blair, the fear that WMD would find their way into the hands of terrorists made Iraqi disarmament essential: Saddam was as dangerous as Bin Laden.

He had a deep personal revulsion for Saddam and was convinced the time had come to teach him a lesson: 'Getting rid of Saddam would be highly desirable, not least for the Iraqi people,' Blair wrote to George Carey, Archbishop of Canterbury, in private, almost confessional correspondence during 2002.[34] In January 1998, he had made a hawkish speech to Labour's 'national policy forum' in Millbank calling Saddam an 'evil dictator' and declaring: 'He must be either persuaded by diplomacy, or made by force to yield up his long-cherished ambition to develop nuclear, chemical and biological weapons . . . If we conclude that the only option to enforce the Security Council's will is military action, we will not shrink from it.'[35] Saddam's repeated obstruction of UN weapons inspectors during 1998 prompted Blair to give Clinton robust support for Operation Desert Fox. In February 2001, Blair readily backed joint US–British air strikes in response to Iraqi attacks on their planes, and spoke out against EU leaders for being critical, describing Saddam as a 'serial sinner when it comes to weapons of mass destruction and a threat to the external world'.[36] Blair believed that the repeated violation by Saddam of UN resolutions was offensive not just to the integrity of that body, but also to the international rule of law. If the West failed to confront Saddam over these violations, he believed, rogue states would feel they could defy the UN with impunity. To Blair, Iraq provided the test case between a 'new world order' and global chaos.[37] Because of Blair's longstanding concerns, 'when Bush popped up soon after 9/11 and said, "Tony, we need to deal with Iraq now that we've dealt with the Taliban", his response was not "Oh my God, do you think we ought to be doing this?" It was "Yeah, right on, I'm with you George,"' said Meyer.[38]

Blair was convinced of the morality of appropriate humanitarian intervention. Revulsion at the brutality of dictators was a regular Blair theme. 'They ask me why we don't get rid of Mugabe,' Peter Stothard recalls him saying in March 2003. 'Why not the Burmese lot? . . . I don't because I can't, but when you can, you should.'[39] 'He saw Saddam as the Pol Pot of the Middle East,' said one close aide.[40] Blair would talk to colleagues enthusiastically about the history of twentieth-century moral intervention and the British left. He would say, 'I can't understand why people on the left oppose it. Hasn't the left always been committed to fighting injustice in the world?'[41] He drew analogies: 'If I'm in this room,' he would say, 'but someone is being killed in the next room, then surely I shouldn't just stay in this room and do nothing?'[42] Blair's rationale for humanitarian intervention had developed in successive speeches since 1997, beginning with the Lord Mayor's Banquet speech that November, and blossoming in his seminal Chicago speech in April 1999, when he tried to blend humanitarian intervention with old-fashioned national interest: 'If we can establish and spread the values of liberty, the rule of law, human rights and an open society . . . then that is in our national interests too.'[43] The fullest expression came at the George Bush Senior Presidential Library in April 2002: 'I have been involved as British Prime Minister in three conflicts involving regime change. Milosevic. The Taliban. And Sierra Leone . . . Britain is immensely proud of the part our forces have played and with the results, but I can honestly say the people most pleased have been the people living under the regime in question. Never forget: they are the true victims.'[44]

Blair's final conviction was that Britain's national interests were best served by standing side-by-side with the US in world politics. He became concerned by the risk of increasing US isolationism towards the end of the Clinton administration, a fear that grew with Bush's victory in 2000. 'Blair always thought it would be disastrous for Europe and Britain to leave the US alone at the time it faced its greatest external challenges in recent history, and when unilateralist voices were at their height,' said Nigel Sheinwald, Manning's successor at Number 10 from 2003.[45] Michael Jay, the Permanent Under-Secretary at the Foreign Office, held several conversations with Blair about whether Britain could be Atlanticist and remain at the heart of Europe. 'He gave you that slightly puzzled look if you queried that there might be a contradiction. He was absolutely determined to be as close to Bush, not because he was particularly enamoured with either Clinton or Bush as a person – I think he became so of both – but because of a very strong belief that it was the right stance for British foreign policy. That's what led him ultimately to support the war.'[46] Blair believed that a close relationship would deliver real influence, which he saw as the key enduring value of the special relationship: 'What we wanted to do was influence American decisions, to be a player in Washington – as Churchill was with Roosevelt, or Macmillan with Kennedy, or Thatcher with Reagan,' said one close Number 10 aide.[47] He saw himself consciously in that historical tradition.

But influence has a price: 'total support in public, total candour in private' became the governing mantra. Blair knew that critical speeches, or leaking against the administration, would close the door to the Oval Office. Number 10 argued in early 2002 that this approach had been vindicated: Bush had not lashed out after 9/11. Instead, just as Blair had urged – although of course they might have acted in the same way anyway – Bush had targeted al-Qaeda in Afghanistan and, with international support, seen military action through to victory. Blair's innermost thoughts can be seen in his March 2002 letter to Archbishop Carey. 'Bluntly, I am the one Western leader the US will really listen to on these issues. That carries a price. It means that I don't grandstand; I don't negotiate publicly; I don't list demands. It is a v. difficult and delicate line to tread. Of course if I disagreed fundamentally with their objectives, I w[oul]d have to say so and w[oul]d.' He concluded his letter to Carey: 'My objectives must be to pull the Americans towards a strategy that is sensible in Iraq, contemplate military action only in the right circumstances; and broaden strategy so that it is about the wider world, including the Middle East peace process, Africa, staying and seeing it through in Afghanistan.'[48]

These four strands of Blair's convictions pulled themselves into a knot of unbreakable strength during the course of 2002. How did this stance translate into a strategy?

Squaring the Circle: January–April 2002

In the weeks after Bush's 'axis of evil' declaration, the world's press was awash with speculation that a US attack on Iraq could be imminent, as 'phase two' of the war on terror. Blair said little in public, unsure himself what the Americans were planning, despite 'endless phone calls' between Washington and London. While trying to discover what the administration was hatching, Whitehall was not planning for war but looking at alternative strategies for dealing with Iraq such as inspectors or more sanctions'.[49] Blair himself thought he should raise awareness in Britain of the threat Saddam posed. At the end of February, just before leaving for the Commonwealth summit in Australia, he spoke out against those 'spreading weapons of mass destruction and engaged in evil trade'. According to *The Times*, 'Tony Blair began preparing Britain for the second phase of the war on terrorism yesterday. In a heightening of the rhetoric against Saddam Hussein Mr Blair virtually lined himself up behind President Bush's portrayal of Iraq as part of an "axis of evil".'[50] On 6 March, the *Daily Express* carried an article with Blair's by-line headlined: 'Why Saddam is still a threat to Britain', and declaring that 'though Iraq seems far away, and Saddam, for the moment, is on the defensive, it is in the interests of us all to face up to these threats with determination and resolve'.[51]

On 11 March Vice-President Cheney visited Downing Street. By then Number 10 had received inklings of the administration's thinking but no detail: 'It was not the first time war was mentioned,' recalled a Number 10 official. 'War had come up before as one option, if we had to go down that particular route.'[52] Cheney met first with Prescott and then attended a wider lunch, including Blair and a range of officials: both events, recalled Meyer, were 'pretty inconsequential'.[53] At a private tête-à-tête, Blair raised the Israeli–Palestinian conflict. 'The Americans claimed to be conscious of the importance of the MEPP,' Campbell noted, 'but we were not really sure they got it.'[54] Cheney then briefed Blair, Powell and Manning on America's latest intelligence on Saddam and WMD and outlined the evolving thinking. Blair struck a hawkish note in the subsequent press conference: 'No decisions have yet been taken on how we deal with this threat, but that there is a threat from Saddam Hussein and the weapons of mass destruction that he has acquired is not in doubt at all.'[55]

This was the time when Blair was beginning to face his first serious opposition from within the Labour Party. On 7 March seventy Labour MPs signed a Commons motion declaring that an Iraq war would be unwise.[56] It followed hard on the heels of a difficult Cabinet discussion on Iraq. Robin Cook wrote in his diary: 'For the first time I can recall in five years, Tony was out on a limb ... The balance of the discussion pointed strongly in the reverse direction of his intentions.'[57] Cook and Clare Short were the most sceptical, though Blunkett also expressed concern. Blair summed up: 'I tell you that we must stand close to America. If we don't, we will lose our influence to shape what they do.'[58] Opposition from deep in his own party, and increasingly the country at large and from EU leaders was a reminder to Blair, if he needed one, of the distance he would have to travel if he was to commit Britain to war. His policy and pronouncements on Iraq needed to be very carefully nuanced.

He was in a quandary. Bush had publicly declared himself in favour of 'regime change'. Inwardly, Blair was sympathetic. In private he said his central aim was less the removal of Iraq's WMD than regime change, because, as Campbell recalled him saying, 'of the threat to the region and the world'.[59] He thought Saddam was evil and he wanted Iraq and the world to be rid of him. But he could not commit himself publicly to it, because of questions over its legality and resistance at home to such naked ambition. 'I think that in his heart of hearts Blair wanted regime change – that's what he was after – he realised that you couldn't deal with the problem of Iraq unless you got shot of Saddam Hussein,' confirmed a senior FCO official. 'So I think that in reality he was in exactly the same position as the President. But he had to present it in public somewhat differently.'[60] So, Blair came up with a 'third way' position. He would tell Bush that he did not support 'open-ended' regime change, as advocated by the Americans, but 'conditional' regime change, *if and only if* all peaceful measures to ensure Iraqi compliance with UN resolutions on WMD had been exhausted. That is, if the UN made Saddam disarm, there would be no war. Of course, if Saddam continued to defy the UN, as he had already done for over a decade, then regime change proper, and military action, would follow. Blair's package of 'conditions' for British support also emerged at this time: there were two core elements, involving the UN and re-engaging America with the MEPP. A lesser ambition was encouraging the US to release a dossier on Saddam to share the intelligence with the public (the 'public relations strategy'). He needed these conditions politically: Britain would not have worn an all-out attempt to depose Saddam without them. But he also believed in them. He had been pressing for progress on the MEPP since early in his premiership, while his wish to internationalise the struggle and to publish a dossier can be seen in his words to Bush within twenty-four hours of 9/11. Blair's conditions blended expediency with personal belief.

Just after the Cheney visit, Manning was dispatched in mid-March to Washington to convey Blair's thinking to his 'opposite number' Rice – they had developed a close working relationship. Blair's position is very clearly set out in a memo Manning wrote back to Blair on 14 March: 'We spent a long time at dinner on Iraq. It is clear that Bush is grateful for your support and has registered that you are getting flak. I said that you would not budge in your support for regime change but you had to manage a press, a Parliament and a public opinion that was very different from anything in the States. And you would not budge either in your insistence that, if we pursued regime change, it must be very carefully done and produce the right result. Failure was not an option . . .' A full year before the invasion, Blair visualised that the military option might not prove successful in achieving the 'right' result: little note was taken of his warning. He would later leave Washington to handle post-war planning with little effective British input. Manning then outlined the conditions for British support: 'I told Condi that we realised that the administration could go it alone if it chose. But if it wanted company, it would have to take account of the concerns of its potential coalition partners. In particular: the UN dimension.' Here Manning recognised the reality of the value of British support to the Americans. While a British military contribution could be helpful, it was not essential. Where Blair's backing mattered was if the administration was looking for allies. 'Without the British, we would have been fighting unilaterally,' conceded one senior State Department official. 'Other countries would have been much less likely to join us had the British not come on board first.'[61] Manning also mentioned the 'paramount importance' of tackling Israel and Palestine. Without these conditions, 'we could find ourselves bombing Iraq and losing the Gulf'.[62]

On 18 March, Meyer had a follow-up talk with Paul Wolfowitz, which he reported to Manning. 'We backed regime change,' Meyer told Wolfowitz, 'but the plan had to be clever and failure was not an option . . . The US could go it alone if it wanted to. But if it wanted to act with partners, there had to be a strategy for building support for military action against Saddam. I then went through the need to wrong-foot Saddam on the inspectors and the UN Security Council Resolutions and the critical importance of the MEPP as an integral part of the anti-Saddam strategy.'[63] Of that conversation, Meyer later commented: 'I didn't beat around the bush. What I was saying was, "Look, we're with you on this. The PM stands four-square behind you." But if you'd gone to the FCO at that time, no Foreign Secretary would have stood up and said, "We've now changed our policy to one of regime change." The policy was regime change, but it was regime change in a more subtle way.'[64] To the administration, the distinction between 'regime change neat' and 'regime change subtle' was largely semantics: 'Regime change would bring about the removal of the WMD. Removal of the WMD would bring about regime change,' said Rove, who believed that the widespread assumption that Saddam had such weapons was essential to his grip on power. 'Same coin, different side.'[65]

In early March Bush had invited Blair to visit him at his private ranch in Crawford, Texas. News of the invitation did not go down well with the Labour Party, nor with Cabinet. Straw wrote a strong letter to Blair. 'The rewards from your visit to Crawford will be few. The risks are high, both for you and for the government. I judge that there is at present no majority inside the PLP for any military action against Iraq (alongside a greater readiness in the PLP to surface their concerns). Colleagues know that Saddam and the Iraqi regime are bad. Making that case is easy. But we have a long way to go to convince them as to: a) the scale of the threat from Iraq and why this has got worse recently; b) what distinguishes the Iraqi threat from that of e.g. Iran and North Korea so as to justify military action; c) the justification for any military action in terms of international law; and d) whether the consequence of military action really would be a compliant, law-abiding replacement government.'[66] Manning was more optimistic about the meeting. 'My talks with Condi convinced me that Bush wants to hear your views on Iraq before taking decisions. He also wants your support. He is still smarting from the comments by other European leaders on his Iraq policy. This gives you real influence: on the public relations strategy; on the UN and weapons inspections; and on US planning for any military campaign. This could be critically important. I think there is a real risk that the administration underestimates the difficulties. They may agree that failure isn't an option, but this does not mean that they will avoid it . . . The talks at the ranch will also give you the chance to push Bush on the Middle East. The Iraq factor means that there may never be a better opportunity to get this administration to give sustained attention to reviving the MEPP.'[67]

Blair processed this advice as he worked out his goals for the Crawford meeting, scheduled for early April. 'TB wanted to be in a position to give GWB a strategy and influence it,' noted Campbell, rather exaggerating the influence Blair was likely to have. 'He believed Bush was in the same position as him, that it would be great to get rid of Saddam and could it be done without terrible unforeseen circumstances?'[68] At a meeting at Chequers on 2 April, Britain's military leadership painted a gloomy picture of the military options for Iraq. Boyce, Chief of the Defence Staff, 'appeared to be trying to shape the meeting towards inaction', while Deputy Chief of Operations Lt-General Sir Anthony Piggott suggested that, while possible, a full-scale invasion 'would be bloody, could take a long time'.[69] Unlike many in the US military, the British armed forces were uneasy about the prospects: 'The war aroused deep concerns among several in the military,' explained one senior source.[70] Britain's top brass were further troubled that their US counterparts were 'planning something for later in the year, maybe the New Year', but they were not yet in the loop.[71]

The British military were not the only ones being excluded from the plans being developed in Washington. Blair's trip to Crawford came at a time of heightened division among Bush's own advisers. The hawks, Cheney, Rumsfeld and Wolfowitz, thought beating Iraq would be an easy contest, which America could undertake alone. 'Cheney's people in particular,' recalled Colin Powell's Chief of Staff Lawrence Wilkerson, believed 'that America didn't need anybody. This was the most blatant, arrogant, insolent type of unilateralism. It just emanated from some of those people's pores.'[72] The 'doves', led by Powell, viewed the invasion as full of hazard and not to be undertaken alone.[73] Powell recalled that the President's advisers 'were split on how far to go to bring about regime change in Iraq. You could say that on one level we all wanted regime change. Saddam was a jerk and we wanted him out. But some of us wondered if the cost of achieving this was going to be worth it. How high a price should we pay for regime change? Was it worth a war?' In early 2002, Bush still had an open mind, but he was inclined towards regime change through military action. Cheney and Rumsfeld – the former more than the latter – pushed single-mindedly for regime change and saw military action as the 'only solution' to this problem.[74]

Blair, accompanied by Manning, Powell, Campbell and Meyer, arrived for the Crawford summit in the early evening of Friday, 5 April. Blair was immediately whisked off by helicopter to Bush's ranch for a private dinner, while the British and American teams dined together at a Tex-Mex restaurant in nearby Waco.[75] The next day Bush and Blair held lengthy discussions at the ranch, sometimes with aides present, sometimes not. Contrary to some accounts, Iraq did not dominate the meeting. Blair worked to get the focus 'off Iraq simply and on to the Middle East'.[76] Here he succeeded. Manning recalled that the two most pressing issues were the MEPP and nuclear stand-off between India and Pakistan.[77] But Iraq was also on the agenda and the discussion proved hugely significant: 'It was when we first began to realise fully how serious they were about it,' said one senior aide present.[78] To maximise his influence, Blair calculated he should impress his support for the policy towards Iraq first before going on to raise his conditions. In this way, Bush was given an 'understanding' of support, albeit a qualified one. 'It didn't feel as if a Rubicon had been crossed,' said one close aide, 'but clearly a serious conversation had taken place.'[79] A Cabinet Office document later recorded that: 'When the Prime Minister discussed Iraq with President Bush at Crawford in April he said that the UK would support military action to bring about regime change, provided that certain conditions were met: efforts had been made to construct a coalition/shape public opinion, the Israeli–Palestine crisis was quiescent, and the options for action to eliminate Iraq's WMD through the UN weapons inspectors had been exhausted.'[80] At Crawford's concluding press conference Blair sounded circumspect, in contrast to Bush's unequivocal assertion that 'we support regime change'. But in his speech at the Bush Senior Presidential Library the following day, Blair spelled out the British position: 'If Saddam refused to co-operate fully, regime change would follow.' Allegations were later made of mendacity on Blair's part, telling Bush one thing in private while dissembling in public. The speech shows that the gulf between his public position and what he was telling Bush in private was not large. '[We] must be prepared to act where terrorism or WMDs threaten us . . . If necessary the action should be military and again, if necessary and justified, it should involve regime change.'[81] The difference between British and American positions, as seen in these public statements, was Blair's insistence on giving Saddam a final chance to co-operate.

According to one British official present at Crawford: 'Blair certainly took the view that we should say to them "we're with you", and he did this because he believed that was what needed to be said to the administration if they were going to take us seriously. But saying "we're with you" is different from saying "we're going to go to war with you".'[82] The problem was that many in the administration failed to register this distinction. Blair's words immediately after 9/11 created a big impression in Washington, which would not be dispelled lightly: 'We . . . here in Britain stand shoulder to shoulder with our American friends . . . And we, like them, will not rest until this evil is driven from our world.'[83] The administration thus had a working hypothesis from September 2001 onwards that Britain was committed to whatever they were going to do: 'It was in their bloodstream.'[84]

Blair's problem at Crawford was that he didn't sufficiently disabuse them of this notion. In fact, his strategy of stressing his support for 'regime change' first before laying out his conditions had the reverse effect. What the Americans *heard* Blair say at Crawford was that he was with them. Blair's crucial mistake was not to make his 'conditions' truly conditional: they 'were our policy but they weren't put in terms of the price for British co-operation', said one aide.[85] As Armitage later confided in Meyer: 'The problem with your "yes, but" is that it is too easy to hear the "yes" and forget the "but".' What happened subsequently was that the 'but' faded away in US thinking, exposing Blair's stark bottom line: 'Come what may, we'll be with you.'[86]

Indeed, senior administration officials, talking in early 2007, confirm the impression that Blair's 'conditions' made little impact at Crawford. 'It was always a given that Blair would back us militarily, should it come to war in Iraq, so far as I was concerned. Right from the start,' said Colin Powell. 'He didn't attach any conditions to that support. Or none that I recall anyway.'[87] 'The President and Prime Minister discussed Iraq and agreed on what needed to be done,' said Rove. 'I don't think it was like, "George, if you don't do this, then I won't do that." But it was like, "We share the same goal. How is it that we can achieve that goal?"'[88]

John Kampfner, senior among the British critics to have written on the war, has argued that, from Crawford onwards, Blair's talk that war was not 'inevitable' was just a 'front', and that he concealed the truth from the Cabinet, FCO and others. Blair, he argues, had committed Britain to war with Iraq as the price worth paying for US friendship.[89] Among his evidence, Kampfner cites Blair's instructions to Brown on his return from Texas: rework your April Budget to take account of expenditure on an Iraq war, which would cost an initial £1 billion.[90] Yet he sees conspiracy where there was no conspiracy. His construction also confuses military preparations, which had to be made for war to be a credible threat, with decisions taken to wage an inevitable war. Diplomacy with Saddam worked better with the threat of force, as even Kofi Annan admitted back in 1998.[91] As Boyce put it: 'I had the impression that Tony Blair wanted to make it sound very real to Saddam, but that he continued to hold out hopes for a peaceful outcome in the end.'[92] However the Americans interpreted Blair's words at Crawford, Blair himself did not believe British involvement in military conflict was inevitable: his understanding of the political forces ranged against war, alone, make it wrong to argue that he was set on war. He wanted to be rid of Saddam but not until the very end did it become clear that peaceful means would not work, with British forces receiving his order to fight.

Proof that Blair had an uphill struggle on his hands, if he needed proof, came when he reported back on Crawford to an apprehensive Cabinet on 11 April, saying, 'I do believe in this country's relations with the US.' Quite, thought Cabinet, but so what? The UN path 'conditions' were far from in the bag and, some, like Patricia Hewitt, spoke up about the necessity of securing UN approval first. Blair sympathised but argued that 'we should not tie ourselves down to doing nothing' without such approval being forthcoming.[93] He realised his line was not winning them over. Elsewhere, support was disappearing. His public remarks from Texas had not gone down well. Fellow EU leaders were not pleased by what they saw as a 'council of war' at Crawford. The Labour Party was increasingly concerned and critical. The FCO and many officials in other departments across Whitehall were sceptical. The media and public opinion were increasingly hostile.[94] It was a lonely time for Blair. The home front was not going well, and in the coming weeks Bush tested his patience greatly in the Middle East.

Taken for Granted: April–July 2002

In the immediate term, in his shopping list of conditions, Blair placed re-engaging the US with the MEPP at the top. Violence in the region was spiralling out of control. In March, in response to repeated Palestinian suicide bombings, Israeli tanks had moved into towns in the West Bank. At this time Straw wrote to Blair of his concerns about where 'the conflict between Israel and the Palestinians' might lead.[95] The casualty count led to growing pressure for an Israeli withdrawal from the Palestinian territories. While Blair advocated this course, the US had remained silent. Blair was worried: 'How do we get the Americans doing more re: the Middle East peace process without it looking like we are criticising them for not doing enough?' he asked ahead of April's Crawford meeting.[96] One answer was traditional diplomacy. 'Unless the Americans called also for Israeli withdrawal, the press would drive a coach and horses between the two leaders,' recalled Meyer.[97] The administration responded on 4 April, when Bush delivered a statement urging Ariel Sharon to withdraw from recently occupied Palestinian cities and halt further incursions into Palestinian-controlled areas. Sharon was not pleased. 'He told Bush to go to hell,' recalled one diplomat, 'and just carried on doing what he wanted to do.'[98] But the British pushed back and Bush responded. The administration now began briefing the media that 'withdrawal' meant 'without delay'. Blair was pleased. Bush's 4 April statement included a crucial reference to a final settlement in the Middle East in which two states, Israel and Palestine, would coexist (the 'two state solution'). And here was evidence that the President would take a firm line with the Israeli Prime Minister.[99]

But the 4 April statement was to prove the highpoint of Bush's toughness with Sharon. When Blair met Bush at Crawford two days later, the Middle East was discussed at length, at Blair's insistence, and Bush subsequently dispatched Colin Powell to the region to convey the President's new stance in person.[100] Yet, while Blair applauded, British diplomats remained unconvinced: 'Hell is likely to freeze over before Bush is ready to treat Sharon with a big stick,' the Embassy in Washington warned London.[101] 'The administration was not at all disposed to do anything that Sharon didn't agree with,' confirmed Wilkerson.[102]

Powell's trip was undermined by the hawks back in Washington. The Vice-President had no enthusiasm for engaging with Blair's peace process. The constant neocon refrain was that the 'only way to unwind the violence in the Middle East was to do Iraq first'.[103] Much talk began to be heard in Washington of the 'strategic importance of Israel' from the influential domestic pro-Israel lobby.[104] Sharon played on his ready supporters within the administration and called Bush's bluff. The 4 April statement came under fierce criticism from the Republican right. Bush was charged with losing 'moral clarity' in the war on terrorism, and 'failing to see that Arafat was the moral equivalent of Bin Laden'.[105] The pursuit of the MEPP was portrayed as giving out mixed messages of fighting a 'war on terrorism' internationally, but appearing to reward Palestinian terrorism against Israel. It was no contest. The Sharon–Cheney axis won the day. On 24 June, Bush delivered a new statement in which he called for the Palestinians to elect leaders 'not compromised by terror'. Bush also reaffirmed his support for a two-state solution, but declared Arafat a roadblock to progress in the Middle East. He 'basically said that Arafat was done', noted Rice. 'We wouldn't deal with Arafat.'[106] According to Meyer: 'The Republican right and the Israelis were cock-a-hoop at the statement. So was Karl Rove. He wanted to raise the Jewish-American vote for Bush from around one-fifth to a third.'[107] 'We may have had the two-state solution,' said a senior State Department official, 'but no one in the administration wanted to do anything about it.'[108]

Despite the 24 June statement being a clear rebuff, Blair had more sympathy with Bush's position than many realised. Campbell noted that Blair was 'in agreement that Arafat was weak, and that there had to be more sympathy for the Israelis'.[109] Two days after Bush's statement, world leaders gathered for the Kananaskis G8 in Canada. The US delegation was braced for a frosty reception. At around 6 A.M. on the first day, Rice came across Blair at the hotel gym. 'I was working out on a treadmill and the Prime Minister was lifting weights,' she recollected. She decided to tackle him on the Arafat statement: 'I said, "Gee, I guess we've kicked up quite a firestorm, haven't we?"' Blair's response surprised her. He backed Bush completely: 'I've tried harder than anybody to work with Arafat,' said the Prime Minister. 'He's done nothing but disappoint, and he's basically a bit corrupt.' Soon after Bush also entered the gym and the two talked through the Arafat issue. 'They came to an understanding about how to handle it in the press conference,' recalled Rice. 'Despite the firestorm, the Prime Minister knew the President was right and he was prepared to say that he was right.'[110] Blair's real concern was with the manner and timing of Bush's announcement, about which he had not been consulted.

Blair had no more luck making progress directly with the Israelis. From 2001, he formally appointed Lord Levy to be his personal envoy to the Middle East, who became a key figure to understanding Blair's actions: 'The Israeli experience of Tony Blair has been mediated by Lord Levy and often the Israelis did not know quite what to make of it,' said an FCO official.[111] Might the Jewish and well-connected Levy be able to achieve a breakthrough with Sharon where diplomacy with Bush had failed? Levy had some early successes. He met with Sharon at his farm in January 2002 and, over tea and cake, took the measure of the new Israeli leader for some three hours. He reported back to Blair that Sharon 'should not be demonised' and that 'provided the circumstances were right, he could make painful concessions'.[112] But Levy was a volatile character, capable of causing Blair great embarrassment. Neither Number 10 nor the Foreign Office were happy with his role. By mid-2002, Levy's personal diplomacy had run into the ground. At the time of the Kananaskis G8 in June, Sharon had a row with him over Arafat, telling him that dealing with Arafat was 'supporting terrorism': 'Levy asked Sharon three times if he was saying Blair had blood on his hands,' recalled one official. 'Sharon exploded, thumped the table and said in Hebrew, "The mandate is over" before throwing him out of the room.'[113] It was not only Levy's manner that grated with Sharon: it was also his association with the left in Israel. Neither did he inspire confidence with the Arabs: Prince Bandar, the well-connected Saudi Ambassador to the US, was one of several Arab leaders to express his distrust of Levy to British officials.[114] Levy proved an unwise choice. Not for the only time when he mixed friendship and work, Blair's judgement of character was at fault.

By the summer of 2002, voices in London and at the British Embassy in Washington became increasingly concerned by the state of the transatlantic relationship. As the Middle East showed, Blair appeared to be getting little back for his support. On 3 July, Meyer wrote a candid letter to Manning. 'We risk being taken for granted in Washington,' the Ambassador declared. 'We are seeing too little for our public support of the US.' Washington had 'an almost automatic assumption' that the UK would keep 'in the American slipstream. What is needed,' Meyer wrote, 'is a plain-speaking conversation. The PM should talk to the President about the damage being done to Britain's reputation and to its interests in the Middle East: we have a fund of political capital in the bank, but it is perishable and we should use it before its sell-by date.'[115] For a while Meyer heard nothing. His letter seemed to have disappeared into a Number 10 void. So later he spoke to Manning about it. There followed a sigh, and a sort of 'What can I do about it?' reaction from the other end of the line.[116] Manning found himself in an increasingly awkward position. Blair did not appear willing to listen.

Concerns were to the fore at a meeting held at Downing Street on 23 July. MI6 head Richard Dearlove opened by reporting on his recent talks with CIA counterparts in Washington. There had been 'a perceptible shift in attitude', and in the US 'military action was now seen as inevitable', which would be 'justified by the conjunction of terrorism and WMD'. In a sentence that has caused much speculation – the record of the meeting leaked – he then said, 'But the intelligence and facts are being fixed around the policy.' On Blair's concerns about exhausting the UN route and making the case against Saddam to win public support, he reported that there was 'no patience with the UN route, and no enthusiasm for publishing material on the Iraqi regime's record'. Dearlove concluded presciently: 'There was little discussion in Washington of the aftermath after military action.' His account provided a clear picture of the way the balance of power within the administration had tilted hawk-side: focused on war – only the timing was in doubt – rather than the UN, post-war planning or the niceties of the intelligence on WMD. Even if Blair had raised the lack of thinking about post-war Iraq at this stage, which he did not, he would not have been heeded.

What then of Blair's thinking in July 2002? The record states that 'we should work on the assumption that the UK would take part in any military action', but we need 'a fuller picture of the US planning before we could taken any firm decisions'.[117] Blair said he 'needed to be convinced first of the workability of a military plan, and second of an equally workable political strategy'.[118] According to the record's author, Matthew Rycroft, Manning's deputy at Number 10: 'The note shows that the PM wanted proper advice from our military on what the exact US military plan was and whether it would work before any decision could be made by Britain.'[119] Far from being a smoking gun pointed at Blair, as has been alleged, the memo shows that he had not yet committed Britain to war, nor would he until the UN route had been exhausted. Blair had nevertheless recognised by July, Michael Jay believes, that if there were to be a war, if all other attempts had failed, he would want Britain to back the Americans, principally because of the importance he attached to the relationship.[120] This was exactly his thinking in response to Straw at the 23 July meeting when he raised the prospect of not going into battle with the US: 'TB said that would be the biggest shift in foreign policy for fifty years and I'm not sure it's very wise. On the tactical level, he felt maximum closeness publicly was the way to maximise influence privately.'[121]

To the political forces ranged against war were added legal objections. Attorney-General Peter Goldsmith made it clear to Downing Street that of the three possible legal bases for British military action – self-defence, humanitarian intervention and a UN Security Council Resolution (SCR) – only the third might hold water. But existing SCRs would be 'difficult' to rely upon as a basis for going to war.[122] This view was not shared by the Bush Administration: 'the British government lawyers were a problem' recalled one Pentagon official. 'They looked at it rather differently to our lawyers.'[123] The FCO sent strict instructions around Whitehall that in any talk of Iraq and any potential planning for war, the words 'removal of Saddam' and 'regime change' could not be used, as neither were justified responses in law.[124] Blair 'did not want any of this "swimming around the system"', noted Campbell.[125]

At the end of July Blair wrote to Bush. Since Blair's memo in the immediate aftermath of 9/11, similar notes flowed from his pen 'pretty frequently' said one Number 10 aide. 'They'd be in his scribbled long hand, usually after a weekend. We sometimes tried to tighten them up, tone them down or even scrap them – usually to no (or strictly limited) avail.'[126] Opposition to a war had grown during July, and Blair now feared that the train was leaving Washington too quickly: he worried that his conditions, without which he realised he would not secure political support at home, would be left on the platform. Blair stressed yet again the need for a UN resolution, to release a dossier on Saddam's WMD, and to kick-start the MEPP. So far, so good. But then Blair faltered. At a time when the currents were swelling so strongly in Washington in the other direction, and he feared that Britain might simply be dumped – a fate he wanted to avoid at all costs – he pulled his punches. To the despair of his officials, he said in effect, 'You know George, that whatever you decide to do, I'll be with you.' Meyer was horrified. 'Why in God's name has he said that again?' he asked Manning. 'Well, we tried to stop him ... but we didn't prevail,' came the weary response.[127] Blair's unwillingness to be more assertive with Bush was arousing comment across Whitehall. 'If you wanted Blair to make a fairly stiff point about something, you'd ask Downing Street in advance,' recalled one official. 'The response was always, "Well, we've put it in his brief. We don't know whether he'll use it." We never, ever saw a record in which he made a confrontational point to the President.'[128]

Manning was sent to Washington on 30 July on the heels of Blair's note to get a feel for the mood of the administration. He told Rice, 'My honest advice is that this has to go the right way. It must go down the inspection route, down the UN route and we must get the context right, i.e., we must endeavour to make real progress on the MEPP.'[129] They both then went to see Bush in the Oval Office, where he repeated the same message. Bush listened intently. Manning was pleased with his response, and reported back to Blair that he believed Bush would follow the UN route.[130] But it wasn't going to be quite as simple as that. Blair had walked headlong into a battle royal raging among Bush's advisers.

Blair Wins His UN Concession: August–September 2002

By August, divisions within the US administration had reached a new intensity. Cheney remained fundamentally opposed to involving the UN in US efforts to deal with Iraq. 'We already had Security Council authority,' insisted John Bolton, one of Cheney's allies then working in the State Department, 'because Iraq was so clearly in violation of the original ceasefire resolution' from the 1991 Gulf War.[131] Powell, at the opposite end of the spectrum, believed a new resolution was essential. All that summer in meetings that appeared in their private schedules as 'Regional Strategies Meetings' to conceal their true import, the administration's top figures debated their approach to Iraq.[132]

Bush himself was in two minds. He had let the hawks carry him forward, but still he felt undecided. Only a year before they had all been so united. What had gone wrong? In a speech at West Point in June, Bush had endorsed America acting alone, but he was now beginning to question whether unilateral action, on the lines Cheney and others advocated, was indeed right. Domestic opinion in the US, so solidly behind him after 9/11, was turning. In Congress, the powerful Senate Foreign Relations Committee, and key Republicans in the House of Representatives, were expressing reservations about a war against Iraq. Memories of the quagmire of Vietnam in the 1970s and humiliation in Lebanon in the 1980s were still fresh. Key figures from his father's administration now made it clear they disagreed with Cheney. James Baker, Secretary of State to Bush senior, and Brent Scowcroft, his

National Security Advisor, both counselled caution, privately and in public.[133]

At this delicate stage, Colin Powell weighed in and spoke to Bush on 5 August. He recalls: 'Over the summer of 2002 I realised that the planning for war was racing ahead and I wasn't sure we'd thought it through enough. I thought to myself, "Jeez, what are we getting ourselves into? Do we understand the implications of what we're planning?" So I arranged to spend an evening with the President in early August, to lay out my concerns. I said to him that he had to understand that a war in Iraq would suck the oxygen out of his presidency and tie up the army for years and years. If we went in and succeeded then we would have a whole country to manage and be the proud owner of some 25 million people. I told him that not only would the Iraqi government collapse, but the civic structure would likely collapse and we would have to deal with the consequences. "Are you really ready to pay that price for getting rid of that jerk Saddam?" Bush listened and said, "Well, what would you do? What's the alternative?" I said, "We have to take this to the UN."'[134] His friend Blair had been banging on for weeks about the same thing. Bush agreed. The decision to go to the UN in principle was ratified at a key National Security Council meeting on 16 August. But the critical question of whether Bush would ask for a new resolution or merely insist the UN enforce existing resolutions, remained unresolved.

Over in London, Straw was fretting. Powell and Straw enjoyed frequent phone calls, and had become friends as well as allies. But the phone had its limits, so Powell suggested they talk face to face. 'Powell wants to talk about this very privately,' Straw told Blair, who agreed that it was a very good idea.[135] On 20 August, in absolute secrecy, and accompanied by just his Private Secretary Simon McDonald, Straw flew across the Atlantic on Concorde. From JFK airport a helicopter flew them down to a waterside home at the Hamptons, where the Powells were staying with some close friends. The British party of two, who were returning to London that night, were struck by the bizarre nature of their lightning visit. 'Because of the security surrounding Powell, particularly at that time, the whole Secretary of State's security team had assembled itself in an adjacent de-sanctified church. I went in and it was straight out of *Mission Impossible* – here was a full operations room.'[136]

Secrecy was vital so that both men could speak in utter candour. The US government machine could not always be trusted: often Powell and Straw would send confidential e-mails to their private addresses 'to stop it getting into the American bureaucracy'.[137] For this meeting, Powell had no State Department official and McDonald was the only note-taker for their three-hour talk. The record was then delivered to Powell 'outside the system'.[138] Efforts were made to limit knowledge of the meeting to a very small circle; for a time it was kept secret even from Meyer.[139] They spoke about whether a UN resolution was needed, and whether the UN resolution was the only way a war could be legitimised to the international community. Both were clear: there had to be a UN route. Without it, Straw stressed, the UK could not be part of American plans.[140] Powell's recollection of the meeting is similar to Straw's and McDonald's. He added this: 'Neither of us had any love for Saddam, but agreed that we had to calculate how much it would cost to remove him. We were worried that our two leaders might not have a strong enough sense of the consequences of removing Saddam militarily. One of us made a quip about regime change – that it might not be regime change in Baghdad that we should be worrying about. If this went badly it would weaken both our governments tremendously.'[141] None realised at the time how accurate that would prove.

Straw and Powell believed strongly that the diplomatic course could yet succeed. One British official spoke to Powell late in the summer, and was told that he and Straw saw it as their job to stop a war.[142] Straw frequently put pen to paper: 'Jack wrote a lot of handwritten minutes throughout these months. What he was writing about was so sensitive he didn't trust his words to the Whitehall computer system. He wrote a double-figure number of letters to Tony Blair at this time, always beginning "Dear Tony".'[143] A difference in outlook on Iraq between them had been obvious through the spring: that summer it became a gulf. 'Jack was pretty unhappy in August 2002,' recalled one senior diplomat. 'A number of us in the FCO reckoned that the Prime Minister had effectively sold the pass.'[144]

Colin Powell, for his part, remained mystified by Blair's attitude: 'In the end Blair would always support the President. I found this very surprising,' he said. 'I never really understood why Blair seemed to be in such harmony with Bush. I thought, well, the Brits haven't been attacked on 9/11. How did he reach the point that he sees Saddam as such a threat? Blair would express his concerns, but he would never lie down on the railroad tracks. Jack and I would get him up all pumped up about an issue. And he'd be ready to say, "Look here, George." But as soon as he saw the President he would lose all his steam.'[145] At the State Department, recalled Powell's Chief of Staff Lawrence Wilkerson, 'There was disappointment that Blair didn't push more. Let's face it, we looked to him as a natural ally.'[146] Number 10, in turn, found Powell's stance disappointing. 'It was as if he was trying to get Blair to do what he should have been pressing for anyway,' said one aide. 'Powell was always phoning Jack and saying, "You've got to get Tony to say this to the President." And our thought was, "Why the hell can't *you* say that to Bush?" We were irritated that he was so ineffective at getting his own point of view across in the White House. It struck us that the Prime Minister had more influence with the President than the US Secretary of State.'[147] Relations with Britain 'began to fray a little' conceded Wilkerson, 'because of Powell's inability to get anything done that the UK felt needed to be done'.[148]

In Washington the hawks were furious to have lost the initiative in August. They resolved to seize it back. On 26 August Cheney delivered his own verdict on the UN. In a bellicose speech in Tennessee, Cheney raised the spectre of Saddam gaining nuclear weapons and poured scorn on the UN inspection process: 'A return of inspectors would provide no assurance whatsoever of his compliance with UN resolutions,' Cheney declared. 'On the contrary, there is a great danger that it would provide false comfort that Saddam was somehow "back in his box".'[149] Cheney's words, high on emotion, low on evidence, were widely reported in Europe, and widely reviled. They made Blair's self-appointed task of holding the EU together much more difficult.

On 29 August an anxious Blair called Bush. 'TB sensed Bush was a bit nervous about the UN route,' noted Campbell. 'He was clearly getting a lot of competing advice. TB still felt confident we could turn the argument.'[150] When Manning met Bush back in July, they had agreed that Blair would visit Bush at Camp David in early September. The British aim, naturally, 'was to get GWB in a more dove-ish position'.[151] 'Tony was very tense on the flight over,' recalled Sally Morgan. 'He worked really hard to get his arguments straight in his head. It was a very big deal for him.'[152] Blair knew that military action would be up for discussion: 'Before his visit, we briefed him on what could happen and the options,' recalled Boyce. 'We sent military advisers on the plane with him.'[153] During the flight, Blair learned more about Saddam's failure to comply with UN resolutions on weapons inspectors and on concerns about Iraq's WMD.[154] They confirmed his deepest apprehensions. From the Washington Embassy, Meyer had submitted his own preparatory brief, in which he warned that the nub of their discussion would lie in what 'exhausting the UN process' actually meant. There was a real danger that the UK would be caught in the middle between the US, whose patience would be short, and the rest of the Security Council, who would be wedded to a longer time-scale. The administration seemed already committed to war, and would fight alone if they had to, though their analysis suggested that the invasion 'will be less perilous if they do it in company'. Hence their desire to get the British on board. Blair was warned that the President seemed to have bought into the 'neocon notion that with the overthrow of Saddam, all will be sweetness and light in Iraq'.[155]

On arrival at the President's retreat on 7 September, the apprehensive British party was disconcerted to find their *bête noire* Cheney waiting sullenly with Bush. At NSC meetings on 6 September, and again on the morning they arrived, Cheney had been lobbying hard against asking for a new UN resolution. Bush had promised to 'think about it'.[156] The two were extremely close, and Cheney's views mattered a great deal to Bush. Blair could hardly hope to match his influence: 'The most important force was Cheney going into the Oval Office and closing the door after Blair left and making sure the President was still on the "straight and narrow",' noted Wilkerson. Cheney's presence was thus hugely significant and suggested to the British he did not trust Bush if left exposed to Blair alone.[157] Blair realised that, if he was to keep Bush on side, he had 'to sell the case for the UN route to Cheney'.[158]

Blair had no fallback position if he lost the argument, so he pushed hard. It would be much easier to 'deliver the Europeans', as well as his own party, if they worked through the UN, he argued. In effect, he was offering Bush a deal based on logic that had been in his mind for many months: 'We must go through the United Nations. If it works, fine. If they won't disarm through the UN, Britain will back you in a war with Iraq.'[159] Bush heard what he needed to hear, and what Cheney wanted to hear: that the British were going to be fighting alongside them. Bush was relieved, and stressed again that Saddam Hussein was a threat, and that the world would be better off without him. Bob Woodward records Blair's response. 'I'm with you,' the Prime Minister replied, 'looking Bush back in the eye, pledging flat-out to commit British military force if necessary, the critical promise Bush had been seeking. "We want you to be part of this," he told the Prime Minister.'[160] Bush was impressed. 'Your guy's got balls,' he later told Campbell.[161] Once the Americans had confirmed this prize, discussion moved on to the UN. Bush was reluctant to go as far as seeking a new resolution. Blair was insistent: 'I remember the Prime Minister saying, "But everybody will be waiting for the punch-line . . . and then what?"' said Rice.[162] In one of his most important sessions of advocacy with Bush, Blair deployed every argument he could think of in favour of a UN resolution. Eventually Bush signalled his assent: 'GWB said he'd decided to go to the UN and put down a new UNSCR, challenge the UN to deal with the problems for its own sake.'[163] Blair was massively relieved. 'I suppose you can tell the story of how Tony flew in and pulled the crazed unilateralist back from the brink,' Bush joked with Campbell as the British left. Even better for Blair, the President also said that he would 'get something on the Middle East. "That's a promise."'[164]

Blair flew home a man with a great weight off his shoulders, stopping off at Balmoral for a truncated audience with the Queen. 'He was very high on the plane. He did not want to go to sleep. He kept talking. We were all exhausted.'[165] While Blair unwound, Bush set to work on his speech to the UN General Assembly five days later, on 12 September. The subject of violent pressure within the administration, it went through a couple of dozen drafts and more. Cheney and the hawks continued to fight against a UN resolution. No one knew quite what Bush would do. 'Despite what was said to us at Camp David, it wasn't clear to us until the last couple of days that he would agree to the UN route, and it was not until the morning of the speech that we were made aware of the wording,' said Jeremy Greenstock, Britain's representative at the UN.[166]

On an auspicious anniversary – 11 September – Number 10 received a draft of the speech which did not feature any request for a new resolution. Manning rushed to send through a new passage from Blair and spoke to Rice, but could not obtain absolute clarification, and Bush's final intentions remained unclear. With hours to go, Number 10 heard that Bush would indeed call for the resolution. But the drama had one final act to play. At the podium in front of the General Assembly, Bush noticed he had been handed an earlier draft of his speech, omitting any request for a resolution. From memory, he reinserted the phrase: 'We will work with the UN Security Council for the necessary resolutions.' But he misremembered it, saying 'resolutions' in the plural even though the final draft referred to only one resolution. 'That caused immediate speculation among other members of the Security Council that the President might support two resolutions,' recalled Greenstock.[167]

Blair and his team stood helpless in front of a television screen in Number 10 watching anxiously as the American President ad-libbed the lines on which so much hinged.[168] But this prevarication and muddle aside, he had spoken the words. After five months of lobbying, Blair now had something concrete – Bush's public agreement to seek UN support against Saddam. Was it Blair who swayed Bush? Or Colin Powell? Or was he minded to do it anyway? Robin Cook, Blair's most vocal critic in Cabinet, later wrote, 'Blair deserves credit for persuading President Bush that he must take Iraq to the United Nations for multilateral agreement. It is the only point in the whole saga where it is possible to pinpoint a clear instance where British influence made any difference to US policy on Iraq.'[169] Number 10 believed that 'Bush would never even have tried to use the UN without Blair'.[170] So do some American officials: 'Aside from Secretary Powell and the State Department,' recalled Marc Grossman, then the number three official at State, 'no one else in the administration would have paid the slightest attention to the UN had it not been for PM Blair.'[171] Another senior US official believed it was the Blair/Powell pressure that made the difference. 'No other allies were taken as seriously as Blair. France and Germany were in the dog house.'[172] Ultimately, one cannot say whether Blair's lobbying was decisive on Bush, but as David Manning puts it, Blair was a highly influential voice in 'a coalition persuading Bush to go down the UN route'.[173]

Advice Blair received from diplomats that autumn was that Britain would hold the key vote on whether or not the US would go to war in Iraq.[174] The offer of British participation in a military campaign seemed to be Blair's trump card. With hindsight, this case looks overstated. Ultimately, the US would have gone to war in Iraq without Britain. They did not need Britain militarily, although diplomatically British support was very useful. It is telling that Britain rarely figures in Woodward's two-volume account of the war and its aftermath. The neocons never felt British participation was particularly important. They sneered at Blair's idealism on MEPP and multilateralism: Lewis 'Scooter' Libby, Cheney's powerful Chief of Staff, would jibe, 'Oh dear, we'd better not do that or we might upset the Prime Minister.'[175] More moderate voices, including Bush, wanted the UK as an ally so long as America continued to call the shots. Blair's leverage was thus always limited, but not insignificant. With a sympathetic but tougher approach, Blair might have pulled the administration closer to his preferred strategy for Iraq and the broader Middle East. The ramifications of his failure to achieve this would be felt for the rest of this premiership and beyond.

5

'Make or Break' at Home

June–December 2002

A year had passed since the General Election. 'If you failed to get into your stride in the first few months after the election, your second term could go the same way as the first!' The stark words of his policy advisers in Number 10 echoed in Blair's mind. The post-election honeymoon and 9/11 glow had evaporated, and he was facing the nastiest press in his premiership. The way forward in Northern Ireland and Europe appeared elusive. Over the summer British entry to the Euro reappeared on his screen, not because he believed deeply in it but because it was at least a distinctive policy that he could ram home, win a referendum on, and then . . . who knew? The distractions of foreign policy, which in many ways he found more enjoyable than domestic policy, were impeding the time he was able to give to his domestic agenda. Where it was fructifying, it was bringing him up against his party and, more particularly, his Chancellor, as in health, and in particular education.

Education: June 2001–October 2002

'No one ever believes that anything happens in education and we will prove them wrong,' Blair declared in 1997.[1] By 2001, some things had happened, not least in primary schools, where a strong drive from Blunkett's DfEE brought together the pioneering work of Michael Barber and Chris Woodhead, Chief Inspector of Schools until 2000.[2]

Blair had taken a keen interest in their progress, but British schooling remained largely untransformed. It was not until Andrew Adonis, who joined Miliband's Number 10 Policy Unit in 1998, applied his mind to the whole of education policy that Blair raised his sights for the second term. Apart from Barber, who shared his views, 'there were simply not enough people in the [renamed Department for Education and Skills] DfES or education world who believed in Andrew's agenda', said a Treasury official. 'It was very much him driving it with the force of his own arguments and position close to the PM.'[3] The February 2001 Green Paper, 'Schools: Building on Success' and the Learning and Skills Act 2000 were early fruits of that new thinking.

Yet little of this radicalism found its way into the 2001 manifesto. Some blame Blunkett; 'Even though we knew he was going, he was still allowed to be the key figure on education in the manifesto. He was not a choice and diversity man.'[4] Despite shining as minister for school standards in the first term, Estelle Morris was expected by aides in Number 10 to be 'cautious with a big C' as Education Secretary.[5] She did not, however, seek to block the new agenda driven by Adonis, newly promoted to head of policy at Number 10, which was the creative force rather than the DfES. In contrast, the new health policy that was emerging in 2001 was driven from the Department of Health. Adonis's relationship with Blair, which blossomed in the second term, was key to establishing the new agenda.[6] 'Adonis and Blair wanted autonomous schools everywhere. Neither of them wanted local authorities to have any control at all,' complained one DfES official.[7]

Relations between Adonis in Number 10 and Morris in the DfES were often strained. She felt she was being harried; Number 10 felt she was ponderous. 'She was not on the same page as people in Number 10 like Heywood, Stevens and Adonis, who understood what Blair wanted to do. Our role was to bring his policies into line with his instincts,' said a close aide.[8] Blair needed people like them because he was not primarily a policy person. He had instincts, but needed others to produce the ideas for him to champion. Adonis, like Blair, did not arrive at Number 10 with his ideas fully formed. He had to work them up from talking to a group of successful heads of secondary schools: from these conversations came the idea of giving schools greater autonomy and self-governance. 'His emerging views chimed with the Prime Minister's instincts. They thought the same. Andrew gave him a lot of his ideas.'[9] Three ideas were to emerge in 2000/01, which were to form Blair's distinctive contribution to education in his second and third terms.

Academies were the first idea. The seed was planted when Adonis visited three City Technology Colleges (CTCs) in Croydon, Telford and Gateshead in 1998. He realised that he was not just looking at individually exceptional schools; here was a model of future schooling which had at its heart four ingredients that were to become the distinctive features of academies: independence from local authority management, successful external sponsors offering inspiring vision, a no-nonsense approach setting high standards, and finally investment in modern buildings. Blunkett was supportive, and in March 2000 he unveiled the 'city academy' programme. His Learning and Skills Act provided the legislative framework for academies to be created. Had further legislation been required after the 2001 election, when academies became highly controversial and disliked by Labour's left, and when Blair's stock fell, it might well have sunk the programme. Morris was initially cautious on academies: 'She believed that we should try out a small number before making them the driving principle of education policy.'[10] So the early second-term drive came from Number 10 and Barber's Delivery Unit. By the beginning of 2001, Adonis was seeking to create at least ten academies a year; his hope was that once that critical number was reached, the model would take off.[11] On 7 January 2002, he wrote to Blair to call 'for greater boldness on secondary school reform, including more city academies'.[12] Morris, and her successor Charles Clarke, wanted academies to be restricted to areas of high deprivation, as did the DfES, whereas Number 10 wanted to build them across the country. Brown was less than enthusiastic about academies at first (shortly before becoming Prime Minister, he embraced them), but 'the Treasury never had a look-in because there was no new policy, and the money was already all allocated to the Education Department.'[13]

Expanding the number of 'specialist schools' was a second policy. The origin here was the 1999 'Excellence in Cities' initiative and followed by the Green Paper, 'Schools: Building on Success' of February 2001. It was at its launch that Campbell spoke the graphic words about disliking the 'bog-standard comprehensive'. 'Alastair does this for Blair. The phrase was a carefully constructed one before. We knew exactly what we were doing,' said a Number 10 aide.[14] Campbell did not readily accept the new thinking. 'All I had been trying to do was make a point in favour of modernised comprehensives, with the emphasis on both parts of that,' he noted in his diary defensively (he was a Labour traditionalist on education, as still more was his partner Fiona Millar).[15] According to an aide, 'The defining moment in going radical in the second term was that 2001 Green Paper.'[16] By encouraging comprehensives to become specialist schools with differing expertises, accompanied by some extra state funding, it helped identify 'choice and diversity' as a core philosophy in Blair's public-service reform principles. But specialist schools became bitterly controversial because the model was regarded as a betrayal of the uniform comprehensive principle, so sacred to old Labour. Blair trod carefully on specialist schools during the 2001 election. Once it was over, Number 10, in league with the feisty Cyril Taylor at the Specialist Schools Trust, campaigned to make every single comprehensive school specialist, which had Blair's enthusiastic support throughout. Barber's monthly stock-takes became the primary way in which Blair was able to monitor the DfES's progress in establishing new academies and specialist schools.[17]

The third strategy was a focus on London, where state schools were seen to be particularly unsuccessful: some 18 per cent of London parents opted out of the state sector to send their children to independent schools, as opposed to only 7 per cent nationwide. 'London Challenge' was the new body set up by Blair to provide a sharp focus on the performance of London schools, with dedicated units to drive improvement, helped by a particular commitment to spread specialist schools and academies across London. Very slowly, standards in London schools began to improve, especially where the 'Excellence in Cities' programme had been introduced, though the numbers opting for private schools continued to rise.[18] The ambition was to transform the teaching profession, over and above increases in pay, by training headteachers better and by opening up new avenues to bring able young graduates and mature workers from other fields into the profession. Thus was created the National College for School Leadership and 'Teach First' in 2002, both with Blair's strong backing. 'It is essential that we reconnect the teaching profession with the top universities, and this needs to be a key mission of yours,' Adonis told him.[19]

By August 2002, Estelle Morris ran into trouble over the publication of that year's A-level results, when it appeared that an exam board had not been marking scripts fairly. Number 10 had already begun to have doubts about her leadership and there were concerns that primary school results were falling short of their targets, but it was her handling of the A-level crisis that sapped confidence in her.[20] 'The PM felt she'd made a mountain out of a molehill out of the A-level circus,' said one Number 10 source.[21] Blair accepted that she was clearly no longer happy in the job, but it was still a shock when she turned up 'out of the blue' to see him on 22 October and said, 'I don't think this is for me.'[22] Blair asked Campbell and Morgan to discuss whether she should stay: 'At times she was close to tears,' Campbell recorded. Blair later told Campbell that he 'didn't think she should go, but that only she could know if she was really up for it'.[23] The following day she had made up her mind to go. Blair had to move quickly and put in someone who would be decisive, quick-footed and strong on the reform agenda at secondary and also higher education. He chose Party Chairman Charles Clarke. 'We put in Clarke because when you have someone like Estelle who says they are not up to it, you demonstrably need to have somebody who is.'[24] It was not an easy position, with policy effectively being driven from Number 10. Education had moved on a lot in the fifteen months since the General Election. There was still much further to go, but it was as though the skies had suddenly cleared and Blair was discovering at last exactly where he wanted to go. Education and health became his two areas during 2002 where his distinctive agenda was being rolled out. It was here that Blairism was born.

The 2002 Wobble

Blair had pushed to the back of his mind the question of whether he would fight a third General Election. He knew Brown expected him to go in 2004, and had carried that clear interpretation away from the Granita dinner in 1994. His unpleasantness was already becoming draining: it would become intolerable if he continued in power. The press, for so long an ally, were turning against him, as in the Black Rod episode. He wanted to have a career after politics, quite what, he did not know: Leo was still a baby, begging the question about bringing up a young family within the confines of Downing Street.[25] Life in Number 10 was losing some of its appeal. He missed the quartet. Mandelson and Hunter had gone from the centre: though he spoke to both regularly by phone, it was not the same. Since late 2000, he felt he could no longer work harmoniously with Brown: deep down, the relationship had changed. And Campbell was now itching to go as well. Blair felt guilty about asking him to stay on, but he was not yet ready to live without his constant contribution. Of the old guard, Powell was a massive support, above all on Washington, Iraq and Northern Ireland, but they were not as close. Morgan had blended back in as Hunter eased herself out, and here was an emotional relationship that he needed. But being Prime Minister felt different to him, and the prospect of Campbell's departure was troubling him.

Since the early summer, Blair had thus been tussling with a crucial question: how long did he want to remain as Prime Minister? Would a decision to leave earlier rather than later actually enhance his ability to enact his growing domestic agenda? On 11 June, Blair invited Powell, Morgan and Campbell into the den. His plan was to announce publicly that he would not fight the next General Election and 'tell Cabinet that if ministers wanted to fight a leadership election, they would have to do it outside'.[26] Morgan feared that it would immediately make him a lame duck, while Campbell told him that 'he had to decide simply whether it was the right thing to do, and that if it wasn't, he was simply caving into psychological warfare [from Brown's camp]'.[27] Campbell pressed him: did he really want to go? Blair replied: 'That's exactly what Cherie would say.'[28] Blair elaborated on this thinking: what he wanted was to win an election, followed by a referendum on the Euro and then leave after 'getting a new leader in place'. If a referendum were possible before the election, he would 'win that, stay to the election and get a new leader in place'.[29] Blair's consultation with the core team broke up without resolution. Although taken by surprise, 'it wasn't high drama,' as on person put it, 'but "do you think this is a sensible thing to be thinking of?"'[30] A fortnight later, on 27 June, Blair wanted to discuss what he now called '*La Grande Stratégie*' with Campbell alone. 'The only question that mattered was whether it strengthened or weakened him,' Campbell recorded in his diaries. 'It was true that he had always imagined only doing two terms, but I wasn't convinced it was remotely time for him to go yet.'[31] Campbell thought that the plan resembled 'one of those things that had a certain immediate appeal, but which would go in the box marked "things I wish I hadn't done"'.[32] Blair insisted that he wasn't 'fed up' but that unless he could achieve real progress in the public services within eight years 'there was a bit of a problem'.[33]

Blair returned to the subject with Campbell in the Number 10 garden in early July. Campbell was almost certain that he had 'settled his view, that he would sometime announce it, say that he was going to stay for the full term, but not go into the election as leader'.[34] Blair then debated the central question about whether his authority would diminish and whether there would be an automatic shift to Brown. He was working through the dilemma that he would eventually impose on himself two years later, when he made the announcement in September 2004 that he would not serve a fourth term. He believed he would be able to move Cabinet ministers 'without saying it was because he feared a rival'. Taking the country into the Euro after winning a referendum would be crucial: 'Not because of a place in history but because I think it is the right thing to do.'[35] Blair had also floated the idea with Mandelson, who, surprisingly, was not hostile,[36] nor was Hunter.[37] It was an audacious plan for a serving Prime Minister: none of his predecessors in the last century had made such a public announcement about their departure plans. But very few had been in power for so long, with every prospect of a future election victory. Campbell again challenged Blair's motives as the two walked in from the terrace to the Cabinet Room: was he really being intimidated by a 'mix of GB and the press?' he asked.[38] Blair thought not: 'You have to know when to go. I also think the history of leaders trying to choose their successor is a very bad one.'[39] But Blair had not made up his mind. As the conversation drew to a close, he asked him pointedly, revealing everything one needs to know about the depth of their relationship: 'Is it the right thing or the wrong thing? I want your best brain on it.'[40]

On 19 July Blair pushed Campbell again. Historical analogies were now on the Prime Minister's mind: 'Bill C. had said to him, "Whatever you do, go when they're still asking for more. Don't go like Thatcher." TB said if she'd gone in '88, it would have been very different for her.'[41] He continued to insist that rather than making him a lame duck, the plan would enhance his authority. But another factor now seemed to argue in favour of leaving the job earlier rather than later: 'I think Cherie is pregnant,' he told Campbell. 'He said they were absolutely gobsmacked by the whole thing. But it did mean it was forcing him to think about the future. "I've effectively got two families with the same woman."'[42] Cherie had wanted to have another child so that baby Leo would not grow up on his own. They were both apprehensive, but very excited about the prospect of having a fifth child, and building a new future beyond politics.[43] But over the summer, Blair's enthusiasm for his *grand projet* waned. On 5 August Cherie suffered a miscarriage. She had been watching the Commonwealth Games in Manchester which closed that day and had started feeling unwell. She was admitted to Chelsea and Westminster Hospital and was discharged the following day after an operation.[44] Had the baby been born, it would have changed his life and hers enormously. For Cherie, aged forty-seven, it was a serious blow, and, with her husband deeply preoccupied, it heightened her reliance on her friend and 'lifestyle' mentor Carole Caplin, with consequences that would explode at the end of the year.

By the time he returned at the end of August from their delayed holiday in France, his mind was made up. There would be no pre-announcement of his departure. Instead, he was determined to reinvigorate his government. And he returned from France with a particularly important holiday note.

Blair Rededicates His Premiership: August–September 2002

Over his three-week summer holiday Blair pondered why his second term had so far failed to make the impact he had hoped for. He wrote his holiday notes while staying at a rented villa near Toulouse in the south of France. They explored the lessons he had learned over the first term and the election period, and envisaged how the twelve months ahead would be much more purposeful. The warning words of Adonis echoed in his mind: he was desperate for his second term to avoid the mistakes of his first. All was not lost. He knew he still had another year to make his mark before he had to begin preparing for the following General Election. 'The year ahead', he wrote, 'would be a year of struggle and challenge, but also a tremendous opportunity.' It was going to be 'make or break' for the government, Blair's twenty-four-page typed memo, sent to his close Number 10 aides on 30 August 2002, was a scouring attack on the limited achievements since 1997. From late spring, aides often heard him using the word 'reconnect' in Number 10; a long, decisive memo he wrote to his Number 10 team in early summer had opened with the words, 'This is the time to revitalise.'[45] 'He had begun to realise that time had been lost in the first term undoing what the Tories had done up till 1997 without saying how he was going to improve or "New Labour-ise" policy. In many ways he realised we'd actually gone backwards. He was a long time clocking that,' said a close aide.[46] 'He told us, "I want you to think the unthinkable, and then let's decide how much of it we can do. Don't worry", he used to say, "whether you think this is deliverable for the party or the government. Tell me what you think is right and let's work out how we can do it."'[47] He would not have said that in 1994–97, or in the first term. He was freeing himself from the thinking of his old guard, and adopting his new paradigms that were to make the second half of his premiership much more successful than his first.

The four challenges in the year ahead, he wrote in his August memo, were public service reform, the Euro, law and order and Iraq/war on terror. The task would be to 'keep the centre ground; to force the Tories out to the right; and to persuade ourselves that radical reform is the answer, not the problem'. New Labour had built its case in the first term on traditional values of social justice and solidarity; now he looked for a 'new formulation for the party in the future', taking it beyond the 'big state' prescription of the 1945 Labour government. Public service reform lay at the heart of what he wanted to achieve in his remaining time as Prime Minister. This entailed 'diversity of supply, choice and an end to old practices'. In health, it meant 'ridding ourselves of the monolithic

NHS . . . Can we make foundation hospitals a reality?' He was pleased with Milburn, who was 'certainly pushing change radically'. In education, specialist schools replacing comprehensives 'just about gets there' but he wanted greater independence for specialist schools from local authorities. He praised Adonis who 'had dreams of a radical agenda' but worried whether the DfES was 'equipped to push it through' because it had a 'real timidity in taking big policy changes on board'. This is the point where the Euro re-enters centre stage. He had played around with it at the General Election and since, ducking and weaving around Brown. This time he was going for it. Northern Ireland too was to see a more serious tone.

Blair's speech to the party conference on 1 October echoed many of the words and sentiments in this memo. New Labour was 'best at its boldest . . . we've not been bold enough'; a 'great push forward' was needed urgently. Education needed to see more choice for parents and 'a post-comprehensive era', while in health, patients should have operations on the NHS 'at the time [they] want with the doctor [they] want', as part of a more 'personalised' NHS. He was irritated by the defeat earlier in the conference over the Private Finance Initiative (PFI): it was time to move on 'from the old ways', he said, goading union leaders and Labour activists unhappy about private finance in the public sector. 'Come on,' he challenged the party. 'This isn't the betrayal of public services. It's their renewal.' On the Euro, he said it was 'about our destiny' and if the economic tests for entry were met 'we go for it' and call a referendum.

It was a vital conference for him to win over, his last easy ride until 2006. Pressure had been building up against him within his party: if he hadn't won them over convincingly, his future would have been much more difficult. 'Tony's speech went down well with the audience,' recorded Cook in his diary. It would not 'have gone down well with the rumbustious conferences of twenty years ago, but Tony has complete mastery over the modern conference'.[48] Blair was happier speaking at Blackpool than at Bournemouth or Brighton, the other two venues for Labour's annual party conference. 'He prefers staying in Brighton, but Blackpool's a great conference hall for delivering a speech. It's far too small but it has a fantastic atmosphere and there's a bit of sentimentality about speaking at Blackpool.'[49] Added colour was provided in 2002 by Blair inviting his old friend Bill Clinton to speak. 'This came directly at Blair's request. "Please help me, I need you" was the message. Clinton was delighted to help out,' said one of Clinton's aides.[50] 'We wanted Clinton to highlight the importance of staying New Labour, not wobbling as the Democrats did under Gore,' said Morgan.[51] The occasion was heightened by Clinton arriving with actor Kevin Spacey, who humoured delegates by his story of the Blackpool McDonald's burger he'd eaten the night before. Clinton charmed the audience, but his nuanced remarks about the Iraq crisis hit the delegates' spot rather too well for Blair's comfort. 'Don't cross bridges we would rather not cross,' Clinton said when urging full support for the UN rather than going to war. 'Saddam needs to have one last chance. As an American, and as a citizen of the world, I'm glad Tony Blair will be central to weighing the risks and making the call,' implying that Blair and Blair alone could make the White House see reason. The applause was spectacular. One Cabinet minister was overheard saying afterwards, 'I've just been outside for a fag. I always like a smoke after being made love to.'[52]

Turbulence in Northern Ireland: June 2001–October 2002

While delegates were packing up to leave Blackpool, with the words of Blair and Clinton ringing in their ears, the police one hundred miles across the water in Belfast were preparing to raid Sinn Féin's offices at the Northern Ireland Assembly at Stormont in full glare of the TV cameras. The cack-handed raid provided an unsettling end to what had otherwise been a very good week for Blair: it was claimed that the raid was 'death to the peace process'.[53] One of Blair's skills was not over-reacting to reverses. He had many opportunities to hone that skill in his first five years of battling to bring lasting peace to Northern Ireland. Jonathan Powell compared him to Gladstone in the way they were both intrigued by Ireland and became personally deeply committed to it. But why had he invested so much time and capital, especially as it was an area which would never bring him much political credit? Powell, who worked by his side on Northern Ireland every step of the way over ten years, believed the genesis of his interest lay in his family background: his grandmother was an Orange woman from Donegal (her last words to him were 'Whatever you do, don't marry a Catholic').[54] This combined with his strong commitment to bring peace to warring parties, the same instinct which informed his zeal to bring peace in the Middle East. He sensed that the province was an area where he should, and could, make an enduring contribution.

After Blair became party leader in 1994, he smartly ended Labour's traditional commitment to a united Ireland. His first major address after becoming Prime Minister in May 1997 quite consciously was at the

Royal Ulster Agricultural Show in Balmoral, on the south side of Belfast: Northern Ireland, he said, was going to be every bit as important to him as it was to his predecessor John Major. Terrorism being perpetrated by both the Republican and the 'Loyalist' (militant Unionists) groups must stop, and he emphasised the need for decommissioning of weapons and movement towards democratic settlement. 'My message to Sinn Féin is clear. The settlement train is leaving. I want you on that train but it is leaving anyway . . . You cannot hold the process to ransom any longer. So end the violence. Now.' His commitment was rewarded ten months later in the Good Friday Agreement of 10 April 1998, when in a frenetic seventy-two hours of activity in Belfast, he helped bring all political parties to agree to a democratic future. A Northern Ireland Assembly at Stormont in Belfast was to be established which saw devolution of power back to the Province. Terrorists on both sides, the IRA (or 'Provisional IRA') on the Republican side, and the various paramilitary groups on the loyalist side, had to lay down their arms by May 2000. It was the IRA who were the real obstacle, not the far less well-organised loyalist groups whose political representatives stood little chance of being in government.

'The difficulties will all now lie ahead, however,' said George Mitchell, the convenor of the Good Friday talks. The challenge was now for Sinn Féin, the political wing of the IRA, and led by Gerry Adams and Martin McGuinness, to show they were committed to the democratic process and not to violence, and for David Trimble, leader of the larger and more moderate of the two Unionist parties, the UUP, to convince fellow Protestants that the Republicans were sincere and that they should enter power-sharing with them. Rejectionists on the Unionist side were given powerful ammunition for breaking off talks when four months later the Omagh bomb on 15 August 1998 committed by a splinter group, the 'Real IRA', killed twenty-nine people and injured and traumatised hundreds. Coming so soon after the euphoria of the Good Friday Agreement, it made Blair deeply worried about how both sides would react.[55] Would Unionists say this would mean the end of the process? In the event Adams swiftly condemned the atrocity, paving the way for both sides to redouble efforts for peace. Elections to the new Assembly at Stormont, held in June 1998, weakened Trimble's position to the gain of the more hard-line Unionist party, the DUP, led by Ian Paisley. Trimble formed a government in November 1999, which was subsequently suspended, then reconvened. In the 2001 General Election, Trimble's UUP again lost seats to Ian Paisley's DUP (holding six MPs to the DUP's five). On the Republican side, the moderate

SDLP retained their three MPs, but Sinn Féin's tally increased to four. It was worrying for Blair to see the more extreme wings on both sides make headway over the more moderate parties.

Once the election was over, Blair again pushed Sinn Féin to agree to decommission arms and to end criminality, while urging the Unionists to share power with them. 'The game was trying to get movement on the Republican side sufficient to make the Unionists feel that it was worth doing something: the whole trick was about maintaining momentum,' said Tom Kelly from Number 10.[56] Policy was driven by Number 10, principally by Blair and Jonathan Powell, who handled the day-to-day papers and many of the meetings. But Kelly, one of Number 10's two official spokesmen, was also deeply involved. Unlike Blair and Powell, he came from the province. The Northern Ireland Office (NIO) was the other principal player, with its succession of Secretaries of State. In practice, however, it was to be officials at the NIO who were to play a bigger part throughout the whole story than the Northern Ireland Secretaries.

'Decommissioning was always seen as the litmus test of the Republicans' sincerity,' said Kelly.[57] Blair thus convened talks the month after the 2001 election at Weston Park in Staffordshire to try to kick-start decommissioning, especially as the latest decommissioning deadline had passed without success two weeks before. 'The purpose of these conferences was to bring the parties to a crisis where they had to make a decision,' said one official.[58] Initially intended to last two days, the talks eventually lasted six. Blair and Powell went for a walk with a vexed Trimble during the discussions. 'We're fairly convinced that [the IRA] is going to do something [on decommissioning],' said Blair. Trimble retorted testily that the Unionists' own intelligence had suggested before that the IRA was going to 'do something' on decommissioning, but they had not delivered. 'Did they have any new intelligence to suggest new thinking?' Trimble asked Blair. He turned to Jonathan Powell. 'Are you optimistic this time?' he asked. 'Yes, I think they are going to do something.'[59] Although Weston Park broke up without immediate agreement, the first IRA act of decommissioning came three months later in October. After brief suspensions of Stormont by Northern Ireland Secretary John Reid, and arrests of suspected IRA terrorists in Colombia on suspicion of links to local terrorist groups in August, devolution survived the rest of the year.

Blair refused to give up. 'Even during the build-up to the Iraq war, barely a week went by when there wasn't a discussion on Ireland in some form. It took a large quantity of Blair's time,' said a Number 10 source.[60] He would see Adams and McGuinness regularly in Number 10. They would often enter the building via the entrance to the Cabinet Office in Whitehall to evade the ever-present cameras watching Number 10's front door. Blair's dealings with them were highly controversial. To some in British politics it was repugnant to be talking to these two men, both of whom were powerful figures in the Republican movement, and had been for many years. It remained an open question how far they were still involved in or aware of IRA operations, and how far the IRA was still involved in paramilitary activities against their wishes. Were they just stringing Blair along? Blair believed that, if he did not give them 'leg room', he would lose them, and the province would be plunged back into civil war. He was fully aware of the risks involved in pursuing such a strategy, but felt he had to in order to make progress.[61]

It wasn't just the political right who were disconcerted about Blair's closeness to both men. Some officials in the NIO worried when Blair met Adams and McGuinness, because they always wanted to see him without officials present. If Powell was not with him no record was taken and they were never certain what had been said.[62] 'I never thought he was tough enough on Sinn Féin,' said one NIO official. 'Adams and McGuinness are very skilful negotiators. They are harder and more professional than he is. Blair likes to be liked. They didn't care about that. They could be very cold and relentless.'[63] Others in London accepted that Adams and McGuinness had a very difficult and sensitive management job bringing the IRA along with them and 'sometimes they had to let their movement play out certain things'.[64]

Cynics about the IRA had their suspicions confirmed when the IRA raided the Castlereagh Special Branch office in east Belfast in March 2002. Highly sensitive intelligence was stolen. Doubts were further heightened when both the IRA and Sinn Féin denied the IRA had been involved, and improbably accused British intelligence of being behind the raid. The Castlereagh raid led the Police Service of Northern Ireland (PSNI), which had replaced the Royal Ulster Constabulary in November 2001, to investigate other alleged Republican operations. Suspicions grew that they had spies inside the NIO in Belfast, and that the IRA 'spy ring' based at Stormont had even penetrated John Reid's own office.[65] A sure response was called for. It came at 5 A.M. on the morning of 4 October, when police officers from the PSNI burst into a number of Republican homes in Belfast, seized documents and made arrests. A few hours later, thirty police arrived at Stormont and raided Sinn Féin's offices: the event that coincided with the end of the Labour party conference in Blackpool.

Northern Ireland officials later spoke about the raid being a 'classic cock-up', which took place probably at a 'shift change' for the police, and with television cameras that happened to be present.[66] The officers burst into the office of Sinn Féin's head of administration and chief spy suspect, Dennis Donaldson, from whom they seized computer disks. Donaldson later confessed in 2005 that he had been a British agent. He was shot dead in a remote spot of Ireland, in suspicious circumstances, on 4 April 2006. Trimble met Blair four days after the raid, threatening to pull his ministers out of power-sharing if Blair did not expel Sinn Féin. Trimble's biographer Dean Godson records his subject telling Blair, 'They've initiated an intelligence operation to gain advantage over you and us.' Blair replied that he thought Adams and McGuinness still 'wanted this to work'. Trimble replied, 'Be careful about putting your faith in them. They are not honest or moral people.'[67] Many in Belfast and London thought similarly. Was Blair indeed being made a fool of by continuing to take them seriously?

Blair and Powell had been thinking for some months that a major speech was required, firmly warning the Republicans that they could not carry on as they were, and that an unequivocal and tangible commitment to peace and democracy was needed. 'We had been debating for some time the need to reassert our position or lose credibility,' said a Number 10 source.[68] In the four and a half years since Good Friday, the hard truth was that little progress had been made since that bright weekend early in his premiership. Blair worried that the peace process was losing momentum. A vicious circle was in play. The less progress there was from Sinn Féin, the more Trimble and the UUP were vulnerable to hard-line Unionists on their own side who wanted to abandon talks. Yet the more Trimble demanded concessions, the more Sinn Féin doubted their sincerity, and the harder it became for Adams and McGuinness to go to the IRA and say 'stop your activities and start decommissioning'. Blair worried that Number 10's authority was being called into question. Unionists were beginning to lose faith in his nuanced line, while at the same time the Conservative Party at Westminster became increasingly critical. Additional pressure on him came from the south, from Taoiseach and close ally Bertie Ahern. Ahern was facing his own elections and had made it clear he was not prepared to go into government in partnership with Sinn Féin, as they had not yet shown sufficient proof of their democratic credentials. 'We were thus in an impossible position where in the north we were saying that Sinn Féin were suitable to be part of the democratic process, but in the south Bertie Ahern was saying that they were not yet ready.'[69]

Blair made his views clear in a major speech on 17 October in Belfast. Time for drafting was short. He wrote it on the way back from an Iraq meeting with Putin: 'It was an extraordinary example of his ability to switch focus,' said an official. 'He wrote it almost from scratch on the plane.'[70] In deliberately stark language, Blair took on Republican thinking, arguing that the movement could no longer be served by its dual strategy of maintaining an armed presence and refusing to decommission arms while also keeping a foot in the democratic camp. A 'fork in the road' had been reached. He demanded that the Republicans make a *full* transition to the democratic path and begin decommissioning of weapons, accompanied by a 'complete end' to IRA activities, including punishment beatings, procurement of weapons and spying. 'There had to be acts of completion' (his own phrase) to show that Sinn Féin was honouring understandings it had given at the Good Friday Agreement.

The speech may only have been a thirty-minute address to a small audience of business and community leaders, but it had a significant impact. In appealing to 'thinking Republicans' and progressive forces on both sides, Blair held out an olive branch to Unionists, and specifically Trimble, who was still threatening to walk out of Stormont if Sinn Féin were not expelled. 'It was Blair at his firmest. He was saying that it was no longer sustainable for Republicans to continue as they were. They had to choose,' said an NIO official.[71] Kelly described it accurately as 'one of the defining Northern Ireland speeches of his premiership'.[72] Some Unionists doubted Blair's sincerity, and thought he would have wooed Sinn Féin back if they had decided to walk out in response to the speech. Blair meant to be tough. But would he really abandon Sinn Féin/IRA if they did not do as he asked in the speech? Would he sacrifice the chances for peace, or would there be no enduring peace without them as partners in government? His patience with the IRA was to be tested even more in 2003.

Europe: June 2001–December 2002

In contrast to Northern Ireland, where Tony Blair got into his stride as early as 1997/98, his ambitions for the EU early on had either been thwarted by resistance at home (Brown) or frustrated by leaders abroad (Chirac and Schröder). He had launched initiatives, made inroads and had setbacks, but enduring personal impetus and direction only came with his speech to the European Parliament in Strasbourg in June 2005. For several years before he had felt impatient with the Europe dominated by Chirac, Schröder and Berlusconi: he thought they were merely recycling the ideas of the 1980s and 1990s. So what was Blair's vision for the role that the EU might play in the twenty-first century? Before he came to power in 1997, he had determined that building a 'modern' relationship with the EU was going to be a central mission of his premiership. In contrast to earlier Prime Ministers, whose thinking was forged by outdated notions of Britain's past, he felt that he had a uniquely fresh vision and stance, unsullied by the mindset of the Second World War and its aftermath. But in the first term, he found it hard to make progress towards achieving that vision. Taking Britain into the Euro at the earliest opportunity had been thwarted by Brown and the Treasury in the autumn of 1997. Though egged on by advisers, principally by Mandelson, it was not a policy he had reflected upon deeply. Indeed, absence of sustained thought characterised his first-term thinking on Europe. Blair then pulled back from boldness in the 2001 election manifesto and in his Edinburgh speech during the campaign for fear of inflaming the Eurosceptic press. Campbell slapped down Cook who had wanted to talk about the Euro with the words, 'You can't talk about it. It's a second-term prospect.'[73] But Straw's appointment as Foreign Secretary did not suggest it would be a more Europhile second term.[74] Evidence of strategic thinking on the Euro, or EU more generally, is hard to discern.

With the election victory under his belt, Blair decided to unveil his thinking in a series of speeches. The first one, his most important on the EU in the second term, was delivered in Birmingham on 23 November 2001. The content was first discussed at a meeting in Number 10 on 15 October and followed up with a meeting on 8 November. His speech-writer leaned heavily on Hugo Young's *This Blessed Plot* (1998), which argued that the history of Britain and the EU from Churchill onwards had showed that Britain's interests had lost out because it had failed to be at the heart of Europe. Close involvement was the only way to exercise Britain's proper influence and power. Stephen Wall, Blair's senior EU adviser, chipped into the speech the argument that the experience of 9/11 helped undermine traditional notions of national sovereignty.[75] The speech was spun as a personal statement of Blair's credo: 'The history of our engagement with Europe is one of opportunities missed in the name of illusions – and Britain is suffering as a result . . . It is time for us to adjust to the facts. Britain's future is in Europe.'[76] His most ringing sentence was, 'First we said it wouldn't happen, then we said it wouldn't work, then we said we wouldn't need it and Britain was left behind at every step of the way.' The speech was an elegant reworking of Young's thesis: but it was not the claimed deeply personal statement of Blair's views for the simple reason that he had yet fully to form those views.

On the Euro, he acknowledged the truism that the final decision rested with the electorate and a referendum, and that the economic tests had to be met, but added, to Brown's intense irritation: 'Britain has no economic future outside Europe.' The *Guardian*, for whom Hugo Young wrote, called it 'the most explicitly pro-European speech of his premiership'.[77] It was deliberately intended to be 'stark and challenging, and to set out his mission for Europe'.[78] The speech was followed by a meeting on 30 November at Number 10 with Blair's pro-EU team Wall, Hyman and Roger Liddle, who 'kicked around ideas' for further speeches to maintain momentum on the EU: on economic performance, on the introduction of the Euro notes and coins (which were introduced on 1 January 2002), and a final speech on sovereignty and national identity.

Blair's EU initiatives in this period, all of which were to evolve later in his premiership, came at four successive European Councils. By late 2001, Blair was in his fifth year as a regular attendee of these two-day meetings for EU leaders. They occurred four times a year (June and December councils at the end of presidencies were more important) and he had grown weary of them. 'They were all frightful, absolutely the most ghastly form of human experience that man has invented,' said one Council-scarred official.[79] Blair disliked being cooped up in one building with fellow EU leaders for forty-eight hours: 'He found it immensely boring and quite a lot of the time he would sneak out of the room and chat to Alastair or talk on the phone to other people.' Officials noted that he used 'to leave quite a lot of business to the "school swat", i.e., to Cook or Straw, but he always had an uncanny sense of when he himself needed to be in the room and when to intervene'.[80]

The first European Council on which Blair focused fully after the General Election was held in Laeken, Belgium on 14–15 December, at the end of the Belgian presidency. The mid-presidency European Council meeting in Brussels on 21 September had been overwhelmed by 9/11, and steps were rushed through to heighten security and to combat terrorism, with bomb or chemical threats to EU buildings a real concern. The chief topic at Laeken was the future shape of the EU after enlargement from fifteen to twenty-five members, due to come into force in 2004 (involving countries from the former Soviet bloc, the Czech Republic, Slovakia, Slovenia, Hungary, Poland, Latvia, Lithuania and Estonia, as well as Cyprus and Malta). In July, at the beginning of their presidency, the Belgian Prime Minister Guy Verhofstadt had set up a group of 'wise men' from France, Belgium, Italy and Britain to produce proposals about how the EU should best adapt in the light of this near doubling of its membership. Everyone in Europe expected Blair to nominate a 'grey beard' like Douglas Hurd to the group, but instead he produced David Miliband, just out of Number 10, to represent his vision of the future Europe.[81] After six months' work, the wise men duly presented their conclusions to the Laeken Council. Out of their deliberations came the 'Laeken Declaration', which entailed establishing a convention, to be chaired by former French President Giscard d'Estaing, to produce proposals on a new structure for the EU. At the time no one in Number 10 foresaw the intense difficulties that would arise from Giscard d'Estaing's convention, with its grandiose vision for a future constitution of Europe.

The Barcelona Council in mid-March 2002 debated the Lisbon economic reform process, which had been cobbled together by Blair, Spanish Prime Minister José María Aznar, who held the presidency, and Portuguese Prime Minister José Manuel Barroso. It aimed to make Europe the world's most competitive currency area by 2010, including the creation of 20 million new jobs. Blair worked hard to advance economic liberalisation across the EU, and, in this, was following in the tradition of Thatcher and Major, both of whom argued that it was essential if the EU was to compete globally. Greater liberalisation would also help pave the way for joining the Euro, as it was dependent on the flexibility of other European economies. In the event, one of the reasons why Brown said 'no' the second time was because he did not judge that flexibility was yet sufficient in European economies at large.[82] In contrast to Barcelona, the Council in June at the end of the Spanish presidency held in Seville, was a non-event. Discussions were overshadowed by ETA car bombs at the resort town of Fuengirola, harbingers of the 3/11 train bombs in Madrid which ended Aznar's premiership in April 2004. The British delegation was less than wholly absorbed in the Council, and avidly watched the World Cup. When the England team lost to Brazil, they were disconcerted to hear a loud cheer go up from all the other EU delegations.[83] Blair was disappointed: he enjoyed watching football, especially with his children, and when England won.

The Danish presidency Council, held in Brussels on 24 and 25 October 2002, took place under the shadow of the Iraq war build-up, and became renowned as one of the most unpleasant EU Councils in recent history. Chirac, who had been convincingly re-elected in May 2002, and

Schröder, who was narrowly re-elected that September, had fallen out badly with each other at the Gothenburg Council in June 2001. Blair saw this as an excellent opportunity to drive a wedge between these two men whose countries had dominated the EU since its inception in 1957. Their row had been over the future EU constitution: Schröder wanted more votes for Germany on the EU Council because of its large population after reunification but Chirac blankly refused, citing the legacy of the Second World War of France and Germany emerging as equal partners. Schröder was deeply offended. Blair made a bid for Schröder's support, casting caution aside and going to Hamburg during the Chancellor's election campaign to help support his cause. 'There were very high hopes for Schröder, and Blair was prepared to take great risks in the hope that he would help us with the French.'[84] They became so chummy that Schröder happily revealed to Blair how disconcerted he was by Chirac, who had been invited to his home and 'had treated me and my wife like the butler and the maid'.[85]

The Council in October was due to debate reform to the Common Agricultural Policy (CAP). The CAP was one of Britain's longstanding and most fraught concerns about the EU, and Blair believed 'he would be able to start moving' with Schröder on a plan to reform the CAP.[86] This would be strongly linked with trade liberalisation at the new round of the World Trade Organization (WTO) at Doha. But it emerged that Chirac had met Schröder in private before the Council and they had agreed on an alternative Franco-German plan for the funding of the CAP until 2013. Blair flew into Brussels late and not in the best humour, having had to reshuffle Cabinet following Estelle Morris's resignation. Chirac calmly told him that evening, 'Gerhard and I have agreed a package.' Blair saw red, and felt double-crossed. The other twelve EU countries fell into line behind the Franco-German plan. 'There wasn't an enormous amount we could do because the majority were in favour of it, but it was presented as a *fait accompli*', recalled one official.[87] When Chirac summed up at the end of the Council, he then announced that the mid-term review of the CAP, due to come into play in 2005, was to be suspended. Blair protested that the Council had not agreed to this, and it should stand. In front of his fellow leaders Chirac had to back down. He felt humiliated and furious. 'The mid-term review is a big deal for us and we had made a clown of Chirac,' said one British official.[88] All hell broke loose.

'This was the moment that we lost faith with Schröder,' said one British official. 'Everybody in Number 10 felt pretty disgusted with him.' 'Schröder was useless at the Brussels Council,' said another. 'We saw it as a betrayal of all the investment we had made in him.'[89] Although Blair continued to work with the German Chancellor, it was downhill from that point on, soured still further by Iraq in 2003, until Schröder was replaced by Angela Merkel in late 2005. Had Schröder deliberately double-crossed Blair? British officials thought that Chirac was the chief villain, and easily won over a hapless Schröder who understood far less about the CAP than him. 'Schröder didn't understand what Chirac was up to: Chirac simply bamboozled him, selling the deal to him and giving him no time to go back to his officials to check it out.'[90]

The media, in what they described as 'Le row', rejoiced in Blair's spectacular spat with Chirac. Blair was livid with the French President: 'How can you defend the CAP and then claim to be a supporter of aid to Africa?' he demanded of Chirac, in a mixture of French and English, after the formal Council was over. 'You are responsible for the starvation of the world's poor,' he finished. Chirac shot back, 'You've been very badly brought up. You are labelling me a demagogue and a hypocrite.' Those present feared Chirac would grab hold of Blair when he yelled, 'No one has ever spoken to me like that before.'[91] The exchange followed one the previous day when Chirac had needled Blair by saying, 'How will you be able to look Leo in the face in twenty years' time if you are the one who unleashes this [Iraq] war?' Chirac knew what he was doing in drawing in Blair's youngest child. He had made a big fuss of baby Leo when he was born in 2000 and sent the Blairs a signed photograph of him with Leo which resided for a time in the Blairs' drawing room at Downing Street. In a fit of pique, Chirac cancelled the Anglo-Franco summit planned for that December. In contrast, Chirac and Schröder were now back as best of friends, and agreed to make a great fuss of each other in January 2003 over Franco-German celebrations for the fortieth anniversary of the Elysée Treaty.

In insisting on the mid-term review of the CAP in 2003, Blair had extracted a concession, but in letting himself be outmanoeuvred by Chirac, he limited Britain's options when it came to negotiations over the EU budget during the British presidency in late 2005, because the CAP deal until 2013 could not be unravelled.[92] The October 2002 stitch-up by Chirac and Schröder was one of the last times that Franco-German domination of the EU was seen: 'The wheels of the Franco-German motor came off shortly after; no longer would the two of them meet, white smoke appear, and everyone fall into the deal,'[93] said a British official. Blair's relationship with Chirac never recovered. It had never been strong: 'I think that Chirac probably disliked Blair from the word go,' said Wall.[94] The difference in age was significant. Chirac had first become Prime Minister of France when Blair was still an undergraduate at Oxford. Their age discrepancy was tactlessly underlined when in 2002 Blair presented Chirac with a cake to mark his seventieth birthday, arousing Chirac's vanity. Early on Blair had been fascinated by the charismatic and quirky Chirac, who would drink beer, have huge plates of *charcuterie* and cheese brought in to him at Council meetings, and speak with his mouth full. Initially they worked well together, conspicuously at the Anglo-French summit at St Malo in December 1998, which launched the European Defence Initiative. At the height of their 'good period', and knowing of Chirac's life-long interest in the East, Blair entertained him at Nobu, one of London's finest Japanese restaurants. But Chirac's suspicion of the young 'upstart' Blair, who had little natural respect for him, or for France's hegemony in the EU, began to tell. It had gone wrong long before 'Le row', and nose-dived over Iraq. The story of Blair's deteriorating relationship with Chirac forms the leitmotif of the EU story in later chapters.

Franco-German hegemony of the EU faltered because of enlargement, which came to the surface at the Copenhagen Council in December 2002. The ten new countries were scheduled to join in sixteen months, and the question was whether they were all fully ready for accession. Chirac was not keen on enlargement and had consistently found pretexts to obstruct it. France feared that the ten would dilute the EU, as well as French influence over it. Blair fought hard at the Council for them, and negotiations were successfully concluded to admit all ten, thereby creating a single market of 420 million people. The Council had more differences over Turkey's accession. Prior to the meeting, Giscard d'Estaing had reiterated his controversial view that Turkey, as a country with a mainly Muslim population, had no place in the EU. Blair in contrast, not least in the post-9/11 world and with the Iraq war brewing, wanted to send out a positive signal to the Muslim world. The US pressed for Turkey's accession, with the argument (not well judged for an EU audience) that Turkey would be a key ally in the 'war on terror'. The decision was taken, however, that further discussions about Turkey's admission would have to be delayed until 2004, and for the country to demonstrate that it had met specific human rights criteria.

The years 2001–02 were not the high point of Blair's relations with the EU. The disillusion Blair felt for Chirac and Schröder at Brussels in October 2002 helped nourish the idea which took a further two years to gestate – a vision for the EU which would leave the world of the Chiracs and Schröders far behind. Blair's position was not aided in those years by his lack of close personal relations among EU leaders: Aznar and Berlusconi were his two closest allies, but neither carried great weight, and Aznar was to depart for good in spring 2004. The new EU that Blair envisaged saw an end to the Franco-German-Benelux dominance, a central role for the ten accession countries, and a policy-focused agenda. Before Blair's new vision was to crystallise, he was to have his worst year yet with the EU, in 2003.

A Bad End to the Year: November–December 2002

It had been a harrowing year for Blair, the most difficult in his premiership so far. Progress on domestic policy had proved painfully slow, while overseas efforts to try to influence the US from the inside had earned him nothing but opprobrium. It was also the year in which Blair's personal safety was seriously called into question for the first time: 'We had to increase security around Number 10 and around him personally because the threat against him was immense,' said Metropolitan Police Commissioner John Stevens.[95] All Prime Ministers are targets for terrorists – there is no bigger prize. The IRA came close to killing both his predecessors in Downing Street. Now, as the threat from Ireland receded, the greater threat from Muslim extremists took its place. In advance of the Queen's Golden Jubilee that summer, Scotland Yard received 'specific and credible' reports of an al-Qaeda plot via Chechnya to assassinate the Prime Minister, while he attended a public street party with the Queen on the Mall on 4 June. 'The intelligence indicated he was going to be shot by a sniper or someone with an automatic weapon.'[96] Stevens briefed Blair personally on the threat at Downing Street. From the start Blair refused to countenance withdrawing from the event. 'John, I am quite sure that you will do everything necessary as you have done in the past,' he told Stevens.[97] Such threats did not faze Blair. 'I remember going to see him once,' recalled Stevens, 'and he asked, "What's your biggest worry?" I said, "You are. If anything happens to you I would have to resign immediately." And he just laughed. There was a feeling around that he took these things lightly.'[98] He showed, in Stevens's view, immense determination to continue as normal.

The security services took every conceivable precaution. Operatives from the counter-terrorism squad walked the Mall late at night. Putting themselves in the shoes of the terrorists, Britain's Special Forces worked out how they would have planned an attack and then developed countermeasures. One was a special screen that would have protected

Blair and Blair alone. But after concerns developed that a frustrated terrorist might then turn his weapon on the Royal Family, a different strategy was adopted. Blair was asked to put on a bullet-proof vest: he refused.[99] Blair knew that that no security measures could provide a 100 per cent guarantee against attack, but on the day of the Mall party he acted as if nothing were amiss. 'I remember sitting with him three or four along the line outside Buckingham Palace, where I knew we were extremely vulnerable,' recalled Stevens. 'I just looked out the side of my eye. There was not a shadow of any kind of fear. He had a job to do and he did it.'[100] In the end the plot did not materialise, or the assassins were frightened off, but the general threat level remained high and would do so for the remainder of his premiership, and beyond. He remained a fatalist, believing that if he was going to be assassinated, he would be, and he was not going to alter his life or worry unduly about it, unless he was putting the lives of others at risk. It was another instance where his faith impacted on his life.

By the late autumn, Blair was badly looking forward to Christmas and time to escape with the family. But in the last few weeks of 2002 he was hit by three difficulties, all of which sapped his energy, and the last his morale also. Relations with Gordon Brown had deteriorated since 2001. The Chancellor had not gone out of his way to be supportive on either facing up to Saddam or on the war on terror. At one COBRA meeting on tightening security measures against al-Qaeda-style terrorism in the wake of 9/11, he sat silent all meeting and, according to one intelligence official, growled at the end: 'Well, you can't do any of these things unless I vote you the money.'[101] He disliked intensely Blair's growing ambitions on the domestic front, and snarled at plans to increase choice and diversity. But it was only when pensions came to the fore in the second half of 2002 that the relationship became truly dysfunctional. Brown believed Blair was moving on to the territory that he regarded as entirely his own. In the first term, Blair and Brown had held similar views on pensions. They both saw the pressures from an ageing society. They believed in focusing attention on the poorest pensioners, with an acceptance of a growing role for means-tested provision in retirement and an increased role for the private sector in pension provision.

Once Frank Field left the government in 1998 after 'thinking the unthinkable' on welfare reform, pensions fell from Blair's attention, and neither did they feature significantly in the 2001 election. It was only in the summer of 2002, aided by thinking from the Number 10 Strategy Unit member Gareth Davies, fresh from PriceWaterhouseCoopers, that Blair began seriously to focus again, and became increasingly worried about the collapse of final-salary pension schemes.[102] The Treasury was bemused. 'They did not quite believe that it was Blair. They thought it was his staff in Number 10 winding him up.'[103] Brown's aides in the Treasury always found it hard to believe that Blair was capable of displaying interest in the detail of any part of domestic policy, particularly welfare. They did not have a high regard for his intellect, nor his capacity for making a sustained contribution to complex policy issues.[104]

In a series of meetings with the Treasury and the Department of Work and Pensions (DWP) in October and November, Blair realised that here was a topic with which he needed to get to grips, and resolved to publish a Green Paper on the subject that autumn. The Treasury agreed, but wanted to dominate its content. At a meeting in Number 10 in November, Blair's economic adviser, Derek Scott, described how 'Gordon arrived at the den with no fewer than seven officials (all of whom remained silent)' and how at subsequent meetings Treasury officials made clear to him that 'pensions was no business of Number 10 or the Prime Minister; Gordon was in control'.[105] Number 10–Treasury discussions revealed profound differences over the Treasury's policy of means-testing and pension credit. Blair decided that a much more fundamental review of the whole pensions issue was required, and proposed a long-term commission to find the way forward. He envisaged a cross-party consensus on pensions removed from party politics and to 'last for fifty years'. To Brown, the idea was anathema – at least initially.

On 19 November the Treasury showed signs of agreeing to the commission, but again wanted to dominate it. Difficult bilaterals took place in mid-December between Blair and Brown. The date of publication of the Green Paper to announce the commission was constantly pushed back from October through November to 'the last day of term' in December.[106] 'Brown's line was, "As Chancellor of the Exchequer, I have responsibility for expenditure and you can't hand that over to an independent review",' said one Number 10 aide.[107] Only very grudgingly did he give his consent to the commission – on the condition that it looked only at private pensions, not state. Terms of reference were finally agreed between Blair and Brown only on the weekend before publication and were inserted at the printers once the final drafts had been signed off. An aide recalled: 'The whole thing had gone to bed and that is why if you read the Green Paper, you suddenly find it talking about the commission in a very bizarre place.'[108] The choice of Adair Turner as chairman was about the only uncontroversial aspect of the commission, but sowed the seeds of future conflict: 'it was immediately obvious to me and my two fellow commissioners that it was impossible to deal with what was wrong in the private pension system without looking at state system as well,' recalled Turner.[109] On timing, Brown insisted it would not report for three years, i.e., in 2005, after a General Election, by which time he imagined he would be Prime Minister and could deal with it how he wanted.

In November, to Number 10's intense irritation, a union dispute arose which reminded it how little some unions had moved on even after eight years of Blair's leadership of the party. Andy Gilchrist was one of the new generation of radical union leaders who were coming to the fore and replacing the moderates who had backed Blair over 'Clause IV' in his early years as leader. Gilchrist became General Secretary of the Fire Brigades Union (FBU) in 2000, and was determined that the fire-fighters would receive a 40 per cent increase in pay. So when a committee into fire service pay under Sir George Bain reported on 11 November, advocating a pay increase of 11 per cent, which Gilchrist thought risible, he started preparing for strike action.[110] On 13 November fire-fighters began a forty-eight-hour strike and on 22 November an eight-day strike, which resulted in the armed forces stepping in with 'Green Goddess' fire engines. The fire-fighters posed a serious challenge, and the most sustained trade union action Blair was to face in his ten years as Prime Minister. 'As a crisis, it was not on the same scale as the 2000 fuel protest or foot and mouth in 2001, but it was nevertheless very important, because it involved issues of government competence, sensitive trade union handling, public sector pay and policy and a potential national crisis in the making,' said Heywood.[111]

This was one for Prescott, Blair decided. '"You can sort this out for me, can't you?" he said rhetorically.'[112] Blair selected him, said Morgan, 'because, if unions are not behaving in the way that he felt that they should be behaving, there's nobody better than John Prescott when he gets cross. Tony was almost having to hold him back.'[113] 'John was out to kill,' said another aide.[114] Blair studiously left Prescott handling it, with minimal micro-management. 'It was probably unique for Blair as a self-denying ordinance, avoiding getting immersed in the detail in a crisis.'[115] The bigger picture did worry him, though, particularly if the strike continued if Britain went to war. It looked as if just that might happen when a third strike took place on 28 January 2003, but then the dispute fizzled out and the fire-fighters finally accepted a deal in June 2003. Gilchrist was replaced two years later. Blair was relieved at how effectively the strike had been handled, with the army playing a pivotal role, which helped show that the fire-fighters were not indispensable, thereby undermining a key part of their case.[116] He thought it showed off 'Prescott at his best', and was relieved that the strike did not poison relations with the union movement at large, nor set a precedent for other pay settlements to follow. With hindsight, it is quite remarkable, especially in comparison to his four Labour predecessors as party leaders, how free Blair's premiership was of union troubles.

If luck played a part in the successful conclusion of the fire dispute, Blair had nothing but bad luck in late 2002 when Cherie's involvement with Carole Caplin suddenly went wrong. Cherie had met the attractive and vivacious Caplin first at a gym in 1990, and her influence subsequently on Cherie was powerful and generally benign. Caplin helped guide Cherie, a woman with little natural dress sense or self-confidence, to portray herself more confidently in public: 'She had not worn make-up until her late thirties,' said a female friend.[117] Blair quite liked having her around and appreciated the positive impact she had on his wife. His tolerance was not shared by Campbell, who periodically ranted, 'What is that bloody woman doing here?' nor by his partner, Fiona Millar, Cherie's long-serving aide in Number 10. Millar neither liked nor trusted Caplin, had no time for her 'weird' lifestyles, and thought Caplin's growing influence over Cherie at the expense of her own would lead to disaster.[118] Caplin's relationship with Cherie had aroused little concern beyond the walls of Downing Street until the end of 2002, but then things suddenly fell apart. Cherie's deep lack of confidence, which dated back to her childhood, extended to an acute anxiety about money. Blair himself had a cavalier attitude towards both money and housing; he was unworried about them. Cherie did, because for her they were profound security issues. After they had sold their Richmond Terrace house in July 1997 for £650,000, and with Myrobella worth at most £250,000, she was concerned that they lacked property assets for their future. She saw an opportunity to get on to the property ladder when their eldest son Euan started at Bristol University in September 2002. To maintain privacy, Caplin agreed discreetly on her behalf to view two flats, one for Euan and the other for an investment.

The house purchase negotiations were conducted not by Caplin, but by her maverick lover Peter Foster, a convicted con man, who bought both flats for her for £260,000 and £265,000. A disaster was waiting to happen. Millar and Campbell first got wind of Foster's involvement on 27 November. According to Campbell's diaries, Blair called Cherie the following day to say that the issue 'had to be gripped and Carole had to understand this was about us every bit as much as it was about her. As he understood it, the guy was a total con man, and dangerous.'[119] The hostile *Mail on Sunday* first got hold of the story on Saturday 30 November, because Foster had allegedly boasted about his role in the purchase negotiations. It promptly phoned Number 10 with a list of more than twenty questions.[120] Campbell phoned Blair, who was at Chequers for the weekend. 'TB admitted to me he was always against the idea of a flat on political grounds, but also that until today he had no idea they had bought two.'[121] Cherie denied Foster was her 'financial adviser', or that he had any role in the purchase, and the Number 10 press office then rebutted the *Mail on Sunday* story. The paper, however, had proof that Foster had been involved in negotiating the price of the flats down. On the evening of Wednesday 4 December all hell let loose when the *Mail* revealed to the Number 10 press office an exchange of e-mails between Foster and Cherie. 'Even though I had half expected this, I was absolutely livid,' Campbell penned in his diary. 'We were being hit again because we didn't get the full facts out.'[122] He was furious that the press office had been allowed to pass on a half-truth to the press on the basis of Cherie's word. He swiftly dictated a note to Blair, who was at the theatre with Cherie, saying the story was 'likely to be big and bad'. Campbell recorded: 'He called me at ten to twelve, said it was ridiculous to say Foster was their financial adviser. He was still in denial about it.'[123] For a time, especially over the weekend of 7 to 8 December, it appeared that Blair might lose Campbell, who was feeling this was the last straw. 'Alastair was always muttering about having had enough,' said one aide.[124]

The episode made Blair angrier than he had ever been in his premiership, because of the way that Cherie was being treated by the press.[125] He always hated it when the media intruded into his family life. Blair was angry with Cherie that she had let herself become involved with such a dubious character as Foster, for not telling him, and then not telling the truth when questioned at Chequers. 'Tony was tearing his hair out. It was a bleak moment in their relationship together.'[126] After a bad night on Saturday 7 December, he was desperate. Who could he turn to? Campbell? He was the very last person, and was on the warpath. Hunter? The coolness between her and Cherie precluded it. Powell and Morgan? They were not part of the quartet, and lacked the deep emotional empathy of those who were. So he turned to his old friend Mandelson, with whom they were both comfortable, and whose love for Blair, though still sore over his second resignation in January 2001, was always there under the surface. He had flown back into Heathrow from New York that Sunday morning, to receive a call on his mobile from Blair asking him to go straight to see them.[127] Mandelson spent much of

Sunday 8 and Monday 9 December up in the Number 10 flat, counselling both of them, and managed 'to restore calm in their hour of need'. 'That's my job,' he said. 'It's called "being Peter".'[128]

To try to bring the matter to an end, it was decided that Cherie should give a speech in the Atrium at London's Number 4 Millbank in which she admitted making 'two mistakes': refusing to answer press enquiries fully, which she felt led to 'misunderstanding in the [Number 10] press office', and allowing Foster, who 'she barely knew, to get involved with my personal affairs'. 'I'm not superwoman,' she declared.[129] She was highly emotional, and at one point close to tears: her mother was angry that she had been made to parade herself in public.[130] Blair was having his weekly audience with the Queen when she made her tearful statement. 'He caught it on the news later and said he was really proud of the way she stood up to it,' Campbell noted: 'TB did for once thank us for what we had done.'[131]

It had been a scouring two weeks, and it re-ordered much in Blair's life. Peter Stothard believed 'the sight of his wife being pilloried for weeks in the press caused miserable stress to Tony Blair', and it marked a very significant downturn in Number 10's relations with the media.[132] It helped bring Mandelson back centre-stage, for a while, in Blair's life. It soured the Blairs' relationship with Campbell and Millar. As Stothard wrote in his diary: 'The four are like friends who have been on holiday together for too long.'[133] Millar's relationship with the Blairs never recovered: she blamed him for keeping Campbell at Number 10 when she wanted him to quit (indeed, she had never wanted him to take the job). Cherie's continuing attachment to Caplin was too much for her, and she left in 2003, as did, eventually, Campbell. For a time, it seemed as if Blair was having to chose between Campbell, his closest friend and biggest prop, and his wife. 'You're married to a woman who is determined to protect and help a woman who is in love with a con man, so you are linked to a con man.' 'I am not linked to a con man!' shouted Blair. 'You think Cherie has done something monstrous and I don't!'[134] It changed his thinking about Cherie, and revealed again his deep love for her. 'His total instinct during the crisis was to protect her. He understood how totally devoted he was to her.'[135] He realised how far he had neglected her in the furious activity since 9/11, a difficult period for her too which included her miscarriage in 2002. It made him understand again how much he needed her. One close friend said, 'They are as much in love, and their relationship is as fresh, as the day they met.'[136] He was going to need all that love in the near future. If 2002 had been difficult, an even harder year was now about to begin.

6

Confronting Saddam

September 2002–March 2003

'Tony Blair has an incredible capacity, no matter how bad the crisis,' said Heywood of the December 2002 turbulence over Cherie and the flats, 'to turn off one issue and move on to the next.'[1] For all his single-mindedness, however, nothing in his life up to that point had prepared him for the challenges he now faced. Foreign policy decisions of the utmost gravity were encroaching on his daily existence. 'Mentally, he was not fully there on domestic policy,' recalled one close aide. 'Iraq took more and more of his emotional energy.'[2] At stake was the threat of a major war; a war that would be deeply unpopular, risked destabilising the Middle East and could lead to terrorist reprisals on British soil. Decisions on Kosovo and Sierra Leone had toughened him considerably, but this was in a different league from anything he had ever encountered before.

Building the Case: The 24 September Dossier

With Bush's call for a new UN resolution in September 2002, Blair appeared to have won the day. But seeking a UN resolution was not the same thing as achieving one. Blair had much work to do in Washington, the UN and foreign capitals. Planning for a military campaign had to continue at the same time, albeit largely under the radar screen. Blair was determined to have a real military option should diplomacy fail. He wanted to make the threat of war credible to Saddam, but he knew that a very public British military mobilisation would risk the appearance of an inevitable war.

To secure backing at the UN, Blair was locked into tackling Iraq's WMD, just one of the many motives he had for taking on Saddam. On the plane back from Camp David on 7 September, Blair shared his fears of WMD with journalists: 'I am not saying it will happen next month, or even next year, but at some point the danger will explode. This is not an American preoccupation. It is our preoccupation. It must be the preoccupation of the entire world.'[3] He was determined to place hard evidence before the public. Back in March 2002, a dossier about WMD around the world had been produced by the FCO but held back from publication. Some felt that the timing was not right,[4] others felt that the evidence on Iraq's WMD, much of which was not based on secret intelligence, was insufficiently convincing.[5] But the situation had evolved considerably in six months. 'He said the debate had got ahead of us,' noted Campbell just before the visit to Camp David, and so wanted a dossier published 'in the next few weeks'.[6] 'He genuinely wanted to inform the public about what he was seeing and hearing from the intelligence community. The idea came from him,' said one Downing Street official.[7] Bush had indicated at Camp David that the Americans too might provide a dossier, but opposition from the CIA and Pentagon prevented this.[8]

The TUC conference on 10 September gave Blair his first public forum since the summer to bang the WMD drum: 'I for one do not want it on my conscience that we knew of the threat, saw it coming and did nothing.'[9] Number 10 had feared walkouts, but he escaped with a sullen silence during the Iraq passage, and a standing ovation of less than a minute. Cook spoke to Blair the next day, recording in his diary that the letter was attaching 'great importance to the forthcoming dossier' in winning back support at home, while 'hopeful that he could turn around international opinion'.[10] Cook told Blair that military action had to be avoided, warned that Bush was doing Iraq 'for the wrong reasons' and feared that it would lead to the end of Blair's government: 'I'll put you down as an unenthusiastic, then,' Blair replied.[11]

Frantic work took place in the intelligence community in September, developing a dossier on Iraq's WMD. Robin Butler, later to chair the inquiry into pre-war intelligence, believes that Blair said, in effect, "you may not have much evidence but for goodness sake go out and find it". So MI6 and GCHQ went out to find it.' Butler thought the intelligence agencies might subsequently have been a little 'over-eager' to believe the intelligence that they came up with because of the pressure. 'Blair wanted to get rid of Saddam. So did the US. He could only do this if Saddam was in breach of UN resolutions. He needed proof. He put a lot of pressure on to find it.'[12]

John Scarlett, Chairman of the JIC, presented the latest intelligence dossier to Number 10 on the morning of 17 September. That evening Powell sent Scarlett an e-mail arguing that the dossier, as it stood, did not do enough to demonstrate an imminent threat from Saddam.[13] Powell relayed his concern to Campbell and Manning that 'we need to make it clear Saddam would not attack us at the moment [his underlining]. The thesis is he would be a threat to the UK in the future if we do not check him.'[14] Blair's own reaction, reported to Scarlett by Campbell, was that the material was 'convincing' – though, as Campbell pointed out to Blair, he had not exactly come to the dossier 'as a "don't know" on the issue'. Blair thought that the dossier did not focus 'enough on human rights', but in general he thought it would do the job.[15]

The fifty-page document, 'Iraq's Weapons of Mass Destruction – The Assessment of the British Government', was published with appropriate fanfare on 24 September, the day of the emergency recall of Parliament to discuss Iraq. The foreword, provided by Number 10 and signed by Blair, stated that 'the document discloses that [Saddam's] military planning allows for some of the WMD to be ready within forty-five minutes of an order to use them'.[16] Attorney-General Goldsmith's advice had made it clear that non-compliance with UN resolutions was the only sound legal justification for war, as reflected in Blair's speech to the Commons: 'Disarmament of all WMD is the demand. One way or another it must be acceded to.'[17] 'Saddam's WMD programme is active, detailed and growing,' Blair told MPs. '[It] is not shut down. It is up and running.'[18] The reaction to the dossier was mixed: 'Chilling reading,' opined the *Jerusalem Post*.[19] 'No compelling evidence that immediate military action is needed,' sniffed the *Financial Times*.[20]

The question on the lips of the sceptics was, 'Why now? Why, all of a sudden, did the issue of Iraq need to be brought to a head?' At Cabinet on 23 September, the day before the debate, Cook had asked this very question. Hoon attempted a response, which was because of 9/11. 'The problem with this,' Cook noted wryly, 'is that no one has a shred of evidence that Saddam was involved in September 11th.' 'Any suggestion of an Iraq/al-Qaeda link was very tenuous,' said one top intelligence official.[21] But as a close Number 10 aide explained, 9/11 was crucial for Blair, not because of a link between Saddam Hussein and Osama bin Laden, but 'because the balance of risk that he was willing to accept

changed dramatically after that day'.[22] At Cabinet Blair also declared that
'it would be folly for Britain to go against the US on a fundamental'
policy, while Prescott, in loyalist mode, saluted his 'brilliant job moving
the US down the UN route'.[23] Blair summed up: 'To carry on being
engaged with the US is vital. The voices on both left and right who want
to pull Europe and the US apart would have a disastrous consequence
if they succeeded.' It had been a 'grim meeting', concluded the jaded
Cook: 'Much of the two hours was taken up with a succession of loyalty
oaths for Tony's line.'[24] He and Clare Short, 'the two rebels', came under
attack for their growing willingness to criticise the government's
approach in public. Prescott had taken the lead: 'We could all do our bit
of positioning to make our views heard and get a few plaudits,' he said,
'but we were in this together . . . Tony had an incredibly difficult job at
times like this and we should support him.'[25]

Most in Britain and around the world believed in Saddam's WMD
stockpiles and active WMD programme. At Cabinet, even Short had
professed 'no doubt Saddam was dedicated to possessing WMD'.[26]
Blair's top advisers were united on the subject. 'If we didn't believe
there had been WMD, we wouldn't have been on board with the
strategy,' insisted Meyer.[27] Cook recalled how perturbed Blair had been
by intelligence reports that Saddam had told his Cabinet that he wanted
to get hold of nuclear weapons 'to pose a threat to the West'.[28] None who
knew Blair doubted the sincerity of his belief. 'It drove him mad when
people questioned his honesty on WMD,' said Morgan.[29] According to
Butler, 'Tony Blair honestly and sincerely thought Saddam was a very
bad and dangerous man who had stockpiled chemical weapons, who may
have biological weapons and was trying to acquire nuclear weapons.'[30]

Michael Boyce, Britain's most senior military officer, skipped the
dossier and went straight to the raw intelligence. He was totally
convinced that Saddam had WMD: 'It was not simply that the
intelligence people were telling Blair what he wanted to hear.'[31] During
the war, Boyce recalled, there was continuing optimism over the WMD
search: 'Dearlove would say, "Tomorrow, we'll find them at this location
or that location," and Blair would say, "Okay, good – they'd better be
there."'[32] Had the government not been totally convinced they would
not have spent the time and money kitting out selected British
embassies, as well as the armed forces, with the appropriate protective
suits. 'There was an absolute conviction, based on intelligence, that
Saddam had WMD – chemical and biological weapons – and would use
them,' insisted Michael Jay.[33] The French, the Russians, the UN, and
even weapons inspector Hans Blix, believed Saddam had WMD.

'We were almost all wrong,' admitted David Kay, the former US inspector, in January 2004, after scouring Iraq unsuccessfully for evidence of WMD stockpiles.[34] Deficiencies in aerial and 'intercept' (e.g., mobile phones) intelligence threw even greater weight on 'Humint', or human intelligence, which was at best flaky.[35] The Butler report revealed that MI6 had six main agents supplying intelligence. Of them, two were discredited. A third, improbably called 'Curveball', was later exposed as a low-level trainee, who had been fired from his job at Iraq's Chemical & Engineering Design and had spent much of his time in Baghdad.[36] Britain's top agent in the field meanwhile lacked first-hand access to the weapons information. As Butler made clear, Iraq was an extremely difficult target to penetrate. Yet considering the extraordinary importance of the task, Britain's intelligence-gathering left much to be desired.

Should Blair have probed the intelligence more deeply? Cook had no doubts: speaking shortly before his death in 2005, he said, 'The reality is that he [Blair] believed in the evidence because he needed to believe in the evidence.'[37] Alas, the truth is not that simple. Much hinges on the relative responsibilities of the Prime Minister and the intelligence community to probe the detail and provenance of incoming intelligence. Ivor Roberts, a seasoned diplomat, believed that MI6 were 'largely to blame for the faulty intelligence'. Breaking a tradition of using outsiders and placing an intelligence officer, Scarlett, as Chairman of the JIC may have been a particular error. 'Insiders are bound to give greater weight to intelligence than it deserves: an outsider would have probed more,' said Roberts.[38] One former intelligence chief squarely blames his former profession. 'I'd exonerate the Prime Minister of not being quizzical enough of the JIC. It's not something which I think you should expect a PM to do.'[39] After all, Scarlett had insisted on taking 'ownership' of the dossier and had cleared everything in it.[40] Blair had learned to have confidence in the intelligence community: they had delivered him a list of successes earlier in his premiership, so he saw no reason to doubt the JIC on its professional judgement now.

Blair, however, must shoulder some of the blame for the presentation of the dossier, in which tentative conclusions from secret JIC reports were presented as gospel truth to the public. Every last drop of intelligence was squeezed from the relatively thin raw material to portray the dossier, and hence the justification for war, as strongly as possible. Dissenting views were dropped and caveats fell away. Blair himself described the intelligence as 'extensive, detailed and authoritative' at the Dispatch Box in the House of Commons on 24 September.[41] Here he may well have crossed the line: 'He should perhaps have been more careful with his words,' admitted one senior official, adding, not entirely convincingly: 'But that's the sort of thing that happens in the rough and tumble of politics.'[42] 'The three words – extensive, detailed, authoritative – were the closest Blair came to the "lie direct",' said Robin Butler. 'He was perfectly aware of what he was saying and I think his tongue ran away with him.'[43]

For all his efforts, the dossier had little effect on the sceptics in his own party, fifty-six of whom voted against the government in the emergency debate in the Commons on 24 September. Even shorn of caveats the dossier was not an overwhelmingly persuasive document. 'There's no smoking gun here,' Conservative Party leader Iain Duncan Smith had said to Scarlett when given a chance to look over the dossier a few days before it was published. 'No,' said Scarlett, 'there isn't.'[44] In many eyes the dossier strengthened the case for the UN inspectors returning to Iraq and being given sufficient time to locate Saddam's WMD. It did not justify military action. Blair's need to tie his policy to the UN was now even stronger.

The Rise and Fall of UNSCR 1441: September 2002–January 2003

The first UN Security Council Resolution – 1441 – took eight weeks of hard slog, rather than the fortnight the British government had expected. 'We all went in knowing the UN route would be agony, and it was real agony,' said Manning.[45] At this stage, there was little talk of unanimity; the target was to carry the resolution with a minimum of abstentions.[46] The minutiae of the negotiations were handled by Colin Powell in Washington, Straw in London and Dominique de Villepin (the French foreign minister) in Paris, backed up by their Permanent Representatives in New York. Blair's role was to help build support among Security Council members while continuing to act as the 'bridge' between Europe and the United States. He and Bush were kept regularly informed, but largely stayed out of the detail.[47] The transatlantic bridge was no more appreciated by EU leaders than it was valued by the hawks in Washington, who cared little for the opinions of Europeans, or indeed, of any other countries. The UN, proclaimed arch-hawk Richard Perle, was little more than a 'looming chatterbox on the River Hudson'.[48] Number 10 believed Bush himself was sincere in trying for a peaceful resolution but they remained concerned by the influence of the neocons who, according to one British official, were now ready 'to go all-out for war'.[49]

The hawks deliberately set about resisting any effort by the UN to limit their freedom of action. 'Scooter' Libby admitted that they were desperate to avoid a new inspection process as they were all but 'locked on' to the spring 2003 window for a military attack.[50] Their hope was that an unrealistically tough resolution would provoke deadlock among the Security Council. A hard-line version of the text was leaked to the *New York Times* in early October. The timing could not have been worse for Blair, coming in the middle of the Labour conference, just as he was squaring up to an increasingly sceptical party. He was forced to secrete himself away with Straw in an airless 'secure room' at Blackpool's Imperial Hotel as they made long phone calls dealing with the fall-out.[51]

A distinction between Bush 'the head', who was willing to see diplomacy through, and Bush 'the gut', who sided with the hawks, became familiar in the British camp. Manning was one who became disconcerted by what he saw happening in Washington. 'He could see the bits of the administration that counted were determined to have their war, and at times feared that he was involved in almost a sham exercise, going through the motions,' said one diplomat.[52] But against this he weighed what he heard directly from the President's lips. 'You do realise, George, that if Saddam does disarm, we will have to take "yes" for an answer from the UN?' Blair said to Bush shortly after the Camp David meeting in September. 'Yes,' said the President, 'I do.'[53] So if the UN judged that Saddam had disarmed there would be no war. It was worrying for the British that the administration was giving such mixed messages.

On 8 November, the UN Security Council passed Resolution 1441 unanimously. Even Syria had agreed to it. The resolution declared Saddam in 'material breach' of his responsibilities under previous UN resolutions, and gave him one final opportunity to comply or face 'serious consequences'. Blair was delighted.[54] It confounded the swelling ranks of sceptics who doubted Blair's influence in Washington and asserted that the hawks alone drove policy.[55] In Number 10, it was considered a 'great triumph for the Prime Minister personally' recalled one aide. 'At the time, it seemed like a major decisive shift in US policy.'[56] 'If Saddam were to be perceived to have met the requirements of Resolution 1441, Bush would have faced tremendous pressure to have called off the invasion, both from within the administration, and from Tony Blair,' admitted one US official.[57] But while London seemed briefly overwhelmed by the euphoria that followed the passage of 1441, seasoned diplomats, particularly Greenstock, knew that the resolution had been forged in ambiguity. This would later prove its undoing.

With the threat of 'serious consequences', military planning continued apace. Towards the end of 2002, the Pentagon was pushing heavily for war in the spring, not the autumn, of 2003. Moderate Arab nations were privately urging the US to get any war over with as quickly as possible, while in the US there were fears that the economy could suffer if uncertainty continued for another six months. Delaying to the autumn would also have left the campaign perilously close to the 2004 presidential election, which was already warming up, with Bush likely to face a fierce challenge at the polls.[58] The US plans were predicated on full British participation, said one senior administration official, 'because of the tremendous military capability value of British forces and because it would be much better politically to go with the UK than to go unilaterally'.[59] That said, powerful voices in Washington countenanced the possibility of war without Britain: it might create some extra diplomatic and logistical problems, but militarily the US could easily go to war alone.

US military leaders visited the British Military Command Centre at Northwood – the British equivalent of CENTCOM at Tampa – to unveil their plans. 'It was a bit like a standard commercial American presentation. You know, "Turn on the PowerPoint and this is what we intend to do,"' said Rob Fry, Northwood's chief of staff. The British service chiefs subsequently gave Blair a presentation at the MoD on what they had learned from their American counterparts. 'I'm pretty sure that in Blair's own mind he thought that we were going to take part in this,' recalled Fry. 'But it was never said. He just took the brief, asked sensible questions and did it at the level of grand narrative.'[60] Blair may have given his senior military advisers the impression that he thought that war was inevitable but, deep in his own mind, he remained undecided. There were still formidable political obstacles to be scaled if he was to take the country to war: his ideal remained getting Saddam out without an invasion. He knew though that the British military had to perform a difficult balancing act: making full preparations for war, including stockpiling ammunition and moving troops into battle positions, while at the same time 'not giving any indication that we were for certain going to be involved in the whole thing'.[61] Even if war was indeed averted, it was still essential to put military pressure on Saddam to force him to comply with the demands of the UN.[62] The more real the threat, Blair felt, the less likely it would have to be acted on.[63]

Yet at this critical point, in early December, the pressure on Saddam eased. A split opened up in the UN on what compliance with 1441 actually meant, and the length of time he had to show that compliance.

The Americans thought it enough for an invasion to follow a 'material breach' of the resolution, while the French and Russians wanted a second UN resolution explicitly authorising force. Herein lay the seed of the future battle about whether the war was or was not legitimate.[64] Saddam played the limited cards at his disposal well. Had he rebuffed 1441 completely, it would have been a clear act of defiance justifying military action. So he did what any common-or-garden tyrant would have done: he complied partially. He claimed he would agree to the tough new inspection regime, but failed to provide the 'full' declaration of Iraqi weapons programmes that the resolution demanded. By exploiting the ambiguities in 1441, Saddam succeeded in splitting the allies straight down the middle.[65]

Saddam's official response of 7 December 2002, an extraordinary 12,000 pages, proved a turning point. According to a Number 10 aide, this was 'the obvious moment when Saddam signalled that non-co-operation would be his chosen way. He gave us only waffle that indicated that he was not serious about co-operating.'[66] Blair told his staff that Saddam's declaration was 'the defining moment. This was his big opportunity. He's blown it.'[67] As late as November, senior figures in the administration had told the British that war was still not inevitable. The best option, Condi Rice said, would be the 'implosion of the Iraqi regime', leading to Saddam's fall and obviating an invasion.[68] 'We were still trying to get Saddam Hussein to behave until the very end or to leave, to avoid our having to go into Iraq,' recalled Donald Rumsfeld.[69] But Saddam's December declaration at once stiffened the wind in the war party's sails. His defiance did not suggest a man ready to 'behave' or leave power any time soon. Cheney pressed Bush to declare Saddam's response the required 'material breach' and thus grounds for war.[70] On 18 December, Bush told the Spanish leader Aznar privately that he considered the Iraqi declaration 'a joke'. Saddam, Bush said, was 'a liar and he's no intention of disarming'.[71] The following day, highly significantly, Colin Powell declared Iraq to be in material breach.

Shortly after the declaration the Washington Embassy warned London that the Americans might now seize upon a *casus belli* that other countries would not accept. The Prime Minister, they warned, would then face an agonising decision over whether to stand with Bush or step back. Given that Bush had precious few allies of significance other than Blair, his views would be crucial and could even, Meyer suggested, prove decisive.[72] By January, however, Bush seemed set upon military action. On 13 January he summoned Powell for a twelve-minute meeting in the Oval Office: 'I think I have to do this,' Bush declared. 'I want you with me.' Powell signalled his assent.[73] In the US, diplomacy now took a back seat. Short of Saddam relinquishing or being forced from power, war was coming.

Early in the New Year of 2003, senior British military officers attended a US 'rock drill' or military briefing in Qatar to advance planning for the invasion: 'They didn't need us for the military power we represented. This was all about political representation,' thought Fry.[74] On 15 January Britain's top brass briefed Blair again on the evolving US plans, saying that they expected Bush to make a decision on 15 February, 'and they would go within twelve days or so to a massive air, sea and land operation'.[75] It was all becoming very real. If war could not be averted, Blair mused, he did not want the US to fight alone: he wanted Britain to be by its side. After the presentation he 'looked more nervous', Campbell recorded, 'particularly about the idea of UK military casualties and the possibility of large numbers of civilian casualties'.[76]

Knowledge of US intentions did little to shake his underlying beliefs. Throughout the latter part of 2002 and early 2003, attendees at the regular Monday meetings in his den recall him saying, 'It's not a question of whether this issue is right or wrong, or which choice might be better or worse; it is a question of do we go with the Americans or do we not? He'd say that there was no other option.'[77] Yet even as the US prepared for war Blair refused to give up on diplomacy. 'We hoped till the end that Saddam would comply. There was no one moment when we knew that war was inevitable,' recalled one Downing Street aide. 'We were desperate for him to co-operate. Even after the 7 December response, we bent over backwards to give him the opportunity to co-operate.'[78] Straw and the FCO clung even more strongly to the hope that war could be avoided, and that Saddam would finally realise that if he did not co-operate, he would face annihilation. 'We thought there was a real chance that he might see the light very late in the day,' said Peter Ricketts, then FCO Political Director.[79] The WMD inspectors were now returning to Iraq – they had to be given time to do their job and, so Blair hoped, deliver proof of Saddam's perfidy.

A Second Resolution and Post-war Planning: January–February 2003

Intense debate within Number 10, and with the Foreign Office, took place in early and mid-January about whether a second UN resolution would be needed before Britain could participate in military action against Iraq. The risk of trying and failing weighed heavily. Where would the defeat of a resolution leave Britain? Blair was influenced by his experience in Kosovo, where he pressed ahead without UN backing on the basis of his own conviction.[80] Blair was in two minds, but in the end consented to pursuing a second resolution. 'It was a calculated risk,' said one aide. 'We were fully aware of what it entailed.'[81] Politics was the decisive factor. By late January Blair accepted that war without UN cover 'would be a very tough call domestically'.[82] Without a new resolution, Labour backing in the Commons would not be guaranteed. From within Number 10, Manning had also been arguing the case for a second resolution from as early as September. His views were critical: 'He now effectively took the decision within the parameters that the Prime Minister had set out,' said one official.[83]

Straw's view of this debate was deeply coloured by his growing concerns over the prospect of war. In late October 2002, a senior diplomat told Straw that British intelligence suggested a 'high likelihood' that the Americans would go to war; 'I can remember Jack going quite white. It wasn't part of his agenda.'[84] On New Year's Day 2003, in a comment he later repeated publicly, Straw said that he thought the chances of war were 60:40 against. His senior official, Michael Jay, was with him at the time. 'I remember thinking "On what basis does he think that?", because it was absolutely clear to the rest of us that it was at least 60:40 on.'[85] 'Colin Powell and I are campaigning to stop this war,' Straw told one Foreign Office official in January 2003.[86] On the 23rd, Straw told Jay that Britain could not take part in military action unless it was clearly in accordance with international law. He personally did not believe that a second resolution was necessary legally, but it would be desirable, verging on essential, for political reasons at home and abroad.[87]

Throughout January, Manning spoke to Rice at least daily, and Blair to Bush weekly.[88] There were increasing anxieties in London over the schedule for military action: 'All the time we were probing to find out what preparations Washington had for actually initiating "armed force" – we didn't call it "war",' said one close adviser.[89] The aim was not only to find out what the Americans had in mind, but to persuade them to delay the start of the campaign long enough to give diplomacy – including a possible second resolution – time to work. Unfortunately for Blair, London's grip on the key levers of power in Washington was to prove shaky. Real power centred around the Vice-President's office and within the Department of Defense. The Washington Embassy's warnings that Cheney was implacably determined to remove Saddam by force had not resulted in London finding a convincing interlocutor to liaise with this unusually powerful Vice-President. Blair found Cheney, who was immune to his charm, more difficult to deal with than Bush. Nominally it was Prescott's job as Deputy PM, but it was no match and he was considered 'hopelessly ineffectual' in dealing with Cheney.[90] Occasionally Straw would try his luck, but he too failed to make any discernable impact. Instead, Number 10 held out hopes that Condi Rice, often receptive to the British viewpoint, would win over the President, and bypass Cheney. Yet by this stage she too was losing influence. British officials despaired as they saw her 'outmanoeuvred time and again'.[91] Rice was outmanoeuvred also at the Pentagon. Hoon did not have the same rapport with Rumsfeld that Straw had with Powell, and little information flowed out of the building to the British. In consequence, the exact timing of the war remained uncertain. Lengthy – and ultimately fruitless – US negotiations with Turkey over access routes meant that a precise start date was set only very late in the day. But, as one British military figure put it, 'They couldn't keep the troops on the boil ad infinitum, and using chemical and biological protective suits in the summer would have been very difficult. So spring 2003 was the time – either we do it or not.'[92] Blair's room for manoeuvre was already looking very small indeed.

On 27 January, Hans Blix delivered his first statement to the UN Security Council. Hawks had hoped for a simple statement that Iraq was not co-operating, so applauded Blix's comment that 'even today Iraq has not come to a genuine acceptance' of the need to disarm. Yet Blix also reported that Iraq was co-operating 'on process' if not fully 'on substance'. His statement seemed designed to open up the prospect of a lengthy inspection process. But the Americans had no time for equivocation. On 29 January, Bush delivered his 2003 State of Union address: 'The dictator of Iraq is not disarming. To the contrary; he is deceiving . . . If Saddam Hussein does not fully disarm, for the safety of our people and for the peace of the world, we will lead a coalition to disarm him.'[93] From the Washington Embassy, Meyer's report was stark: 'It is politically impossible for Bush to back down from going to war against Iraq in the spring unless Saddam suddenly falls. If he had any room, he lost it with his State of the Union speech.'[94] Meyer's report was most unwelcome in Number 10. 'TB clear that he wanted to try to get GWB to a second UNSCR,' noted Campbell. 'Pretty clear we couldn't do without one. He felt we needed two or three Blix reports, and more time for Arab leaders to push Saddam out.'[95] 'Blair was desperate to buy time,' recalled one aide.[96] He knew that the Pentagon war planning and the Blix inspections were now on hopelessly different timetables: 'How in God's name are we going to make Blix synchronise with the US for war in February/March 2003?' Meyer asked his colleagues despairingly.[97] Blair rued to Campbell that by stressing the inspections 'we had allowed the goalposts to be moved to the smoking gun issue', so that instead of Saddam being judged by whether or not he co-operated with the UN, the key test had become whether Blix could unearth his WMD. Blair now wanted the focus to return to the co-operation issue: 'If the Iraqis didn't co-operate and Blix makes that clear repeatedly, we should say so and then we go for a second resolution and action could follow.'[98] The second resolution suddenly became the Holy Grail.

To sell the plan to Bush, Blair crossed the Atlantic on 31 January. The night before he arrived, Meyer warned the Prime Minister that Bush remained very cool towards both a second resolution and a delay to the start of the campaign.[99] These were nervous times for the Prime Minister. 'He was under huge pressure,' recalled Morgan. 'He spent a lot of the time on his own. He was absolutely determined he had to get Bush to agree, but was worried that he might not be able to persuade him.'[100] Originally scheduled for Camp David, bad weather forced a change, so he met Bush in the White House. The weather seemed an omen. During three hours of intense and difficult meetings, Blair found Bush, Cheney and even Powell united in opposition to a second resolution. 'Blair's the one who wanted the second resolution and he alone,' Powell recalled. 'No one else in the US government wanted it. I certainly didn't want it. But Blair pushed us very hard on this.'[101] Blair won the President over with a personal plea, stressing that a second resolution was absolutely necessary for him domestically: Blair was asking for it as 'a favour', to help him get the political backing to allow Britain to fight alongside. 'If that's what you need,' Woodward recounts the President saying, 'we will go flat-out to try to help you get it.'[102] But how important were British forces to the US? Bush told him that 'the US . . . would twist arms and even threaten . . . But he had to say that if we ultimately failed, military action would follow anyway.'[103] Blair's tenacity, and the logic of his plight, won the day. Bush realised that no second resolution might mean, thanks to parliamentary opposition, no Britain. 'PM Blair was very influential on the second resolution,' said the State Department's Marc Grossman. 'It was much harder to get the second through the administration than it was the first.'[104]

Blair's second objective from the talks, delay on timing, proved much more difficult. 'We came up against the full might of the US military planners and a President who had adopted their mindset,' recalled one official present. 'Bush was very sceptical.'[105] Blair argued for the end of April but Bush would not budge later than March. According to Meyer,

Bush showed flexibility 'for the simple reason that the Americans were not ready to go until March.'[106] 'Let's not kid ourselves,' said a senior British official. 'We were always tied to the US timetable. Blair felt that March was still too soon, but we knew perfectly well that the US could go it alone. Ultimately he resolved to back the US because he was not going to be seen as a "fair weather" friend.'[107] In a minute of their meeting Manning wrote 'our diplomatic strategy had to be arranged around the military planning . . . the start date for the military campaign was now pencilled in for 10 March.'[108] The closing press conference reflected the tensions that had preceded it. Bush gave only perfunctory and lukewarm backing for a second resolution, having been talked out of a broader statement of support at the last minute by his press secretary Ari Fleischer.[109] Blair returned to London knowing the chances of extracting a second resolution from the UN would now be significantly hampered by Bush's refusal to delay military action beyond March. He was about to enter some of his most challenging days.

Post-war planning for Iraq – if there was to be a war – was another subject raised by Blair during his visit. With his experience in the aftermath of the Kosovo and Afghanistan campaigns in mind, Blair had strong feelings. The official record says: 'The Prime Minister asked about aftermath planning . . . Condi Rice said that a great deal of work was now in hand.' Bush predicted, incredibly, that it was 'unlikely there would be internecine warfare between the different religious and ethnic groups'. Blair did not dissent.[110] In the FCO, it was commonplace that 'Iraq would split into three, a Shia, a Sunni and a Kurdish area'. It was one of the biggest lacunae of Blair's premiership. For all his humanitarian concerns and experience, he fell in – fatally – with American confidence that civil conflict between Shias and Sunnis would not erupt, and that they had the topic under control. 'The Prime Minister was not really involved in the post-war planning,' Manning recalled. 'Whenever he asked the Americans, he was told that "We have plans for this". He accepted their assurances.'[111]

Whitehall did make some effort to get in on the post-war planning act. Ideas about post-war Iraq were being developed in the FCO as early as the autumn of 2002 and gathered pace from January to March 2003. 'The presumption was that the invasion would work and there would be a relatively straightforward reconstruction,' recalled Michael Jay. 'We were not planning for the worst case.'[112] These efforts were subject to important limitations. One senior official deeply involved in the process rued 'the extent to which open or visible planning was held back by ministers not wanting to admit that war was a possibility'.[113] Clare Short and her Department for International Development (DfID) emerged as particularly culpable, according to Number 10. 'Clare complained about the Americans' lack of preparedness, but the situation was not helped by the same problem in her own department,' recalled Straw.[114] 'I remember having conferences at Northwood,' said Rob Fry, 'at which DfID made completely clear its profound moral disdain for what we were planning – both the operation and its aftermath.'[115] According to Andrew Turnbull, Wilson's successor as Cabinet Secretary, Short finally agreed to the development of post-war plans only *after* the conflict was under way,[116] although her own account suggests DfID planning had begun in late 2002, and her decision not to follow through on her first threatened resignation was based on Blair's promise that she would be involved in post-war reconstruction.[117] In addition to the refugee plans, detailed strategies were also put in place for dealing with oil wells set alight, attacks on British civilians living in Israel and WMD being used against troops: all contingencies that did not occur. 'We didn't plan for the right sort of aftermath,' Hoon admitted later.[118] Very little thought had been given to the more complicated issues of civilian and constitutional reconstruction – particularly if things went wrong. 'We underestimated the way the Sunnis and Shias would turn on each other,' recalled one senior Number 10 official, 'and we underestimated the extent that Iran would meddle. Those were our two big failures.'[119]

Number 10 took some interest in the planning efforts, but its attention was elsewhere: 'In reality their minds were focused on the run-up to military action, the UN Security Council and the dynamics in the Labour Party,' said one senior official, 'the problems of post-war reconstruction were not their number-one concern.'[120] Even if Blair had given this issue far higher priority, British efforts would have counted for little without major US engagement. Colin Powell reassured Straw in mid-February that the Americans were 'on the case' of post-war reconstruction, and he relayed how they had long experience of nation-building: 'We rebuilt Japan from ruins, we rebuilt Germany from ruins and we have the capability and the determination to do the same again.'[121] During 2002 and early 2003, the State Department had worked hard and well on the 'Future of Iraq Project', which gathered specialists together to plan post-war government, education and health structures.[122] It was not a comprehensive post-war plan, but it was at least a starting point. There was also considerable British involvement, with FCO officials travelling regularly to Washington to take part in inter-agency meetings chaired by the NSC. A range of issues were discussed, including the importance of the UN in a post-war environment.[123]

In late 2002, the Pentagon – with the backing of Rumsfeld – persuaded the President to sign a directive giving them the lead in the post-war effort. Colin Powell supported the idea: the wealth of resources available to the Department of Defense made them the obvious choice. 'Powell had no idea that subsequently the State Department would be deliberately cut out of all post-war activities,' recalled his chief of staff, Lawrence Wilkerson.[124] The 'Future of Iraq' project and other existing planning efforts were now shelved. 'Rumsfeld's people were determined to be in charge and didn't consult much with their own people, let alone close allies,' recalled one British official. 'It became hard to see that our contributions, which were all very politely received, had any impact at all on US thinking.'[125] Rumsfeld's assumption was that 'he and his department would not be organising a massive nation-building program, but facilitating Iraqi efforts to secure and reconstruct their own country, using their oil exports to finance whatever was needed'.[126] He was fixated on the Afghanistan experience. According to Fry, 'Afghanistan was seen as his model of this kind of intervention. You didn't need to think about what came afterwards. It was to be a relatively short-duration, clear-cut, military outcome. The only thing he was looking for was a bunch of compliant Iraqi politicians to hand the whole thing over to.'[127] General Sir Mike Jackson, who took command of the British Army one month before the invasion of Iraq, later rued the Pentagon's failure to plan for a major nation-building exercise in Iraq. Rumsfeld's approach, said Jackson, was 'intellectually bankrupt'.[128]

Dossiers, Jitters, Morality and the Pope: February 2003

Blair's failure to acquire more time for diplomacy now placed almost impossible pressure on the system, leaving him next to no time to lobby for the second resolution. And public support was wavering. By late January, 'the anti-war mood was definitely growing', noted Campbell, who complained to the Americans that their efforts to sell the war domestically to their right wing were causing problems in the UK.[129] Something needed to be done to bring public opinion more on side, and quickly. On 3 February Campbell fired the latest salvo in the UK public relations war, providing journalists with a hastily cobbled together second 'dossier' on the threat from Iraq and Saddam's efforts to obstruct the UN inspectors. 'It was an Alastair Campbell stunt,' recalled one official, 'saying, here are the facts that people still haven't grasped yet, let's reissue them once more.'[130]

The dossier was seized on by Colin Powell, who was laying out the US intelligence 'proving' that Saddam was involved in WMD-related activities before the UN Security Council. 'I would call my colleagues' attention to the fine paper that the United Kingdom distributed yesterday, which describes in exquisite detail Iraqi deception activities.'[131] The dossier aroused little interest among journalists until three days later, when it was exposed as containing large chunks of material directly lifted from the internet (including erroneous grammar and typographical errors). Scenting a spin story of major proportions, the media pounced. Number 10 admitted the provenance of the material but insisted that the fact that it was plagiarised did not 'take away from the core argument'.[132] But given the publicity shone on it by Colin Powell, the damage was immense. The intelligence community were furious: 'The second dossier came as a complete surprise,' recalled one official.[133] The FCO meanwhile saw it as a 'cock-up by Number 10'.[134] In fact the second dossier was originally produced by a relatively junior Foreign Office official, working in the 'Coalition Information Centre'. Although based in the FCO, this body reported direct to Campbell, with little oversight. 'The Number 10 press people were just over-eager,' insisted Turnbull. 'In the process they bypassed proper channels and made complete fools of themselves.'[135] The clamour surrounding the second dossier 'contaminated the whole perception of the government's use of intelligence', rued Godric Smith, 'and forever after, the first dossier was seen through its prism. This was unfortunate given the painstaking work by the intelligence services in putting the first dossier together. We suffered very badly. The public thought that we were playing fast and loose with the intelligence, and lacked appropriate checks and balances. That perception went straight into the public bloodstream.'[136] It was 'a bad own-goal' admitted Campbell, particularly as Blair needed public opinion onside now more than ever. 'Definitely no more dossiers for a while.'[137]

Inside the FCO, Straw's disquiet at the growing possibility of war was becoming widely known – and shared. On 6 February Michael Jay held an open forum in the Locarno Room, one of the large meeting rooms in the building, to attempt to allay these fears. All staff were invited for what turned out to be a tense hour-long meeting: 'It was absolutely packed, standing room only,' Jay recalled. 'I spoke, then we had questions and answers. There was clearly unease.'[138] Subsequent meetings were addressed by Peter Ricketts, as well as again by Jay. 'There was a widespread recognition that we needed to put the views of the PM across,' said one senior diplomat, 'and allow the staff to speak about their own concerns. And a lot did just this.'[139] Discontent among the public at large welled up on 15 February when, in the biggest protest the country had ever seen, up to a million men, women and children marched against the war. Speakers at the rally in Hyde Park included Tony Benn, Charles Kennedy, Harold Pinter and Bianca Jagger. Blair found the protest, and its scale, threatening. 'Even I am a bit worried about this one,' he declared.[140] 'The problem', according to Campbell, 'was that for the moment it looked as if every part of the strategy was in tatters – re: the EU, re: the UN, re: the US, re: the party, re: the country.'[141] This protest dwarfed any other anti-war demonstration in British history. Most unnerving for Blair was the reaction of his closest allies in Downing Street. 'My brother was on the march,' said one; 'My sister too,' said another, 'and my children.' 'The Prime Minister was surprised, shocked that the people closest to him had not been persuaded,' said one aide.[142] The American Embassy in London's Grosvenor Square, the focus for the anti-Vietnam war protests, was closed down as a precaution. A senior US diplomat, who remained holed up in his office to e-mail progress reports back to Washington, recalled, 'What struck me was the broad coalition out there. They were all pressing their own agendas, but Iraq had brought them all together. It was a watershed moment for us. We thought that it might trigger a fundamental change in policy.'[143]

Tony Blair was not in London for the protest. Instead, in Glasgow he sought to answer his critics even as the march unfolded. He was 'visibly stressed' as he prepared for his speech. Morgan had been hoping to take the weekend off but, seeing how uptight he was, and knowing that Campbell was also planning to be away, she decided to head to Scotland anyway. Arriving in Blair's suite she was taken aback to hear Campbell's familiar northern vowels emanating from within. Campbell had shared Morgan's anxieties and also come to help out, but neither had told the other.[144]

'There was a sense that the Prime Minister regretted that we hadn't spoken more about the brutal nature of the Saddam regime before that,' thought Godric Smith.[145] 'He'd been so focused on the UN and on inspectors, that he had not given enough attention to the emotional case,' said another aide.[146] He was pleased that Glasgow now offered him such a platform. The speech was Blair at his rawest yet most eloquent: 'I do not seek unpopularity as a badge of honour. But sometimes it is the price of leadership and the cost of conviction.' Having acknowledged the strength of the anti-war protest, he focused on Saddam's regime. 'Ridding the world of Saddam would be an act of humanity. It is leaving him there that is in truth inhumane . . . The moral case against war has a moral answer: it is the moral case for removing Saddam.' Blair's difficulty was that Saddam's inhumanity seemed a more convincing case for war than the increasingly problematic WMD argument, but there was no legal basis for attacking Saddam for immorality. The best Blair could offer was that it meant Britain could go to war 'with a clear conscience'. In a voice heavy with emotion Blair declared, 'As you watch your TV pictures of the march, ponder this: if there are 500,000 on that march, that is still less than the number of people whose deaths Saddam has been responsible for. If there are one million, that is still less than the number who died in the wars he started.' The speech moved the audience, and some of the media. Sky News and News 24 juxtaposed live images of Blair's speech and the protest, making his remarks all the more striking. The press too was encouraging: 'we got as many front-page leads as the march, which was a surprise' noted Campbell.[147] The *Observer* said Blair 'laid his political future on the line'.[148] One gain from the Glasgow speech was the succour it gave those in Number 10, like Morgan, who were battling with the prospect of war. They became increasingly comfortable the more the moral argument was deployed.[149]

Glasgow helped reconnect Blair with his moral and religious side, which had underpinned his actions in Kosovo. Blair's faith had been central to his life since his days as an Oxford undergraduate. It was one of the first issues the Protestant Blair discussed with Cherie, a Catholic, after they first met in 1976. Blair's faith only deepened during his time in Number 10.[150] At first he would attend Mass regularly with the family, but after 9/11 security concerns made this more difficult. Instead, the Blairs arranged for a Catholic RAF Chaplain to visit Chequers virtually every Saturday to say Mass for the family in private. Visiting family friends and Catholics on the staff at Chequers would always be invited to join them if they wished. The arrangement endured until the end of Blair's premiership.[151]

Catholicism was the Christian denomination with which Blair felt most instinctively in sympathy, but he always considered his faith an intensely personal matter. In Downing Street he would say his prayers every night without fail, although never aloud.[152] His personal relationship with God mattered more to him than the views of high religious authorities. Archbishop of Canterbury George Carey and Catholic leader Cardinal Murphy O'Connor spoke out publicly against the war before it started. Their disapproval made no appreciable impact on Blair. According to one Number 10 aide, 'This is a man who, in terms of judgement of right and wrong, would think that his own judgement was at least as good as that of the Archbishop of Canterbury, of the Cardinal of Westminster and the Pope combined.'[153]

With the pressure on Blair mounting and the war drawing ever closer, Blair spent the weekend of 21–23 February 2003 visiting the Vatican. An audience with the Pope – Cherie's wish – had been in the pipeline for many months. Some in Number 10 resisted strongly because they did not want the visit to fuel speculation about Blair being a closet Catholic.[154] Reservations were not confined to Downing Street. The Vatican's line was very clear: total opposition to war in Iraq. Would seeing Blair, an arch-exponent of standing up to Saddam, not send the wrong message? The Vatican assented to the audience, but 'wanted to be very, very clear that it was neutral on the war'.[155] So a visit was arranged with Iraqi Deputy Prime Minister Tariq Aziz a week before, to provide balance.

Blair flew into Rome early on Friday 21 February for a summit on Iraq and the EU with Berlusconi. Cherie and three of the four children flew in that evening (Nicholas was on a skiing holiday), and the family spent the night at the Irish College ('Pontificio Collegio Irlandese'), a seminary judged sufficiently secure, where Cherie knew the Rector. On the Saturday morning, the Blairs arrived at the Vatican for the audience, the first of two meetings with the Pope, John Paul II, who by then was very frail (he died two years later after a long illness). Accompanied by heavy security, they arrived twenty minutes early, and had to be driven round the Vatican gardens. When the Pope was ready, they were brought into the Court of St Damasos (the courtyard of the Apostolic Palace) and greeted by the Swiss Guard, who escorted them to the second loggia where the Pope resides. As with most guests, the Pontiff received the party in his library. Blair was the first to be brought in, alone, for an audience of twenty minutes. No record of their discussion was kept. Cherie then joined them for a further ten minutes, before the children were summoned. 'The real interaction', said one witness, 'was between the Pope and Leo, then aged two and a half.'[156] Cherie was more at ease than her husband during the audience and seemed quite unphased by Leo scampering around the room. But the Prime Minister seemed off his game. To colleagues, he appeared discomforted by this personal audience. John Paul II was a known critic of the war. 'There were some people saying to him in advance that you weren't going to be able to go in there and turn that man's view around.'[157] He knew this, but he still harboured hopes of some understanding for the moral position he believed he was taking. It was not to be. The Pope acknowledged that Blair's intentions were good, but he would go no further.[158] One aide formed a clear impression that the Pope had 'laid into him about Iraq, making clear that he was against the coming war'.[159] That afternoon, Blair's party were treated to a private visit to St Peter's, including visits to the Apostolic Palace and the Raphael rooms. Blair remained troubled and out of sorts.[160]

Despite the serene surroundings, there was also business for the Prime Minister to transact. He took a series of calls that afternoon, and again on the Sunday, from President Bush, Chirac, Putin and Berlusconi. Finally he heard some good news. In a four-way conversation with Bush, Aznar and Berlusconi, they agreed formally on introducing a second resolution declaring that Saddam had 'failed to' comply with UNSCR 1441.[161] Even as war loomed, frenetic diplomacy continued.

Sunday proved less angst-ridden, with a second encounter with the Pope for morning Mass. The intervention of Cardinal Murphy O'Connor had been significant in swaying the Vatican to hold the Mass. He said, in effect, 'This is a couple who send their children to Catholic schools and are regular attendees at Catholic Mass. He is an Anglican, she is a Catholic, but the children are being raised as Catholic. So you are dealing with genuine faith.'[162] Two final matters were only resolved at the last minute. As late as the Saturday night, it was still not clear whether Blair himself would receive communion. In the end it was decided that the Pope's private secretary, Archbishop Dziwisz (now Cardinal of Kraków), should give communion to all in the Prime Minister's party, including Blair.[163] The second issue involved less soul-searching: should toddler Leo attend? Blair in particular was nervous at the prospect of keeping Leo quiet for that length of time. The answer back from the Pope's private office, and Number 10 thought from the Pope himself, was strongly that Leo should be there.

The service was held in the Pope's private chapel, a small oratory located within his personal apartments. At the end is a modern stained-glass window with white marble. The chapel is lit by electricity, having no natural light. They were greeted by Dziwisz who brought them in to an ante-chamber accompanied by the Rector of the Irish College. The Pope remained in private meditation for thirty minutes after the party arrived at 7 A.M. It had been arranged that Cherie would read, as would two of their children. But the Pontiff intervened. 'The Pope said specifically that he wanted the Prime Minister to be given the first reading and Cherie should choose the music,' said one aide.[164] The two children were assigned the second reading and the psalm. When the party was shown in, the Pope was already sitting down in front in white, with his back to them. On to the three rows of pews on either side of the

aisle were shown members of the Prime Ministerial party, who joined
the Mass; and a group of Polish sisters. Blair and Cherie sat in pews in
the front on the left, with the family immediately in front of them on
stools. Leo was placed at the back of the chapel with his nanny and a
little bag of sweets. 'Every now and then you would hear this little echo
round the chapel, there'd be a rattle of plastic and a sweet would go into
his mouth and there'd be silence again for about three or four minutes,'
said one observer.[165] Blair found solace in the Mass and took comfort
from the Pope's recognition that his motivation was good. But beyond
some initial discomfort, the Pope's implacable opposition to the war had
little effect. Blair pressed on regardless.

The Dangerous Demise of the Second Resolution: February–March 2003

Agreement from Bush to introduce a second resolution at the UN was
a start, but gaining support for it was never going to be easy. Germany
and France were two Security Council votes he had little hope of
winning. 'It was Iraq that really drew Chirac and Schröder together,' said
one close aide. 'And when they were pulled together with Putin it was
calamitous. It split Europe in two.'[166] On 22 January – the fortieth
anniversary of the Elysée Treaty, Chirac and Schröder held their joint
press conference foreshadowed at the disastrous EU Council in October
2002. In a moment of high drama they 'stood together' in opposition to
what Bush and Blair were planning in Iraq. With weapons inspections
still under way, they wanted any second resolution to wait until the work
was completed, a process that could take months.

From Washington, Rumsfeld's response was swift. 'You're thinking of
Europe as Germany and France. I don't,' he told an interviewer. 'I think
that's old Europe. If you look at the entire NATO Europe today, the
centre of gravity is shifting to the east and there are a lot of new
members.' His comments, which certainly captured the truth about the
EU, were widely picked up. Following this lead, the *Wall Street Journal*
asked Aznar if he would consider writing an article responding to Chirac
and Schröder? Aznar spoke to Blair who was enthusiastic, and called
Berlusconi to bring him on board. Several EU 'candidate countries' were
also very keen to be part of any statement distancing themselves from
the Franco-German position. This was how the 'Letter of 8', pledging
support for the US position in Iraq, came to be published on 29 January
2003 in the *Wall Street Journal*: 'Europe and America must stand united.'
Number 10 decided to give Chirac and Schröder's office a courtesy call

the evening before publication. The response was frosty. A week later, on 6 February, the 'Vilnius letter' was published, signed by Eastern European 'accession' countries who resented the idea that Chirac and Schröder spoke for the whole of Europe. Power was indeed visibly seeping away from France and Germany. The stakes were high. Chirac lambasted the Vilnius letter as 'not well-brought-up behaviour. They missed a good opportunity to keep quiet.'[167]

Blair was still optimistic in late February that he could achieve UN backing. With Spain and Bulgaria's support in the Security Council guaranteed, on top of the US and UK vote, he needed only five more non-permanent UN members to secure the nine necessary for the resolution to pass, assuming no permanent member dared veto it (a veto from any of the five permanent members sinks a resolution). On the rejectionist side stood five states: Syria and China joined France, Germany and Russia. That left six 'middle ground' members – three African states, Angola, Cameroon, and Guinea, together with Mexico, Chile and Pakistan. Blair could afford to lose just one. The battle for votes was on. 'It was a hugely complex negotiation. Just as you felt progress was being made with one country, it fell away with another,' said one aide.[168] While Greenstock lobbied at the UN, Blair and Manning focused initially on Mexico and Chile. 'These were the most stressful moments,' recalled one Number 10 official. 'Every hour was being spent trying to track down those leaders, fighting for those votes.'[169]

Blair was so focused on this struggle, recalled a close aide, because of the 'huge stakes. It wasn't only Iraq. It was also the future unity of Europe. There were lots of big "globals" attached to this.'[170] Without the second resolution, Blair's risk of losing a vote in Parliament was much higher. Over the next few days the balance of opinion on the Security Council seemed to be moving against war. Whereas Blix's first report of 27 January had been critical of Iraq, a second report on 14 February was more positive. 'We had not anticipated that Blix, having been faced by non-co-operation, would not describe it as non-co-operation,' said one exasperated aide.[171] 'You definitely got the impression that [Blix] was deliberately siding with France,' thought Campbell.[172] Number 10 concluded Blix wanted to avoid war at all costs, and hopes of a resolution began to fade. On 25 February, a fraught Blair called Campbell: 'He said it was going to be really tough from now on in. The truth was we may well have to go without a second UNSCR, or even without a majority on the UNSC. The Bush poodle problem would get bigger.'[173]

On 7 March came further worrying news. Blix's third report suggested an accelerated pace of Iraqi co-operation, while Manning received word that Putin had told Bush that Russia would veto a second resolution.[174] The deadline for war was fast approaching. What could Number 10 do? A crisis meeting took place over the weekend of 8/9 March. Blair, Manning and Scarlett, with telephone input from Greenstock in New York, came up with the idea of 'six tests' to ascertain whether Saddam genuinely was beginning to comply with inspectors. Why? 'We wanted him to comply, but also wanted to appear reasonable for the sake of the domestic and the international market,' said one official.[175] Manning was dispatched to see President Fox of Mexico and President Lagos of Chile, while Baroness Amos was sent off to the three African states to try to win support for the tests more broadly.[176] Black humour began to set in at Number 10: 'TB said his future was now in the hands of the ailing President of Guinea [Lansana Conte] and the diplomatic judgement of [waverer Labour MP] Jeff Ennis.'[177] Cabinet Secretary Turnbull began to consider how a caretaker government led by Prescott would operate, lest Blair fell. Campbell tried to quantify the situation: 'I reckoned the chances of [Blair] being out within a week or two were about 20:1.'[178]

Monday 10 March was the moment of maximum danger for Blair. It began with Clare Short breaking cover on the airwaves: 'The whole atmosphere of the current situation is deeply reckless,' she proclaimed, 'reckless for the world, reckless for the undermining of the UN in this disorderly world, which is wider than Iraq, reckless with our government, reckless with his own future, position and place in history.'[179] No one in Number 10 had expected so public an outburst; she was, after all, still a Cabinet minister, tied by conventions of loyalty. Blair 'viewed it as an act of personal betrayal'.[180] 'There was a sense that everything was precarious,' recalled one Blairite. 'All of us in Number 10 were concerned about what would happen in the next twenty-four hours.'[181] Adding to their worry was their constant paranoia about Brown: 'When Clare spoke out, was Gordon behind it? We really didn't know.'[182] Deep apprehension gripped Number 10, but Blair held firm: 'It is remarkable how little "conviction deficit" the PM suffered,' said one aide.[183] Blunkett told Blair that Short should be sacked. Blair replied he 'didn't want to make a martyr of her'.[184]

A Cabinet coup was not Blair's only danger. He had been persuaded that a parliamentary vote, although not technically necessary, should precede a declaration of war. Many in Number 10, including Campbell, had not been keen. Their instinct was to avoid sensitive parliamentary votes where possible: 'If you could get away without a vote, then you should.'[185] Cook, as Leader of the House, argued that a vote was essential. But Straw's voice was the decisive one: 'I'd always thought it was eccentric to make decisions to go to war without a vote,' he recalled. 'People would have gone berserk if we didn't observe proper process. I said, "Tony, we'll end up with a disaster. You can't do this. This is a discretionary war."'[186] 'Jack in effect committed us without very much in the way of a Cabinet discussion,' recalled one Cabinet colleague.[187] The case was bolstered by three earlier parliamentary votes on the crisis – in September and November 2002, and February 2003. 'We had crossed the Rubicon that September,' said Straw.[188] Blair asked Chief Whip Armstrong what she thought might happen. 'I was fairly clear that it would be a very difficult vote,' she replied. 'But in the end he just thought it was the right thing to do.'[189] Campbell warned that 100 Labour MPs might vote against the government: 'He said fine, they're mainly the dispossessed and the disaffected.' Blair added that he knew it was more serious than that, 'but was pushing the argument that those against us had to face up to the fact that the consequence of their actions was Saddam staying in power'.[190]

If there was to be a vote, Blair had to win it, or risk resignation. Straw discussed Blair's predicament with Jay that same Monday (10 March) in Straw's office at the FCO. Here were Britain's two top foreign policy figures (outside of Number 10) deep in thought. 'If he gets the nine votes and no veto, no problem,' said Jay. 'If he gets nine and a French veto, he can probably get parliamentary support for action, though it would weaken the UN.' Other outcomes they felt would be much trickier, but the real danger for Blair would be to seek parliamentary authority and not achieve it. In those circumstances British troops would not be able to support the US.[191] It would make a nonsense of Blair's entire foreign policy. Would Blair have to resign? Not going in with America would 'be a bitter blow', they agreed, 'but he would recover'. This blow could be lessened by a pledge to assist the US as far as possible, by offering use of the bases at RAF Fairford and Diego Garcia, and help with reconstruction. The bottom line was that Britain could not support the US militarily without UN or parliamentary support.[192]

On the Monday evening, Chirac made a startling announcement on French TV. The wording is important: 'Whatever the circumstances, France will vote "No" because we believe, tonight, that there are no grounds to wage war, to achieve the objective we have set – the disarmament of Iraq.'[193] If France was indeed to exercise its veto, it would kill a second resolution stone dead. Number 10's reaction was swift: they announced publicly that by his televised pronouncement,

Chirac had sabotaged the prospect of diplomacy working at the UN. Sceptics, including Number 10's Stephen Wall, say that Chirac's words were cynically manipulated to make France the scapegoat for the collapse of the UN process. One aide recalls Blair and Campbell in a corridor at Number 10 talking almost gleefully about Chirac giving them a way out with someone to blame.[194] Chirac, explained Wall, 'did not say that France would always veto such a resolution, but the story was spun by Number 10 as if that's what indeed he had said, i.e., that France would never ever agree to the overthrow of Saddam Hussein'.[195] This was certainly the line London fed the Embassy in Washington.[196] Rupert Murdoch's *Sun* also lapped up this take on events, comparing Chirac to a 'cheap tart who puts price before principle, money before honour'.[197] It later emerged that Blair had spoken to Murdoch personally the day after Chirac's announcement, and twice more before military action began.[198] Wall insisted that Chirac's revenge had a lot more depth to it: 'What Chirac was trying to say was exactly what he had said on several occasions to Blair, which is that "I served in Algeria, I know war, war is bloody and if you go in to Iraq you risk a civil war. You talk about democracy but a Shia majority is not the same thing as democracy." Tony Blair would roll his eyes and say, "Poor Jacques, he doesn't really understand things, does he?"'[199] Chirac certainly provided a very convenient excuse, but Blair's line was not entirely cynical. He later phoned Chirac, who confirmed that there was no possible second resolution he would agree with.[200] Stothard recorded Blair's reaction to the news from Chirac. 'The Prime Minister does not like to be angry, still less to show anger. But he is angry now. "This is just a foolish thing to do at this moment in the world's history."'[201]

Although Number 10 now had a scapegoat at the ready, it was agreed on the Monday night that diplomatic efforts should continue, in part due to Straw's strengthening conviction that without a second resolution Britain could not take part in military action. The next morning he went to see Blair and they agreed to split the lobbying of key Security Council votes between them. Jay described an 'intense effort still to get a second resolution' but with the prospect of success 'only 50:50'.[202] Number 10 still had hopes of declaring any Chirac veto 'unacceptable', but as Manning later said, 'After Chirac made that pronouncement, the game was really up. Why should middle-ground members like Chile and Mexico take huge risks with their own public opinions at home when any resolution would be vetoed anyway?'[203]

On Tuesday, Greenstock reported to Downing Street that the second resolution attempt was losing ground. 'I'm not sure we are going to get it through,' Blair told his four most senior aides in Number 10, Manning, Powell, Campbell and Morgan. 'Hell, we are stuck then!' declared one of them.[204] How viable would the Prime Minister's position be if he took the country to war without a second resolution, they asked? Those at the dove end thought that if a second resolution indeed were to collapse, it gave him the pretext to explain to Bush that it would now be impossible for British troops to participate. But those who could see the force of such an argument, like Manning and Morgan, held no sway against a Blair who *believed in* military action if diplomacy was to fail. If the US was going in, so should Britain. Despite the urgings of his aides and his precarious position within the party, Blair now was to spurn at least two chances to back out.

The first opportunity had come privately on 9 March in a phone call with Bush. The US Embassy in London was sending Washington worrying accounts of Blair's position: 'We were talking to backbenchers. What we heard was a fairly strident message that there was only so far that we could go, and the UN was extremely important. We heard some very ominous analyses of what could happen,' said one senior official.[205] Bush too was worried. 'I remember standing in the Oval Office,' recalled Condi Rice, 'and the President said "We can't have the British government fall because of this decision over war." I said, "So what are you saying?" He said, "I have to tell Tony that he doesn't have to do this."' Rice's first thought was to call Manning and 'grease the skids ahead'. But there was no time. 'I'm going to call him right now,' said Bush.[206] 'What I want to say to you is that my last choice is to have your government go down,' Bush told Blair. 'We don't want that to happen under any circumstances. I really mean that.'[207] 'It was, I think, very emotional for the President,' said Rice.[208] If it would help, Bush suggested, he would let Blair 'drop out of the coalition' and they would find some other way for Britain to participate. 'I said I'm with you. I mean it,' Blair replied.[209] 'Having taken it so far,' explained one confidant, 'backing out seemed to him a rather pathetic thing to do.'[210]

On the evening of 11 March, Rumsfeld offered Blair a second escape route. Early that day Rumsfeld had spoken with his opposite number, Defence Secretary Hoon: 'I felt that I should point out to him that if we lost the vote, we could not commit troops,' Hoon recalled.[211] Straw passed on a similar message to Powell: 'I said to Colin, "Don't bank on this. This is very tight."'[212] But Rumsfeld's response was not what the British had envisaged. Shortly after speaking with Hoon, he held a press conference at which he declared brazenly that the US could go it alone without Britain. At the State Department at Foggy Bottom there was sharp intake of breath: 'It was just plain thoughtless arrogance,' said Elizabeth Jones. 'It was to me stunning that there could be such disregard for the British. Rumsfeld was still on his kick about how much we could do militarily with very few troops.'[213] British service chiefs were equally appalled. Boyce had repeatedly told his American counterparts, on direct instructions from Number 10, that 'we are not with you until we say we are'. These cautious overtures had always received the knowing response: 'Yeah, yeah, Mike, we know, whatever . . .' The implicit American assumption was that British forces were integral to the whole operation. So when Boyce heard Rumsfeld's comments, he thought, 'Bullshit. They couldn't have gone in without us without a major overhaul of their operational plan.'[214] With the UK's commitment of aircraft, amphibious and land forces in the south, and US access to UK bases elsewhere, it was inconceivable the US could have attacked as planned without the British: 'To pull out would have scuppered the whole thing,' said one senior official, 'and the Americans would have been left like the bride at the altar.'[215] British non-participation might not have stopped the war, Boyce admitted, but it would have delayed the US advance by a good few weeks.[216] General Mike Jackson, the army head, believed it would only have been a matter of days.[217]

So what was Rumsfeld playing at? Some interpreted the comments as an effort to push Blair out of the coalition before he jumped. 'Tommy Franks [the US Commander in Iraq] had no time for allies,' insisted Wilkerson, 'and it permeated the whole operation: allies got in the way, they didn't help.'[218] Some in the Pentagon resented any external constraints of their freedom of action, and Blair – and his need to secure parliamentary approval – threatened to limit their room for manoeuvre. '"Does it constrain us?" That was their analysis,' recalled Jones, 'and if it constrains us, it's bad.'[219] 'There were indeed some concerns that our coalition with the Brits could limit our freedom of action operationally,' admitted one senior Pentagon official, 'particularly given their input on the rules of engagement. But there was no mindset at all in the Pentagon that it would be better if the British fell off the wagon. Accommodating the British was the price you paid for a coalition and the associated gain in credibility.'[220] Rumsfeld's comment was in fact an *ad hoc* answer to a journalist rather than a pre-prepared statement. 'I felt very badly about the twist that was put on it,' Rumsfeld said later. 'My attitude was, look, the President said what he said, he believes what he said, he's on a certain track and my impression was that he would continue on that track.' Rumsfeld's remarks were targeted not at London but at Baghdad.

'I wasn't speaking to the British people,' insisted Rumsfeld. 'I was speaking to Saddam Hussein [and] I didn't want to take the pressure off and leave him with the impression that the US was going to toss it in if we didn't have all the capabilities we hoped for.'[221]

Whatever his intention, Rumsfeld's comments ignited a firestorm at the heart of British government. 'TB went bonkers about it,' recorded Campbell, 'he couldn't believe how the US kept fucking things up.'[222] 'We had to put something out straight away saying that we were completely committed to this,' recalled Godric Smith.[223] It took two late-night phone calls to Bush to establish that Rumsfeld was 'only trying to help'.[224] Not everyone at the heart of the British government 'went bonkers' at Rumsfeld's comments: 'My private view was that we should have grabbed the offer and not done it,' said one senior Number 10 aide.[225] Straw had already written a series of handwritten letters to Blair outlining his concerns. If he followed Bush into Iraq 'without a second resolution', he had warned him face-to-face on 5 March, 'the only regime change that will be taking place is in this room'.[226] He now felt that Rumsfeld's comments could offer Britain a lifeline. They met privately in the Downing Street flat. 'Jack said, "Here is an opportunity for the UK not to participate",' recalled one witness. 'I don't recall anybody else saying the same thing. Blair would have none of it; he dismissed his suggestion out of hand. I remember thinking that he had already made his mind up at a very deep level that he was going to go ahead.'[227]

On 12 March Blair and Straw met again. For all their differences over military action, both realised that, barring a miracle, the second resolution was no longer viable. They resolved not to put it to a vote in the Security Council: 'Mexico and Chile were not playing.'[228] Without the resolution Number 10 worried that they would either fail to secure parliamentary approval for military action, or that the majority in favour would be so small that it would cripple Blair personally. Some began to suggest that the whole strategy needed a radical rethink. 'Certain people in Number 10 were urging the Prime Minister to go for military action without seeking parliamentary approval,' recalled one FCO official, 'and daring Parliament to say "no" when our soldiers were in action.'[229] This argument did not go far. 'It was in my view completely inconceivable that this would not have gone to a vote in the Commons,' said Turnbull. 'There would have been an absolute riot.'[230]

That evening the second resolution, already holed below the waterline, slid further under the waves. Bush and Blair had two sombre phone calls. At Blair's direct request, Bush agreed to phone Lagos and Fox to push for their support. Bush agreed, albeit half-heartedly. Neither would play along. Bush later called Blair back and delivered the news: 'It's over.'[231] On 13 March the 'six tests' fizzled out: 'Greenstock put down the six tests at the UN at 2 A.M.,' noted Campbell. 'Before anyone had even had time properly to discuss them, de Villepin rejected them.'[232] The next day Greenstock confirmed to Blair that the second resolution attempt had, as he fatally put it, 'lost traction'. In an attempt to forestall a counter resolution the British kept the discussions going for several days, until it was formally withdrawn on 17 March. It had been a close-run affair. At the State Department, considerable effort had been expended in trying to round up votes: 'I don't think I ever saw Secretary Powell work as hard on anything as I saw him work on the second resolution,' recalled Jones, 'because he knew how much Blair wanted it in order to survive.'[233] But elsewhere, particularly in the White House, the work rate was less impressive. Had the President engaged more he might have tipped the balance. As Greenstock said, 'All the middle-ground members came on board at different times, but never together. It was very, very close.'[234]

End Game: 12–18 March 2003

Blair now had no fall-back position: it had to be war, or withdrawal of British military support. Cook thought he was suddenly 'mystified as to how he got into such a hole'.[235] 'It was all much scarier than taking big decisions during a General Election campaign,' said one of his inner team.[236] It was also far less clear cut: 'All of us, I think, had had pretty severe moments of doubt,' noted Campbell later, 'but [Blair] hadn't really, or if he had he had hidden them even from us.'[237] The toll on Blair was beginning to tell in other ways. 'I think he was at his lowest ebb in the run-up to the Iraq war,' said Wall, 'and he looked awful, partly because of his fitness regime, which contributed to his loss of weight.'[238] His political position remained shaky. Cabinet Ministers were not the least of his anxieties. Short's ('reckless') outburst on Monday 10th had been followed by a phone conversation the next day. 'I said happy to go now or agree now to go later, whatever he wanted,' she noted in her diary. 'He said no, need you for reconstruction.'[239] The impact of her speech, and the encouragement it might offer to others to rebel, was still being assessed. Cook was teetering on the brink of resignation, though he had little personal following. Straw's concerns were potentially far graver for Blair, but he kept his counsel. Brown's sullen response throughout had continued to worry Number 10 greatly, but he chose not to strike at the vulnerable PM. Blair held a private dinner on Tuesday 11 March with him and Prescott to shore up support. It was almost the first time that Blair had actively sought advice on Iraq. If he was to carry the Cabinet and the party, he needed them bound tightly to him.[240] If Brown was negative, Blair's strategy was finished, and there would be no British troops in Iraq. But he raised no fundamental objections at the dinner, though he expressed concern that no option was being presented to the party other than all-out support for America. Blair was relieved – but still not sure.

The Cabinet meeting on Thursday 13 March would be critical. This was the moment Number 10 believed that Brown could have brought their boss down.[241] One insider described this week as 'the most vulnerable of the entire Blair premiership'. Brown had decided at the eleventh hour to come off the fence. He persuaded Short to stay, and from now on played a very straight bat. 'As ever, it was the case that Gordon didn't strike when he could have done,' said one Blairite. 'He was thinking of his political future, and he didn't want to be associated with anti-Americanism.'[242] Brown could not have been more supportive at Cabinet: 'Gordon launched a long and passionate statement of support for Tony's strategy,' Cook recorded. 'The contribution was rather marred by an outspoken attack on France: "The message that must go out from this Cabinet is that we pin the blame on France for its isolated refusal to agree in the Security Council."'[243] For Brown, Chirac's intervention provided the hook on which to hang his new coat of outspoken loyalty. 'Brown would have been troubled to have found himself on the side of the French against the Americans,' recalled Turnbull. Brown's quiet approach hitherto did not mean he disagreed with Blair's line: 'Gordon was not against the war. He was pro the US. After all, even the Democrat leadership was supporting the war.'[244] But at the time the Blairites took nothing for granted. Only later did they learn that their apprehensions about him had been ill-grounded. 'Balls *et al.* were studious, punctilious indeed about not ever rocking the boat on the topic,' said one top official.[245]

Blair took meticulous care in preparing for the Cabinet. One present recalled his emphatic delivery: '"The problem you [the Cabinet] have got, is that I absolutely believe we have *got to do* this" … He was passionate in his delivery of this line – I remember it distinctly. He was saying "I believe this" and "I believe that".'[246] The gravity of the issue was clear: 'Everyone in Cabinet knew it was the hardest decision you can possibly take,' said Milburn.[247] Those who think Blair bounced the Cabinet are wrong: it had discussed Iraq every time it met from

September 2002 onwards. 'We all sought out the evidence, interrogated it and decided accordingly.' Hoon would typically open the Iraq discussion and, in Cook's opinion, 'reflected the thinking of the Pentagon and would be pretty pro-war'. Straw followed, reflecting the concerns of the State Department and concentrating on the diplomatic position. 'The great majority of the Cabinet rarely spoke.'[248] Cook was the main one who argued. Prescott's line was 'I've come in with them, and I'll see them through': he was 'hugely supportive all the way through'.[249] The tone of the meeting that Thursday was serious, concerned but favourable to the Prime Minister: 'Everyone had worries, but it was the general worry of sending the country to war,' said Milburn.[250] Blair had passed this test, but had to gird himself up for one final Cabinet the following Tuesday, at which the decision on war, underpinned by the all-important advice on the war's legality, would be formally taken.

On 27 February, Attorney-General Goldsmith had met Manning and Morgan to discuss the legality of war, particularly without a second UN resolution. He was asked to put his views in writing and on 7 March he presented Blair with a thirteen-page detailed, and often nuanced, statement of the legal position.[251] The document implied that the war could be considered legal, but appeared equivocal. On 14 March, at the request of the MoD, Goldsmith produced a second statement of the position, a one-page document confirming that he believed the war to be legal on the basis of UNSCR 1441. This view was later published in answer to a parliamentary question on 17 March. It was an absolutely crucial step on the road to war, because both Boyce (as head of the military) and Jay (as head of the FCO) needed a clear legal opinion. 'All I needed was a one-liner,' said Boyce. 'Legal approval is bread and butter for military operations – every bomb that is dropped has to be cleared by the Attorney-General.'[252] Jay concurred, 'There was no way I could associate the diplomatic service with the conduct of conflict unless I could be absolutely certain the war was legal.'[253] Turnbull too, as head of the home civil service, needed confirmation as no government department could commit money or make decisions without legal approval.[254]

The enduring bone of contention concerns the emergence of Goldsmith's one-page opinion of 14 March.[255] Was the Attorney-General 'leant on' to produce this more certain and less nuanced brief? Goldsmith denies the charge completely. Even at the time of the 7 March legal advice, he later suggested, he was 'clear that there could be a green light for military action'.[256] But conspiracy theorists point to a meeting Goldsmith held with Morgan and Lord Falconer on 13 March, at which Goldsmith stated unequivocally for the first time that war would be legal, and suggest here is evidence of Number 10 pressure. Morgan disputes this: there was no discussion of the advice, merely an opportunity for him to air the burden he was carrying. 'Peter is a proud man and a very good lawyer: he took his own counsel from fellow lawyers.'[257] Turnbull insists that the original thirteen-page document was not advice at all but a snapshot of Goldsmith's thoughts at that time, put down in a working paper: 'He was refining it all the time and talking to people about it. Eventually he persuaded himself that he could make a good enough case for war.'[258] But even some inside Number 10 disagreed with Goldsmith's conclusions. 'We stretched the legal argument to breaking point in my view,' Wall later commented.[259] The FCO's mounting concerns now burst cover over the legal question. Michael Wood, the FCO's legal adviser, was thought to be sceptical about the legal arguments expressed, but decided not to object in public.[260] A deputy legal adviser, Elizabeth Wilmshurst, felt differently and resigned. 'The rules governing the use of force are at the heart of international law. What they did showed contempt for the UN. I did not want to continue to work for a government that thought so little of international law and of the UN.'[261] Blair himself does not appear to have taken great interest in the niceties of the legal argument. In Goldsmith's single-sided judgement, he had what he needed. 'Tony Blair never had much time for lawyers,' recalled one Downing Street aide, 'and certainly not in terms of their driving a policy. Perhaps because he was a lawyer himself he didn't have that much respect for what they had to say.'[262]

War was only days away. Blair became for a time 'much calmer than one could possibly imagine anyone in his position to be'.[263] Blair's total conviction that his actions were right for the country, and morally right, partly explains his composure. So too was his experience. When he first considered using military force in Iraq in 1998 and Kosovo in 1999, he had been very anxious. He would 'count the aircraft out and count them back in again' and was hugely alert to loss of life and the military risk. But after successful actions in Kosovo in 1999, Sierra Leone, Indonesia and East Timor in 2000, and Afghanistan in 2001, his focus shifted from the risks to the soldiers and pilots to the effectiveness of their actions. 'However tough was the decision to deploy forces in domestic terms, he gained confidence that, once they were in action, they would produce the results he wanted,' said Sawers.[264] Over the space of four years, from late 1998 to 2002/3, he had changed to a leader who was usually confident about the use of military action. 'Tony Blair didn't back down at this point because he didn't want to back out,' stressed Nigel Sheinwald, Manning's successor in Number 10. 'Even if he had known all the consequences that have happened since, I suspect he would still have gone for it.'[265] Although he regretted bitterly not having secured UN support, this omission 'fell within the parameters' of what he was prepared to stomach to stick with his convictions.[266] 'Tony Blair took Britain to war because he was convinced that the multilateral option was finally exhausted after twelve years, and he believed Iraq under Saddam posed a serious threat that now had to be confronted. It was as simple as that,' said Manning.[267]

Blair still had to win the vote in the Commons on Tuesday 18 March. After the decision to go to war, agreeing to a parliamentary vote had been Blair's 'second biggest' decision during the crisis.[268] Following the 13 March Cabinet, Number 10 had mounted a ferocious lobbying effort, mobilising not only Blair but Prescott and Brown too. Armstrong recalled the challenge: 'I had staff in all weekend, and we did endless phoning and talking to people ahead of the vote.'[269] Bush's eleventh-hour announcement on 14 March that he would publish the 'road map' for peace in the Middle East, on which Blair had been pushing him hard for many weeks, helped bring some back into the fold. 'It was never a quid pro quo,' said Rice. 'We knew it would make it easier for the Prime Minister, but frankly it would make it easier for us too.'[270]

On Sunday, 16 March, Blair flew to the Azores to meet Bush and Aznar. To Stothard, it was the day of the crisis when Blair seemed the most grave.[271] It was a bizarre 'day trip', intended to demonstrate to the Security Council the strength of the alliance.[272] 'There was a more than slight feeling of going though the motions,' felt Campbell.[273] A 3,300-mile round trip with eight hours in the air was long for a non-event, and the British team left early in order to get back on the phones ahead of the Commons vote. They had only time to eat the salad course before boarding the plane. By this stage the Americans were well aware of the risks Blair was facing. As the British delegation said hasty goodbyes, Rice turned to Andy Card, Bush's Chief of Staff: 'I hope that's not the last time I see them,' she said.[274]

Returning to Downing Street at midnight, Blair knew he faced the most historic and challenging week of his premiership. Straw had become desperately unhappy over the weekend. After an anguished conversation with his close friend and adviser Jay, he took up his pen one final time to write Blair a 'personal minute', urging him to think about alternatives.[275] And not only Straw. Both Morgan and Manning held separate conversations with Blair, even at this late stage, to 'try to persuade him to say to Bush that we couldn't go in without the second resolution'.[276] Their chief concern was not the wrongness or rightness of the conflict, which had already been debated exhaustively, but the likely ramifications for Blair's long-term position. But he was not in listening mood. 'The Prime Minister at that stage was clear that he was going to do it and he believed very strongly that that was the right thing to do,' recalled one witness.[277]

As war neared, some within the FCO felt their oft-repeated concerns had not been acted upon. 'There was a collective failure of the Chiefs of Staff and the Foreign Office to present a coherent case that would make Blair think again,' complained one diplomat.[278] Why did more not break cover? Blair's closest advisers, for all their doubts, would never have dreamed of criticising the Prime Minister publicly. Straw too chose to keep his concerns private. 'I never saw any doubts from Jack, nor did he express in my recollection any doubts in Cabinet,' Hoon recalled.[279] To colleagues, Straw explained his post-Azores letter to Blair as part of his 'duty' as Foreign Secretary.[280] Yet Straw's reservations went far further than that, and are a matter of record. To some, his failure to speak out in Cabinet was weak; to others it was a fine demonstration of service.

Cook felt no such compunction, and resigned on 17 March. He had co-ordinated his departure with Campbell some days earlier, insisting that he wanted Blair to stay in office: 'I do not want to be part of a process that sees Gordon become Prime Minister,' he declared.[281] At Blair's request Cook did not attend the final Cabinet meeting on the day of his resignation.[282] This was the Cabinet where Goldsmith's one-page statement was presented. One unpublished diarist recorded: 'Jack . . . looked pretty tense. Ministers have been helped by Peter Goldsmith coming off the fence and saying military action would be legal.'[283] Short was unhappy at the way Goldsmith's legal opinion was handled: 'The Attorney started to read the statement. We murmured that there was no need to read it aloud [each Cabinet minister had a copy in front of them] and he stopped. I tried to start a discussion and asked why it was so late, had he had doubts? The Cabinet was impatient with me. They didn't want such a discussion. His advice was that war was legal under 1441 and that was it.'[284] Hewitt had considered resigning if she was not convinced of the war's legality. 'I thought if this is unlawful then I'm going,' she commented later. But, having spoken privately with Goldsmith, she felt confident on the legality, well in advance of this meeting.[285] So did Straw. 'I was never in any doubt once we got 1441 that military action was lawful,' he later claimed.[286] Hoon too. As a lawyer, he had scrutinised not only the one-page brief but also Goldsmith's thirteen-page document: 'Although it was quite complicated in terms of its legal arguments, in my mind it clearly gave us the legal authority to take military action.'[287] By this stage, 'they were all in solidarity mode', said one observer. The mood in Cabinet was 'we've got to stick together and stand behind the forces that we are committing to battle'.[288] Short alone held out, saying that she needed to reflect further: 'I'm going to have my little agonising overnight. I owe it to you,' she said.[289] She fell into line early the next day, writing a letter to every Labour MP explaining that, although she remained 'very critical of the way the Iraq crisis has been handled', she backed the government over the war.[290]

The Commons vote was now the only hurdle before Britain could go to war. Government business on the Monday and Tuesday virtually ground to a halt as Cabinet ministers were enlisted in last-minute lobbying of Labour MPs. 'It was "Right, it's all hands on deck",' said one aide. 'Gordon was clearly on side, as was the entire Cabinet.'[291] Conservative leader Iain Duncan Smith came to Number 10 and pledged his party's backing for the war: Blair said afterwards how very supportive he felt he had been.[292] Lady Thatcher's vocal support for war also encouraged Blair, while Dick Cheney and Karl Rove at the White House intervened with key Tories to urge support for the government.[293] 'I knew we would win it with the Tories,' said Armstrong, 'but our concern was to get the Labour opposition down as much as possible.'[294] And while the Tories were willing to back Blair on the substantive vote on the war, should it come to a vote of no-confidence, their support would fall away: 'In the event of a confidence motion, we weren't in the business of saving Blair,' said Duncan Smith.[295] 'I think I can win,' Blair told Bush around lunchtime on Monday 17 March, '[but] I'm concerned about the margin of victory. I don't want to depend on Tory votes.'[296] The stakes were very high: 'Everyone believed in the run-up to that vote that Tony had put his premiership on the line, and those who are very close to him would go down with him,' said Blunkett.[297] Those in Number 10 were 'examining what was in their drawers to see how easily it was portable', recalled Greenstock, 'because he was on a knife edge'.[298] Turnbull probed a little deeper into the procedure for a Prime Ministerial resignation. As Thatcher's top official aide, Turnbull had been closely involved in her resignation as Prime Minister in November 1990. This was the resignation template Turnbull now mulled over in his mind.[299]

Blair gave two speeches on Tuesday 18 March. The first, to Labour MPs in private, was the more impressive: 'He desperately wanted to win the vote inside the Labour Party,' said Milburn.[300] His second, in the Commons debate, was still one of the most accomplished parliamentary performances of his premiership, and one of his most meticulously prepared. He removed himself from the office to work in total concentration upstairs in the flat. 'A number of the team went up and worked on it while others of us worked on the politics over at the House,' recalled Godric Smith.[301] Blair told the Commons that the dangers of the Iraqi WMD threat were real and growing, and that he was ready to stake his career on Britain going to war on the basis of Saddam's repeatedly ignoring the UN. 'To retreat now, I believe,' he said, 'would put at hazard all that we hold dearest, turn the UN back into a talking shop, stifle the first steps of progress in the Middle East; leave the Iraqi people to the mercy of events on which we would have relinquished all power to influence for the better.' He spoke up for the importance of working with the US: 'There is fear of US unilateralism. I tell you what Europe should have said last September to the US. With one voice it should have said: we understand your strategic anxiety over terrorism and WMD and we will help you meet it.' It won him admirers if only a few extra votes from MPs, who had mostly made up their minds before he rose to speak. The backbench Labour rebellion, a larger than expected 139, still gave him a majority among Labour MPs: 'He was relieved. He knew that we'd got the rebellion to as low as we possibly could.'[302] Campbell immediately sold it to the media as a great victory, a line they mostly bought. 'Had we not got a reasonable majority among Labour MPs,' said Straw, 'we wouldn't have gone to war. It would have been like Neville Chamberlain in 1940, who won the vote, but lost office: it was that serious.'[303] 'If he had lost, he would have resigned,' confirmed John Burton, Blair's long-standing Sedgefield mentor.[304] Blair had psyched himself up to 'stare defeat in the face and go'. It had not happened.

Boyce, waiting by the telephone, had the green light: 'When the vote came through we told the Americans that we were in.'[305] Blair returned to Number 10 that Tuesday night, his mood relieved but sober.[306] At times of high strain, he wanted to be alone with his close circle and family, where he felt most at peace. Three thousand miles away along the borders of Iraq, British soldiers were stirring themselves for battle.

7

Iraq: From Agonising to Vindication

March–July 2003

After months of talk and negotiation, Blair had committed his country to war. His concern now was to ensure that good came out of the inevitable loss of life once the guns started firing. This meant ensuring a democratic country emerged from post-Saddam Iraq; persuading Bush that serious progress had to be made on peace between the Palestinians and Israel; and healing divisions among the allies, in particular France, Germany and Russia.

Blair at War: 19 March–4 April

'Let's go,' said the President. The time was 7:12 P.M. Eastern Standard Time (EST) on Wednesday 19 March. For two hours Bush and his closest advisers had been debating whether to launch a pre-emptive strike in an effort to kill Saddam Hussein and end the war before it had begun. Intelligence had reached the CIA that Saddam, together with his two sons and their families, would be spending the night at Dora Farm, a complex south-east of Baghdad on the bank of the Tigris river. The information was considered reliable: 'I can't give you 100 per cent assurance,' said CIA Director George Tenet, 'but this is as good as it gets.'[1] None of Bush's advisers opposed a pre-emptive strike, and after some fretting about the possibility of 'collateral' civilian casualties, Bush agreed. Stealth bombers went into action, followed by a barrage of thirty-six cruise missiles. At 9:30 A.M. EST, air-raid sirens sounded in Baghdad. Fifteen minutes later Ari Fleischer, Bush's spokesman, took the podium in the White House press room: 'The opening stages of the disarmament of the Iraqi regime have begun.'[2]

Tony Blair, the Cabinet and military had been expecting war to begin some twenty-four hours later, on Thursday evening, UK time. Bush did not call Blair to consult him, nor even to brief him on the change of plan. Instead Rice phoned David Manning shortly after the decision was taken on Wednesday. 'David, I know this is going to come as a surprise . . .' she began before explaining that Bush had just authorised the action against Saddam. 'Well, it seems to me that you have to take the shot,' Manning replied.[3] He then woke the Prime Minister around 12:15 A.M. London time to tell him that the attacks were about to begin.[4] The advance in timing caused problems in London. 'All the politics, the communication, and military thinking had been very carefully planned on a set timetable,' recalled one Downing Street aide. 'The early start added an extra layer of confusion. The atmosphere was tense and strained.'[5] After a short night, Blair met with the 'War Cabinet' at 8 A.M. on Thursday morning and then the full Cabinet at 10 A.M., where he imparted the news. Bush called at 4 P.M. London time, by which time it was becoming clear that Saddam had survived. 'Thank you for understanding that plans change,' Bush told him. 'My opinion is that if the military comes with an option and highly recommends it, then everybody adjusts to the plan. And that's what happened.' The Americans recalled Blair's mood as optimistic: 'I kind of think that the decisions taken in the next few weeks will determine the rest of the world for years to come,' he said.[6]

Blair's principal task that Thursday was to prepare a broadcast to the nation, announcing that, from that evening, British troops would be at war. Peter Stothard, allowed privileged access to the inner circles of Number 10 (for non-sensitive discussions) to write a diary subsequently published as *30 Days*, caught the atmosphere in the den while Blair pondered how to open his speech: '"My fellow Americans . . ." suggests Campbell. Tony Blair does not even begin to laugh. There follows a testy discussion of whether "tonight" will seem the right word when the address is broadcast in Korea. "It doesn't matter if the Koreans misunderstand the bloody time." "What about the end?" asks the Prime Minister, impatiently scratching the side of his face . . . "I want to end with 'God bless you'," he says. There is a noisy team revolt in which every player appears to be complaining at once. "That's not a good idea." "You are the most ungodly lot I have ever—" Tony Blair's words fade away into the make-up artist's flannel.'[7]

In the end he resolved to end safely on 'Thank you'. The godless den had prevailed. Unwittingly, they had saved him from repeating John Major's conclusion of his television broadcast to the nation on 17 January 1991, at the start of 'Operation Desert Storm', ousting Saddam from Kuwait: 'God bless,' he had signed off.[8] Instead, Blair's words echoed an earlier Prime Minister, Churchill: 'Tonight British servicemen and women are engaged from air, land and sea. Their mission: to remove Saddam Hussein from power, and disarm Iraq of its weapons of mass destruction. I know this course of action has produced deep divisions of opinion in our country. But I know also the British people will now be united in sending our armed forces our thoughts and prayers.'[9] That evening, British Royal Marines seized the al-Faw peninsula while the Special Boat Service captured two offshore oil tanker moorings.[10] Meanwhile some 4,000 Royal Marine commandos supported by heavy armour launched an 'aerial and amphibious assault' on 'Red Beach' in the south.[11] The British wanted the capture of nearby Basra, Iraq's only port, to act as a model for how the rest of the campaign should be conducted, with professionalism and humanity. The war had begun in earnest.

Number 10 is a political and diplomacy machine, not a war-fighting one. War beginning on 19 March was a watershed. Incumbents spoke of 'a sense of relief that it was no longer our responsibility. We've done our bit. Now it's over to others. Suddenly the lead passed from us in Number 10.'[12] But with the transition came a sense of powerlessness. Staff spoke of an 'eerie feeling', finding that Number 10 was no longer in the driving seat. 'To a large (and perhaps surprising) extent for a Prime Minister, Blair was powerless to do anything about it,' said an official.[13] Blair himself experienced mixed emotions. He worked hard to maintain routines: 'I don't think we missed a beat, really. We carried on having our regular Monday business and Thursday Cabinet meetings. He's a fantastic handler of stress,' said a senior official.[14] But Blair remained anxious about the widespread objections among the public and the Labour Party. Although he believed that once British troops were in action the public would swing round and support them, at the back of his mind he still worried about the risks of having moved ahead without the second resolution.[15] Supposing the war involved heavy casualties and protracted fighting? Or WMD attacks in or beyond Iraq? How would he convince the nation that the war had still been justified?

From day one, Blair knew the tremendous risk he had taken. Normally a sound sleeper, he found himself lying awake at night. The burden of leading the country into such a contentious war and the daily expectation of casualties left their mark: 'It was to him a completely different level of responsibility,' commented Morgan.[16] For relief, he worked out even harder in the Downing Street gym and spent time with Cherie and the children, and with his closest allies in the den. During these crisis weeks Blair worked hard to keep his life in perspective. Solace was always found in religion: 'it gave him inner strength' explained one confidant.[17] He prayed regularly, and spoke of being ready 'to meet my maker' and answer for 'those who have died or have been horribly maimed as a result of my decisions'.[18] Despite his brave face, and the image he projected of a battle-hardened leader now on his fifth war, news of casualties still troubled him. He had become more steely in taking decisions, but 'didn't divorce himself from the war. He demanded more and more information,' said one close aide. 'I really couldn't exaggerate the extent to which news of British casualties affected the PM personally. I don't think he was able to distance himself from it.'[19]

The early days of the campaign were blighted by incidents of 'friendly fire' and unexpected pockets of resistance, but it was the helicopter crashes that affected him most deeply. In the early hours of Friday 21 March, eight British marines and four Americans were killed when a US helicopter crashed in Kuwait. Blair was given the news as he met with European leaders in Brussels for a European Council. Schröder was the first to offer his condolences, followed by other leaders. Chirac wrote a personal note calling for an end to 'mutual aggression' on the diplomatic circuit and in press briefings. 'They agreed it was time to make up,' Campbell recorded.[20] On the way back to London, Blair turned to Campbell and said: 'God, it is awful, this war business.' 'Yes, that's why it is usually best to avoid it,' was Campbell's curt reply.[21]

The next day, 22 March, six British servicemen and one American died when two British Sea King helicopters collided in the Gulf – 'The biggest single blow,' one senior official said.[22] When told the news he became 'very, very thoughtful. It had a big impact on him. That was the most down I ever saw him.'[23] Just how grim the situation could yet become was now sinking in. Blair's reaction to bad news could rarely be detected readily by those present. This occasion was different. Boyce thought that he felt 'responsible', as he did for the 'other casualties that occurred afterwards'.[24] Blair's peculiarly intense involvement was seen in his writing personal letters to the next of kin of all British casualties. Blair had to do battle with the MoD, who argued that the next of kin would only want to hear from the commanding officer, 'They wouldn't want to hear from the Prime Minister.' But Blair insisted and won the argument.[25]

Once the fighting began, Blair soon wanted to resort to his 'default position' in crises, taking personal charge himself. He became increasingly drawn into monitoring the war closely, even if there was nothing for him to do. In unconscious imitation of Churchill, whose Cabinet War Rooms still lurked in the bowels of Whitehall under Downing Street, he asked for big maps to be placed on the wall of the den so he could follow the progress of the troops.[26] Like many Prime Ministers, he became impatient with the traditional apparatus the British state devised for managing wars, and found the War Cabinet (technically 'OPD', the Overseas Policy and Defence Committee), which met daily during the fighting, too formal and insufficiently focused.

Blair thus leaned on the smaller group that met in the den at 8:15 A.M., comprising himself, intelligence chiefs Scarlett and Dearlove, defence chief Boyce, the home team of Powell, Campbell, Morgan, Manning and Rycroft, as well as Straw and Hoon. Scarlett would open with an update on intelligence, and Blair would decide what he wanted them to discuss. The dominant voice depended on the issue: if diplomatic, it was Powell and Manning; if politics or Parliament, it was Morgan; if communications, it was Campbell. Once their meetings were over they took a circuitous route through Number 10 to join the OPD meetings in the Cabinet Room, to avoid their colleagues becoming suspicious of a stitch-up in their earlier gathering.[27] At OPD, at 8:45 A.M., where they were joined by Brown, Prescott, Beckett, Reid, Short and Turnbull, the inner team would usually be quiet and let the others speak. Turnbull recalled: 'There weren't a lot of decisions to be taken, and it was often a question of understanding what was happening, and trying to foresee trouble ahead.'[28] When Boyce was away, Mike Jackson would take his place. He found 'the sofa politics in the den very interesting. They would troop into the Cabinet room and it was a sort of *fait accompli*. It drove Short mad because she wasn't part of the smaller cabal.'[29] Some were equally unimpressed by Short's conduct in the War Cabinet: Brown thought that she was 'just blathering away', while Prescott told Blair on 26 March that her behaviour was 'intolerable and he should not put up with her for too long'.[30] Campbell records that Blair went 'out of his way to keep her involved and on board, as much as she ever would be'.[31]

If the high military decisions were being taken in the Pentagon or at CENTCOM in Tampa, in Britain the delegated military decisions were taken at the MoD or at the military command centre at Northwood, where Fry ran operations on a day-to-day basis. Blair 'wasn't pushing, petulant or impatient about the way that things were going. He understood that this was a complex business and was perfectly happy to invest his faith in those who were prosecuting the war on his behalf,' Fry said.[32] Turnbull could not recall 'any point at which the Prime Minister needed to intervene to get anything done differently'.[33] Military forecasts had indicated the war could last as long as eight to ten weeks.[34] So there was initially 'a genuine astonishment at the speed', said Godric Smith. 'But there was a real fear that when we got to Baghdad things would be far harder than they proved.'[35]

The 'sudden collapse' which Blair had told Cook would transpire, had not yet come to pass.[36] Around day four of the campaign, military chiefs recall Blair becoming anxious when the US advance halted briefly.[37] A greater concern was soon to emerge: British progress in achieving their key objective – taking control of Basra. By 25 March, as British forces started to shell targets in the city, the question in Number 10 was how long it would take for it to fall. Stothard recorded: 'Tony Blair is on his way back to the flat from his morning military report in the den. The news from Basra has been bad. "We do not have real access," said Boyce. "A humanitarian horror is looming," fear those who like to match what they hear in Cabinet against what they read in the newspapers. Resistance from Fedayeen militia, as predicted by Scarlett's intelligence men, is "patchy but fierce".'[38] On 26 March, Blair was told by Boyce that progress was 'slow . . . but so far without disaster'.[39] Fry and Boyce met Blair and Manning to discuss the situation. The chief concern was that, in a large city like Basra, the British did not know how many of its population would remain loyal to the regime. The great fear the military had was protracted fighting in built-up areas, because of its high cost in casualty and material terms. 'Blair asked sensible questions. There were no Hitlerian rages. It was all pretty calm and well modulated stuff,' Fry recalled.[40]

Blair's biggest concern lay with the timetable for taking the city. 'How long will it take?' the Prime Minister probed. 'A week or thereabouts,' said Fry. After a reflective pause Boyce offered, 'two weeks, at least'. As the two officers walked back from Number 10 to the MoD, Boyce turned to Fry and muttered wryly, 'Don't encourage him.'[41] Boyce knew only too well that fears of a protracted campaign with heavy casualties weighed heavily on Blair. At the height of this anxious time Blair made a fleeting visit to Camp David to see Bush on 27 March. 'There is no point trying to set a time limit, or to speculate on it. It is not set by time. It is set by the nature of the job,' Blair declared at their press conference in an effort to defuse the tension.[42] Despite this philosophical stance in public, in private Stothard records a clear concern on 1 April that the war was taking longer than expected: 'In the Campbell zone it is necessary continually to say that "We have always known it could go on this long" . . . In the diplomatic knights' zone [Manning, Wall, Rycroft] they have genuinely envisaged a war of many weeks, not days.' Stothard picked up also on the mounting concerns among Cabinet: 'The worrying is real. They had hoped it might be over now. They would not admit that. But that is what they hoped.'[43] As his ink was drying, however, fortunes turned. On 2 April the US military began its full assault on the Republican Guard outside Baghdad and, by 3 April, Saddam's forces were retreating. 'Things were also going a lot better in Basra and the mood was much improved all round,' Campbell noted in his diary.[44] On 4 April, US forces took Baghdad airport. Basra too was looking less worrying. Stothard recorded almost a holiday atmosphere: 'The War Cabinet has become like breakfast on the last days of an ocean cruise. Suspicions have broken down. Friendships have been made. Even the people who would not choose each other's company can be civil in the knowledge that they need not be together every morning for much longer.'[45] The fall of Basra and indeed Baghdad would now be only days away. Blair remained focused on the military progress, not wanting to take victory for granted any more than he did in General Elections. But his mind was already working overtime on his priorities for the post-war period.

Looking to Bush for Payback: April

Blair badly needed movement on the Middle East Peace Process (MEPP) and a US commitment to involving the UN in post-war Iraq. He believed deeply in both, but he also needed to show domestic and world opinion that he was extracting something tangible from Bush in return for British support. As in the pre-war period, conviction and expediency were inseparable in Blair's mind. He took Britain to war with a promise from Bush to publish the 'road map' for the MEPP as soon as a new Palestinian Prime Minister took office. Extracting this commitment had been no mean feat, and owed much to him personally. He was serious about wanting to see progress.

At the party conference in October 2002, his speech had ramped up the pressure on the US administration: 'Some say the issue is Iraq. Some say it is the Middle East peace process. It's both.' Serious talks, he demanded, must begin before the end of 2002 towards achieving 'an Israeli state free from terror, recognised by the Arab world, and a viable Palestinian state based on the boundaries of 1967'.[46] The tight deadline for progress had been inserted at the last minute by Blair and Jonathan Powell, without apparently consulting Straw or Sherard Cowper-Coles, the British Ambassador in Tel Aviv.[47] Sceptics like Short were appalled by his haste, finding it 'completely shocking' that Blair should make such a commitment when there was 'no substance in the promise'.[48] More significantly, Bush was not pleased, and let it be known he did not believe in tight deadlines: Blair and Powell did, and had used this strategy in Northern Ireland. 'It's not like the President and Prime Minister to come at the Middle East from different poles,' recalled Karl Rove, 'but the President thought this process was not susceptible to a time frame.'[49] Blair and Powell were disconcerted to hear through unofficial channels that Bush was not keen to discuss anything as sensitive as the MEPP until after his mid-term elections were over that November.

Bush prevailed. The December deadline came and went. To give the peace process another kick, Blair organised an Israeli–Palestinian conference in London on 14 January 2003. Sharon refused point-blank to accept a Palestinian presence, having imposed a travel ban on all Palestinian leaders after a suicide bomb attack in Tel Aviv on 5 January had killed twenty-five Israelis. To break the impasse, Number 10 dispatched Cowper-Coles to see Sharon with a personal letter from Blair asking him to assent to Palestinian participation. Sharon refused to see him, and then kept Cowper-Coles waiting on tenterhooks for several days, before finally turning down the request flat. In the end a face-saving formula was decided whereby the Palestinians took part in the London conference by telephone: but the impetus of the event had been lost.[50] Blair subsequently dispatched Lord Levy, his Middle East envoy, to press Arafat to appoint a new Palestinian Prime Minister, in view of Bush's stipulation. Levy surprised sceptics by returning with a written agreement from Arafat. Blair now pushed Bush to agree to publish the so-called 'road map', a series of internationally backed steps that would eventually make the 'two-state solution' a reality. But still Bush stalled. The mid-term elections were over: what was stopping him now? At their meeting at the White House on 31 January, Bush remained hesitant over the road map. But he left with the firm belief that the President had promised him 'that once Iraq was over, the road map would be published'.[51]

As British support for war deteriorated, it became clear that Blair was going to need something rather earlier from Bush. Short was particularly voluble, telling Blair on 13 March that she would stay in the government only on certain conditions, which included the publication of the road map.[52] Blair knew that a public commitment from Bush along these lines would help him significantly with the party. The road map was also something he believed in deeply. All available channels of the special relationship were now working at full capacity: Manning spoke to Rice, and Straw to Colin Powell, saying that Blair's future could hinge on this issue.[53] Bush was finally forced to accept the logic. Here at least, Blair's influence had been decisive, as Colin Powell admitted: 'Try as I might, I couldn't get the President to say the words "road map". It was finally Blair who said to Bush, "You have got to do this. You have got to say this." And Bush agreed.'[54] On the afternoon of 14 March the President duly stepped out on to the lawn of the White House and, flanked by Powell and Rumsfeld, announced his readiness to publish the road map as soon as a new Palestinian Prime Minister with 'governing authority' took office, his favoured choice being Abu Mazen. After the announcement there was discussion in Downing Street as to whether his statement amounted to anything new. They concluded it did because, as Blair and Powell found repeatedly in Northern Ireland, it was the sense of momentum that counted.[55]

Bush's position on Blair's second campaign at this time, a role for the UN in post-war reconstruction, was to prove still more fraught; with the unilateralists in the administration wanting nothing to do with it. At the polar opposite were internationalists in the UK and elsewhere, championed by Short. They wanted a new UN resolution to be passed immediately after the war, turning over total authority and control in Iraq to Kofi Annan and the UN, who would then supervise reconstruction. To some, who believed the invasion had been dictated by US economic interests, including oil, the case for such a transfer was obvious. Short predicted major civil disruption and displaced refugees, and argued for the UN to be involved as a way of legitimising the invasion.[56] Blair's own position fell somewhere in between both poles. 'He spent quite a lot of time arguing with both extremes, pulling them towards the centre,' recalled an official. With the internationalists he argued that reality would dictate that certain functions in post-war Iraq would inevitably end up not being managed by the UN. With the American unilateralists he argued that the best way to broaden out the post-military coalition was for the UN to be involved as early and fully as possible.[57]

The issue blazed to the fore only days after the fighting began. The post-war situation suddenly moved centre-stage. What would happen once the fighting was over? Blair's Number 10 team discussed the UN issue on 25 March: 'We want more Kofi,' said Sally Morgan. 'We seriously have to have Kofi now.'[58] Morgan was a dove on post-war, as she had been on the war. Stothard captured a debate as Blair prepared to meet the press: '"Look," says Campbell, beginning to lose his patience again. "The main issue on their minds is the role that the UN is going to play when the war is over." "The UN is determined to have at least an umbrella role," says Manning. "And the Americans are dead against that," he continues, like a tutor answering his own question in a class. Tony Blair gets up . . . "That is only a matter of timing," he says, with a confidence that is not widely shared.'[59] When questioned repeatedly in the House the following day before heading to Washington, Blair was sufficiently confident to declare that he did 'not believe that there is a need to persuade the President about UN involvement. We made it clear in the statement that we issued that any post-conflict Iraqi administration must be specifically accepted and endorsed by the UN.'[60]

As Blair flew across the Atlantic later that day, the full extent of the gulf began to dawn on him. Campbell learned that Bush had been irritated by a story in the *Financial Times*, suggesting that Blair was preparing to push Bush on a more substantial role for the UN.[61] Stothard recorded the scene on the plane: 'Tony Blair is impatient. He and the President agreed in the Azores [the summit in mid-March] on a post-war place for the UN. Surely they can build on that, not bury it? Suddenly the problem seemed much more than the mere "matter of timing" that he described to his team yesterday in the den.'[62] Blair used the remainder of his plane journey to work on a twelve-page note for Bush, explaining that the manner in which the US put over their views and intentions was fuelling fears of US unilateralism. Bush needed to reach out to Germany, Russia and France and 'seize the moment for a new global agenda, one to unite the world rather than divide it'.[63]

When Bush and Blair met at Camp David on 27 March, they went through Blair's note 'virtually line by line'.[64] There was some good news: Bush was 'fairly strong on the MEPP', noted Campbell.[65] At the press conference that closed the summit he declared, 'Soon we will release the road map . . . both America and Great Britain are strongly committed to implementing [it].'[66] So far, so good. But there was little movement on the UN. Blair met a blank wall. Whatever may have been said in the Azores, the administration now had little time for the UN. 'The argument was that it was too lame, and that if the UN were involved that would restrict US activities,' recalled Elizabeth Jones. 'There was just a juggernaut of antipathy to the UN.'[67] Pentagon adviser Ken Adelman recalls a sense that 'these guys [the UN] weren't with us before, and why should they get the contracts and part of the glory now? We're not going to do a goddamn thing to help French businesses, or German businesses. Screw 'em.'[68] Colin Powell accepted that the UN were 'absolutely indispensable', and felt that 'you've got to have them there', but it was a view he expounded with little enthusiasm.[69]

Blair's task was immense. He had to wrestle very hard 'to pull the US towards a policy of involving the UN far, far more than they would otherwise have done', recalled one close aide.[70] 'He had frank and tough conversations with Bush, who largely seemed receptive,' recalled Morgan.[71] But, as ever, Blair's influence only went so far. 'The problem was not so much with Bush himself,' felt one Blair confidant, 'rather it was the combination of Cheney, with all his contacts, and Rumsfeld, which was pretty cataclysmic.'[72] At the press conference Blair tried to paper over the cracks. Nothing had changed since the Azores, he said: 'We will seek new UN Security Council resolutions to affirm Iraq's territorial integrity, to ensure a rapid delivery of humanitarian relief, and endorse an appropriate post-conflict administration for Iraq.'[73] But the magic words of commitment from Bush were missing. 'Blair just wasn't getting anything,' recalled Wilkerson, 'but he was having to come out to the podium and act as if he had.'[74] The already suspicious press scented difficulties. 'If [Mr Blair] went to resolve the differences of opinion between him and Mr Bush about aspects of the post-conflict settlement ... he failed,' said the *Independent*.[75] According to the *Financial Times*, Blair failed to secure a clear role for Britain in post-war reconstruction, and to persuade Bush to pledge that the UN would have supreme authority over the post-war arrangements: 'The limits of Mr Blair's influence over the US are apparent.'[76]

A frustrated Blair headed to New York later that day to meet Kofi Annan. The symbolism of his visit was important, showing those still bruised by the lack of a second resolution his commitment to the UN. But substance mattered too. Annan's deputy had already signalled to the Americans that the UN did not want any role in Iraq beyond immediate humanitarian relief.[77] That did not bode well for Blair. He faced an uphill struggle when he saw Annan in his room at UN HQ on Manhattan's east side. The UN had to have a major role, he said, and he was 'disappointed that the UN were not pushing to have that role'.[78] But several prominent Security Council members, including France and Germany, wanted no such involvement for the UN. It was payback time for Chirac and Schröder. 'This was not our war,' they were saying, 'and it is not going to be our post-war either.'

The US trip had not gone well. The US did not want the UN in, and neither did the UN itself. He was caught in the middle. With Annan under such heavy pressure, he realised his best chance still was to win Bush. Another opportunity presented itself just ten days later when Bush visited Hillsborough Castle in Northern Ireland. Arriving in his extravagant convoy on the afternoon of Monday 7 April, the President caused amusement in the British camp by his shaky grasp of geography: 'I go to sleep, wake up, and here I am in Merry Old Ireland,' he declared on arrival.[79] They hoped his command of politics proved more secure. 'TB felt today's meeting with Bush was going to be tough,' noted Campbell.[80] Blair battered away at Bush, on a private evening walk in Hillsborough's gardens, for a strong US commitment to the UN's role in post-war Iraq. Bush could not simply say that the UN was 'important': he must describe it as of 'vital' importance. The battering was successful, but his persistence was causing the administration to divide: 'A big fight ensued over whether the President should use the word "vital",' said a senior administration official present.[81] The British hope was that Condi Rice, the 'casting vote', would support the Blair line. All eyes now turned to her. Number 10 had long seen her as their best ally in the Bush court. Would she support Blair now? Mindful of what her colleagues back in Washington thought, she played safe. Bush lost his patience, and in front of the advisers, said, 'Look, I'm going to say it.'[82] During the press conference Bush mentioned the word 'vital', as if to goad his team, no less than eight times. Rice started to protest to Bush, as overheard by Stothard: 'The President leads her away from the crowd towards the garden, where he can be ear-whacked more discreetly. He looks at first concerned, then a bit frosty . . . After the commemorative snapshots, Rice continues her commentary on the excess vitality of the press conference. "Ease it, Condi, ease it," says the President. The dispute ceases.'[83]

Blair had gained as much from Bush on the UN at Hillsborough as he could have hoped – assuming he was prepared to deliver. Bush went further on the MEPP also. By being in Northern Ireland, Number 10 aides hoped Bush would absorb the 'subliminal message' that a peace process could work.[84] It seemed to do the trick. In their six and a half years together, Bush was rarely more accommodating to Blair than he was at Hillsborough. He was unaccompanied by Cheney, Rumsfeld or other top hawks. It was 'no coincidence that Bush said what he did because Cheney wasn't there', said Lawrence Wilkerson.[85] 'There was a bit of a view that whoever was the last one in the room with the President was the one whose view he would articulate,' was the enlightening comment from the State Department's Jones. 'I cannot underscore enough the importance we all ascribed to Blair's ability to bring Bush around on issues that we knew that Cheney *et al.* were pushing him on. Blair was the kingpin in persuading Bush to do the right thing.'[86] Over dinner at Hillsborough, Bush told Blair and his aides 'in a way we had not heard from him before', that he was 'deadly serious about the MEPP'.[87] And not only in private. At the concluding press conference on 8 April, the President declared: 'Being here in Northern Ireland makes me even more firm in my belief that peace is possible. I've talked at length with the Prime Minister about how hard he had to work to bring the process this far. I'm willing to spend the same amount of energy in the Middle East.'[88] Bush was now way ahead of his hawks. The reaction in Washington was electric, and divided. Doves like Jones in the State Department sat bolt upright: 'I don't think he knows how much time Blair has spent on Northern Ireland. There's no way he's going to spend as much time on the Middle East.' Some wondered, 'Does he know what he's saying?'[89] Many were sceptical: 'If Bush was saying anything, giving anything, showing any ankle to Tony, it was simply to get Tony out of his hair,' said Wilkerson. 'I don't think he ever intended to follow up on it.'[90] But the hawks were rattled, and not only in Washington. Israeli officials attempted to play down Bush's promise on the MEPP, saying he only expressed such views under pressure from Blair.[91] Blair himself was delighted. He was 'full of himself on the flight home', noted Campbell, 'really felt it had been good and positive, pretty much on all fronts'.[92] Blair began to believe that he at last had the President close to where he wanted him.

The enduring question was how bankable Bush's words would prove once the war was over. They would not have long to wait to find out. Within days of the Hillsborough meeting, British troops had captured most of Basra. On 9 April, American forces stormed into Baghdad, where they helped Iraqis topple the ubiquitous statues of Saddam Hussein. Some in Downing Street recall the famous TV images of the statue in Baghdad's Fargus Square being pulled down. 'It's just one statue,' said Blair. 'I don't know what all the fuss is about.'[93] For a very brief period, however, there was a hint of euphoria in Downing Street and in the FCO. 'There was a feeling that we had done it,' recalled one diplomat. 'The worst had not happened and there was no humanitarian disaster.'[94] WMD had not been used in Iraq or beyond. Very quickly a second thought struck: 'Oh fuck. The war's over already and we've only just started thinking about what we should do afterwards.'[95] But there was no immediate panic. After all, Blair and the British government had been told that Washington was handling 'post-war'. They were about to learn whether their faith had been well placed.

Post-War: Critical Weeks in Iraq: April–May 2003

On 9 April, in the immediate aftermath of victory, Blair and Bush talked over the challenges of post-war Iraq. 'We've got to win the story in the peacetime era,' Bush told Blair. 'We've won the war. We cannot have people define the peacetime era for us.'[96] Blair agreed wholeheartedly. It went to the crux of the whole case for the war. 'There is upon us a heavy responsibility to make the peace worth the war,' Blair told the House of Commons five days later.[97] These were fine words, but already they seemed dangerously disconnected from the emerging reality in the cities and provinces of Iraq.

Within days of the fall of Baghdad, the capital was gripped by a looting frenzy. Shops, offices, hospitals and even Iraq's National Museum were stripped of valuables. 'No one, it seems to me,' said Britain's man at the UN, Jeremy Greenstock, 'was instructed to put the security of Iraq first, to put law and order on the streets.'[98] Rumsfeld, America's supremo of post-war Iraq, seemed unruffled. 'Stuff happens!' he famously declared on 11 April. 'Freedom's untidy, and free people are free to make mistakes and commit crimes and do bad things. They're also free to live their lives and do wonderful things, and that's what's going to happen here.'[99] While Short called for American troops to do more to protect hospitals against the rampaging mobs, Number 10 announced that some looting was to be expected. Straw concurred: 'Wherever totalitarian regimes have collapsed,' said the Foreign Secretary, 'there is always a period of some disorder.'[100]

In private, recalled one aide, Blair had been 'dismayed' by the looting and 'found Rumsfeld's apparently relaxed attitude deeply disquieting'.[101] On 14 April, a week after British troops arrived in Basra, Blair addressed the Commons to present his vision for post-war Iraq: 'Just as we had a strategy for war, so we have a strategy for peace. Iraq will be better, better for the region, better for the world, better, above all, for the Iraqi people.'[102] Blair explained to MPs that the process of Iraqi reconstruction would begin shortly, and that it would have three distinct phases: ensuring immediate security and humanitarian needs were met, establishing an 'interim authority' involving Iraqi leaders to take up some of the reins of governing, and finally, a fully representative and elected Iraqi government, once a new constitution had been approved, which he said would occur after about a year. 'In each phase, the UN will, as President Bush and I have said, have a vital role.'[103]

Blair used the word 'vital' deliberately, reflecting concerns in Number 10 that 'although Bush used the phrase "vital" several times at the Hillsborough press conference, it didn't really sink into the US system as a whole'.[104] He found himself over the weeks ahead having to press the US hard to back a new UN resolution, and all the more urgently as his concerns grew over the deteriorating situation in Iraq. The Pentagon jealously guarded its control of post-war Iraq. In January Rumsfeld had selected a retired three-star army general, Jay Garner, to run the Office for Reconstruction and Humanitarian Aid (ORHA). The British had concerns from the outset: 'The very fact that Jay Garner was taken from nowhere – with none of the depths of resources of the State Department, the Foreign Office, DfID or any of the international organisations – alerted us very early on to the paucity of American post-war planning,' said one British military figure.[105] Garner, selected because he had successfully led the operation to protect the Kurds after the first Gulf War, in fact realised the scale of the challenge he faced. He told Rumsfeld how several years had been spent planning for the post-war situations in Germany and the Far East before war ended in 1945. He was being asked to provide a solution within five to ten weeks. 'I know,' Rumsfeld said. 'We'll get somewhere. We'll get somewhere on this. Just maximise the time available.' Garner found himself waking up at 2 A.M. writing 'to do' lists.[106]

Jack Straw met Garner at his temporary base in Kuwait on 16 April. Although Baghdad had fallen a full week before, Garner had not yet been permitted by the military to enter Iraq, which it insisted remained unsafe. The meeting was a major wake-up call for the Foreign Secretary. Straw was 'completely taken aback by how little had been done, even after the victory, and how hamstrung the allegedly key American player in theatre was'.[107] For the first time Straw appreciated the extent to which the post-war planning worked on by the FCO and State Department had been allowed to 'turn to dust'. He was shocked to find there were some twenty American staff under Garner working in a small room in Kuwait trying to run a country of 20 million. He thought to himself: 'Wow, is this it? They didn't really seem to know what they were going to do.'[108] Britain's senior military figure, Michael Boyce, was utterly contemptuous: 'We realised the Americans were in disarray. General Garner was not up to it. He thought that he could go into Baghdad with a suitcase of money. He had a pretty fuzzy idea of how to apply it, thinking we'll buy ourselves friends and influence.'[109] 'The dramatic ousting of Saddam, it was assumed, would create a "*Wizard of Oz* moment" ... After the wicked dictator was deposed, throngs of cheering Iraqis would hail their liberators and go back to work under the tutelage of Garner's post-war organisation,' was how one American general characterised the American approach.[110]

Garner did not encounter lines of flag-waving and grateful Iraqis, nor a series of government officers ready to start work for the new bosses, but a demoralised and confused population, with administration in chaos – government offices ransacked, communications destroyed and the police absent. Straw was not alone among the British in being shocked. 'The extent of the collapse of the Iraq system was not expected,' said Sawers. 'The tasking of the military after the war was not given any sustained thought by the Americans.'[111] At the Pentagon, they remained optimistic. Donald Rumsfeld considered post-war plans to be just the starting point for what would unfold on the ground: 'war is unpredictable. Post-war stabilisation is unpredictable,' he said later. 'The enemy has a brain. They think. They see what you're doing and they adapt and adjust. Any war plan, any post-war plan has always been something that has had to be adjusted, refined, and modified as you go along.'[112] But in the White House, Rumsfeld's nonchalance was causing unease. 'Within two weeks of taking Baghdad, real worries were heard in the NSC about the situation on the ground,' said an official.[113] A new thought began to take hold in Washington: 'At that point you really had to run the country,' said National Security Advisor Rice. 'Frankly, I think we were more resistant to the idea than Britain. We didn't even want to use the word "occupation", but I think the British lawyers told us we had to.'[114] Rumsfeld's promise of 'wonderful things' was not happening.

Efforts were soon under way to replace the hapless Garner. Rumsfeld began trying to identify a 'presidential envoy', a more senior rank than had been given to Garner, to take over. Later in April, he selected Paul Bremer, sixty-one years old, with twenty-three years' experience in the US foreign service and an expert in counter-terrorism. These considerations were an unwelcome distraction to many hawks in Washington. This was a time to celebrate victory over Iraq. On 1 May, Bush was flown on to the deck of the aircraft carrier USS *Abraham Lincoln*, for a ceremony that imitated the formal surrender of Japan to General MacArthur on the deck of the battleship USS *Missouri* at the end of the Second World War. Standing in front of the 5,000 crew, under a huge banner reading 'Mission Accomplished', Bush announced: 'The war on terror is not over . . . We do not know the day of final victory, but we have seen the turning of the tide . . . We have removed an ally of al-Qaeda. That regime is no more . . . You are going home.'[115] As the British in Whitehall watched Bush make his announcement, they experienced a profound disquiet. In Britain, any euphoria evident at the quick conclusion of the war had speedily evaporated. 'We expected we would win, but we didn't know that it would be with the brevity and elegance with which it happened,' said Rob Fry. 'So there was a certain amount of perplexity on everybody's part: "Why doesn't it feel better than it does?"'[116] In Number 10, a new concern began to be heard. They were caught off-guard by how quickly domestic approval of the war evaporated. Support for the war had risen from 56 per cent to 63 per cent in the week fighting ended, but sank in May. Questions were increasingly being asked about what was happening on the ground. The answers were thin.

Blair's antennae told him all was not well. He decided he wanted someone of more senior rank than the existing British Ambassador, who could relay high-grade intelligence direct back to him and weigh in with the Americans on the ground. So important did he regard the mission that he wanted someone personally known to him for it. His solution was to enlist John Sawers, Manning's predecessor, then serving as Ambassador to Egypt: on 1 May, the call came summoning him back home from Cairo. 'We need someone who can work really closely alongside the Americans, and be a channel of communication back to us so that we can work with people in the White House,' the Prime Minister told him. Sawers found Blair still fairly optimistic, but concerned that the transition to the peace-building had made a poor start. He was beginning to appreciate that it was going to be a more demanding task than anyone had envisaged, but Sawers saw no sign that Blair thought Iraq was not going to work out, or that there was anything fundamentally wrong.[117]

On 7 May Sawers arrived in Baghdad. He quickly discovered that London's concerns were an underestimate. Just four days after getting his feet behind the desk, he fired a stark telegram back to London. 'Garner's outfit, ORHA, is an unbelievable mess. No leadership, no strategy, no co-ordination, no structure, and inaccessible to ordinary Iraqis . . . Garner and his top team of sixty-year-old retired generals are well-meaning but out of their depth.'[118] He advocated a 'Baghdad first' strategy, concentrating resources where the problems were worst: 'The one place we can't afford to get wrong.' But it was the Americans, not the British, who commanded Baghdad, so the prime burden fell on them: 'The clock is ticking.'[119] Further reports followed in similar vein. They were a wake-up call for Blair: 'He would devour the political reporting that John sent back,' recalled an official. Very soon, Blair was demanding updates from every Whitehall department with any responsibility in Iraq.[120] Blair was not the only person who poured over Sawers's reports. US reporting from Iraq was patchy at best and what did emerge often disappeared into a black hole in the Pentagon. 'Colin Powell really appreciates your reports,' Sawers was once told by a State Department official. 'They're the only ones he gets on Iraq.' He had not realised that they were being copied to the Americans through the Embassy in Washington.[121] His reports were read avidly by Rice at the White House: 'They were observations from the front on things that we didn't know anything about,' recalled one NSC staffer.[122] The White House realised that whereas Garner had lacked the infrastructure to do political reporting, Bremer did not, but he simply refused.

Sawers's dispatches sometimes reported alarming American heavy-handedness. In one telegram he wrote: 'Our Paras at the Embassy witnessed a US tank respond to (harmless) Kalashnikov fire into the air from a block of residential flats by firing three tank rounds into the building . . . Frankly, the 3rd Inf. Div. need to go home now, and be garlanded as victors, but sadly that isn't due for several weeks. Can it be brought forward?'[123] From very early on, a sharp clash was evident between the British and American military approaches. 'We believed in peacekeeping,' Boyce had explained to Blair shortly after Baghdad fell. 'They believed in war-fighting. We were good at both. They were really only focused on one, so didn't adapt quickly enough to changed circumstances.'[124] The British approach was characterised as 'all floppy hats and hearts-and-minds stuff. "We've got this right," they were saying, "and we'll be out within months. If only the Americans could change their approach, then they'd be out too!"'[125] In the years ahead, even the British would come to realise that it wasn't quite as simple as that. But in the early months the British military believed that they had much to offer the Americans, particularly in kick-starting the development of the Iraqi police force. From this emerged the idea that the British presence should be extended to the Iraqi capital: 'We Brits do not have all the answers,' Sawers wrote, 'but an operational UK presence in Baghdad is worth considering.'[126]

This idea would have been a major new British commitment, with implications for British casualties and continued troop deployment down the line, but it had support among military leaders on the ground. One put his views directly to Manning during a conversation about British casualties: 'British soldiers did not die to make Basra a better place,' said the senior officer. 'They died to transform Iraq, so we mustn't limit where British forces are by an artificial boundary. You can be incredibly successful in Basra and it'll make no difference at all to the structure of Iraq.'[127] Manning agreed. A plan to move troops north to Baghdad now gathered support, not least among senior army generals. It was also backed by Sawers and the FCO and MI6, because they felt it would improve UK intelligence access into Iraq. When Blair heard of the plan, he gave his full backing. But nothing happened. It ran into the implacable opposition of Michael Walker, who succeeded Boyce as Chief of the Defence Staff in May 2003. He had been heavily influenced by his time as a divisional commander in the Balkans, where conditions had been relatively benign compared to Iraq: yet some serving on the ground in Basra felt that he underestimated what could have been achieved.[128] Walker's response was that the redeployment north ran against the military's grand strategic plan, which was to reduce forces as quickly as possible: having British forces deployed all around Iraq was not a route to a quick withdrawal. Instead, it was resolved that the British would try harder to make Basra 'an exemplar' and use this success to influence the Americans and their *modus operandi*. How successful this strategy would prove remained to be seen.

On 11 May, Bremer arrived in Baghdad. 'Not a day too soon,' Sawers reported. He was 'much better organised' than Garner and 'ran meetings better and with more intellectual rigour', and he brought in better people.[129] But where Garner was minimalist in ambition, Bremer was maximalist. Concerns soon were heard about what became one of the cardinal errors of post-war Iraq, and one that Blair later admitted in public.[130] On 16 May, Bremer issued an order – 'De-Ba'athification of Iraqi Society' – which barred the top four levels of former Ba'ath party members from public employment. Under Saddam, virtually everyone who worked for the government had been forced to join the Ba'ath party. The allies were broadly in agreement that the most senior Ba'athists should be denied any role in post-war Iraq. But they disagreed over how many levels down de-Ba'athification should go. Garner was fundamentally opposed to the depth Bremer proposed: 'You won't be able to run anything if you go this deep.'[131] One of Sawers's earliest meetings with Bremer concerned this very question: Sawers argued it should only be the first three levels, but not down to the extensive fourth level, which consisted of 20–30,000 middle-ranking administrators. He was the only one to express caution at the meeting, and failed to convince Bremer. 'I didn't press on with it after I reported back to London that Bremer wouldn't do it,' he said, adding 'my instructions from London were simply to question the wisdom of taking de-Ba'athification too far, not to block the decision.' The Americans had been listening to the advice of Ahmed Chalabi, the Iraqi exile close to the neocons, and had made up their minds based primarily on that advice.[132] The British, rightly or wrongly, did not believe they knew enough about the Ba'ath party to contest it.

Bremer had arrived in Iraq with a clear strategy of pulling everything down and building the state up again from the roots. His model was

Germany in 1945, where the edifice of the Nazi party structures had been dismantled and built again piece by piece. Number 10 and the FCO saw it differently, with Manning in particular very clear that the allies should preserve what they could of the old and to give as much responsibility to Iraqis as possible, and as soon as possible. Manning's analogy was not Nazi Germany in 1945, but Communist Russia after the end of the Cold War: he would say, 'Imagine if you forbade any member of the Communist Party to have had any role in the new Russia.'[133] Fry was one of many soldiers who saw Bremer's wholesale de-Ba'athification as aggressively neocon. 'It wasn't about doing what was right for Iraq. It was about doing whatever the neocon handbook said you did in these circumstances.'[134] Bremer retorted that 'the White House, DoD, and State all signed off on this'.[135] This assertion is disputed by others in the administration, who claim Bremer personally was driving the policy and paying little heed to views in Washington.[136] 'It was Bremer's way or the highway,' said Wilkerson.[137]

A week after his de-Ba'athification order on 23 May, Bremer issued another order, disbanding the Iraqi army. Again, it seemed Bremer was fired up by his idea of rebuilding Iraq from scratch. He even removed the army's pension rights, which later had to be restored. Hindsight suggests this was another grave error. Why did London not try to stop it? The British 'didn't fight his decision, because the Iraqi army didn't really exist any more. It had completely disintegrated and dispersed,' said Sawers, although he added, 'We could have taken the decision to recall certain units.'[138] Boyce, by now retired, was contemptuous. British post-war military thinking, for which he had been responsible, had visualised the preservation of the Iraqi army with strict instructions for it not to be destroyed. 'We knew we'd need it afterwards. It was idiotic to get rid of it.'[139] What was Blair's thinking on all this? He had no choice but to accept Bush's decision that the Pentagon would be running the post war show, with what appeared to be 'only a very loose hand from the White House'.[140] He had the clear presumption that Rumsfeld and the Pentagon knew what they were doing. Officials testify that Blair had no direct input on de-Ba'athification or the disbandment of the army, content that Manning and Sawers should represent him.[141] One official said, 'His mind was elsewhere. He was not up with the pace of what was happening at this point,'[142] while another recalled, 'I don't think that the Prime Minister felt he had to take any more of a personal interest in stabilising Iraq. He was leaving it all to the Americans.'[143] 'Look, you know, I can't do everything,' he said to Mandelson around this time. 'That's chiefly America's responsibility, not ours.'[144]

Where Blair did believe he could contribute best to post-war Iraq was maintaining momentum for a new UN resolution. Now the war was over, he wanted to bring the international community together behind the lifting of UN sanctions on Iraq, to help funds flow back into the country, and the economy to recover. Chirac and Schröder remained cool, but 'the main sourness was with Putin'.[145] So Blair travelled to Moscow on 29 April to seek to mend fences. Putin was being 'very difficult', recalled one Number 10 aide.[146] At their press conference, the Russian President declared that Russia and its partners 'believe until clarity is achieved over whether weapons of mass destruction exist in Iraq, sanctions should be kept in place'. He then asked pointedly: 'Where is Saddam? Where are those arsenals of weapons of mass destruction, if indeed they ever existed?' Rubbing salt into the wound, he goaded Blair, 'Perhaps Saddam is still hiding somewhere in a bunker underground, sitting on cases of weapons of mass destruction.'[147] At the dinner that followed Blair and Putin clashed repeatedly over Britain's support for the US in the post-9/11 world. Blair was left fighting off Putin's claims that the US was bent on world domination. 'TB was pretty taken aback by the vehemence,' noted Campbell. 'I said [to Manning] that was the death of diplomacy.'[148]

Blair, as ever, refused to be discouraged. Continued pressure on the US resulted on 9 May in a draft resolution being introduced into the Security Council. This ambitious resolution proposed that the coalition authority running Iraq be recognised, sanctions be lifted, the UN have a key role in reconstruction, and a special representative be appointed to co-ordinate the UN's role in Iraq. While Blair was pleased to have pulled such a resolution out of the bag, it did not go far enough for Short. She complained that Blair and Straw had begun to behave secretly over the draft resolution, and that when she eventually saw it, she was appalled it gave only 'a minor role to the UN'.[149] She resigned on 12 May. One senior official recalled how 'she had already started behaving rather oddly in going AWOL on things. She'd almost gone on strike.'[150] By the time she left, her dithering had damaged her standing in the party, and she lost significant credibility. Blair himself was unperturbed. He had long been irritated with her. At a War Cabinet meeting in April, during one of her lengthy contributions, Campbell had slipped Blair a note reminding him of the time Saddam had shot his health minister during a meeting because he had annoyed him. Did Blair want Campbell to 'get a gun?' he asked. 'Yes,' Blair scribbled.[151]

On 22 May, UNSCR 1483 was passed unanimously: fourteen votes to nil. For Blair it was a moment of rejoicing. It locked the UN into a central – if still indeterminate – role in post-war Iraq. The geopolitics were even more important to him. 'He wanted to find a way of bringing the Security Council back together again,' recalled one aide. 'Fourteen–nil gave a very strong signal, after the bickering of the previous weeks, that the Security Council had come together again.'[152] Success at the UN invigorated Blair. He hoped it would be the turning point in the Iraq story. Of course, with hindsight, he was mistaken. But at the time those close to him sensed a more upbeat mood: 'He hadn't got the unanimity on military action he wanted, but at least, he thought, we can now bring everybody together,' recalled one aide. 'At the time we thought it would be the beginning of a new chapter.'[153] Blair's pleasure was mirrored by Bremer's distaste. 'I wanted our coalition, not the United Nations – with its murky political agendas – to take the lead in pushing this process forward,' noted Bremer.[154] The hawks were not going to take the defeat lying down.

Vindication at Last: May–July 2003

The increasingly negative press and sceptical public opinion in May did not dent Blair's fundamental belief that the Iraqis wanted freedom and would adapt to democracy because it was essentially what all people wanted. The problems emerging in Iraq would, he believed, be overcome.[155] His natural optimism was nevertheless tested by what he was hearing on the ground. The picture from Sawers's telegrams was now confirmed by Manning and Scarlett when they visited Bremer in Baghdad. Their report spoke of communication problems between the allies and the Iraqis and the difficulties for American forces in switching from 'war-fighting' to 'peace-building'.[156] Another growing concern was highlighted by Putin's taunt: where were Saddam's WMD? Finding them had become a top priority for Blair. As soon as Baghdad fell, an elite team from Britain's Special Forces worked with the Americans to search high and low for the elusive weapons. Pressure was applied to all parts of British intelligence as well as military and civil apparatus to provide him with information. Blair required a written update every week, with verbal updates on almost a daily basis. The news from the ground was not encouraging. After six weeks, the British search team began to conclude that the most they could find was evidence of a dormant programme. Nothing active and no stockpiles. Manning, Scarlett and Dearlove were briefed at an MI6 station in Baghdad in early June. 'I remember watching poor old John Scarlett's face just drop,' recalled one of the weapons team. 'I said, "Look, I'm really sorry but there's nothing we can present to the press to meet the claims made."'[157] This, however, was only an interim report: they were instructed 'to keep looking'.

Blair was facing increasing heat at home, particularly after Rumsfeld declared on 28 May that Saddam's WMD might never be found. It fuelled a media frenzy over the apparent inability to find WMD that would rumble on for most of the summer. 'I spoke to TB, who said it was grotesque,' Campbell recorded in early June. 'There was no story here at all, but it was being driven by the BBC as a huge crisis for us.'[158] 'Had Britain been taken to war on a false prospective?' many were now asking. Blair remained absolutely convinced that WMD would be found, and resented the media questioning it. 'So certain was he,' recalled one official, 'that it was a very gradual process of realisation that they might not exist.'[159] In the meantime, Number 10 worked to publicise the benefits of the invasion to counter what it saw as one-sided and negative reporting, especially from the distrusted BBC. From Iraq, Sawers's point of contact became as much with Campbell as with Manning, with the former working hard to ensure that the media operation in Iraq was upgraded to focus on producing 'good' news stories. He urged Sawers to give regular media interviews, including on BBC Television's *Newsnight* and Radio 4's *Today* programme.[160]

Number 10's concerns over America's handling of Iraq were not going away. They concluded that 'Bush wasn't really gripping during this period.' [161] A fresh approach was required, Blair believed. On 29 May, he decided he needed to see Iraq for himself, in part so he could promulgate the benefits of victory. It was the first visit to post-war Iraq by a Western leader, and included a stop off at the Kahdija-al-Kubra primary school in Basra, which had been rebuilt quickly with British money. In the full glare of the cameras a young boy planted a grateful kiss on Blair's cheek. He enjoyed mixing with soldiers and chatted happily with them on the veranda of one of Saddam's former palaces, signing their khaki shirts, before thanking them for their work. 'Blair knows absolutely how to speak, communicate and empathise with soldiers and their families,' recalled one senior military officer. 'He spends 95 per cent of his time either telling you how marvellous what you're doing is, or listening. That's perfect because you feel appreciated.'[162] In an emotional speech, intended also for domestic consumption, he told them that their relatively bloodless victory and reconstruction work were now 'famous throughout the world . . . When people look back on this time, I honestly believe they will see this as one of the finest moments of our century, and you did it.'[163] This was quite a claim, and it reflected how he felt about the invasion, and those who were trying to belittle it.

His six-hour trip did not include a trip to Baghdad, so what he saw was limited. Blair was keen to size up Bremer who flew down to meet him for himself, and he fired a stream of questions at him. Sawers thought 'they got on pretty well: he thought Bremer had a grip and was offering clear direction'. Showing off British soldiering as 'exemplary' was another purpose of the trip in contrast to reports of American occupation tactics. He asked Sawers 'What are the police like?' Sawers replied that it would take a full eighteen months to train them up. 'Ridiculous,' he replied. 'Let me know what it takes to train them in six weeks. We must do it.'[164] It was to prove a sobering trip. 'He realised the huge task in front of us, much bigger than we had imagined.' The lack of Iraqi enthusiasm for the invasion and the problems of establishing civilian government were two aspects that troubled him. 'He was clearly agitated and frustrated by the slow pace of progress,' concluded Sawers, 'though the idea that a new police force could be trained up in six weeks showed that he didn't yet appreciate the full depth of the problem'.[165] Here was a moment when Blair could have raised fundamental concerns with Bremer, and with Bush, but he did not, partly because he believed that the UN resolution passed the week before would broaden out responsibility and give others more of an input.

A more pressing problem was an allegation made at 6:07 A.M. on the day of his Iraq visit on Radio 4's *Today* programme. Referring to the claim in the September 2002 dossier that some of Saddam's WMD could be ready for use within 'forty-five minutes', BBC journalist Andrew Gilligan alleged that, on the basis of confidential information from a senior official in charge of drawing up the dossier, 'The government probably knew that that forty-five-minute figure was wrong, even before it decided to put it in.' Someone in Downing Street, he said, had ordered that the dossier be 'sexed up'.[166] Gilligan followed up his report with an article in the *Mail on Sunday* on 1 June, naming Campbell as the official who intervened to make the dossier 'sexier'.[167] Blair was with Campbell in Kuwait, where his plane had landed en route to Basra, when Gilligan's report was broadcast. Both saw red when they were told what Gilligan had said. 'Blair is not often angry,' said an official, 'but on this occasion he was extremely angry.'[168] What concerned Blair so much was that he had specifically insisted on the dossier being factual and 'as far removed from the spinners as possible', recalled one aide. 'His instructions were that he wanted it to be empirical and dry.'[169] What was 'so corrosive' said

Number 10 spokesman Godric Smith, was that Gilligan's broadcast 'went right to the heart of the Prime Minister's integrity'.[170] Blair drew breath before responding, resisting the temptation to react immediately. Before delivering his riposte, at a press conference with the Polish Prime Minister on 30 May, he checked his words very carefully with the intelligence community. The evidence that Saddam had WMD was drawn on and verified by the JIC, evidence 'I have absolutely no doubt about at all', he said. The idea that Number 10 or the intelligence agencies had invented evidence was 'completely absurd'. His conclusion was clear: 'What is happening here is that people who have opposed this action throughout are now trying to find a fresh reason for saying why it wasn't the right thing to do.'[171]

Blair was even more explicit three days later in Evian for the French G8, when he said, 'I stand absolutely 100 per cent behind the evidence, based on intelligence.' Blair's conviction that Gilligan was plain wrong prevented him being obsessed by the reporter: 'He's endlessly phlegmatic about these things,' said Heywood. 'He never really gets down in a ditch over one particular thing, and certainly not one piece of press reporting.'[172] But for Campbell, the rawest of nerves had been touched. Months of suppressed emotion welled up. His long-standing hostility towards the BBC became a vendetta overnight: 'Number 10's response was very much something that was being driven by Alastair,' said one aide.[173] It had felt for several weeks that 'there had been a clear BBC agenda on Iraq, that it was hopelessly biased', so no one was too upset initially that Campbell, its prize fighter, was taking to the ring.[174] Over the weeks that followed Campbell relentlessly pushed the BBC for a retraction both in private and in public. On 25 June, although Blair was sceptical about the benefits, Campbell insisted on testifying before the House of Commons Foreign Affairs Committee, which was investigating the WMD allegations, further raising awareness of the clash between Number 10 and the BBC.

While Campbell was obsessed with Gilligan, Blair's attention was elsewhere. He was fixated on the MEPP, the litmus test, together with UN involvement, of British influence in Washington. Evidence of real progress here would help pacify domestic critics of the war and heal wounds with France and Germany. On 29 April came a promising development – the swearing-in of the new Palestinian Prime Minister Abu Mazen (Mahmoud Abbas), who was committed to curbing Palestinian attacks on Israeli civilians. With an alternative interlocutor to the administration's *bête noire* Yasser Arafat in place, Bush had delivered on his pledge to publish the 'road map'. On 4 June, he agreed to fly to the Jordanian town of Aqaba to meet with Sharon and Abbas. Blair believed that his labours were beginning to pay off. As with the UN resolution, active American enthusiasm was the *sine qua non* of persuading Israel to play ball. The 'Middle East peace process is now moving forward. This is of fantastic importance,' Blair told reporters. 'A few months ago . . . if I had said I think that President Bush will be seeing Palestinian leaders and Israeli leaders out in the region in order to push the Middle East peace process forward, I think most of you would have said I was being extremely, if not wildly, optimistic.'[175]

The meeting was indeed a breakthrough. For the first time Sharon endorsed a Palestinian state and all three leaders pledged support for the 'road map'. Bush's personal commitment was underlined by Rice's visit to the region later that month and by Colin Powell's public reassurance to America's three partners in the 'Quartet' – the UN, the EU and Russia – that the administration was united behind the President's commitment to achieving a peaceful resolution. But the administration was not united. The neocons remained unconvinced: 'I don't think anyone who had a realistic appreciation of where the Vice-President and President sat on this issue, including my boss Powell, thought that any progress was going to be made while they were in the White House,' said Wilkerson.[176] Cynicism also prevailed among some in Sharon's Cabinet, who dismissed Bush's new-found enthusiasm as a mere transitory reward to Blair for Iraq.[177] Nonetheless, in accordance with the road map, Sharon began to withdraw from parts of Gaza, relinquishing control of much of its main motorway, and pulling troops out of the northern Gaza town of Beit Hanoun.[178] On 14 July, Blair met Sharon in London. The time had come to build bridges. Over a family dinner at Number 10 with Sharon's right-hand man Dov Weissglass and Manning,[179] the leaders smoothed over their differences. The love-in was judged a success: the *Jerusalem Post* said Sharon returned with a 'satisfied glow' and that relations with a key European power were 'back on track'.[180] Blair said that he was 'more than ever convinced' that progress towards the two-state solution would be possible.[181] That indeed would have been the holy grail, an extraordinary diplomatic and personal achievement if he could help pull it off.

On 25 June, the US House of Representatives decreed that 'in recognition of his outstanding and enduring contributions to maintaining the security of all freedom-loving nations' Blair would be awarded the Congressional Gold Medal. Even more of an honour, he was invited to address a joint session of Congress, only the fourth Prime Minister to have been asked. The other three premiers, Churchill, Attlee and

Thatcher, were exactly the class with whom Blair wanted to be bracketed. These were heady days for Tony Blair: 'The days before the speech in Congress was a very positive time; the Prime Minister was in upbeat mood,' recalled one Downing Street aide.[182] Negative press and political comment about the whereabouts of Saddam's WMD remained the principal cloud on the horizon. 'Blair changed imperceptibly in these weeks from a 100 per cent certainty that WMD would be found, to "surely they will get their act together and find them soon", to the realisation that deeper issues had been misjudged,' said one close observer.[183] In the immediate term, news even looked brighter on the Gilligan front. On 7 July, the House of Commons Foreign Affairs Committee issued a report clearing Campbell of exerting 'improper influence' on the drafting of the September WMD dossier. There was more. Part of Number 10 had been on a 'war footing' ever since Gilligan's report and they now believed they had discovered the source of his story, a WMD expert named Dr David Kelly. Because Kelly apparently denied some of the accusations in Gilligan's claims, Number 10 felt it had the upper hand, as Campbell recorded in his diary: 'Spoke to Hoon who said that a man had come forward who felt he was possibly Gilligan's source . . . GH and I agreed it would fuck Gilligan if that was his source.'[184] Even the news from Iraq was more positive. On 13 July, Bremer assisted by Sawers had finally succeeded in setting up the 'Iraqi Governing Council', an ethnically and geographically diverse twenty-five-member council, which would work with Bremer to restore sovereignty. Here was the second step on the road to establishing self-government for the Iraqi people, according to the timetable Blair had announced on 14 April. Things were looking up.

Blair took great pains over his speech to Congress – Godric Smith recalled 'how anxious he was about getting it right. He booked out real time to prepare for it, like for his party conference speech. This wasn't one of those he wrote on a plane.'[185] The night before he flew to Washington, he spoke to an aide at the annual summer party for Downing Street staff and said, 'I've cracked it, I'm very pleased I've sorted it.' He saw his core theme as 'the importance of building a coalition rather than going it alone. He offered them a powerful philosophy of multilateralism.'[186] On the afternoon of 17 July, Blair arrived in Washington. Before delivering the speech he was uncustomarily anxious: 'He was even more nervous and fussy than usual about what tie and shirt he should wear for the occasion. It was a huge thing for him.'[187] Standing before Congress that evening Blair delivered a thirty-two-minute address which received nineteen standing ovations.

He opened self-disparagingly, with words not present in the distributed text of his speech: 'Mr Speaker and Mr Vice-President, honourable members of Congress, I'm deeply touched by that warm and generous welcome. That's more than I deserve and more than I'm used to, quite frankly.'[188] His speech attacked the 'virus' of terrorism, and used language he knew would chime with Middle America. 'Members of Congress, ours are not Western values, they are the universal values of the human spirit. And anywhere, any time ordinary people are given the chance to choose, the choice is the same: freedom, not tyranny; democracy, not dictatorship; the rule of law, not the rule of the secret police.'[189] It was thus a strong pro-US speech, but Blair also managed to tackle less palatable themes, telling his audience to put working in coalition above acting alone; and about the central importance of the MEPP, 'I want to be very plain: this terrorism will not be defeated without peace in the Middle East between Israel and Palestine.'[190] More, he stressed the importance of tackling two issues that were to dominate the final four years of his premiership: poverty in Africa and climate change. 'The world's security cannot be protected without the world's heart being won. So: America must listen as well as lead.'[191]

Blair was very happy. He considered it one of the most powerful and best-delivered speeches of his premiership. He had said everything that he wanted to say, and pulled no punches in doing so.[192] Reaction from the British media was largely cynical. 'Claptrap', said the *Mirror*,[193] while in the *Daily Mail* Stephen Glover labelled it a 'kind of fantasy which bears no relationship to the true state of affairs', and predicted it to be a 'pivotal moment after which everything turned from bad to worse'.[194] The *Daily Telegraph* and *The Times* were more appreciative. Peter Riddell wrote that 'Tony Blair engaged last night in an elegant form of transatlantic triangulation'.[195] In America the reception was much warmer: 'Tony Blair Brings Down The House' read a headline in the *Washington Post*, which noted that by the time Blair had finished speaking, 'the assembled members seemed ready to weep with gratitude'.[196]

Immediately after the speech, Blair headed to the White House for dinner, a light-hearted affair: 'It was very jolly and not at all worky. He felt a real release of tension,' recalled one witness.[197] Blair's party split: Powell stayed in town briefly on personal business, Campbell and Morgan flew direct back to London, while Blair, Manning and press spokesman Godric Smith were driven to Andrews Air Force base to fly off to the Far East in a chartered Boeing 747 with the press corps in the cabins behind ('the *Mail* and *Sun* reporters were paid for to fly business class, most of the rest went economy').[198] Blair relaxed back into his seat after the strain of his seven-hour visit, and had a drink. After months of intense stress, he felt the clouds at last beginning to clear. The coalition had reformed around the UN resolution for post-war Iraq, real strides had been made on the MEPP; anyone who claimed he was 'Bush's poodle' could now see the gains that his support for America was bringing. After chatting to Manning and Smith, he looked at the speech he was due to deliver in Japan the next day, before stretching out to sleep. His rest was frequently interrupted by 'absolutely diabolical' turbulence. Before he landed, however, he was to receive news that would prove infinitely more unsettling.

8

Losing My Agenda

April–November 2003

Cruising at 36,000 feet over the Pacific Ocean, the Prime Minister's plane received a call with disturbing news from a quiet corner of Oxfordshire. David Kelly had committed suicide on 17 July. It was an event that would shake Blair to the core. The high successes of Washington suddenly felt utterly distant. Cherie remembers it as one of the most shocking reversals of the premiership (the other being 7/7).[1] Kelly's death was to cast a shadow over the summer and for much of the rest of the year: the conduct of the government in the run-up to the war would be placed under intense scrutiny, distracting Blair from matters closer to home. The second year of his second term was meant to be about domestic policy: public service reform, the single currency, law and order. The time he spent on Iraq, and the attendant diminution of political capital, impacted negatively on that ambition. In these months, Blair battled to maintain domestic direction, with limited success. 'Once the war began, we lose sight of him for months: he switches back on a bit for the party conference, then we lose him again,' observed one Number 10 confidant.[2] By the summer of 2003 Blair was encountering sustained hostility: as a political leader, who had known only adulation and the aura of success from the moment he entered Parliament twenty years before, he found this hard. At the same time, his closest supporters in Number 10 and Cabinet were seeping away, and his integrity was being called into question. Again, he contemplated departing, but could he find a high point on which to leave? Had he put the solid work in on his domestic agenda, he might have been able to drive it through. But had he done enough?

Constitutional Apathy

Blair was no more interested in constitutional reform than in 'management'. Neither set him alight. Most of the major constitutional issues, notably devolution to Scotland and Wales and human rights, had been resolved in his first term. Removing all but 92 hereditary peers from the House of Lords in 1999 was a significant step, but reform was far from complete. In January 1999, the government published a White Paper proposing to abolish 'hereditary peers with no democratic legitimacy'. But in January 2000, the then Leader of the Commons, Margaret Beckett, announced that reform would not be introduced until after the General Election. The 2001 manifesto duly included the promise to conclude House of Lords reform, and during the campaign Adonis worked in Number 10 to produce proposals for reform, reasoning that unless the government moved on it immediately, progress would stall again. Blair's own attitude was not encouraging. 'He was bored absolutely rigid by it,' said one aide.[3] 'Supremely uninterested in the details,' said a senior official.[4] So when a victorious Blair returning to Number 10 was presented with a draft bill ready to be introduced into the first session, he groaned, and gave it no priority. What he did do, fatally, was hand it over to the new Leader of the House, Robin Cook.

Cook had plans for radical reform involving an elected second chamber. Blair accepted his recommendation that the matter should be discussed by a Cabinet committee. Never totally sure of Cook, he wanted him to work on it in league with his old mentor, Lord Chancellor Derry Irvine. It proved one of New Labour's less happy couplings. Cook wanted to be radical while Irvine was urging caution, and a wholly appointed House. They started fighting, and their rows frequently came up on Blair's radar. His instinct was to back Irvine, 'but without particularly wanting to engage'.[5] After three months of slugging it out, a disenchanted Cook unveiled a White Paper in November 2001, visualising just 20 per cent of peers being elected. He never believed in its proposals, and resented Irvine's taming influence over them. 'He effectively disowned it. Making it clear that it was all Derry's work, and he didn't believe a word of it,' said an aide.[6] To try to unlock progress, Adonis proposed to Blair that the House of Commons should be given a free vote. Cook seized this because he thought MPs would choose radical reform. Following pressure from all parties to increase the proportion of elected peers, the White Paper was effectively abandoned, and a joint committee of both Houses was set up in May 2002 to produce proposals on the powers and structure of the House of Lords, with members to be allowed a free vote on their findings.

The committee produced a range of proposals, from a wholly appointed upper House to a wholly elected one. In the January 2003 debate, Irvine spoke strongly in favour of a wholly appointed House of Lords, deriding the 'nonsense of hybridity'.[7] To the surprise of many, an Iraq-distracted Blair decided to go with the easiest option, and back his former mentor, arguing that a hybrid upper House with a mixture of elected and appointed members would fail.[8] Cook, already soured because of the Iraq war, was livid, telling MPs that in his 'own, personal, very humble opinion', Blair's idea for an unelected second chamber would not gain public confidence. On 4 February, MPs voted, rejecting all of the five options put before them. House of Lords reform was thus killed off for the second term, to be revived in 2006/07. Had Blair given a lead, reform could have been achieved in the second term. But in his mind he had no clear preference for the kind of upper House he wanted to see. In any event, this was a political battle he wanted to avoid.

Elected mayors were different. Here was a constitutional reform that did induce some excitement in Blair. It was all about leadership. His criticism of local authorities was that they were often dull and conservative. 'Charismatic leadership was what was needed to revive local government, he believed,' said an aide.[9] By 2002, *bête noire* of the first term, Ken Livingstone, had been translated into something of a hero in Number 10. His advocacy of congestion charging was more radical than anything that Blair's transport ministers were proposing. (Blair's thinking on this had been shaped by Birt's work on transport, which had forecast a 'grim future of gridlock' within 25 years. His desire for a proper plan met with distinct apathy from the Treasury.)[10] He also admired the Mayor for his galvanising effect on London. In May that year, Blair and Livingstone had the first of a series of meetings that continued throughout the rest of Blair's premiership, latterly on London's 2012 Olympic bid. 'I think we both came to quite like each other, after a very difficult start,' Livingstone said.[11] By summer 2003, Blair made overtures to Livingstone, through Morgan, to return to the Labour fold, which he duly did the following year. If every town and city across the country had an elected mayor like Ken, Blair reasoned, local government would be a far more dynamic force. But he did not reckon on the implacable hostility of Prescott, who saw elected mayors as a threat to the powers and position of traditional local councillors, and from Labour councillors themselves. Blair weighed the situation and decided he did not want to take on Prescott at a time when he needed his backing on the more important issue of public-sector reform. For all his attraction to elected mayors, in the final analysis, he simply did not care enough.

Prescott also carried the day on another pet project – regional assemblies. Blair, like many of the Cabinet, had thought they were 'stupid', but he let Prescott do what he wanted, arguing they were 'Prescott's toy'.[12] In his heart, he knew that Prescott's ambitions for the English regions would be bound to fail, and was therefore happy to humour him. Regional assemblies duly fell apart in 2004 when a referendum on one in the north-east was rejected by an extraordinary 78 per cent of voters. So poor was the result that the government cancelled plans to hold similar referenda in England's other eight regions. Second-term battles can be divided into those about which Blair did not care (House of Lords reform); those he did, but would not fight over (elected mayors); those on which he was prepared to fight hard but accept defeat (the Euro); and those on which he was prepared to fight to the death (Iraq, tuition fees and foundation hospitals). It is to the Euro that we now turn.

The Euro – Dead and Buried: June 2001–June 2003

The Euro saw Blair at his most enigmatic. Private memos for his inner circle from 2001 and 2002 stress the importance he gave to entry in his second term. He told the Euro enthusiasts in Number 10, several of whom held key positions, how important it was to him. 'Tony Blair was completely up for this,' said Hyman. 'He realised it was going to be the battle of his second term.'[13] He even sent signals to Brown (the exact nature of which is contested) that he would leave office early in return for the Chancellor's support over British entry. Brown thought he was deadly serious. So too did the Euro-enthusiasts in Number 10. But was he?

In October 1997, Blair's efforts to push for early Euro entry had been beaten off by Brown and the Treasury. But Brown's statement of 27 October included a lifeline: 'Britain will be in a position to join a single currency, should we wish to, early in the next Parliament.' At the same time, Brown had specified five 'economic tests' which needed to be met prior to any decision about Britain joining: this had the effect of ceding complete control over entry to the Treasury. Blair was not going to give up without a fight, however, and, on 7 February 2001, he announced that Brown's words 'early in the next Parliament' entailed a decision being reached 'within two years' of re-election. From 1999 he had been thinking about how to achieve his goal, and the topic had come up in several meetings with a reluctant Brown. By 2000, Number 10 was pressing for preparatory work, saying it was a question not of 'whether' but of 'when'.[14] Brown had different ideas: as FCO head John Kerr said, 'The Treasury made it very clear that they were the sole determinants of the five tests, and simply closed down discussions.'[15] When Number 10 persisted, the Treasury set up an analytical team under David Ramsden, a formidable intellect who was head of economic and monetary policy. Blair knew he had to match the Treasury's top guns. He was reassured by Wall's presence in Number 10 as his EU specialist, not least because he was on good terms with Ramsden who others viewed as a 'technocrat in a white coat'.[16] Apart from Britain, only two other members of the EU (after Greece joined in 2001), Denmark and Sweden, were not members of the Euro-zone, and Blair believed that Britain's future lay with the twelve who were. 'He fundamentally couldn't see how Britain could be Europe's leader if it wasn't a member of the Euro. He had a fifty-year view: it was Britain's destiny,' said an official.[17] The political case thus ranked highest with Blair: he did not worry unduly about the economics, which he never fully grasped. Brown in contrast saw the political advantages too, but became increasingly concerned about the economics, especially as, by 2001, the Euro-zone economies like Germany were in trouble.[18] The British economy, meanwhile, was riding high. It led many to question whether the potential benefits of entry still exceeded the costs.

Blair was in bullish mood immediately after the 2001 election. In late June he told Gavyn Davies, Goldman Sachs economist and husband of Sue Nye, Brown's gatekeeper, that 'everyone wanted us in apart from the French. If we wait four to five years we will not be able to extract as good a deal and we will have less influence.'[19] His comments inevitably filtered back to the Brown camp. But by not talking about the Euro during the election campaign (for fear of arousing an adverse press reaction) Blair had denied himself the opportunity to claim a mandate for entry, which would have proved a valuable battering ram against the doors of the Treasury. The odds were stacked heavily against him. In the summer of 2001, an uncustomary period of warmth broke out with the Treasury. Heywood worked closely with his opposite number Ed Balls to explore how they could best tackle the Euro assessment.[20] Collegiality was also the order of the day as Blair prepared for his keynote speech on the EU in Birmingham on 23 November. When he met Brown to discuss the speech (itself a rare event), Brown told him he was concerned about the two pages which dealt with the issue of entry. In an otherwise bold speech on the EU, Blair's pronouncements on the Euro were bland, a direct result of Brown's intervention.[21]

The Euro became very tied up in Blair's mind with his ideas about the future. Nothing in Blair's entire premiership is so hard to penetrate as his intentions about when to quit Number 10, because he was not sure himself, and he told different people different things at different times. The events of 9/11 and ramifications had shaken him and made him realise how little time he would have to give to achieve his key objectives, including the Euro. Although evasive as ever about his departure, one thought in his mind was to go halfway or towards the end of the second term – perhaps in late 2004. Sally Morgan describes it as 'just a vague assumption around the place, although his focus remained very much on the immediate future'.[22] But it certainly chimed with what Gordon Brown wanted, and thought Blair had promised him. Blair fretted that the Euro, which he considered central at the time to his desire to build a new relationship with the EU, would be thwarted by Brown. Anji Hunter, now at BP, suggested to her close friend Sue Nye that Blair would quit for Brown as long as 'he delivers on the Euro', a message that was allegedly repeated by Blair to Brown at a dinner at Downing Street on 18 December 2001.[23] Campbell's account of the dinner does not mention this offer, but he records on the Euro that Blair felt Brown was 'more open-minded but that Balls was pouring opposition into his head the whole time'.[24] But Blair said things to Brown he did not tell even Campbell. The history of the Blair–Brown relationship is littered with occasions where both men gained very different understandings from meetings. Brown's camp tended to take Blair literally: Blair was inclined to say what he thought his interlocutor wanted to hear, but then would only remember what he wanted to remember. Brown would return to his camp and tell them exactly what Blair had said, not what Blair had maybe meant. Blair would fudge what he said to his camp, or not tell them. Many in Blair's camp, however, thought the problem was that Brown heard not what Blair said, but what he wanted Blair to say. 'I saw it happening a million times with Gordon,' said one.[25]

The Euro issue was being played out in the full public glare. 'There was tension because Tony was making it public repeatedly that he wanted to join, and Gordon was responding on the other side,' said one of Brown's closest allies in the Cabinet.[26] Blair mentioned the Euro and his future at one of his regular sessions with Prescott, knowing that he would pass it on to the Chancellor. According to Clare Short, Blair confided in her on a flight back from Africa in February 2002: 'I really wish Gordon would let me join the Euro. If he would . . . I don't want a third term, I would hand over to him,' and he asked her to speak to him. When she did so, Brown (according to his camp) responded that he could not conceive of recommending that Britain join the Euro to advance his own prospects at the expense of the economic interests of the country.[27] Blair's aides, naturally, deny this interpretation of his motivation: would Blair seriously suggest to Brown he sacrifice his principles for the sake of his own glory? What they say he said was 'if you are genuinely on the same agenda, and are fully co-operative, and we are running a government together, obviously I will be minded to go sooner than if we're not doing that'.[28]

A distracted Blair had come under strong pressure from aides in Number 10. 'There are so many people pressing Tony to see this as his legacy,' Blunkett wrote in his diary after dinner with him on 20 May 2002.[29] Chief advocates were Wall, Hyman, and Roger Liddle, with Jonathan Powell strongly supportive, and none more influential than Mandelson from the wings. Optimism among the group was at a high point in the summer of 2002: 'There was a real belief that the Euro was the way forward and that people would return from their summer holidays in Europe much more ready to see it in Britain.'[30] The Euro notes and coins had been introduced on 1 January 2002, and 'there was a feeling of inevitability in Britain that we would be in the Euro within ten years'. Hyman and Steve Morris, a Number 10 official, prepared a 'massive dossier' of reading material on the Euro and Euro referenda for Blair to digest during summer holidays in the Lake District and the south of France.[31] A note from Hyman at the dossier's front said: 'This is the big one: never before has a Prime Minister voluntarily risked a commanding majority, on an issue about which the country was lukewarm, the Treasury and his own party sceptical.'[32] Discussion took place within Number 10 on the form the referendum should take. Some saw it as a battle between the progressives led by Blair and the Euro-sceptics, led by the Conservatives. But Blair insisted he wanted it to be a broad-based campaign, including key figures from all parties. Liberal Democrat leader Charles Kennedy and former Conservative Chancellor Ken Clarke were summoned to private meetings with Blair in the Cabinet Office to avoid attracting attention: Clarke was still viewed as a potential future Conservative leader and the last thing he needed was to be seen to be having confidential meetings with Blair on such a sensitive topic.[33]

The veneer of collegiality between Number 10 and the Treasury began to break down during the summer of 2002. The former began to press for a decision before the June 2003 deadline, while the latter began to take the measure of Blair's determination. Heywood was dispatched to talk timetables with Balls and Treasury Permanent Secretary Gus O'Donnell. But Brown was very reluctant to engage, arguing that Blair had ceded economic decisions to him.[34] 'I think Jeremy's sympathies were with us over all of this,' said one Treasury official. 'But he did his best to help Blair present a half-decent case from a useless brief.'[35] When Blair met Brown in October, the latter again refused to discuss the Euro, claiming that to do so would pre-empt the Treasury's assessment of the five tests: 'An absurdly prickly response to the man who was after all Prime Minister,' commented Blair's economic adviser Derek Scott.[36]

By Christmas, the Treasury had completed its analysis, on which twenty-five officials had worked full-time under Ramsden producing eighteen separate 'background studies' at a cost of £5 million. So all-absorbing was it that this task left 'little space in the Treasury for other significant policy initiatives'.[37] On 4 December, Balls delivered a coded lecture in Oxford as 'a final, futile attempt to persuade the Prime Minister and his pro-Euro allies in Downing Street that it would be foolhardy to fix or distort the outcome of Ramsden's assessment'.[38] To underline the point, a deliberate leak to Larry Elliott, economics editor of the *Guardian*, said that the two most important economic tests had not been met and that the overall assessment would be negative.[39] Number 10 refused to be discouraged. 'In late 2002, our thinking was that the tests would be debated in early 2003 and once they were out of the way, we would hold the referendum in May, or at the latest, the autumn,' said one aide.[40] Most in Number 10 did not see, or did not choose to see, the Treasury's implacable opposition.

O'Donnell and Balls read Ramsden's eighteen studies over Christmas 2002. Their conclusion was that they were negative. There was 'plenty here arguing against entry to the Euro'. How should they now proceed? Blair's lack of economic expertise was an open secret: even a well-disposed Treasury official described him as 'pretty hopeless at economics'.[41] Heywood thrashed out with Balls how Blair and Number 10 might best digest the eighteen studies, and came up with the device of a series of five or six 'seminars' leading up to the Budget.[42] It was to be 'an education of sorts'. Balls pricked up his ears at this notion: 'Ed thinks the Prime Minister is a moron, so the idea that he needed educating appealed to him.'[43] Blair proved a reluctant student and did not understand why the seminars were necessary. They proved hard to arrange during the build-up to Iraq and often had to be re-scheduled at the last minute.

At this stage the Number 10 team comprised Powell, Wall and Heywood while the Treasury's representatives were Brown, Balls, O'Donnell and Jon Cunliffe, head of international finance. The meetings were conducted in great secrecy and even the Prime Minister's economic adviser, Scott, was forbidden by the Treasury to see the papers.[44] 'It was totally ludicrous,' said one of the Number 10 team, 'because we never got the papers until a day or two before the meetings, and they were highly detailed and complex.'[45] Heywood's job was 'highlighting to the Prime Minister what was in the papers and the key arguments for and against, so that he could make some intelligent comments at the meetings'.[46] Blair dreaded the ninety-minute sessions and found them every bit as excruciating as he expected. 'The white-coated David Ramsden sedated us all with his lengthy technical papers,' recalled one Number 10 aide.[47] Ramsden had little inkling that his meticulous projections, graphs and data were not making more of an impact.

Number 10 found the whole exercise disingenuous: 'It was fairly clear that Brown was presenting all the findings in a negative light, almost regardless of the evidence,' said Wall, who felt the Treasury were downplaying the inward investment and trade benefits of Eurozone membership.[48] Blair himself became 'utterly infuriated' by the 'insouciance' with which Brown 'got to the punch-line as if it were the product of a deeply technical and intellectual process, rather than a political judgement that he could have stated at the beginning'.[49] Even Number 10 officials sympathetic to the Treasury regarded the meetings as 'a charade'.[50] Blair remained bullish, however, saying to his unconvinced aides, 'leave Gordon to me'.[51] The Treasury, meanwhile, was adamant that the tests were indeed objective and scientific, and that Brown had exerted no influence whatsoever on the process.[52] By the second term, Number 10 had begun to see Brown's hand behind much that they did not like, and discounted his protestations to the contrary.

Both sides displayed ill-concealed relief when the seminars ground to a halt with what was intended to be their final meeting on Tuesday, 1 April. Its purpose was to consider the overall assessment and what the recommendation would be. Ramsden geared himself up to deliver his final presentation, consisting of a fifty-page slide show. Ramsden's final sentence concluded that 'a decision to join now would not be in the national economic interest', as a 'clear and unambiguous case' for British membership of the single currency has not been made (a deliberate mimicking of words that Blair had used in 1997 when he said that the case for joining had to be 'clear and unambiguous'). The Number 10 team were disappointed; shocked, even. Blair said, 'I don't agree,' and demanded that the summary assessment, which Number 10 thought 'one-sided and unbalanced', should be modified to reflect better the overall tenor of the eighteen papers.[53] The meeting broke up and Heywood wrote a twenty-five-point note for Blair for insertion into the final assessment, to make it more balanced.[54] A second meeting took place later that Tuesday afternoon, which proved short and tense. Brown was at his most rude and blunt, and declared that there would be no changes in the assessment. 'This is a Treasury assessment,' he insisted and tried to swat the revisions aside, but Number 10 persisted. The Treasury finally agreed to make some modifications, which they considered minor. 'When Tony Blair saw it in the final form he was still disappointed that more had not changed,' recalled a close aide.[55]

Imperceptibly, Blair's views were deviating from those of his largely pro-Euro team in Number 10. 'In his heart of hearts, he realised that taking Britain into the Euro in 2003 was not going to work,' said one aide.[56] He may not have understood all the economic arguments, but he realised that to take Britain into a referendum when the Chancellor was not prepared to endorse it enthusiastically was a non-starter. As one of his closest colleagues said, 'I suspect he always realised that Brown effectively had a veto because of the grip he had over the referendum.'[57] But Blair played his cards very close to his chest, leaving his pro-Euro colleagues to continue to believe he was totally on their side. Without sharing it with them, he 'realised at that stage there was no question of going in immediately', and that he would return to it in 2004 once the Iraq war was safely out of the way.[58] What he required therefore was an assessment which allowed him to return to the Euro in a year or two's time, stating that it remained the government's policy to join. So while most of his colleagues were still fighting tooth and claw to join the Euro at once, he was one step ahead, thinking about how best to position the government for a deferred entry.

The showdown with the Treasury came at their meeting on 2 April. Blair fought hard for the assessment not ruling out delaying the referendum, to keep open the chances of Britain joining the Euro before the next General Election. Brown, deeply irritated, argued that the conclusions should be published in the Budget exactly one week later. To put it in the Budget in the middle of the Iraq war, Blair said, and without proper Cabinet discussion, was totally unacceptable.[59] The temperature rose rapidly and Blair lost his temper, a rare occurrence.

Both sides agree that the meeting concluded with him saying to Brown that, if he was not prepared to concede, 'You will have to consider your position,' and with Brown replying, 'I'll do just that,' before leaving abruptly with his team.[60] Where both sides disagree is in the import of what Blair had said at their most fraught public encounter of his decade in office. As ever, Brown and his camp took Blair's words at face value. They were not certain whether the Chancellor had just been sacked or whether he had resigned.[61] Number 10 did not think Blair was seriously asking his Chancellor to resign. 'I didn't come out of that meeting thinking, "Right, we'd better start planning for a new Chancellor." None of us thought he was about to walk out,' said one of the Prime Minister's party.[62] While some urged Blair in private to sack Brown if he was not prepared to be more accommodating on the assessment, Blair and his more reflective colleagues realised that if he were to go ahead on this basis, the chances of him remaining in power for long were slender.[63]

Once their camps had simmered down, Blair and Brown realised that they had to pull back from the brink urgently and find a way forward before news of the bust-up leaked. Heywood and Balls were nominated to hammer out a mutually acceptable wording of the assessment, meeting in Balls's room at the Treasury at 9 P.M.[64] They worked until shortly after midnight. 'Heywood negotiated a few changes to the assessment, taking out some things which would have made it very difficult for us to revisit it in a year's time,' said an official.[65] Out therefore went passages implying that the exchange rate would have to move a long way before Britain could join; in went the conclusion that sterling had converged as least as much as some currencies which had already joined the Euro.[66] Balls believed these interventions were mere tinkering, according to the account that Brown's camp gave Robert Peston for his biography of Brown.[67] Balls rang Brown at 12:30 A.M. to assure him he was happy with the changes. From 12:45 to 1:45 in the morning, Balls then briefed Ramsden, who went straight to the printers to oversee the alterations to the assessment, which were ready by 7 A.M. A final proof copy was immediately delivered to Number 10.

It was not well received. At 9 A.M. a message was sent to the Treasury that Blair forbade Brown to mention the assessment in the Budget. The Iraq war was now under way and Blair insisted the government could not appear to be using the conflict as 'cover' for announcing a decision of such importance. The Treasury had no more shells left to fire back and consented that the Budget should make no reference to the Euro assessment. Brown still harboured hopes of getting his own way, according to Blunkett, who the next day wrote in his diary, 'It is quite clear that Gordon wants to make an announcement [in the Budget] to settle the thing once and for all . . . I don't think Tony will want to do that, so it should be interesting.'[68] But Brown followed Blair's command in his 9 April Budget. Fears in Number 10 that when Gordon 'got to the dispatch box he might still make an ad-lib announcement' did not materialise.[69]

Four weeks of what were described as 'highly secretive' conversations now ensued, with Blair and Brown thrashing out what should be said and when. Neither had aides with him and no minutes were taken. 'Blair wouldn't give an account afterwards, not even to Jonathan,' said Wall.[70] Brown was not so coy with his team. He remained adamant that the assessment was not only a 'not yet' but also a bald 'no'. Blair fought back: when the assessment was published, it should be a 'yes, but not yet'. But the ground was slipping away from Blair more widely, with the argument being lost in the City. Michael Butler, formerly of the FCO, was spokesman for the traditional banks who argued that if Britain did not go into the Euro, business would desert to Frankfurt. Nonsense, said banks like Citigroup, Goldman Sachs and JP Morgan, whose viewpoint was vindicated. In May, Cabinet began to discuss the issue. Brown had initially wanted to deliver the verdict without Cabinet discussion. Blair prevailed. Brown then wanted to see all Cabinet ministers individually to talk to them on his own. Blair would not allow that either.[71] Brown yielded, judging correctly that the balance in Cabinet was against a referendum. The principal Euro enthusiasts were Clarke, Hain, Hewitt and party chairman, Ian McCartney. Prescott was neutral, while Straw, Darling and Blunkett were firmly against. The decision to lay the full matter before Cabinet had the merit for both camps that it could then be presented as a collective decision, thereby concealing the fundamental differences in opinion. Cabinet ministers were presented with Ramsden's entire assessment documents – a total of 1,982 pages – and they were offered 'tutorials' with Blair and Brown. Some like Milburn complained that they were given just ten minutes, but Blunkett was pleased, 'I went straight to Number 10 to see Gordon and Tony about the Euro. It was a very good meeting, and it was clear they were getting their act together.'[72] 'By and large there was a favourable response from Cabinet ministers,' Wall said.[73]

The 9th of June was decreed as the date the statement should be made to the House of Commons. A 'huge debate' took place between Number 10 and the Treasury over wording. It had now come down to the Treasury wanting the word 'if' and Number 10 wanting to use the word 'when'.[74] A further quarrel was over whether Blair or Brown should make the statement to the House. It is doubtful whether Blair himself ever seriously contemplated making it, but many in Number 10 wanted him to do so to ensure he set the tone for the future. Brown had had enough. The stark message came back from Brown's office that 'if the Prime Minister makes a statement, he can get himself a new Chancellor of the Exchequer', recalled Wall.[75] Blair pulled back and Brown duly made the statement, supported by a 246-page report, 'UK Membership and the Single Currency – An Assessment of the Five Economic Tests'. As a concession to Blair, the statement did say there would be a review at the next Budget on whether to conduct a further assessment in the light of fresh circumstances. An 'Enabling Bill' was also to be published in the autumn of 2003 for a referendum on the Euro, should one be needed. A gruesome joint press conference followed the statement, at which Blair's and Brown's body language made clear the Grand Canyon of their differences: 'Tony fiddling with a pencil when Gordon spoke and Gordon gazing into the middle distance when the Prime Minister was answering a question.'[76] They announced there was to be a 'road show' campaign to begin in the autumn to make the case for the Euro. This was window-dressing. 'I probably said to Jonathan, "What about it?"' recalled Wall. 'I think Jonathan replied, "Forget it." Certainly none of us did any work on the road show.'[77] By the time the statement was delivered, Blair had even given up any lingering hopes of taking Britain into the single currency before the next General Election. The Treasury's trump card was its belief that, if interest rates were to be reduced as required to European levels during the life of the Parliament, politically unacceptable rises in taxes or cuts in spending would be needed to compensate.[78] As Blunkett recorded in his diary, 'I think the issue is dead for some years to come.'[79]

After the 9 June statement, Blair did not press Brown to deliver even on the limited concessions he had obtained. He even refused to act on the advice from his Number 10 aides to set up a formal Cabinet committee to examine sterling convergence and the conditions that Brown stipulated would be required to meet the tests. 'Frankly, after the statement was made, the energy just left,' an official recalled. 'We could not get the Prime Minister to put any real weight behind the process. It just fizzled out.'[80] The Euro was a clear Brown win, and one on which he was unequivocally on the right side. Many in Number 10 as well as in the FCO thought that Britain would lose influence in Europe if it did not join the single currency and that 'joining the Euro was the litmus test of whether we would be considered to be good Europeans'.[81] Mandelson, who had pressed Blair all the way, thought Blair had already missed the boat: 'He should have gone into government and very early held a referendum on the principle, not the timing . . . If he had won the argument when he was strong enough to do so, he would have been much better off.'[82] He was angry and disillusioned that Blair had lost the argument. The ultras in Number 10 were also disappointed. Wall recalls that at a certain point: 'I realised that this relationship was not breakable. There was never a moment that Blair was actually going to say, "I'm going to get myself a new Chancellor."'[83] When Wall left Downing Street a short while later, Blair paid a rare visit to his office in Number 10. He said, '"You must feel disappointed how things have turned out over Europe." I do not think I said anything in reply.'[84]

So what did Blair truly think about the Euro? The answer is that, whereas Britain's role in the EU was of major importance to him, the Euro was merely a means to an end. 'His paramount concern was Britain's political position, and if the Euro was necessary for that then that was where he came from,' recalled one close aide.[85] When he was uncertain over his future in late 2001–02, he even saw victory on British entry in a referendum as providing the high point on which he could depart. But during 2002–03 he began to think differently. Partly he realised he would not shift Brown, and without his willing support, the project was dead in the water. With Brown on the backbenches and given his influence in the party and over opinion outside, a referendum would never have been won. He may have begun to sense that membership of the Euro was not essential to exercising influence in the EU: enlargement was shifting power eastwards and away from France and Germany, affording new opportunities for British leadership. If he had been as deeply committed to the Euro as he had led his supporters to believe, he would not have walked away so lightly after Brown's 9 June statement. The truth is that, with his domestic agenda so incomplete, he seized on the Euro as a great defining issue on which he could win over a sceptical Treasury and nation. He convinced all parties it mattered greatly to him. It did not. He had other battles to fight, and other, better ways of exerting British influence in the EU.

Messy Reshuffle: June 2003

The Euro was not the only issue preoccupying the Prime Minister on 9 June. The week was to prove a bloody one for Blair. It should have heralded what Turnbull described as 'one of the greatest and most successful constitutional changes the country's ever seen', and one that

had been many months in the planning.[86] Instead, the week finished
with a botched reshuffle, widespread recrimination and accusations that
Number 10 had lost its way. The weekend before, Blair had been in his
Sedgefield constituency at a party given by his local Trimdon Labour
club to celebrate his twentieth anniversary as an MP. Alan Milburn, a
guest, told him ominously that he needed to see him urgently in London
the next day. That Monday he told Blair that he had to resign
immediately. Blair was horrified. Having already lost Estelle Morris and
Stephen Byers, this was now the third of the four 'delivery' Cabinet
ministers who he had wanted to remain in their posts for the whole of his
second term. On Thursday 12 June came the messiest reshuffle of Blair's
premiership.

Blair was as uninterested in reshuffles as he was in constitutional
reform. The thinking behind this one, which had at its heart a
fundamental change to the position of the Lord Chancellor, had been in
the ether since 1997. Pat McFadden, his first constitutional adviser in
the Policy Unit, articulated a view widely shared across government.
Surely, he argued, it was no longer sustainable to have the Lord
Chancellor heading both the legislature and the judiciary, while also
holding a dominant position in the executive running the Lord
Chancellor's Department and occupying a seat in Cabinet. Cabinet
Secretary Wilson, and later his successor Turnbull, agreed
wholeheartedly, and pressure on Blair began to mount.

At the 2001 General Election, a Wilson/Heywood plan to give direct
administrative control of the courts to the Home Office had been foiled
by Irvine, who argued forcibly that to separate the courts from the judges
would undermine judicial independence. Blair bided his time but
became increasingly susceptible to the arguments of his advisers, now
joined by Adonis, that the 'three in one' role of the Lord Chancellor was
a constitutional anachronism for a progressive government. Blair wanted
Irvine to mastermind the change, but Irvine resisted. He 'was an ardent
believer in the "Holy Trinity" and, moreover, he believed that the Holy
Trinity must be him', noted one senior official wryly.[87] If the change was
to be made, Blair realised he had no option but to sack Irvine. This was
not easy: he was his long-standing mentor, the head of chambers when
he first became a barrister, and the man who had introduced him to
Cherie. Irvine fought to stay, insisting he had much to do in the second
term, including work on criminal justice and House of Lords reform.
Blair wavered: he was never good at standing up to powerful men. But
the bonds were loosening. His faith in Irvine had weakened in his first
term, and by 2003 he had become exasperated by his lack of political

nous and his resistance to the reform agenda on criminal justice. The final straw came with Irvine's appearance on the BBC's *Today* programme in January 2003 when he argued that the public were happy to see burglars kept out of jail for second offences. At a meeting at Number 10 to discuss their differences over criminal justice, Blair was 'deeply irritated' with Irvine, but surprised those present by 'how strongly he stood up for him'. Shortly afterwards Irvine accepted a £22,000 pay rise with greatly enhanced pension rights. This led to a re-circulation of the 'trouble with Derry' stories, which had proved damaging during the first term. Blair realised that the game was up. 'It was just time for him to go,' said one senior aide.[88]

In the early summer, Heywood, Adonis and Turnbull concluded plans for a supreme court, a new Department of Constitutional Affairs (DCA), and a separate appointing body for all judges. Irvine would accept there was a need only for limited reform. Blair tried one last time to convince him that change had to come. There were 'harrowing' meetings at which Irvine refused to budge. Blair protested: 'Why on earth do you sit on the Wool Sack in the House of Lords every day? It's a complete waste of your time.'[89] Insiders recall 'terrible battles' in which Irvine would say, 'You are wrong, Blair,' at which 'Blair' had to remind him, 'I am the Prime Minister.' He eventually realised he would never compromise – 'Derry was not even one-tenth of the way towards where the PM was' – and sacking him was inevitable.[90] Charles Falconer was pencilled in to replace him. Blair's aides breathed a huge sigh of relief. Less contentiously, Blair accepted official advice that, following devolution in the first term, it was anomalous to have separate Secretaries of State for Wales and Scotland. Fears that Labour would be hammered if the change took place before the Scottish and Welsh elections dictated the timing of the announcement, while Brown suggested an alternative to outright abolition of the ancient posts. 'Gordon had always spoken of the idea of a Secretary of State for Scotland having another job as well in the Cabinet,' said Falconer.[91] Darling duly took over Whitehall's remaining responsibility for Scotland on top of running Transport, while Peter Hain combined the residual functions of Welsh Secretary with his post as Leader of the Commons.

The plan had been to execute the reshuffle shortly before the summer recess in July, but incessant press speculation about it and Milburn's pronouncement disastrously advanced the timetable to 12 June. It left too little time for all bases to be covered. Blair had pleaded with Milburn to stay, to no avail. 'Alan's departure was a complete shock to us, and a very bad one,' said Morgan. Blair returned from Paris on the morning of 12 June to chair Cabinet, Milburn's and Irvine's last, which discussed Iraq and the EU.[92] Blair asked Irvine to remain behind after the meeting and saw him alone in his room. After all his prevarication, his resolve still had to be stiffened at the eleventh hour, something often needed on dismissals, thwarting a rearguard plan to allow Irvine to remain.[93] 'TB was dreading the Derry discussion,' noted Campbell.[94] Irvine was incandescent: 'You are getting rid of me and putting in another peer,' he fumed.[95] Milburn's news was already out, and for six hours, until the official announcement of the reshuffle at 5:45 P.M., the media was left to speculate why a leading Blairite had resigned. Infuriated Number 10 officials saw their long-standing constitutional changes being picked apart before their eyes. 'The journalists were not properly briefed, which pissed them off and led to the poor headlines, especially when the Conservatives egged it on, as did the judiciary,' said one.[96] Aides lamented that the lessons of the 2001 reshuffle had not been learned, when just one figure, Cook, had knocked the plan off course. 'It took one person in 2003 – Milburn – to make it all go wrong again.'[97] Blunkett ascribed the confusion to the departure from Number 10 of Hunter, who would have sorted out the diary. 'The result is the reshuffle is just shoe-horned into everything else that is already there . . . The media have presented the reshuffle as a fiasco, but how could they not?'[98] Some in Number 10 blamed Turnbull. It was an orgy of recrimination.

With the media storm growing, Blair had to spend two hours hosting a lunch for BBC executives at Number 10, and only at 2:30 P.M. could he return to the reshuffle, to call in John Reid to persuade him to become Milburn's successor. But could the Scottish Reid take over as English Health Secretary? He had held three separate Cabinet posts within the previous year: was it a move too soon for him? Blair needed him badly, given the importance he was investing in his health reforms. He had few options among his ministers, and knew he could take no chances. 'Tony thought he would be tough and continue with Alan's work.'[99] With some hesitation, Reid agreed. Irvine's successor was less angst-ridden. Blair asked his old friend Falconer to head the DCA, and temporarily become Lord Chancellor until its functions could be dispersed. 'The critical factor was that Tony thought I would be much more emollient than Derry in dealing with other members of the government – which is to my discredit, I suspect,' said an emollient Falconer.[100]

That afternoon Blair sat on the terrace at Number 10 with Powell, Campbell, Morgan and Chief Whip Armstrong, considering how they might regain some control. The press had to be briefed at 5:45 P.M. in time for the six o'clock news bulletins, which left insufficient time to explain that there would be legislation and further pronouncements on the detail of the constitutional and judicial changes. Problems were compounded because Number 10 failed to do its homework properly. Having taken soundings with senior figures, including Lord Bingham, they expected that the House of Lords judiciary would relish the task of becoming the Supreme Court. But they did not. Neither was the House of Lords pleased to be appointing its own speaker: 'Oddly enough, we learned that they didn't really want a speaker, but preferred their traditional working methods.'[101] The judiciary was offended by the abolition of the post of Lord Chancellor, which Falconer later admitted had been unnecessary, with the loss of its 'champion' in Cabinet. It was also angry that it had not been consulted: Number 10's riposte was that they could hardly have been asked their views when the departure of Irvine was integral to the whole thinking. Even the Queen was said to be 'hopping' about it.[102] Brown too was far from delighted with the reshuffle, but he stayed 'relatively quiet'. Blair had sacked Brown's closest acolyte in Cabinet, Nick Brown, but the Chancellor's attempts to save him had been 'pretty half-hearted'. Neither did Brown succeed in securing promotion for Douglas Alexander or Yvette Cooper, wife of Ed Balls.[103] While Brown had taken succour from his triumph in the Euro decision and the departure of arch-enemy Milburn, the reshuffle brought him back down to earth. Blair was still Prime Minister. At least for the time being.

Kelly's Death and Campbell's Departure: July–August

No one could have foreseen how quickly Falconer and his department's advice would be required at the highest level. Blair's flight from Washington to Tokyo was well over its halfway point when, 8,000 miles away, news was received in Number 10 that David Kelly had gone missing: there was 'a very deep sense of shock in Number 10, with huddled conversations going on all round the building', recalled one.[104] Through the plane's satellite communications, the duty clerk travelling with Blair was phoned; he then woke Godric Smith. Soon afterwards, a second call was received to say that Kelly's body had been found. The police did not at first say that the body was David Kelly's, and it took some time for Number 10 to get confirmation. Smith's task was to tell Blair, who was already awake and having breakfast with Cherie.[105] His reaction was deep shock. He knew at once what it would mean in terms of blame being pointed at Number 10: 'Here was a man who had been hounded by the media for several weeks on the basis of intelligence he might have been leaking, who then commits suicide wrapped up in the biggest issue of the decade.'[106] Blair talked it over with Manning and Smith on the plane, and by phone with Heywood and Turnbull in London, saying, 'When I arrive in Tokyo, I need to be able to say what we are going to do about this. We will need an inquiry, we need to decide what terms of reference it will have, who is going to head it, who will give evidence, etc.'[107] Heywood recalls the frustration of listening properly through a very crackly communication system, but clearly remembers Blair's calm and resolve. He spoke to Falconer, and Hayden Phillips, the Permanent Secretary of the DCA, for their advice on who should head the inquiry.[108] Speed of reaction was deemed essential by Blair: it was now Friday morning in Britain, and Blair was determined to announce the inquiry before anyone could call for one, and make it seem that he had been forced into it.[109] Falconer was in no doubt who to select. 'Lord Hutton had proved himself to be utterly independent amidst the great political pressures of Northern Ireland. I knew he would command respect.'[110]

With the differences in time zone, it was late on Friday evening when Blair's flight touched down in Tokyo. While he was in bed that night, rushed arrangements were made across London finalising details for the inquiry. With further details of the story breaking all the time, it was a desperate race against time. On Saturday morning, Blair announced what would happen. It had been a bad night. 'TB called. It was 5 A.M. there,' Campbell recorded, 'He said he couldn't sleep, he felt grim.'[111] It was as bad a moment as he had in his premiership. Disorientated by the change in time zone, he looked strained and gaunt, and chose a moment when there was only one reporter present to deliver what he wanted to be his definitive statement. 'I am profoundly sad for David Kelly and his family. He was a fine public servant . . . There is now, however, going to be a due process and a proper independent inquiry. I believe that it should be allowed to establish the facts. We shall set aside speculation, claims and counter-claims and allow the due process to take its proper course: and in the meantime, all of us, politicians, media alike, should show some restraint and respect. That is all I am going to say.'[112] His entourage were under such pressure they omitted to include in the final copy of a pro-EU speech he delivered later that day the three most sensitive passages on the Euro: rather than disturb him in front of cameras mid-speech and risk speculation it was related to Kelly, they took the decision that he would have to 'fudge it'. Much as his handlers tried to keep him away from the media, they could not help Blair during the joint press conference with Japanese Prime Minister Junichiro Koizumi. Jonathan Oliver, from the despised *Mail on Sunday*, asked the question most in the media's mind about whether Number 10 had leaked Kelly's name to the press, which built up the pressure in him which led to his suicide. 'Have you got blood on your hands, Prime Minister? Are you going to resign?' Blair was momentarily lost for words. To those observing him, he appeared to be ashen, exhausted and beaten.[113]

The very purpose of the Far East trip had already come under fire. Labour backbench critic Alice Mahon had asked why Blair was letting himself be used as 'Bush's envoy yet again', in particular over the story that he was to threaten North Korea over its nuclear weapons. Blair was aching to return to London to exert his authority, but had to visit China, South Korea and Hong Kong before returning a day early on 23 July. By shifting the focus on to a real concern over WMD, North Korea's nuclear weapons, Blair had hoped the trip would draw a line under the dossiers and WMD before the summer recess. It was a forlorn attempt. Compounding Blair's distress throughout the trip was the hysterical reaction of Campbell. On the morning of Friday 18 July, Sally Morgan and Campbell had arrived back at London Heathrow overnight from Washington. When Campbell switched his phone back on there was an urgent message to call the Number 10 duty clerk. He was told that Kelly had gone missing. 'I felt sick,' Campbell noted in his diary. 'I could sense a juggernaut heading my way.'[114] Campbell rang Morgan, Hoon and Prescott on the way back to London. Tom Kelly at Number 10 informed him that a body had been found shortly before 11 A.M.[115] Campbell's instinct was to quit at once: in a series of fraught conversations from the Far East, Blair told him to calm down. Some of their most difficult discussions took place over the weekend when Blair was staying in the hot-spring resort of Hakone. Campbell had spoken to him about his depression. He had had suicidal thoughts in the past. Cut off deep in the Japanese countryside, Blair had no idea what to think. For Campbell, Kelly's death brought back to the surface all his cravings to leave Number 10: the two years since the 2001 election, when Blair had enticed him to remain, had been the least happy of the nine he had spent with him since 1994. The highly personal way that Campbell had reacted to Gilligan's broadcast, and his increasing anger at the media and his treatment by it, made Blair realise the time had finally come for him to go. 'They had both reached the conclusion that it had gone too far,' said one aide.[116] Campbell's value was long past. His aggression with the media, if necessary once, was no longer needed and it damaged Blair. So too did Campbell's obsession with the short-term when what Blair needed was someone at his shoulder urging him to think about policy, not presentation. With Campbell still there, Blair would never blossom fully as a person or as Prime Minister.

Blair and Campbell agreed that his retirement should be announced on the day after Blair gave evidence to the Hutton Inquiry, Friday 29 August. Blair knew that the press would give him a critical send-off, and his own words about him were nuanced, 'He is a strong character who can make enemies, but those who know him best like him best.' Campbell's friends think he never fully recovered from the shock of Kelly's death.[117] For Blair himself, the shock of Kelly's death would also linger. Resolution had to be found on a personal level. In great secrecy, he and Cherie met Kelly's widow Janice and daughter at Chequers. 'Tony wanted to meet them and to say how sorry he was about what had happened,' said one confidante.[118]

Re-thinking the Power House

Within two years of the General Election, Blair's Number 10 and Cabinet team, on which the success of the second term had been predicted, had collapsed. Hunter left in late 2001, now to be joined by Campbell, Milburn, Irvine and, at the end of the year, Heywood. Simon Stevens, Number 10's health expert, was shortly to depart. Adonis's future was uncertain. By the summer, relations with Brown had reached their lowest point. Brown had become a figure who he no longer trusted and who he believed was determined to do him down. A friend had been replaced by an avowed enemy. Of all the departures, the one Blair minded the most – albeit for the wrong reasons – was Campbell's. 'He was his greatest confidant, his strategist, his PR adviser, his mate, his ally and his counsellor,' said Milburn.[119] He galvanised Number 10 and gave it focus, for better or worse: 'He was a big character – his moods could influence the building one way or another.'[120] But he had become over-powerful. Someone would be needed to take his place, or drift, never far away since 2001, would become even more marked.

Since the spring, Morgan and Political Secretary McFadden had become concerned about the growing opposition to Blair from within the PLP. Adonis became the chief target of hostility from within Number 10 and outside. Those who had never been comfortable with his appointment as head of policy in 2001 now blamed him (rightly) for being the prime influence on Blair's radical thinking on the public services. Attacking him was a way of attacking Blair. It was not only the backbenchers who were challenging Blair's authority. He had to pull back from introducing three-year devolution of fund-raising to schools because he did not believe he would get it past Brown and Prescott in Cabinet: 'He was finding it very hard getting things through that summer,' said Barber. 'If he was not certain of success in Cabinet, he would pull back.'[121]

Blair's premiership was in danger. He had sustained two potentially serious challenges. Cook's resignation on 17 March presented for the first time in his premiership the possibility of a serious heavyweight focus for dissent within the PLP. But Cook deliberately chose not to act as Geoffrey Howe had with Thatcher, and although his resignation speech was a powerful critique of Blair's approach on Iraq, it was a *sotto* exit the day before the major Iraq debate in the House of Commons. Had he spoken soon after Blair in the debate, his resignation would have had a very different impact. Cook had authority, but he never chose to strike or let himself become the focus of dissent. Short had missed her chance of a devastating impact by not resigning on the cusp of war: when she eventually resigned on 12 May she had lost credibility.

The role of spearheading dissent passed to the Brownites. From the spring onwards, and particularly after his dismissal on 12 June, Nick Brown, coupled by George Mudie, led the dissenters. Their roles as Blair's initial Chief Whip and Deputy Chief Whip gave them added leverage within the PLP. What the growing numbers of anti-Blair MPs lacked at this stage, however, was an obvious leader. Brown played the loyalist, at least (Number 10 thought) on the surface. Other potential challengers like Michael Meacher were still in the government. Unrest in the party focused on the dislike of Blair's public service reforms, particularly foundation trusts and tuition fees. But Kelly's death pushed Iraq to near the top of the PLP's concerns about Blair, piling on pressure in the immediate pre-summer period, which was always frenetic. Some colleagues thought the end of July was the lowest they had ever seen the Prime Minister.[122] 'I could feel . . . him destroying himself physically and emotionally. The strain was palpable,' a Cabinet ally recalled.[123]

Late July was traditionally when Blair sat down with his team to conduct brain-storming sessions at Chequers about the autumn, and themes for the party conference and beyond. With Campbell about to depart, Blair felt at such a time he had no choice but to turn to the one member of his 'quartet' who was available: twice-departed Peter Mandelson, whose strengths as a communicator and strategist he hoped would help compensate for Campbell's loss. Mandelson shared the view that Adonis had to go and Matthew Taylor, then running the Institute for Public Policy Research (IPPR), be brought in to run policy, along with Geoff Mulgan, then heading the strategy unit. Taylor was close to Morgan, and well-regarded by mainstream Labour MPs: he was an authentic Labourite in a way that Adonis and Stevens were not. Adonis, worried that the panic gripping those around Blair was about to lead to the abandonment of public service reform, offered Blair his resignation at the end of July. Adonis was not a political operator and others were left to defend him, notably Powell, who argued that he was needed as the best interpreter of the Prime Minister's wishes and that the Policy Directorate did not need yet more figures who 'understood Labour Party politics'. Some close to Blair even questioned whether Powell was 'the right person to be Chief of Staff' on the grounds that he lacked the strategic ability to manage Number 10 for him as Prime Minister.[124] Birt was one of the most scathing about Number 10's lack of strategy: with his experience of managing the BBC behind him, he thought Number 10 was amateurish.[125] Birt's views aroused strong feelings: Number 10 was divided on how it should be run, and over the direction of policy. If Powell, Adonis and Stevens lay on the progressive wing of Number 10, on the other was Morgan, McFadden, Campbell and his partner, Fiona Millar, who had also had enough and was to quit. Millar's departure was also full of regret. She had protected Cherie for many years with some conspicuous success, never more so than over the handling of the birth of Leo. But she resented the creeping influence of Carole Caplin, which reached a climax during the Bristol flats débâcle, and Cherie's refusal to dispense with Caplin after it. The final straw was Cherie's defiantly letting *Marie Claire* magazine photograph Caplin applying lipstick to her mouth while sitting on her conjugal bed, the epitome of all Millar had fought to avoid.[126]

Blair turned to Mandelson and Birt in July to write him a long dossier on how to 'sharpen up' the whole Number 10 operation, which was 'to be on his desk' on his return from holiday.[127] They laboured hard throughout August to produce a blue folder with some twenty-five appendices, outlining not only how Number 10 could operate better in the future but also how the strategy could be improved over the following five years. On 2 August 2003, Blair became the longest continuous-serving Labour Prime Minister, surpassing Clement Attlee's 1945–51 record, which cast an unwelcome spotlight on the state of his achievements to date. Unfavourable comment too was made on his holiday location, Cliff Richards' home in Barbados. The holiday did at least provide the tonic Blair badly needed: 'It vastly energised him – he came back wanting to go flat out.'[128] As soon as Blair returned, the dossier's authors, along with Heywood and Powell, went to Chequers to discuss it with him. He expressed himself 'pleased' with the report ('You knew that you had arrived in the close team if Blair didn't thank you').[129] Blair also persuaded Adonis to remain, but to move 'sideways' to oversee education and public service reform within the Policy Directorate.

Number 10's communications operations post-Campbell was one of the topics tackled in the summer dossier. The question neatly coincided with the publication of the Phillis report into improvements in government communications. David Hill was an obvious and successful choice to take over from Campbell, known to Blair for twenty years, and with long and deep roots in the Labour Party, but also trusted and respected by journalists. A more measured figure than Campbell, though lacking his charisma, ambition and speech-writing skills, Blair thought him none the worse for that. 'The perception of Number 10 as a place of spin had to change, and be put on a calmer footing,' Hill said.[130] To help improve co-ordination further, the dossier proposed a plethora of meetings: at 8 A.M. for all Number 10 unit heads; Monday afternoons, chaired by Mandelson, on short-term strategy; and on Wednesdays with Blair to review and plan longer-term strategy. These were in addition to the regular Monday morning meetings in the den, a staple of Blair's since 1997. The intellect and experience of the fathers of this new regime were not in doubt. But in practice the new grid did not survive long as the politics changed, and Blair's erratic management style proved as impervious as ever to systematic planning. 'Virtually none of the Birt–Mandelson proposals were ever implemented,' recalled one aide.[131] Many in Number 10 also thought Mandelson's return was 'a bit of a joke and embarrassing'.[132] Things had moved on since the heroic early days of New Labour. 'He chaired the meetings and treated everybody like small children,' recalled one aide. 'We were deeply irritated by him, but not scared of him. He'd lost his hold.'[133] Further confusion came because Taylor thought he had been appointed to take over from Adonis[134] and Mulgan to run both policy and strategy.[135] With Heywood not leaving until the end of the year, and Adonis with ambitions that extended far beyond education – and as sceptical of Mulgan's and Taylor's Labourite politics as they were of his – it had all the ingredients for another Number 10 fudge. A more successful appointment was making Pat McFadden director of political operations, with a brief to rebuild relations with the party. Blair had rarely found a steadier hand.

'Five-year plans', the brainchild of Birt, were a successful innovation proposed in the August document. He believed, two years after the General Election, that the initial focus had begun to fade and fresh impetus was required.[136] Indeed, bar the passage of the foundation hospitals and tuition fees legislation, much of the rather thin 2001–03 agenda had been completed. Providing a forum for backbenchers to become 'reconnected' with drawing up the policy agenda was an obvious attraction, though modernisers worried it carried with it the 'risk of retrenchment'.[137] In September, a series of meetings took place at Chequers and Number 10 to discuss the five-year plan model, which it was decided should encompass education, health, the Home Office and pensions. Many of Number 10's 'old guard' wanted the Treasury excluded from the process, especially following their attrition over foundation trusts and school reform, arguing that its habit of briefing the press against anything they did not like would stymie the process. It would be futile to exclude the Treasury, countered Taylor, Mulgan and Heywood, as Number 10 would ultimately need its support. A compromise was reached whereby the Treasury would be treated in similar fashion to the way it treated Number 10 on Budget and spending plans: 'Two weeks before we were shown half of what was going to be in it, a week before we were shown more, and a couple of days before the announcement we more or less got the whole lot.'[138] Involving the Cabinet fully in the plans was to be another strategy to circumvent Treasury obstructionism, as well as signalling a return to Cabinet government to counter the criticism that Blair was becoming too presidential and was replacing Cabinet government by 'sofa government' or 'denocracy', i.e., decision-making in 'the den'.

The 'big conversation', a further initiative, this time authored by Taylor, sought to 'reconnect' Number 10 with the party. The modernisers in Number 10 again sniffed retrenchment, and worried that the big conversation would be a device to water down Blair's radical zeal. Such fears proved misplaced. Taylor posed a series of questions designed to provoke new policies. The format appealed to Blair and played to his great strength of talking openly with people and debating ideas with them, which he was to do in open meetings across Britain. 'What we wanted to do was encourage people to engage with us,' said the aide in charge of the exercise.[139] Blair launched the big conversation in his party conference speech at Bournemouth on 30 September. To try to build bridges with the party, the tag 'New Labour' was subtly down-played at the conference while the prefix 'new' was dropped altogether from party membership cards. Blair was in defiant mood as he approached the conference. His principal aim was to show that the government was not being overwhelmed by the Hutton Inquiry, or by the Iraq war, and that he was uniquely capable of driving it ahead. On Sunday 28 September, in his pre-conference interview on television's *Breakfast With Frost*, he admitted that 'we are in a fight' over public services and Iraq. As soon as the interview was over he told Hyman, 'I just want to get on with the speech.'[140]

On the Monday, with Blair absent from the conference at the funeral of Lords Leader Gareth Williams, Brown delivered a *coup de théâtre*. Parodying Blair's soundbite at the 2002 party conference 'We're best when we are at our boldest', he ended his speech with: 'We are . . . best when we are Labour'. 'Gordon was saying to the world, "I'm here, I'm ready, I've won",' said one of his close followers. 'It was the speech that he had been planning to give ever since he became Chancellor in 1997.'[141] Brown believed that he had won 'on the battlefield of ideas, personality, policy and even publicity'. 'He saw himself as a palpably stronger figure than the shrunken and weakened Prime Minister. This was his moment.'[142] Another Brownite expounded on his great fear. He never doubted that he would succeed: his obsession, 'his nightmare', was that he would inherit a shell of a party that had effectively been destroyed by Blair. 'In the speech he was reaching out to the party's heartlands, to the unions, and alerting them.'[143] Kelly's death and the setting up of Hutton, the Brown camp had concluded, had fatally wounded Blair. It would only need one more thrust and he would be finished. Brown basked in the applause of the audience, and his camp were delighted by the speech's reception. When one of Brown's aides was asked why he had referred to 'Labour' forty times in the speech, but never once to 'new' Labour, the response was, bristling with confidence, 'It was a long speech: something had to give.'[144]

Number 10 was alarmed. How should they respond? First up, they let it be known that they believed Brown had made a significant mistake in trying to engineer a coalition of the left and centre-left against Blair. He had become the champion of the left, the trade unions, Compass and 'a vast array of disparate groups of the dispossessed and never possessed'.[145] Blair feigned a relaxed manner when, returning from the funeral, he commented that it was not an ignoble ambition of Brown's to be Prime Minister. His aides were seething: they thought Brown's speech at best 'crass and clumsy' and at worst treacherous.[146] Reports filtered back to them that Yvette Cooper had been one of those whipping up support at the conference against foundation trusts,[147] while Nick Brown was said to be mobilising opposition to tuition fees. Gordon Brown protested, as he always did, that he was not responsible for any of these actions. All eyes were on Blair to see how he would respond to that first ever challenge to his leadership.

He asked his aides to research a biblical quotation that was in his mind; it was Proverbs 24, v. 10: 'If thou faint in the day of adversity, thy strength is small.'[148] He drew inspiration from this message to justify his uncompromising stance on Iraq and public service reform. 'I would make the same decision on Iraq again today,' he said. At one point he appeared close to tears: 'During the past few months on Iraq, I have received letters from parents whose sons have died as soldiers. One who believed their son had died in vain and hating me for my decision. Another, a beautiful letter, said . . . though their son was dead, whom they loved dearly, they still thought it was right.' Nor would Blair pull back from his thrust on public service reform, regardless of opposition within the party: 'I don't have a reverse gear.' The over-riding tone of his speech, however, was conciliatory, which played well with both Blairites and mainstream Labour voters, and helped him win them back round. He warned them of the real dangers of dissent when he spoke about how Labour's history had been characterised by long periods of opposition, punctuated by only brief periods of government which were then curtailed by internal divisions and accusations that the leadership had 'betrayed' the party. Avoid such accusations against him now, he was saying, if a third election victory was to be won.

Was it enough? Number 10 judged that he had seen off the Brownite challenge and made the case, firmly but reasonably, for moving ahead with the reform agenda. The party conference paved the way for the Queen's Speech on 27 November, which introduced what was expected to be the last full parliamentary session before the next General Election. The most controversial item was the Higher Education Bill, which introduced top-up fees, with other major Bills on asylum and immigration. Number 10 expected Hutton to report in late November. It hoped that its publication would provide 'a major cathartic moment', allowing it at last to leave WMD dossiers and spin behind, and move forward confidently with a new agenda into Christmas and the New Year. It hoped, after a terrible six months, that the worst was over.

Admiralty House Dinner – Black or Brown?: November 2003

The aspect of Blair's kitchen Cabinet reshuffle that spread most alarm in the Brown camp was the return centre-stage of the hated and mistrusted Mandelson, who they saw as behind every slur and reversal from day one of Blair's premiership. 'He's all over Tony like a cheap suit; Gordon hates his guts,' was the uncompromising verdict of one Brownite. Even more cuttingly (and ahistorically), 'he's like a camp version of Rasputin: every time you think he's dead he comes back'.[149] The arrival in Number 10 of Taylor and Mulgan did nothing to compensate for his arrival, even though Taylor was not a Blairite and Mulgan had earlier worked for Brown. Balls regarded Mulgan as quirky and jargon-ridden and Brown's camp refused outright to deal with Taylor. The only person who they would continue to engage with in Number 10 was Heywood.[150] 'The mood music between Brown and Blair was, post-conference, very bad,' said one in Blair's camp.[151] Balls had long been the focus of Number 10's suspicions: Blair had held discussions with Brown on what he regarded as Balls's inappropriate behaviour and exalted position. It had no effect.[152] By the autumn of 2003, Number 10's focus had changed anyway from a loathing of Brown's acolytes, principally Balls, to Brown himself. 'Gordon was a bully in all kinds of ways, sending out his hacks to brief against Number 10, pretending he wasn't doing so, and putting all kinds of pressure on MPs. The damage he did was immense,' said one Blairite.[153] In October, Brown positioned himself as a sceptic in relation to the plan for identity cards, advocated by his foe, the one remaining 'big four' delivery minister of 2001, Blunkett. The relationship between Blair and Brown remained remarkably tense. Blair bided his time. It was obvious he would strike. No one knew when or how. 'You must retaliate and show you are not weak,' was how one close Cabinet minister described his mindset.[154]

Blair's response came on 5 November, when he had the opportunity to make three nominations to Labour's NEC: he proposed Ian McCartney, the party chairman, Hazel Blears and the Brownite minister, Douglas Alexander. Brown was excluded and only confirmed the news when he visited the Labour Party website. The story rapidly moved into brief and counter-brief. Brown felt he had been 'taken advantage of' while on paternity leave for his son, John, born on 17 October, it was said.[155] Number 10 feigned surprise that Brown even wanted to be on the NEC in the first place. 'The notion that Gordon suddenly wanted to be on the NEC so that he could come along and speak at a meeting just irritated him,' said an aide. Blair's response was 'this is ridiculous'.[156] Number 10 said that Blair had always made it clear that he would not nominate Brown. This may have been true, but it was also a snub, and was taken as such by the Brown camp.[157] On television the following day, Brown bounced back and defiantly made it clear that he 'expected to be put in charge once again of Labour's General Election campaign', which he believed the Granita deal of 1994 entitled him to.[158] Blair did not react at first. It was the same day that Michael Howard was confirmed as Conservative Party leader. Number 10 put out that Blair respected Howard since they had sparred together ten years earlier when Blair was Shadow Home Secretary, and he expected Howard to provide far firmer leadership than the departed Duncan Smith. In fact, Howard's succession was regarded with 'tremendous enthusiasm' by a 'delighted' Number 10. Blair was convinced that Howard would push the Tories to the right – which, after an initial speech indicating that he would be a pragmatic leader, he did.

At Cabinet that morning, Brown's counter-attack went down badly, as did his scathing criticism of Blunkett's case for ID cards. 'Gordon more or less told us that if we were going to support this, we'd better look at our own budgets in the spending round that was coming up. It was appalling bullying by the Chancellor,' said one Cabinet minister.[159] Brown's behaviour was placing Cabinet ministers in an impossible dilemma: whereas in the first term, the Treasury and Number 10 had worked together for most of the time, it was obvious to all that a deep fissure had now opened up. 'It confused Whitehall no end. Secretaries of State had to achieve their core aim of getting their money, but should they try to please Number 10 or the Treasury? It was very bad,' said a free-thinking Treasury official.[160]

On 6 November, to resolve the impasse, Prescott had Brown and Blair to dinner at his residence in Admiralty House, on Whitehall between Downing Street and Trafalgar Square. Much was made by the media of this as a one-off event, but while it was important, it was only one of several such gatherings between the three men, sometimes over a drink and food, at Admiralty House, Number 10 or at Number 11. The first time they met was at Prescott's official residence at Dorneywood, on 24 February 2002, when Blair and Brown were at odds over academies and foundation trusts, after the relationship first started to deteriorate.[161] 'I invited them both to come along and have a chat to me about the politics, and putting their heads together.'[162] Prescott was also brought in as a mediator in early May 2003 to help quell the row over the Euro: he codenamed the meetings 'Bed and Breakfast', standing for Blair and Brown.[163] 'Tony would moan about them, and found them a chore, but he could also see their purpose,' said one Number 10 aide.[164] Prescott, in contrast, was in his element, and was left to brief about them to the press. 'John rather liked to see himself in the role of peacemaker,' said one Number 10 aide.[165] He saw himself as the conscience of the Labour

Party, with a unique role in holding the party together and preventing it splitting into two camps. Blair had a soft spot for Prescott: 'The fact that Prezza loathed Balls, as he did almost all political advisers, also commended him to Number 10.'[166] Blair knew he was not personally happy with the 'choice and diversity' agenda, but he felt he could always win him over by ensuring that the proper processes were followed by taking decisions through Cabinet and Cabinet committees.[167] In the second term, Prescott was vital to Blair. Without his support he would have fallen.

Initially, the intention on 6 November had been to discuss the Queen's Speech and the political outlook in the run-up to the New Year. But the spat over the NEC and Brown's reaction gave the meeting added piquancy. The Brown camp firmly believe that Blair said, 'I'm not going to turn this round for a very long time, therefore I'm going to stand down before the election. I need your help to get me through the next year.'[168] 'Pure fantasy,' say the Blairites. One pressed him: 'I kept asking him afterwards, "Are you sure you didn't say it?", and he kept on saying again and again "No".'[169] Brown had long said, 'Blair's got seven years in power, and that's enough. He will win two elections and then that's it, and he will pass it on.' Brown was so clear in his mind that Blair would do this that he did not always read the signals correctly.

So what was Blair's thinking about his future? Much of Blair's urgency with his domestic agenda after 2001 was because he might only have two or three years to make a difference, should he depart some time in 2004. But he was going on his own terms. At a dinner between the two men in December 2001, Blair had told Brown that 'he still believed he was easily the best person to follow him, but he was not going to support him in circumstances where he felt he was being forced out'.[170] He toyed with the idea of pre-announcing his departure in early 2002, but mothballed the idea that summer. The Euro came and went as a possible issue where he could resign after a referendum 'yes' vote. A heart flutter in October 2003 that required a brief hospital visit was more significant than was admitted at the time. Doctors blamed it on too much coffee, but it certainly contributed to the state of anxiety in Blair's mind about his health. Did anxieties about his health influence what he told Brown and Prescott that evening?

But Blair clearly gave Brown *some* understanding: 'The higher up the food chain that you go to those close to Blair's mind, the more likely they are to admit that their boss did say something,' said a mutual friend of both men.[171] After all, he had been thinking for some time about leaving before another election. Prescott believes Blair said he would go sooner rather than later, and he would 'endorse Brown as his successor, thereby reducing the risk of a contested take-over'.[172] Morgan asserts he would have been thinking of 2005, 'but he would have said nothing categorical about a date'.[173] What is clear is that the three agreed that a public statement should be made drawing a line under the acrimony of the week that had just ended. Brown should be allowed to attend NEC meetings whenever he chose, and was to be placed in charge of the coming election campaign. In return, he would cease to attack Blair's policy in public.[174] It was the thinnest of compromises. Brown went back and told his supporters to prepare to take over Number 10 in the following year. The dinner had settled nothing, although it did lead to a brief period of conciliation between the two camps.[175] It was short-lived. When Blair was to think about it, would he really conclude he had achieved enough to quit before he had to? The skirmishes in the first term, which had become battles in 2001–03, were now set to become open warfare.

9

The Descent

November 2003–April 2004

The period from the summer of 2003 to the summer of 2004 proved the most difficult year of Blair's premiership. It saw two intensely bruising parliamentary battles on foundation hospitals and tuition fees, the loss of the initiative in Iraq and forced Blair to contend with enduring hostility, if not contempt, in the country at large. Number 10 was continually under the spotlight from two separate inquiries into Iraq. Relations with Brown continued to be draining. Despite these difficulties, some Number 10 insiders recall a sense of resilient optimism, of 'fun' even, in Downing Street as they rode out these storms and stayed ahead in the polls. But, in private, Blair's mood was darkening. After the long-awaited Hutton Inquiry into the death of David Kelly failed to clear the air, he began to wonder whether it might not be better for him and the party if he simply quitted Downing Street.

Iraq Wobbles, Bush Visits: August–December 2003

Tony Blair returned from holiday in late August to find Iraq in real difficulty. For the first time, the word 'insurgency' began to dominate the airwaves. On 19 August there was particularly worrying news: UN Headquarters at the Canal Hotel in Baghdad had been hit by a massive truck bomb, killing twenty-three people, including the UN's chief envoy to Iraq, Sergio Vieira de Mello. 'We're in trouble here,' Paul Bremer told his staff. 'The terrorists have arrived in a deadly serious way.'[1] On 29 August, the Iman Ali mosque in Najaf was bombed, leaving eighty-three dead. 'The scale of bombing came as a real blow to us,' said a Number 10 aide.[2] On 22 September a second car bomb exploded outside the central Baghdad hotel housing relocated UN staff. Kofi Annan concluded that a UN presence in Iraq had become untenable: shortly afterwards the UN's 600 staff withdrew. 'The departure of the UN was even more serious than it appeared at the time: lack of UN cover made the whole post-war allied operation much more difficult,' said the FCO's Middle East Director, Edward Chaplin.[3] Blair had pressed hard for the UN to be involved. It had come to nothing. The British and the Americans were now effectively on their own.

Nigel Sheinwald succeeded Manning as foreign policy adviser in Number 10 that August, at a time of dawning realisation that Britain was going to be in Iraq for the long haul. 'We have a massive problem on our hands,' he concluded after the bombing of the UN building and other attacks. 'There will be no easy solutions.'[4] Blair's response was to push for more information from the ground and more action. Sheinwald and Sawers, now back in the FCO, spoke regularly to Jeremy Greenstock, who had left the UN to become the senior British figure in Iraq from September.[5] Real frustration was evident in Number 10: '"Why aren't you doing more, why isn't the electricity working, why isn't security working?" Blair would ask. There was a sense that if only we would put more effort into it then it would become right.'[6] 'He was tearing his hair from time to time at things that couldn't be done more quickly,' recalled Greenstock.[7] But in Baghdad, the American military were in control, and the British continued to have little leverage. This worried Blair deeply. For him, the priority for Iraq had shifted from the legitimacy of the invasion to the competence of the allies to be nation-builders. It was essential, he believed, to string together the economic, political and military strands of the occupation. His anxiety remained that the US lacked a suitable command structure to carry it out. 'We tried every trick in the book to persuade them to create an effective structure,' recalled one senior official, 'but instead we were seeing the American machine flounder.'[8] To the south, Number 10 worried about the shaky situation in Basra, and badgered the British military about progress. 'Nigel [Sheinwald] does outrage very well,' recalled Rob Fry.[9] The military too, were frustrated by their inability to quell the insurgency. 'We were struggling to find the levers to pull, but it was against a background of disunity and uncertainty. They were difficult times.'[10]

Blair realised he needed to engage Bush himself if nation-building was to make real progress in Iraq. The quest was aided by a technological innovation that would shape the Bush–Blair relationship for the remainder of his time in Downing Street: the video telephone conference (VTC). VTCs made use of large flat-screen monitors in the White House and Number 10 to allow the participants to see as well as hear each other. The first VTC took place in July 2003 and by the autumn they had become a regular means of communication.[11] Lasting forty-five to fifty minutes, they took place at least fortnightly and often weekly, usually around Tuesday lunchtime, UK time.[12] Bush would be joined by Cheney, the National Security Adviser (Rice, then Hadley) and his Chief of Staff (Andy Card, then Josh Bolten). Blair was accompanied by Sheinwald and Powell. Other officials would join the calls on an *ad hoc* basis and traditional memos (not verbatim transcripts) would be circulated promptly.[13] For over three years, Blair was the only leader with whom Bush would hold these sessions. Only in late 2006 did the White House set up a similar system with the new German Chancellor, Angela Merkel. No other leader had such privileged access.[14] Speaking with the President regularly over so many years led to a certain intimacy: 'The body language was always very friendly. These were people who knew each other well.'[15] 'Typically Bush would start off by saying something like, "Hi buddy, how's it going? I see you've had problems with X",' recalled one British official, 'but in the end the Prime Minister ended up speaking more.'[16] According to Stephen Hadley, the VTCs were less formal venues and more an 'opportunity to share perspectives on problems and develop a common approach'.[17] 'The relationship the Prime Minister had with President Bush gave him an opportunity to get things into his mind and vice versa,' recalled Donald Rumsfeld. 'It works both ways when you have that kind of a friendly and confident relationship.'[18] 'Quite often the PM would put something to the President,' recalled one Downing Street aide, 'and Bush would say, "Okay, I'll think about that." And then you would know you'd won half the battle.'[19] But, for all the warmth and the closeness, was winning 'half the battle' enough?

Blair hoped the VTCs would give him leverage with the President in his concerns about post-war Iraq.[20] His approach was non-confrontational. 'On no occasion did Blair say, "Look, George, we've got a real problem here and this is what we have got to do",' recalled one witness. 'It was always much more, "Well, George, what do you think we can do about this?"'[21] An exception came on concerns over communications from the ground in Iraq. In one VTC exchange, Blair berated Bush, 'Look, we're not getting the message across.' Bush replied smartly: 'We'll get on to it. Condi, we've got to fix this.' He told Rice that 'if we don't get this improved by December then we'll hand over the communications responsibility to the UK'. But the transfer did not happen. Blair did not push for it, and neither did Bush.[22] Part of the problem was that Bush's own writ did not run as far in Washington as he would have liked, and neither did Number 10's reach extend into the Pentagon, where Rumsfeld continued to take his own decisions. 'We couldn't get the Americans to see what they needed to do,' said a senior official.[23] Blair found the Pentagon unreceptive to his enthusiasm for internationalising the reconstruction of Iraq, which became an ever greater priority after Annan's decision to quit Iraq in the early autumn. Blair badly wanted wider US support as he struggled to engage the international community. On 23 October, Blair argued strongly at the 'Donors' Conference' in Madrid that, whatever different countries thought of the initial invasion, it was now their duty to help put Iraq back on its feet and establish a proper democracy. But of a desired target of $56 billion, only $33 billion was raised, most of it in pledges that never came through.[24]

Britain's continuing involvement in Iraq was losing popular support. Whereas 51 per cent polled by ICM thought the war was justified in mid-July, by late September it had fallen to 38 per cent. It provided an unsettling backdrop to Bush's State visit to Britain in November, the first – surprisingly – since President Woodrow Wilson in 1918. For a US President to visit Britain was not unusual. Ronald Reagan had done so three times as President, staying at Windsor Castle in 1982 and addressing MPs in the Royal Gallery at Westminster. But in the past these trips had always been arranged as 'official visits', one rank below a 'State visit', the most formal engagement in protocol terms. In the aftermath of 9/11, but before the Iraq war, Blair had been keen to demonstrate Britain's solidarity with America and thus set wheels in motion for a 'State visit', in the hope that it would appear more significant than previous Presidential visits.[25] These plans were now coming to fruition in rather different circumstances to those at their conception. From the start, the Americans accepted that, given Bush's and his war's unpopularity, the visit would have to be carefully controlled: 'A lot of the traditional trappings of a State visit fell off the radar screen as possibilities fairly early on,' admitted one State Department official.[26] But for Washington, the visit was about more than ceremony. 'It was a vital operational meeting,' recalled one of Bush's top advisers. 'There was around this time a sober realisation of the depth and breadth of damage inside Iraq and how difficult it would be to make the transition to democracy. The visit was a chance, at a critical moment, to reaffirm our joint strategy.'[27]

Blair knew that many in Britain were deeply unhappy at the prospect of Bush arriving on British soil, and addressed the issue head-on at the Lord Mayor's Banquet on 10 November. 'A battle of seminal importance for the twenty-first century' was being played out in Iraq – the battle for democracy, he said, arguing that it was exactly the right time for Britain's ally to visit.[28] Bush's sojourn was unpopular even in some quarters of Number 10: 'The more the problems started to develop on Iraq, the less we wanted to be constantly attached to Bush,' said one aide.[29] Morgan (and Campbell before he left at the end of August) were especially cool, given the antipathy in the party to the war and to Bush. They tried unsuccessfully to limit the duration of the visit, and the time Bush spent with Blair, fearing the administration would exploit the visit for images to bolster the President's flagging ratings ahead of the presidential election in November 2004. Blair refused to budge. Some in Number 10 felt he was deliberately digging his heels in and being perverse: 'He has this streak in him when he says, "I'm not going to let them stop me: if you think I'm going to give in because of public opinion, you're quite wrong."' They noticed a strange contradiction in him: on one level highly attuned to what his advisers thought, yet on another stubborn and perverse.[30] On 15 November, just before Bush arrived, came a very welcome boost. An agreement was signed between the Coalition Provisional Authority (CPA), run by the allies, and the Iraqi Interim Governing Council (IGC), which called for the transfer of sovereignty to a new Iraqi government by 30 June 2004. Perhaps, Blair hoped, there might still be light at the end of the tunnel.

On 19 November, the first full day of the State visit, the anti-war demonstrations were smaller than feared. George and Laura Bush attended a lunchtime banquet with the Queen, reportedly cooked by Nigella Lawson, before the President went on to give a speech at the Banqueting House laying out a 'forward strategy for freedom'. The speech stressed the importance of encouraging democracy in the Middle East as part of the war on terror and providing encouraging language for Blair on the Israeli–Palestinian conflict: 'We seek a viable, independent state for the Palestinian people,' Bush declared, 'who have been betrayed by others for too long.'[31] 'It was seen by us as one of the President's more important foreign policy speeches,' recalled a senior administration official.[32] Bush also met families who had lost loved-ones on 9/11 to express his appreciation for their sacrifice. The President and First Lady then attended the state banquet in their honour at

Buckingham Palace that evening, with Andrew Lloyd Webber performing at the piano, which went down very well with the President's party.[33] The smooth choreography was rudely disturbed the next day, however, when two bombs exploded at the British Consulate in Istanbul, killing the British Consul-General and twenty-six others.

Blair was chairing the Thursday Cabinet when the news came through. An emergency meeting of COBRA was called immediately. Scarlett and Dearlove attended to review the risks to Britons at home and abroad, and to debate whether al-Qaeda were responsible. It was decided that Straw would leave for Turkey the next day. Bush was at Westminster Abbey visiting the tomb of the Unknown Warrior when he heard the news. Fifteen minutes later his motorcade was on its way to Downing Street, where Blair greeted him. As both men posed for photographers on the steps of Number 10, Bush laid his hand on Blair's shoulder in front of the cameras in a gesture of solidarity.[34] 'The bombing cast a shadow over the rest of the visit,' recalled Karl Rove, 'and clearly summed up the threat about which the President had spoken the day before.'[35] Suspicions that the bomb had been timed to coincide with the President's visit were rapidly confirmed, reigniting the debate about whether British involvement in Iraq had decreased or increased the risk to British citizens from terrorism. Blair was stoical, maintaining, implausibly, that there was no connection. To many, the connection was undeniable: Blair's adventurism had bought Britons into the front line. That afternoon, in the largest mid-week protest in British history, an estimated 300,000 demonstrators marched across Westminster Bridge and on to Trafalgar Square, where an eighteen-foot statue of Bush was pulled down to thunderous cheers in conscious emulation of the iconic felling of Saddam's statue in the immediate aftermath of hostilities in Baghdad.[36]

The 'working' part of the trip took place that day in Downing Street. 'We worked really hard to counteract the notion that Blair was just the poodle sitting on Bush's lap,' said Elizabeth Jones.[37] Part of this effort included a round-table discussion on HIV/AIDS, an important topic to Blair, hosted jointly by both men, and said to be 'full of energy'.[38] Over a working lunch, they talked at length about Putin. Blair started: 'He's really getting off track, don't you think, George?'[39] Bush agreed. They then 'waxed lyrical' about his growing authoritarian tendencies, until Rice stepped in. 'But he's really trying,' she said, launching into an eloquent defence of the Russian President. 'Come off it, Condi,' said Bush.[40] 'They both then turned to her,' recalled one witness, 'and said "No, we've got the measure of this guy; he's a problem".'[41] It was 'a surprisingly substantive discussion', recalled one witness.[42] There was less common ground, though, when they got on to Iraq, where Bush's enthusiasm for a greater UN role remained limited. The fate of the nine British citizens held at Guantánamo Bay, Cuba, also provided a fault-line: Blair wanted the release of some of the detainees, in part to show his influence with the President. Straw had also been battering away. Colin Powell intervened directly with Bush after Straw's intense lobbying, but to no avail: 'I hear you, Jack,' he would say. 'I'm trying, I'm trying, but I can't make any headway.'[43] It was only in March 2004 that the first of the British detainees were returned.

On 21 November, Bush's final day in the UK, The President received a formal farewell from the Queen at Buckingham Palace before flying on Air Force One to the north of England and then on to Sedgefield, the part of the trip critics in the den thought particularly unnecessary. Two presidential helicopters swooped down on the residents of Trimdon supported by three Apache helicopters. It was 'awesome', said Blair's agent, John Burton.[44] In the unlikely venue of the Dun Cow pub in Sedgefield village, the teetotal Bush found himself in a 'snug' with Blair's most loyal local party supporters. 'We couldn't believe we were spending an hour and a half with the President of the United States, talking about all kinds of things,' said Burton.[45] The menu of potato soup, fish and chips and lemon brûlé contrasted with the *Délice de Flétan Rôti aux Herbes* and *Suprême de Poulet Fermier au Basilic*, washed down with 1996 Puligny-Montrachet and 1995 Veuve Clicquot, at the state banquet at Buckingham Palace. But Bush seemed pleased, as he was by the schoolchildren waving the American flag at Sedgefield Community College after lunch. In the distance, securely behind barriers one hundred metres away, the protestors shouted out anti-war slogans. For the Americans the State visit had been a success. The BBC's Justin Webb observed Karl Rove with a broad smile on his face: 'Domestically, for the President, the pictures, images and progress he's made in solidifying his relationship with Tony Blair were all of a very high order, he thought.'[46] It suited Blair less well. Critics within Number 10 felt vindicated when the trip delivered no immediate results for Britain. No progress on the UN. None on Guantánamo. If Bush's team really were intent on counteracting the poodle image, their efforts made little impact on most people in Britain.

Better news arrived, however, just before Christmas, and from an unexpected quarter. The UK had broken off relations with Libya in 1984 following the shooting of WPC Yvonne Fletcher outside the Libyan Embassy in London. Relations deteriorated further following the seizure of a boat loaded with arms and explosives for the IRA and the blowing-up of the airliner PanAm 103 over Lockerbie on 21 December 1988. Diplomatic relations were restored by Blair on 7 July 1999 and the first British Ambassador to Tripoli for fifteen years arrived in December 1999. The Libyan leader Muammar Gaddafi had decided that Libya had more to gain from co-operating with the West than in maintaining his position as a pariah or 'rogue' state. Relinquishing his WMD plans would be the price for his reacceptance. In the autumn of 2002, as news of the Libyan leader's new thinking reached Downing Street, Blair wrote a letter to Gaddafi, and pressed Bush at Camp David in September to reappraise the Libyan. 'Blair saw this as a major strategic opportunity and worked hard to persuade the President that Gaddafi was sincere,' said Sawers.[47] Bush agreed that the CIA should collaborate with MI6 on it. In March 2003, British intelligence received a phone call to say that Gaddafi was willing to put his WMD on the table and that his son, Saif al-Islam Gaddafi, would be the interlocutor. On Saturday, 15 March 2003, an MI6 agent and a colleague met Saif at a Mayfair hotel. The MI6 man had phoned Manning in Number 10 to ask if Blair would give his agreement to such discussions. It took Blair just three minutes to say 'yes'. 'He was very much for it.'[48]

Three days later, on the day that fighting in Iraq began, a secret plane left London bearing a small team bound for Libya for the first of many meetings between British and American intelligence and the Libyan authorities. The net was drawn very tight. John Bolton, in charge of arms control at the State Department before being appointed UN Ambassador, was kept out of the loop. A proud hardliner on 'rogue states', London feared that Bolton would leak the news and destroy the negotiations.[49] A deal was crystallising that if Gaddafi would publicly admit that he had renounced his WMD programme, Bush and Blair would simultaneously declare that Libya could now bring an end to its international isolation. Gaddafi's big worry was that he would be double-crossed at the last minute. On 18 December, Sheinwald summoned the negotiating team to Downing Street, where a phone call was arranged between Blair and Gaddafi – the first time they had spoken. Blair reassured Gaddafi that if he stuck to the text that had been provided about relinquishing WMD, he would respond immediately. Gaddafi's announcement was due at 9 P.M. the following evening on Libyan television, but a live football match over-ran, creating anxious moments in London and Washington about his sincerity. But at 9:55 P.M. Libyan television confirmed his statement. Blair went before the cameras at 10:15 P.M. from Durham, fifteen minutes before Bush made his own statement. Blair praised Gaddafi's decision as both 'historic' and 'courageous', which he said showed that 'the problems of proliferation can be tackled through discussions and engagement'.[50] A rogue state coming in from the cold on WMD was a rare piece of good news for Blair to offset against the continued difficulties in Iraq.

Foundation Hospitals: The First Brownite Rebellion

The hit Blair took over Iraq seeped into his anxiety domestically, and his ability to win disputes with Brown. Some Brownites had been on the warpath since mid-2003 but the first open rebellion did not come until the row over foundation hospitals. The opening shot had been fired the day after the April 2002 Budget, when the Treasury wrote to Milburn at the Department of Health to say that foundation hospitals would not be able to raise their own money privately, but would have to borrow money as part of government spending. The Treasury's chief concern was that if hospitals were to borrow freely, it would break down public spending discipline and undermine the Private Finance Initiative (PFI).[51] Opposition to Milburn's plans began to grow in the PLP, fuelled by briefings from Brownites which caught the reformers in Number 10 and at Health off-guard: 'We were surprised. We had expected a centre-left policy to offend those on the right, but we didn't foresee that it would also offend those on the centre-left,' said Paul Corrigan, Milburn's special adviser, later to move into Number 10.[52] Milburn was not one to be deterred, and decided to fight Brown. According to one Number 10 record from the end of June, 'Alan has really started to drive NHS reform in the way that we wanted. It has opened debate, created momentum and the policy agenda has started to move in a far more radical direction.'[53]

By July 2002, the Treasury was becoming alarmed. Milburn wanted foundation hospitals to be able to borrow money against their assets to allow them to expand, and for them also to be able to perform some private work.[54] This was, after all, the model used in many other parts of Europe.[55] The Treasury objected on the grounds that if a hospital faced bankruptcy, the government would have to step in to forestall it closing, thereby accepting liability while sacrificing political control. The Department of Health response was that they had already planned for this eventuality by preventing the assets of a local hospital from being sacrificed.[56] Brown argued further that an increase in hospitals treating private patients could lead to inflation in healthcare costs, and he feared that they could become like NHS dental practices, offering a premium service to those who could pay and a basic one to those receiving just the standard NHS service. Milburn countered that there should be a cap on private work to ensure foundation hospitals focused on NHS patients.[57]

This was not only a battle over hospitals and healthcare: there was a larger struggle for the soul of the party. Milburn kicked off the debate with a provocative article in *The Times* in early August, in which he wrote that 'the battle in the party is now between consolidators and transformers'.[58] Labour must break away from its 'overtly centralised fraternalistic history' in its approach to NHS reform, he said, and he warned that Labour risked losing the next General Election if it allowed 'cautious consolidators' to block proposed reforms of public services. The article touched a deep nerve in the Brown camp. 'A deliberate attempt was made to characterise Gordon and the rest of us as centralisers and anti-reform,' said a Brown aide.[59] One line of counter-attack, dubbed 'ludicrous' by Number 10, was that Milburn and Blair were trying to introduce choice and a market into the NHS which would lead to a US-style insurance model.[60] In the vanguard of the defence of the status quo was Blair's first Health Secretary turned arch-critic, Frank Dobson, who spoke on 9 September 2002 at a fringe meeting at the TUC's annual conference in Brighton: 'The Labour government's health policies will mean the end of the NHS . . . It should stop criticising the NHS and stick up for it instead.'[61] The PLP became notably more negative about foundation trusts and Blair's modernising agenda than they had been before the summer recess. Number 10 believed that Brown and his acolytes were deliberately orchestrating the unrest. To counter it, Milburn and his deputies John Hutton and Jacqui Smith regularly saw MPs across the party in an organised campaign to head off the negative propaganda.[62]

Brown and Balls held meetings throughout the summer with Blair and Heywood, in which Brown argued that if foundation trusts went ahead with the free borrowing envisaged in the plan, it would jeopardise the government's economic credibility. In this Kafka-esque world, Brown and Balls began to speculate about Blair's motivation. Balls in particular had no respect for Blair as an economist or as a thinker, and assumed that he merely took his script from Heywood. They suspected, rightly, that Heywood was a sceptic on allowing foundation hospitals to borrow, and that he had conveyed his scepticism to Blair. So why was he banging on about foundation trusts? They concluded the only reason he was doing so was to cause difficulty for Brown.[63] What they did not allow for sufficiently was that Blair had been a genuine advocate of greater choice and independence in health since 2001. An ideological, political and personal gulf now divided the two camps. 'Usually we managed to iron out the differences between the Treasury and Number 10 by Jeremy Heywood and Andrew Adonis sitting down with Ed Miliband and Ed Balls,' said one official, 'but on foundation hospitals this usual channel broke down.'[64] One episode that particularly appalled Blair's aides was the paper sent by Brown to Blair on the eve of the party conference at the end of September 2002, and copied to every member of the Cabinet, setting out in considerable detail the Treasury's objection to foundation hospitals. Blair was furious, as was Prescott.[65] Brown very rarely committed himself to paper. Why had he this time? Number 10 concluded it had been written with the intention that it should be leaked, to maximise concern away from the wider party.[66]

The issue exploded at the party conference, when it was a principal source of conversation and the subject of many debates on the fringe, though not on the floor of the conference itself. At a fringe meeting organised by the IPPR, Milburn declared, 'I passionately believe that it is right to create NHS foundation hospitals . . . A service employing one million people in thousands of hospitals and health centres . . . can't be run from Whitehall.'[67] In the next-door room, Brown presented the opposite view: 'Balance-sheet borrowing usually ends up in the same way, with the government having to pick up the bills.'[68] Balls briefed journalists on 30 September before Brown's speech, saying categorically that 'NHS hospitals would remain in the public sector and that borrowing by foundation hospitals would be included in the public sector accounts'.[69] Blair counter-attacked in his speech, described by journalist Don Macintyre as 'the most uncompromising challenge Mr Blair has issued the party since he stunned it in the same hall nine years ago' over Clause IV.[70] Blair declared that the age of 'monolithic public services' was in the past. Antagonism between both camps rose to fever pitch. Milburn believed that Brown and Balls were briefing not only the press against his plans, but also trade union general secretaries, because they suddenly had a wealth of detailed information about his thinking that 'could only have come from the inside track'.[71] The conflict between Milburn and Brown was intensely personal. 'Hatred' best described how they felt about each other. Suggestions that Blair might prefer Milburn as his successor added to the bitterness. Briefings emanated from the Treasury that Milburn and Blair were trying to introduce privatisation behind the back of the Treasury across all public services. 'Utter nonsense: there was no generic plan, and at all stages we tried to engage the Treasury,' said one Number 10 source.[72]

To break the impasse Heywood hit on the idea of involving Andrew Turnbull, knowing that he 'understood money and was sound'. Turnbull, as Cabinet Secretary, and an ex-Treasury man, did not look favourably on the campaign on foundation hospitals, and suspected that Milburn was pushing it so hard partly 'because he wanted to poke Gordon in the eye'.[73] His mediation came in a series of meetings culminating in one on Monday 7 October with the key permanent secretaries.[74] A compromise was hammered out whereby 'top performing' hospitals would become independent 'public interest' companies for largely NHS patients, though not run or owned by the NHS. They would have the right to borrow money, but the Treasury retained the right to decide how much money they could all borrow (which would be limited), and the money would remain on the public sector balance sheet. The more the hospitals borrowed, however, the less money the Department of Health would have to spend on other parts of the NHS. Critical to winning this point was the argument that if a hospital borrowed too much and went bankrupt, the Treasury would have to bail them out, which justified the Treasury having ultimate authority on borrowing limits.

On Wednesday 9 October, Blair met Brown, Milburn and Prescott in the den to decide whether the Turnbull compromise should be accepted.[75] Tempers flared, with Milburn saying to Brown, 'Don't be so ridiculous, you know full well this isn't policy; it's just politics which you're arguing.' Brown swung round on him and said, 'You shouldn't have written what you wrote in the summer,' referring to his 'consolidator versus transformer' article in *The Times*, which still rankled.[76] Milburn was angry and frustrated that he had no room for manoeuvre, and was annoyed when Blair had phoned him the Sunday before to say, 'We're going to have to reach an accommodation on this.' 'You must be bloody well joking,' he had replied. Blair told him there was no alternative. 'Oh, fine then, you reach an accommodation if that's what you want, but you must understand that we are never going to get all the advantages if we concede on this point.'[77] To Milburn, Blair had caved in.

After the meeting in the den, Simon Stevens was delegated to draft the minute of the decision, which he did with Turnbull at his shoulder. While the meeting was still in progress, Campbell briefed the press about the compromise plan, to stop the Treasury twisting it in their favour. The mistrust was so great that Number 10 believed that as soon as Brown and his aides returned to the Treasury, they would brief it as a total Treasury victory. 'That's how bloody it was,' said one aide.[78] Milburn consoled himself by pressing ahead with increasing choice for patients and payment by results in the NHS, which he believed were more significant reforms than the more politically high-profile foundation trusts. Some months later, Blair told him that he regretted having made the concession on borrowing to Brown: it was the example in his mind when, at the 2005 party conference, he said that every time he had introduced a reform in government, in retrospect he wished he had gone further. In the short term, however, 'The Treasury had achieved their main aim of killing the "Milburn vision thing",' recalled one senior official. 'By the time it reached Parliament the proposal had been thoroughly emasculated.'[79]

Achieving a settlement in Whitehall was one thing. It was another to persuade the party at Westminster to agree to it. When Parliament reconvened on 15 October, it was immediately clear that backbenchers were very restless. The left was further inflamed by a speech Milburn gave the next day when he said that the 'old-style public service monoliths' were no longer relevant to meeting the challenges of the modern world. He called for new 'local partnerships' to bring services much closer to the people being served.[80] Balls responded from the Brown side in the same vocabulary by calling for his own brand of 'new localism'. Suspicions grew that Number 10 was promoting Milburn as Blair's successor, further needling the Chancellor's camp.[81] Dobson continued as the chief backbench critic, warning that 'elitists' were now trying to shape health policy, and dismissing foundation hospitals as the first wave of a 'two-tier' NHS.[82] Heated debate followed the Queen's Speech on 13 November. On 11 December, the government produced further detail on foundation hospitals in *A Guide to NHS Foundation Trusts*. To try to reduce opportunities for fractious debate, the government decided not to publish a White Paper on the grounds that the proposal had been foreseen in the NHS White Paper of 2000. But it still sparked furious debate, and Dobson was prominent among some 124 Labour MPs who signed an 'early day motion' in protest. To the government, it was a worryingly high number.

On 3 February 2003 Brown delivered a speech at the Social Market Foundation designed to 'demolish' what he perceived to be the Blair/Milburn/Number 10 vision of a 'privatised' future for public services. Milburn's article in *The Times* remained a sore, and he wanted to redress the notion that if one was not a Blairite moderniser, one was anti-reform: 'We risk giving the impression that the only kind of reform that is valuable is a form of privatisation.'[83] On 4 March, Milburn came back on the Dobson argument that his proposals would lead to a 'two-tier' system. At the Health Select Committee of the House of Commons, he provocatively suggested that *all* trusts would achieve foundation status within five years: all hospitals would thus be in the 'top tier'. The briefing and counter-briefing continued throughout March and April and provided a backdrop for the other debate raging in the party at the time: the Iraq war.

On 7 May came a critical test, a vote to give a second reading to Milburn's Health and Social Care Bill, which advocated foundation hospitals. Before the vote the whips were worried that Michael Howard's Tories opposed the Bill because the proposals were 'so hemmed in with restrictions and so limited that I thought we would have to tear it up and start again'.[84] Blair too was worried: 'This is classic. The Labour Party making historic errors that will help put us out of power and leave others to do the reforms we should have done,' he complained before the vote.[85] Despite intensive pressure on backbenchers to vote with the government, 65 rebelled, which was concerning for Blair as it meant they had voted against the Bill in its entirety. The main motion was carried through by 304 votes to 230, with the government's majority cut to 74. Even without unrest over the Iraq war, there would have been a substantial rebellion: the anti-war feeling merely added to the number and audacity of the rebels. There followed six months of further parliamentary battle. Number 10 was convinced that 'Gordon's surrogates were using the Bill as a way of doing in Milburn. It was obvious they were acting with permission or under cover of Gordon.'[86] It viewed the debate over hospital governance as a 'proxy' for a wider struggle over the control of the party: 'It was personal and political, with policy being a distant third in the whole battle,' asserted one aide.[87] With Blair's own future cast into doubt because of the war, Brown's camp was buoyant, but even more concerned that Milburn might be a potential leadership candidate in the future. They wanted their man to succeed not only quickly, but to a united, and grateful, party, not one that had been through a painful leadership election.

Milburn's sudden resignation in June 2003 was thus greeted with relief and joy by the Brownites. Even though his successor, John Reid, was to prove as determined an advocate of health reform, and better able to connect with the party, he was not a credible leadership challenger, and neither did the Blair camp have another champion in the wings. Reid was to develop his own interesting line on reform: that Labour had reached a point in its history where it had to modernise its understanding of 'public ownership'. In a speech soon after he took over, which Number 10 saw as a 'straight attack on Brown, and stunning',[88] he argued that the 'ambitions of ordinary people' should be listened to, and 'the old structures and systems . . . must be reformed'.[89] It had always been an article of faith with Blair that 'ordinary voters' understood and wanted choice, and that the vested interests in the traditional NHS (and other bastions for the welfare state) did not meet their needs. Rarely for Blair did he have ministers who advanced its argument: Reid was an exception.

On a more immediate level, the future of foundation hospitals hung in the balance. Blair realised he would have to do some trading. Chief Whip Armstrong advised him that 'if he didn't bring back the Hunting Bill for a third reading soon we would not have a hope in hell of winning the foundation hospital vote'.[90] The Bill to outlaw foxhunting had first been introduced in 2000. Blair was not a 'countryman' – his interests were essentially urban and cosmopolitan – but he was not an advocate of the Bill, and wanted to find any device to avoid an outright ban. He wasted his authority on unworkable 'middle way' schemes. Labour MPs became increasingly determined to have a full ban, and in the end, he had to concede. Campbell observed that Blair didn't 'understand how we can put at risk our whole public service agenda over hunting'.[91] Armstrong replied that hunting 'went deep . . . even with it we couldn't be sure of winning on foundation hospitals'.[92] She was right: although the Hunting Bill received its third reading on 9 July, it was not enough to put the rebels off the scent.

Nine separate rebellions occurred during the six-month passage of the health Bill, threatening its survival all the way through to the final vote on 19/20 November 2003. In total, eighty-seven Labour MPs voted against it at various points; had they united on the same vote, they would have defeated Blair, but dissenters ebbed and flowed. At 5 P.M. on 19 November, the Commons finally agreed, by a majority of just seventeen, to the proposals for foundation hospitals, with the government having to rely on the votes of Scottish and Welsh MPs despite the proposals only affecting hospitals in England. At 10:30 that evening, the Lords rejected the plans by a majority of sixty-eight. At 2:15 A.M., the Commons backed the Bill in a second vote, returning it to the Lords unchanged, and the upper chamber was forced to agree to it at 11:30 the following morning. Brown was enlisted as a supporter at the last minute. Number 10 believed this *volte face* only occurred because he was frightened about the government being defeated and him then being portrayed as 'anti-reform'.[93] 'To say Gordon came on board is an exaggeration. We gave him a list of his own people who we wanted him to influence. It was not altruism,' said a Whip.[94] Not until the absolute end did Blair know whether he would win. Working closely with Armstrong in the Whips' Office, they were frustrated when they were unable to find several MPs:

'People disappear when there's a difficult vote.' Some thirty-five indeed abstained from the vote. Blair had worked frantically up to the end, seeing MPs in his room in the House of Commons. When Armstrong told him that they had carried the vote, he was delighted, and appeared unworried by the small size of the majority.[95] Had he been defeated, it is uncertain what he would have done: a confidence motion would have been the probable response, on which most of the rebels and abstainers would have returned to the government's side. Insiders agree: 'He never countenanced losing. There was no Plan B.'[96] Blair had won the first big onslaught of his premiership on his domestic reform agenda, albeit on a much watered-down piece of legislation. As rebel Labour MPs licked their wounds, they plotted how to make their next strike more deadly. They had only to wait two months.

Tuition Fees: January 2004

As the New Year beckoned, 'We seemed to be coming to a "perfect storm" moment,' recalled Number 10 spokesman Godric Smith.[97] The higher education funding debate and the debate following the publication of the Hutton report, were scheduled on consecutive days at the end of January. A defeat on either could have been a resignation issue. It was a moment of great jeopardy.

Tuition fees proved even more fraught within the party than the battle over foundation hospitals, largely because unlike foundation hospitals, it was a big concern with voters. The issue went back to Blair's early days as Prime Minister, when he had given his consent to introducing tuition fees for higher education courses. Leading universities subsequently argued that they should be able to levy 'top-up' or variable fees above the £1,000 per annum cap introduced in 1997. Blair initially was keen, but Education Secretary Blunkett and Number 10 policy chief Miliband were not.[98] As the 2001 election approached, caution overtook Blair, and he even considered abolishing tuition fees altogether because they were so unpopular with the middle-class voters who were vital to his winning a second term. The manifesto thus stated that 'we will not introduce top-up fees and will legislate to prevent them'. But once the second term began, pressure mounted again from the Vice-Chancellors in the form of the '94 group', 'University UK' and the 'Russell group' of universities, which all campaigned for Blair to let them introduce top-up fees to supplement their income. 'The PM knew that he'd have to do something if he was to keep higher education internationally competitive,' said political secretary Robert Hill.[99] Lord Browne, then chief executive of BP, was one of several powerful voices urging him in this direction.[100] They were pushing at an open door. Within Number 10, Heywood and Adonis (a late convert to top-up fees) set to work to advise him on workable schemes. On 3 December Blair met with Adonis to agree the way ahead. Number 10 had not reckoned on the Treasury. They came up against a Chancellor 'virulently against top-up fees'.[101]

The Treasury favoured a graduate tax, which would rise progressively and be linked to the income of graduates, to replace up-front fees and loans for maintenance. Heywood and Adonis met Balls and Ed Miliband in late 2001 and again in early 2002 to explore forging a common path. The Treasury were adamantly opposed to student loans, which they thought would deter the less well-off from going to university, but were more open to the differential element in the Number 10 proposals. 'But we simply couldn't get the Treasury off the graduate tax. We tried very hard with Balls and Ed Miliband, arguing that it was unworkable, but we couldn't budge them,' recalled one Blairite.[102] When the Treasury examined the graduate tax plan in detail, however, they discovered it would be 'prohibitively expensive'. That avenue blocked, the Treasury's next gambit was to argue that a wholesale review of higher education funding was needed, a course they advocated for several months.[103] Number 10 became irritated that the Chancellor offered no practical alternative to top-up fees. 'Brown was not being perverse,' remonstrated a Treasury official. 'What he wanted was for universities to reform their admissions procedure to give increasing opportunities for less privileged students to attend them before they received any extra money.'[104] Brown's views on many subjects are well formed: but on several topics, including education, they were not. 'He was, however, moved by visceral instincts, about social justice and access to higher education for those from less advantaged backgrounds. You saw Gordon's true feelings over the Laura Spence episode,' when he lashed out at Oxford University for not admitting Spence, a state school pupil, to read Medicine in 2000 (an error in this case, as it transpired that her rejection had been entirely fair).[105]

The government's clarity was not helped by Education Secretary Morris being unable to make up her mind: Number 10 thought her 'aimless' at this time. On 21 March 2002 an acrimonious meeting between Blair, Brown and Morris failed to find a way forward. After a month of unproductive discussions, Blair decided that he had to apply more pressure. Morris was persuaded to sign up to the top-up fees principle and she committed herself to an autumn White Paper. Adonis went to Australia to look at differential fees, and returned an even greater advocate. When Blair met Morris on 20 June, she accepted the thrust of where Blair and Adonis were going, but still no specific proposals were agreed.[106] Blair was too distracted by the Iraq build-up to push her further. Brown argued that if the top-up fee plan was to go ahead, so many 'sweeteners' would have to be offered it would increase spending unacceptably in the first three or four years before any future benefits would kick in.

The air cleared when on 24 October Charles Clarke replaced Morris, her departure prompted in part by her misgivings over the direction of higher education reform. Much to the surprise of the DfES, Blair gave Clarke no clear instruction to deliver on top-up fees. 'He arrived in the department very obviously not having had any direct instructions. It was very baffling,' said one senior civil servant.[107] All Blair had told him was that raising more money for universities was 'his bottom line': if Clarke could persuade him of any better way forward than top-up fees, he would accept it.[108] On his first evening in his new job, Clarke indeed told journalists that he was far from persuaded about top-up fees. To his officials he said, 'I know you've been looking at it for eighteen months, but I'm going to start the whole process over again. You should know that I start with a pre-disposition towards a graduate tax.'[109] One of Clarke's first demands was to delay the White Paper promised for the autumn: on 30 October, Blair duly announced it would not be published until January 2003. Brown hoped that Clarke would see sense and come down on his side. Clarke spent his first eight weeks working intensively through the various schemes. He realised quickly that a graduate tax would not work.[110] Notes on his 19 December meeting with Blair record that 'CC soon persuaded the reform should proceed on the basis of a capped fee paid after graduation on a fair basis through the tax system, including the £3,000 ceiling'.[111]

With Clarke and Blair both now on the same page, Brown became agitated, and he wrote a rare letter to Cabinet expressing his worries that top-up fees would deter less well-off students going on to higher education. Another worry in the Brown camp was that forging ahead with top-up fees would 'split the PLP and turn Labour-voting students and their families against us at the next general [election]'.[112] Number 10 viewed this objection cynically and thought that those responsible for creating the splits were Brown and his acolytes. Clarke returned from the Christmas break recharged and ready to drive ahead.[113] In early January, with opinion finely balanced, he tried to talk to every member of

Cabinet, either in his own office or in their department. The timetable was very tight. His aim was to get as many on side as he could before the imminent Cabinet committee which would agree the proposals before the White Paper was published later that month.

Blair needed more heavyweight support if he was to carry the day. In early January, he brought Prescott round to supporting tuition fees, and chair the key Cabinet committee on the issue which met in the Cabinet Office on 16 January.[114] 'John was fine as long as he felt the proper Cabinet procedures were followed,' said one Number 10 aide.[115] It was to prove one of the most significant Cabinet committee meetings of Blair's premiership. Clarke opened, and was followed by Brown, who gave an 'implacable statement of opposition to the whole policy'.[116] Most of the Cabinet were present, and many were swayed by him. An hour of discussion followed, with the balance going one way then the other, and the meeting concluded with a strong counter-attack from Clarke defending his proposals. Prescott summed up the meeting by saying that he would 'report to the Prime Minister'.[117] His role was pivotal. Had he not in effect over-ruled the Treasury's objections by leaving it to Blair to decide the way ahead, tuition fees could have toppled at that point.[118] Blair's unsurprising response was that they must forge ahead. A further round of talks took place over the weekend of 18/19 January, when Cabinet ministers met Clarke and key figures from Number 10 to try to convert them ahead of the publication of the White Paper. The Treasury responded with a volley of memos describing the proposals as 'ridiculous' and 'dangerous', which resulted in a string of counter notes and memos flashing around the system from Number 10.[119]

Monday 20 January saw Blair and Prescott working in a closely co-ordinated manoeuvre to procure either written agreement, or at least tacit consent, from Cabinet ministers. Much of that night was spent re-drafting the White Paper, with Clarke, Adonis and advisers closeted in Clarke's office at the DfES, correcting the final draft and fending off a barrage of last-minute Treasury objections.[120] By the early hours of Tuesday morning, they had come up with a workable document. Blair resolved outstanding Treasury/DfES disagreements that day, after which he authorised Clarke to proceed with the paper, over-riding Brown's objections. On Wednesday 22 January, Clarke announced the tuition fees proposal in a Commons statement.

The year that followed was a comparatively quiet time on the tuition fees front. Below the surface, intensive work was taking place among a large team writing the legislation. Modifications were made to ease the

Bill through the committee stage, though Number 10 felt nothing of principle was being sacrificed. The Treasury posed constantly difficult and searching questions throughout. With attention on Iraq in the first part of the year and Hutton and foundation hospitals in the second, the political and media spotlight was off top-up fees. The lights were switched back on with a vengeance as the year ended. On 4 December, Clarke spoke about tuition fees in Cabinet, and was grilled about the plans by colleagues for almost an hour.[121] He argued that, although many in the PLP did not like the proposals, the party in the country, the balance of university opinion and the electorate did.[122] Cabinet by now was almost wholly supportive. Brown was not happy that he had lost the argument and refused to accept that top-up fees were popular with the public when the Treasury's own focus groups – organised, Number 10 said, along sympathetic lines – were telling him they were not.[123] Relations between Brown and Blair reached a low in December and January 2004. An official who entered Number 10 at this period was stunned by how dysfunctional the relationship was. He found that his stock went up in Number 10 every time he said anything against the Treasury: 'Indeed, if someone told the Treasury to "Fuck off", their standing shot up. Exactly the opposite happened in the Treasury.'[124]

It was an uncomfortable Christmas and New Year for Blair, holidaying in Egypt. He knew the forthcoming vote was going to be 'very dicey'. In early January 2004, over 160 backbenchers signed an 'early day motion' opposing the introduction of top-up fees. Intensive lobbying took place in the three-week build-up to the vote scheduled on 27 January: initially pencilled in for December, the debate was put back 'because we needed more time to win the votes'.[125] Blair became re-engaged in domestic policy in a way that he had not been since before the Afghanistan war in late 2002. Clarke played the role of tough guy while Alan Johnson, the minister for higher education since the previous June, played the nice guy.[126] The Whips' Office was not always convinced by their double-act, and Armstrong had to persuade Clarke that a full-scale whipping operation was required if the legislation was not to be lost. Johnson was stoical: 'It was, as I used to say, not mission impossible, but mission bloody difficult. It caused huge ructions within the party.'[127]

The weekend 24–25 January witnessed a constant flow of phone calls between the key parties. Number 10 were convinced that Brown had a direct influence over the two leading rebels, Nick Brown and George Mudie, and that had he wanted to, he could have persuaded them to drop their opposition. Some went further, and believed he was deliberately trying to get Blair out. Brown's support for the rebellion, tacit or otherwise, is fundamental because Blair was later to cite Brown's untrustworthiness as a reason for reneging on his plan to leave before the following General Election. Brown's camp reject all charges of plotting or manipulation. They argued that he had no influence at all over Nick Brown or George Mudie, and maintain that he had 'a clear conscience'. Although he disapproved of 'the entire venture as a matter of principle', he was powerless to do anything to stop the rebels. They cite in his defence Brown trying twice over the weekend to persuade Mudie and Nick Brown to support the government, without success, as evidence of his lack of power.[128] 'Rubbish,' says Number 10: if he had wanted to rein them in, he would have done. Prescott was enlisted on Blair's side to try to win over Brown, which may have had some influence.[129] In his heart, Brown faced a dilemma. Was he so intractably opposed to the Bill? Or to Blair? Far more important was Brown's calculation of his self-interest: he realised that if Blair lost the vote, he would be blamed.[130] Had he not intervened, Brown also risked being branded anti-reform in the press, his constant worry. Of all the papers, Brown was most obsessed by the Murdoch press, and especially the *Sun* and *The Times*, which were supporting the reform. Over that weekend, Blunkett sensed a new worry: that Nick Brown and Mudie would realise they effectively had a veto on any future item of reform which came to a vote in Parliament. It gives them, Blunkett wrote in his diary, 'real power against any other measures that they don't like'.[131]

On Monday 26 January the outcome of the vote remained unclear. Number 10, the DfES and the Whips' Office continued working to try to bring round rebel MPs.[132] It was a key moment in Brown's career, with potentially massive consequences for him and the party. Some urged him on, believing that the crown was there for the taking. But he did not want Blair to have to resign quite yet, were he to lose the vote. Sally Morgan believed that 'he would have had to go before long if he'd lost: he would not have been able to stay on after losing on something so major'.[133] With Blair's authority already so weakened, and after the near-defeat of foundation hospitals, continued leadership would not have been feasible. Geoff Mulgan agreed: 'If he'd lost he'd have had to resign.'[134] 'He gambled his entire premiership on it,' as one aide put it.[135] With defeat for the government the most likely outcome on the Monday, a worried Chancellor invited Nick Brown to his Westminster flat to urge him again not to vote against the government. This time Brown was utterly serious. A face-saver was extracted: a review to be set up into the impact of top-up fees on the professions. Brown's camp tried to paint this as a major concession. It was not, and the Longlands report, as it became known, had no major influence.[136] Nick Brown later alleged that he changed his mind because he feared that Blair, if defeated, would reintroduce the bill as a confidence motion, but withdrawing any concessions, which would make the rebels worse off.[137] Brown's camp ensured that his eleventh-hour lobbying was well known in Westminster, so anxious were they by now not to appear to be destabilising the government.

Even with Nick Brown on board, the government still looked as if it might be defeated. During the debate itself on Tuesday 27 January, further concessions were made by Clarke to try to win over the final rebels. At lunchtime, the Whips estimated that they were still eight votes short of a majority. Brown saw over forty potential rebels that afternoon.[138] 'Right until the very end, we didn't know whether we'd won or lost,' said Armstrong. She discussed with Clarke what he would say at the despatch box should the vote be lost: whether he should call a confidence vote, and whether the Tories themselves might call one, which they deemed unlikely.[139] 'Blair would have forced a confidence vote, but he never countenanced defeat,' said an aide.[140] At the eleventh hour, however, two Labour MPs decided to support the government and three agreed to abstain. The vote at 7 P.M. that evening constituted the largest backbench rebellion at second reading since 1945. As Blunkett recorded in his diary, 'Hell's bells, it couldn't have been closer. We won by five, which is really too close for comfort.'[141] Johnson concurred: 'People think the UK government was almost brought down by Iraq. No, it wasn't. It was almost brought down by higher education. We survived by the skin of our teeth.'[142] 'A win is a win,' a very happy Blair declared.

When the dust settled, Blair reflected on how unimpressed he had been by Brown's conduct. 'Effectively Gordon attempted to bring down the government. He had tried everything in his power to undermine the policy,' said one Number 10 source.[143] One close aide remarked some years later that Brown was trying to 'stop Tony developing a forward agenda by process arguments – not on principle'. (As Prime Minister, Brown's first announcement on higher education did not in any way question the principle of tuition fees.)[144] Though not defeated, Blair was, as Blunkett anticipated, weakened. As Anatole Kaletsky put it in *The Times*: 'The Chancellor has shown that he is the only man who can save the Prime Minister in his hour of need,' while the anti-Blairite MPs showed that they could 'undermine the government at almost any moment on almost any issue'.[145] After two nightmare votes in just two months, Number 10 resolved it would do

all it could to avoid parliamentary votes on his domestic programme in
the future. For the time being, Blair had won through on a bold piece
of legislation, and he had other reasons too for being very happy that
evening.

Hutton Reports: January 2004

'He was jubilant, and I remember thinking that he must have already
known what the Hutton report was going to say,' said one present when
Blair arrived shortly after 7 P.M. for drinks in his Commons office after
the tuition fee vote. The Hutton report had preyed on Blair's mind
more than he revealed. He had given a display of consummate
confidence in his appearance before Hutton on 28 August 2003, and on
the surface he showed little sign of anxiety. 'He said on his return he
had felt totally robust, and the facts didn't frighten him on this,'
Campbell recorded in the penultimate entry of his published diaries.[146]
But he hated the idea that his integrity was being called into question.
For the country at large, however, it was court-room political drama at
its height, as a succession of juicy e-mails were unearthed and star
witnesses appeared before the inquiry. The nation revelled in the
spectacle of Campbell and Blair being called to account for allegedly
bullying the BBC and for the death of David Kelly, and the media gave
the inquiry prime coverage. The mood in Number 10 swung over the
six months about what might be said. 'We all felt that if Hutton was in
any way going to reflect the reality of what happened, we would be all
right. But we didn't know how far the inquiry would be affected by the
strongly negative coverage from the media, so a sense of foreboding
came and went,' said David Hill.[147] Hutton troubled Number 10 far
more than the Butler Report, which followed hard on its heels from
February to July 2004. The inquiry was due to report in November, but
its delay led to a sense of stasis: 'We needed to have closure on Hutton
before we could move forward on the domestic agenda,' said Godric
Smith.[148]

An advance copy of the report arrived at Number 10 at midday on
Tuesday 27 January, giving Blair's aides twenty-four hours to prepare
their response. It was agreed that teams should spread out around
Number 10, to examine different aspects of the report, and that they
should then reconvene in the Cabinet Room at 3 P.M. Yellow and pink
highlighter pens were given out: yellow was to be used to highlight
positive passages, and pink negative ones.[149] Consternation was caused

by Jonathan Powell having confused his pinks and yellows: when he arrived at the Cabinet Room and people saw his marked-up copy, panic surged momentarily.[150] Any anxiety was short-lived: the report exonerated key figures in Number 10 and the government. One described their thought processes: 'When we read the report our first thought was, "What will the media do to get their own back on us?" Our mood very rapidly changed from "it could be disastrous" to "goodness me, this is very, very solidly our case being upheld", to "would it not have been better if it had made some criticism?"'[151] Blair returned from lobbying in the Commons mid-afternoon and walked into the Cabinet Room. His aides had debated whether they should tell him solemnly when he came through the door that it was 'bad news', but very quickly thought the better of it. Powell merely said to him, 'It's a positive for us,' adding 'there's even clarity in respect of what was said on the plane'. Blair was definitely of the view that it was much better that the report did not contain criticism, because the media would have focussed on those sections alone and given them disproportionate attention.[152] While Powell disappeared with Blair into the den to brief him further, those left in the Cabinet Room planned how Blair would respond the next day.

Early editions of the *Sun* revealed that the Hutton report had cleared Blair and it suggested that the report would be highly critical of the BBC. The suspicion was that the pent-up Campbell was so keen to get his interpretation (some said revenge) out first that he leaked the report to his friends on the paper. Those intimately involved say that it was categorically not him.[153] Blair was calm when he went to a packed House at 2 P.M. that Wednesday. A windfall was that the report helped reunite the Labour Party after all the divisions and recriminations of the day before, with the opening chord struck during Prime Minister's Questions when Labour MP Siôn Simon described the BBC as 'the enemy within, which should be privatised sooner rather than later'.[154] Blair's case was strengthened greatly by a tepid performance by Conservative leader Howard. His advisers had not been expecting a report so favourable to the government, and he was unable to adjust his attack in time. Hissing and booing greeted his speech from the Labour benches. Blair was at his rhetorical best: 'What you should understand is that being nasty is not the same as being effective.' And in a comment which summed up his bitterness about the insincere way he believed Howard had behaved over the tuition fee votes, he added 'and opportunism is not the same as leadership'.[155]

Within two days Blair had sailed through the perfect storm,

successfully pushing through landmark reform on higher education tuition fees and emerging initially unscathed from Hutton. 'It was a massive cloud-lifting. There was a tremendous sense of relief all round the building,' said one aide.[156] But the expected 'lift off' was not to be achieved. As Mandelson said, 'We had planned to give a number of interviews and that would be it. Chapter closed.'[157] But instead, a new chapter was about to open. In the euphoria of the hour, the popularity and public support for the BBC, which had underpinned the saga of the six months of the inquiry, now re-emerged. Campbell's rant against the BBC shortly after 4 P.M. on the day of publication caused widespread revulsion: 'If the government had faced the level of criticism that today Lord Hutton has directed to the BBC, there would clearly have been resignations by now – several resignations at several levels.' He did not have to wait long. The report plunged the BBC into crisis, prompting the resignations of Chairman Gavyn Davies and Director-General Greg Dyke, further shifting public sympathy to the BBC and against Number 10. The perception grew that Hutton had been a whitewash, which annoyed many in Number 10 who blamed a hostile media. Blair later regretted that he had not stopped Campbell from making his outburst in front of the television cameras: Number 10 understood that he wanted to vent his frustration, but there was consternation that he did it in such an aggressive manner. 'It was the beginning of Alastair really losing it,' said one aide. 'It had become deeply personal to him. Then when he'd been cleared and it seemed to make no difference to him, he became very dark and it affected Tony because they were so close.'[158] Within days of the report's publication, the dark clouds gathered again and hovered over Number 10. 'The result was that Tony had no "post-Hutton moment". No catharsis,' said Mandelson.[159] The demand grew for a further inquiry into intelligence and WMD in the run-up to the Iraq war. On 2 February Blair's hand was forced from across the Atlantic when Bush announced a presidential commission to review US intelligence on Iraq's WMD in the run-up to the war. Blair now felt compelled to follow suit and, on 4 February, announced a further inquiry under Lord Butler to investigate the quality of British intelligence. By the end of 2003, it was widely accepted that WMD were not going to be found in Iraq. How had Britain allowed itself to go to war on incorrect information? Was it down to ineptitude? Or had the government lied about WMD? It was around this time, as the domestic politics for Blair on Iraq were deteriorating, that the Prime Minister's much-vaunted optimism over the position on the ground also began to fade.

Optimism Drains Away in Iraq: December 2003–April 2004

On 2 December, Blair declared: 'I am optimistic . . . about the long-term situation in Iraq . . . There is a lot happening within the economy and society there that is immensely positive.'[160] On 14 December, his persistent optimism seemed vindicated. 'Ladies and gentlemen, we got him,' a breathless Paul Bremer announced to the press in Iraq, revealing that Saddam Hussein had been captured in a 'spider hole' in the town of al-Dwar, ten miles south of Tikrit.[161] The underground hideout was a six-foot-deep vertical tunnel, with a shorter tunnel branching out horizontally from one side, with just enough space for a man to lie down. 'He was caught like a rat,' said Major-General Odierno at the press conference.[162] Some $750,000 (£430,000) in $100 notes, two AK-47s and a taxi were also found in the compound, but no mobile phones or other communication equipment to suggest that Saddam was still co-ordinating Iraqi resistance.

Capturing Saddam provided a rare 'high point' for Blair in the Iraq story. 'He was buoyed, but not jubilant,' said Morgan.[163] Intelligence reports received in Number 10 suggested that it could have an impact on the morale and effectiveness of the insurgency.[164] 'Saddam's capture gave us temporary relief and hope; but its impact on the violence was regrettably short-lived,' recalled a senior official.[165] 'Iraq is deeply complex,' said Rob Fry. 'Every now and again we had positive news and all of a sudden we thought that one event was going to change everything. Looking back on it now, I regard that as a symbol of desperation.'[166] But at the time, certainly in Downing Street, hope sprang eternal. Over the winter, Sawers, now overseeing Iraq at the FCO, reported that progress was being made on restoring electricity, and there were signs that normality was returning.[167] In February, Blair declared: 'What is happening in Iraq, despite the appalling acts of terrorism, is that the Iraqi people are reasserting their ability and their right to a proper economy and a proper way of life, even though the political process is difficult.'[168] The hope was that the economy would begin to recover, the oil would flow again, confidence would grow and the Iraqis would be in a virtuous cycle back towards stability. Intensive negotiations took place throughout the first half of 2004 to keep the country on track for the return to sovereignty in June 2004. On 8 March, despite opposition from Ayatollah al-Sistani, the 'Transitional Administration Law' was finally signed by Iraq's Governing Council. This was, in effect, an interim constitution, which guaranteed Iraqis certain fundamental democratic rights, including freedom of religion and speech, and freedom from torture. It also contained provisions that could be considered advanced by Western standards: 25 per cent of those elected to the Iraqi Parliament, for example, would be required by law to be women.

But beneath the surface, Blair was being advised that all was not well. By early 2004, 'We began to understand that this wasn't going to be something you just whip in and out of, leaving the international community and domestic political process to take up the slack,' said Rob Fry.[169] Perplexity was now turning into alarm. Concerns over the American military had deepened. General Sanchez, Commander of US forces in Iraq from June 2003 to June 2004, seemed out of his depth and 'just fighting to avoid drowning'. The British military thought it a 'revealing' indicator of America's grasp of post-war Iraq that they gave an ordinary divisional commander responsibility for their largest foreign policy operation since Vietnam. 'They just didn't get it. Sanchez was just burnt to a frazzle, and it wasn't his fault.'[170] The relationship between Bremer and the senior British figure on the ground from September 2003 to March 2004, Jeremy Greenstock, began to break down. Greenstock saw himself as Bremer's equal. Bremer did not. As the senior representative in Iraq, Bremer alone was responsible not only for US but also for British policy in the country. When Greenstock began to highlight differences in American and British viewpoints, the Americans became increasingly disinclined to seek British views. 'It soon became apparent to the Prime Minister that it was not working out as he wanted and that Jeremy was not forging the close relationship on the ground,' said an observer.[171] Greenstock believed his differences with Bremer had been 'overplayed', yet he agreed that this independence of thought was not appreciated by the Americans. 'I often questioned their decisions, which is the kind of discussion you have in every Foreign Office corridor on any issue. But it's not natural in the American style, which is to know what the President wants and to go for it.'[172] More worrying than differences in style was the clash over the situation on the ground. While Bremer's reports to Washington remained upbeat, feedback from Greenstock became increasingly gloomy in tone over his six months in Baghdad. Senior Americans would express their concerns to him rather than to Bremer or to Washington, 'because it's not done in the American system to talk the mission down'.[173] Not all American reports from Iraq were positive. The first shock to the American system came with a report from the CIA chief in Baghdad at the end of the summer of 2003: 'It was the most dismal report you'd ever want to read,' recalled Wilkerson. 'It predicted everything.'[174] The response from the

US military was to distance itself from the report. Greenstock knew that his views would have been unwelcome in Washington: 'They would have said "pessimistic Greenstock thinks we're not getting it right, he always was a bit of a wet – let's ignore him".'[175]

Within the British camp, cracks began to appear in early 2004. Greenstock had also been considered too pessimistic by Number 10, while he thought London too ready to accept the American interpretation of what was happening on the ground. His reports regularly warned of insufficient resources and troops, and the danger of the position escalating out of control. Yet Number 10's implicit reaction, he contended, was 'the Americans seem to think they're making progress and will be difficult to confront, so let's stick with them'.[176] Greenstock was particularly disappointed that Blair did not make more of his second visit to Basra in early January 2004. Whereas Bush had visited troops in Baghdad at Thanksgiving in November 2003, Blair was not scheduled to visit the capital, so Greenstock flew down to Basra with Bremer to see him. Greenstock felt that Blair's heart was not in it. 'I sensed it was just getting too difficult: he couldn't get any traction, so his mind went off elsewhere,' he recalled. 'He didn't want to understand the full horror of what he was beginning to hear from us.'[177] Bremer's own account of Blair's visit has the Prime Minister running down a checklist of questions, but contains little evidence of Blair pushing Bremer or trying to put him on the spot.[178] Blair, who had come straight from a family holiday in Sharm el-Sheikh, appeared relaxed on the trip, though he had tuition fees and Hutton on his mind. Dressed in faded black jeans, blue blazer and open-necked shirt, he spoke to British soldiers from an improvised platform at the logistical base at Shaibah, outside Basra.[179] 'I would like you to know that . . . people . . . in years to come . . . will look back on what you have done and give thanks and recognise that they owe you a tremendous debt of gratitude.'[180]

Soon after Blair's visit, Number 10 finally lost faith in Greenstock's reports, which were concluding that Iraq was sliding out of control. 'They couldn't cope with my analysis,' said Greenstock. Nor his demands, which included asking Washington for another 50,000 to 100,000 troops.[181] Greenstock was not the only source of information London relied on. Michael Jay, for example, visited Iraq in February/March 2004. 'I didn't have the sense that it was doomed,' Jay recalled, 'only a sense that it was more difficult than we'd thought.'[182] Secretly, Blair now began to harbour doubts. That spring was when his closest aides first began to hear him say things like: 'I didn't think it was going to be like this.'[183] The unpalatable reality of post-war Iraq was beginning to dawn.

'Unbelievably bad days' were ahead for Iraq: 'It may well get worse before it gets better,' Greenstock told Reuters when he left Iraq at the end of March.[184] Blair had to wait just days for this prophecy to come true. On 31 March, a car carrying security contractors from Blackwater USA was ambushed in the centre of Fallujah. Bremer later recalled the horror of the situation and detestation towards Americans: 'The gunmen raked the Americans' car with AK-47s. Then the vehicle was set alight. Dancing in frenzy, a mob of townsmen dragged the smouldering corpses from the wreckage and ripped at the charred flesh with shovels. Then two blackened, dismembered bodies were strung from the girders of the city's main bridge across the river.'[185] Bush was alarmed and horrified by this attack on American citizens. 'We still face thugs and terrorists in Iraq who would rather go on killing the innocent than accept the advance of liberty,' he said on the evening of the attack. 'Their deaths will not go unpunished,' Bremer promised.[186]

The US envoy was as good as his word. He unleashed, without prior British discussion, a major offensive against 'insurgents' in the towns of Fallujah and Najaf. These knee-jerk actions proved intensely destabilising to the political process. Members of the IGC spoke out against the US offensive, which they believed was leading to the deaths of innocent civilians and constituted, in effect, collective punishment for the towns involved. On 9 April Bremer asked Generals Abizaid and Sanchez to consider a temporary cessation in Fallujah: 'The IGC is fracturing over operations in Fallujah,' he told them.[187] At noon that day the Americans announced a unilateral 'suspension of operations'. But the battle was far from over: 'We needed to recognize that we were simply postponing the inevitable showdown with the insurgents and terrorists there,' Bremer wrote.[188] The threat of a US offensive thus continued to lurk over Fallujah. Unilateral US military campaigns had been exactly what Blair had been so keen to avoid, and it made him redouble his determination to re-engage the UN.

Blair recognised the threat American action posed to the planned handover of sovereignty on 30 June, and the damage it was doing to public opinion. A mid-April visit to the US could be used to tackle both concerns. He travelled first to New York and met with Kofi Annan over dinner on 16 April at the Manhattan residence of British UN Ambassador Emyr Jones Parry. The meeting was 'partly substance, partly optics', said one present.[189] Ever since the UN had been bombed out of Iraq the previous summer, the British had laboured hard to get them back, with the topic raised regularly by him in his VTCs with Bush. On the surface the administration offered no resistance. Blair tried to persuade Annan that the UN should help with the formation of the interim government in Iraq, and back a new UN resolution, which the British had been developing, on gaining wider international involvement in Iraq. The 'optic' aspect of their meeting was that entering into dialogue with the 'saintly' figure of Annan would help Blair's position in Britain, given the widespread unpopularity of the war and his relationship with Bush: 'Domestic politics dictated that we needed the UN re-involved in a very public way, even more than the Americans did, though they needed it too for legal and other reasons,' said a Number 10 official.[190]

The next day, Blair headed to the White House against a background of graphic television images of continued American operations in Iraq as the US military continued to 'squeeze' Iraqi insurgents across the country.[191] The temporary cessation of the Fallujah offensive continued, but it was no secret that the administration was considering resuming it in the near future. Blair pulled no punches. The British party worried that plans to resume the assault had not been fully thought through, that the allies risked for the first time fighting not only the insurgency, but also the Shia. In meetings that were unusually sensitive and which saw officials later imprisoned for leaking its minutes, the British argued that 'it was a very dangerous moment to be fighting on two fronts'. The British repeated their view to the Americans that they feared excessive US military zeal would jeopardise the handover of power to an interim Iraqi administration two months later. As a result of their efforts, the US military did pause and went in softer. 'We pressed hard on this and we discussed the nature of the attack that was being proposed. We judged at the time that we'd been successful.'[192] Blair thought he had also been successful in achieving Bush's support for the proposed UN resolution, whose aim was to win wider international support for the coalition's strategy in Iraq.[193] Solidarity was much in evidence at the joint press conference on 17 April. Bush heaped on the praise: 'The American people know that we have no more valuable friend than Prime Minister Tony Blair. As we like to say in Crawford, he's a stand-up kind of guy. He shows backbone and courage and strong leadership.' Blair responded by stressing the strength of the alliance: 'For many years, but particularly most recently since September the 11th, our two countries have been friends and allies standing side by side and we will continue to do so.'[194]

Blair may have temporarily convinced the administration in Washington of the folly of escalating the operation in Fallujah and Najaf, but just three days after he left, the possibility remained on the table. On 21 April, Rice called Bremer to ask his opinion: 'What if the President orders a full-scale assault?' 'I'm conflicted,' he reported. 'Sooner or later, we've got to get back in there and get those guys. But frankly, the President must assume that if he orders an assault now, it will lead to the collapse of the entire political process.'[195] Caution prevailed, and the Americans resolved to tread lightly in Fallujah until after the scheduled transfer of sovereignty on 30 June. This decision helped keep the political process on track. Returning to the UK after his Washington visit, Blair reported to the House of Commons, explaining where he thought the resistance in Fallujah and Najaf was coming from: 'All those who think they will lose out when Iraq becomes democratic – former Saddam supporters, foreign terrorists, militias led by extremist clerics – have a vested interest in seeking to delay or disrupt the transition towards democracy . . . of allowing the Iraqi people the chance to choose their own leaders in free and fair elections.'[196] For all this upbeat tone, it was Fallujah that shook Whitehall's confidence in Iraq's future. As Turnbull recalled, 'That's the point when you suddenly realised that this thing was going seriously wrong. Up to that point, lots of things had gone right.'[197] In May, Blair, concerned at the political problems the allies faced after Fallujah and Najaf, dispatched Sawers to Iraq to evaluate. 'I brought back a very negative report. It was sent to Number 10, the Foreign Secretary, and a very limited number of people. The possibility of strategic failure was first glimpsed in the spring of 2004.'[198]

Coming hard on the heels of Greenstock's repeated warnings, here was yet another warning to Blair that Iraq was in trouble. He had done all he could to engage the US. With the Americans calling the shots on the ground, he could do little more than pray that the planned handover of sovereignty on 30 June would provide the turning point. In public he maintained his optimism. But Iraq had begun to weigh him seriously down and caused him deep inner anxiety. It was to prove one of several factors that would bring him to the brink of resignation.

10

The Recovery

April–June 2004

Blair was brought so low in the spring of 2004 that he contemplated leaving that autumn. Though he had continually evaded the question of his departure (despite briefly raising it with the inner circle in mid-2002), he never contemplated that he would be hounded out of office. He had become a pale shadow of the strong, confident leader of 2001–03, dominant not only in Britain but in world politics also. Iraq, health, the party, criticism at home and Gordon Brown all combined to bring him to the lowest point of his premiership. For a few weeks, he lost his self-confidence. Rediscovering his inner strength and resolve was fundamental to his decision to fight on – and face up to the inevitable fury that Brown and his circle would unleash.

EU Constitution Débâcle: April 2004

At the European Council meeting at Laeken in December 2001, Europe's leaders agreed that the EU needed a new constitution, and spawned the convention chaired by Giscard d'Estaing. Blair and Straw were distracted from its work in the immediate build-up to the war: Straw admitted, 'I found I simply did not have time to be involved in its detail with so much else going on.'[1] Blair's chief ally was Aznar of Spain: both were strongly opposed to a 'federalist' constitution. Only after the Iraq war broke out in March and Blair lost the argument over the Euro in April 2003 did he begin seriously to study what exactly was being proposed. It was 'in the long term the most important thing the Foreign Office is doing', he told Straw, 'including Iraq'.[2] He worked for the next three months to counteract Franco-German and Belgian attempts to skew the constitution in a federalist direction. Despite his efforts, the convention produced just such a draft in July. It conceived a 'single legal personality' for the EU, a permanent president for the Council of Ministers and a new EU foreign minister. Responses by EU countries lined up along the 'old' and 'new' Europe lines, with the former (apart from Italy) favouring a federalist constitution, and the latter a looser one.

A new focus of debate now came to the fore: should the electorate of member states be able to vote on the constitution in a referendum, or should national parliaments decide? Blair was adamant that he did not want a referendum because 'his strong strategic sense was that it would be very tough to win', said one aide.[3] More importantly, he feared that the referendum debate would drag on over several months if not years, and with the Eurosceptic press making the most of it, this would compromise his whole strategic direction. 'He worried that the whole political agenda would be dominated by that one issue and distract from the real business of government,' said Stephen Wall.[4] So he argued that a matter of this importance should be decided by Parliament, as had been the case with all previous EU treaties. He did so believing that Parliament would vote in favour, and with the support of leading Conservative pro-Europeans (Clarke, Patten, Heseltine) who were anti-referendum.

In September 2003, Straw went to Chequers to see Blair. He had been an early enthusiast for the constitution, but now alarm bells were ringing in his head. Giscard's draft was not the pocketbook publication he thought would be useful, but had grown 'to the size of a telephone directory'. It was also far more federalist than he had imagined. He told Blair that demands from Conservatives and Liberal Democrats for a referendum meant Labour risked losing seats at the next election against candidates who had pledged themselves to vote for one.[5] The treaty did not justify the cost and disruption of a referendum, Blair said. Straw replied that the very fact that it was a called a 'constitution' and that it proposed fundamental new rights, meant that Labour could look very vulnerable in the election if it had not given the electorate the chance to vote directly on it. Blair responded sharply that this was a negative strategy. 'Jack saw the politics of it – could we go into a General Election saying that we wouldn't have a referendum,' recalled one Cabinet colleague.[6] The government had to hold one 'otherwise we will be in the shit' – and forced to yield on a referendum in the worst possible circumstances. Blair would not be moved. Straw was disappointed he had not shifted the Prime Minister, and subsequently wrote long handwritten notes to try to persuade him, becoming convinced that Blair was movable.[7] Number 10 was equally convinced that Straw, and Brown as well, were keen to show off 'their Eurosceptic credentials to the public and media'.[8]

The convention's proposals were formally discussed at the EU Council meeting in Brussels on 12–13 December 2003, held at the end of Italy's presidency under Berlusconi's chairmanship. Blair had made it clear that some of the proposals were not going to be acceptable to Britain. His 'red lines' included Britain retaining control of foreign and defence policy, tax, justice and some other matters. He met with Chirac and Schröder for breakfast on the first day, where the French President surprised them by saying he was not prepared to do a deal on the constitution at the Council under any circumstances. Some in the British delegation suspected this was because he was not prepared to let his rival Berlusconi enjoy the success of achieving a deal. More importantly, he did not think there was sufficient backing for the federalist constitution he wanted. The Italian leader nevertheless worked throughout the night to try to produce a compromise, and the next day the big four leaders met. He told them that he believed that he had the elements of an agreement. 'There's not going to be an agreement,' Chirac replied. 'We're not prepared to have one.'[9]

Number 10 was appalled by Chirac's behaviour. One aide commented, 'Although Berlusconi's a rascal, he's a polite rascal with manners, which Chirac doesn't have.'[10] Blair concluded that with no possibility of a compromise between the parties, he had most to gain by acting as a healer, 'pouring oil on troubled waters'. The Council broke up in stalemate, with the blame being placed on anti-federalist Spain and Poland rather than on Britain. 'Tony Blair was left insisting that a new constitution could still be made to work despite such an embarrassing setback,' reported the *Observer*.[11] On the fraught subject of a referendum, Blair bought time, saying publicly that Britain should wait to see what was finally proposed in the constitution before deciding whether it should call a referendum. In the secrecy of the Council, Chirac had broached with Schröder and Blair the possibility of a 'mutual pact' where they all agreed not to hold one. Chirac had earlier promised a referendum to the French people but realised that his political situation would make it too difficult. Schröder declared outright, 'We don't have referendums in Germany.' Blair restated his view that he did not think one in Britain was justified. So Chirac left the Council believing that the three largest countries of the EU were pledged not to hold a referendum. The stage was set for another 'British betrayal'.

It seemed in early 2004 that the constitution was on the back-burner. But then following the al-Qaeda bombings at Madrid's Atocha station on 11 March 2004, Spain's ruling Popular Party fell. The new left-of-centre government wanted to rebuild relations with France and Germany. Their first step was to drop Spain's objections to the constitution. Suddenly, the constitution shot to the top of the agenda. At the Brussels summit on 25–26 March, EU leaders agreed that a deal on the constitution should be reached at the mid-June Council, under the Irish presidency of Bertie Ahern. The pressure on Blair continued to build. In December, thirty-one Labour MPs had written an open letter to the Prime Minister demanding a referendum; now the pressure for one spread across the party. The Conservatives under Howard seized on it as a chance to beat Blair, believing that any referendum would be lost but that the democratic appeal in calling for one would be applauded. From the top of Labour, Straw and Brown's pressure for a referendum mounted. In private Prescott told Blair, 'You can't maintain your position going into the coming European, local and General Elections with Europe dominating everything if the constitution treaty is going through Parliament.'[12] The Eurosceptic press rallied to the cause. From the Murdoch press came the headline: 'Traitor Tony Blair is to let Britain be run by ten unelected bodies in his EU splendour' in the *News of the World*.[13] Murdoch had personally argued for the use of the word 'traitor', it later emerged.[14] The *Daily Mail* also turned up the heat by organising its own campaign for a referendum.

At Prime Minister's Questions in the House of Commons before the Easter recess, Blair found himself having to repel a barrage of questions about why he was not holding a referendum. He realised he was getting the worst of the argument. He told one aide: 'This argument about the referendum is a huge distraction. We are just being cast as against the voice of the people and it is preventing us making the real argument about Britain's place in Europe.'[15] Though remaining cynical about the motives of many of those pressing for a referendum, very subtly he began to change his thinking. Number 10 had already girded itself up to fight a referendum on the Euro: he was told that it would be very simple for the 'pro-Euro' referendum campaign to switch to the 'pro-constitution' campaign. 'It was not that difficult psychologically for him to make the transition,' said one official.[16] Sally Morgan was also giving him strong advice that, from the party's perspective, a referendum made perfect sense.[17] But he still had qualms to overcome, not the least upsetting his staunchly pro-EU colleagues in Number 10, and in particular Mandelson. At such a vulnerable time, he was also concerned not to be conspicuously caving in to pressure. He had held his nerve on foundation hospitals and top-up fees, after all. But close colleagues now noticed a change: 'I know when Blair is about to change his mind on something, because he starts to make rather pompous remarks like, "I never make any U-turns",' recalled John Prescott. 'That's when you know.'[18]

Powell and Wall went up to see him in the flat just before he flew off to Bermuda with the family on 9 April for their Easter holiday. He was now under conflicting pressure. Prescott advised him to go public about the referendum before flying off, arguing that 'people will start talking about it while you're away',[19] while Brown argued that he should delay any announcement on the grounds that it would look like a U-turn being made under pressure.[20] Blair took two memos to Bermuda. One from Straw argued that if he did not declare a referendum before the elections to the European Parliament on 10 June, Labour would fare badly. He argued that, as a constitutional treaty, it would go before the House of Lords where the Conservative majority would be bound to say that it could only be ratified on the back of a 'yes' vote in a British referendum. There would be insufficient time to use the Parliament Act to overturn the Lords' judgement before the coming General Election, which would result in a reduced majority and the government being forced to concede a referendum following it.[21] The second paper, which was from Wall, took the opposite view. Although Wall did not waste time repeating all the arguments against the referendum, which Blair knew well, he suggested that the Prime Minister wait for the constitution to emerge from the EU Council in June. This would demonstrate that the Eurosceptic press and the Conservatives had grossly distorted any 'dangers' to British sovereignty.[22] But had Blair made up his mind before he left for Bermuda? The signs are that he had, in all but name. Close Number 10 aides testify to the fact that 'Tony gave rather more than just a nudge and a wink to Jack'.[23] It was convenient for him that pro-Europeans like Hain even to this day blamed Straw for 'bouncing' Blair into the referendum.

After Blair left on Good Friday, speculation and uncertainty intensified. Press stories appeared, claiming that 'leading' members of the Cabinet were pushing Blair towards a referendum.[24] Pressure from

Straw was a factor, but not as great as the inexorable logic of public and political opinion. With his personal position so vulnerable with Iraq, and with Brown rampant, something had to give. He could no longer fight on all fronts.[25] By the time that Blair saw Kofi Annan in New York on 16 April, he had decided that he had to concede on the referendum. The debate then shifted to the timing of the announcement. Prescott wanted to wait until after Cabinet on Thursday 22 April, but that would have meant Blair warding off embarrassing questions at PMQs the day before. Straw favoured the announcement on the first working day after he returned, Monday 19 April.

At this point, a story was leaked to the *Sun*[26] and then to *The Times*[27] that Blair was about to announce his U-turn. Number 10 believed that Straw (or someone close to him) was responsible for the leak to lock down the decision before Europhiles in Cabinet could persuade him to change his mind.[28] Straw denies any knowledge of the leak: 'It did not come from the FCO. I don't know where it came from.'[29] The leak was to prove deeply embarrassing. The first Number 10 or the Cabinet at large knew about it was when they read the story in the press. Understandably they felt bounced. 'There wasn't nearly enough discussion,' said a senior Brownite in the Cabinet. 'The decision to have a referendum was announced and then we were invited to agree with it afterwards.'[30] Mandelson, confirming his reduced influence on Blair, had not been consulted beforehand, and was both cross and offended. One of his acolytes reflected ruefully to the press a few days later, 'Tony regrets this already. But then again that is typical Tony.'[31]

Blair had only the Sunday and Monday to prepare for his statement, which he decided could wait no longer than Tuesday 20 April. 'Are you sure you're right about this?' one aide asked him, wondering where he and the government would stand if, as seemed highly possible, the referendum roundly rejected the EU constitution. 'There'll be a lot of water that will flow under the bridge before we get to a British referendum: mark my words,' said the Prime Minister thoughtfully.[32] Ever the optimist, to the House of Commons Blair presented the referendum as 'a historic' opportunity for the British people to vote for a bold, confident Europe: if it was to be a 'no' vote, it would see Britain being forced into the margins of Europe. The debate over whether to hold the referendum, Blair announced in his speech, had been allowed to muddy the real debate over the EU. Attention should now turn to the constitution and whether it was in the interests of Britain. 'Let the issue be put and let the battle be joined' were the final words of a bravura performance.[33]

Cabinet was not the only group the Prime Minister failed to consult. Blair had not talked it over with his EU colleagues. When taking the decision, he realised that there would be a domino effect on other EU countries. Number 10 predicted that the French, Dutch and Swedes, among others, would all have to hold referenda.[34] Blair was persuaded by his staff that he ought at least to call Chirac, given the understandings he had given the French President in December 2003. When he did so, Chirac had already picked up hints of Blair's decision from the British press. The call was not harmonious: 'Chirac kept his cool but he must have been pretty pissed off,' said one aide,[35] not the least because he had to confirm that France too would hold a referendum. Coming almost one year to the day after the invasion of Iraq, it was another body-blow to Blair's standing with the leaders of old Europe.

Blair's decision on the referendum, albeit taken on the back foot, would prove to be a blessing in disguise. In the short term, it neutralised the hysteria from the Murdoch press and the *Mail* group. In the longer term, he believed that he had a bomb-proof strategy for avoiding the humiliation of a referendum defeat. Other EU countries would be holding their referenda before Britain. If they all voted 'yes', he would deploy the argument that if Britain did not vote 'yes' it would be utterly isolated in Europe. If they voted 'no', he would be let off the hook.[36] Not even he foresaw quite how prescient that judgement was to be.

The Wobble: March–June

In as far as Blair had any definite thoughts, some point mid-to-late in the second term seemed to him to be the likely date for his departure. 'I didn't necessarily want to fight a third term,' he later told friends, such as Tessa Jowell.[37] Following the Prescott dinner in November 2003, the Brown camp were geared up for a 2004 handover, and they clearly saw Ivan Rogers, Heywood's successor at Number 10 from December 2003, as their 'advance guard' to help oversee the transition.[38] 'Absurd,' say Number 10. 'That was never part of his appointment.'[39] Ed Miliband began meetings with Philip Gould to plan how a transition might take place. Number 10 deny this was ever a serious 'transition exercise'.[40] Blair was constantly changing his own thinking about his departure date. Because he did not know exactly what he thought, and told intimates different things at different times, it is difficult to piece together exactly what happened in this most 'murky' period of Blair's premiership, the first half of 2004. A combination of factors, however, came together to incline him towards quitting, without ever pushing him to the brink.

The deteriorating position in Iraq ground him down. It was clear to him that mistakes were being made and that the early consequences of these mistakes were now being felt. He was having to accept that WMD would never be found, which opened him up to the accusation that he had taken Britain into war on false pretences: either he was a liar, as many believed, or he was incompetent. Sally Morgan places his lowest point in January/February, earlier than most others. 'The depth came in the immediate aftermath of Hutton.'[41] Dr Brian Jones, formerly of the MoD intelligence branch, had cast doubts on Hutton's findings which were widely taken up. 'There we were, we'd been cleared, and then he realised that he wasn't clear at all. It was the utterly low point.'[42] At the end of February, Clare Short alleged that British intelligence routinely bugged the offices of Kofi Annan at the UN. The accusation contributed to the toxic atmosphere of mistrust in Blair. In March, he told Brown, 'I can't get through on Iraq. I'll never turn it around.'[43] One Number 10 aide confirmed, 'After Iraq started to go badly wrong . . . he started thinking about his future.'[44] Philip Gould agreed that 'it was Iraq that really got him down in early 2004'.[45] Tessa Jowell commented how 'Iraq turned his hair grey. It was in early 2004 that you first saw a big physical change in his appearance.'[46]

On 28 April, the first pictures showing abuse of detainees by US soldiers at the Abu Ghraib prison appeared in the American media. The reaction in Number 10 was 'pretty dismal'. 'Tony thought it was terrible, but I think some us wanted him to be angrier than he was. He kept saying, "Well, we've got to be careful, we can't go over the top on this." The rest of us just saw it as an outrage and a chance to be heavily publicly shocked.'[47] Shortly afterwards similar photographs, allegedly depicting abuse by British troops, were splashed across the front page of the *Mirror*. The military quickly assured Number 10 that they were almost certainly fakes, but public vindication took a little longer. On 15 May the paper apologised and its editor, Piers Morgan, was forced to resign. By then the British images had done their damage and, coupled with the enduring pictures from Abu Ghraib, they cast further doubts on the moral case for war. Blair had always seen himself as the moral agent in the Iraq conflict. Surveying the fall-out from the abuse revelations he realised that his initial private reaction had been too cautious. He had laid so much store on taking what he thought was the right action morally, that to be attacked as a liar, who had helped create a barbaric country, shook him to the core.

He began to ask himself whether staying in office was the right course of action.[48] Constant attrition from Brown further ground him down. 'Relations were very, very bad at this time,' said one observer.[49] Scenting blood, the Brownites kept up the pressure which they hoped would destroy him. 'It was the endless psychological drain of the warfare with Gordon that got him down. It went on and on, and it sucked his energy dry,' said one aide.[50] The high hopes of 2001–02, or of the autumn of 2003, that at last he would be able to command the second-term domestic agenda had disappeared. He now doubted whether he would ever be able to achieve his ambitions at home, while abroad, the first-term successes of Kosovo and Sierra Leone had become the second-term abysses of Iraq and increasingly, he feared, Afghanistan.

Family matters had been brewing for some time and started now to prey seriously on his mind, adding to his stress. Throughout his premiership, Blair and Cherie had been always deeply concerned about the pressure that his job brought to their children. They worked very hard to protect their family from the assaults of office and to try to give them as normal a life as possible. They took great pride in their success in doing this and in bringing up four happy children. 'He's a wonderful father. Very loving and demonstrative. He has brought up lovely children,' said a close friend.[51] But the job inevitably took its toll on them all. From 1997 to 2002 the children basked in having a charismatic, popular father. The Iraq war and its aftermath changed that: it is never easy for children if their father is unpopular and under attack. The change also brought new stresses to their marriage, which had seen periods of great happiness and some stress, with the Bristol flats episode in December 2002 their lowest point. Another difficult period came this spring. Leo, aged nearly four, was not sleeping well which resulted in many broken nights. The night Blair came back from the European Council on 25/26 March, for example, Leo had woken up and got into their bed. Blair could not sleep so he climbed into Leo's little nursery bed, but was still exhausted in the morning. By mid-April Blair become worried about the three older children as well, with one incident in particular leaving him upset and despondent. It also began to make Cherie, his most stalwart supporter, wonder whether remaining at Number 10 was really worthwhile.[52] Brown's camp thought family concerns might provide Blair with 'an honourable exit strategy that would win public sympathy'.[53]

The very day when Blair was battling over what to say to Parliament about his U-turn on the referendum coincided with a particularly bloody meeting of the PLP. Opinion polls in February and March had Labour level-pegging with the Tories, while Blair's own ratings remained obstinately negative. The party was not happy. Neither at home, nor abroad, did they like where he was taking them. A clear contender was in the wings with the promise of policies that sounded much more congenial. Blunkett recorded in his diary, 'Tony was clearly tired at the PLP meeting on the Monday evening – no wonder. It's been a difficult three months.'[54] Those close to him began to wonder how much more punishment he could take. He suffered further afflictions too, which only a handful knew about.

The pressure had begun to take its toll physically. On 19 October 2003, he had been rushed to hospital after complaining of chest pains while at Chequers, and was diagnosed with an irregular heartbeat. An emergency cardioversion was administered, and he remained in hospital for almost five hours before being driven back to Number 10. The official bulletin insisted there was no reason why the condition should recur, and Blair himself was blasé about it, such that even close colleagues thought it had ceased to be an issue. But intimates confirmed that his heart continued to trouble him well after the October 2003 episode. 'He felt unwell quite a lot during the year that followed,' said one confidant. 'After he told me, I began to watch him carefully. He was generally not very well in 2004.'[55] He would feel his heart beginning to pound and it made him feel 'strange and disconcerted'. Though no one spotted it, the pounding happened twice during PMQs in 2004.

Blair needed the comfort and stimulus of his closest allies, and missed the company of his personal 'quartet'. By the spring of 2004, he was very despondent. 'On top of everything he was missing key people, principally Alastair and Anji,' said Milburn.[56] He spoke regularly to Hunter and Campbell on the phone, but Campbell had become depressed and erratic following Hutton and his blackness weighed Blair down.[57] Hunter was always available on the phone, but she was busy with her new job at BP, and preoccupied with her new partner, Sky Television's Adam Boulton, to whom she became married in 2006. Mandelson was in and out of Number 10, but Blair was moving away from him. His sights were set on a job in the EU. Brown, the fourth member of the quartet, had meanwhile become the enemy next door. In their place in 2003–04 emerged Morgan and Powell as the key friends and counsellors to Blair. But if Powell's strength was in handling the detail of the issues surrounding Blair, Morgan was the natural leader: 'Sally imposed herself more and more,' recalled one Number 10 aide, 'and became the effective leader of Downing Street.'[58]

Blair's friends in Cabinet – Jowell, Reid, Falconer, Armstrong, Clarke and Blunkett – and Milburn and Byers outside, began to pick up on Blair's sense of isolation. They shared another concern: might he suddenly announce he was going to leave? In late April, Jowell talked to him in the den. 'You're going to get through this and you're not on your own,' she told him. 'Never think that there's nobody there with you.'[59] His friends organised a series of dinners at Chequers, in the flat at Number 10 or in their own homes to remind him 'that they were there for him'.[60] In contrast to the group around Brown, the Blairites in Cabinet were always inchoate and had never seen themselves as part of a tribal group. 'We didn't organise and had no clear plan, in marked contrast to the way Gordon operated. He always had an operation and he's always thrown his cloak around his people when they've got into trouble, which is why they survived.'[61] They now felt their champion was under threat and they made it clear to him that they wanted him to stay. Even those on the penumbra of the group contacted him. Patricia Hewitt wrote to him offering her support[62] and Peter Hain went to see him to tell him he should stay. 'He's a remarkably resilient person, but he wasn't particularly resilient at that time,' said Hain.[63]

Did his Cabinet colleagues have any effect? Close aides in Number 10 doubt it. 'Any influence they might have had would have been pretty minimal. The people who would have influenced him were his oldest friends, Anji, Alastair and Peter. These are the people who really count with him,' said one.[64] But not only were they now one step removed from him: they also gave him conflicting advice. At different times, Campbell and Hunter both counselled following their example and leaving Number 10. Morgan and Powell were staunch, however: he should stay. Most significant of all was Cherie. 'She's always been massively in favour of him staying on. She's never wanted to pack it in and that's why she's so furious with Gordon Brown,' said Blair's agent and close friend, John Burton.[65] 'Cherie couldn't stand the neighbour,' said a senior official. 'She begged Tony to stay on. She simply couldn't bear the prospect of Brown taking over.'[66]

But how close was he to quitting? There is no doubt that he was very down. As Falconer said, 'It was his first period of unremitting unpopularity. He found it very hard.'[67] He stopped reading the press at this point, so 'demoralised' was he by the constant criticism.[68] In March, he floated the idea again with Brown of making an imminent announcement that he would be leaving Number 10 later, specifying that autumn as the date. 'Don't do that, it would be crazy,' Brown told him. 'You'll make yourself a lame duck. You'll send the Labour Party into turmoil.'[69] The Brownites were to rue Brown's response, and said that it was motivated by a desire not to damage the party with important elections coming up in June. They favoured instead Blair signing up to a private deal that he was going to go in the autumn. But this time, to avoid any more betrayals, the deal would have to be 'concrete'. Blair baulked at this. 'The perception of Tony's was that it was not possible to have any private deal without it becoming public,' said Blunkett.[70] The Blairites, who could not count Blunkett among their number, believed that Brown was not motivated by concern for the party but, as ever, for his own position: a public announcement that Blair was going in the autumn would give rival candidates six months to gather support, and risk the coveted prize being sacrificed. Blair told his close aides that it was unlikely that Reid and Clarke would give Brown a clear run.[71] By early April, Brown's camp were certain that Blair's days in office were numbered. That month, one Brownite described Blair as a 'shrunken and weakened Prime Minister, who might go as early as July, or by the autumn at the latest'.[72]

As early as April, Brown had begun to grow suspicious that Blair might change his mind. Over the Easter holiday some of Brown's allies concluded that Blair was 'already well on his way to reneging once again on his promise to stand down before the election'.[73] In fact Blair was still undecided in April over what he would do. 'What he had was a wobble, a loss of confidence,' confirmed one of his closest aides. 'He thought, "What the hell's the point of going on?", but he never reached the stage of saying, "Well, I'm going now."'[74] Instead, Blair played his cards remarkably close to his chest, which is why insiders are so confused about what he was thinking. Only Cherie knew the full truth. 'The wobble was not visible to me at the time,' recollected Cabinet Secretary Turnbull. 'It was only when I read about it in the press that I knew what might be happening.'[75] Blair oddly said nothing to his agent Burton. 'He would have told me. He had always said to me, "When I am to go, you'll be the first one I tell."'[76] As Campbell's successor, David Hill, admitted, 'I can see why some people in the building were unaware of anything going on.'[77]

The pressure was at its height from his return from the US on Sunday 18 April until the elections on 10 June. He pulled himself together and gave a strong performance when announcing the decision on the referendum on 20 April, but was then plunged back into gloom. At Cabinet on Thursday 29 April, he was at sea. 'I was in despair. We didn't seem to have a strategy for the imminent elections. We appeared to be drifting and we were back-biting each other,' wrote one present.[78] 'The Prime Minister's vulnerability was very visible,' recalled Mulgan.[79] A crisis meeting in Number 10 was convened on 2 May. Mandelson tried to reassert control, attacking aides for having 'no grip' following Campbell's departure. The Prime Minister, he said, 'had been badly served by those around him'.[80] It did nothing to enhance Mandelson's own position, nor morale in a building that was already reeling from one blow after another.[81] Early May brought even worse news. A YouGov poll suggested that Labour would fail to win a workable majority at the next General Election under Blair, but that it would be seventy-seven seats clear if Brown was at the helm. Blair began to wonder again whether he had become a liability to the party. More worrying for Number 10, it showed that forty-one Labour MPs would lose their seats if Blair remained as leader.[82] In the febrile atmosphere, much speculation followed a discussion on 9 May between Brown and Prescott in the back of the latter's official Jaguar, in the car park of the Loch Fyne Oyster Bar in Argyll. The conversation was merely one of many that Brown and Prescott had during this period about the succession. What is clear is that Prescott said to the press that 'the plates appear to be moving', which was interpreted as him saying that a change of premier was imminent.[83] 'John later apologised to Number 10 that he had not meant to say what he said, but he was describing a general feeling around the place,' a Number 10 aide said.[84] Blair had always taken Prescott's loyalty for granted. He had to depend on him.

The Turning Point

The rallying moment came when Blair was in Ankara, seeing Turkish premier Recep Tayyip Erdoğan on 17 May 2004 about Turkey joining the EU. At the press conference, he said he would be 'staying the course, not . . . cutting and running, or ducking out, but for staying the course and getting the job done'.[85] Those travelling with him felt convinced that, though he was talking about the allies not quitting Iraq in the face of increased bombs and assassinations, 'he was really talking about his own intentions to stay on as Prime Minister. It was a signal.'[86]

Blair's mood went into an upswing in late May. He began to talk about how, if he left before the General Election, his own reform agenda would have barely left the drawing board, while Iraq remained bleak. He was horrified at the prospect of his premiership being viewed exclusively through the prism of Iraq: he was sure it would come right, but it would take more time.[87] Everything now hinged on the local and European election results on 10 June. A very bad result might thwart his ambitions to remain. Polls in the run-up to the elections looked bleak. On 9 June Gould warned Blair that private polling suggested the Conservatives could achieve over 40 per cent of the vote. 'We focused the campaign on Michael Howard and made it very negative,' said one aide. 'We attacked him very hard.'[88] Blair was under no illusions, though, that it would be anything but a black day. The results were indeed poor. Labour lost over 450 seats, sliding into third place with 26 per cent of the vote, behind the Liberal Democrats on 27 per cent. In the European elections Labour received a miserable 23 per cent. Crucially, however, the Conservatives only achieved 37 per cent in the local elections and 27 per cent in the European elections (with the UK Independence Party scoring 16 per cent). Blair, much to his concern, had to be in Washington for the funeral of President Ronald Reagan, and was unable to be there for the results. He had flown direct from the G8 summit at Sea Island under the Americans' presidency which Number 10 had found disappointingly bland: it played its part in making Blair realise that the British G8 summit the following year would have to be far richer in content. 'You could tell by the way he responded to the results that he meant to stay on,' said Tom Kelly, who was with him in Washington.[89]

The results could indeed have been worse for Labour: they were not the 'white out' some had predicted. Cabinet loyalists had been instructed to get on the airwaves and play down the results. Number 10 was thus extremely irritated when Blunkett went on Radio 4's *Today* programme and said he was 'mortified' by the losses. He was phoned at 6 A.M. Washington time by one of Blair's aides to tell him that he had made a *faux pas*.[90] Number 10 was even more angered by the Brown camp, who briefed that the elections were bad for Blair and for the party. 'It was typical, boring and pathetic,' said one aide in Number 10.

Philip Gould's take on the results was relentlessly positive: 'This means you can win a three-figure majority at the next General Election,' he told the Prime Minister, his face beaming.[91] The Tory recovery under Howard had stalled. That weekend, the Number 10 aides rallied around Blair. According to one, the clinching argument for Blair was 'do you think the UK would be better without you? And secondly would the country be better run with Gordon?'[92] The Brownites thought it was the local and European elections that had 'finally convinced' Blair that he should stay.[93] They were right, although it was a further two months before he irrevocably made up his mind that he would fight a third General Election. His mood picked up. 'There was a definite change of his morale in the early summer,' said a senior official.[94] The Brownites were livid. Ed Miliband marched in to see Sally Morgan and demanded,

'Why haven't you packed up yet to go? There's a deal and he's got to go.' Morgan was heard to reply, 'I don't know anything of the sort.'[95] Miliband returned later to relay the story about the dinner in November. When Blair heard about Miliband's outburst, he told Prescott, who reportedly 'went mad'.[96] The Brown camp were in meltdown. Brown came over to Number 10 and stormed into Blair's study. 'When are you going to F off and give me a date?' he shouted. 'I want the job now!'[97]

II

Back in Charge

June–September 2004

Blair's decision to remain in office begged further questions. How would he put his fight-back into effect? How long would he remain at Number 10? How would he plan his third-term strategy and ensure that it would not be hijacked by the Treasury? The immediate backdrop did not appear encouraging. The Butler Inquiry, an awkward reshuffle, an angry PLP and some troublesome by-elections were all lurking ominously. If he could survive until September, he should be safe; but could he? Although he did not know it, he had just passed the lowest point of his premiership. From now on it would be upwards for his final three years. He would buck the rules of British premiership which say that achievement comes early on, not at the end. He had still to define policy in key areas that would become important to him – climate change, Africa and the EU – while in other areas, notably public service reform and Northern Ireland, he still had much work to do. His first task, though, was to come through the immediate storms and rebuild some political capital.

Victory in Europe: June 2004

Blair needed a victory to kick-start his recovery. His attention shifted to the EU, where efforts were under way to choose a successor to Romano Prodi as President of the European Commission, an appointment that would last for five years. Europe's leaders also needed to finalise their approach to the new EU constitution. Both issues were to be determined at a heavy EU Council meeting in Brussels on 17/18 June, under the chairmanship of Bertie Ahern. Blair had patched up his relations with Chirac and Schröder in the second half of 2003. In the face of the imminent enlargement of the EU, both Chirac and Schröder had concluded that unless the three largest countries worked together, it would be unmanageable. Their *détente* of a kind reached a new high when they met in Berlin in September; here Sheinwald and Wall negotiated a deal on European defence issues with their opposite numbers.[1] The Americans from the outset had been suspicious of this idea despite British efforts to win them over: 'You know you say all the right things,' Manning had said to Condi Rice, 'but your body language is awful.'[2] But Blair, speaking effectively on behalf of Europe, was now able to sell the deal to Bush. Here was an occasion, recalled one senior official, when 'the Prime Minister was able to convince the President to be more charitable'.[3]

The new European accord would not endure for long, however, as Chirac and Schröder's vision for the EU was fundamentally different from Blair's: 'I think the Prime Minister felt that they were holding Europe back from making progress towards a competitive market and liberalisation,' recalled Kim Darroch, who was to succeed Wall at Number 10 in June 2004.[4] Chirac and Schröder believed in a strongly federalist EU, controlled from the centre. They 'expected to be able to ring up the President of the Commission and tell him what to do', according to one of Blair's team. That meant that they wanted 'somebody as president who would do their bidding, and knew their place. The British wanted someone who would be genuinely independent and who would apply the rules vigorously,' while also sharing Blair's vision of a looser, free-market Europe.[5] Chirac and Schröder concluded between themselves that the Belgian Prime Minister, Guy Verhofstadt, was their man; their second choice would be Luxembourg Prime Minister, Jean-Claude Juncker, both renowned Benelux federalists. Number 10 was aghast. Though he liked Verhofstadt at the time personally, Blair regarded him as 'a crack-pot federalist with appalling ideas', and 'in the pocket of France and Germany'.[6]

Blair had discussed the topic with Schröder at the December 2003 EU Council, but not wanting to unsettle their new accord, he pulled his punches. Schröder told him that he wanted Verhofstadt, to which Blair replied, 'He's not my favourite candidate. I'll think about it.' Schröder took this as a grudging acquiescence. Wall had to intervene with his opposite number in Berlin: 'Be in no doubt – Blair does not want this guy.'[7] Subsequently, Verhofstadt arranged a meeting with Blair to seek his approval. 'I want to run, but I won't if you tell me you won't support me,' he told Blair, who replied, 'Well, I don't actually, you're not my candidate for the job, but we're not in veto territory here.' Verhofstadt left their meeting thinking that, in the last analysis, Blair would not stop him. He then went and spoke to Schröder's people to say that he had got a 'fair wind' from Blair. Again, it was left to British officials to convey Blair's true feelings. The matter was thus left to be resolved at the June Council. Ahern made it clear that he wanted the issue settled at dinner on the first night, Thursday 17 June, so that negotiations over the constitution could proceed the following day.

Schröder and Chirac sprang into action. The decision on the presidency was to be made on the basis of 'qualified majority voting'. This meant that all the Germans and French had to do was to build a sufficiently large majority behind Verhofstadt, which they tried to do by offering the new member states (who had joined on 1 May) a deal over funding, and they would have their man.[8] To Blair, it was a classic EU moment: either he had to acquiesce in the traditional Franco-German hegemony, or fight.[9] Blair chose the latter, and picked his friend Berlusconi as his comrade-in-arms. Chirac and Schröder, they both thought, were effectively saying to the accession countries, 'This would be a very good time for you to shut up and do what you are told.' 'The Prime Minister is meek and mild most of the time at EU Councils,' said one British official. 'But he doesn't react well to that kind of thing.'[10] He had fought hard against 'old' Europe for enlargement, and now saw an opportunity for the accession countries to come to his aid.

The atmosphere on the Thursday evening rapidly became poisonous. It reminded one in the Number 10 party of watching the film *Zulu*, 'There were wave upon wave of Franco-German attempts to steamroller their candidate through. One after another, their waves got mown down.'[11] Working with Berlusconi, Blair worked to achieve the 'blocking minority' necessary to stop Verhofstadt, and managed to win support from Poland, Portugal, Greece and Slovakia. But was it enough? Throughout the evening, the British delegation remained unsure if they had secured enough votes.[12] While Wall went around the delegations making notes on the back of an envelope of supporting countries, FCO lawyers worked out the legality of the complex counting procedure and what exactly would constitute a blocking vote.

But who to back if not Verhofstadt? Blair spoke to the centre-right leaders at the Council (the group to whom he was closest) and by phone to Angela Merkel (though it was to be another year before she was to become German Chancellor). Attention fell on Chris Patten, ex-EU Commissioner, former Hong Kong Governor and Conservative Cabinet minister. Chirac had some months before blocked the suggestion of Patten, but Blair now advanced his name again as a ploy. 'Patten was put up as an Aunt Sally,' said Wall. 'The French had made it clear they would not accept him so it was an entirely tactical manoeuvre: they got to block our candidate and we would get to block theirs.'[13] Patten was aware of this, but duly waited in his room until about midnight. When the call did not come, he slipped quietly away.[14] Meanwhile, over dinner, boasting the finest fare of Ahern's land – wild Irish salmon, Wicklow lamb and Chateau MacCarthy red wine – the atmosphere was far from congenial. Blair and Schröder became involved in a heated dispute. 'What are you doing?' the German demanded. Before Blair could offer any explanation the Chancellor interrupted. 'You and I are finished,' he said, looking Blair in the eye.[15] The dinner proved the lowest point in their relations, though Schröder later retracted his remark.

Long after midnight, Ahern decided that his hopes of a deal were dead: some member states were so openly opposed to the Belgian Prime Minister that he saw little point even in calling for a vote. 'Ahern reached the private conclusion that it wasn't going to work and the best thing was to bring the shutters down,' said a British official.[16] The Verhofstadt candidacy was dead, and everyone was now too tired to agree a successor. Before Blair went to bed, he tried to talk to Chirac and Schröder. Schröder turned on him, refusing to shake his hand.[17] Rumours started to percolate around the corridors that France and Germany would go home that very night. 'It could not have been more dramatic,' said one in the British party.[18] Without naming France or Germany for their bullying tactics, Blair authorised a barbed press briefing. The task fell to official spokesman, Tom Kelly: 'Normally we are quite diplomatic at Councils. This time we decided not to be. It is rare to hear a sucking-in of breath from journalists, but that's what I heard when I addressed the news conference.'[19] Kelly said that the EU had to accept that it was now a union not of six or even two member countries, but of twenty-five, and that there would be no second-class citizens in the new Europe. When Schröder heard about this briefing, his officials said that he was 'spitting blood'.[20] In Chirac's press conference, he alluded to Thatcher's tactics of twenty years before, and said that the EU could not again allow itself to be blocked by a single country.

The next day, 18 June, Blair prevailed again. He successfully defended Britain's 'red lines' on the proposed EU constitution, on taxation, foreign policy, defence, immigration and social security, averting Franco-German efforts to push the constitution in a federalist direction. It was a moment of reckoning for Chirac and Schröder: 'France and Germany realised they had finally lost control of the EU,' said one British official.[21] Coming after their failed attempts to mould the European convention in their own way, to rally the EU against Iraq and to secure their candidate as president, they had even lost on the constitution. The atmosphere was toxic. At the concluding press conference at 11 P.M. on Friday evening, Blair set out his emerging vision for the future of Europe: the drive from the Franco-German axis towards a federalist super-state was dead, he declared. The 'new Europe, including the new members, did not favour the integrationist policies pursued by the Benelux countries for so long'.[22] A normally restrained official said 'it was a fantastic performance . . . I came out of his press conference thinking, "That was bloody brilliant"'.[23] The European press largely agreed, with *Le Monde* concluding that 'whatever people say, this remains a British victory'.[24] *Der Spiegel* said 'the vote in favour of the constitutional treaty means victory for British Europe',[25] while *El Mundo* reported that 'Blair, the winner of the summit, achieved everything he wanted'.[26]

The British party left that night for RAF Northolt, north-west of London. There was 'a certain amount of celebration', as officials described it. Champagne flowed and Blair toasted Wall, who was shortly to leave his post at Downing Street.[27] But Blair was also pensive. 'No one must underestimate the anger and resentment now of France and Germany,' he told Wall, and spoke about the need to avoid his own 'Zidane moment', a reference to the football match between England and France two weeks before in the European Cup when Zinedine Zidane had scored twice for France in injury time to beat England. Blair's great fear was that France and Germany would default to their second choice, Juncker. 'We will have to endure him for five years if they succeed. They're absolutely burning and will go all-out to recover it on a rematch over the president. Tomorrow we'll need to hit the phones,' Blair said.[28] He had already alighted on Portuguese premier José Manuel Barroso as his favoured choice, and secured Merkel's backing for him. Barroso was a kindred spirit of Blair's, described by his team as 'a global thinker, trans-Atlanticist and non-federalist', who was just as much in favour of economic reform as Blair.

Before the Brussels summit broke, Ahern had called for a 'special summit' in late June to resolve the outstanding presidency issues: agreement on the constitution would have to await another Council. At that meeting on 29 June, Blair's telephone diplomacy bore fruit: Barroso became the compromise choice for President of the Commission. It meant that from July 2004, seven years into his premiership, the focus of the EU began to flow in Blair's direction. John Grant, Britain's permanent EU representative, regarded Blair's stance on the presidency as 'his single biggest achievement in Europe: had it not been for Blair, the President of the Commission today would be Guy Verhofstadt'.[29] The full significance of Blair's victory was not apparent in Britain at the time, but it significantly boosted his morale. He began to look ahead with greater confidence.

Good News on Iraq: June–July

The first half of 2004 had been bloody in Iraq: a constant stream of bad news, culminating in Abu Ghraib in May, had led Blair to the verge of despair. Now there was to be a break in the clouds. On 8 June, the Security Council passed the resolution for which Blair had long lobbied, UNSCR 1546, endorsing the appointment of the interim government from the end of June, and authorising US and allied military forces to remain in the country until January 2006. Blair had toiled hard to bring the UN back: 'It is an important milestone for the new Iraq,' he said. 'We all want to put the divisions of the past behind us, and unite behind the vision of a modern, democratic and stable Iraq.'[30] In the FCO, however, Jay was concerned, and asked his senior staff: 'Look, shouldn't we be producing contingencies for the worst case?' 'In theory, yes,' came the reply, 'but there's a real danger that if we produce worst-case-scenario planning it will leak and become a self-fulfilling prophecy.'[31] Instead, hopes were pinned on the handover of sovereignty (scheduled for 30 June) as the possible turning point in Iraq's fortunes. From the time of the invasion the British had argued that the allies should remain in Iraq not 'a second longer than was necessary', and that power should be handed over to the Iraqis.[32] With hindsight, some close to Blair questioned whether retaining control of Iraq for a full year had been wise: 'In retrospect I would have gone for a much dirtier and shorter transition,' said one Number 10 official. 'I would have handed power back to people about whom we had completely legitimate suspicions, but I would have done it just to get it off our hands.'[33] Arch-hawk John Bolton agreed. 'It would have been better if there'd never been a Coalition Provisional Authority,' he said, because it allowed the US to become 'perceived as an occupying power'.[34] In mid-June, under conditions of utmost secrecy, the Americans resolved to move the date forward to 28 June;[35] the British were not told until the last minute.[36] The change was partly to pre-empt bombs in Iraq, but also to maximise the political impact of Bush and Blair being together in Istanbul for a NATO summit.[37]

Blair and Bush discussed the timing of the announcement on 27 June in Istanbul over a private dinner. At midnight, Rice called Bremer: 'Blair is okay with the transfer tomorrow.'[38] The next day, the coalition provisional authority handed power over to acting Prime Minister Allawi. Bremer formally announced in Baghdad that 'the occupation will end and the Iraqi interim government will assume and exercise full sovereign authority on behalf of the Iraqi people'.[39] In Istanbul Rice scribbled a hurried note for Bush: 'Iraq is sovereign.' Bush showed the note to Blair and scrawled across it, 'Let Freedom Reign!'[40] After months of almost intolerable strain, Blair's relief was intense. His hope was that, at long last, Iraq would assume a more stable footing. His words from outside Istanbul's Hilton hotel, nevertheless, contrasted sharply with Bush's jubilation. Avoiding hyperbole, he described the transfer of sovereignty as 'an important staging post, as democracy replaces dictatorship'.[41]

In mid-July, Blair cleared another Iraq hurdle, the publication of the Butler report. Number 10 had fought hard to avoid the further inquiry, but Hutton's publication at the end of January had failed to close the chapter on whether Blair had led Britain into war on a false prospectus. 'The media pressure was so great that we had to find a way of lancing it,' said David Hill. 'We did it in the belief that the Prime Minister had acted responsibly and would be cleared.'[42] A precedent for such an inquiry had been established when Lord Franks investigated the circumstances surrounding Argentina's invasion of the Falkland Islands in 1982, which the Thatcher government had failed to predict or prevent. Number 10 fought a rearguard action to constrain the terms of reference of this inquiry purely to intelligence, rather than the wider issue of why Britain had gone to war.[43] Butler received notification of his terms of reference at 9 A.M. local time (2 P.M. London time) on 3 February, when he arrived in Atlanta in the US on a flight from Mexico City. Before he could discuss them with anyone in London, they had been announced publicly.[44] Several weighty figures in Whitehall wondered whether the 'tightly defined inquiry' was not in fact too restrictive.[45] Its scope was also limited by the timescale. In the US, the commission was set up to report only after the presidential election in November; in Britain, Butler would report long before the next General Election.[46] But while Butler's findings being published in July was good news for Blair, it was bad timing for the Bush administration. Overtures were made to London requesting that the inquiry report after the November elections. The British response was that the timing of America's own inquiry 'was not entirely convenient for Blair'.[47]

The composition of the inquiry was Blair's choice, as it was his decision to set it up. Number 10 suggested that it should have figures from the three main political parties. The Liberal Democrats refused to participate, the Conservatives nominated Michael Mates and Labour put forward Ann Taylor, who had previously served as Chief Whip. The other two members were Sir John Chilcot, a former Permanent Secretary at the Northern Ireland Office, and Lord Inge, formerly Chief of the Defence Staff. The committee's diverse composition led Butler to conclude that his best strategy would be 'simply to tell the story'.[48] Others could then draw their own conclusions.

Butler was not the automatic choice of chairman: at one time it was thought it might be Inge, but together they decided that it should be Butler.[49] This set off alarm bells in Number 10. Butler had served as Cabinet Secretary for only the first few months of Blair's premiership, overseeing the transition from John Major. At the time, the Blairites had few complaints; Butler was considered positively helpful in arranging for Campbell and Powell (both technically 'special advisers') to wield powers previously reserved to civil servants.[50] Butler, who Blair thanked repeatedly for the success of the transition, had no sense at the time that the relationship was difficult.[51] But there was an inevitable difference in outlook between the traditionalist Butler, at the climax of his distinguished career in the civil service, and his New Labour Young Turks who arrived in Number 10 with their own ideas on how to run government. Butler 'never really made the jump', said one aide. 'He never really got what we were on about.'[52] Indeed, many traditionally schooled civil servants in Whitehall in 1997 didn't know what the incomers were on about or didn't like what they were on about. Those who felt that the relationship with Butler had been awkward now feared there might be 'a bit of him wanting to get his own back. "I'll show them" kind of thing.'[53] The main Number 10 concern was, however, directed at the Conservative nominee on the committee, former minister Michael Mates, who they hoped would be a 'typical' Tory grandee, 'pro the establishment and pro security'. They came to believe, however, that he was 'playing political games'.[54] Mates and Inge in particular felt that the wealth of material that the committee had uncovered, some of which leaked to the press, justified hard-hitting conclusions. Ann Taylor resisted tenaciously.

In the last few weeks before the report was published, there was feverish speculation that pressure was being exerted on the committee to tone down its conclusions. Various sections were indeed shown by Butler to the individuals directly involved, and passages were amended. But Butler denies that there was any undue influence, or changes of substance. 'We did amend passages where individuals made representations which we felt were justified. But any changes were not very significant, and my broad conclusions were not affected.'[55] For all this, it was only in the immediate run-up to the inquiry's publication that Number 10 became jittery. 'We never felt that Butler was likely to come up with anything that would seriously worry us. This created much less of a cloud for us than Hutton,' said David Hill.[56] The arrival of the report at Number 10 contrasted starkly with the frenetic activity and suspense over Hutton: 'There was no burning of the midnight oil as there had been [then],' said one aide.[57]

On perhaps the most crucial question, the report supported the Prime Minister. Neither Blair nor Number 10, it said, had lied: 'We should record in particular that we found no evidence of deliberate distortion or of culpable negligence.'[58] Nevertheless, the report implied that Blair exaggerated the strength of the intelligence, in particular when he spoke to the House of Commons on the day the dossier was published.[59] It was 'over the strength of the evidence', Butler later said, that he thought that Blair had 'misled the public, Parliament and the world'.[60] On the morning of 14 July, before the post-publication press conference, Butler met with his committee. They considered the issues and questions likely to arise and discussed how Butler should react if asked whether the Prime Minister should resign. His response, they agreed, would be to say 'that question is not for us, but for Parliament and the people'.[61] That reply would very likely have been contrasted with the report's explicit recommendation that John Scarlett should be allowed to keep his new job as head of SIS. But – to the committee's astonishment – no journalist asked whether Blair should keep his job. Where Butler's punches did land, however, was in his criticism of the Blairite style of leadership and governance, where he saw traditional Cabinet government being replaced by aides meeting informally in Number 10 and deciding great issues of state without properly minuted discussions or prior paperwork. The government knew this was coming. 'It was perfectly obvious that Robin Butler had reservations about the style of government,' said one Cabinet minister.[62] But Number 10 still 'vehemently disliked all the stuff about "sofa government" in the report', said one insider. 'They were pretty bitter.'[63] This in particular was where one aide thought 'you could feel the personal animus'.[64] Nevertheless, Butler's concerns were widely recognised, and played their part in a limited revival of Cabinet government in Blair's remaining years.

Deep inside Number 10 there was a regular joke about how often the media could keep saying this is the 'worst week ever for Blair'.[65] The *Guardian* duly billed the week beginning Monday 12 July as 'Tony's week from hell'.[66] Once he escaped fatal censure from Butler, all eyes turned to by-elections in two apparently safe Labour seats to be held on 15 July. This, his detractors hoped, would deal Blair's premiership a final blow. A swing of 26 per cent handed Leicester South to the Liberal Democrats. But Labour held on Birmingham Hodge Hill – just. Number 10 breathed a sigh of relief. 'If that was the Prime Minister's worst week,' one of his advisers joked, 'then let's have more of them.'[67] Blair went into the weekend in buoyant form. Word came out that he was 'playing a hard game of tennis at Chequers and contemplating a Cabinet reshuffle'.[68]

Taking on the Treasury: March–July

Blair was regaining control, but he still needed to clarify his own agenda and see off incursions from the Treasury. The next battleground was to be his 'five-year plans', with Brown's counter-attack coming with his biennial 'comprehensive spending review' (CSR). The decision to produce a series of five-year plans had been taken at Chequers in September 2003, but it was only with the tuition fee vote out of the way that Blair began seriously to engage. He considered the plans essential to driving through public service reform. They also said a great deal about his future intentions: 'I saw the whole five-year-plan agenda as clear, uncontroversial evidence that he wanted to go for a third term,' said a close aide.[69] A strategic approach to policy was relatively new territory for the British government: 'When the PM started in 1997,' recalled Lord Birt, 'no department did strategy work, if you define strategy as an all-embracing look at the total environment in which you operate. So this was a learning experience for everyone, including, frankly, the PM.'[70] Birt's work aimed to create a 'modern corporate centre', ensuring world-class capacities for strategy, delivery, marketing and communication and the management of human resources.[71] Blair tried to gird up the Whitehall machine for the task ahead in a speech on 24 February, when he called for 'a transformed civil service' driving change in an era of globalisation, as opposed to maintaining the *status quo*, which he claimed had been Whitehall's purpose in the past.[72] Throughout his premiership, Blair had felt let down by the civil service. They were 'the single biggest thing standing in the way of Blair achieving his vision', said one aide. 'They weren't skilled enough to help deliver.'[73] Blair's speech, drafted by Barber, was his latest effort to 'push the mandarins to raise their game'.[74]

Despite his concerns, and in part to help enhance their capacity, Blair was now convinced that he needed to make use of as many government departments as possible in producing his five-year plans. He did not want them to be seen as something driven from the centre: the goal was to secure far broader 'buy-in'. A heavy reliance on three Cabinet ministers was a crucial component of these efforts: Reid at Health, Clarke at Education and Blunkett at the Home Office (his fourth 'key' department of 2001, Transport, had fallen by the wayside). Initially, this inclusive strategy helped overcome Whitehall's antipathy. That spring, Number 10 worked through the ideas that came back from the departments, even though it was thought they were often 'complicated and confused'.[75] As Number 10 began to critique the plans and insist on revisions, tensions grew. 'The growing power of the centre was often resented deeply by the politicians concerned, and of course by the civil service,' said Birt.[76] They co-operated with different degrees of enthusiasm but 'it was never believed that they would really write [the plans] on their own without heavy guidance and input' from Number 10, recalled Blair's PPS, Ivan Rogers.[77] In the end, Birt judged the effort to involve the departments a 'valuable but not wholly perfect process in terms of getting buy-in'.[78]

Blair also worked hard to build support among Cabinet colleagues. The plans as they developed would be discussed not only with the Secretary of State responsible, but also with small groups of ministers and aides who gathered at Chequers.[79] The fruit of these works would then be presented to Cabinet and discussed at length. Cabinet government indeed was rarely more in evidence than it was in these few months. The balance of Cabinet had been concerned by Blair's apparent lack of confidence and grip in early/mid-2004, but ministers remained essentially supportive of him and his ideas to improve public services. 'What he did was to ensure the five-year plans were truly owned by the Cabinet. He played them brilliantly.'[80]

Cabinet support was essential if Blair was to make headway against the Treasury. Brown's suspicions of the plans were both personal and political. Their very existence (and title) suggested to him that Blair might be reneging on what he thought was a 'commitment' to quit before the next General Election. The Treasury at large was also worried by the spending implications. 'I can't trust the Treasury to be with me,' said Blair. 'If we have them in on the process, they'll endlessly nit-pick and create difficulties and it will go nowhere.'[81] The decision to keep the Treasury at arm's length led to confusion across Whitehall.[82] Within Number 10 some senior officials thought the decision 'ludicrous', while Turnbull thought excluding the Treasury was 'madness'.[83] It meant that for the first half of 2004, there were two parallel processes in Whitehall: five-year plans driven from Number 10, and the CSR, which incorporated the Gershon efficiency review, driven by the Treasury. The view at Number 11 was that 'Blair's five-year plans wouldn't happen. Our spending review is the real five-year plan.'[84] The Treasury could not, however, prevent the plans being published.

They were published in two waves, before and after the summer break. The three to which Blair gave most time, and which bore his imprint most heavily, were the three staples: health, education and law and order. The health plan was published on 24 June. Reid remained every bit as fiery a champion for reform in health as had Milburn. The proposals bore the imprint of the powerful Number 10 operator, Simon Stevens, as well as his even more radical successor in the Policy Directorate, LSE academic Julian Le Grand. The plan proposed no less than 'trying to turn downtrodden patients into savvy consumers'.[85] 'The key idea in the plan,' one insider said, 'was the principle that the money followed the patient.'[86] The plan announced that patients would have the right to choose from a wide range of public and private hospitals, which would be able to match the NHS in quality and in price.

The education plan proved more troublesome. Clarke had barely engaged with the plans in the autumn or in January because of his focus on tuition fees.[87] When he did, Number 10 was disconcerted to discover that he did not share their enthusiasms. 'Clarke was never really a Blairite on education. The only true believers on education were Andrew [Adonis], the Prime Minister and me,' said Barber.[88] Clarke's officials at the DfES were 'hostile because they feared the argument with local authorities, unions and the left wing education establishment.'[89] From the Permanent Secretary, David Normington, downwards, the Department's strategy was 'not really in tune' with Number 10.[90] Consequently Adonis was far from impressed when he saw the draft plan the weekend before it was due to be published, and a frantic redrafting effort began.[91] Adonis had not been idle in his new perch in Number 10: his menu included radically 'expanding the number of academies, and more freedom for all state secondary schools, including over the employment of staff, ownership of assets and composition of their governing bodies'. His vision was to make them more independent of local authorities, with funding coming direct from Whitehall. Popular schools should be allowed to expand, and private school managers, churches and parents' groups encouraged to open and run new schools. It was an ambitious list, and he won over a sympathetically inclined Blair to it by sheer persistence and by writing 'brilliantly timed notes' to him that pressed 'all the right triggers'.[92]

But without Clarke's willing support, Blair was always going to find it more difficult to get the education plan through Cabinet. A crisis point was reached on 1 July, with Prescott and party chairman McCartney being the chief critics. Blair would not compromise and in one of his most emphatic performances he drove the plan through largely unaltered by Cabinet. Some critics, though, kept their powder dry: there would be time enough later to fight if the plans ever moved towards policy. The education plan was published on 8 July. Differences with Clarke again emerged over the way that Blair presented the White Paper on education. Blair favoured a tub-thumping launch; Charles Clarke did not. But Blair knew that education was fast emerging as his most distinctive contribution in domestic policy, and now he was beginning to feel the blood surge again through his veins, he was not going to go *sotto* on it for anyone.

In health and education, Blair was arguing against the views of many in the PLP. On his law and order plans, he was far more in tune with them, except for its libertarian wing. Nor did the Treasury share his enthusiasm. Brown's disdain for elements of Blunkett's populism was in part responsible for his fighting the proposals to the limit, resulting in the Home Office plan being the last of the big three to be released, on 19 July.[93] 'But the PM loved Blunkett on Home Office matters: they were entirely on the same wavelength,' said Barber.[94] The proposals reflected the three strands along which Blair's mind always ran: serious and organised crime, high-volume crime, and anti-social behaviour.

The publication of the plans lifted Blair's morale and enhanced his authority at Westminster and in Whitehall. 'Taken with the situation in Iraq, which all thought would improve quite rapidly that summer, it was a case of "glad confident morning again",' said one aide.[95] But where Number 10 saw bright weather, the Treasury saw only storm clouds. Brown, as predicted, fell back on his fourth CSR as his response. CSRs traditionally saw vicious behind-the-scenes battles, with Cabinet ministers trying to maximise their department's funding for the following two or three years, and the Treasury and Number 10 fighting each other over budgets and priorities. Brown relied on the CSRs as one of his main levers to control domestic policy. The power to grant money gave him influence over departmental ministers, and the 2004 round was to see the bloodiest fight yet between Number 10 and the Treasury. The process had kicked off relatively well in January, though Number 10 complained that it could not get hold of the Treasury model and had to devise its own.[96] The Treasury's particular priorities were tax credits, poverty alleviation, social programmes, sustainable communities and housing; Blair's were the Home Office and defence (as health and education had already been fixed). Brown was acutely aware that he would be shaping the spending priorities for his own premiership, which he expected to begin imminently. This made him all the more insistent on getting his own way.

Over the spring and early summer, discussions took place between Rogers at Number 10 and Balls and Macpherson for the Treasury. In July, the discussions suddenly turned sour. Military expenditure was the cause. Brown thought that Blair was being too soft with the top brass: 'You're giving away too much and are being outrun by those military bastards,' he said.[97] Brown was never entirely at ease with the cost of 'Blair's wars', and Hoon and the MoD were largely bypassed as it came down to a personal tussle between Blair and Brown. At one meeting late in their exchanges, Brown said, 'You've brought this all on yourself by making the service chiefs believe that if they press you'd give way.'[98] Blair replied that the service chiefs were in open revolt. Indeed on 3 July, Chief of the Defence Staff Mike Walker, who had earlier written to Blair, exercised his constitutional right to see the Prime Minister. He travelled to Chequers and threatened to consider his position if the services did not get the money he demanded. This pressure resulted directly in the most generous settlement the MoD received for twenty years, achieving some £800 million extra from the Treasury in the final week of the spending review.[99] Brown was furious. Blair himself was irritated that the Treasury and Brown failed to 'signal a bit more flexibility earlier in the process.'[100] One official added: 'He blamed the Treasury for screwing up the process and presumed that Brown was doing so further to ratchet up the pressure on him.'[101]

Disagreements over Home Office spending were even more intense. Blair ended up fighting for even more than Blunkett was requesting. His priorities were for prison financing, where he succeeded in raising the money to finance a prison population of 80,000 a year, which he thought would be enough (the accommodation crisis in 2006/07 revealed that even this figure was too low). Blair also fought for extra money for additional Community Support Officers. It resulted in a 'final, gory weekend' on 10/11 July, with the Treasury eventually coming up with several hundred million pounds extra. Blunkett was repeatedly frustrated during it because Brown had gone to ground and would not talk to him, nor would Blair, who was in the gym at Chequers. His Permanent Secretary, John Gieve, was no more successful in finding out from the Treasury or Number 10 what was going on.[102] The atmosphere was vitriolic: Number 10 accused the Brown camp of trying to destabilise them, Mandelson was 'going around spreading poison' and loyalists on both sides were briefing and counter-briefing against each other.[103]

Brown delivered his CSR statement to the House of Commons on Monday 12 July. By largely endorsing the Gershon efficiency review, which included cuts of 84,150 civil service jobs, it put him directly in the firing line of the civil service unions. These unions were not affiliated to the Labour Party, however, and their opposition proved relatively insignificant. Within a week the Treasury rage at Number 10 had subsided and it accepted that the spending review had been 'pretty fair'. Some in Whitehall nevertheless felt that Blair had been overly generous with the public finances, which had seen public spending as a percentage of GDP rise from 37.4 per cent in 1997 to 42.3 per cent.[104] One Treasury official described Blair as 'the most fiscally profligate Prime Minister I've ever met'.[105] Number 10 said Brown was the Chancellor: blame him.

Delaying the Killer Reshuffle: July–September

Blair was '80 per cent sure by July that he was going to carry on as PM, but he still wasn't absolutely decided when he went off on his summer holiday', said one of the inner circle.[106] Much had still to be clarified. Should he pre-announce his departure at a future point, bring in a big-hitter in a reshuffle and, most delicate of all, how would he tell Brown that he was not going to be departing imminently? Would they orchestrate a firestorm in the party and media for him to go? Blair resorted to his 2001/02 idea of announcing that he would be going, but at a future date, which he had yet to decide. By doing so he hoped to bring to an end the debilitating speculation over his future and stem some of the poison dripping daily from the Brown camp. 'Blair's view was that he would never have got through the 2005 election had he not set a date in 2004,' said one aide. 'If he hadn't, he knew the election would have been a complete nightmare.'[107] Given that Brown had made it very clear he no longer believed what he was saying in private, Blair hoped that a 'public' announcement that he would step down within a stated time frame, even if that time frame was not to Brown's liking, might be enough to placate the Chancellor. It was all 'an attempt to stop the attack from Brown's people', confirmed John Burton.[108]

Many of Blair's allies put the idea down to Mandelson: 'Everyone suspected it was Peter, but no one knew for certain,' said one senior colleague.[109] But Mandelson was not the game-maker he had once been. Blair's closest advisers confirm that it was pure Blair, inspired largely by Aznar's announcement of his own intended departure, which Blair had talked with the Spanish leader about personally.[110] He discussed the idea in strictest confidence with Powell and Morgan who backed his instinct, seeing it as an essential part of his fight-back strategy.[111] In major decisions Blair's style was always to consult a number of close confidants and then to make up his own mind. Byers was one who counselled against: '"Don't do it," I told him. "It will only mean more questions, because people will then want to know when you are going to be going in the third term."'[112]

Blair's third-term strategy would require a powerful figure to work alongside him to counterbalance Brown. He thought he could not prevail over him, and drive through his agenda, without some such figure (in fact he was to show he could do it alone). But who should he have? Mandelson was out of the question. Blair favoured him, but Prescott and Straw made it clear that his return for a third time would be wholly unacceptable, not least because of the instability it would cause with Brown.[113] It highlighted Blair's desperation, and the lack of credible alternatives, that he could be contemplating a figure with such little support across Cabinet.[114] He had still not realised he was much better off without him. Blair instead nominated Mandelson to become Britain's next European Commissioner on 23 July, a post for which Hoon had been widely tipped. Who else was there? Blunkett, Clarke and Reid were deemed not suitable as Blair's big-hitters for different reasons. One obvious candidate, however, kept cropping up in Blair's mind: Milburn. He had been an irregular presence in Number 10 and confidant of Blair's since his resignation in 2003. 'Some of us had long felt that we needed to have another politician in and around Number 10, not least because so many of the political figures from the first term had dispersed,' said Mulgan.[115] Milburn told Blair that Number 10, for all its re-engineering in 2003, 'lacked coherence and direction, lacked mission, and thus the agenda was lost at a time when public support was visibly disintegrating'.[116] Blair warmed to the sound of this. He also liked

Milburn personally. 'They were on the same wavelength,' explained one senior minister. 'They instinctively felt the same about the big issues and Tony badly needed another male around with whom he felt comfortable.'[117]

Blair had hoped to announce a pre-summer reshuffle on 21 July. Milburn, who he had already asked to return to Cabinet on several occasions, now came under intense pressure again from him, as well as from Morgan and McFadden. 'We knew persuading him would be an uphill task, but equally we knew he'd been missing it,' said a Number 10 aide.[118] Milburn had reached an understanding with his family that he would not return to government, and when Blair asked him in the week beginning Monday 19 July, he prevaricated. He was walking on the street beside the House of Commons when Blair called his mobile phone to offer him the job of chairman of the party with a role overseeing policy. To Blair's intense disappointment, especially given the absence of a Plan B, or indeed time to construct one, he said 'no'. 'Fine,' Blair replied, carefully keeping his cool.[119] He now had no option but to postpone the whole reshuffle until after the summer.

Most difficult of all for Blair was telling Brown that he was planning to stay on until after the General Election. The two men met for dinner with Prescott on 18 July. Brown's aides had been planning intently throughout the early summer for the transition. Ed Miliband had drawn up lists of who would serve as ministers in the new government.[120] Orders had even gone out to key Brownites to cancel their summer plans to prepare for the imminent transition. Was the moment at long last about to happen? Brown was suspicious. He had a hunch another 'betrayal' might be imminent. At the dinner he pushed Blair hard for a precise date. Then Blair unleashed the bombshell. Butler had just reported, he said, and with the inquiry's attacks on intelligence failings and his style of leadership, and with Iraq delicately poised with its own government barely three weeks old, it would be a mistake to go now. 'It would look like I've been defeated over Iraq. I need more time, I can't be bounced.'[121] Brown was horrified and the meeting broke up fractiously. The following day Brown's nightmare deepened: he learned about the imminent reshuffle and the plan to bring back Milburn.[122]

By the end of July, Blair was tired and drawn, but he did not strike close aides as approaching 'meltdown'. 'He was knackered as he went away, but nothing worse,' said one.[123] He had decided to take an unusually long break, lasting twenty-six days, including a fortnight at Cliff Richards' home in Barbados, a visit to Athens to see some of the Olympic Games, a passion of Cherie's, a visit to Berlusconi at his holiday home in Sardinia, and a stay at the Villa Cusona, a Tuscan palace belonging to Prince Girolamo Strozzi.[124] Burton recalled a conversation in the garden at the Blairs' home in Sedgefield, when he told him that he was not going to stand for a fourth term, but would be carrying on.[125] But others insist that only during the holiday in Barbados did he finally decide that he would be fighting the next General Election, and that he would announce that he wouldn't fight a fourth.[126]

Any lingering doubts in Blair's mind evaporated under the heat of the Barbadian sun. Cherie was completely clear that he should fight on and not cave in to the pressure from Brown, or leave with his work far from complete.[127] From her own, and the family's point of view, staying on was the right course. The idea of a pre-announcement came back to him strongly: it seemed the ideal solution to keep his enemies at bay while avoiding Thatcher's statement, which he found shrill, that she was going to 'go on and on'.[128] 'He sat in the sun for a couple of weeks and refreshed himself. His powers of recovery are strong. He returned as though the wobble had never happened,' said Turnbull.[129] 'It was perfectly obvious on his return from holiday that he intended to stay on as Prime Minister,' recalled Rogers.[130] He returned to Britain on 25 August, with an unusually long list of notes. 'He was very fired up,' said one of his inner circle.[131] At the heart of the fight-back strategy stood Milburn. Blair had spoken to him again over the summer, as had Morgan, and had succeeded in making him re-consider his 'no' of July.[132] The key piece of the jigsaw was now ready to fall into place.

Blair now had to decide exactly what form his announcement would take. He wanted Milburn to spearhead the election campaign and ensure that the manifesto, unlike in 2001, or 1997, would be solidly New Labour. But what precise job should he fill? Blair still wanted him to be party chairman. But Prescott refused to let McCartney, blamed for the disappointing summer election results, be replaced. 'The party and the trade unions would never have let it happen,' added Blunkett.[133] Blair was left to muse what other niche he could offer Milburn, who had made it clear he wanted a job overseeing both policy and party. It would be delicate. Brown had also returned from holiday fired-up and with detailed notes of his own. 'The difference between them is that whereas the Prime Minister writes his painful longhand by pen, Gordon bashes away furiously at his computer in his inimitable two-fingered typing style. The common factor is that they both return more anti the other than when they went away,' said one official.[134]

Brown's camp did not react at all well to the news that Milburn was about to return. The story was leaked to the *Sunday Times* on 5

September,[135] when the front page spoke of Milburn returning as joint party chairman alongside McCartney. 'There is enough speculation to last a lifetime . . . You'd have to be a political hermit not to be aware of the force that is ranged against the idea,' recorded Blunkett in his diary.[136] The atmosphere in Westminster and Whitehall became every bit as fetid as it had been in June and July. Milburn became worried that his appointment was being portrayed as a trial of strength and a way of doing down Brown. He questioned whether he should come back, especially after Blair told him early in the week beginning Monday 6 September that the party chairmanship was a step too far.[137]

A new plan emerged. Milburn would now become 'election co-ordinator' instead of party chairman. This post was currently held by Douglas Alexander, an arch-Brownite, but Blair told aides that Alexander was not a big enough political figure to handle running the campaign. He wanted Milburn instead.[138] On 7 September Blair saw Brown to break the news. 'Why's Milburn coming back? Is it about cooking the manifesto against me?' Brown demanded. 'This is symptomatic of the way you behave,' he shouted, in a difficult half-hour meeting.[139] Blair was disconcerted by Brown's reaction, but even more so when Milburn told him that the job of 'election co-ordinator' was not enough. He wanted a 'real job'. Blair hadn't reckoned on bargaining for his own side. On 8 September, Milburn met with the 'ultra-Blairites', including Jowell, Reid and Byers, in Byers' office in the House of Commons. 'We were very clear that it was going to be a very different role from what the Prime Minister originally offered. Alan needed to know exactly what power and authority he would have in his new position,' said one witness.[140] They wanted something sufficiently bombproof to withstand the expected assaults from Brown. The job description they hatched gave Milburn oversight of Downing Street's policy and strategy units in addition to being in charge of the election campaign and having a seat on Labour's National Executive Committee.[141] Short of Brown's job in the Treasury, there wasn't much they'd left off.

Early the next evening, Milburn saw Blair with his ambitious job description in hand. Milburn still had one more demand: securing Blair's promise that he would remain Prime Minister at least until the General Election.[142] Milburn insisted they agree an official statement on his status. It was not only Brown, it seemed, who didn't trust Blair's spoken word. Formalities over, both men relaxed over beer watching an England–Poland football match in the den.[143] Milburn told Blair that he wanted to speak to Brown himself about the position. The opportunity came after Cabinet the next day, Thursday 9 September, the day of the reshuffle. The conversation had been sabotaged, he felt, by the press portrayal of his return as a humiliation for Brown. It was difficult and uncomfortable. Milburn tried to be constructive. Brown's attitude was 'you've been given the job and now you're going to get on with it'.[144]

Alexander was furious when Blair told him about his demotion to Minister of Trade to make way for Milburn. 'Sharply raised voices' were heard emanating from Blair's study.[145] Another disillusioned Brownite, Andrew Smith, fell on his sword before he could be pushed. He resigned three days before the reshuffle and Blair appointed Alan Johnson in his place as Secretary of State at Work and Pensions. 'We appointed Alan because he was a bit Milburn-ish, the voice of C1 and C2 voters,' said a close aide.[146] Johnson had impressed Number 10 over his support for tuition fees, and his reforming zeal and skill in front of the media were highly regarded. As a concession to Brown, his ally Ruth Kelly was promoted from his Treasury team to Minister of State in the Cabinet Office to assist Milburn. Even this went down badly because it meant Brown losing her from the Treasury.[147] By bringing back Milburn, 'Blair had crossed the Rubicon', said one Brown ally.[148] 'It was a deliberate affront to Gordon as he had always been seen as campaign co-ordinator,' said a senior official. Brown's Treasury team interpreted the reshuffle as Blair saying, 'I'm going to run this election campaign with my own man at the helm and I'm going to win it, take the spoils and then I'll be able to dictate terms to Gordon. Then I'll be able to do the things I want in the third term or be powerful enough to sack him if he won't let me.'[149] They had it spot on. 'You've appointed that fucker Milburn!' Brown raged at Blair.[150] The atmosphere hit rock bottom. The Treasury moved into a policy of non-co-operation. '"You're on your own and you can piss off" was their attitude,' said one Number 10 aide.[151] But even as Brown's camp were reeling from Milburn's return, Blair was plotting an announcement that would inflame them still further.

The September Surprise

The reverberations of the reshuffle continued until the party conference, which opened on Sunday 26 September in Brighton. It was the tensest run-up to this annual event in Blair's years as leader, worse even than 2003. Everyone expected an epic, gladiatorial Blair–Brown conflict to unfold. Brown set the tone by publicly declining to acknowledge whether or not he 'trusted' the Prime Minister.[152] Pundits predicted that Brown would use his speech to declare himself the authentic leader of the Labour Party, followed by a strong Blair slap-down, reasserting his own credentials. Brown's team settled on a more subtle strategy. Instead of a full-frontal, they would characterise Blair and Milburn as 'espousing divisive and damaging policies' with their pushing of the market, choice and privatisation. In contrast, Brown gave primacy to party unity and to social justice.[153] Sympathy welled for Brown as he rose to speak on 27 September, not least because he had recently returned from the funeral of his mother. In his nuanced speech, he attacked the 'choice and diversity' agenda: 'There are values far beyond those of contracts, markets and exchange,' he memorably said, to considerable resonance. He heaped praise on the government's achievements while his call for party unity was almost self-consciously underlined at the end of his speech when he did not take his applause at the podium, but walked back to be beside Blair instead. 'The speech was judged to be a unifying force and not the feared assault on Blairism,' declared the *Guardian*'s Michael White.[154] Here was Brown, loyal but also expounding Labour values, waiting for the call.

Blair's speech was equally the fruit of prolonged debate. His supporters knew that something had to be said about Iraq, and he decided to do so early on. The doves wanted him to be apologetic and conciliatory, but he refused. 'The problem is I can apologise for the information that turned out to be wrong, but I can't, sincerely at least, apologise for removing Saddam,' he told delegates.[155] Twice his speech was interrupted by hecklers shouting, 'You've got blood on your hands.' Many delegates wanted his apology to go further. On Brown's challenge, he decided to answer it head-on: 'Choice is not a Tory word. Choice dependent on wealth: those are Tory words. The right to demand the best and refuse the worst and do so not by virtue of your wealth, but your equal status as a citizen, that's precisely what the modern Labour Party should stand for,' he asserted. Blair too could play games. In a display of public support for Brown, he praised Labour's economic record, saying the election would be fought in part on it, as the Brownites wanted, as well as, crucially, his own radical new agenda. He described Brown as 'a personal friend for twenty years and the best Chancellor this country has ever had'.[156] The speech received a mixed response. Jonathan Freedland wrote, 'Mainly Brighton gave a warm, if not wild, embrace for a leader who many assumed would either be gone or in deep peril by now',[157] while *The Times* thought his speech sounded 'more like a collection of worthy ideas than a compelling programme . . . Blair will need a stronger message before embarking on the hustings.'[158] If Blair's camp were slightly disappointed by the way their leader emerged from the conference, Brown's team were pleased. 'They tried to kill us at conference by painting us as dinosaurs. It didn't work. We out-manoeuvred them.'[159]

As conference was drawing to a close on Wednesday, 29 September, Brown went to see Blair at 3 P.M. in his suite at the Brighton Metropole Hotel. Blair accused him of conducting a deliberate campaign to undermine him throughout the conference week and before. How could their relationship be re-established, Brown asked? 'You've got to work with me,' Blair said. The Brownites interpreted what Blair said as code for 'he would stay in the top job until Brown had helped him earn his place in history'.[160] As always, both sides have different understandings of what was said. Brown certainly raised his irritation at Milburn's return to which Blair replied, 'You know I've got to be able to bring my people in. Milburn's very talented, we need campaigning people.' The Brownites believe this was the meeting at which the Chancellor lost any residual belief that Blair was sincere in wanting them to work together.[161] Of many alleged 'rock bottom' and 'worst ever' moments, this was the lowest, and worst. 'Tony thought he could work with Gordon until this point. It's been civil war ever since,' said one man close to both.[162]

Blair deliberately chose not to share with Brown his now well-developed plan to pre-announce his departure. Blair did not believe he could trust Brown to keep it to himself. The final details were only agreed by those closest to him, Morgan, Powell and Cherie, when in Brighton.[163] The key announcement was that he would serve a 'full third term', but not fight a fourth General Election. There were two other strands. Some months before, the Blairs had bought a £3.6 million house in Connaught Square, in London's Mayfair. 'The house purchase said, "We're thinking of going and need to have somewhere to live." The house was saying there'd been more than just a wobble,' recalled one aide.[164] The civil servant who oversaw the house purchase ensured that the Blairs had an ordinary mortgage and avoided anything that could be interpreted as a special deal because of who they were. It was not a risk that had occurred to either of the Blairs,[165] and proved a wise precaution, with some Brownites later implying that the Blairs' ability to afford such a house was suspect.[166] They had managed to keep the purchase secret: even Morgan did not know about it until she was told at the conference. But news of it was about to leak: Number 10 knew that Andy Grice, of the *Independent*, had got hold of the story, which helped dictate the timing of the announcement.[167] The third element was an announcement that he would be going into hospital on 1 October to have an operation to eliminate his atrial flutter or irregular heart beat, which had been a source of concern to him for a year.[168] 'Let's do a triple whammy,' Blair told his close team at Brighton. They could all see the sense of it.[169]

On his return to London, Blair called a meeting in the den that Thursday afternoon, 30 September, where he told the wider group, 'I'm contemplating doing all three at once. I'm thinking of saying I'll stay on for a full third term, what do you think?' 'He explained that he had needed to get the conference out of the way, and now needed to set out his stall for the future,' said David Hill. Everyone present knew he had made his mind up so there was no point in them expressing reservations. 'There wasn't a lot of discussion about it.'[170] Number 10's task was to ensure that the story was broken flawlessly. 'We assembled the most detailed description of what was going to happen,' said one. 'This was the second time we had spoken about the Prime Minister's heart and so we were going to make absolutely certain there could be no complaint whatsoever about people being properly informed.'[171] The ever-efficient Hill had set up the media for an important announcement to be made that evening. Godric Smith and Tom Kelly were deputed to call the broadcasters, who were rendered almost speechless by the news.[172] Blair now rushed to inform selected Cabinet colleagues, before they heard about it on the news. Some he phoned personally; for others he arranged Number 10 to call their private offices. It came as news even to the Cabinet Secretary. He was hosting a permanent secretaries conference in Sunningdale and received a message to call Number 10, just a couple of hours before the news was made public. He passed on the news to the other permanent secretaries and that evening they debated the impact it would have on the way their departments operated.[173] Blair himself phoned Byers. He had kept so many of his closest political colleagues out of the loop, Blair explained, because he 'didn't want to get talked out of it again'.[174] Several were disconcerted that they were only being told when it was a *fait accompli*: Peter Hain had seen him in his room in Brighton in his capacity as Leader of the House to discuss the forthcoming Queen's Speech and had found him distracted. They discussed the run-up to the General Election, but not a word was spoken about the grand plan.[175]

'Don't you have to phone Gordon yourself?' Powell said to Blair in the study that afternoon. 'No, you tell Gordon,' he responded. There was general ribaldry throughout the den before Blair said to Rogers, 'Come on, it's your job to phone Gordon's private office and tell them.'[176] Brown had flown off that day to an IMF meeting in Washington. There is no evidence that Blair deliberately planned his announcement to coincide with Brown's absence, but it was 'a bloody convenient time', admitted one aide.[177] Rogers tracked down James Bowler, Brown's new PPS, at a hotel in Georgetown. 'I've got three interesting pieces of news, and you'll have to think carefully how you're going to relay this to your boss,' Rogers told him, before wishing him luck.[178] Predictably, Brown went 'berserk': his lieutenants later branded Blair's action 'an African coup'.[179] It was indeed Blair at his most brutal. In the short term, Brown could do little other than send a telegram wishing Blair well with his heart operation. But he was determined to exact vengeance.

Television crews from the BBC, ITN and Sky arrived at Downing Street at 7 P.M. for broadcasts to go out later that evening. 'If I am elected I will serve a full term. I do not want to serve a fourth term – I don't think the British people would want a Prime Minister to go on that long,' Blair declared. Mindful of the need to defuse the likely counter-attack, Blair said, 'I don't think it rules Gordon out in any shape or form at all, because he will be younger than many Prime Ministers have been if he took over at the end of a third term. I'm not going on and on for ever,' he concluded, deliberately mimicking Thatcher's words. When he met his team shortly after the announcement, Matthew Taylor joked, 'There were a couple of protestors in here, Tony, but we cleared them out for you.'[180]

The atmosphere soon soured. 'Some of his closest colleagues felt deeply angry,' said Hain.[181] None more so than the Blairites in Cabinet, Milburn, Reid, Clarke and Jowell. All thought it was a serious misjudgement in both tactics and substance. 'From day one of the third term, the clock will tick,' Blair was warned.[182] 'It was a very foolish, indeed, mad thing to do,' said Milburn. 'You never pronounce your own demise.'[183] Turnbull thought that the announcement had the effect of turning Blair into the equivalent of a second-term US President. 'Over time he began to do things to secure his legacy which diverged inevitably from what Labour needed to do to be elected. The Labour Party was slow to wake up to that.'[184] A factor that all Blair's entourage underestimated was the 'relentless barrage that the Brownites would unleash after the General Election', said one close aide.[185] As the Brownites viewed the prospect that their champion might not take over until 2009, by which time the country might be feeling tired of Labour after twelve years in power, they realised they had been humiliated and outmanoeuvred. A premiership equivalent to that of Alec Douglas-Home (1963–64) at the end of a long period of Tory rule was an awful prospect, when they had all held such high hopes of what could be achieved. They retreated to their tent to plan their next move.

12

Crafting a Bold Future

October 2004–March 2005

Now that Blair knew he was going to be remaining in power, he set about planning in earnest for the next few years. He had one last chance to get his premiership right. What would he do? The first priority was to ensure victory in the General Election, and on his own manifesto, giving him a clear mandate for a third term. Early summer had served Labour very well in the past, and all eyes were fixed on May 2005 as the likely polling day, though technically he could have continued until 2006. Helping the new Iraqi government build a stable democracy was a high priority, as was gaining the upper hand in the war on terror at home and abroad. Northern Ireland had seen little solid progress since the Good Friday Agreement in 1998: he now planned a major initiative at Leeds Castle to kick-start talks. The chance coincidence of British presidencies of the G8 and the European Union falling in 2005 gave him major opportunities to advance his own agenda on climate change and Africa. His third principal foreign policy objective, progress on the MEPP, would be pursued bilaterally with the Americans once November's presidential election was out of the way. Deep within the bowels of Number 10, work was taking place on its own weapon of mass destruction: a nuclear option that would involve moving Brown at the election and splitting the Treasury. If his third term was to be more successful than the first two, the 'Brown problem' would have to be dealt with once and for all.

Dealing With Gordon, Part I: October–December 2004

Brown demanded the earliest possible meeting after he returned from the IMF in Washington and a three-day tour to Africa. He met Blair in Number 10 on 5 October. Blair was anxious to build bridges after his 30 September announcement, and worried about the damage Brown and his camp might cause in the run-up to the election. He offered Brown the chairmanship of Labour's press conferences during the General Election campaign, an offer that Brown thought 'contemptible'.[1] Brown told him that he was not interested in any job at the centre, but would travel around the country rallying Labour support. He demanded to know why Blair had not given him prior notice of the announcement before he left for Washington, especially since they had had a personal meeting at the end of the Brighton conference. Blair, clearly uncomfortable, replied disingenuously, 'I told you that before.'[2] Brown left the meeting making no secret of his utter contempt for Blair. Exasperated by what he considered to be Blair's repeated lying to him over departure dates, it was the occasion when Brown said to him, 'There is nothing that you could ever say to me now that I could ever believe,' sixteen words which three months later were to explode across national headlines in Britain.[3] 'Gordon didn't really believe he would be going,' rued one of Blair's aides. 'He always thought Tony would find some reason for staying on.'[4] Among Brown's many grievances, bringing back Milburn was at the top. The Treasury refused to co-operate with Milburn's policy exercise: their attitude to Number 10, according to one official, was 'You can do what you like; we'll not have anything to do with Milburn.'[5] 'It was an insult to Gordon. It was a deliberate downgrading,' fumed one Brownite. 'So Gordon sat back and said, "Okay, if that's how they play, they can win the campaign on their own."'[6]

Milburn, assisted by his deputy, Ruth Kelly, took to the task of preparing the manifesto with high seriousness. Sticking to the letter of the 'contract' on his appointment on 9 September, he made himself in effect the supremo of policy and strategy within Number 10. A memo of 28 October shows how he and Kelly had carved up domestic policy, and were insisting on a very strict modus operandi: 'We need to ensure a coherent approach to commissioning advice from departments on the PM's behalf and communicating his decisions,' it said. 'The experience of ministerial colleagues is that too often they receive conflicting and inconsistent messages from different sources within Number 10.'[7] Milburn regarded Number 10 as having been largely dysfunctional since the 2001 General Election, and he now relegated Matthew Taylor and Geoff Mulgan to subordinate positions.[8]

The Queen's Speech on 23 November was an early fruit of Milburn's approach. With Blair's other two domestic priorities, education and health, forging ahead with no need for further legislation, the programme included thirty-two bills, an increase of nine on 2003, and included eight on law and order. It brought the number of crime bills introduced into Parliament since 2001 to thirty-four.[9] Among the new bills was one establishing a Serious Organised Crime Agency (SOCA) – an idea conceived by John Birt and championed by Turnbull and Heywood – which was presented as a British-style FBI. Another bill provided for the introduction of identity cards. In response, Michael Howard came up with perhaps his wittiest and most damning response, berating Blair for not achieving more since 1997: 'If it took Winston Churchill five years to win the Second World War and it took Clement Attlee six years to build the welfare state, surely seven and a half years is more than enough for you to get a grip on the problems that face Britain today.'[10] The Queen's Speech received a mixed response. Simon Jenkins dubbed the measures 'The Big Fear'[11] while Johann Hari said it was 'a programme that any pragmatic centre-right government could be proud of'.[12] Such comment stoked fires among Blair's critics in the PLP.

Despite an increasing focus on the short-term politics of election planning, Blair also made it clear that work on 'delivery' would persist, and he continued his regular meetings with Barber's Delivery Unit. Barber, meanwhile, had become concerned that progress was not proceeding as swiftly as planned. In the jargon of the Delivery Unit, there were too many 'reds' in departmental reports on delivery objectives and too few 'greens'. In mid-October, Barber raised this with Blair: 'I suggested to him that he should remind Cabinet ministers of the need to do everything they could to shift their delivery priorities from red to green by the end of the year.' Blair, concerned by the danger of 'slippage', agreed and pushed the point at the next Cabinet meeting.[13] With Blair's continued support, the Delivery Unit redoubled its efforts. By early December improvements were beginning to show. On 9 December Barber made a final presentation to Cabinet, and was able to report real progress across the board, even if the public remained unimpressed. Time lags in improving performance, uneven improvements across the country, hostility from public service leaders, the media climate and the distraction of the Iraq war all had negative impacts on the success of this most central plank of Blair's second-term domestic agenda. Barber concluded: 'By the end of a gruelling and controversial second term, the public were no longer prepared to give the government the benefit of the doubt.'[14]

If this conclusion did not bode well for the forthcoming election, Brown's conduct was scarcely more encouraging. The Chancellor was widely expected to use his 'pre-Budget report' on 2 December, his first major parliamentary statement since Milburn's return, to lay out a personal manifesto in advance of the General Election, which Number 10 feared would be an attempt to distance Number 11 from Number 10, with media support. 'Mr Blair was taken to task last week for promoting the so-called politics of fear; this week the Chancellor wanted to claim as his own the politics of hope,' wrote Matthew d'Ancona.[15] Against expectations, Brown remained largely on-message. His report included extra money for anti-terror measures, a ten-year childcare strategy and an increase in the period of maternity pay. This disconcerted Number 10 considerably. At least they knew where they were when Brown was being difficult. Now they had no idea what he was thinking or planning. Aides speculated that Brown had slipped into 'one of his depressions'. 'He may have been fed up rather than angry by then,' said one of Blair's inner circle. 'I think he's often depressed. He goes within himself and total gloom descends. Deep dark gloom.'[16]

Instead of suffering at Brown's hands, Blair took a broadside from another quarter, and it was friendly fire. The lack of Blairite big-hitters in Cabinet was one of the themes of his second term; David Blunkett was a rare exception. But it was as if there was a jinx on them: Blunkett had been conducting a three-year affair with Kimberly Quinn, the American publisher of the *Spectator* and wife of the millionaire publisher of *Vogue*, and news of this unlikely liaison broke in mid-August. Hitherto only a very small circle knew of its existence, and that they had a child. On 14 August reports appeared in the press of Mrs Quinn being pregnant with her second child, and on 27 November that Blunkett had fast-tracked Quinn's nanny's visa application. Blunkett flatly denied that he had abused his position. The former government economist, Sir Alan Budd, now Provost of The Queen's College, Oxford, was asked to chair an inquiry into the alleged wrong-doing. While this work was in train, journalist Stephen Pollard's biography of Blunkett began to be serialised in the press on 6 December, containing inflammatory remarks about Blair and Cabinet colleagues, reportedly spoken by Blunkett himself: Blair was portrayed as weak for not standing up more to Brown; Straw of having left the Home Office in a 'giant mess' in 2001; Clarke of having 'gone soft at education'; Cook of being a 'snob'; Beckett a 'time server' and so on. While Blunkett had the ignominy of telephoning round

Cabinet colleagues to apologise, Blair prepared for what became a trying Questions session later that week.[17] 'PMQs were horrible and I regretted every moment that he had to deal with it,' Blunkett later acknowledged. 'It put him under pressure from obvious opponents and also opponents from within the government.'[18]

On the evening of 14 December, Budd phoned Blunkett with the news that his investigation had unearthed an e-mail suggesting that Blunkett had indeed fast-tracked the visa application.[19] Blunkett and his special adviser Huw Evans went to Number 10 the next day at 3 P.M. He and Blair were both shocked at Budd's finding, not least because Blunkett had asked for the inquiry and had told Blair very clearly that he had done nothing wrong. Powell, Morgan and Hill were summoned to take part in the meeting in the den. When Blair asked Blunkett for his decision, Blunkett said that he was 'very sorry' to have let Blair down.[20] Blair then turned to Huw Evans, who was known and trusted by Number 10. 'What do you think?' the Prime Minister asked. Evans turned to Blunkett and told his boss, 'You know what I think. You have to resign.'[21] Blair was reaching the same decision. 'If David hadn't resigned at that meeting, Tony would have pushed him,' confirmed one of the Number 10 team present.[22] Blair told him that resignation now meant that 'he'd be able to bring him back at some future point', said Evans.[23]

After everyone left, Blair and Blunkett hugged each other. Blunkett choked up, and repeated how sorry he was. Blair replied, 'Not as sorry as I am. I was relying on you in the build-up to the General Election.'[24] Although Blair thought Blunkett had behaved unwisely in allowing himself to be captivated by Quinn, he strongly disliked seeing his colleagues pushed out of office on personal issues, and regarded this case as a 'particularly grotesque' example of a woman's revenge.[25] Blair was losing Blunkett at the very moment that the Home Office's legislation was top of his agenda, and was deprived of a 'very loyal lieutenant, an authentic working-class man in the Cabinet and a remarkable communicator', said one senior mandarin.[26] 'Tony was just very sorry for him. He [Blunkett] was falling to pieces with the woman and the child. He was in emotional turmoil,' said an aide.[27]

Blair was forced to focus on an immediate successor. There were only two possible candidates, the remaining loyalists in Cabinet good enough to have the department: Clarke and Reid. Neither were shoo-ins. Some in Number 10 favoured the latter, because they did not believe that Clarke would support Blunkett's very tough policies. But they were over-ruled by Blair, who wanted a more subtle and emollient figure than

Reid to carry the agenda forward, even though he had been disappointed by Clarke's lack of reforming zeal at Education.[28] The Conservatives had announced that they were hiring Lynton Crosby, John Howard's hard-hitting electoral strategist from Australia, which implied a particularly aggressive campaign was in prospect. Labour's record at the Home Office would be a target. 'We all thought we needed someone with Charles's thick skin and experience, who already had a grasp of the Home Office,' said one aide.[29] Clarke proved tougher than predicted, though over the coming months Number 10 worried he had become too much his own man. He was 'never going to go populist in the Blunkett mould', said a senior official. Instinctively, as on the 'Muslim question', 'he was more liberal than Blair'.[30] Clarke's vacancy at Education was filled by Ruth Kelly, who had impressed Number 10 greatly in the two months she had been at the Cabinet Office with her loyalty, grasp of detail and ease of communication. Only later did Number 10 appreciate 'that she was not yet ready for it',[31] with her 'politics not equalling her skills at policy'.[32] So Blair was to go into a General Election with his public service team utterly different from the four champions of 2001. But Blair had high hopes that Kelly, whom he initially thought might be too close to Brown, could turn into a radical at Education. No sooner did everything appear settled by Christmas, than another volcano erupted.

The journalist Robert Peston had been working on a biography of Brown for three years. The book vividly detailed Blair's thinking on standing down in 2004 or 2005. Peston spoke with those closest to Brown at the Treasury, including Ed Balls, Ed Miliband, Tom Scholar, Gus O'Donnell, Shriti Vadera and Nicholas Macpherson, several times, and had several substantial meetings with Brown in 2004.[33] The supposition on Brown's part was that by the time the book was published, he would be in Number 10: 'The book was timed to come out after the transfer,' said one close to him.[34] It would help explain, at the onset of his premiership, why he had been so frustrated and angry with Blair and how and why he had driven so much of domestic policy, way beyond the normal remit of a Chancellor. But even when it became clear to Brown's camp that Blair was not going, Peston's informants carried on talking. Peston's evidence is meticulous, suggesting that his informants had consulted their documentary records before they saw him. What emerged was the fullest and most accurate book to appear in the ten years of Blair's premiership, albeit one which Blair's camp hotly contests. In December 2004, just a few weeks before Peston was due to publish, Brown asked him to delay: its inflammatory material would create a storm in the run-up to the election. Peston refused. He had reached no understanding with Brown; publication was all set for early in the New Year, and delay was not possible.[35]

Blair was scheduled for an interview on BBC Television's *Breakfast With Frost* on 9 January 2005. Two days before the programme, Blair called Brown: 'There had better not be anything to destabilise me on Frost.'[36] Only on the Saturday did both men discover that the serialisation of Peston's book would begin the following day in the *Sunday Telegraph*. Shocked, they spoke again for thirty minutes to work out a strategy for getting them through the following few days: they could work well even in this phase if they had a common aim. On the Sunday morning, Frost came into the studio waving his copy of the *Sunday Telegraph*, and persistently asked whether the 'killer' quotation in Peston's book was true, that Brown had asserted, 'There is nothing that you could ever say to me now that I could ever believe.' Blair tried to palm the question off, but refused outright to deny that Brown had said it. How could he? He had heard him say it, and worse, more than once.

Neither man came out of the biography well. In John Kampfner's words, Brown emerged as 'a man ... consumed with grievance', while for the public to be told that Blair could not be trusted by his Chancellor was 'devastating'.[37] Nick Brown said he could very well imagine Brown saying that he would never trust Blair again: 'I think it got things fairly right.'[38] It was Blair's turn now to be furious, believing (wrongly) that the Brownites had egged Peston on to publish at this point as a way of exacting revenge over the return of Milburn. On Monday 10 January, Brown and Blair addressed a fractious meeting of the PLP. MPs accepted that they were not going to see the end of Blair this side of the General Election without grave destabilisation, but they were angry that the squabbling was damaging their electoral prospects. They made it plain that the fighting had to stop. 'I think we've got the message,' Blair announced as the meeting was ending. 'He means that Gordon's got the message,' one backbencher was overheard saying.[39] The PLP's concerns were given added weight by one of Philip Gould's focus groups finding that the Blair/Brown rows were having a negative effect on voters. But once the genie had been let out of the bottle, and Brown's lack of trust in and contempt for Blair had become public knowledge, there was no going back.

Hope and Despair in Ulster: October 2004–January 2005

Blair had let Northern Ireland politics drift somewhat in the first half of 2004. Now he knew that he would be fighting a third term, it returned to the top of his list. Together with Powell, he convened talks at Leeds Castle in Kent from 16 to 18 September, as soon after the summer 'marching season' in Ulster as could be arranged. Before the conference, he spoke of 'the yearning of the people of Northern Ireland for a peace that . . . is complete and lasting', and urged all parties to 'complete the process' that had been begun with the Good Friday Agreement six and a half years earlier. He referred to his speech in October 2002 in which he urged that the Good Friday process be concluded and which spoke of a 'fork in the road', with the need for Sinn Féin/IRA to choose either peace or violence.[40] That speech had not, to his regret, led to any dramatic change in paramilitary activity from either side. Blair and Ahern had held an abortive meeting with the Northern Ireland parties at Hillsborough Castle in March 2003 to restore devolution, suspended in October 2002, but it foundered on IRA unwillingness to give a firm declaration that their weapons would be destroyed. A day later Blair and Ahern decided to postpone for four weeks the Assembly elections scheduled for 1 May.

Number 10 worried that Trimble's position as leader of the more moderate Unionist party, the UUP, was being undermined by the repeated failure of the IRA to deliver: Unionists were increasingly looking to Paisley and the DUP, which had maintained all along that the IRA were not to be trusted and that it had been an error to enter into negotiations with them. The elections were delayed again until the autumn. Blair's concern to protect Trimble led to a fall-out with Ahern over the postponements.[41] He could postpone the elections no longer and when they came on 26 November, the result was a victory for the extremes. Blair admired Trimble as the man who had taken the Unionists into the Good Friday Agreement.[42] Now, after five and a half years of working with Blair, his political career was at an end.

Despite acknowledging the new mandates of both the DUP and Sinn Féin, Blair was disturbed by the results and took time to react to Paisley's success. Not knowing him well personally, 'stuck in his mind was the Paisley of old, who had resisted the Good Friday Agreement.'[43] He had also made unpleasant remarks about Cherie and Catholicism.[44] Ahern had similar difficulties: Paisley had made a point of never shaking his hand and had made insulting comments about him too.[45] As if in denial, 'The Prime Minister did not want to deal with Paisley and continued to deal with Trimble for several months,' said a senior official.[46] Fortunately, the nine months following the Assembly elections were a quiet time in Northern Ireland. Gradually Blair realised that he could not hold off indefinitely, and meetings began to take place with

Paisley at Number 10 as well as in the DUP leader's office in the House of Commons.[47] But in general in early/mid-2004, Number 10 took a back seat while the Northern Ireland Office (NIO) oversaw the province largely on its own.

Blair saw the talks at Leeds Castle in September 2004 as the opportunity to forge a close working relationship with the DUP leader. The picturesque castle in Kent was chosen because it was secure, 'but also boasted sufficient quiet corners for people to have private words'.[48] Blair was all too conscious of the emotional and political gulf between the DUP and Sinn Féin. Would their leaders really be calling to engage in real dialogue as opposed to grandstanding? Worse, it became known that Paisley was ill: questions now emerged about whether he would be fit enough to travel to Leeds Castle, and whether he would have the strength to lead the Unionists on returning to Ulster. 'The Prime Minister was very insistent that everything be done to make sure that Ian was comfortable, and he responded well to that attention,' said Tom Kelly.[49]

Adams and McGuinness turned up at Leeds Castle in upbeat mode, declaring 'we want to do business with Ian Paisley'.[50] They even injected humour on the first day by arriving with a three-foot bugging device which they had uncovered at Sinn Féin's headquarters in Belfast. 'This is an offering to the mighty god of British intelligence. We brought it here to return to Mr Blair,' Adams said. The gesture, as was intended, made it into the headlines. Blair's response, after they had left the room: looking at the old chunky bug, was, 'I thought we could do better than that!'[51] The bonhomie was to disappear once hard talking began: the Republicans became disillusioned when the Unionists were not prepared to jump straight into power-sharing, while the DUP felt that Sinn Féin was again not playing fair over decommissioning. Both parties came close to achieving a breakthrough, but in the end it was the DUP stipulation about requiring 'visual proof' of IRA decommissioning that proved the obstacle. Blair tirelessly used his personality and diplomacy to coax the delegates along, and was disappointed, though not unduly, when the talks broke up without hard agreement. Just having the leaders of both sides sitting down and talking in earnest was an achievement on which to build. In the final press conference on 18 September Blair said he thought that the prospect of an agreement had been brought much closer and that the conference achieved clarity about what needed to be done.[52] Hopes of a breakthrough were heightened when Blair and Ahern met in Downing Street on 24 November. December saw the government pressing the DUP behind the scenes to accept power-sharing and Sinn

Féin to provide the incontrovertible evidence of decommissioning that would allow the process to move forward. The 'comprehensive proposals' on the future had been published, and many felt agreement was within reach. Blair's mood was 'more determined and upbeat than it had been for many months on Northern Ireland', said a senior NIO official.[53] But at that promising moment, as so often in Northern Ireland, disaster struck.

On the morning of Monday 20 December, Powell was in Belfast to attend a meeting with Adams and McGuinness at the secluded Clonard Monastery. For several years, Powell had held meetings with Republicans at this quiet location in west Belfast as it provided the confidential and secure venue for the talks which had seen Republicans' views progressively soften. As Powell, NIO officials Robert Hannigan and Jonathan Phillips were about to walk into the monastery, they received a call from security to say, 'Before you go in, you need to realise that a robbery has just happened, and it looks like it was the IRA.'[54] It was the biggest bank robbery in Irish and British history: £26.5 million had been stolen from the Northern Bank. Intelligence was suggesting that the Provisional IRA was responsible.[55] 'If it's the IRA, the process is in deep shit,' commented Powell.[56] They chose not to broach the robbery, and went ahead with the meeting with the unnerving feeling that they had no strategy. 'Emotionally and intellectually, we were stunned,' said one of the party.[57] The meeting over, the British team regrouped to assess where they now stood. 'What the hell do we do now?' they asked themselves.[58] The NIO promptly rang Tom Kelly, who was about to board a flight leaving Bosnia after his pre-Christmas visit. He broke the news to Blair: Kelly described his reaction as 'deeply dejected: it was like taking a cold shower.'[59] Within forty-eight hours, British intelligence was confirming the IRA was responsible: unlike the Omagh bomb in 1998, this was not the work of a splinter group. The NIO now had problems convincing Blair.[60] 'There was a pattern of Blair not believing us. There were various occasions during this period when we had to gently remind him we were quite well-informed about what the IRA was up to.'[61]

In fact, Blair and Powell were under no illusions about the IRA, but they worried about provoking a backlash from the Republicans: if pushed too far, they might return to war. 'We may not just lose the talks process: we might lose the peace process too. We have to give the Republicans a ladder to climb back up,' Blair declared.[62] Powell, who worked intensively on finding a way forward, said, 'There's no point in being angry. We just have to work out where to go from here.'[63] What had the bank robbery signified? Was it sanctioned by Adams and McGuinness? The British were genuinely confused over the motive. 'I'm afraid none of us know the answer,' said a Number 10 official. 'Our assumption was always that Sinn Féin and the Provisional IRA were inextricably linked over it. It was sanctioned at a certain, possibly high, level.'[64] One theory was that militant voices within the movement thought that the pressure to produce photographic evidence of decommissioning during Leeds Castle and after was pushing the Republicans too far, and that the British needed a reminder of the power they still possessed. Number 10 concluded it was either a release valve or a sign of frustration.[65]

While 'rejectionist' Unionists were claiming the robbery proved that they had been right all along, and that Republicans could never be trusted, there was worse still to come. On 30 January 2005, a Catholic father of two children, Robert McCartney, was murdered, allegedly by members of the Provisional IRA. A fight had broken out in a bar in central Belfast which culminated in McCartney being stabbed. Revulsion grew when witnesses refused to co-operate with the police investigation and systematically all traces of what had happened were covered up. 'Robert McCartney's murder put everything into a state of free-fall in the early part of 2005,' said a senior official.[66] 'Blair himself was appalled, and still more so by the reaction to the murder: the notion that you could clear up a murder scene with such care and precision that the whole incident was denied revolted him,' said another.[67] Blair now had to tread a tight rope. He had to make it clear to Adams and McGuinness that this kind of behaviour would never again be tolerated, without pushing them over the edge.[68] The McCartney sisters launched a campaign to end sectarian violence, which was to have a major effect internationally, particularly in the United States.

While the British were still reeling from the episode, a bizarre offer was made on 8 March by the IRA to shoot those directly involved in McCartney's murder. Blair's reaction was disbelief on two levels. 'One, that the IRA could think that this was an appropriate way to behave; two, that if that was indeed what they intended to do, they were naïve enough to announce it.'[69] Again the British were unclear about IRA thinking. Number 10 thought it a 'monumental' political miscalculation and a throwback to the past, and speculated whether it was a cack-handed attempt by the IRA to portray themselves in a better light.[70] 'The age of the IRA thinking it was a state within a state, and could usurp the police, was over,' said a Number 10 source.[71] The only sign of optimism was that the Northern Bank robbery and the McCartney murder might act as a 'moment of catharsis', waking up the Republican movement to the fact that its old ways were finally over. Blair's speech in October 2002 had not *forced* the Republicans to choose their path. The best hope Blair had as the General Election approached was that the choice of which road to follow could no longer be avoided.

Despair and Hope in the Middle East: September 2003–March 2005

The Middle East was also showing signs of disturbing change. Following some hopeful months in mid-2003, the region had plunged again into crisis when, on 6 September 2003, the new Palestinian Prime Minister Abu Mazen resigned after pressure from a jealous Arafat made his job impossible. The US, after such a promising period of engagement over the summer, became less focused on the region. 'It was one of those cases where we probably didn't seize the moment,' explained Condi Rice. 'You couldn't have launched negotiations if Arafat was still in power but probably we didn't shoot high enough . . . so much was caught up now in Iraq and trying to move that forward that I think we lost a little momentum.'[72] Through calls and the regular VTCs Blair tried to keep up the pressure, but to little avail. 'Blair was pushing us,' recalled the NSC's Dan Fried, 'and I remember the phone calls thinking, "He's just asked a bunch of questions that I can't answer . . . Shit!" I think he was right.'[73]

The Israeli government were not sorry that the US were backing off, and had never been keen on the road map. Instead, they developed a unilateral plan, which they unveiled at a conference in the Mediterranean resort of Herzliya on 18 December. They insisted that the plan was a bold attempt to advance the peace process, particularly given that Sharon faced major opposition from his own supporters to any surrender of land. But there were also clear structural pressures for disengaging from Palestinian-occupied territories. While Arabs within Israel's original borders form only 18–20 per cent of the population, the percentage rises sharply when the territories occupied since the 1967 war are included. The Israelis calculated that within the next five to seven years the Jews would lose their majority 'between the Mediterranean and the River Jordan'. If this happened, the Palestinians would no longer be clamouring for Israeli withdrawal, but for 'one man, one vote': the country would be theirs. Sharon thus proposed removing 40 per cent of the Palestinian population from Israeli responsibility by a total withdrawal from Gaza, and a much smaller withdrawal from the strategically sensitive West Bank. Bush's advisers applauded the plan: 'It showed an enormous amount of courage on Sharon's part,' said one.[74] For Bush's political operatives, supporting the plan had the added bonus of placating Jewish voters in the key battleground states of Florida, Ohio and Pennsylvania in the upcoming November 2004 presidential election.

On 14 April 2004, Sharon visited the White House, where he pushed his plan strongly. After Sharon agreed to withdraw further from the West Bank than originally envisaged, Bush readily endorsed the plan. This went down very badly with the Arab states, as well as with the EU, who called for an urgent meeting of the Quartet – the EU, the UN, the US and Russia – to revive the road map, which they feared Sharon had now abandoned. When Blair himself arrived at the White House on 16 April, his support for Sharon's disengagement plan gratified some on the American side. 'I was happy that Blair was backing our position, but curious. I just couldn't understand why he would do this,' recalled Colin Powell. 'It seemed to me that Bush and Blair were drawn together by some force.'[75] To Condi Rice, the situation was a little simpler: 'The Prime Minister knew we were right, so he came in to help us.'[76] British officials assert that, in fact, Blair's support for Sharon was less fulsome than some suggested at the time. Nevertheless, 'The media played it as if he supported the whole Bush/Sharon line, which we did not,' rued one senior aide.[77] Sharon's response to the green light from Washington was immediate. Israeli rockets tore into the car of Hamas leader Abdel-Aziz al-Rantissi, killing him. The Palestinians interpreted this as a consequence of American support for Sharon, adding further to the tension. A few days later, Sharon warned that Arafat could be the next Palestinian leader in the Israelis' sights. The Middle East was once again spiralling out of control. A letter to the *Guardian* signed by fifty-two retired British diplomats in April, criticising Britain and the other sponsors of the road map for 'merely waiting on American leadership' and not doing more independently,' now appeared prophetic.[78] According to an internal FCO document, the main problem lay in 'a lack of effective international engagement on the MEPP due to other international priorities'.[79] For Blair, gaining US support for the UN resolution on Iraq and handling the proposed EU constitution at home were among his bigger priorities: he did not have the capacity during the spring to press harder on the MEPP.

For the US, the chief 'priority' was the November presidential election, which by the late summer was in full swing. In July, Senator John F. Kerry from Massachusetts had emerged as the Democrat challenger. Blair was in difficulty: traditionally the Labour Party was close to the Democrats, but where did this leave his relationship with the Republican Bush? Fortunately for Blair, Kerry did not want to be photographed with the British Prime Minister (due to his association in America with Bush and the Iraq war) any more than Blair wanted to be seen to be aiding the Democrats and risk incurring the wrath of the White House. Manning at the British Embassy, and Sheinwald, advised that, if elected, Kerry would quickly establish a rapport with Blair. They sent out feelers and received assurances that Blair would be invited over to Washington straight after a Kerry inauguration in January 2005. Many in Downing Street looked longingly on the possibility of a Kerry victory. Blair had more in common with Kerry on his approach to climate change, Africa and the Middle East than he did with Bush. On Iraq, Kerry had been more critical, warning that the US risked being dragged into a quagmire like Vietnam, but his comments remained tame compared to those on the anti-war side of the Democratic Party like Howard Dean.

As November approached, Bush and Kerry seemed neck and neck in the polls. The advice from the British Embassy was that the election was 'too close to call'. The German and French Embassies in Washington told their capitals that Kerry was going to win, but the British Embassy thought, given the intense antipathy between Chirac and Schröder and the right-wing Bush, that they were merely 'giving the message that their bosses wanted to hear'.[80] In Number 10, the fear grew, even among Bush critics, that a Kerry victory would be interpreted as 'a slap in the face for Blair', and that it would make 'life very difficult for him in the run-up to the General Election'.[81] Commentators' pens were poised to pour scorn on Blair for his support for a defeated President who had dragged Britain low. Blair went to bed on 2 November, US election night, thinking that Kerry had won. He woke up to find that, with one state still to declare, Bush was the likely winner.[82] They spoke to each other by phone. 'The latest I've been up since college,' confessed Bush, who was still waiting for Ohio to declare.[83] Kerry conceded on the morning of 3 November. Blair called him that day and they spoke for half an hour. Kerry took the call straight from his farewell rally in Boston and Blair was gratified at how friendly and relaxed he was with him, as he chatted away, 'unwinding about the issues of the campaign'.[84] The same day, Sheinwald phoned Rice and said that Blair 'would like to come over'. She went into the Oval Office to see Bush, and 'it was sorted out very quickly'.[85] 'Bush told Blair, "I want you to come over and talk to me about what I should do in my second term, and about what I should do on my foreign policy."'[86] Never before had an American President appeared so eager to see a British Prime Minister just after his election with such a wide-ranging brief. It was quite an invitation. There was, however, an element of flattery in the President's proposal. Bush was not quite the blank slate some in Downing Street believed: 'Sure the President wanted to take the PM's views into account,' said Condi Rice. 'He valued the PM's counsel, but I think he already knew what he wanted to do.'[87] Bush had previously confided in his aides that he intended to use his second term to re-engage on the MEPP. He also stressed that while Iraq and Afghanistan remained crucial, he wanted to re-emphasize the importance of Latin America and keep the pressure on Iran and North Korea.[88] So although Bush already had an agenda, the chance for Blair to help Bush develop these ideas and add some of his own was hugely significant.

Blair's visit to Washington on 11 November was to prove one of the most successful Bush meetings of his premiership. That evening he had dinner with Bush alone in the White House's Old Family Dining Room, while Sheinwald dined separately with Rice, who would be nominated to replace Powell as Secretary of State a few days later. Bush had grown to like talking to Blair privately one on one, without officials or record-takers. He found him learned, supportive and discreet. They now talked about Bush's election campaign and victory and Blair spoke with him at length about how he thought Bush should run his second term, and in particular what he could achieve on foreign policy.[89] They touched on Iraq, Iran, Russia, Guantánamo Bay, climate change and Africa, but Blair's principal focus was on restoring the transatlantic relationship between the US and Europe, and on reinvigorating the MEPP. Blair urged him to 'get on to the front foot' and rebuild bridges with EU leaders, principally with the distrusted Schröder and Chirac. They both knew that Germany and France had ardently wanted a Kerry victory; equally they knew that Schröder and Chirac were pragmatists who would respond to the right message from Bush. Blair's advice was for him to say, 'We can differ about the rights and wrongs of Iraq, but we've got to work together towards common objectives in the future.' Bush sent Rice to Europe in January 2005, and he himself went to Brussels in February and returned again to Europe that spring. The Number 10 team saw Blair's hand in evidence here and judged that 'the transatlantic stuff was very successful'. The decision to reach out to Europe was 'quite deliberate' confirmed Dan Fried, who noted that although Blair was pushing this course of action it was also being advocated from within the administration.[90] That night, he went back to the Embassy where he sat up with Sheinwald and Manning reviewing how the talks had gone so far. Manning thought there had been a 'defining moment' because, hugely significant though it still was, from this point onwards 'Iraq ceased to be the prism through which all other transatlantic issues were seen'.[91]

Blair returned to the White House the next morning with a note he had scribbled out overnight. He had plotted three to four elements that would provide practical assistance with the creation of a Palestinian state and for which he sought American support. Yasser Arafat had died on 11 November, the very day that he had arrived in Washington. Blair immediately recognised his death as a great opportunity, and decided to make a 'comprehensive pitch' on the Middle East.[92] To the Americans, Arafat ('the grandfather of terrorism') had been an insuperable block to the road map. The Israelis too regarded him as beyond the pale, so his death opened up new opportunities on the ground in Israel also. For four years, Blair had tried to convince Bush that a resolution of the Arab/Israeli conflict was fundamental to bringing about a wider peace between the West and the Muslim world. The earlier high point at Hillsborough in April 2003 was about to be trumped.

That morning, the persuasive Sheinwald worked hard selling Blair's note to Rice. She had always had Bush's ear, and even more so now as she prepared to join the President's Cabinet. The plan was then discussed in the Oval Office with the five or six key figures from each side. Bush, in expansive mood, agreed the text, which foresaw five steps to reach 'a just and peaceful resolution of the Arab/Israeli conflict, based on two democratic states – Israel and Palestine – living side by side'.[93] Even more remarkable was Bush's comment, at the press conference, that 'the creation of a Palestinian state is possible within four years', and he pledged to 'spend the capital of the United States on such a state'.[94] Although the British party thought that achieving this by 2008 was 'pretty optimistic', they were pleased by Bush's agreement for Blair to chair an international meeting in the spring of 2005, to include the Palestinians.[95] This was important for Blair politically, and a boost to the efforts of the Quartet. Blair failed to win Bush's support for the appointment of a special US envoy to the region with full presidential authority, and it disappointed him, given his belief that the problem demanded a high-ranking figure who gave it his priority (one can see the origins here of his post-PM Middle East job). Overall, though, Number 10 were pleased with the visit. They returned to London believing that a new era was beginning, with the tribulations of 2004 laid to rest. 'The best moment for four years' on the Middle East peace process, declared one senior British official.[96]

Optimism, albeit guarded, flowed also from Iraq. On 30 January, the first elections were held since the Iraq invasion nearly two years before. Blair followed progress intently and had been keen to do all he could to support the interim Prime Minister, Allawi. Blair liked him: 'He was very Anglophile, British-educated, the same age as the Prime Minister, a real politician who knew his stuff on the economy,' said his foreign affairs private secretary at the time, John Sawers.[97] Number 10 had the idea of sending one of its officials, Charles Heatly, to work in Allawi's private office in Baghdad as part of the British institution building efforts. The Labour Party also seconded figures to help run Allawi's machine and to assist his communications. 'Their task was to help prop up the moderate secular centre of Iraqi politics,' said a senior official.[98] Bush took a phlegmatic view of the election: 'We're not going to pick winners,' he told Blair. 'Let the chips fall where they may.'[99] The chips fell badly for Allawi, whose party failed to win sufficient seats for him to remain as Prime Minister, and he was succeeded in April 2005 by Ibrahim Jaafari. To Blair, the very fact that elections had been conducted successfully, with an estimated turnout of 58 per cent, was a cause for celebration: the Iraqis had come within a whisker of equalling the turnout in the 2001 British General Election (59.5%). The elections struck 'a blow right to the heart of global terrorism', Blair proclaimed.[100] 'There was initially great optimism,' recalled a senior mandarin, 'and for a time it looked as if something really would happen. If we could establish a secular democratic state, then that would serve as a model at the heart of the Middle East.'[101] Was Blair about to see his critics vanquished?

Elections took place that month also in the Palestinian territories. On 9 January, the British/American preferred candidate, Abu Mazen, was elected President of the Palestinian authority. From early 2005, however, the high hopes began to fade. The new Palestinian leadership proved incapable of either controlling terrorism against the Israelis or of providing united leadership for the Palestinian people. 'After Arafat's death, there needed to be a clear Palestinian leadership, but they were deeply divided and not prepared to rule out terror,' said Manning.[102] 'I don't think there was any opportunity to make progress,' was the verdict of arch-hawk John Bolton, because all the disagreements between the Palestinians that had been suppressed for so long under Arafat now burst out into the open.[103] Number 10 began to realise more than ever that, with a half-hearted Israeli government and growing internal conflicts among the Palestinians, there was a limit to what they could do by themselves.[104] At this point, Bush now began to disappoint them once again, as he proved unable or unwilling to deliver on his high aspirations of November 2004. 'We had difficulty getting the President to translate his positive words into real change on the ground,' admitted a senior British official.[105] 'It's like a stone that you push up the hill for a bit and then you go away and it rolls down the hill,' said another Number 10 figure, 'but you can't be there all the time. Bush does mean what he says but then events intervene or other people get to him. He's not a very executive President. He decides things but there's always a problem with implementation.'[106]

In an ideal world Blair would have liked the London Middle East conference of 1 March to have been a major affair, at which both Israeli and Palestinian representatives engaged in serious peace talks. But the Palestinians were not ready for a major negotiation and needed time to adjust to life without Arafat. It was equally clear that the Israelis would not play ball and that the Americans had no intention of pushing them. 'I don't think that there was ever any sense in it trying to be a major peace conference,' recalled a senior administration official.[107] 'The Israelis were never going to come,' explained one British official, 'because that would have then looked like a peace conference.'[108] But Sharon's assent was still needed if the Palestinians were to attend, given Israeli control over the Palestinian territories. Sheinwald thus sold the idea of a conference to Sharon's office on the basis that it would focus on Palestinian institution-building. 'It was a real heave to get the Israelis to agree,' recalled one involved, but eventually they promised not to block the conference taking place.[109] The US was also supportive: 'we've always felt that the capacity building issue and the financial issues for the Palestinians were critical in getting the peace process moving', said a senior administration official.[110] At the eleventh hour Shimon Peres, Sharon's rival, then deputy Prime Minister, sought an invitation from the British government. But Number 10 felt that without Sharon's asking they had no option but to stick to an exclusive Palestinian focus, and so Peres' request was declined.[111] The aim for the conference was seen in Number 10 as 'catalysing a new degree of American engagement and getting the Israelis to accept a new level of international involvement'.[112] Attended by twenty international delegations, including Abbas, Rice and Annan the conference focused on how the international community could help the Palestinians prepare for statehood. It was a step forward, but nowhere near as far forward as Blair had originally hoped. Blair's inability to make more progress in the Middle East would gnaw away at him for the remainder of his premiership.

Preparing for the Presidencies: EU and G8

Now he knew he would be around to chair them, Blair looked forward with real excitement to the possibilities presented by the presidencies of the EU and the G8, coinciding in the second half of 2005. Whitehall spends much longer preparing for an EU presidency than for a G8, because almost every department is involved with Europe. Since 2003, the Whitehall machine had been grinding away, but it was not until mid-2004, after he knew he was staying, that he began seriously to engage with his presidency. Number 10 feared that it would be overshadowed by his need to campaign for the referendum on the constitution. Europhiles in the building thought that Blair's high profile during the presidency would help their campaign. But Blair worried that the job of playing a neutral president would conflict with his task of heading the British 'yes' vote. No one at the time foresaw that the French would vote 'no', which, on the very eve of the British presidency, would change everything.

On the G8, some work had taken place since 2003, but it was only after the Sea Island G8 summit in June 2004 that Blair started really engaging. He wanted to make it a much more business-like presidency than when Britain had last held the chair in 1998, when it had been glitzy but light on substance. It was a sign of how much Blair had matured as a politician that he wanted this G8 to tackle major and hard issues. To the surprise of many, he announced in 2003 that his two objectives would be increasing aid to Africa and tackling climate change. These were not new issues for him, but there had been little prior to this to suggest they would make it to the top of the G8 agenda: it was an example of 'pure Blair instinct', said Sawers.[113] He realised after Iraq 'that he had a problem', said one Number 10 aide. 'He needed to open up another flank where he could reconnect with his natural supporters who had drifted away from him.'[114] He believed in a moral obligation to tackle such long-term issues: 'He's never been a short-term politician,' said Jay. 'He would say it is really important that my generation of politicians takes seriously the issues that are going to matter for future generations.'[115] Blair believed that climate change and Africa were 'the new agenda' and intended to take advantage of this.[116] His argument was that 'the G8 would only have legitimacy if it focused on the issues that really mattered to people'.[117]

Whitehall was less convinced. 'Are you sure?' officials probed. 'You know that these are two issues on which the Americans are going to be absolutely on the other side.' 'I know,' he said. 'Don't worry, I'll bring them round,' Jay recalled him promising.[118] But several Whitehall departments, including the FCO and DfID, argued that the G8 was intrinsically the wrong forum for such topics. Blair's response was that 'if we are serious about seeing a big shift on both, it can only be done at

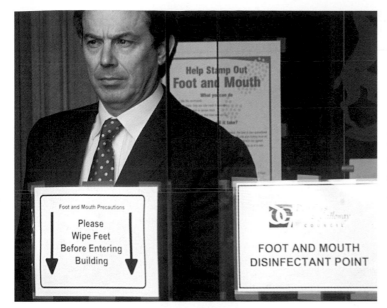

Blair arrives for a meeting with farmers affected by the Foot and Mouth crisis in Dumfries on 30 March 2001.

Blair with Andrew Adonis, who did more than any other single figure to shape Blair's domestic policy agenda.

Blair shares a casual moment with President Bush at Camp David on 27 March 2003: the warmth was genuine. Blair's decision to tie himself so closely to Bush infuriated most of the Labour Party and many in the country at large, but Blair refused to distance himself, even to the end.

Difficult relations. From left to right: French President Jacques Chirac, Tony Blair, and German Chancellor Gerhard Schröder.

Gordon Brown, John Prescott and other ministers listen, aware of the cameras seeking to capture their every reaction, as Blair delivers his speech to the Labour Party Conference on 28 September 2004. Two days later he would announce to the country his decision to stand down as Prime Minister after serving a 'full third term'.

Dick Cheney, whose opposition to much of Blair's agenda repeatedly frustrated Number 10, sat in several crucial meetings between Bush and Blair impassively, rarely saying a word. Here he listens, motionless, to a White House press conference on 12 November 2004, at which President Bush, standing alongside Blair, pledged to 'spend the capital of the United States' to create a Palestinian state over the next four years. Cheney's companions (from left to right, Secretary of State Colin Powell, British Ambassador to the US Sir David Manning and National Security Advisor Condoleezza Rice) were cheered by the announcement. Cheney was not.

Blair meets with Palestinian President Mahmood Abbas in Ramallah in December 2004. For a time the death of Yasser Arafat, whose picture hovers over them, seemed to offer an opportunity for real progress in the Middle East peace process.

The 'ice cream moment'. Blair and Brown put on a united front during the election campaign on 2 May 2005.

Blair joins forces with Sebastian Coe at the London 2012 Olympic bid press conference at the Carlton Hotel, Singapore on 5 July 2005.

Having just heard news of the terrorist attack in London on 7 July 2005, G8 and other leaders break off from their discussions at the Gleneagles summit to show solidarity with the Prime Minister.

The Prime Minister signs a book of condolence at City Hall in London on 12 July 2005, in memory of the victims of the 7 July bombings. He wrote: 'With my deep condolences for all those who lost their lives and for their families who mourn. And with heartfelt admiration for London, the greatest capital city in the world.'

Following a meeting of foreign ministers on the Iranian nuclear issue, Foreign Secretary, Jack Straw, and US Secretary of State, Condoleezza Rice, attend a press conference in Berlin on 30 March 2006. Rice and Straw became close, but Rice's most established British relationship was with Ambassador Sir David Manning, which gave him access in Washington that few ambassadors could match.

Blair and the Governor of California, Arnold Schwarzenegger, talk with reporters at the Port of Long Beach, California, on 31 July 2006; the same day they signed an innovative agreement to tackle climate change.

Blair attends the State Opening of Parliament on 15 November 2006 in London with his deputy, John Prescott, and his successor in-waiting, Gordon Brown.

Blair is welcomed to the fortified Green Zone in Baghdad by Iraqi Prime Minister Nouri
al-Maliki on 17 December 2006 as he embarks on a five-day visit to the Middle East.
Despite the smiles, Blair found al-Maliki's inability to get a grip on his government a
source of increasing frustration.

Blair preferred to write his speeches long-hand. A casually-dressed Prime Minister writes a speech on the role of British armed forces in the 21st century at the Bovey Castle Hotel, Dartmoor National Park, on 12 January 2007.

Blair and his advisers en route to Berlin to meet Chancellor Merkel, 13 February 2007. From left to right: Kim Darroch, EU adviser to the Prime Minister; Tom Kelly, Prime Minister's official spokesman; Caroline Wilson, private secretary; Justin Forsyth, special adviser on foreign policy; James Roscoe, press officer; Tony Blair; David Hill, Director of Communications.

Blair met Presidential hopeful, Nicholas Sarkozy several times in the run-up to the French Presidential Election. He later wondered how very different his relations with Europe would have played out had Sarkozy, not Chirac, been President for most of his premiership. From left to right: Sarkozy, Blair, Powell.

Blair walks into Downing Street with Ruth Turner, Head of Government Relations in the third term and one of his aides involved in the 'cash for peerages' inquiry, on 2 May 2007. In July Crown Prosecution Service confirmed that no charges would be brought.

A new era of power-sharing begins in Northern Ireland as previously mortal enemies feel able to share a joke. From left to right: Martin McGuinness; the Irish Taoiseach, Bertie Ahern; Tony Blair; Peter Hain and Ian Paisley in the First Minister's office of the Northern Ireland Assembly on 8 May 2007.

Blair is made an Honorary Paramount Chief of Mahera Village near Freetown in Sierra Leone on 30 May 2007, during his final five-day visit to meet with African leaders.

On 19 June 2007, during his final visit to Iraq, Blair chats to British forces in the coffee bar in Basra, Iraq.

G8 leaders en route to the official photograph on 7 June 2007, in Heiligendamm, Germany. From left to right: Canadian Prime Minister Stephen Harper; Tony Blair; Jose Manuel Barroso, President of the European Commission; French President Nicolas Sarkozy; Russian President Vladimir Putin; Japanese Prime Minister Shinzo Abe; German Chancellor Angela Merkel; Italian Prime Minister Romano Prodi, and Bush.

Blair prepares his final speech in Sedgefield on Friday 22 June, supported by Number 10 aides, David Hill, Liz Lloyd, Jonathan Powell and his agent John Burton (seated).

'That's it. The End.' Wednesday, 27 June: a day of mixed emotions for the Blair family as they say goodbye to Number 10 Downing Street.

national-leader level, and the G8 is the obvious place to raise them given we have the presidency', said Number 10's Liz Lloyd.[119] Some others expected him to use the G8 as a forum to advance his third major overseas passion, the MEPP, especially after Arafat's death pushed the peace process up Blair's priority list. 'Gleneagles would not have been the right forum for this,' insisted a close aide. 'You had people there like the Canadians and Italians who are not players. In fact the Europeans are barely players. The Americans wouldn't have it, and you wouldn't get very far.'[120] Blair believed that a surer route to success on the Middle East would be working stealthily with the Americans.[121]

Blair outlined his thinking at Chequers, before he went on holiday in July 2004, to representatives from several departments. 'It was very clear at that meeting that he wanted to be as ambitious as possible on both agendas,' said one present.[122] In contrast to the traditionally limited ambitions of G8 meetings, Blair deliberately set the bar high. Too high, for many in the FCO.[123] On 7 October he announced his agenda publicly in a speech to the African Union in Addis Ababa, emphasising, amid some cynicism, that 'partnership' was going to be essential for future progress. He primed Bush on both topics when he saw him in the White House on 11–12 November. The administration regarded climate change as a particularly unfortunate choice.[124] From the start of his presidency, Bush had seemed dismissive of the climate change arguments and unremittingly opposed to the Kyoto treaty and, according to the State Department's Wilkerson, 'it was just downhill from there.'[125] During Bush and Blair's first meeting, at Camp David in February 2001, his hostility had been clear to the British side. 'We tried to get the administration to at least make a polite remark in public about Kyoto,' recalled one official. 'Condi made it absolutely clear that they wouldn't play ball on this. Blair then said, "Okay, we'll drop it."'[126] The US view was that there was too much uncertainty in the science to justify the tough targets in the Kyoto agreement. Criticism in Britain, however, suggested the Texan Bush was overly influenced by oil and business interests, though not even the Democrats were sympathetic to Kyoto. In the US climate change 'was just radioactive for a while', admitted Dan Fried.[127] In the run-up to Gleneagles, however, the Bush administration became acutely aware that Blair was deadly seriously over his agenda: 'I remember saying to people on the NSC, "Look, you've got to suck this up. The Brits are going to push it and you're going to have to find a way to be positive about this,"' recalled the State Department's Elizabeth Jones.[128]

The focus on Africa, by contrast, was received more positively. There was some irritation at the White House that its own efforts, in particular in spending far more on aid than the Clinton administration, was not receiving greater recognition. Administration officials now saw a chance to get their message across. President Bush was 'very pleased' by the Africa focus recalled Condi Rice. This was an issue on which the two leaders shared common goals. 'The President thought that he had led on Africa and had the results to show it,' continued Rice. 'He felt that what the PM was doing was bringing others on board.'[129] But underlying Bush's approach, was a deeper motivation, forged by Blair's longstanding support for his administration. The President was 'absolutely determined that the Gleneagles G8 had to be a success for Blair', said Karl Rove.[130] One reason was because Bush thought Blair's standing would rise among their fellow G8 leaders if Gleneagles was a success for him. Given the Prime Minister's enduring support for US policy, this could prove valuable to Bush in the future. But, as one State Department official recalls there was a genuine debt of gratitude: 'We frankly all agreed that we did owe our British colleagues this one.'[131] The administration was struck, in contrast to their own G8 at Sea Island, by how early and how visibly Blair began to prepare: 'It wasn't until the end of the first quarter that we set out to the other 8 countries what we would focus on and, even then, we strenuously avoided any publicity regarding what was being discussed in the run up to our Summit,' said Faryar Shirzad, the US sherpa.[132]

Blair needed high-calibre staff in addition to a long run-in if he was to make the G8 work. Justin Forsyth was one such recruit, joining from Oxfam in December 2004, and on Africa and development, his main figure was Laurie Lee, from DfID. As his 'sherpa', or right-hand man, he selected the PUS at the Foreign Office, Michael Jay. Though unusual to have such a senior figure, it proved an inspired choice.

At this point, an episode threatened to unsettle Blair's plans and to insert a new priority for the G8. On Boxing Day 2004, just after 8 A.M. Indonesian time, the world's most powerful earthquake in forty years measuring 9.0 on the Richter scale, occurred underneath the Indian Ocean, causing the earth to wobble on its axis.[133] The Blair family were on their way to their Christmas holiday in Sharm el-Sheikh when the tsunami struck coastal areas in the Far East. Number 10 was slow to realise the full extent of the disaster, which led to some 300,000 people dying, of whom a suspected 141 were British.[134] 'He didn't really have a holiday at all,' said one Number 10 official, because of the lengthy phone calls that took place between him and Downing Street.[135] Prescott and Straw ran the British response from London and gave him firm advice when he asked whether he should come back. 'No, you've got to have a break some time. We can handle things this end.'[136] 'A terrible tragedy had now become a global catastrophe,' Blair said from Egypt on 1 January. The media created a furore about why he had not returned. 'Mr Blair has failed to grasp the essence of leadership,' said a headline in the *Independent*.[137] The story developed a new twist when Brown announced aid packages off his own bat. 'The appearance of two leading politicians apparently attempting to outbid each other for ownership of disaster relief on aid for the Third World is little short of obscene,' said *The Times*.[138] What such comments missed was the genuine and deep commitment shared by both men to alleviate global poverty. Blair later confided that if he had realised how serious the disaster was going to prove, he would have returned, though Number 10 thought he would have been condemned equally if he had come back.[139] By mid-January, Number 10 had a new worry. How would the tsunami affect the G8 presidency? Was it wrong to select Africa and climate change when the attention of the world was so focused on Asia?[140] Pressure built for the issues to change. But then the situation stabilised, and by February, Number 10 considered that the focus the tsunami was giving to poverty in Thailand, India and Sri Lanka would complement the priority Blair was giving to poverty in Africa.

Blair had been interested in helping the African continent since before he became Prime Minister: at Oxford in the 1970s, the priest Peter Thomson had first opened his eyes to politics by talking about the 'social gospel' and the need to alleviate suffering in the world. His Christianity deeply informed his zeal to help Africa. In 1995, at the party conference, he had alluded to the parable of the Good Samaritan and its centrality to his mission as a politician: 'I am my brother's keeper and I will not walk by on the other side.' He made two visits to South Africa in 1999, where he was shocked by the levels of poverty and deprivation. John Sawers believes that Blair's Millennium Summit speech on 6 September 2000 was a core staging post in cementing his commitment to Africa.[141] 'There is a dismal record of failure in Africa on the part of the developed world, that shocks and shames our civilisation,' he said. Many were dying needlessly from starvation, disease and conflict made worse by 'bad governments, factional rivalries, state-sponsored theft and corruption'. He urged the conference to begin the process 'of agreeing a way forward for Africa'.[142] September 11 also had a major impact on his thinking, leading to his 'scar on the conscience of the world' passage and his highlighting the need to help Africa in his seminal speech at the party conference in Brighton that autumn. In private the Blairs began to sponsor a child in an HIV orphanage in Cape Town.[143]

In June 2003, while at France's G8 at Evian, Blair received a call. 'It's happening again,' his interlocutor exploded. 'Calm down,' Blair said, 'and tell me what the problem is.' 'I can't calm down,' said Bob Geldof. He went on to explain that, twenty years after *Live Aid*, conditions in Africa were still no better.[144] Blair told him to come and see him on his return. Out of their discussions came the 'Commission for Africa', launched on 26 February 2004. 'Blair always saw it as a partnership, with half the members African; this is a real partnership and not about a donor–recipient relationship.'[145] The 'Make Poverty History' (MPH) campaign further helped Blair's cause: he worked most closely on it with Geldof, Bono of the rock group U2, and screenwriter Richard Curtis. The involvement of these popular and well known figures led to real excitement in Number 10. Blair held regular meetings with MPH leaders on strategy, but, said Forsyth, 'They were never in our pockets, and we were never in their pockets.'[146] Number 10 valued their ability to mobilise voters in the US, where Bono was influential on Capitol Hill and in Japan, where he had a big following, as well as in France, Germany and Italy. Because of the leverage MPH could exert on G8 leaders over poverty, Number 10 thought it could raise the bar higher on Africa than on climate change, which lacked the same organised mobilisation of public opinion.[147]

The Commission for Africa reported on 11 March, corroborating Blair's analysis that the solutions to Africa's problems encompassed good governance and the reduction of war, and it was not just about pumping in extra money. Coming out four months before the G8, it focused the attention of its leaders on the need to help Africans help themselves, a message that went down well in Washington.[148] Blair's task was much helped by Brown sharing his own commitment: 'Gordon's absolutely passionate about Africa and always has been,' said Nick Brown.[149] Their relationship on Africa during 2005 was helped by Forsyth's personal link with Brown's economic adviser, Shriti Vadera.[150] Brown and Blair's joint belief that they should be as ambitious as possible in their demands helped ensure Whitehall would not water down their aims, particularly during the election period. The senior mandarins might feel they were aiming too high and annoying all the UK's allies. Blair and Brown always felt something big was possible if the UK kept its nerve and gave no ground until the leaders met.[151] Brown helped further by setting the 2004 spending review's ambitious aid target of 0.7 per cent of GDP. Britain was the first G8 country to set a timetable to reach this figure. 'In some ways our early declaration on this target weakened our bargaining hand, but it also allowed us to say, "We've set this figure. Why can't you do this?"'[152] The target helped development secretary Hilary Benn pressure EU development ministers to deliver on ambitious European aid targets.

In marked contrast to their relationship on domestic policy, Brown also facilitated Blair's second priority, climate change. Blair had been slow to pick up on climate change in the first term and had left work on implementing the Kyoto summit to Beckett and Prescott as well as to Brown, who introduced a climate change levy to reduce British emissions. 'Tony Blair certainly supported Kyoto, but his own interest in climate change only came mid-way through the second term,' said one close adviser.[153] His epiphany came when preparing for his speech on 2 September 2002 to the 'Earth Summit' in Johannesburg. Just after his return from his summer holidays that year, he held a meeting on the terrace outside the Cabinet Room. Those present detected an air of *ennui* about him. 'Surely the main issue has got to be CO_2,' he said. 'Well, no, actually, that's not really the issue that's around now,' they said. Jonathan Powell and Liz Lloyd patiently explained to him that the agenda had moved on, but Blair seemed unconvinced. As Lloyd left the room she muttered something about Blair not having read her earlier briefing notes on the subject.[154] But Blair's mind was now open. And the government's chief scientific adviser, David King, managed to capitalise on it. When King delivered the Zuckerman lecture at the Royal Society on 31 October 2002, Blair asked for a briefing on what he had said, and took it away with him to Chequers to read closely. King thought it had a big effect in 'bringing him round to an understanding of what the issues were'.[155] Blair felt inclined to trust King as his advice during the foot and mouth crisis in 2001 had been so sound.[156]

'I want a bloody big wodge of material on climate change,' he said in July 2004 to an official helping prepare his summer reading. 'I want to understand its impact on the environment and the full scope of the threat. Whack in a really good book from Hatchards and some interesting articles from *The Economist*,' he continued, 'and I'm really going to think about it.'[157] So captivated was he by the material that he wrote a handwritten request to Nick Rowley, another specialist recruited earlier in the year, asking still further questions and requesting more material before he left.[158] Jay recalled how he returned from the summer break 'absolutely convinced by the science and that the world faced a serious threat that his own generation and politicians had a duty to take seriously'.[159] He began to say that climate change was *the* most important problem that the world faced.[160] The response from Whitehall remained discouraging: the FCO argued that it would be unlikely for Russia or the

USA to ratify anything, while there was even less hope of the rapidly developing economies, above all China, accepting the case for doing more.[161]

Blair delivered his credo at the Banqueting House on 14 September 2004. It was one of those speeches on which he lavished immense care, writing it in the Downing Street flat over the two days prior to delivery. He wanted it to be a highly personal message. 'Tell me if this sounds stupid,' he said to Rowley as he experimented with different sentences.[162] 'He wanted to come up with something on climate change that would change the terms of debate,' said one aide.[163] The speech's aims were to boost acceptance of the scientific case for climate change, to seek agreement over technology transfer leading to low carbon growth and, finally, to make the case for the 'rapidly developing countries' signing up if any agreement was to be successful. This last objective explains his decision to invite the full 'G8 + 5' to Gleneagles, the 'five' being the emerging markets of China, India, Brazil, South Africa and Mexico.[164] The speech was one of the most personal of his premiership. He argued that with a six-fold population growth in 200 years, global warming had become 'simply unsustainable' for the planet within 'the lifetime of my children certainly', and 'possibly within my own'. The challenge, he said, was 'so far-reaching in its impact to be irreversible in its destructive power, that it alters radically human existence'.[165]

At the end of the speech, he departed from his text to offer a challenge to the businessmen in the audience. 'You as business leaders might also accept that there may be more that you can do.' Economic life need not suffer from climate change measures, he stressed. Indeed, he saw major business opportunities from the technologies that were being developed, an argument that was to play well in the White House. The speech helped spawn the corporate leaders' group on climate change. Blair knew that Britain only emitted 2 per cent of the world's carbon dioxide, so if he was to make any difference, he had to reach out to business people worldwide.[166] He thus used his speech to the World Economic Forum at Davos on 26 January 2005 to proselytise more widely, and he helped catalyse a spin-off group of 'leading world CEOs'. A meeting in Number 10 that spring of British and world chief executives encouraged further momentum. From an innocent to a serious believer within two years, he was on fire on the topic. The previous December, he wrote a passionate article in *The Economist*, which up to that point had been sceptical on climate change, and which subsequently was to soften its line.[167]

The scientific community, however, was far from convinced in early

2005 about the threat posed by climate change. To try to bring them round, King suggested to Blair that they initiate a conference at the Meteorological Office's Hadleigh Centre in Exeter, which was arranged for February. Number 10 deliberately stayed at arm's length, and Blair, to remove any suggestion that politics was influencing science, did not himself participate. Number 10 were nevertheless delighted by the consensus that emerged: that the world was far more at risk through human-generated climate change than had hitherto been assumed. Convincing the Americans of this was to prove harder than swaying the business and scientific communities in Britain. Blair had a breakfast meeting with Bush in Brussels on 22 February 2005 during his two-day visit to Europe. On Africa, the US had agreed to put money into malaria drugs, but differences over debt relief remained. On climate change, progress had been glacial, but by early spring, Blair detected some movement, despite some resentment within the administration that 'he was putting into place all these mechanisms, and then it would be our job to show up and just rubber-stamp all he had done'.[168] Other preoccupations were now pressing in on him. He summoned Jay to see him. 'You're going to have to get on with it on your own for a while. I have a General Election to run, and I won't return to all this until after it's over.'[169]

Dealing With Gordon, Part II: January–March 2005

'Your big mistake in 2001 was not to move Brown. If you want to have a serious third term, you've got to go for it now.' It was a common line among the Blair 'ultras' in Number 10, led by Birt and Powell.[170] Several senior civil servants too believed that no Prime Minister should allow a Chancellor to be in place for so long that he becomes a second centre of power in government.[171] By mid-January 2005, Blair was describing his first term as a 'lost opportunity', and was even regarding the coming General Election as the start of his 'real' second term.[172] Alongside Milburn's work on preparing the manifesto, a parallel and more covert operation was in train deep inside Number 10. Blair asked his 'blue skies' thinker, John Birt, to help him define his main domestic policy priorities and an ideal government structure for delivery so he could hit the ground running with very precise plans for the first twelve or eighteen months after the 2005 election.[173] To this end, a special project team was set up from January 2005, reporting regularly to the PM. It was spearheaded by Birt and Cabinet Secretary Turnbull, aided by Principal

Private Secretary Ivan Rogers and Gareth Davies from the Policy Directorate. When Birt looked back at the second term, he saw that insufficient work in Number 10 had been put in before the 2001 election to map out what would happen after it. They could not afford a similar mistake now. They would also need people of the highest calibre to drive policy in the third term. A leading head-hunting firm was brought in, on a strictly covert basis, to trawl for talent. The most senior appointment from the search was David Bennett, formerly at McKinsey's management consultancy, as Head of Policy in June 2005.[174] The Birt team now developed detailed proposals on health, education, law and order, pensions, welfare reform and energy, including a precise grid on how to implement the policy.[175] 'We wanted to go into the third term with absolute clarity about what the objectives were and how they were going to be achieved,' said Birt.[176] 'It was all done very much within Number 10, not involving any other department, and certainly not the Treasury,' said one official.[177] Blair was presented with these ideas at a series of meetings at Chequers from January to March, culminating in two final meetings during the campaign in April.

The team also spent considerable time examining the optimal structure for the centre of British government, exploiting Birt's experience of re-engineering the BBC, and Turnbull's reputation as an iconoclastic thinker within Whitehall. 'The basic processes at the centre of government were not right, not least the relationship between Number 10 and the Treasury,' said Birt. 'We plainly all understood we had a dysfunctional set-up.'[178] The emerging proposals included revamping the office of the Deputy Prime Minister, and an ambitious plan to strengthen and revive the Cabinet committee structure. In his first two terms, Blair had largely ignored Cabinet committees. 'Tony was never keen on them,' confirmed one Cabinet colleague, 'but after Butler it became much more formal.'[179] Despite their distaste for Butler's criticism of Blair's 'denocracy', at least some in Number 10 had taken his recommendations to heart. Blair also now realised, as he had found with the five-year plans, that the best way to lock in Cabinet ministers (and negotiate with the Treasury) was to use Cabinet and its committees structure.[180] In the autumn of 2004, a serious attempt was made to revive Cabinet Committee, and to give Blair a meaningful role. Turnbull was particularly concerned that the economic affairs committee barely met, and when it did, Brown would not let it have any information. He wanted all this to change. Barber was resistant, believing the existing structure of stock-takes and informal exchanges with ministers suited Blair better, but Whitehall had the upper hand. After the election, the new Cabinet Committee structure swung into operation. Despite approving the change, Blair never felt comfortable with the new model: 'What's happened to my stock-takes?' he exclaimed after one of the first new committee meetings. According to Peter Riddell, many of the committees were 'largely moribund under Mr Blair, including several chaired by him'.[181] 'His enthusiasm for chairing those committees waned very rapidly,' confirmed Rogers. 'He soon wanted to go back to more bilateral processes with the people he most trusted.'[182] As Blair said, 'These things don't really function for me, and they don't enable me to have the sort of discussions I want to have.'[183]

A more dramatic proposal was designed to deal with the problem of the 'over-mighty' Treasury. Turnbull, Birt and Rogers examined various models, including creating a new 'Office of Management and Budget' (OMB) distinct from the Treasury, as in several developed countries, with the Australian and Canadian models being considered especially attractive. The OMB would have responsibility for economic productivity and domestic spending, while the Treasury would be left in control of macro-economic policy. One plan was to compensate the Treasury for its loss by the 'sweetener' of absorbing trade and competition policy from the DTI.[184] The recommendation in their final report, which become known as the 'third term plan', was that the Chief Secretary's domain in the Treasury should be given more status, and that the incumbent should sit on a committee consisting of the PM and Deputy PM, to which he or she should present spending plans. The ultras hoped that Blair would not only adopt such a plan, but also move Brown out to the FCO. 'Everybody involved saw clearly that this could not happen unless Brown moved, and you had somebody in there who was going to be ready to operate in a different kind of way,' said one Downing Street aide.[185] Some saw this as setting Brown up for a fall, believing he would not be able to make a success of running foreign policy.[186] Comparisons were made with Anthony Eden, whose premiership was a failure because he lacked the breadth to operate outside his specialist area: foreign policy. Blair certainly gave serious consideration to the OMB plan and of moving Brown. He 'licensed and encouraged this work', said one Number 10 aide, 'and was highly interested in where it was going'.[187]

But Blair kept his own counsel, and never indicated whether he would accept the plan. The ultras urged him on: 'You must sort out this problem with Gordon.'[188] They were fervent that if Brown did not leave the Treasury, he would ruin Blair's remaining years. Brown would have to accept it or resign.[189] One draft of the plan, which leaked in July 2007, notes that the 'new Chancellor' must have a 'lack of personal investment in previous policies' and excel at 'teamwork', a quality that Blairites often claimed that Brown lacked.[190] Birt had wanted Blair to move Brown in 2001: with Blair at his most powerful, it would have been easier. Powell detested Brown and wanted him out. Adonis blamed him for persistently blocking the reform agenda in the second term. Like Birt, Turnbull felt that the Treasury's influence under Brown had become too all-pervasive across Whitehall: it had become a policy department and needed to be cut back to a classical finance department.[191] Across Whitehall many agreed, including some prominent officials in the Treasury itself.[192] In Number 10 a standard joke was that the Treasury was the biggest spending department in Whitehall. Whereas some like Turnbull and Powell questioned whether Blair would 'bite the bullet', when the time came, Blair was giving out positive signals that he was serious.[193] In January and February 2005, when relations were particularly bad with Brown, Blair would say, 'I'm going to drive my public service agenda and not let myself be blackmailed or blocked any more by the bloody Treasury.'[194] One close aide would often ask Blair, 'Are you really up for this?' to which he replied, 'I'm going to take no more shit from over the road, I'm going to do it.'[195] Blair had further concerns about Brown, and they were personal. 'He was worried about Gordon's character and personality, the dark side of his nature, his paranoia and his inability to collaborate.'[196] There is no doubting Blair would have wanted to move Brown, if he thought he had the necessary political capital.

Many in Number 10 subsequently claim to have known nothing about the 'nuclear option'. But as Matthew Taylor said, 'Even though it was labelled "top secret", it wasn't top secret.' He suspects that a couple of civil servants learned about it. And 'if a couple of civil servants knew about it, then all the civil servants would know about it'.[197] Indeed, the first reports of the plan, complete with speculation that Ruth Kelly would be the enhanced Chief Secretary in charge of the new OMB, began to appear in the press in January 2005.[198] By mid-March, the talk was that Blair was determined to move Brown from the Treasury after the election.[199] With polling day fast approaching, Blair came under pressure to speak to Brown about his thinking. He made up his mind that he was going to speak to him. 'He was very clear that he was going to see Gordon on his own.'[200] The outcome of that conversation was to come as a surprise to many.

13

General Election, 2005

Blair had pulled himself back from the brink, and now had to put himself at the head of the radical reforming government he had always wanted to lead. For the third term to be more successful than the first two, he believed he needed to win the General Election in his own right. He alone had to triumph. A victory in league with Brown, as in 1997 and 2001, would not suffice. The 'dual premiership', in so far as it had ever existed, had to be in the past. He needed a manifesto based on his own ideas, and he needed a post-election reshuffle lodging Blairite reformers in all the key Cabinet posts and with a remodelled government structure. Encouraged by the Number 10 'ultras', Blair pushed forward, but was still not overly confident of success.

The manifesto

'Tony Blair likes a competition over ideas. It helps him to choose the best,' said one involved in creating Labour's manifesto.[1] Blair had charged Alan Milburn with preparing the document, and he set to work to weld Number 10 into an efficient policy operation while ensuring that the Labour Party was in a fit state to fight the election. 'I was very concerned by the dysfunctionality of the relationship between Number 10, the government and the Labour Party, and I saw my job as binding them in,' Milburn remarked.[2] A series of meetings were organised between Secretaries of State and Blair, as well as arranging special Cabinets, ensuring that the ideas flowed and that ministers were all on-side. Based in the Cabinet Office, Milburn also set up an office within Number 10, at the top of the back stairs,[3] keen to be within close proximity to the centre of power.

Milburn was more than disconcerted, however, when he discovered that Blair had asked John Birt to organise his own policy operation. Birt believed that his own task was to work alongside Turnbull to develop the third-term agenda, in league with the strategy and policy units, and that Milburn had been brought in to work solely on election planning.[4] It soon became evident that these two forceful characters were not going to work harmoniously together. Their spats became common knowledge throughout the building.[5] 'From their very first meeting that autumn it was obvious that they couldn't stand each other: it was even more about alpha-male behaviour than disagreements over policy,' said one official.[6] By Christmas 2004, it reached crisis point. Birt was in despair, believing that the manifesto was thin, and that Blair ran the risk of repeating the errors of the second term, which he characterised as reactive, short-termist and Treasury-driven. 'We're going to get ourselves in exactly the same mess in the third term if we don't get this sorted out now,' he would say regularly.[7] Milburn wanted a 'rich' manifesto that chimed with what Blair really wanted. What we need is new policy, new policy, new policy,' he declared.[8] He was particularly concerned that there were still vulnerable areas, such as crime, where the Conservatives were establishing a lead. Although Birt felt he was ranging outside his brief, Milburn drove relentlessly on. One senior official felt the turf war was hindering progress: 'Blair, as ever, seemed to license the spat rather than taking sides and putting a stop to it. The result was that by Christmas, policy was not as coherent as it should have been.'[9]

In an increasingly acrid atmosphere in early 2005, criticism focused on Matthew Taylor, whose job it was to draft the manifesto. Taylor had proved a more than capable political strategist. But could the Blairites trust him? Was he really 'one of them'? Was he trying to ride both 'Gordon' and 'Tony' horses at the same time? Taylor was not a true Blairite at this time; his politics were closer to those of Mulgan, head of strategy: only in the third term did Taylor become more of a true believer.[10] To thrash out and finalise policy ideas, seminars were held in January and February. Birt controversially demanded a further one in March, 'because we need to get all of this sorted out', even though it was getting perilously close to the beginning of the campaign. For all their differences, the manifesto that emerged, meshed together by Taylor, had many of the new ideas for which Milburn worked as well as much of Birt's long-term thinking, such as on crime, energy and pensions.

Blair's focus in the manifesto centred on his three priority areas, education, health and law and order. On education, he wanted policy pushed beyond even the radical five-year schools plan, and certainly further than Clarke had gone or his successor, Kelly, was prepared to go. Blair had a telling conversation with his first-term policy chief, David Miliband, who asked him in early 2005, 'Are you diverging from the 1997 mantra of "standards not structures"?' Blair replied, 'That was right then, but not now. If we're going to get long-term change, self-sustaining change, we've got to get the structures and incentives right. We can only do so much from the centre.'[11] Blair saw academies, trust schools and greater school autonomy lying at the heart of his third-term plans.[12] Labour's draft manifestos, however, have to gain approval of a joint meeting of the unions and party members. To them, talk of greater school autonomy was anathema. Tactics were going to be paramount. 'We made sure the language in the manifesto included enough hooks to allow us to move to what we wanted to do on both academies and trust schools,' said one senior DfES aide.[13] The policy went through.

On health, Blair gave a major speech on 13 January in Chatham in which he advocated more personalised service and choice, and spoke of 'breaking the monolith' of the NHS.[14] Before the campaign began he wanted to state loudly and clearly that public service reform was going to be fundamental in the third term, and that the tone would most definitely be New Labour.[15] He personally inserted the eighteen-week maximum time pledge for patients to see a specialist from the date of referral. The dynamism he was getting from Reid impressed him, though he thought Alan Johnson was overly cautious on welfare.[16]

One area on which the Conservatives had a clear lead was on crime, immigration and law and order. As early as 2004, Blair had recognised this would be the central background for the election, and had begun to position himself accordingly. With six months to go before the election, he worked hard to 'close down' the potential 'negatives', making strong statements on immigration, asylum, prisons and security. 'It was straight out of a classic campaigning handbook about what to do in the medium term before the election,' said Byers.[17] The advice from his electoral strategists chimed strongly with his own inner conviction. His old confidants Campbell and Gould were also advising Labour, and their experience, especially after two successful General Election campaigns, was considerable. He would need every ounce of their expertise in the weeks ahead.

In some areas, Blair retreated from radicalism. Milburn advocated that housing association tenants be allowed to buy their own houses, an extension of Mrs Thatcher's policy on allowing council house tenants to buy their own homes. Prescott was strongly against and Brown equivocated: 'Prescott at the time was a powerful figure: Blair decided he did not want to stand up to him,' said Milburn.[18] On transport, Blair 'didn't have an intuitive feel for what the right answer was and he didn't care quite enough about it to really work it out for himself', according to one involved.[19] In the end he seemed to lean towards road pricing but again retreated from a fight, this time with the Treasury: the manifesto included only a weak commitment to examine the idea.[20]

Britain: Forward Not Back, the 112-page manifesto, was launched on 13 April. For all the agonies that had gone into its construction, it was the most detailed of Blair's three election manifestos, and a more persuasive document than that produced by either the Conservatives or the Liberal Democrats. The economic sections had been written by Brown. Number 10 was unimpressed by his efforts, however: 'Five times longer than it should have been and written in unintelligible "Brown-ese",' according to one insider. They tried hacking it down but without great success: the published version was 'longer and more incoherent' than it needed to have been.[21] The rest of the manifesto, far more so than in 1997 and 2001, offered an action plan for the third term, not a mere campaign tool, and also captured better Blair's own thinking. Blair wrote the introduction himself almost word for word, his principal theme being that of rights and responsibilities and opportunities in society.[22] At last the machine appeared to be working well. Milburn was sorting out the politics, strategy was coming from Birt, while Turnbull was commenting that there was a more systematic approach to planning a new term than he had ever witnessed before.[23] One unspoken question was, how long would the Prime Minister be remaining in power? 'Nobody talked openly about timing, but there was an implicit sense that it would be only half a term,' said Taylor. 'We were thinking all the time, "What can we achieve in two years?"'[24] Powell, Adonis and others felt Blair would have at least three.[25] Technically, he had pledged himself on 30 September to 'a full term', i.e., four years. The other unspoken question was: whither Brown?

Campaign – The First Three Weeks: 5–27 April

Blair was expected to announce the dissolution of Parliament on 4 April, but delayed his visit to the Queen by twenty-four hours out of respect for the Pope's death, an event of personal significance to him, on 2 April. He finally went to Buckingham Palace at 11:05 A.M. on Tuesday 5 April. An hour later, he stood outside Downing Street and announced the election date. 'It is a big choice, a fundamental choice,' he declared. 'The challenge is to build on the progress made, to accelerate the changes, to widen still further the opportunities available to the British people and above all else to take that hard-won economic stability, the investment in our public services, and entrench it.'[26] Parliament was prorogued on 10 April, leaving just four weeks for the formal campaign before polling day on Thursday 5 May. The date had long been agreed: though less than four years since the 2001 General Election, it was understood by all that the second term had run its course, and a fresh mandate was required.

Throughout February and March, before the campaign formally began, there had been growing concern among Labour's high command. The polls, which had shown a ten-point Labour lead in October, had shifted little since early March when Labour's lead had fallen to 2 or 3 per cent.[27] Concerns were expressed about the schism at the heart of the imminent Labour campaign between Brown and Blair/Milburn. 'Alan had been planning the campaign,' said one Brownite, 'and it became obvious that it wasn't working.'[28] A harbinger was Labour's response to the James Report, which the Conservatives had published on 17 January, identifying savings of £35 billion that could be made by a Tory government. Blair, Powell and even Campbell tried to persuade the Treasury to produce a riposte, 'But Gordon's line was "I'm not playing any part in it".'[29] The impasse continued throughout February. Brown would come to the General Election strategy group but would sit sullenly, apart from the periodic interjection of a highly critical comment. 'Gordon was in a negative frame [of mind] and that was very damaging,' said one insider.[30] One wag dubbed it the 'group of death'.[31] Reports began to appear in the press that Brown was 'sulking' and refusing to play any part in the official campaign.[32] 'He was even talking of going on his own tour,' recalled one aide.[33] Number 10's behaviour was 'utterly stupid and destructive', said Nick Brown. 'Their obvious plan was to run a campaign without Gordon, win without Gordon and not be beholden to Gordon afterwards.'[34] This was indeed exactly what the 'ultras' in Number 10, including Milburn as well as arch-Blairite politicians like Byers and Reid, wanted. A Labour victory with Blair solely at the helm was the *sine qua non* for them of a successful third term.

But Campbell and Gould thought differently. Campbell began to worry that the General Election could be lost; Gould never thought this was on the cards, but feared the majority could be cut as low as forty or fifty, though he thought it unlikely that it would be less than eighty. From late 2004, Gould had pushed for Milburn to work closely with Douglas Alexander, the Brownite who had held the post of election co-ordinator before Milburn's return, in the hope of bridging the Blair/Brown divide.[35] But Blair's lieutenants would not countenance it. Brown remained aloof and his allies reluctant to engage. From February onwards there were repeated efforts – 'endless discussions' – to mend fences. Campbell and Gould spoke regularly to Blair and to Brown, but never to both together. Both principals began to realise they had to get back together, but neither wanted to make the first move: 'It was a frustrating dance,' said one involved.[36] Within Number 10, Morgan advised that if Blair brought Brown back in, it should be with his eyes wide open. Blair should realise that Brown's power would only grow.[37] Early peace overtures by Blair to Brown had been rebuffed: Brown made it clear that Blair had appointed Milburn to run the campaign, and no more needed to be said. He would exact a heavy price.[38] Blair's response was that Milburn was merely in charge of 'day-to-day management', not strategy, which was Brown's great strength, but he got nowhere.[39] 'They were desperately trying to get Gordon back on board,' said Prescott.[40] Milburn was the sticking point. A steady flow of negative briefings emanated from the Treasury to undermine him and make his life difficult. 'Allies of Brown were determined to down him,' said Taylor.[41] Milburn kept pushing for the campaign to focus on Blair's bright new ideas for a third term, whereas the Treasury fought for it to be on Brown's record of economic success. It was getting very bloody. Something had to give.

Campbell says he spoke to Blair on 3 March at St Andrews before the Scottish conference, and again on 18 March before the Welsh conference, and told him, 'You've got to do something about this.'[42] Gould and Campbell were agreed that the focus did need to be more on the economy, and that the flagging campaign needed a major jolt to wake it up: bringing Brown back in would achieve both objectives.[43] 'It was not about sidelining Alan, but making the best of a tough situation,' said one involved. In the end, Campbell decided to take the law into his own hands in a move only 'half sanctioned' by Number 10.[44] The previous year, Campbell and Gould had taken an Easter holiday in Scotland together and had called in to see Brown at his home during it. This year Gould felt he had to remain in London with the campaign and Campbell decided to call in again on his Easter holiday to see Brown. During the visit on 29 March, he persuaded Brown – in what became known in

Whitehall as the 'settlement of North Queensferry' – to change his mind.[45] Campbell's message was stark, and went beyond appealing just to Brown's better nature. If he carried on sulking in his tent, he ran the risk not only of the party losing marginal seats and damaging his own economic legacy, but also undermining his case to become Prime Minister in a third term.

Brown bided his time after Campbell's visit. There would be no sudden change of mind. 'Gordon wasn't particularly happy, though, with what was offered,' said one Brownite.[46] After heavy consultation with his team in early April, he decided he would come back into the campaign, but on his own terms.[47] 'The condition,' said one Brownite, 'was that Alan Milburn vanish into the wings.'[48] Brown wanted his 'own people, Ed Balls, Ed Miliband and Douglas Alexander, moving into campaign headquarters, a cast-iron guarantee he would remain Chancellor in the third term and have a major role not only over appointments but also policy until such time as he took over'.[49] 'I think that Gordon genuinely believed it was going to be a genuine joint premiership from now on,' said one close Blair aide.[50]

To Gould, Brown's return to the fold marked a crucial moment in the campaign, when discord dissolved into unity. At the first campaign meeting proper, at 7 A.M. on 4 April, Gould recalled Blair and Brown present with both of their key lieutenants, ready to get down to work. It was 'both moving and impressive', he wrote. 'A campaign unified as the battle was about to commence. It felt like New Labour had come home.'[51] Not everyone in campaign HQ quite shared the new mood: some ribbed Gould and Campbell over their so-called 'appeasement.'[52] However one insider insisted that Brown's return was 'no kind of defeat for Blair, but a bringing together of two great campaigning forces'.[53] Blair gave a signal of this new accord on 6 April when he said in public that Brown would not only keep his job but that he was 'the most successful Chancellor in a hundred years. We would be crazy to put that at risk.'[54] Election plans were restructured to ensure that both men were seen and filmed together as often as possible during the campaign. 'It made it much more difficult for people to say that they were at each other's throats when they were seen to be clearly getting on and dealing with the same issues together,' said Huw Evans, who had joined the campaign in mid-March to work on Labour's press grid.[55] On 11 April came a joint party political broadcast shot by the Oscar-winning director, Anthony Minghella, with Blair and Brown the only characters, 'depicted as old friends and equals, looking back on their common ideals and achievements and pondering the future', said Kavanagh and Butler, the veteran election-watchers.[56] Hill remembers the impact that the broadcast had on morale in campaign HQ: 'The more emotional coming together happened over the next few days.'[57] Operationally, Brown lost no time in getting his feet back under the table: 'I remember coming down to London one Sunday and it was quite obvious that the balance of power had changed very dramatically to Gordon,' recalled one Brownite.[58] The moment in the campaign that summed up their new deal came near the very end when, on 2 May, Blair bought Brown a '99' ice cream cone as well as one for himself. It was too much for some in Number 10, whose stomachs churned. 'Bloody nauseating,' was Powell's comment.[59] Others observed with distaste, 'They're virtually holding hands.' 'People were almost vomiting,' said one Number 10 official of their love-in.[60]

Unity is always crucial to a successful election campaign, but it was particularly important in 2005, as Gould saw it. He knew that Labour faced a very tough political landscape. With the electorate inevitably beginning to tire of familiar faces after eight years of the same government, winning a third term would always be tougher than winning a second or a first, but the problem was made more acute by the prevalent negative public mood towards the government. Looking at the 2004 US presidential election for guidance, Gould believed that the only route to success was to stick to one single and constant message (as Bush had done) and avoid the impression of uncertainty and inconsistency radiated by John Kerry. And while Bush had chosen security, for Labour the focus would be the economy, because 'the economy was robustly strong, it was our most important issue, and a huge strategic advantage over the Conservatives'.[61] With Brown's support it became, at least in Gould's eyes, the trump card: 'When we campaigned on the economy we did well,' said one involved; 'when we did not we did badly. It was as simple as that.'[62] Gould believed that from the moment Brown and Blair came back together victory was assured.[63]

Blair never enjoyed campaigning, and found 2005 easily the least pleasant of his three elections as leader.[64] 'So often he would look tired and stressed,' recalled one party official.[65] He had geared himself up for the campaign, knowing it was going to be hard, but 'he believed his case was right and that it would get through if he focused on getting it across'.[66] Iraq and persistent rumblings over tuition fees provided a challenging backdrop. Both frustrated him: he believed Iraq would come right and he would be vindicated, and that tuition fees would be accepted within two years. Some of his advisers suggested that this latter issue alone cost Labour twenty seats, a view Gould dismissed as 'nonsense'.[67] Overall, the party was far less confident than it had been in the two earlier elections. The party was no longer the toast of the chattering classes or the commentariat. 'The media wanted to damage us in 2005 in a way they hadn't in 2001,' said Hill.[68] Blair also found the Conservatives' tactics unpleasant. 'If he's prepared to lie to take us to war, he's prepared to lie to win an election,' proclaimed one Tory poster.[69] Through it all, however, Blair 'always felt he had Howard's measure'.[70] He was not troubled by his policies: the Conservative manifesto launched on 11 April was dismissed as 'just a magazine'. Blair was surprised that it contained so little detailed policy work.[71] What did trouble him was the Conservatives' strong organisation at ground level and its funding. 'We were not able to match them on their resources. The threat was clearly there,' said Huw Evans.[72] The perception quickly grew that the Conservatives were fixated on the issues of immigration and asylum. In Dover on 22 April, in one of his main campaign speeches, Blair addressed this head-on, and dismissed the Tories' highlighting of both issues as 'an attempt deliberately to exploit people's fears'.[73] In Downing Street, the timing of the speech had been carefully calibrated. Blair 'waited until the public saw Howard's constant immigration focus as opportunist', explained one insider, 'and then went for the kill with his speech'.[74]

A key campaign strategy was to expose Blair to as much media publicity as possible and show him confronting his critics. The party's 'war' book, the bible on how the election should be fought, said that 'TB must connect with the electorate, particularly with the hard-working majority, and make it clear he is not abandoning them'.[75] Dubbed the 'masochism strategy', opportunities were positively sought for him to appear on television and admit 'we've made mistakes, we can do better and I'm aware of that'. Campbell and Gould thought it important for him to be seen to be 'taking some hits'.[76] One such came on 20 April in Leeds during an organised 'Q & A' session. Blair was confronted by student Jessica Haigh, who told him, 'It's heartbreaking when you work so long to get a Labour government in power and then they turn into a Conservative one.' Blair swallowed and said he had heard many similar complaints: 'If you measure any government against perfection, you would vote for someone else,' he retorted. 'But you must measure us against the alternative, which is the Conservatives.'[77] 'Operation Matrix' was a parallel strategy, to promote Blair's popular touch by placing him on mass audience programmes such as *Richard and Judy*, in which he had to answer a complaint from Cherie that he never bought her any flowers, and an appearance on *Ant and Dec's Saturday Night Take-Away* on 2 April.

On this occasion he was presented with a pair of Union Jack panties for Cherie by 'Mini Ant' and 'Mini Dec', both then ten years old. 'I don't believe this,' he said.[78]

With Brown back in the campaign, life for Milburn became extremely difficult. He did not 'vanish into the wings' as the Brownites had insisted, but tried to continue with his job as planned. 'Alan was very strong, very determined and did a fantastic job in difficult circumstances,' said one campaign insider.[79] He said he had always viewed Brown's involvement as inevitable: indeed, he had wanted Brown to play a role in the campaign from the start, and tried to build bridges after his appointment was announced in September. But he wanted Brown to understand that he had to come back on side, for reasons of obvious self-interest, of his own volition. He absolutely did not want it to be at Blair's behest. 'Milburn felt squelched and very badly treated,' insiders confirm.[80] Milburn regretted the way Brown's return was handled: 'It was engineered so clumsily that Gordon was allowed to present it as a victory, as the white knight sailing to the rescue. It was presented as Tony having sold the pass. That weakened him.'[81] Hain concurred, saying that 'there was a sense that Gordon's return was bringing credibility to a wounded Prime Minister'.[82] Of Blair's political allies, Reid was markedly angry. He had often been the minister who had spoken out against Brown in Cabinet and other forums, and Brown had made his life difficult and unpleasant. Reid now felt 'particularly outraged that Gordon was brought back into the campaign'. He thought Labour would have won the election anyway, and that Blair had lost his nerve.[83] Many of Blair's loyalists thought he had panicked needlessly. 'All of those working on the 'third-term plan' instantaneously realised that Gordon was going to be the Chancellor,' recalled one. 'All our work was dead.'[84]

A Bloody Final Week: 27 April–5 May

'The last week of the campaign was absolutely dreadful. He was called a liar almost every day. He absolutely hates having his integrity questioned,' said Morgan.[85] The final week began badly. On Wednesday 27 April, *Channel 4 News* presented by Jon Snow aired leaked documents about the Attorney-General's opinion on the legality of going to war in Iraq. It was categorically the last subject that Blair wanted raised now. Although the advice itself was less damaging than some had expected, the 'leak' gave the media an open goal. The party believed that political editors were 'desperate' to lead on Iraq, particularly the BBC, which Evans, like Number 10, thought was 'absolutely obsessed with Iraq'.[86] The story was that Goldsmith's advice said that 'while a "reasonable" case could be made for going to war, he was not confident that a court of law would necessarily agree'.[87] The Channel 4 report included reaction from the respected historian Peter Hennessy, who said that the findings established Goldsmith's reputation as the most 'pliable' Attorney-General in recent history. Still more damning was Philippe Sands QC, who delivered a comprehensive condemnation of the government's actions in going to war. Politicians, including Liberal Democrat Menzies Campbell, immediately claimed that Blair had been 'caught out' in misleading the public over the gravest possible issue. Blair found the accusations 'wounding' and 'very unpleasant'. Morgan described it as the 'worst' media treatment that Blair received during the campaign.[88]

Iraq dominated Blair's press conference the following morning, which had been intended to showcase the launch of Labour's 'business' manifesto. He was bombarded with questions. The most dramatic moment was when Brown was asked whether he would have gone to war on the legal advice. Brown's measured response was that it was the most difficult decision any Cabinet could make, 'but the decision was made in an honest, principled and clear way with the evidence before them'. He continued, 'I not only trust Tony Blair but I respect Tony Blair for the way he went about that decision.'[89] His statements silenced all those who doubted the strength of Brown's commitment to fighting alongside Blair. 'What could have been the worst moment of the campaign, became one of the most encouraging,' said a senior party official.[90] For a few seconds, Brown held Blair's political future, and credibility, in the palm of his hand. Blair emerged unscathed. It confirmed that Brown coming on-side had been the turning point of the campaign, and also cemented the image of Brown as Blair's saviour. That night, Blair went before David Dimbleby on a special edition of BBC One's *Question Time*, in which the three main party leaders were asked questions individually for thirty minutes. Blair came last after Howard and Kennedy. The audience's blood was up. He took a string of angry questions on the NHS, tuition fees and Iraq. He asserted again that the Attorney-General's advice showed that the war had indeed been lawful: the decision was whether to leave Saddam in power or put him in prison, and he said he thought it right for the country to choose the latter. He found the studio unbearably hot, and by the end of the grilling, he was drained, with sweat running down his face. One of his team later described it as 'cruel'.[91]

The onslaughts took their toll. Towards the end, he began to think he would lose the election and worried that he was throwing away his legacy on the back of Iraq, said Blunkett. 'He was utterly exhausted and drained,' he added.[92] Pain in his lower back dogged him, which resulted in him walking in an angular way: he desperately tried to avoid the ailment being picked up by the media.[93] Gould later estimated that Iraq cost Labour around 2 per cent of their support in the last ten days of the campaign.[94] The war was even becoming an issue in the place where Blair felt the most politically secure: his constituency. Reg Keys, whose soldier son had been killed in Iraq in June 2003, had chosen to stand in Sedgefield on a single 'anti-Iraq-Blair' ticket. Keys picked up support from disaffected left-wingers while high-profile anti-war figures including former journalist and independent MP Martin Bell came to the constituency to speak for him, with the world's press in tow. Blair phoned up Burton mid-election to ask how it was going. '"I think we'll do all right," I said. "Do all right, John? Is that all?" I did my best to reassure him, but it did get him down,' said Burton.[95] That evening Blair went before a hostile audience on ITV's *Ask the Leader* election programme, hosted by Jonathan Dimbleby. He was forced to say, 'I'm not going to stand here and beg for my own character. People can make up their own minds whether they trust me or not.'[96]

The rapprochement with Brown was at least one source of strength for Blair. 'Thank God I've got Gordon back on side,' he declared. 'You could see the relief throughout his body,' said one aide.[97] For the last few days of the campaign, it was like old times again. They laughed and joked together, and observers could see that a deep bond existed between them. 'Gordon really now believes in reform,' Blair began to say in private.[98] He made many warm and positive comments about Brown, and he seemed to forget, or disbelieve, that Brown had ever tried to rally the party against him. 'Tony is good at making himself believe things,' said one close aide.[99] Brown became equally positive, and for a time believed that the battles of the second term had passed and that a new era had begun.[100] All passions were spent, and he visualised a brief period of joint premiership leading up to his take-over of power. But was Blair just playing him along? That was what the Brownites later came to believe. What would happen when they no longer had a common enemy to bring them together?

The final day of campaigning was Wednesday 4 May. Blair travelled around the country on a final sweep, covering London, the Midlands, the west of Scotland and then Scarborough. He returned to Sedgefield in the evening, where he enjoyed the comfort of his closest allies –

Campbell, Powell and Morgan, and was encouraged, but not greatly, to hear of Gould's prediction of a 'worst case' scenario of a 3-point lead and a 70-seat majority and a 'best case' of 6 points and 120 seats. 'Had the Tories fought a more positive campaign, they'd have done better. Iraq knocked some of our seats down,' said one Labour insider.[101] Blair did not want to hear that.

Campbell, Powell and Morgan stayed in a local hotel that night because the Blairs' house, Myrobella, was too small to accommodate them, and returned the next morning. The plan was to put in much-needed final work on the reshuffle. Gareth Davies arrived from Number 10 with various plans for government changes for the third term, including the re-arrangement of the Treasury. Blair glanced at the plans on and off, and signed off on some of the less controversial changes, but was constantly distracted and kept looking at a list of marginal constituencies. 'We were all twitchy about how the election was going, but he was incredibly tense,' said one present. 'We did none of the work we meant to do.'[102] Blair kept asking his team to phone party headquarters for the latest updates. Messages back were patchy, with no clear overall picture. Blair disconsolately went off for a tour of the constituency, leaving the others at Myrobella to find out more in the afternoon. At one point in the early evening Morgan received reports from south-east and university constituencies, and thought the election might be lost.[103] Blair slipped upstairs and sat on his bed, the only light coming from the landing outside. Campbell and Morgan followed him up and reassured him through the open door that it was going to be all right.[104]

The house started filling up by the middle of the evening with friends and aides from the constituency and London. They were all glued to the television as Big Ben struck 10 P.M. and polls closed. The official joint BBC/ITN exit poll predicted a Labour majority of sixty-six (which was spot on). Blair did not appear in the least comforted, and at one point turned the television off, saying he could not bear it.[105] The first results came in from London, indicating a modest Conservative recovery. Then at 12:35 A.M. they heard that Labour had lost Putney to the Conservatives. It completely unnerved him. 'He walked out and went into the dining room by himself,' said Burton. 'The old gang went in to see him. He was sitting there and wasn't saying anything but was looking at the sheet that Jonathan had given him, and said, "If we lose this, we're going to lose the lot."'[106] At another point, he went out into the garden, taking Campbell and Morgan with him. It was 'freezing cold' but he needed to get away. He started muttering things like 'it's all my fault' and 'Iraq'.[107] 'It was a pretty grim hour or so,' admitted Morgan.[108] At 1:30 A.M., an anxious Blair left the house for his count in Sedgefield. By this time, they were confident that they had won, and the debate was on what size of majority would ensure that his leadership was secure. They agreed that if he achieved less than forty, life was going to be hard. The ideal would be to win a majority of over a hundred.[109] In his own mind he thought a majority of only forty to forty-five would be unsustainable.[110]

Blair's own result in the Sedgefield constituency was declared at 2:17 A.M. His majority had increased, but his share of the vote had fallen from 65 to 59 per cent; not significant, but it troubled him. Reg Keys narrowly missed third place. With Tony and Cherie Blair standing directly behind him, and with the world's television cameras beaming in on them, Keys said, 'I hope in my heart that one day the Prime Minister will be able to say "Sorry", he will say sorry to the family of the bereaved and one day the Prime Minister will feel able to visit wounded soldiers in hospital.'[111] With Cherie on the edge of tears, 'It clearly impacted very badly on him: it was the most visibly weak I'd ever seen him,' said one close aide.[112] What neither Keys nor the world knew was that Blair had already visited and would continue to visit the wounded from Iraq and Afghanistan. He had, however, taken extraordinary steps to ensure that the media did not report this information: 'I don't want it to become political,' he told one military officer, 'and because I don't want it to become political I'm prepared to take the hit from people that think I don't visit.'[113] He did it 'for the sake of his own conscience', said one official.[114]

At the Sedgefield count Blair spoke only a few words: 'The British people wanted to return a Labour government but with a reduced majority. I know too that Iraq has been a divisive issue . . . But I hope that we can now unite again and look forward to the future.'[115] He left with his party before 3 A.M. for Teesside airport, with results coming through to them all the time. 'We lost some very good people, it was sobering,' Morgan said. One such was the ousting of Oona King by the anti-war 'Respect' candidate George Galloway in Bethnal Green and Bow, and Steven Twigg in Enfield South, who had famously taken the seat from Michael Portillo in 1997. Milburn joined them at the airport from his own constituency, having announced that he wanted to return to the backbenches. On the plane he told Blair, 'For God's sake, we've won', to little effect. Blair was in pensive mood throughout the flight south, which subdued those who wanted to celebrate.[116] Cars whisked them from the airport to the National Portrait Gallery by Trafalgar Square where they arrived about 5 A.M. to the accompaniment of the party's campaign theme, 'Beautiful Day' by U2. 'There are good comrades that have fallen,' he said, in a rare slippage into the language of old Labour. 'It was really emotional. There were people in the room in tears. He was great,' said Peter Watt, who went on to become Labour's General Secretary.[117] But those who cheered him now had only minutes before debated whether he would be able to survive the next few days. 'Most seemed to think his departure would be sooner rather than later.'[118] He returned to Downing Street at 7 A.M., had a shower and an hour's sleep, and was back from seeing the Queen at the Palace by 11:30. The first appointment in his diary was with Turnbull and Birt in the den, where the Prime Minister seemed to behave as if he had lost the election: 'He felt in some part rejected,' said one witness.[119] 'Here was a man who had barely slept: he was very demoralised. We should have said, "Go to bed, don't form a government until you have rested,"' said Birt. 'I very much regret not being quick-witted enough at the time to say that.'[120]

The overall results became clear by late morning. Labour had won 356 seats (with 47 losses) to the Conservatives' 198 (up 36) and the Liberal Democrats' 62 (up 11), yielding Blair the overall majority of 66. David Hill thought that the way Blair had been treated by the media and its portrayal of his third-term victory as close to a defeat left him depressed.[121] 'Good God, we've won. Getting in with sixty-six seats and achieving a third term is fantastic for any Prime Minister. Anyone who doesn't see that is crazy,' Gould told Blair the next day.[122] The questions churning through Blair's mind were, would he be able to govern? Would the PLP let him? Would he be able to do what he wanted to do or would Brown again stop him? The challenge Blair now faced was whether he had the personal and political strength to take on Brown, either with the nuclear option of moving him, or at least excluding him from any part in the reshuffle. All eyes were now on him.

The Vultures Circle: Victory and Aftermath

'The Prime Minister was dog-tired, and felt very bad about the result,' said one of his close team.[123] It was Friday 6 May, his birthday, but not his happiest. He rallied himself in an effort to put his stamp on the reshuffle, and to show who was in charge. Letters to ministers, including some significant switches, had been drafted and were ready for him to sign.[124] The first meeting that morning was with Prescott. Blair planned to tell him that he would have to relinquish the communities and local government briefs in their entirety but he could remain as Deputy Prime

Minister. Prescott refused point-blank. 'He took advantage of the Prime Minister feeling politically weak,' said an observer. 'Blair didn't have the stomach for a fight.'[125] His second meeting was with Brown. He put to him a watered-down 'third plan' of splitting the Treasury, but with the OMB reporting up through him. According to one Treasury official, 'The Prime Minister genuinely seemed to think that Gordon might have gone along with it.'[126] Brown rejected the idea outright.[127] He had already made it clear, as part of his 'price' for returning, that he was not going to be moved to 'gain experience' of foreign policy. Blair's much-reduced majority had squashed once and for all his hopes of doing anything to Brown against his will. Powell told an official in Number 10 that, because of the results, 'You can forget the plans now. They won't work.'[128] Birt's and Turnbull's meticulous planning went the same way as much of Birt's innovative thinking on transport and health. 'A lot of the radical stuff had to be put straight in the bin,' said Taylor.[129] As it turned out, more survived than initially thought, particularly on energy and pensions.[130]

Blair still had some leeway, however, and was adamant that he was going to promote modernisers in the reshuffle. This would be a Blairite government. The 'dual leadership' of the preceding three weeks was now over. Number 10 became enraged on Friday after the Brownites briefed the press that the results were bad for Labour, and for Blair: 'There was a pretty big rubbishing of it from the Brownites. That is what they do,' said one of Blair's team, who even went as far as to speculate that Brown wanted the reshuffle to fail.[131] Brown had expected to be consulted fully in the reshuffle, and considered it part of the 'deal' of his returning to the front line. 'He really believed that he had been told in the General Election campaign that it was going to be different from now,' said a Treasury official.[132] He was right, he had been. Before the election results were known, Brown's office had phoned Number 10 to offer his services in the reshuffle. That Friday, after their bilateral, a number of subsequent phone calls took place between Blair and Brown. They were not the conversations Brown had been expecting. Blair had decided that he was going to move in on the Treasury appointments. 'Isn't it at last time to sack Dawn Primarolo?' Brown reacted strongly to protect her. According to one official, the conversation followed their typical pattern at the time: 'The Prime Minister would start off the conversation on the front foot and Gordon would respond simply by saying, "F off".'[133] Blair said he wanted his own nominee, John Hutton, to become Chief Secretary to the Treasury. Brown flatly refused, considering it an affront as Hutton was such a Blairite. Blair tried pushing John Denham, who had left government in 2003 over Iraq: Number 10 wanted to reach out and show all was forgiven. Brown again flatly rejected him, but that evening a story appeared that he had wanted Denham back but Blair had stood in his way.[134] 'It was unbelievable,' said an official.[135] After a lot of persuasion, Brown accepted the compromised candidature of Des Browne (a Brownite, who was seen as more palatable in Number 10 because of his closeness to John Reid).[136]

'Is my team all you're going to talk to me about? I thought you said you'd consult me over the whole government. You promised me. So this is it?' said an indignant Brown. 'Gordon, it's got to be my reshuffle,' Blair responded. 'I am the Prime Minister.'[137] In fact, Blair's team had never even discussed whether Brown should have been involved in the construction of the new government.[138] Instead, Blair relied on the counsel of Morgan and Powell above all, with Turnbull and David Hill both present, though neither expressing strong views.[139] The Treasury very quickly got the message that the Chancellor was not going to be involved at all. 'Their response was, "You bastards." We were straight back to where we were. "We can't ever trust you and we won't trust you again" kind of territory,' said an official.[140] 'After the election, Brown defaulted to "betrayal mode",' said one observer.[141] 'Gordon felt let down and frustrated and things settled at a low point,' agreed Nick Brown.[142] One Number 10 official recalled 'from the Monday following the General Election, the usual state of war with the Treasury resumed'.[143] The reality of the political position meant that Brown nevertheless was the 'silent' influence in the reshuffle, as ministers were all too aware that it would be Brown not Blair who would be their political master in the – perhaps very near – future.

When Blair examined his options, he realised his scope in the reshuffle was not that large. Beckett was too powerful to move against her will, and Prescott's refusal to budge denied him another slot. Blair was happy enough with Clarke at the Home Office, though he toyed with the idea of moving him to the Foreign Office, shifting Straw sideways. Straw was granted a reprieve because in the run-up to the Gleneagles G8, his relations with key figures abroad would be useful. Also, with the referendum on the EU constitution imminent, Blair had at the back of his mind that if it failed, 'Jack would be a useful fall-guy.'[144] The dearth of committed Blairites at the very top level constrained him. Reid was a rare exception, and he decided to move him to the job he coveted: Defence. Hewitt replaced him at Health. Efforts to persuade Milburn to return came to nothing.[145] A return for Byers was never considered. Blunkett was one Blairite who Blair could bring back, and he was slotted into the Department for Work and Pensions (DWP), an important department for the third term and a position for which Blair thought him ideally suited.[146] He had wanted Miliband promoted to succeed Prescott, had the latter been prepared to go. Miliband had been far from a true Blairite, whether heading policy at Number 10 in the first term or as a minister in the second, but Number 10 felt that his modernising credentials had grown over time and Blair rated him. Aides in Number 10 had pressed for him to be given a bigger job, but in the end he was promoted to Cabinet as only Communities and Local Government minister under Prescott's realm. Here he could 'make sense of Prescott', who 'made it clear he would reject almost everybody else who was proposed'.[147]

Andrew Adonis was one reformer whom Blair was determined to promote: he had hopes of appointing him Minister of State at Education as number two to Ruth Kelly. Adonis was the epitome of Blairism. The Brownites rapidly moved into action and hit the phones to block it. 'Gordon will never let this happen,' the *Observer* cited one of his team saying.[148] Again Blair had to give way, and Adonis was appointed to the more junior rank of Parliamentary Under-Secretary, promoting him to the House of Lords as he was not an MP. 'The sense that he couldn't even appoint junior ministers without his Chancellor's approval made him look weak,' admitted one aide.[149] Rather than proclaiming that the reshuffle was seeing Blair assert his authority, as Number 10 had wanted, the headlines boomed out that the reshuffle was a bungle and had been taking place under duress. The Birt plan to give 'productivity' a higher profile after the election was another casualty: as part of this thinking, the DTI on 9 May had its name changed to the Department of Productivity, Energy and Industry. The new Secretary of State, Alan Johnson, did not think much of his new title and came to see Blair the week after the reshuffle. Speaking on the terrace outside the Cabinet Room, he told Blair, 'I understand your wish to re-brand and re-launch the department,' but he added, 'it is not playing well: people are inventing acronyms for it like DIPPY and PENIS.' 'Okay, okay, change it back if that's what you want,' Blair replied.[150] Johnson reverted its name to DTI on 13 May. Birt was incandescent. 'It was just typical of his quixotic change of mind,' said one official. 'I don't suppose deep down he ever really believed it.'[151] With hindsight, Blair would indeed have done better to have waited until he was fresher. As with the reshuffle after the 2001 General Election, he failed to grip the appointments and dictate the agenda.

Brown, not Blair, emerged as the primary victor of the 2005 election. '"It was Brown what won it." Those are the headlines he wanted, and he's had plenty of them,' wrote Andrew Rawnsley.[152] Blair had slept well over the weekend and was much more in command on the Monday morning. But the impression in Westminster and Whitehall had formed by then of a weakened Prime Minister. The conversation in both locations was how long he would be able to continue in power: three MPs (John Austin, Clive Efford and Jon Trickett) even called for his swift departure to allow the party to restore itself.[153] On Wednesday 11 May, Blair went before the PLP for a meeting billed 'as a post-election showdown'.[154] Before it, an apprehensive Blair met his aides in the den to discuss what, if anything, he should say about the succession. 'Given those actively saying it has been a disastrous election, he worried about the meeting,' recalls a Number 10 aide.[155] The formulation they came up with was that he should say he would stress the need for a 'stable and orderly' transition before the General Election. He would add that the party should give him 'the time and space to ensure that happens.'[156] Sitting at the front of the meeting in the Commons, alongside Brown, Blair had a stark but very clear message for MPs: if they remained united behind his modernising agenda, 'the fourth term is there for us'. But if the party moved to the left, it would 'cede the centre ground to the Tories, and that's where elections are won in this country'.[157] For the first time in a PLP meeting, MPs openly stood up and challenged his leadership, saying that MPs had lost their seats because of his continuation as leader. Former minister Peter Kilfoyle put it to him directly that 'the sooner he stood down, the better off the party would be as he had become a negative factor.' There was deadly silence.[158] The mood was sombre and confused, reminiscent of Major's bruising encounters at his own backbencher meetings. Blair responded that he needed 'time and space', and MPs owed it to him to be loyal until the handover took place, adding that he had been loyal to the Labour Party through three election defeats in the 1980s and early 1990s. 'It's only fair to ask for some loyalty in return.' It did little to calm the unrest.[159]

Blair was reluctant to say any more about when he would go. Even with his most senior colleagues in Number 10, 'He didn't want to get into a conversation about when he was going, because he worried that it would set hares running,' said Taylor.[160] Blair may have performed well enough before the PLP to stave off his harshest critics, but it would not be long before the storm clouds would gather again. Blairites like Milburn, Reid and Byers, who had said it was a mistake for him to have made his 30 September announcement about not fighting a fourth term, now saw the chickens coming home to roost. From the very beginning of the third term, winning General Elections had been his greatest single quality and function in the eyes of many in the party. But he would not now be fighting any more elections. The stories began about how long he could and should survive. Coming on top of the unemphatic election results and the half-cock reshuffle, it was the worst possible start to the third term. After all the determination and work to avoid the errors of the first and second terms, it was doubly galling. If he was to make headway, he would need his third term to start with a zest that his earlier terms had lacked. That seemed, at best, unlikely.

14

Second Honeymoon

May–August 2005

As the implications of Labour's 2005 electoral showing began to sink in, one question emerged on the lips of friend and foe alike: 'What is the point of Tony Blair?' It was a question that would not go away. He began his third term without the considerable advantages with which he embarked on his first and second terms. Even within Number 10, it was far from clear whether he could survive for long. His detractors had failed to prise him out at the General Election: the referendum on the EU constitution would be their next chance. If Britain voted 'yes', it would give him the face-saving opportunity to leave on a high: if, as seemed more likely, the vote was lost, his authority would slip away, and he would be forced to stand down. His premiership hung at the end of a very thin cord.

Europe Rides to the Rescue: May–June

Britain's referendum on the EU constitution was scheduled to take place in May 2006. On 25 January 2005, to pave the way, the government had introduced a referendum bill in the Commons with the question: 'Should the United Kingdom approve the treaty establishing a constitution for Europe?' Number 10 had been keenly planning for the referendum itself. Blair's advisers had looked in detail at the 1975 referendum on whether Britain should remain a member of the

European Economic Community (as it was then called). Prime Minister
Harold Wilson was in a precarious position and offered the government
an 'agreement to differ', allowing Cabinet ministers to vote according to
conscience. In Number 10 they pondered the same recommendation,
thirty years on, but came down in favour of urging that any minister who
did not support Blair's 'yes' line would have to resign. 'We hadn't
identified anyone specifically, but if anybody emerged, we felt that they
would have to go,' said one number 10 aide.[1] Into Blair's Christmas bag
in December 2004 was placed a thick file on the intricacies of the
campaign.[2] The referendum was seen as a core feature for Blair's re-
galvanised third term. The polls were inconsistent but Number 10's best
guess was that the British public were 60:40 against, a situation they
judged could be turned around with an effective campaign. 'He was sure
he could do it,' said Byers.[3]

Essential to victory, Blair thought, was a broad coalition in support of
a 'yes' vote. In January and March 2005, further meetings were held in
Number 10 with Ken Clarke and Charles Kennedy. Plans to launch a
'yes' campaign immediately following the French and Dutch referenda
two months later were discussed. They agreed at the second meeting
that although they would have to fight each other 'hammer and tongs'
over the six weeks that followed, as soon as the election was out of the
way they would unite for the common battle. Blair worried that the
'Britain in Europe' campaign would be much weaker than the campaign
being organised by the 'no' lobby.[5] In the past Blair had been
disappointed that the 'Tory grandees', Heseltine, Hurd and Patten, had
never given him the kind of support over Europe that he thought the
cause demanded. They, in turn, were dismayed by what they considered
Blair's timid attitude towards greater engagement with the EU and
concluded they were being used to make trouble for the Tory
leadership.[4] From the spring of 2005, Number 10 took a far more
proactive attitude. Jonathan Powell was put in charge of chairing regular
meetings on referendum preparations, while Straw chaired a group of
officials and Hewitt a body of outside experts.[6] After the fraught May
General Election, Number 10 became even more concerned about the
consequences of a British 'no' vote. The FCO believed a 'no' would
pose a major strategic threat to the EU, though it was unclear what might
happen as a result, and whether it would require a renegotiation of EU
membership. Earnest weekend discussions took place at the Foreign
Secretary's official residence at Chevening in Kent. Number 10's
concern was additionally what a 'no' would mean for Blair himself, and
whether he could possibly survive.

A further worry in May was how exactly the French would vote on Sunday 29 May. Blair asked Number 10's Steven Morris, an EU specialist, how it looked. 'It'll probably be the worst possible result – a yes by a whisker,' he reported. 'Yes, you're probably right,' Blair replied.[7] The accepted wisdom was that the French electorate would bounce back in favour of the referendum in the final days of the campaign. Straw had convened a gathering in his office when the news of the result came through at 7:30 P.M. With 55 per cent of the French voting against, there was a sense of shock and surprise. Straw laughed uproariously. He was 'exultant', recalled one present, and appeared full of *schadenfreude* for Chirac. Straw's guests clustered around the television in the Private Secretary's office adjoining the grand Foreign Secretary's room. 'There was a surreal moment when Chirac came on television and we thought he was about to resign. He looked very shocked,' said one witness.[8] Blair was at a Tuscan villa on half-term holiday with the children. He had steeled himself for a French 'no', and his statement from Italy, which he settled on himself, asked for a 'time for reflection': the 'no' vote was a wake-up call for EU leaders to reconnect with the voters, he said, rather than the EU bureaucrats.[9]

The next day, he was in very cautious mood. He warned Straw directly not to be too triumphalist about the result. Advice he received from Darroch, his EU specialist in Number 10, was that the French 'no' meant the constitution was 'dead in the water'. There would now be no British referendum. 'Blair didn't buy that. He thought that the British people would demand a referendum. His concern was that public opinion would react badly if he immediately announced he was dropping it,' said an official.[10] The emphatic Dutch rejection of the constitution on 1 June, however, with 62 per cent voting against, strengthened the hand of those who called for the British referendum to be buried. A 'tremendous argument' with Straw about the statement to be delivered to Parliament on Monday 6 June now ensued. Blair asserted that no statement was needed. 'We do not need to go out there and declare it dead, nailing down the coffin and dancing on top of it as if to say "We told you so",' he argued.[11] Straw, who the previous year had pushed so hard for Britain to have a referendum, responded that political reality dictated otherwise. On Sunday 5 June, a draft statement arrived in Number 10 from the FCO. Arguments over the language continued until the early hours of the morning. Straw fought hard against Number 10's modifications before finally agreeing to a compromise.[12] In the statement, Straw stopped short of declaring the constitution dead and argued for 'a pause' to allow EU leaders to think through their response, and for the French and Dutch to say whether they thought they could reverse their 'no' votes.[13] But it was increasingly clear that this was window-dressing: the British referendum was indeed dead.

Those who had worked for months on the referendum were distraught, although others reasoned that at least the British presidency would not be dominated by Blair fighting for an unpopular and, to many, a marginal cause, which in all likelihood would have resulted in a 'no' vote and still more questions about his political future.[14] Some considered it would have been the 'third term's 9/11', every bit as distracting to Blair's domestic agenda. Instead it was a time of 'glee at the French catastrophe – neighbourly love and all that'.[15] Brown's views were mixed. 'There was relief in Number 11 that the French had voted "no" because we'd have lost the campaign: Gordon did not want to take over in a disastrous situation,' said one of Brown's camp.[16] But it also meant Blair's immediate position became more secure.

Blair had mixed emotions of his own. The pugilist in him had been relishing a fight over the constitution in the third term. Equally, he saw all the problems a referendum would have brought. With characteristic opportunism, his mind moved like quicksilver – as it often did after reversals – to exploring gains from the predicament. He latched on to the prospects for building a different *kind* of EU. He had always been ambivalent about whether the constitution addressed the real needs of Europe: 'He never thought, "Wow, the constitution means Europe is saved: we've got it."'[17] He realised he had the chance to shift the EU agenda away from an obsession with internal structures and 'social' Europe to an EU that worried less about institutional apparatus and more about policy and advancing a more liberal economic model.

But this was not a propitious moment for him to launch new ideas. Chirac was on the warpath and blamed him, a little unfairly, for bouncing him into holding his own referendum. Schröder was equally hostile. Together with Jean-Claude Juncker, the Luxembourg president chairing the Council, they planned their revenge. They hatched a plot that would demonstrate the continued vitality of the EU, constitution or no constitution, centred on the settlement of the EU budget for the following seven years. Resolving the budget had been given added urgency by the demands for cash from the 'accession' states in Eastern and Central Europe. Blair had known all along that he would have to give up a proportion of the British rebate, famously negotiated by Mrs Thatcher at Fontainebleau in 1984, to help fund this new, larger EU. He was eager for the budget to be settled at the June summit before the British presidency began on 1 July. British eyes were off the EU ball because of the General Election and subsequent planning for a British referendum, but he had not envisaged any great dramatics. On to an empty stage walked the three strutting figures of Chirac, Schröder and Juncker.

On 14 June, Blair was invited to meet Juncker in Luxembourg in advance of the summit. Together with his unwitting party, he met the chain-smoking politician in a villa on the outskirts of the city. Juncker got straight to the point. 'Tony, you've got to give away more of the rebate,' he insisted. Blair kept his cool. 'Give me some figures, Jean-Claude,' he responded.[18] Juncker produced his calculations, which the Treasury officials accompanying Blair immediately pored over. They were fundamentally flawed. 'It was complete chaos,' recalled one official. 'It proved an utterly useless meeting.'[19] Juncker claimed to be arguing for some €10 billion off the British rebate, but the British party calculated that his demands amounted to some €30 billion, which would have wiped out at a stroke Thatcher's rebate. The British smelled a rat. Was Juncker simply out of his depth? Or was he dissembling? They calculated that Chirac and Schröder must have said to him, 'Tony Blair is the biggest supporter of enlargement. Very well. We're going to make him pay for it out of the British rebate.' The plan indeed had a certain logic. Fears grew in Whitehall of a summit ambush, with many EU countries having a vested interest in seeing the British humiliated. Chirac was believed to be particularly motivated because of the longstanding French hatred of the British rebate, Blair's ditching of Verhofstadt and because he was still smarting from his referendum humiliation. Finally, here was a glorious opportunity for him to play the hero to the new EU countries. Blair was suspicious when he met Chirac in Paris that month – there was no meeting of minds, nor even the customary joint press conference. Blair left saying that there had been 'obviously a sharp disagreement' over the budget and the constitution.[20] The two men were as far apart as they had ever been.

The scene was set for a grim council. Blair arrived in Brussels on Thursday 16 June. Matters came to a head on the Friday, the big day at councils, when Britain's isolation quickly became apparent. Blair had just two allies in Jan Peter Balkenende and Göran Persson, prime ministers of Holland and Sweden respectively. At 10 A.M., they came to see him on the seventh floor of the Justus Lipsius building, where councils meet. Blair, always eager to conduct business alfresco, spoke to them on the balcony. Neither leader was keen on Juncker's expansive proposals, as both were under considerable domestic pressure to reduce their own budget contributions. But they knew they were not powerful enough to block the deal by themselves. 'Tony, we don't want to do a deal today,' said Persson. 'I just don't like the atmosphere. There is plotting everywhere.'[21] After their departure, Blair sat on the balcony pondering his next move. Neither Number 10 nor Number 11 felt Britain should do a deal at the summit, but Blair had not yet given up hope. If Juncker was serious about reaching agreement, Blair was still prepared to accommodate him.[22] The omens were not promising. 'It was classic European Council stuff,' said one of the British party. 'No one really knew what was going on. Everyone was waiting to be summoned to the plenary meeting while all the time covert meetings were going on in private offices.'[23] Juncker appeared to be meeting everyone else systematically, leaving the 'awkward squad' of Britain, Sweden and Holland to last.[24] Intelligence filtered back to the British delegation that he was promising the British rebate to every member state 'several times over'.[25]

At 7 P.M. Blair was finally summoned for his bilateral with Juncker in the Presidency office two floors below. He arrived flanked by Straw, Darroch, Sheinwald and the Treasury's Jon Cunliffe. Juncker got straight down to business. He advocated his plan, declaring that it would cut only €10 billion from the British rebate. Blair turned to Cunliffe, 'Is that what we think?' Cunliffe replied, 'My calculation is that to do what the president is asking will cost at least €25 billion over seven years.'[26] Blair turned back to Juncker and said, 'It's inconceivable. We could not possibly do as you ask.' Juncker looked defeated, but to the surprise of the British delegation, barely argued. His financial aide did, to whom Blair responded, 'Look, there's no way I can go back to Britain and say I've given away €25 billion off the British rebate. It just won't work.'[27] The meeting broke up after about twenty minutes. On leaving, the British team were immediately besieged by the Dutch and Swedish. 'Have you done a deal?' they asked nervously. Blair's aides reassured them that they had nothing to fear.[28] The mood in the corridors was becoming very bleak indeed. Late that night, the plenary session, which had not met since the previous afternoon, was convened.

With all the leaders gathered, Juncker admitted defeat. He did not mention Britain by name, but implied as much by saying that 'a few' countries had not accepted their 'responsibilities'. Blair was outraged. Officials described him as 'as angry as we have ever seen him'.[29] The plenary broke up in disarray, the leaders filing off to their separate press conferences. Chirac condemned Blair in uncompromising tones, and Schröder was equally belligerent. Blair was measured but clearly very angry when he addressed the press some time after midnight. 'I gather that already people have been saying that it is all because the UK was unable to reach agreement,' he said. The process, he argued, had been shambolic; Britain was willing to negotiate on its rebate but not in the way that was being proposed.[30] Blair was still angry when, in the early hours, he flew back with the British delegation to Northolt. The budget was now going to have to be resolved during the British presidency. And Blair had no clear idea how to handle it.

'It happens, sooner or later, to all British Prime Ministers,' said the *Daily Telegraph*. 'They begin with hopeful talk about putting Britain at the heart of Europe. They end up isolated.'[31] Blair found himself the darling of the Euro-sceptic press on his return, particularly after his statement to the Commons on the afternoon of Monday, 20 June. The Conservatives taunted him. 'I congratulate the Prime Minister on treading the familiar path for British Prime Ministers from uncritical acceptance to a realistic Euro-scepticism,' jibed David Heathcoat-Amory.[32] They revelled in his obvious discomfort. Not for the first time, Blair felt wrong-footed to find himself in the Euro-sceptic camp. His line of defence was that the reviled Common Agricultural Policy (CAP) needed changing, and that it was 'absurd' for the EU to spend 40 per cent of its budget on the CAP when it produced less than 2 per cent of its output: 'This isn't a budget fit for purpose in the twenty-first century,' he told the House.[33] It carried that day, but he knew he would have to come up with a stronger position than this.

Ever since his return from Brussels he had been mulling over not only how to resolve the EU budget but also its wider purpose and relevance in the new century. Late in the day, he hit on the idea of using the speech given by incoming presidents to the European Parliament in Brussels as the opportunity to lay out his stall.[34] Traditionally, such speeches are anodyne: Blair, still riled by the way he had been ambushed over the budget, did not feel in the mood to be anodyne. It was another example of where he was at his most creative when he was boxed into a corner, and where he was forced to crystallise thoughts that had been forming in his mind for several months. Over the next few hours he produced the seeds of not only his own EU policy, but what would become a main part of EU rethinking overall for the next few years. He cancelled all appointments from lunchtime on Wednesday, 22 June, and went up to the Downing Street flat to study the drafts he had been given for the speech. 'The golden rule on speeches in Number 10 was that not a single word from any first draft would survive,' said one involved.[35] This was even truer when Blair's blood was up. He sat down at his desk in the corner of the sitting room with fountain pen in hand

and began work on his own draft. 'He wrote the body of his argument from scratch,' said speechwriter Phil Collins, with the offerings from his officials and aides strewn all over the carpet 'like a chess board'.[36]

Nothing interrupted his flow until Juncker struck again. At around 3 P.M. reports reached Number 10, via British officials in Brussels, that Juncker was using his farewell speech as president to attack Blair personally. There was worse to come. 'We hate to say this,' the officials reported, 'but Juncker's speech was greeted by a standing ovation from MEPs.' Convention dictates that a retiring president delivers a neutral speech on behalf of the Council as a whole. His was not a neutral speech. Emotions now ran high within the walls of Number 10. 'The European Parliament are a bunch of nitwits and second-raters,' declared one aide. 'It's no surprise they gave him a standing ovation.'[37] News came in that Reuters had branded Juncker's speech a 'withering account', which 'accused Prime Minister Tony Blair of distorting the presidency's proposals . . . and using misleading arguments'.[38] Number 10 officials and aides ran upstairs to the flat. 'This is outrageous,' they told Blair. 'It's not true, he's used the wrong figures again . . . What has Luxembourg ever done for the EU?' they protested.[39] 'Bloody hell!' Blair said as he read over Juncker's text. But then he surprised those present by saying, 'I'm not going to get involved in any tit-for-tat. He's merely upset because his presidency did not end well for him.'[40] In that Zen-like mood, he carried on working until early evening when officials tore him away to leave for the short flight to Brussels. All journey, he carried on writing, head buried in his papers.[41]

It was already dark by the time the party checked in to 'a very grim hotel' by Brussels airport, and traipsed up to Blair's suite. There they were joined by EU Commissioner Mandelson for a meeting on the state of the text. Blair listened to the views of his old friend, who said it was the most 'head-banging' speech he had ever read, and suggested changes and subtleties which Blair duly adopted. At around midnight, Blair said, 'Thanks, guys. I know what I'm going to do. I'll get up at five and rewrite it myself. I'll have the speech ready before we go.'[42] His team, including Powell, Darroch and Hill, all left worried that there was still no definitive text. After a few hours' sleep, Blair rose early and worked with Powell to produce the final text. While the clerks brought them coffee, the Garden Room Girls typed up the latest drafts. At 8:15 A.M., Blair appeared for breakfast with the wider group still wearing the shorts and T-shirt that he had slept in. 'That's it,' he said. 'I've done it. I'd better have a shower.' Aides scrambled with the final logistics. But their printer jammed after the first final draft came off so, as they hurried down into the cars, there was still only one text. Numerous phone calls were made between the cars in his convoy as they sorted out the final figures on competitiveness. Only at this late stage, when it proved difficult to ascertain the correct figures, did Blair appear to show any stress.

He arrived to a packed European Parliament seething with gossip. Following Juncker's speech, no one quite knew how Blair would respond. And how would the MEPs receive the British Prime Minister? It became clear after only five minutes into the speech, even with the dead acoustics in the chamber, that Blair had made a connection with his audience.[43] 'He's one of the best communicators on the world stage and they realised that they were listening to a top-level speech. It blew them away,' said one aide.[44] 'It is time to give ourselves a reality check. To receive the wake-up call,' Blair told his audience. 'The people are blowing the trumpets around the city walls. Are we listening?' It was much more important to refine the policies of the EU for the twenty-first century, in line with the concerns of people throughout member states, he told them, than to devise a new constitution, which should not be rushed into.[45] The speech could have been a disaster, but it was greeted by rapt applause and a standing ovation at the end. 'Tony Blair held MEPs rapt yesterday . . . The European Parliament had been in no mood to be lectured by the PM, but as he left MEPs queued up to shake his hand [and] the press corps were drafting rave reviews,' said the *Guardian*.[46] The effect on Blair himself was powerful. 'It lifted him to somewhere else,' said Collins. 'The success of that speech dispelled the post-election gloom and gave everyone a big positive feeling.'[47] Six weeks into his third term, it was the first significant success he had achieved. Within the next few weeks, out of a blue sky, there were to be three more significant boosts.

Olympic Victory in Singapore: July

Rivalry with Chirac provided the backdrop for another event that summer, the competition to host the Olympic Games in 2012. Paris was the clear favourite to win. Chirac was confident of victory and viewed it as an excellent opportunity to put Blair back in his box. In early 2003 Blair had decided that the government should back London's bid, encouraged by Culture Secretary Jowell. Iraq then intervened and, as London Mayor Livingstone complained, 'You couldn't get decisions.'[48] Cabinet debated whether to bid on 15 May that year, when the balance of opinion in favour. When it came to the point of formal decision Blair was called out to take a phone call from Bush (a strange echo of the first term when Blair had been called out of Cabinet during the debate on whether to proceed with the Millennium Dome) and Cabinet again decided to be bold. In January 2004, at a launch at the Royal Opera House, London officially became an 'applicant city'.

After early criticism from the International Olympic Committee (IOC) president that Britain was behind France and Spain with London's 'obsolete' transport system, the time came for a more dynamic approach to the bid. On 19 May, Olympic gold medallist Sebastian Coe took over as chairman of London's bid. Coe worked closely with Keith Mills, the father of the Airmiles concept, to deliver a winning lobbying strategy. Coe quickly realised that 'we needed Blair on board', as the bid would be thought much stronger if the government was seen to be underwriting it.[49] The turning point for Blair, Coe thought, the moment he began to feel genuinely excited about the bid, was when he visited the Athens Olympic Games in August 2004. Coe wanted him to realise the sheer scale of what was being envisaged: 'For one city to host twenty-eight individual championships puts the World Cup in the foothills.'[50] The Olympic quest gave Blair the opportunity to do what he enjoyed most, being a national leader rather than head of just one party. When the IOC evaluation team came to London, he invited Michael Howard and Charles Kennedy to the Cabinet Room to meet them. Bridges were rapidly mended with Livingstone, one-time New Labour *enfant terrible*. During the course of 2004, and particularly after he knew he was staying, Blair began to believe that London had an outside chance. It had not hosted the Olympics since 1948, when the competition had done much to rejuvenate London after the war: he saw wonderful opportunities flowing from a return sixty-four years on.

In early 2005, Blair began to hold discreet, informal conversations with both IOC members and their political leaders trying to win support for the British bid. The Olympic team considered this work invaluable, and believed Blair's close relationship with Berlusconi had been particularly significant in reaching the Italian IOC member. The extent of Blair's support can be seen in his decision to shift the date of the upcoming G8 at Gleneagles to allow him to attend what would be the decisive IOC meeting in Singapore. In Blair's inner circle, debate had raged about whether he should travel to the Far East for it. Those against said it would weaken his authority if he gave his all and lost: it would be particularly damaging if Chirac beat him, and it risked exhausting him before the G8, long planned as the centrepiece of Blair's foreign policy that year. The 'no' camp had the better arguments, but Blair favoured taking the risk, and when it became clear that Chirac was going to Singapore, the case for him going too was undeniable. On the weekend before he left on 3 July, Chirac remained as disdainful as ever: 'The only thing [the British] have ever given European farming is mad cow disease,' he scoffed before pouring scorn on British cuisine.[51] 'There are some things that are just not responded to,' responded Number 10.[52] Blair's flight left on Saturday 2 July. He was still in high spirits after his speech to the European Parliament.

Blair was greeted at Singapore airport by Coe. The groundwork that had been laid by Coe, Mills and others was impressive. 'We really do have a chance of winning,' he told the Prime Minister, 'but the deciding factor will be you.' Blair replied, 'I'll give it all I can, but let's not kid ourselves.'[53] Livingstone found Blair 'at the top of his form, a global superstar. It seemed as if anything was possible.'[54] They were driven to Raffles Hotel on the Sunday evening and immediately started to lobby. The IOC had been jumpy about several aspects of the British effort, including the presence of David Beckham and the role that Blair personally could play. But they conceded that he should be allowed to hold individual meetings with the IOC delegates, who were to vote on the winning city on 6 July.[55] Coe, who had flown out the week before, had mapped out hour by hour how to maximise the value of Blair's time, to include thirty-four one-on-one meetings with the IOC members regarded as the most influential or who were the floating voters. Each meeting lasted for fifteen minutes.[56] 'My team and I would prime him with verbal pen-portraits of those people he was just about to meet. That was all he needed,' said Coe.[57] His team from Number 10 choreographed it carefully so that IOC delegates avoided bumping into each other on the stairs heading up to Blair's suite. 'We wanted to make each one feel they were getting the special treatment,' said one in the team.[58]

Coe admired the way Blair handled the delegates: 'He never asked them for their votes. Often he would just talk to them about issues unrelated to the Olympics, and was just very attentive and warm with them. In that way he won some over,' said Coe.[59] Into the forty-eight hours, Blair also fitted a reception on the Monday evening at the British High Commission, with guests including the Beckhams, and a party in Blair's suite on Tuesday for London's faithful. 'We wanted to ensure that our loyal supporters didn't feel that we'd forgotten them as we were spending so much of his energy winning new voters over,' said Tom Kelly.[60] There was even time for dinner out at a restaurant on the quay in Singapore. The local police had been jumpy throughout his stay: at one point in the meal, he caught sight of a boat full of police with mounted machine guns cruising up and down in front of them. 'Do you think that's for me?' he enquired.[61]

Cherie arrived on the Monday. A fan of athletics, particularly track and field, she had attended the Commonwealth Games in Manchester in early 2002. She visited the World Indoor Athletics Championships and the World Championships in Paris, as well as travelling with Blair to the Athens Olympics in 2004. She was as passionate as he was about London winning. She worked closely with Jowell, but also lobbied on her own, acting as an informal ambassador.[62] The Coe team had decided that once in Singapore she should concentrate on shoring up the safe votes. She also acted as a sounding board: 'Is there anything that Tony needs to know?' she would regularly ask Coe. He found this very helpful.[63]

By late on the evening of Tuesday 5 July, it was time for Blair's party to leave Singapore for the G8 in Scotland, while Chirac stayed behind for last-minute lobbying. Antipathy between the two camps was high. Livingstone, no neutral observer, thought that the French President 'had the smell of death about him, with no one believing that he could be re-elected'.[64] The British party thought Chirac's approach arrogant, with a 'we deserve this' attitude.[65] They began to see a victory for London as a real possibility. 'We had come from nowhere to a position where Paris looked as if they might lose it, aided and abetted by Chirac,' said Jowell.[66] Blair had managed some G8 preparation on Africa in between meetings at Singapore, but the moment he got on board the chartered Boeing 777, jet lag and exhaustion caught up with him. 'He did a small bit of G8 work on the plane, but fell asleep very quickly. He hadn't slept much in Singapore,' said one aide.[67]

With the time difference travelling west, they arrived in Scotland early on the morning of Wednesday 6 July. As the tarmac at Edinburgh airport had been deemed incapable of handling the weight of the G8 planes coming in, particularly Air Force One, the decision had been taken that all the leaders' planes should land at Glasgow airport, and journey from there to Gleneagles by helicopter.[68] Feeling fresher for the sleep, though still a little dazed, Blair went straight into preparatory meetings at Gleneagles. One of his first was with Bush. 'You could tell his mind was half on Singapore,' said one aide. His whole party were fully aware that a defeat for London would 'be a real dampener on the whole G8. It was very knife-edge stuff.'[69] While Blair spoke with half a mind in Gleneagles, he spoke with a full voice in Singapore, where his pre-recorded speech was played to IOC members at the voting ceremony. He began in French, 'Athens inspired me – and taught me much about the Olympic movement. Our goal is to witness its power in London,' before reverting to English and saying, 'It is that unique combination of strengths which London offers – a global platform for the Olympic message to young people. Not just for the seventeen days of the competition, but for the years leading up to the Games, and beyond.'[70]

Tension mounted all morning before the announcement, which was expected around 1 P.M. 'I don't want to watch it on television,' Blair said. 'I'll be in the garden.'[71] As he strode outside with Powell and Michael Jay they gave him a briefing about the Kyoto framework. 'Despite all the excitement, he still asked serious questions about the protocol, and how it affected climate change,' said Jay.[72] The team meanwhile began to gather around a television inside.[73] Unable to bear the pressure any longer, Blair put in a call to Coe's mobile in Singapore. 'What's happened?' the Prime Minister asked anxiously. Coe replied that he was on his way to the hall to find out. 'Yeah, yeah, I know, but what's happened?' Coe explained that they had no local intelligence and no idea what the outcome would be. 'Look, I don't want to be rude, but they're just about to close the doors and I don't think it would be very good if I'm not in the conference hall when the result comes in,' said Coe as he hurried into the hall.[74] Minutes later, at 7:49 P.M. local time in Singapore, 12:49 P.M. in Britain, IOC president Jacques Rogge took the podium. 'The International Olympic Committee has the honour of announcing that the Games of the thirtieth Olympiad in 2012 are awarded to the city of . . . London!' The switchboard at Number 10 immediately called Powell; he passed his mobile to Blair saying, 'I think this will be the news we didn't want to hear.' But Powell's pessimism was misplaced. 'We've won!' the jubilant switchboard operator told the Prime Minister.[75] Blair immediately hugged Powell. 'It's not often in this job that you punch the air and do a little jig and embrace the person next to you,' he said later.[76] 'We ran down the stairs as Tony and Jonathan ran in from outside and converged in a massive screaming hysteria,' recalled one aide. 'Everyone was on a complete high.'[77] They all hugged him. For a moment, recalled Nick Rowley, 'All the training in restraint of the upper echelons of the civil service was forgotten. But after twenty seconds or so decorum was re-established.'[78]

In Singapore, on the floor below the British delegation, there was a different atmosphere. The French heard the wild British euphoria above. It was a bitter blow for them. For Chirac personally, it was especially sad. He had failed to achieve the Olympics first as Mayor of Paris, secondly as Prime Minister, and finally as President. Coe and

Jowell were clear that Blair's forty-eight-hour visit had tipped the balance against him. Livingstone was equally in no doubt. 'He was absolutely decisive. I can't think of another leader who would have subordinated themselves in a team in that way, just doing as he was asked.'[79] It had been close, a victory by just four votes, but a victory nonetheless. The dark days of April and early May receded further into the background. A 'no' would have made Blair look personally weak, and foolhardy. 'Hubris' and 'come-uppance' would have been two of the attacks made against him. But these same jibes could have been made against his ambitious plans for Gleneagles, which were still far from safe. Much work needed to be done if he was to secure the outcome he needed.

Final Preparations for the G8

While Blair had been preoccupied by the General Election, senior civil servants had put pressure on Jay, who was left carrying the torch, to lower Blair's ambition and go for a more consensual outcome. 'Some very strong words were spoken to Whitehall departments about why the Prime Minister and Chancellor shouldn't have to put up with this when they were campaigning, and it wasn't for the civil servants to decide,' said Forsyth.[80] Blair and Jay agreed that, as soon as possible after the election, they should go across and see Bush to align on climate change and Africa.[81] Blair never doubted his own persuasive powers: 'Don't worry, I'll bring them round,' he told Jay.[82] In advance of Blair's visit, Straw visited Washington shortly after the election. 'I know the Gleneagles summit is all about kicking American ass,' Bush told him, mixing banter with defensiveness. 'But we'll play our part and I'll make it okay for Tony.' Straw replied, memorably, 'Sometimes, Mr President, you present your ass to be kicked.' Straw thought the visit reassured Bush that Blair was absolutely genuine in his wish to advance the issues, rather than trying to isolate the US publicly as some of his advisers suspected.[83]

Blair himself left for Washington on 6 June. For all his earlier optimism, once on the plane he knew it was going to be a hard sell. 'How am I going to approach this? You know, George isn't going to like this, is he?' He rehearsed his arguments again and again, in what one senior aide described as 'a nervy and hesitant fashion'.[84] They arrived in Washington to pelting June rain and called in to see Manning at the Embassy before heading to the White House. 'We worried that if we couldn't get Bush on side, Gleneagles wasn't going to work,' said Forsyth.[85] As with most multinational conferences, the key understandings had to be thrashed out in advance, and this was by far the most significant of all Blair's mandatory pre-Gleneagles conversations with G8 leaders. The US wanted to help the Prime Minister, stressed the NSC's John Simon, but 'we had to make certain that our own policies wouldn't be undermined.'[86]

Blair's first objective was to secure American agreement over debt relief. The Chancellor had already made significant progress with his G8 finance ministers but there were still significant UK/US differences about how a deal would be characterised. Originally the US had argued for the debts of the poorest countries to be simply cancelled. Brown, fearing change to the international institutions who held these debts (such as the World Bank and IMF), argued that debt relief would be better achieved by the G8 countries agreeing to cover the debt payments of the poorest countries for ten years. Only after the US agreed to commit to additional funding to the international institutions concerned had Brown given his assent to debt cancellation in principle. But the details remained in dispute. Downing Street believed this was a tactical ploy on the part of the administration: 'US officials wanted to hold out on debt relief until the summit itself, so it became the main prize they conceded,' suggested Number 10's Forsyth. 'But we wanted to bank the debt relief in advance and push for a doubling of aid and universal access to AIDS treatment. We knew our best bet was to get the President to focus on this.'[87] While Number 10 blamed the US for stalling, White House aides believed that the problem lay in London at Number 11 Downing Street. 'We had already reached a compromise intellectually,' said one senior administration official, 'but for whatever reason the UK Treasury kept blocking it. I suspect they didn't want this to be a Blair success. They wanted to make it a Brown success.'[88] Before Blair arrived in Washington, British officials made it clear to their American counterparts that the Prime Minister was absolutely determined to reach an agreement. Nothing would stand in his way.

Just before Blair's arrival at the White House, Bush was briefed on the situation: 'Mr President, the truth is that our Treasury's getting nowhere on the debt relief language. Our guys seem to think that we can reach a compromise but we've seen nothing.' Bush replied, 'Well, the Prime Minister's going to be here in half an hour. You'd better fix it.' NSC staffer John Simon left the Oval Office immediately and tracked down his counterpart at Number 10, Laurie Lee. He said, 'Look, your guy's going to be here any second and we don't have a deal on this. Isn't this insane?' Lee replied, 'Let's work this out.' By the time Blair arrived at the White House, a text had been drafted and approved by Steve Hadley. Faryar Shirzad, Bush's 'sherpa', rushed to find the British group in the Roosevelt Room to ensure that Nigel Sheinwald was also happy with the text. But Blair, assuming Shirzad was there to welcome him, began to engage him in polite conversation. Shirzad extricated himself, saying, 'Prime Minister, we have to talk to your people about the new debt relief text.' No sooner had he located Sheinwald and begun to run over the text than he was floored again. The White House head of protocol announced that the British party was due in the Oval Office immediately: 'Faryar continued to talk to Nigel as the group assembled,' recalled one witness, 'and as they walked from one room to the other, reached agreement just a foot away from the threshold of the Oval Office.'[89] The deal provided for the Americans to fund $15 billion (£8 billion) of debt 'cancellation' as part of a comprehensive package that would ensure international institutions were not 'penalised'. The British also secured American agreement that the new money not be financed out of existing aid programmes. Five days later, building on Bush's pledge, G8 finance ministers reached an agreement promising £22 billion worth of debt relief to the world's eighteen poorest countries, fourteen of which were in Africa.

Blair spent a lot of time at the White House on a second Africa goal: trying to persuade the US to double overall aid to the continent. This particular focus did not go unnoticed among administration officials who developed their own theories: 'the only way we could explain the PM's relatively dismissive attitude to the debt deal (which we estimated was worth up to $60 billion) was that it was a Brown victory,' said one, 'while the aid increase would be Number 10's achievement.'[90] In fact, Blair chose not to dwell on debt forgiveness because he knew Brown had this under control. To ensure his goals for Gleneagles were as ambitious as possible, Blair pushed ahead with aid volumes, which he knew would be the more difficult issue for the US. The British had already signalled their intent to increase their aid to the UN target of 0.7 per cent of GDP by 2013. For Gleneagles, Blair wanted the G8 to agree to increase aid by $50 billion a year by 2010, with half of this increase going to Africa. But Blair highlighting the figure in the build-up to the visit had 'royally pissed off the administration', reported one senior British Embassy official.[91] 'We had already been involved with the global funds for AIDS which was worth over $15 billion over five years,' said National Security Adviser Hadley.[92] And to many in the administration, talk of increasing aid without linking it to the effectiveness of spending was fatuous. 'The last time we wrote off several billion dollars of debt to Tanzania their President went off and bought a private jet' the British were told.[93] The Americans were fundamentally opposed to aid targets, either in dollar figures or as percentages of GDP, preferring instead to evaluate each proposed project on its effectiveness: 'Numbers don't matter,' insisted one NSC staffer. 'What matters is what we do.'[94] Whereas British aid spending stood at 0.47 per cent of GDP in 2005, US spending was only 0.2 per cent. Against a total US aid budget of $25 billion, Blair pushed hard for the Americans to double aid specifically to Africa in dollar terms, from $4 to $8 billion. But the administration was adamant. 'Our opinion was that you don't throw money at the problem. There need to be sound programmes that make sense. And you need to use the power of free markets and free trade to lift people out of poverty,' said Hadley.[95] 'The focus on money threatened to demean, diminish or ignore the fundamental reforms and policy actions that were taking place in Africa and were necessary for Africa to fulfil its potential,' stressed Shirzad.[96] Number 10 saw such reasoning as a smokescreen. 'The package Blair was putting on the table included all these elements,' insisted one British official. 'It was never just about aid. But without new aid and debt relief the commitments on governance, health and education would be meaningless.'[97] The Americans recall it differently, suggesting that Blair's proposal included a stress on policy reform only after repeated prodding from Washington. During Blair's visit Bush agreed to a unilateral increase in US aid of £370 million to Ethiopia and Eritrea, but it was unclear if this was new money or simply a re-allocation of existing US aid. Although the money saved countless lives in helping avert famine, the headline numbers fell far short of what Blair was hoping for. And the NGOs knew it. 'It's a slap in the face for Tony Blair,' said War on Want's John Hilary.[98] But Blair knew that this was not the final throw of the dice. He kept up the pressure.

Bush's tough stance was reflected at the sherpa level, where Shirzad, with the support of the other sherpas, refused point-blank to discuss aid volumes in the run-up to the summit. 'If we tried to pretend that a G8 statement was a funding document we would inevitably build expectations that were ultimately going to be dashed,' one senior administration official explained.[99] It seemed to the Americans that, contrary to usual practice, Jay did not intend to negotiate the issues involved, but simply impose the British line. Consequently they resolved that Shirzad would need to play 'bad cop' in the Sherpa negotiations and maintain an extremely hard line up until the very end. Once Jay signalled that he might be ready to compromise, the Americans would respond in kind. But for now, 'We had to meet British intransigence with our own intransigence,' explained one senior administration official.[100]

Blair achieved least in the early June Washington visit on climate change. Jay put it down to 'the White House not believing that governments should interfere in market principles'.[101] Bush had listened carefully to his chief climate change adviser Jim Connaughton, who persistently told him that the science far from proved that human behaviour was leading to climate change.[102] For all Bush's desire to give Blair 'a good G8', here was a red line. Blair left Washington far from sure how much he could shift Bush before Gleneagles.[103] Blair was philosophical, but his team were not. 'The Prime Minister tends to accept these things and move on, but people who had sweated blood for months were hugely deflated by Washington,' said Rowley.[104] Knowing that he would not immediately budge Bush on the science, and that this would go to the wire, Blair tried a new tack, based on the advantages for US companies from developing alternative fuel sources.[105] With only four weeks to go, Blair wanted to pull any lever that might work. The chances of a deal on climate change hung in the balance. As Number 10's Lee said, 'Our strategy was to keep as much as possible on the table until the very last moment.'[106] The wisdom of this approach was now to be tested.

Apart from the US, there were six other G8 countries to be brought on side. 'Germany, Canada and Japan were really annoyed with us,' said Forsyth. 'They thought that we had broken the G8 way of working because we weren't compromising and the G8 was all about consensus.'[107] Blair pledged to spend late May and June squaring G8 leaders. On 27 May, he flew to Italy to see Berlusconi in his palatial headquarters. The Italian leader quickly came round. 'I assured Mr Blair of my personal support and my country's support [for] sound and viable proposals,' he said.[108] On 13 June, he was off to Moscow to see Putin. Relations with the Russian leader were already sour, and were further damaged by the perceived snub of Blair not attending the fiftieth anniversary VE Day commemorations in Red Square in May. Blair went into overdrive as he lavished praise on the Russian people for their resistance to Nazism, and he exalted the quality of Putin's leadership. His reward came with Putin's 'full support'.[109] The next day he faced another meeting he was not looking forward to, with Chirac. Given all their recent differences, Blair was delighted with the outcome: 'France was a fantastic ally throughout the whole G8 process,' said Lee. France had a history of commitment to Africa and development, so Blair was working with the grain. Bad blood with Schröder, however, was seen as principally responsible for his failure to move the Germans further. The lack of a German representative on the Commission for Africa 'really pissed the Germans off. But to be honest, it was a lot about personalities,' said one aide.[110] Video conferences with Paul Martin of Canada and Junichiro Koizumi of Japan, culminating in conversations on 27 June, showed how much further Blair still had to move them. 'He made clear his determination, but he didn't manage to move either completely,' said Forsyth.[111]

While Blair laboured with the leaders, Jay was having a torrid time with his fellow sherpas. On 15/16 June, in the room in which the G8 leaders were to meet at Gleneagles, he chaired what was intended to be the 'final' sherpa gathering. Sherpas liked to reach agreement on what their leaders were to say at the annual G8, but on this occasion, it was not to be. Particular sticking points were the British insistence on the extra $50 billion in aid pledges and the commitment to provide universal access to AIDS drugs. At their working dinner, at which the intention had been for the sherpas to relax over Scottish whiskies with their task complete, Jay waved around the unfinished text, saying, 'This is outrageous. What will the people campaigning on Africa think if we don't reach agreement?' At that point, the text caught alight from one of the table candles. 'It's a pity it's not the climate change text too,' one disillusioned sherpa mumbled.[112] 'Everyone was basically against us,' recalled Jay, 'because nobody else really wanted Gleneagles to be a pledging conference.'[113]

On 30 June, with just a week to go to the conference, movement came from the US. Ever since his Washington visit earlier that month, Blair had continued to push the Americans to double their aid to Africa. Bush asked Hadley how close he felt they could go. Including new commitments already in the pipeline, he reckoned they were only $400 million out of $4 billion short of Blair's target. Hadley advised that, for all the administration's opposition to aid targets in principle, there was little point in holding out for the sake of $400 million.[114] 'It was important to the Prime Minister and we felt that we could do it.'[115] Hence, Bush's 30 June announcement that the US would indeed be doubling aid to Africa. 'It never would have happened with any other leader apart from Blair,' said the NSC's John Simon.[116]

An apprehensive British team assembled at Chequers on Saturday 2 July, hours before Blair was due to fly off to Singapore. Despite Bush's commitment on the aid pledge, major problems remained.[117] Blair began to lose patience and said he wanted to take over control of the negotiations himself. 'If we push too hard, we'll isolate the Americans,' Jay warned him. 'I'm prepared to do that,' he said, uncharacteristically.[118] He broke off the meeting to speak to Bush to plead for progress on a principal sticking point, universal access to AIDS drugs.[119] Their difficult conversation was not helped by the weather: Chequers was struck by lightning during the conversation and the phone line went dead several times. 'The President was increasingly nervous and worried about how the summit would turn out for Blair,' recalled one administration official. He couldn't understand why Blair was handling the preparations in such a public way, with the effect of only painting himself further into a political corner. 'He feared that it could become a fiasco.'[120] Further US compromises were still slow in coming. Some White House advisers felt Bush had already gone far enough. By the time Blair left for Heathrow, agreement had still not been reached. 'Okay, all right, do it your own way' were his departing words, leaving many to wonder about the wisdom of the decision to go to Singapore.

A hastily convened final meeting of sherpas was taking place consecutively at London's Lancaster House to try to secure the agreement that had eluded them so far. 'All the sherpas hated leaving it to the last minute. Their biggest fear was actually letting their leaders discuss real issues,' said Forsyth. They worried that, if they left it to their bosses, Blair's persuasive charms might result in more being given away than they thought wise. Despite the pleas of his seven colleagues, Jay remained unmovable: 'It was seven against one on virtually everything from beginning to end,' recalled one witness. 'Michael would keep coming back saying, "I understand, but the Prime Minister wants . . .".'[121] Ultimately his negotiating strategy came down to a game of brinkmanship with Shirzad: 'We didn't see that Michael was given any room to negotiate and so our view was, we can't negotiate when our counterpart isn't authorised to negotiate,' said one US official. 'And all the time the others were largely watching this spectacle of the "special relationship" under test.'[122]

While they met, the warm-up music from the 'Live 8' concert in nearby Hyde Park drifted through the windows. It was one of those rare occasions in world history where collective public pressure moved politicians. The Live 8/Make Poverty History campaign that weekend helped shift some G8 leaders, who feared the impact on their domestic public opinion if they returned from Gleneagles empty-handed. Blair was pleased that work with Geldof and Bono *et al.* was paying off, if, on a personal note, he was disappointed to be missing the concert. 'Being given the video and the tapes was scant consolation for the guitar-playing

Blair,' said one aide.[123] This was his kind of music: he was a world apart
from Chirac, Schröder and Bush in his musical taste. The music may not
have swayed the sherpas, but a reception for them at Number 10
addressed by Blair and Bono had more effect: Bono asked them to think
how proud their grandchildren would be if they did the right thing.
Some considered the overture in poor taste, others that they were being
bounced. Vital matters were left by them unresolved: the language on
universal access to AIDS drugs had not been agreed by the Americans,
while a number of countries, including the US, continued to resist the
plan to include a firm commitment to boost aid by $50 billion in the
summit communiqué. Worse, Washington refused to confirm whether
their 'additional' $4 billion for Africa would be a commitment on top of
their existing $25 billion aid budget, or merely a re-ordering of priorities
within it. Gleneagles was not going to be a typical G8: the leaders were
going to have to take the final decisions themselves.

On Wednesday 6 July came the news that Bush had moved a little on
climate change. 'The surface of the earth is warmer,' the President
confirmed, 'and an increase in greenhouse gases caused by humans is
contributing to the problem,' though he stressed that leaders needed to
move beyond the distrusted Kyoto framework.[124] Even as the leaders'
planes were circling to land at Glasgow airport, conversations hammered
on. While Jay spoke to Shirzad on board Air Force One, Laurie Lee
spoke to John Simon. Jay, Sheinwald and Forsyth made the bottom line
very clear: 'The Prime Minister wanted the President's support and that
was it.' The Americans remained unhappy with the demand for
'universal access' on AIDS treatment, which they considered impossible.
'Look, Laurie,' said Simon from Air Force One, 'if you can get a
technical person to tell you this can be done, we'll run with it, but my
technical people say "universal access" can't be done.'[125] Finally, a deal
was reached: 'The Brits agreed to the "as close as possible" on AIDS
treatment, as well as several other changes in various texts, in return for
our agreement to put a dollar amount in the declaration,' recalled an
American official.[126]

That evening, as they settled into Gleneagles, Jay went round the
delegations and told them that the US had agreed to double aid to Africa
and the EU had already agreed to increase aid by €42 billion. 'We want
the G8 collectively to pledge an extra $50 billion in aid by 2010,' he
insisted.[127] The British told each delegation in turn that the other seven
had effectively signed off on it and so they should fall into line too. It was
an unusual ploy for such a correct diplomat, but it worked with most.
Not all. 'The nice cuddly Canadians and the Germans were being

complete bastards,' said one official. 'The Germans in particular had to be dragged kicking and screaming to sign up to it.'[128] Concerns about money played a part in their reticence, though the British felt that 'Schröder hated Blair so much, he simply didn't want to give in to him'.[129] 'Schröder was the one leader about whom the British party would ever hear their Prime Minister being rude. He regarded the German Chancellor as a man of no principle and was unusually intemperate in the way he dismissed him,' said Sally Morgan.[130] Blair knew he still had to outflank him, but by the time of his arrival that morning, he felt reasonably confident about the rest. That evening, the Queen hosted a dinner for the G8 leaders and their spouses, cooked by Andrew Fairlie, the Michelin-starred chef trained in the south-west of France. As the leaders settled down to dinner, far in the distance in Edinburgh, Make Poverty History held a noisy rally. The summiteers tucked into smoked salmon with roasted langoustine, followed by fillet of lamb with aubergine caviar and parmesan polenta, finished off with a pudding called 'textures of chocolate' accompanied by a 1990 Château Climens Sauternes. As the satisfied leaders padded back to their bedrooms that night running through the day ahead in their minds, 400 miles away in London, four young men were making their own preparations.

Terror Strikes London: 7/7

After breakfast at 7:30 A.M. on Thursday 7 July, Blair and Bush went for a stroll in the gardens. Now a five-star golf resort set in 850 acres of open scenery, Gleneagles Hotel opened in 1924 and is described as a 'Riviera in the Highlands'. Blair's team had chosen well. Both men were in good spirits as they strolled around the gardens within the heavily guarded security perimeter, admiring the rolling hills of the Perthshire countryside, 'bathed in bright sunshine'.[131] In London, the morning rush hour was just getting into full swing as commuters journeyed to work, some having celebrated the news of the Olympic win the night before. At 8:50 A.M., three British-born Islamic fundamentalist suicide bombers blew themselves up simultaneously at different points on the London Underground: Mohammad Sidique Khan (aged thirty, from Dewsbury, West Yorkshire) at Edgware Road; Shehzad Tanweer (twenty-two, from Leeds) at Aldgate; and Germaine Lindsay (nineteen, from Aylesbury) between King's Cross and Russell Square. Just under an hour later Hasib Hussain (eighteen, also from Leeds), unable to detonate his bomb underground, exploded it on the Number 30 bus as it journeyed through Tavistock Square. It was not until 9:17 A.M. that the Underground's network control centre knew that it was dealing with a series of explosions, and issued a 'Code Amber' alert to commence the immediate shutdown of the entire network, with trains told to terminate at the next station while passengers evacuated.[132]

At almost the same moment that the Underground bombs were detonated, Blair finished his stroll with Bush and went to greet Chinese President Hu Jintao in a reception room at the front of the hotel overlooking the lawns.[133] Over coffee, the Chinese leader congratulated Blair on the successful 2012 Olympic bid, and Blair reciprocated by saying he was sure the 2008 Beijing Olympics would be spectacular.[134] David Hill and Tom Kelly were preparing for the day ahead watching television upstairs when the first news came through shortly after 9 A.M. of a 'power surge' on the London Underground. Their suspicions aroused, they phoned Number 10 to ask for more details. Number 10 were already talking to London Transport, but as yet there was no clear picture. It looked suspicious enough for them to decide Blair had to be told. Kelly went downstairs and passed Blair a note mid-conversation with Hu Jintao. Blair hurriedly read it and told the interpreter, 'There are reports of what may be terrorist bombs in London. Do you mind if we adjourn?'[135] The meeting with the Chinese premier broke up at 9:35 A.M. and Blair, now joined by Powell, Kelly and Hill, debated what to do. When the news came through of the bus bomb, any lingering hopes that it might not be the work of terrorists disappeared. Were those the only bombs, or might London, and other cities, be under attack also? No one could tell. The immediate question was whether or not Blair should make a broadcast. But with little detail as yet to go on, they thought that it might cause panic unless a fuller picture could be ascertained. Blair seemed 'clearly rattled', said one witness, 'and unnerved by what had happened'.[136] Cherie believed that along with David Kelly's death in 2003, the bombings were 'the other shocking reversal of the premiership'.[137] With the leaders already making their way to the main conference room, and the prospect of the long-awaited G8 and months of preparation being wrecked by terrorists, it required all his strengths of composure to remain calm and focused. He decided to proceed with the formal opening ceremony and await further news.

The official opening consisted of Blair greeting each leader one by one as they came into the room, with the formal ceremony caught on camera. The leaders then began the business of the summit, though all were conscious that something serious was happening in London. Blair tried to keep them to the agenda, with each delivering their opening statements, but with more notes being brought in to him, he decided he had to act. 'Look, guys, I think we need to focus on this because it is quite clear to me now this is a serious attack,' he said gravely. 'There have been four bombs and a number of people killed. We've got to decide how to react.' It was obvious to all of them that this was a concerted attempt, probably al-Qaeda-inspired, to disrupt their conference. Some present thought it resembled one of the many films when terrorists attack a conference for the leaders of the most powerful nations on earth. The G8 leaders were swift to offer their support: 'There were enormous amounts of very heartfelt sympathy from all of them,' said one present, particularly from those leaders who 'had been tested by similar challenges of their own'.[138] As the leaders groped towards how they should react, it became obvious that just three possessed the presence of mind to come up with the right response and words – Blair, Bush and Chirac. 'None of the others seemed capable of rising to the occasion in the same way,' said one senior official.[139] Even among these leaders who had risen to the top of their countries, hierarchies still emerged.

'This is the G8,' Blair said from the chair. 'I've spent a year preparing for it and now this has happened.' He was faced with a dilemma. This was the biggest conference of his premiership. Did his duty lie in continuing to chair it, or leaving to take control of the response to the attacks? Berlusconi suggested, 'Let us all go to London with you.' But Bush intervened to say, 'No, we shouldn't do that. If we go to London, all the security personnel will need to be siphoned off to protect us. We don't know what else could be in store. The rest of the capital might be vulnerable. We stay here. You go, Tony.' The President had more to say, revealing how much he had learned since 9/11. 'You need to go soon, but not immediately. You need to know exactly what is going to happen first, before you get on that plane.' But Berlusconi, moved by the passion of the events, reiterated his suggestion: 'Look, we can go down,' he said.[140] Blair thanked his peers for their condolences and their suggestions. He knew Bush was right and resolved to prepare to leave for London alone. But he was anxious for the summit to continue without him: 'Will you stop talking?' he asked. Bush replied, 'No, we're going to keep going. We can't stop. We need to do something concrete, of value.'[141] Blair's team had independently reached the same conclusion, that they could not let the terrorists be seen to win by wiping out the summit. 'We had a hunch that was their goal,' said one of Blair's team. But with Blair leaving, who would take over? From the ranks of world leaders came the answer: 'Your guy [Jay] is really good, why don't we have him, he can lead us, and we will take his command,' said Chirac; a suggestion Bush echoed.[142] Blair then hurried from the meeting leaving Michael Jay in charge. Jay's note, which he wrote on his computer tablet linked to the logistics room, recorded the following: 'Prime Minister addressed meeting. Prime Minister informs meeting of events in London. Prime Minister informs meeting he will be leaving to go to London and will return. Prime Minister informs meeting that G8 sherpa will take over chairing of meeting.' After which he wrote one word: 'HELP'.[143]

In Downing Street that Thursday morning, Cabinet was being chaired by Prescott with a lightweight agenda. Ivan Rogers, the senior official on duty, went in to alert him that something was awry, telling him of reports of the electrical surge. While Cabinet continued, Rogers went back to watching the story unfold on Sky Television. 'It was bizarre that Number 10's best source of information was Sky,' he later said.[144] Soon after Rogers' exit Darling received a message on his pager and announced, 'I don't think this is an electrical surge.' The decision was taken to adjourn immediately and go downstairs to COBRA. Assembling shortly after 10 A.M. they were swiftly joined by Dame Eliza Manningham-Buller, the new head of MI5; John Scarlett, head of MI6; and Ian Blair, Commissioner of the Metropolitan Police. At 11 A.M. Blair spoke to them by conference call. Home Secretary Clarke confirmed that several bombs had been detonated and it was almost certainly terrorism. Blair's advisers in Gleneagles had urged him to signal very clearly to the public what he was going to do next. 'You might not be in control of events, but you could be in control of the response,' he was told.[145] Shortly after 11 A.M. Blair announced that the explosions were 'probably a major terrorist attack', indicating that the police had already found evidence of explosives at one of the blast sites. Blair's team at Gleneagles knew that operationally he did not have to return to London to be in control of the situation, but the symbolism was deemed important. He would not, however, visit the sites of the blast because 'there was nothing that the terrorists would want more than to have pictures blazed over the world's media of the Prime Minister standing in front of a bombed capital'.[146]

It was judged that the authorities now had enough of a picture of events for Blair to speak to the country, which he did before leaving for London. Speaking at midday from the G8 press conference room, on the same spot where twenty-four hours before he had waxed euphorically about the Olympic news, he delivered his first statement on the attacks: 'The purpose of terrorism is just that. It is to terrorise, and we will not

be terrorised.'[147] The G8 + 5 leaders then broke their morning session
to join Blair in a show of unity, with all the leaders standing on hastily
constructed staging just behind him. Blair spoke movingly about how
'our determination to defend our values and our way of life is greater
than their determination to cause death and destruction to innocent
people in a desire to impose extremism on the world. Whatever they do,
it is our determination that they will never succeed in destroying what
we hold dear in this country and in other civilised nations throughout the
world.'[148] Blair was hurried out into his black Daimler and driven to the
eighteenth hole of the King's Course where he was taken by Chinook
helicopter to Dundee airport accompanied by Powell, Sheinwald, Hill
and Kelly. They landed at Northolt and unusually were then flown by
helicopter to Chelsea Barracks because of the need for extreme speed
and security: the custom almost always was for him to be driven with
police escort from Northolt to Downing Street.[149]

Blair had long expected such an attack. 'It was a tactical surprise
because it was not forecast,' explained one intelligence official, 'but it
was not a strategic surprise. It was exactly what we had expected.'[150] To
help prepare for what was feared to be in the pipeline, shortly after 9/11
Blair had established the London Resilience Forum. Livingstone, the
vice-chair, believed its scenario planning made a significant difference
on 7/7 (as the 7 July attacks rapidly became known). 'The fact that we'd
anticipated it, war-gamed it, most probably saved many lives. Everyone
knew what to do,' he said.[151] 'He knew it was coming at some point,'
said John Burton. 'But the magnitude of it hit him hard, especially as the
terrorists were British.'[152] For most of Blair's premiership, Britain's
intelligence agencies had been concerned, but it was 9/11 that put them
on high alert. During 2000–05, the five years John Stevens, Ian Blair's
predecessor as Metropolitan Police Commissioner, was in charge, twelve
separate plots were foiled. 'The Prime Minister was well aware before
the 7/7 bombs that home-grown terrorists had become a real threat:
intelligence was increasingly showing that they were a bigger problem
than we'd initially thought,' said one senior official.[153] Intelligence
indicated that young British males had been at training camps in
Afghanistan. 'The changing nature of suicide bombing techniques was
really alarming,' said Stevens. 'But I never saw the Prime Minister panic,
even in his body language. We kept him briefed of all our concerns but
he was always in full control of himself.'[154]

In February 2003, intelligence reported 'credible information' alerting
them to a possible al-Qaeda attack on Heathrow airport. The threat was
of a ground-to-air missile attack launched on a British, American or

Israeli jet taking off from Heathrow and flying low over Windsor. The terrorists planned to observe the runway and identify a suitable target, phoning through the plane's details to their fellow terrorists under the flight path. Special Branch and the SAS were deployed to Windsor and other high-risk locations but were appalled when orders were given for tanks to be sent to Heathrow, alerting the terrorists and preventing the possibility of them being captured.[155] The media reaction was cynical, saying that it had been a put-up job for political purposes. Recognising this widespread perception, a saddened Blair said to Stevens, 'They'll believe what you say, but not what I say.'[156] One year later, on 30 March 2004, police raids in 'Operation Crevice' resulted in the seizure of 1,300 lb of ammonium nitrate, a key bomb component. Intelligence had been monitoring an Islamic extremist network, and had picked up the information that al-Qaeda attacks were imminent on the Ministry of Sound nightclub in London, the Bluewater shopping complex near Dartford in Kent, various synagogues and the gas and electricity network. Stevens described it as 'the most worrying of the twelve foiled plots'.[157] In April 2007, after one of the most expensive trials in British criminal history, five British men were given life sentences.[158] Increasingly, the public and media argued that Blair's policy in Iraq had made Britain more vulnerable to terrorist attacks, a claim Blair repeatedly denied. Uncertainty nevertheless lingered at the back of his mind about whether the accusation might have justice.

Blair arrived at COBRA in the early afternoon and took over the chairmanship from Charles Clarke, who had already confirmed to the House of Commons that there had been 'a number of terrorist attacks in central London'.[159] Intelligence pointed to the significant risk of further attacks, he learned. Those present sensed his deep concern, but also his resolve: 'He was absolutely calm; my impression was of a man who was very good in a crisis,' said Ian Blair.[160] The full horror of the attacks emerged throughout the day: 52 people and the 4 bombers killed, with 700 injured. It was the deadliest single act of terrorism in the United Kingdom since Lockerbie, when PanAm's flight 103 was downed with the loss of 270 lives, and the deadliest bombing in London since the Second World War. The meeting debated how best the police should cope with the attacks, the likelihood of further bombings, and how to respond.[161] The meeting over, Blair delivered a statement from Downing Street. 'When they try to intimidate us, we will not be intimidated. When they seek to change our country or our way of life by these methods, we'll not be changed. When they try to divide our people or weaken our resolve, we will not be divided and our resolve will hold firm.'[162] It was Blair's oratory at its best, expressing how the country felt and offering reassurance and a sense of belonging. In the late afternoon, before returning to the G8, he visited New Scotland Yard, Metropolitan Police HQ, to observe work at the operations centre and to thank the police.

As he made his way back up to Gleneagles, weariness began to bite. 'He was still intensely jet-lagged, he'd had the triumph on Wednesday and the shock today. He was still trying to absorb everything that had happened. On top of it all, he was just very hungry,' recounted Tom Kelly.[163] Just before he took off he learned that Edinburgh's Princes Street had been cleared because of the suspicion of a bomb, which made for an anxious flight. Not until they landed in Scotland did they find out it was a hoax. By 9:30 P.M. he was back at Gleneagles. With the flags flying at half-mast Blair delivered his final statement of the day. 'We will not allow violence to change our society or our values. Nor will we allow it to stop the work of this summit ... Here the world's leaders are striving to combat world poverty and save and improve life. The perpetrators of today's attacks are intent on destroying human life. The terrorists will not succeed.'[164] Later that evening Blair shared his perspective on what he had seen in London with the other leaders informally. Berlusconi repeated his earlier suggestion the G8 leaders should all descend on London in solidarity. Bush again intervened to stress the practical difficulties of such a course. Given Blair's desire for the G8 to continue at full throttle, an elaborate photo call in London was the last thing he wanted. He thanked his Italian friend but politely demurred, and then winked at Bush knowingly.

Success at Gleneagles

Thursday 7 July was to have been the big day on climate change at Gleneagles, while behind the scenes intense talks continued to try to reach final agreement on the Africa text. Discussions pushed on in Blair's absence, but in a desultory way. The leaders' eyes were in part on London, and on the risk of parallel attacks in their own countries, a real concern given al-Qaeda's liking for simultaneous terror. Not for the first time Blair was thankful that so much work had been done before the summit. 'If leaders had not been able to reach agreement, after the bombings, on such an important set of issues for the world, it would have sent an awful message,' said Forsyth.[165] Blair was far from confident of success, however, when he discussed with his team that night how to re-jig the remaining hours of the summit to derive maximum benefit. Was there any way they could turn the loss of time, and unity of purpose, to their advantage? Reshuffling the timetable was an obvious decision. The original plan had been to have two separate communiqués, climate change on the Thursday, and Africa on the Friday. Insufficient progress had been made to justify one on climate change that day so it was decided to issue both on the Friday. Trade, though, would be a casualty. Although not originally on the agenda, Blair had decided to try to reach agreement on export subsidies, hoping to give the World Trade Organization (WTO) talks a push. Blair spoke to Bush about this personally and secured the President's support for the effort to phase out agricultural subsidies, which the two leaders later announced publicly. This was the first Bush's staff heard of the pledge: 'it really was a big deal,' said one US official, 'and it was set in motion by Blair's direct intervention with the President, who gave us no warning at all.[166] With Bush on side, a full agreement was close, but in the end proved a step too far. Instead, the G8 agreed to support a range of measures to help build Africa's trade capacity.

Blair was more determined than ever to knock heads together to achieve the outcomes he wanted. Disagreement over the overall aid package remained a stumbling block. Japan was one of the last to hold out, but eventually came into line. Germany did not. Blair decided he had to confront Schröder himself, who was saying he wanted to exempt Germany from the communiqué. 'He literally had to get Schröder into a corner on the Friday morning and tell him he was going to wreck the whole conference and the prospects of progress. He almost pushed him up against the wall and squeezed agreement out of him. He was very insistent,' said one Number 10 source.[167] The final disagreement came over the annex to the Africa text, in which each country detailed their plans for meeting the pledge to double aid. Chirac insisted on inclusion of an airline tax as part of a European-wide effort. Initially the Germans and Italians resisted, but eventually they came round. All was now set for the communiqué to be issued. Here Blair was to pull off another ploy: by having all the leaders sign it under the full gaze of the media, it helped lock them into the commitment. He controversially insisted on the African leaders being integrated into the concluding proceedings. 'We speak today in the shadow of terrorism,' he said at the close. 'There is no hope in terrorism, nor any future in it worth living, and it is hope that is the alternative to this hatred. So we offer today this contrast for the politics of terror.'[168]

Gleneagles was Blair's most successful international conference. 'He achieved things which officials didn't think were possible,' said Turnbull.[169] It was a rare example in the late Blair premiership of him working productively with Brown, whose marshalling of finance ministers and his links to the NGOs were vital to the achievement. For the remaining two years of his premiership, Blair continued to drive the Gleneagles agenda forward, particularly on trade, and he invested considerable energy in WTO negotiations. With Bush's support, he tried to establish a mechanism to hold the G8 to account for what they had promised, much to the irritation of their fellow leaders. 'We've got to keep people to the communiqué: Gleneagles must not just be a piece of paper. It's a series of commitments which we must hold people to,' he would say regularly.[170] Blair's impact was also felt on the G8 as an institution. Gleneagles was a major staging post, transforming what had initially been a meeting of finance ministers and then of national leaders to talk about economic issues into the most important annual forum for world leaders to discuss major issues. Making the lead up to the summit such a public affair was a particular innovation that endured, ensuring a far greater role for NGOs in subsequent G8s than had been the case in the past. It was also the first time that the G8 had tackled two major issues with a determination to achieve agreement, and was a formula that Merkel returned to with her G8 at Heiligendamm in June 2007. Blair was also largely responsible for the emergence of the G8 '+ 5', broadening out membership to include all of the world's major powers. Kofi Annan would later call it the 'greatest summit for Africa ever'.[170] John Simon believed that on development issues it had been 'much more united and coherent than any G8 that there has ever been'.[171] Bush's support had indeed been crucial: 'Under the leadership of the President and the Prime Minister, we were able to bridge differences of opinion and come up with a statement that all countries could endorse,' was the Washington view from Hadley.[173] Blair had sweated blood for Bush, and the support that he received at Gleneagles was the most significant 'pay-back' he received.

When Bush returned to Washington from Gleneagles, he took a helicopter to the Vice-President's house which lies on the hill just above the British Embassy in Washington, and went straight to the Embassy to sign a book of condolence for the victims of 7/7, and lay a wreath in the garden. The entire US Cabinet came to sign, including Cheney, Rumsfeld and Rice. An Embassy official described it as 'a very sombre time'.[174] Even the arch-sceptics among the neocons regarded Blair for a time as 'one of us'. The question now was whether the President's support for Blair's agenda, which had helped make advances possible at

Gleneagles, would continue to flow, especially with London itself joining New York and Washington in the front line of the war against terror. Without continuing active support from the White House, Blair's high aspirations on climate change and Africa, as indeed in the Middle East, would go nowhere.

15

Promise Fades

September–December 2005

In the space of just two months, from May to July, Blair's third term had been transformed after its near-stillborn birth. His pre-summer success had enhanced both his authority and his self-confidence. His hope was that the corner had been turned, and that he could use his mandate to complete his agenda at home and abroad. He had promised his successor a 'stable and orderly' transition before the next election. Would that be enough to pacify his critics once they returned from the summer? The Brownites had never accepted that the 2005 General Election victory was Blair's alone, nor that he had a personal mandate for public service reform. Would they work to unpick it as they had his reform agenda in the second term? Would even previously loyal ministers look increasingly to life beyond Blair, rendering him in effect a lame duck? Blair's resolute response on 7/7 had been applauded. He would now need to show real progress towards democracy in Iraq, and troop reductions, if he was to avoid the war becoming the septic issue in the third term that it had been in the second. On the positive side, he began his third term a wiser and more autonomous figure than he was at the start of his previous two terms. Finally he knew what he wanted to achieve.

Battling for the Initiative: September 2005

At the heart of a successful third term would be a Number 10 that would enable him to deliver on his policies, while keeping the PLP and other key stakeholders on side. Considerable work had gone into bolstering Blair's office accordingly. Matthew Taylor, who had experienced a mixed time since his arrival in the volatile Number 10 of 2003, remained, with an enhanced brief over political strategy, until he left in November 2006 to run the Royal Society of Arts. David Bennett, a wily strategic thinker, had arrived to head the Policy Directorate. Appointed to direct the Strategic Communications Unit was Benjamin Wegg-Prosser, one-time aide to Peter Mandelson, who had been working since for the *Guardian*. Ruth Turner was appointed head of government relations: she had been a co-founder of the *Big Issue* in the north of England and a member of Labour's NEC. She was felt to have the personal skills and experience to deal with the party although, significantly, she was not well known in the PLP. Philip Collins, who had hitherto run the Social Market Foundation, became Blair's chief speechwriter. These newcomers joined the proven team of Jonathan Powell, David Hill and Liz Lloyd, who became deputy chief of staff to Powell, and an increasingly important figure. Birt remained in situ as an unpaid adviser until he left in December 2005. Two core figures departed at the election, though both continued to have important advisory roles: Sally Morgan and Pat McFadden. Among the civil servants, Nigel Sheinwald continued to advise on foreign policy and Kim Darroch European policy, while Ivan Rogers remained Principal Private Secretary until March 2006. Gus O'Donnell succeeded Andrew Turnbull as Cabinet Secretary on 1 August, fending off competition from Nigel Crisp, Permanent Secretary at the Department of Health, and John Gieve at the Home Office. O'Donnell had been Permanent Secretary to the Treasury and close to Brown, but contrary to speculation at the time, he was not appointed to ease the transition 'because Blair did not see himself departing for several years'.[1] Neither was Blair suspicious about appointing a Treasury man: the key factor in his appointment was him being seen as more of a believer in public service reform than the other contenders.[2] His easy charm and 'bloke-ish' manner also appealed to Blair, and he was to enjoy the happiest personal relationship with O'Donnell of his four Cabinet Secretaries. Although, significantly, it lacked a seasoned PLP operative, collectively, this was the most experienced team Blair would have in Number 10.

Blair began the third term with easily the most coherent body of policy planning he had ever had, derived from the manifesto, the strategy unit, from Birt personally and from Cabinet ministers. The problem was that there was too much of it, and it lacked definition. On his return from holiday Blair fired off a memo to senior officials telling them that the next six months would be vital.[3] 'He came back from holiday fizzing with energy, saying that there's a packed agenda, we have to focus on it,' recalled one aide.[4] But focus on what in particular? When Bennett arrived, he collated a list of the policies that Blair had indicated he wanted to achieve in his remaining time. The total came to some eighteen objectives: far too many. Bennett suggested, gently at first, that he would need to be more focused. 'Tony Blair's a man who finds it hard to say "no",' he said.[5] After meetings at Number 10 and Chequers, Bennett whittled the list down to Blair's traditional trio at the top – education, health and crime, followed by welfare reform and pensions, energy and the environment, social exclusion, housing and planning. On the list also were 'democratic reform' (including local government and the House of Lords) and a fundamental review of how the government spent its money. Unlike after 1997 and 2001, Blair now had finite time. But, used wisely, that constraint could play to his advantage.

Not everything was running in his favour, Blair's relationship with Bush was increasingly under the spotlight. The President's inept response to Hurricane Katrina and the flooding of New Orleans in August 2005 cast further doubt on the judgement of Blair's closest overseas ally. Blair's July successes had spread alarm throughout the Brownite camp. Did it mean that Blair would try to stay on until 2008 or even 2009? In May, the Brownites had him exactly where they wanted him. Had all this now been reversed, especially as widespread press reports were saying Brown had not fared well since the General Election? Number 10 was now to rue Blair's absence for the first half of September in India, China and at the UN in New York, when it was felt he lost momentum to Brown. 'We always lost ground when he was away,' said one aide: in future Blair's non-mandatory overseas tours were to be curtailed.[6] Number 10 believed that the Brownites were planning over the summer holidays to undermine Blair. They were not entirely certain who was organising the agitation but they believed ring-leaders included George Mudie, Nick Brown, John Healey and Angela Eagle: at the heart, they believed, was their absolute *bête noire*, Ed Balls. 'They wanted to stir things up. They never wanted it to be good for Blair,' said one close Blair aide.[7] 'They worked to bring those who were "slightly off-side, moaning" more squarely into their camp,' said another.[8] The absence of an agreed timetable was the core Brownite concern. They wanted Blair out in 2006. The question was how much pressure they would need to get rid of him. Their fear, on which ultra-Blairites played, was that an alternative candidate to Brown would be put up, either to challenge Brown in a divisive campaign or even to rob him of his inheritance. 'When the time comes Alan [Milburn] will be very well positioned to challenge Gordon,' one Blair friend told the *Sunday Telegraph* in early October.[9] As ever, Mandelson was thought to be behind the stirring, while another principal hate figure of the Brown camp, Cherie Blair, was reported to be saying that her husband would be in power 'a long way into the future'.[10] The Brownites identified an inner circle of Blairite provocateurs, which included Mandelson, Milburn, Cherie, Adonis, Powell and Byers, and an outer circle that included Hilary Armstrong, Paul Corrigan, Taylor and Birt.[11]

One aspect of Blair's July successes began to be seen in a different light. Part of Blair's genius was in handling the 7/7 bombings in a way that boosted his support in the country at large: the reaction against Aznar for his mishandling of the bombings in Madrid in 2004 had shown how terrorism could rebound against leaders. When, two weeks later, on Thursday 21 July, attempted suicide bombers returned to London, the mood began to change. 'There was this sense that the attack had happened, exactly echoing the first one; things were starting to connect,' said Met chief Ian Blair.[12] Apprehensions were heightened when it appeared that a 'dirty bomb' might have been detonated at one of the sites. This had long been one of Blair's nightmares: a conventional explosion dispersing radioactive material, with the intention of causing radioactive disease. The second wave of bombings caused widespread alarm among Londoners. 'Terrorists have a habit of coming back to the same place: it was an absolute manhunt,' said Ian Blair.[13] Anxiety was further heightened when, on 22 July, Brazilian-born electrician Jean Charles de Menezes was shot dead at Stockwell tube station. The next day, the Metropolitan Police released a statement admitting that the man they had shot dead was not linked to the failed attacks. Civil liberty groups were outraged, as were many in the PLP, who increasingly asked about the price to British civil liberties from the war on terror.

Blair had ardently hoped to prevent the Iraq war being an issue that autumn. At best, he hoped that the country would settle; at worst, he hoped that the spotlight would no longer fall on it. But on 19 September, British troops stormed an Iraqi police compound in Basra fearing that two captured SAS soldiers were in danger of being summarily executed by Shia militiamen. It transpired that the men had been handed over to insurgents by Iraqi police in Basra. The suggestion that police in the secure British zone had been infiltrated by extremists torpedoed claims that the south of the country was being pacified. Iraq shot back to the top of the headlines. Blair had wanted to skate over Iraq in his party conference speech: he had no choice now but to expand the brief section on it. 'The long-term damage from Iraq neutralised Blair's ability to impose anything that the party didn't want,' argued Demos director Tom Bentley.[14]

At difficult times in the second term, Blair had been able to rely upon the powerful ballast of John Prescott. But even before the 2005 election, he was shifting. 'Prescott was being wound up mightily by Gordon,' said one Blairite.[15] The deputy PM was particularly antagonised by the plans to introduce the private sector further into education, which he considered went too far.[16] He never completely switched his allegiance to Brown, but he was becoming increasingly critical of Blair, and he wanted a timetable for his departure. On the eve of the party conference, Prescott's views were exposed publicly in a new biography of the deputy Prime Minister by journalist Colin Brown. 'Prescott forcefully relayed the message to Blair that he did not think the party would allow him to carry on, regardless of the election result, for another three or more years,' the author wrote.[17] For the second time in twelve months, a biography rocked the delicate political balance at the top. Number 10 detected a pattern where they believed Brown goaded Prescott, who would march in to see Blair and say, 'I really think it would be better if you gave a date; it would get Gordon off your back.' Blair would then talk him round and 'Prescott would sort of remember why Tony was so important and he would walk out with a different attitude'.[18]

But Prescott was not the only member of Cabinet to be raising the temperature in the volatile pre-conference atmosphere. Cabinet was split into three camps: the loyalists on whom Blair could always depend: Reid, Clarke, Blunkett, Jowell, Falconer, Hewitt (mostly), Ruth Kelly, Valerie Amos, David Miliband and Chief Whip Armstrong; the middle-ground: Straw, Beckett, Prescott, Johnson, Benn and Des Browne; and the Brown group: Douglas Alexander, Darling, Hain and Hoon, though Brown could only depend firmly on the first two. But even the loyalists were finding themselves in a dilemma, for a variety of reasons including securing funding from the Treasury, and their own futures. On 23 September, the ultra-loyalist Jowell was taken to be anointing Brown as Blair's successor (and auditioning for the role of Brown's deputy) when she predicted that he would carry the torch for New Labour's market-based reforms.[19] On the same day in the *New Statesman*, Charles Clarke declared that 'Gordon would be a very good PM'.[20] 'It's a real problem for my generation,' one Cabinet minister said that month. 'We want to advance our careers. But who do we talk to? Should we be thinking what Gordon wants, or what would please Tony?'[21]

A torn Cabinet was mirrored in the Parliamentary Labour Party.

'Handling the PLP in the third term compared to in the second term was continually more difficult,' recalled one Cabinet minister.[22] Some of Blair's most reliable allies in the PLP had been defeated in the 2005 General Election, leaving only some fifty loyalists on the backbenches on whom Number 10 could utterly depend. Several had won their seats in 1997, and were conscious that they owed their position to him. Those who entered in 2001 and 2005 had different outlooks. In the middle was a group who were traditionally loyal but who had genuine concerns on the direction of public service reform, and who had supported Blair in the past because he had been so successful electorally. But with no more General Elections to fight, and with Blair pushing radical reform against their instincts, why should they remain loyal? 'They weren't anti-him in any meaningful sense, they just felt Gordon's coming in, Tony's going, why don't they just get it over with,' said one senior minister.[23] 'Tony had not issued a strong statement saying "Look, I'm damn well staying!"' noted one Labour MP, 'so potential supporters had nothing to rally round.'[24] A final group of some eighty Labour MPs were consistently against him, and included the Campaign Group epitomised by backbenchers Jeremy Corbyn and John McDonnell.[25] Number 10 reckoned it could rely on most of their support in a crisis, but little more. The group included a rump of some twenty-five who wanted Blair out under any circumstances. Brownites were to be found in both the middle and the hostile group, and their numbers were growing.[26]

As usual, the media could be relied upon to inflame existing divisions. Even during Blair's summer holiday he was troubled by adverse criticism from the press, especially the *Mail*, about staying at Cliff Richards' home. 'His holidays had become a regular stick for the media to beat him with,' said one aide.[27] Even with David Hill's emollient management the media became one notch more hostile after the 2005 election. The press persistently aired the question of when Blair would and should stand down. To Number 10 the blame fell squarely on the Brownites for 'constantly telling the press there was instability in the party on the succession, and Blair had to go'.[28] A successful party conference was imperative if Blair was to retain the initiative throughout the autumn, and much work had been put into planning his strategy for it. Delegates were in nervous mood when they assembled in Brighton on Sunday 25 September. In public, Blair and Brown appeared at ease with each other. Both camps battled to play down the speculation that Brown was going to be launching an assault on Blair.[29]

Brown was not in a strong position vis-à-vis Blair after the summer. The tone had been set by a provocative article in the *Sunday Times* at the end of August which opened: 'Tony Blair returns from holiday tomorrow in a position he could only have dreamed of in the aftermath of the General Election. While Gordon Brown's position has deteriorated . . . Blair has rebounded.'[30] Brown's speech on 26 September reflected that fact. It turned out to be a traditional Brownite mixed message. He signalled his preparedness to take over, as in his announcement that he would be travelling the length of the country to 'listen, hear and to discuss and learn about the changes that we need to build the future'.[31] This was balanced by a more placatory tone: 'I believe Tony Blair deserves huge credit, not just for winning three elections but for leading the Labour Party for more than a decade,' he said. He wanted to make clear his loyalist credentials in public. Blair was not in a mood for any nuanced message. There was to be no return compliment to Brown when he spoke the next day. Instead, there was a steely clarity, evident from his very first sentence: 'I stand before you as the first leader in the Labour Party's history to win three full consecutive terms in office.'[32] The operative word, which did not escape the delegates, was 'full'. His intention had been foreshadowed the night before by Hill, who told journalists, to the absolute fury of Brownites, that 'Mr Blair would outline a programme that would take several years to complete'.[33] Not only his views on his tenure, but also his declared policies, were anathema to many in the PLP. The programme of introducing more choice and marketisation in the public services would continue, he declared, and in a clear rebuff to Brown, he said, 'Every time I ever introduce a reform in government, I wish in retrospect I'd gone further.' As the *Daily Telegraph* put it, this was Blair saying, 'I wish I'd stood up to Gordon more often, more robustly.'[34] The speech offered one of his most powerful statements of the case for reform to monolithic state provision. 'Today is not the era of the big state . . . [It is about] empowering, enabling, putting decision-making in the hands of people, not government.' He defended his choice agenda again robustly, stating: 'There's a great myth here, which is that we don't have a market in services now; we do. It's called private schools and private healthcare. But it is only open to the well-off . . . But for Labour, choice is too important to be in the monopoly of the wealthy.' His argument won applause from the *Guardian*: 'At long last, he made a progressive case for the policy he cherishes which aroused such suspicion: choice in public services,' it said.[35] Blair himself was very pleased by his speech, and its reception.[36] No one listening had any doubt that Blair meant to carry on as far into the third term as he could.

Rumblings, however, spread throughout the conference. The

education debate on 28 September showed 'exactly how hard we would need to work to get through what Tony wanted', said Ruth Turner.[37] With a major Schools Bill in the pipeline, this debate was a worrying harbinger for Number 10. Unions tabled a motion demanding a halt to privatisation in health, but with no health legislation to go before Parliament around which opposition could coalesce, Number 10 was less concerned. The state of middle-ground opinion was seen when, in the foreign policy debate, 82-year-old party veteran Walter Wolfgang was forcibly ejected after he heckled Straw as he explained why British troops should stay in Iraq. TV cameras caught Wolfgang being grabbed by the collar and manhandled out of the conference hall, along with another delegate who tried to protect him. When Wolfgang was allowed to return the next day, a loud round of applause echoed around the conference hall. 'We are really, really sorry . . . I apologise completely and it should not have happened,' said Blair on 29 September. But the damage was done, and the depth of the party's resentment about Iraq, and macho party management, was made abundantly clear to all. Blair had wanted the conference to be about making the party realise it was in the historically uncharted waters of a third term and that it needed 'to hold its nerve at an altitude it had never been at before'.[38] He only partially succeeded. The conference was dominated by speculation about his future, but he did emerge stronger from it. The July honeymoon was over, and it was clear that he would have no easy ride in the autumn and beyond.

Progress in Iraq; Escalation in Afghanistan: July–December 2005

Blair desperately needed the optimism of early 2005 in Iraq to be sustained. His policy in Kosovo had been criticised for excessive risk-taking, but never in his wildest moments had Blair imagined the duration of the criticism that he would suffer over Iraq. Nothing in his premiership was more important to him than a positive closure. Seeing Afghanistan established as a stable and independent nation before he left Number 10 was another core foreign policy objective. These were high ambitions, but with the election over, and a successful G8 under his belt, Blair's overseas optimism was growing once again.

The year 2005 did indeed prove encouraging in Iraq. Following the January elections, Allawi's provisional government drew up the new constitution which was put to Iraqi voters in a referendum on 25 October. Despite heavy opposition in Sunni areas, the Iraqi electoral commission recorded 78 per cent of voters in support on a turnout of 63 per cent.[39] The Sunni vote, some 20 per cent of the population, was largely against, but the constitution received a massive endorsement from the Shi'ites and the Kurds. The positive result provided a much-needed boost for Blair and Bush in Iraq and paved the way for the national elections on 15 December 2005. Fears that suicide attacks would blight the campaign came to little, although mortar rounds struck the Green Zone in Baghdad, and Abu Musab al-Zarqawi, the al-Qaeda leader in Iraq, dismissed the election as 'a satanic project'.[40] Blair himself followed the election 'intensely closely'.[41] Intelligence had suggested that the Sunnis would not participate, but their boycott of the January elections was not repeated; indeed turnout in Sunni areas was particularly high. Blair was in Brussels for the EU Council when the news came through, and he was excited and relieved. The final election results were not confirmed until 20 January 2006, and had the Shia (United Iraqi Alliance) on 128 of the 275 parliamentary seats, while the Iraqi Accord Front, the Sunni coalition, won 44 seats, with Allawi's party, the Iraqi National List, coming fourth with 25 seats behind the Kurdistan Alliance with 53. That Christmas, he believed that a real corner had been turned, and that perhaps the agonies of the preceding two and a half years were now behind him. On 12 February, Ibrahim al-Jaafari was chosen by the reigning Shia alliance as the Prime Minister of the transitional government.

Hope that Iraq was at last on the road to a stable democracy influenced Blair in a critical new foreign policy decision, supporting increased British troop deployment to Afghanistan in 2006. 'There was no sense in holding Baghdad but losing Kabul,' explained one official.'[42] For much of the period 2003–05, Afghanistan had played second fiddle: 'We would certainly have focused more on Afghanistan in 2003–05 had it not been for Iraq, because there's a limit to the focus of any organisation,' said Jay. 'But the PM never let up on driving the policy forwards.'[43] By 2005, with evidence of a resurgent Taliban, particularly in the south of the country, 'there was a rising sense that Afghanistan needed some radical treatment,' recalled one top British official.[44] Following his election victory in May 2005, Blair knew he had one more chance to get Afghanistan right.[45] Across Whitehall 'there was a general consensus that we needed to make a transition from a main effort in Iraq, to a main effort in Afghanistan,' recalled Rob Fry.[46] Since 2001, British troops had served in Afghanistan as an integral part of NATO's ISAF force, which had operated in parallel with US forces in the country. 'There had been an uneasy relationship between the two,' noted a senior British official, 'leading to mixed messages over what needed to be done.'[47] While ISAF activities centred largely on reconstruction assistance, US forces had focused on offensive operations and the fruitless hunt for bin Laden. The two forces did not coordinate their activities particularly well, nor work to maximise their joint resources. According to Rob Fry, 'the Americans were having one of those periods where they said "this is somebody else's problem", or "we've done our bit and we're not going to invest any further into it."'[48] The British had particular difficulties with the Pentagon: 'it seemed to me that Rumsfeld was much more dismissive about Afghanistan than either Bush or Rice,' said a senior British official. 'Quite frankly, it was easier when Rumsfeld left.'[49] The EU, in British eyes, had been scarcely more accommodating: 'It was largely a British effort to see ISAF expand,' noted one Number 10 aide, 'and it was very uncomfortable for us, because we didn't have the support from our major western European partners that we should have done.'[50] In mid-2005, with the situation in Afghanistan deteriorating, the British chiefs of staff presented the Prime Minister with a bold plan. They proposed a significant increase in British troops in Afghanistan which would allow a British-led ISAF force to be deployed to the troublesome south. At the same time there would be a reorganisation of the NATO and American forces in Afghanistan, bringing a significant number of the US troops under ISAF command.

Blair responded positively. His driving motivation was to prevent Afghanistan sliding into anarchy under Taliban rule: 'The PM had in his mind that it could all slip through our fingers if we failed to consolidate what we already had.'[51] The impact of 7/7 further shaped his thinking: 'There was a belief that the ungoverned space that straddled the Durand Line [the Pakistan–Afghanistan border, first imposed by Britain in 1893] was the UK's front doorstep in security terms,' said Chief of the Defence Staff Jock Stirrup. 'We knew that thousands of British citizens visited this area every year. Most were perfectly ordinary, law-abiding people, but some went for indoctrination and training in terrorism: we couldn't afford to ignore that.'[52] Blair's focus on drugs was another factor, if subsidiary behind his enthusiasm for the plan. At a minimum, the narcotics issue gave Blair 'a wonderful bid on an ethical foreign policy'.[53] The majority of opium narcotics sold on the streets of Britain are grown in the lawless south and eastern areas of Afghanistan, and Blair wanted the production slashed. The British had also discreetly made contact with the governor of Helmand province, who indicated his willingness to be helpful.[54]

In principle, the Americans were pleased by the additional British commitment: 'to have one of our closest allies, in whom we had probably the most confidence, taking greater responsibility in the south was very reassuring and very welcome,' said a senior administration official.[55] 'Given their involvement in Iraq, the US did not have any spare capacity of its own,' explained one British official. 'There was also a sense that the job that needed to be done in Afghanistan was better suited to British expertise in dealing with the locals, skills we had developed in Northern Ireland.'[56] In the Pentagon there was considerable unease at the second part of the plan, placing US troops under ISAF command. Lengthy negotiations now began over the NATO command structure for the new ISAF force, a particular concern of Rumsfeld's. 'It was a matter of getting major allies either to hand over responsibility to us, in the case of the Americans, or to come as part of the force, in the case of the Canadians, the Dutch, and a few others.'[57] Despite these difficulties, overall the plan received a green light in Washington.

Blair now worked closely with Defence Secretary John Reid, and intensive planning took place in the MoD that autumn: 'It probably would have happened without Reid's group, but it would have happened more slowly and without the policy clarity that comes only with ministerial leadership,' noted Rob Fry.[58] By January, the plans had been finalised, and Reid presented the case to Cabinet supported by Straw and Hilary Benn, who spoke about the humanitarian case for moving into the south. Des Browne raised caution about the financial implications, and the corresponding need to reduce troops elsewhere to pay for it. Overall, there was concern, but little dissent.[59] 'We were pretty sober about it . . . We did recognise that there was a hell of a problem and if we did nothing it would get worse. If we did something it would be difficult, but we needed to engage,' said Straw.[60] Blair himself broached the matter with 'utter clarity', adamant that if additional measures were required to secure a stable and peaceful Afghanistan, he would not shirk from providing them.[61]

On 26 January Reid told the Commons that the 2,000 British troops already in Afghanistan would rise to 5,700 over the following months. The 3,300-strong deployment to Helmand province would be led by 16 Air Assault Brigade, and completed by July 2006.[62] The commitment proved more difficult than envisaged: 'Our expected trajectory in Iraq suggested that we could reduce our troops more quickly,' admitted a Number 10 aide. 'We thought that we had a bit more of a cushion for drawing down in Iraq and building up troops in Afghanistan than turned out to be the case.'[63] But the military kept the deployment largely on track, albeit at the expense of over-extension. Britain's General David

Richards took command of ISAF on 4 May, as the new troops began to come on line. But problems with the Pentagon over the command structure persisted. 'General Richards wanted all US forces chopped under him almost the day he arrived,' recalled Donald Rumsfeld. 'Had I been in his position I suspect I would have felt the same. However, we wanted to have the transition take place over a longer period for several reasons: to see how it went, to make sure the US and NATO militaries had thought through every aspect of the new command structure, and importantly, to allow time for the Afghan government to get comfortable with NATO assuming that set of responsibilities.'[64] The full transfer of command to NATO took place only in October 2006. The extra British troops altered the British role in Afghanistan fundamentally, relieving pressure on the Americans who had hitherto taken the brunt of the battle in the south and east, and very significantly escalating British presence. The Taliban, based in Kandahar, responded by increasing their activity. Blair knew that it would be a difficult battle, but he was prepared. With highly trained British troops now in the front line he was optimistic that 2006 would bring good news.

Discipline Breaks Down: October–November 2005

When MPs returned to Parliament after the conference season, Blair had been hoping for a quiet autumn to allow progress to be made on implementing his domestic policies. But out of a blue sky, the corridors of Whitehall suddenly filled with smoke. 'The smoking ban furore was horrible. Cabinet just fell apart. I felt terrible about it. It exploded everywhere. Almost everyone behaved really badly,' said Matthew Taylor.[65] The Republic of Ireland had imposed an outright ban on smoking in public places in March 2004, the Scottish Parliament had voted for a ban in June 2005, followed by similar votes by the devolved assemblies in Wales and Northern Ireland. Pressure on England inevitably grew. In June 2004, Reid, then Health Secretary, argued against an outright ban, with Straw, a powerful voice, taking a similar line. The White Paper on public health that November included a compromise proposal to ban smoking in most enclosed public areas, including offices and factories, but to allow smoking in private clubs and pubs which did not serve food. This approach was reflected in the 2005 manifesto. After the election, Hewitt, Reid's successor, had different views, and pressed for an outright ban on smoking in public places. In Cabinet, she received strong support from Jowell, whose Culture

Department oversaw pubs, and from Gordon Brown and Alan Johnson.[66] Within Number 10, Taylor, a purist on this subject, powerfully drove the policy in favour of an outright ban. He ran right up against Jonathan Powell. 'This is all madness. It is interfering with personal liberties. It's unpopular with business,' Powell complained.[67] Blair had no strong views on the issue: initially he had supported Reid's compromise line, dismissed by Taylor as 'weird social democratic libertarianism'.[68] During the course of 2005, his view shifted to believing an outright ban would be inevitable at some point, given the policy elsewhere in the British Isles. Morgan was one of those persuading him to change his mind: she made several phone calls in which she said this was exactly the kind of issue on which he should be seen to be doing the right thing. It was a 'New Labour policy initiative', she told him.[69] Blair conceded to Taylor: 'Okay, I'm happy to have a complete ban, and let's get on with it. But you're going to have to deal with John [Reid] and Jack [Straw].'[70]

The issue exploded in Cabinet in October. In what was seen as a test of her authority, the still new Health Secretary Hewitt argued strongly for the outright ban but was unable to budge Reid and Straw, now working together. 'It became very brittle and was totally unnecessary, because it was so obvious where it was going to end up,' said Taylor.[71] Not everyone saw it that way. To Reid, it was ridiculous to open up a policy that had been agreed in the manifesto less than six months before. The episode was reminiscent of previous Labour and Tory governments in decline before 1997, with ministers briefing their positions to the press. Reports appeared of Reid being angry that Hewitt was overturning his own policy, while her aides briefed that she had inherited a department from Reid in a state of 'meltdown'.[72] The trusty arbiter, Prescott, was summoned to bang heads together, and on 18 October, Reid wrote him a four-page letter to settle the issue, in which he claimed to demolish arguments for a complete ban. On 24 October, at a key meeting, Straw took over the chair of the committee from Prescott, who was out of the country, and made it plain that he would not accept any move away from the recent manifesto commitment. Committee members looked to Blair for a steer: 'He'd stepped back, wanting the chair of the Cabinet committee to resolve the issue. When it became clear that consensus could not be reached chaos ensued,' said Wegg-Prosser.[73] The chaos extended to Number 10 which divided into a 'Taylor camp' and a '[Geoffrey] Norris camp', which argued that an outright ban made the government susceptible to the charges of nanny state-ism. When it became clear that Reid and Straw had triumphed, and Hewitt was left as a Health Secretary having to argue for a policy that she did not believe in, fury spread. The anti-smoking pressure group Action on Smoking and Health (ASH) said it was 'outrageous' that rogue Cabinet ministers had been allowed to 'stamp around Whitehall trying to wreck the most important public health reform for thirty years'.[74] The decision was subsequently put to a free vote in the House of Commons on 14 February 2006, when it decided by an overwhelming margin of 200 for an outright smoking ban in all closed public spaces, which became operational in July 2007.

The issue was always going to arouse strong passions on either side, but its inept handling made the government look incompetent. Number 10 had no effective response to the jibe of one of its *bêtes noires*, former Health Secretary Dobson: 'It's one of the growing products of the fact that the Prime Minister is going and his authority isn't as strong as it used to be.'[75] The very public spat had not been on an issue of any importance to Blair's agenda. To have allowed so much distraction to have occurred on something not mainstream revealed his lack of grasp. 'It was not his fault, but ours, because he was not really engaged. He was concerned with the European budget,' said a defender in Number 10.[76] But such spats were symptomatic of Prime Ministers losing control, as had occurred in the latter days of Thatcher and Major. Blair knew it. One of the most troubling aspects for him of the smoking débâcle was that it set three of his loyalist supporters, Reid, Jowell and Hewitt, at each other's throats. It gave great encouragement and amusement to the Brownite camp.[77]

The last thing Blair needed was more dramas amongst the select band of Blairite Cabinet ministers. Yet, as the smoking furore cleared, it gave way to the whiff of scandal. On Monday 31 October, it became known in Number 10 that Blunkett had become embroiled in further personal trouble. He failed to inform the Advisory Committee on Business Appointments about his two-week-old directorship of a company called DNA Bioscience and his purchase of £15,000 worth of shares in the company. The alleged impropriety was made worse when it emerged that DNA Bioscience were potential bidders for a contract from Blunkett's own department. Blair refused to believe that Blunkett had done anything serious enough to warrant him going, and he felt terribly sorry for his old friend. He simply didn't have the heart to put the dagger in. Powell thought differently. 'He's got to go,' he stated flatly. Blair protested. Powell, backed up by Godric Smith and Ivan Rogers, told him categorically that he was wrong, and eventually prevailed. 'Okay, I get it, he's got to go,' Blair said.[78] Early on Wednesday 2 November, the message duly went out to Whitehall that Blunkett would be leaving the government that very day.

Blunkett was due to go to a meeting of the Commons Work and Pensions Select Committee at 9:30 that morning, but Powell insisted that he cancel it to come immediately to Number 10. Blunkett refused but agreed to come to Downing Street before the meeting. When he arrived he was confronted by Blair, accompanied by Powell, David Hill and Ruth Turner. It was obvious to Blunkett that Blair was being pressured to sack him. He put his side of the case forcefully, saying he did not think he had done anything wrong, before asking whether he could be left alone with the Prime Minister. After the others filed out, Blunkett pleaded with him. Blair was silent for a long time, and then went and hugged Blunkett and said, 'Go and do the select committee.'[79] The civil servant who had gone to inform O'Donnell that Blunkett was leaving was horrified to learn of the last-minute volte-face.[80] He spluttered out to Blair, 'The information is already in the system. We've reached the point of no return.' Blair replied, 'Oh my God. Stop it.'[81] Frantic efforts were made to close down the story. It was too late. Once the information had seeped out from the den into the Whitehall system, there could be no stopping it.

Oblivious to all this, Blunkett, thinking he was still in the job, turned up at the select committee meeting at Portcullis House. The chairman, Terry Rooney, was baffled to see him as he had already received news that he was no longer the minister.[82] Pandemonium broke out. Blunkett rushed back to Downing Street demanding to know what on earth was going on. An embarrassed Blair had to tell him what had happened. A distraught Blunkett realised the game was up and they agreed that Blair would announce his resignation at Prime Minister's Questions at midday.[83] 'He is a decent and honourable man who has contributed a great deal to his country and who has overcome immense challenges,' Blair told the House a short while later.[84] Of all Blair's mishandlings of departures, this was one of the worst. As one official observed, 'He's utterly useless with bad news and can be easily overturned.'[85] Michael Howard's question in the House of Commons struck home: 'Does he think that in his handling of this affair, his judgement has been at fault in any way?'[86] 'It was the most spectacular cock-up,' said one seasoned official. 'He likes to make people happy and he's no good at getting rid of people, especially face to face.'[87] Another close aide detected a deeper malaise: 'It was another illustration of the government being buffeted by events.'[88] At his best, Blunkett was Blair's star ministerial performer: but the David Blunkett of November 2005 was a pale shadow of the Education and Home Secretary Blunkett. Into his place, Blair promoted John Hutton from the Duchy of Lancaster, where he had been safe but unspectacular. It was to prove one of the most serendipitous appointments of his premiership.

Blair now needed stability more than anything. Yet only one week later he suffered his first defeat in the Commons as Prime Minister over his Terrorism Bill and its proposal to hold terror suspects without charge for up to ninety days. The original trigger for the bill came on 16 December 2004 as the Law Lords ruled that the incarceration of nine foreign suspects at Belmarsh prison, held indefinitely without trial since 2001, contravened the European Convention on Human Rights.[89] Blair 'refused to accept in his heart that this was the right judgement',[90] and soon there was talk of introducing new legislation to provide the power to intern without trial. 'A number of us who lived through internment without trial in the early 1970s in Northern Ireland, thought that was a very bad route to go down,' said a Cabinet Office official.[91] To bridge the gap, control orders, which granted police enhanced powers to restrict the behaviour and movement of terror suspects, were introduced in March 2005 as a 'not very satisfactory' stop-gap solution.[92]

The issue of terror suspects was reignited with the 7/7 bombs and the 21/7 failed attacks. Blair responded with a determined effort to extend 'outreach' links with the Muslim community. In parallel, he became convinced that a new terrorism bill was required to deal with the threat regularly described to him by the police and intelligence services. Before he went away that August, he worried that progress on anti-terror legislation was too slow and thought the Home Office bureaucracy ponderous.[93] 'Their people are just being bloody-minded,' he told a colleague. 'I want to make some announcements before I go away for a break.'[94] The moment was not deemed right, which frustrated him all the more. The police and intelligence services, he believed, should be given every conceivable power to avert any future attacks, which could easily eclipse the 7/7 horror. He knew he would upset the civil liberty *Guardian/Observer* lobby but this left him unphased. '7/7 attacked people who were travelling to a normal day's work, and didn't come home. I think he felt that very deeply indeed,' said Hazel Blears.[95] He believed that 'if only the public knew what I knew about all the people out there who want to hurt and kill British citizens, they would understand what I'm trying to do'.[96] At regular meetings to discuss the security situation, Met Commissioner Ian Blair emphasised that the threat facing the UK from terrorism was considerably greater than anything before the IRA ceasefire: '[The IRA] didn't want to die planting bombs; they usually gave warnings; with the exception of Omagh, they very rarely went for mass casualties and certainly by the end they were heavily penetrated by British intelligence,' said a senior official. He would repeatedly ask the police, 'Is there anything else that you need from me? Is there any more legislation?'[97] Their response, he believed, was that they needed to hold terrorist suspects without charge for ninety days.[98] They disputed later that they had asked for such a long period.

When the Terrorism Bill was published on 12 October, even though some in Number 10 argued forcefully that he was going too far, it contained the 'ninety days' clause for detention without trial for terrorist suspects – a six-fold increase on the existing fourteen-day limit. He stressed that the police needed this period because it took time 'to get the evidence necessary to charge them properly'.[99] Getting the information on suspects out of the Pakistani authorities was a particular reason for the extra time he sought. 'He was determined that he was going to show people that the government stood firmly by what the security services wanted,' said a Cabinet minister.[100] His tough stance led him headlong into friction with the Home Office and notably with Clarke and John Gieve, who resented being jolted and pushed by Number 10, especially into positions that they considered unsustainable.[101] The crucial vote came on Wednesday 9 November. By the weekend before, it was becoming clear that Blair would be in real difficulty. On the morning of Monday 7 November, the press reported that Clarke, in discussions with opposition parties, said that ninety days was not 'crucial'. At the PLP meeting that Monday evening, discussion was acrimonious. Despite widespread criticism of the figure of ninety days, perhaps even in part because of it, Blair said, 'I think we should go for it' as he left the room. Those who suggested reducing the time to sixty or even forty-five days were swept aside. At 8 P.M. that evening, Blair met Clarke and managed to convince him to support the full ninety days.[102] 'I don't think there was a kind of intellectual difference between them . . . it was more practicality,' recalled one Home Office minister.[103] Blair was in a defiant mood: 'I don't mind being defeated on this. I don't mind being defeated by their lordships. Don't mind being on the other side to the judges. I think the Conservatives have read it wrongly.'[104] One confidant felt it was Blair saying, 'I'm doing this because I am the Prime Minister, not because I am a Labour Prime Minister.'[105] Last-minute pleas from the Whips to compromise on ninety days were brushed aside. 'Tony wants this to be a binary issue,' one source said, meaning a polarised issue on which there can be no possible compromise.[106]

Blair felt let down by the unwillingness of the police and the intelligence services to make the case in public for why the ninety days was justified, despite pressure from Number 10.[107] 'The police did their usual thing of having said behind the scenes they wanted this, then as soon as it got hot in the kitchen and became controversial they said, "Oh well, we didn't say it really,"' remarked an infuriated aide.[108] Ian Blair's response was that the police had never proposed going as far as ninety days, but rather advocated a series of seven-day extensions under judicial supervision, with ninety days to be the maximum period possible.[109] The intelligence services even considered detention for ninety days without trial as counterproductive to the strategy of eliciting volunteered intelligence from within the community, which ultimately rested on a perception that rights and liberties were being fairly protected by the government. Whatever the truth, and it seems likely that Blair heard what he wanted to hear, it is extraordinary that he allowed himself to become so isolated.

In the final hours before the vote, Blair's position was looking increasingly bleak. Brown was to travel to Israel on a well-publicised visit during the week of the vote. Before leaving, he had been reassured that a deal was to be struck with the Tories over 'pairing', allowing his vote to be cancelled out by an absent Tory MP. Brown then learned that the deal had collapsed. On 8 November, the day before the vote, he spoke to Hilary Armstrong on his way to the airport, demanding to be found another pair. 'Look, Gordon, this isn't just about your vote. It's more serious than that,' she was forced to say. Despairing of the Conservatives, he extracted a promise of support from a Liberal Democrat MP, allowing him to board the plane with a clean conscience.[110] Within minutes of landing in Israel, however, he was told that he had to return, because his support was needed to lobby rebellious MPs. 'He didn't believe in the policy of ninety days,' said one Brownite.[111] Indeed, as Nick Brown said, 'He resented the whole business as stupid gamesmanship.'[112] When Gordon Brown returned with his team to London, they were 'completely knackered'. He was handed a list of twenty wavering MPs to phone at once. 'I've never seen him so exhausted in my life,' said one witness.[113] He thought that Blair and the whips had 'bungled the whole thing badly'.[114] Brown was portrayed as the white knight, loyally riding to the rescue of the leader. But is that picture correct? 'Tosh,' believe some Blairites, who say it was all a charade. 'The Chancellor stage-managed the whole thing to make him look indispensable in a crisis.'[115] They assert that Brown turning around his plane on the runway was a stunt to make Blair look weak.

The morning of 9 November saw Number 10 and the Whips' office involved in an operation not unlike that on foundation hospitals and tuition fees. 'We worked as hard as we did on any other close vote,' said Armstrong, even though this was not an ideological issue, like the two earlier votes.[116] Veteran Whip Tommy McAvoy warned Armstrong that they were still forty-one votes short of victory, and that rebellion was growing. 'Tony says we've got to get them back,' she told him.[117] Confounding their problems was the publication that morning of a bill granting amnesty to IRA men on the run: the DUP response was to cast its nine votes against the government. At Prime Minister's Questions that lunchtime, Blair already sensed the game was up, and said it was better to lose and do the right thing than win and be wrong.[118] After the vote, Armstrong whispered the figure to Blair, who was seen to nod bleakly: a loss by 332 to 291, with 49 Labour MPs voting against the ninety days. A subsidiary backbench proposal extending the existing detention period from fourteen to twenty-eight days was subsequently carried by 323 votes to 290.[119] The government opposed this measure and voted against, but 51 Labour MPs joined a broad coalition of opposition MPs to ensure the vote passed.[120]

Blair was surprisingly philosophical.[121] 'Funny thing, I think Tony was quite relaxed about it,' said Taylor.[122] Pundits portrayed losing his first vote in Parliament as a massive personal blow and a weakening of his authority. On one level 'it was a great rebuff because he had talked so much about the legislation "sending signals" into the system,' said one Home Office official.[123] But he felt he had done the right thing. 'They'll regret it,' Blears recalled him saying afterwards.[124] 'If there's another terrorist attack and people think I didn't do all I could to prevent it because I was frightened of my own side, where would that have left me?'[125]

The next day in Cabinet, he was calm and self-assured. His decision not to dramatise the defeat limited the personal damage: 'He was absolutely clear he wanted to move on,' said one aide.[126] 'He was unmoved . ... He felt he'd done what was right.'[127] The Brown camp was not alone in believing that he had stuck so stubbornly to ninety days for party political reasons: Nick Brown points to Milburn saying, 'Wouldn't it be good for us to say we're harder on law and order than the other parties?'[128] Some high up in the civil service thought similarly: 'If they'd picked thirty days, sixty days, they'd probably have got it through the House of Commons. But it was tied up with politics and outflanking the opposition was too good an opportunity to miss. I think [Number 10] got too tactical,' said a senior official.[129] Even some Number 10 aides concur: 'Wrong-footing the Tories was what it was mostly about. It was one of those classic campaigns where the issues in the debate were less important than getting one over the Tories.'[130] Howard was convinced that Blair sought to portray the Tories as 'soft on terror'. 'I'm sure he saw it as a battle of wills between us and he was convinced I would cave in.'[131] But it was Blair's own cause that ended up losing out. Forty-nine Labour backbenchers had brought him to defeat. The rebels now walked taller. They talked in corridors and huddled in rooms about where next to strike. They would not have long to wait.

Blair and Brown on Pensions: November–December 2005

Blair was a late convert to pensions. From 2004, he began to view the subject as a legacy issue on which he could take difficult but effective decisions. But his interest ran into a roadblock: as one Number 10 aide said, 'with the Brownite Andrew Smith as Secretary of State at the Department for Work and Pensions (DWP), as with Darling before, we really got nowhere.'[132] 'The Chancellor liked to run the DWP as a fiefdom,' said a Cabinet minister.[133] The climate changed when Alan Johnson replaced Smith in the September 2004 reshuffle. Brown, as ever, resented Blair's interest in welfare issues, and had been unhappy with the setting up of the Turner Commission in December 2002, partly because the Treasury didn't want important decisions to be taken on Blair's watch. But for Blair, Turner would provide 'his legacy material', and would provide a body of ideas for Blair to act on in the run-up to and after the 2005 General Election.[134] In their darker moments, the Brown camp feared that Blair wanted to claim the pension solution for himself, 'to bequeath maximum mayhem to his successor, so that his own premiership would appear more glittering by comparison'.[135] Brown's view was that Turner was being 'egged on to rubbish what the Treasury had done'.[136] 'Nonsense,' said Number 10. 'No one was trying to interfere with Turner, he was totally independent and reached his own conclusions – which is exactly why the Treasury was unhappy.'[137] The key issue was whether there should be a restoration of the earnings link to pensions. Blair was increasingly attracted to restoring this link, which would make the basic state pension considerably more generous.[138] His 2004 party conference speech argued that means-testing had gone too far and that support for the elderly should be centred on a basic state pension. Brown flatly disagreed.

By early 2005 'a train crash was imminent' because the Turner Commission, which produced its first report in October 2004, seemed ready to recommend restoring the earnings link, and thereby 'light the

Chancellor's blue touch paper', as a senior minister put it.[139] But Brown's position was problematic. Restoration of the link was popular with many in the party, and he did not want to be seen to be blocking it. To find a way out of the impossible, some in Number 10 thought that Brown's camp resorted to sabotage.[140] 'What they tried to do was undermine it during the 2005 election campaign.'[141] Pressed on when Labour might act on pensions, Ed Balls said 'future elections will be fought' before any of Turner's proposals being examined were implemented.[142] Blair was not deterred. He told his team in Number 10 that pensions reform was one of his key third-term priorities, and in his choice of Blunkett to run DWP in the third term, he antagonised the Treasury – deliberately, some said.[143]

Before the summer holidays, Blunkett had tried to convene a meeting with Brown and Turner to find an amicable way forward. He was going to say to Turner in Brown's presence, 'You're totally independent: you must come up with whatever recommendations you think are right.' But Brown failed to show up. In his diaries, Blunkett referred to it as an 'abortive meeting'.[144] When he reported the news to Blair, 'Tony was very calm about it and said, "Don't get angry. Talk to Gordon about it and see whether there can be another joint get-together on it."'[145] To Number 10 aides, the fact that Brown shunned the meeting 'symbolised his level of engagement'.[146] At a series of meetings at Chequers over the summer, Blair refined his thinking, concluding that people should be given a simple base pension from the state which kept them out of poverty, to be funded by increasing the pension age, while allowing them to save on top of the basic level if they chose so to do. In September and October he held meetings with Turner at which he outlined these thoughts.

On 2 November, only three weeks before Turner's final report was due to be published, the ground shifted again with Blunkett's departure. John Hutton, his successor, found a difficult mood at DWP. 'Very fraught would be the words I'd use to describe the thinking of officials when John started,' said one witness. 'They dreaded the Treasury condemning the proposals as unaffordable and wrong.'[147] Blair's reluctance to see Blunkett go was partly down to fear that, without him, the battle against the Treasury would be much more difficult. Hutton thus arrived at a pivotal moment when the argument could easily have been lost. He met Turner on only his second day in the office and discussed the issues: 'There was a great sense that we had to get John up to speed very quickly,' said an official.[148] All eyes in Westminster and Whitehall were on Hutton. Presiding over the most contentious issue of the day, to which the Chancellor and in all likelihood the next Prime Minister was deeply opposed, was a tough assignment for a fledgling secretary of state. Would Hutton equivocate and inch towards the Treasury's line, as some of colleagues were doing? No one was entirely certain, but he rapidly won admiration for his fierce independence of mind: 'Hutton took the decision to be his own man and to earn respect for being such a good minister that for Gordon to have dropped him would have looked like a petty act of sectarianism.'[149] Brown was beside himself. He could just about live with Blunkett, who had been a pale shadow of his best at DWP, but Hutton was rapidly showing himself to be the most autonomous DWP head since Labour came to power. In despair, Brown came up with increasingly exaggerated figures of what it might cost if Turner was to propose the restoration of the earnings link. Number 10 were reminded of Dr Evil in the first *Austin Powers* film, when he raised his ransom fee to 'one hundred billion dollars'. The joke in Number 10 was that almost every day Brown seemed to come up with a newer and bigger figure for the cost – £8 billion, £10 billion, even up to £30 billion: 'It was ridiculous, the numbers kept going up. It was the classic Gordon attack on Tony about the black hole,' said one official.[150]

The Turner report was scheduled for publication at the end of November. The week before saw a new twist, with the leaking of a letter that Brown sent to Turner to Nicholas Timmins of the *Financial Times*.[151] This was splashed on the paper's front page on Wednesday 23 November. To spread out the story, Turner's reply to Brown was published by the paper in the next day's edition.[152] Brown's letter criticised Turner's figures and suggested that he would not be able to accept his recommendations should he indeed propose linking state pensions to earnings. Number 10 blamed the Treasury, which they believed had a history of selective leaking: they saw it as a last-ditch strike to undermine the Turner report prior to publication, after all their other ploys had failed. The Treasury meanwhile accused Number 10 of leaking the letters in an effort to discredit the Chancellor and blame him as the wrecker of the proposals.[153] Matthew Taylor became the focus of Treasury suspicion: when he threatened legal action for slander, they backed off.[154] Turner was dumbfounded by it all. 'We all knew that the letters would make no difference because, by the time they were published, it was all set in stone anyway,' he recalled. 'The leak of the letters was not trying to stop the report or change it; it was about the battle between Number 10 and Number 11. We were caught in the middle of a game between the Chancellor and the Prime Minister, and we just had to play it as straight at we could,' said Turner.[155] On Friday

25 November, Powell rang Turner, having spoken to Blair who was attending a Commonwealth Heads of Government Meeting in Malta. 'We think you should stick to what you said,' Powell told him.[156] Turner said there was no question of him changing what he was going to say. Turner thought it bizarre that Powell thought that he should be getting on to the front foot and going to the media, which wasn't remotely the way he worked.[157]

The furore overshadowed the report's publication on Wednesday 30 November, but its message was clear: the value of state pensions had been falling and the link had to be restored. It was the recommendation the Treasury dreaded. To date, pensions had just seen skirmishing between Number 10 and the Treasury. A battle royal was inevitable in 2006 when the government debated whether or not to act on Turner's recommendations.

President of Europe: September–December 2005

Much of Whitehall planning for the British presidency from July to December 2005 had to be discarded after the French 'no' and the cancellation of the referendum. Initially, in contrast to the G8 presidency, Number 10 had viewed the EU presidency with trepidation, fearing that it would be overshadowed by the referendum and constant press criticism, above all from the *Mail* and *Telegraph* groups. In the first half of 2005 there was even talk of making it a 'limited presidency' and cancelling the optional early autumn Council on the grounds of insufficient work for the heads of government.[158] The French '*non*' and then Blair's speech on 23 June to the European Parliament changed everything. 'The question suddenly became for us, "How would we follow that up, and what should we now do with the presidency?"' recalled one Number 10 aide. The problem, common to a number of Blair's major speeches, was that Blair has given little thought to their questions. 'We would ask about the process for follow through,' said one top official, 'but it simply wasn't there.'[159] By early September, however, Blair had finally turned his mind to the upcoming October Council. He wanted it to be a different kind of meeting from the norm, held in the UK rather than in Brussels. From meetings with Barroso emerged the idea of a new format, more a seminar debating real issues than the traditional approach. 'He hated Councils in the ghastly Brussels Justus Lipsius building, and thought there were far too many hangers-on to have any kind of worthwhile discussion,' said one Number 10 aide.[160] Blair decreed there should be no prepared papers or 'officials bursting in and out'. An urgent search took place for the ideal location. The initial thought was Lancaster House, but it was busy and anyway deemed over-utilised. The picturesque Leeds Castle in Kent was booked for a wedding and the government concluded it was too expensive to 'buy them out'. Hampton Court was another venue on the list. One Number 10 official, sent to check it out, found it 'empty, drab, unlit and grisly, like a draughty old barn'.[161] But it was thought to be an exciting option, and it appealed to Blair. An events organiser was brought in to bring out the best in the fourteenth-century former royal palace, making sure it was suitable for a one-day conference. The planning, however, managed to upset almost everyone involved. Whitehall was not happy at Number 10 commandeering what traditionally was a cross-department event. Bureaucrats in the EU were angry that officials were not being invited.[162] Some EU leaders were suspicious about 'what Blair was up to', while the translators' unions wanted to veto the meeting after they were told they could not work in the conference room: 'ugly interpreters' boxes' scattered across the room were considered unsightly and out of sympathy with the intimate atmosphere Blair wanted. A crisis was only assembled by the cameras from the *Big Brother* television series being erected on a gantry above the table to relay the images of the leaders to the translators in a specially erected marquee outside.[163]

Blair's beef with EU Councils was in part that they too rarely discussed fresh policy ideas. A focus on policy rather than on 'designing fixes' was to be another feature of the meeting. Top of his list for discussion was the future security of the EU's energy supplies. Darroch warned him that Britain had traditionally been against considering action at EU level on energy.[164] 'We've moved on, believe me,' Blair replied.[165] Research and Development (R&D) was another subject he wanted on the agenda. He had been fired up by a recent table showing that of the top fifty universities in the world, only six were in Europe, and all six of those were British. 'Europe is crap at R&D in contrast to America and Japan,' he said. 'We're not good at developing high-tech products into the market place. That is one reason why the EU economies are not doing better. Higher education needs to focus on it more.'[166] Demographics, foreign policy and defence were added to the list at the request of Chirac. Blair flew off to see him at the Elysée on 10 October and they had a 'surprisingly successful' meeting. The French President had recently had a minor stroke, and had put behind him his anger at Blair's blocking the EU budget in June and the British victory of the Olympics in July. Number 10 were delighted that he 'threw his support behind the whole Hampton Court idea', though they remained wary: 'The thing with Jacques is that he can just switch it on and off.'[167] The policy ideas for the conference were brought together in a paper written by Barroso in his capacity as Commission President, entitled 'European Values in the Globalised World', which reflected much of Blair's thinking.

A final, naked motive of Hampton Court was to throw the EU heads of government off the scent of the still-undecided EU budget until Number 10 could launch its proposals later in the year, at a time more likely to secure its objectives. Delay did not play at all well with Britain's partners and for a time it seemed possible the Council might be boycotted. The eastern Europeans were particularly incensed. 'Sorry, guys, we're not going to play this game of coming along to the British summit and talking about your policy agenda, because all we're really interested in is finalising the budget deal that you single-handedly blocked,' was how one official characterised their viewpoint.[168] Chirac, for all his bonhomie with Blair, was indeed playing a double game. He tried to 'box Britain into a corner' and whip up the European media into a frenzy, asserting that Hampton Court was merely designed as a distraction from the real issue.[169] Eventually, agreement to the summit was only secured on the back of 'a very clear commitment' that Blair would in good faith work for a budget deal at the December European Council.[170]

For all the cynicism, all twenty-five EU leaders rolled up to Hampton Court on 27 October. 'It was a gorgeous sunny day. All the flowers were out as the leaders' limousines swept down the long drive. The buildings looked stunning, it helped put everyone in a good mood from the start,' said Darroch.[171] A thirty-minute speech from Barroso on his paper opened proceedings. The leaders then responded in turn, almost all positively. Even Chirac spoke enthusiastically, in part because he had been won over by being given an extra time allocation. When Verhofstadt spoke about the need for tax harmonisation, he was roundly squashed. After a break for lunch, discussion focused on the challenges ahead, with the eastern Europeans emphasising growth, competition and innovation. After five hours of fairly free-ranging discussion throughout the day, Blair summed up. Eschewing traditional written conclusions, he said instead, 'This is what I plan to say to the press after the conference. Are you broadly happy for me to sum up the meeting as follows?' All agreed apart from Schröder, who was the one sour figure throughout the day.

Schröder had lost the German General Election in September, and there ensued a long transition period of three months while a coalition government was cobbled together. Blair hoped and prayed that Schröder would not be attending the conference, and that Angela Merkel would do so instead. But she had still to be installed as Chancellor. So, to woo Schröder ahead of the summit, Blair went to see him in Berlin. The wooing backfired spectacularly. He was scheduled to have an early dinner meeting with Schröder and then to go on and have after-dinner drinks with Merkel. But, partly because Schröder's staff got wind of the scheme, they kept pushing the time for the dinner back to squeeze any time Blair and Merkel would have together that evening. So, Number 10 changed their plan and decided he should see Merkel first. So much did he find in common with her in this euphoric meeting, that he overshot on timing.[172] As a result, he was late arriving at the German Chancellery to see Schröder, and kept the journalist pack waiting which left them speculating about Blair's preferences. Schröder was fizzing with annoyance at the perceived snub. 'It was a cock-up in the machinery,' pleaded one official, 'I don't think anyone had explained the scheduling to Blair.'[173] In the dinner that followed the press conference, the absence of rapport between them was palpable.[174] A cynical Schröder thus pitched up at Hampton Court telling the press, to the intense irritation of Number 10, that the conference was merely a British delaying tactic on the budget. As it was to be Schröder's last summit, Blair had to make a short speech about him from the chair. He was typically gracious: 'I cannot say that we have always agreed on everything, because very clearly we haven't, but I do admire you greatly for the economic reforms you have introduced to Germany,' and presented him with a 'very distinguished' French Bordeaux which had been drunk at lunch. Thus ended their long and dysfunctional relationship.

Hampton Court was judged a significant success. Even Chirac told his officials afterwards, 'We should have one of these every couple of months.'[175] The 'Hampton Court Agenda', and methodology, were to have profound effects on the work of the EU in the future. It helped heal the divisions after the clashes over the CAP, Iraq and the budget. According to John Grant, Britain's permanent representative at the EU: 'Without the common purpose generated by Hampton Court, a budget deal in December probably wouldn't have been possible.'[176] Once the immediate afterglow of the conference died away, Blair knew that he had indeed less than two months to decide on one of the biggest European issues of his premiership: the budget.

Before Blair could focus on it, the question of Turkey's accession to the EU had to be settled. Achieving enlargement of the EU was one of

Blair's principal achievements in Europe, for which he received little recognition during his premiership. 'He saw it as righting a historic wrong,' said Sawers. 'Europe needed to integrate countries such as Poland, Hungary and the Baltic states as part of a unified and stable Europe.'[177] In his first British presidency in 1998, Blair had pushed hard on enlarging the EU to eastern and central Europe beyond the five countries deemed most advanced, against a lukewarm reaction from other EU countries, notably the founding six.[178] Ten new 'accession' countries officially joined on 1 May 2004: the Czech Republic, the Slovak Republic, Slovenia, Hungary, Poland, Latvia, Lithuania, Estonia, Cyprus and Malta. Blair had also pushed hard at Helsinki in December 1999 for the accession of Bulgaria and Romania against most EU leaders who thought neither country was ready. They formally joined on 1 January 2007, increasing the EU from twenty-five to twenty-seven.

Turkey was Blair's final push on enlargement: 'Without Blair we wouldn't have had accession negotiations with Turkey,' insisted a senior British official.[179] The desire to bring a predominantly Muslim country into the EU, to help show the international community that the Muslims and the Western world could work together, was critical to him. 'If you have Turkey as a stable democracy within the EU, he hoped it would have a useful demonstrative effect on other Muslim countries,' said Wall.[180] A crunch point on Turkish entry had come at the Council in December 2004. Blair, Schröder, Chirac and Dutch Prime Minister Jan Peter Balkenende worked together to bring round the two principal sceptics, Greece and Austria. Greek-Cypriot President Tassos Papadopoulos was particularly intransigent. Blair tried reasoning, whereas Chirac tried shouting: 'We've given you accession and everything, what more do you want?'[181] In the end the opposition was cajoled or bought off. The price for gaining the acceptance of Austrian Chancellor Wolfgang Schüssel was the promise of opening accession talks with Croatia, to which Blair happily assented as he regarded accession by the Balkan states as essential to his vision of the EU. Agreement on Turkey's accession was finally resolved at the December 2005 Council in Brussels. Straw had done much of the final work in the foreign ministers' Council which was also meeting in Brussels, but at the eleventh hour, Turkey was still quibbling with the text. Straw could get no further. He phoned Blair and asked him to speak to Prime Minister Erdoğan, with whom he has a strong personal rapport. Straw gave Blair the various options and drafting fixes. 'Blair phoned Erdoğan, and within about five minutes had persuaded Erdoğan to accept one of them. It was a great moment,' recalled an official.[182]

'Great moments' were one commodity no one expected Blair to experience in the final challenge of the British presidency: resolution on the budget. Pressure to achieve an outcome built up to a frenzy in October and November. He had been slow to involve himself in EU budgetary matters in the early summer of 2005. 'We couldn't get ministerial attention in the post-election period,' said one aide. 'He hadn't really taken seriously the fact that Juncker was prepared to try and shaft him.'[183] Juncker set a higher bar at the June 2005 Council: 'Every member state would be doing its calculations on the basis of comparison with what the Luxembourg deal had been.'[184] Against that, Blair realised that with the advantages of holding the chair, Britain could obtain a much more favourable deal now than if the matter was passed on to the Austrian presidency to resolve in the new year.[185] With the central European accession countries now desperate for a deal to allow their new EU funding to come on line from 2007 as planned, Blair also believed that Britain, as a champion of enlargement, had a moral responsibility to reach a deal by the end of the year.[186]

First he had to square the Treasury. Blair spoke to Brown at Number 10 in September, and decided to put him on the spot. 'Do you want to do the budget yourself, using ECOFIN [the European Council of Finance Ministers] as a kind of Chancellors' business?' he asked disingenuously. 'No, ECOFIN shouldn't be in the lead on it, it is for the Prime Minister to decide,' replied Brown.[187] It was one of those occasions when they danced around the main issue and never mentioned hard figures: 'Like ships passing in the night,' said one official.[188] The traditional Treasury argument that 40 per cent of the EU budget goes on the CAP, and that Blair should at last fight hard to reduce it, was the principal point Brown made to Blair at the meeting, which broke up without agreement. 'The PM hadn't wanted papers circulated, nor did he want to be pinned down to any particular outcome. It wasn't a satisfactory meeting,' said one.[189] Blair saw the attraction of persuading the EU to end the CAP altogether in return for sacrificing the British rebate, a course to which the Treasury were not entirely averse. 'In fairness to Brown, he said, "I don't rule out using the rebate and the leverage of the rebate, and I am prepared to give bits of it away only in parallel with a genuine reform process,"' recalled one official.[190] But he knew such thinking on the CAP was unrealistic. Chirac would never accept it, and nor would several other countries: 'It became clear that unless we could completely isolate France, such a plan was a chimera.'[191] Moreover, the UK had, albeit reluctantly, accepted the 2003 CAP deal and would be accused of bad faith if they tried to go back on it.[192] The third key British actor in the budget process was Foreign Secretary Straw, who gave Number 10 the impression of 'supporting the last person he'd spoken to: he flip-flopped between Gordon and Tony', said one.[193] One aide recalled how he would 'cuddle up to Brown and say, "We've got to put some lead in their pencil. Number 10 will cave in if we don't." And then he'd cross the road and say to the Prime Minister, "Gordon is in his own world." The FCO were shameless in equivocating between both camps.'[194]

By early November, with only six weeks to the Council, and no agreement forthcoming with the Treasury, Number 10 still had to agree on the budget figures they were to propose. Blair kept on prevaricating, telling his staff that the politics and his domestic position were not right.[195] His principal advisers, Darroch in Number 10 and Grant at the EU, however, were becoming alarmed that the greater the pressure from EU countries to produce the figures, the less leverage the British might have. Relationships between Number 10 and the Treasury deteriorated in November. 'It was inevitable that Number 10 and Number 11 were going to be in a head-on collision,' said one Treasury official.[196] Jon Cunliffe, the Treasury lead on the budget, was 'under instructions not to talk to anybody in Number 10', with the exception of Ivan Rogers.[197] The Treasury then let it be known that the Chancellor did not want to do a deal during the British presidency, arguing that Blair should play hardball until the French gave up the CAP. Blair and Brown had several telephone conversations in November which were described as 'nasty and intemperate'. 'Why are you proposing to do a deal? It doesn't move the EU forwards. It is weak and pathetic,' said Brown. 'This is just you domestic grand-standing,' Blair replied, 'and as the biggest supporter of enlargement in the EU we will have to be prepared to pay our fair share of the costs.'[198] Officials on both sides were caught in the middle of one of the most poisonous of their clashes.[199]

With the Treasury instructed not to co-operate, Darroch settled down to work with the Cabinet Office to produce a first set of figures.[200] As the long-standing EU states were not willing to face reductions in their own money from the EU budget, it became clear that the British would have to persuade the ten new countries to accept a smaller sum than they had been promised in June 2005. The British proposals were finally launched on 5 December, envisaging a reduction in money for the central and eastern Europeans of approximately €14 billion, as well as a reduction of some €10 billion from the old EU states' rural development fund. The proposals deliberately did not reveal how much Britain intended to cut its own rebate. 'It was merely an opening bid. It's the way you do it.

You then let people win concessions off you,' said one official.[201] Blair then set off to see the eastern and central Europeans to try to win them round, with the threat that if they were to hold out for too much money, there would be no settlement during the British presidency and they would not receive their money in 2007. The morning after he saw the Hungarian Prime Minister at his home, Blair was having breakfast in his hotel when David Hill walked in with a copy of the *Daily Telegraph*. Its headline announced 'Day of surrender'. Underneath was laid out in considerable detail Britain's whole negotiating strategy, including its willingness to make a concession on the rebate. 'We believed it was the Treasury that had leaked it to the press. The detail clearly meant it had come from a very close inside source,' said one official.[202] It meant that when Blair went on to see other heads of government, he was stymied because it revealed Britain's whole negotiating tactics. 'The timing of the leak from London was very, very bad for us,' said one of the Prime Minister's party.[203] Number 10 regarded it as a betrayal and, coming on the heels of the pensions leak, as outrageous: they held Brown personally responsible, believing he wanted to undermine Blair for conceding too much, as well as to impress Paul Dacre of the *Mail* and Rupert Murdoch with his Eurosceptic credentials.[204] 'At the morning meeting every day, the political team from Number 10 could see Gordon's hand behind every move going wrong,' recalled one official.[205] Blair was livid. 'I'm simply not interested in getting the Treasury on board any longer,' he proclaimed, with only days to go to the Council. When one official tried faxing a compromise deal to the Treasury the weekend before, his response was, 'They can bugger off. I will settle on the terms I want.'[206]

The Council in Brussels on 15/16 December did not begin well. On the first evening, the President of the European Parliament gave a speech criticising the British offer for being too small: 'To be honest, we didn't care what the European Parliament thought because they had no vote,' said one in the British party.[207] At the opening dinner, the atmosphere was described as 'nasty'. The British delegation were in a box: 'If we conceded and offered more, more would have been demanded of us.'[208] From the chair, Blair gave all the heads of government the chance to speak. Verhofstadt gave a 'deeply bitter talk', consisting of a 'long rant' against the British. 'If I'd been in the chair I'd have gone up and punched him,' said a Number 10 official. Blair remained calm and merely said, 'Thank you very much, Guy.' Verhofstadt was nonplussed, expecting Blair to rise to his challenge.[209] Chirac used his speech also to attack the British: he was clearly still unwell and feeling isolated in his first Council without Schröder present.[210] The evening's most significant contribution came from the new presence on the block, Merkel. Blair had been pleased by his meeting with her two weeks earlier, and by the common understanding they had reached. When she said that the British needed to put forward a slightly bigger package, it sent a very clear signal to all that the Germans were now working with the British.[211] Even with her intervention, however, the British still wondered whether a budget agreement could be reached. After dinner, Darroch and Grant went to talk to the Commission and the French until 2 A.M., edging towards a closer understanding.

The next day, 16 December, Darroch and Grant had breakfast with Blair at 7A.M. They were struck by his optimism as he told them exactly how much Britain would have to concede in its rebate to secure agreement, over which he was remarkably prescient. Blair's two critical allies were Merkel and Barroso, with whom he agreed a figure for the concession that morning. 'Will you persuade Chirac?' Blair asked. 'Yes, we will,' they replied. Merkel was in her element. 'She went around with a mischievous grin, listening to Chirac with apparent sympathy after he confided in her, "This is just a British trick." She would then trot off to Tony Blair and tell him everything that the old boy had been saying,' recalled one witness.[212] By 11 A.M. Merkel, supported by Barroso, had worked her magic on Chirac. The deal they shook hands on was a British concession of £7.1 billion spread over seven years, which was approximately £1 billion off the British rebate each year. Yet, given the complicated way in which the rebate is calculated, even after this concession the rebate would still rise in value in gross terms in the years ahead, albeit by far less than it would otherwise have done. This was an important point for Blair.[213] 'The whole business is like gambling,' said one. 'It's really just a kind of elaborate game which you have to play well.'[214] A buzz shot around the Justus Lipsius building that Britain, France and Germany had settled. 'Everyone suddenly went mad. We were besieged by officials of all member states demanding meetings with the Prime Minister. It was like a bazaar with everyone trying to get an extra few million euros from him.'[215] In drafting the EU budget Blair had a pot of €861 billion to give away. All afternoon and evening, the British team tried to achieve realistic settlements with everyone while not exceeding the figures. 'We desperately tried to keep track of how much money we were doling out. It took so long that all the different countries got knackered and just wanted to get home. Fatigue helps close these negotiations,' said one official.[216]

At 11:30 P.M. the plenary session was convened. Blair outlined the final package and invited all heads of government to say whether they were in agreement. The Poles worried him the most, as they had been persistently obstructive. Blair had given Merkel an extra €400 million for Germany and, to unblock the impasse, she volunteered to give the Poles €200 million of it to ensure that a settlement could be reached. That clinched it and, an hour later, Blair announced that the budget had been settled. Even Juncker made a little speech paying tribute to Blair. A spontaneous round of applause echoed around the room. 'About half the leaders, being continental types, came up and hugged the Prime Minister,' said one marginally disapproving official.[217] Blair faced a more difficult audience at the press conference: hardest to answer was the Treasury line – why had he given away so much of British taxpayers' money without achieving any change to the CAP? In his response, he highlighted the promise of a fundamental review of all EU spending, including CAP, by 2009: the date was chosen because it would be in a post-Chirac Europe, when the British believed it would be much easier to make headway.[218] He was in upbeat mood when the British party boarded the plane about 2 A.M., already thinking ahead to the Commons statement, and asking officials for a draft to be sent to him at Chequers by the Saturday evening. The British delegation – which had no senior Treasury figure – believed that the deal he had secured on the rebate was the absolute minimum that would have been necessary to demonstrate that the UK, as the biggest supporter of enlargement, was paying its fair share of the costs. This was the *sine qua non* of achieving an agreement and for getting the French on board. 'They wouldn't have done the deal for anything less on the rebate,' said Grant. 'They would simply have blamed us, because every other European country hates the British rebate and nobody would have blamed the French for sabotaging it.'[219]

Blair was driven straight from Northolt to Chequers in the early hours of Saturday 17 December. He was up early and at 9 A.M. phoned Darroch, who was already in Number 10. The press that morning was almost universally hostile ('Now Blair gives up £7 billion for nothing in return,' screamed the *Daily Telegraph*[220]) yet he felt positive about being able to sell the deal, and he was pleased that Straw had ended up being very supportive. Overnight, he had honed his 'killer argument', that it would have been morally and politically indefensible for Britain, having been the major country pushing enlargement, to have refused to provide the money to pay for it.[221] Blair was so confident of his case that he did little more than tweak the draft of the parliamentary statement that was sent through to him at Chequers. 'Will it work?' Darroch asked Keith Hill, Blair's Parliamentary Private Secretary on Monday morning. 'Yes, it will be all right,' was the response.[222] The atmosphere in the House of Commons that afternoon was bleak. The Treasury view that Blair had given away too much percolated through to the PLP, and made many restless: Number 11 continued for months after to try to claw back some of the money. The Conservative benches were bursting and MPs, sensing a victory, were in high spirits, waving their order papers. The mood on the Labour benches was tense: the PLP was full of apprehension. Cameron spoke well, but Blair was on top of his game as he argued the case about having to pay for enlargement. The atmosphere in the Commons suddenly changed. Now it was the Labour benches who were buoyant and the Conservative benches quiet: by the end of the debate, their benches had started emptying. Blair left for his Christmas holidays a few days later. 'Thanks for all your help with all this stuff on the presidency, guys,' he said jokingly to his EU team in Number 10. 'I'll never see you again, ever.'[223] But Europe was to return with a vengeance at the end of his premiership, while his backbenchers, who applauded him so vigorously on this final Monday before Christmas, were baying for his blood before January was barely half over.

16

Losing His Authority

January–April 2006

In early 2006 Blair's authority plummeted, and reached its moment of greatest vulnerability to date. During this period the last of Blair's third-term millstones, 'cash for honours', emerged. Together with Iraq and the succession question, these milestones constantly gnawed away at his position. Yet they were also the months when, with the G8 and EU presidencies behind him, Blair needed to concentrate on pushing his domestic agenda. His flagship education bill had to go through the Commons, and he needed to forge ahead with his other core initiatives, including health, welfare reform, energy and criminal justice, while bringing a fresh sense of purpose to Northern Ireland. But would he have sufficient time to do all he wanted? And would his enemies in the PLP strike against him by foiling his reform agenda in Parliament or forcing him to curtail the time before he stood down?

The Push for Respect: January–February 2006

The last few months of 2005 had been difficult for Blair at home, and his top aides now thought carefully about how to recapture the initiative as soon as the New Year began. Before Christmas, Taylor, Wegg-Prosser and Turner persuaded the Prime Minister to launch a swathe of administrative and constitutional proposals early in January, including reform of the House of Lords, a review of party funding, expanding elected mayors and a Green Paper on citizens' juries. Brown fumed against these proposals (egged on, Number 10 suspected, by Harriet Harman) and, together with Prescott, he convinced Blair to pull the plug.[1] 'I'm not quite sure how much he was really persuaded it was the right thing to do,' said one Number 10 aide of Blair's commitment to the package. 'His eyes always glazed over a bit at all local government and constitutional stuff.'[2] But dropping the proposals left a gap, and placed a heavy onus on the launch, on 10 January, of what became Blair's biggest new initiative in the third term, the 'Respect Action Plan'. During the 2005 election campaign Blair had repeatedly heard about a 'loss of respect' in society and an increase in anti-social behaviour. From the steps of Downing Street the morning after the election, he spoke of making the issue 'a particular priority for this government, how we bring back a proper sense of respect in our schools, in our communities, in our towns and villages.'[3] After the election, he created the Anti-Social Behaviour/Respect Cabinet committee, which first met on 30 June 2005. Blair's tone at the meeting was 'very insistent and urgent', recalled Louise Casey.[4] His frustration with ministers for not sharing his enthusiasm for driving it forward in their departments was evident. Some were mindful that this was a Blair, not a Brown, enthusiasm, which made the Prime Minister all the more intent on making it work. When Jonathan Powell broke into the meeting to tell him he was running late, he raised his voice, 'I'll finish when I finish.'[5]

On 29 July a 'respect summit' was convened at Chequers, to which a wide spectrum of organisations and charities were invited to present findings on their work on anti-social behaviour. Blair interrogated them forensically: his thinking shifted away from ASBOs and crackdowns to looking more at the causes of anti-social behaviour. The conversation led him into discussing 'problem families' or 'neighbours from hell', parenting issues and neglected children.[6] Out of these discussions came the Anti-Social Behaviour (Respect) Task Force in September under Casey, reporting directly to him. Casey was Blair's kind of civil servant: 'she can be rude and very forceful', said one Number 10 source.[7] Not everyone appreciated her unconventional methods: 'She would sit at the head of the table next to the Prime Minister and shout at ministers,' recalled one official.[8] But Blair saw that she made things happen.

At the launch on 10 January 2006, Blair called for a 'radical new approach' and a 'genuine intellectual debate' about the nature of liberty in modern society, concerned not purely with the freedom of the individual but also 'their freedom to be safe from fear'. There were echoes here of Blair's encounter with the philosopher John Macmurray from his days at Oxford and his early passion for 'community'. In one of the most personal speeches of his late premiership, Blair cited the socialist historian R. H. Tawney, who raised the danger of 'rights divorced from obligations'. He sought to bring about a 'fundamental shift' in society to give 'people control of their communities' so that they could rebuild 'the bonds of community for the modern age'. Richard Sennett, the LSE academic, had been brought to his attention, and he referred to Sennett's work on the decline of 'basic courtesies' in modern society. Blair's overall aim was no less than to 'eradicate the scourge of anti-social behaviour' and to 'restore respect' to communities of Britain.[9] Not everybody appreciated his thinking. Shami Chakrabarti, director of Liberty, delivered a speech on the same day entitled 'ASBO-mania: from social and natural justice to mob rule?' Another attack came from the Children's Society, whose chief executive said, 'The respect action plan fails to offer much more than a cocktail of policies that have already been launched, minor tweaks to existing anti-social behaviour measures, and shock tactics.' Blair nevertheless thought the launch helped regain the initiative, and he dismissed the criticism as coming from the minority of 'usual suspects' on the libertarian wing who had little experience of the woes he was addressing.[10] The *Guardian*, unusually, chose to lavishly praise the government's initiative: 'The government was right – and brave – to seize the issue. There is nothing harder for a government to achieve than changing human behaviour.'[11]

By the end of his premiership, Blair considered the 'respect' agenda one of his clear domestic success stories: a substantial response to a problem that Labour MPs reported was continually a top issue with voters. He was particularly proud of the real changes it brought to life on working-class estates.[12] But by this stage, the press gave him little credit, and the respect agenda failed to give the fresh impetus he needed. The 'tricks that we'd used in the past to get out of problems, such as new initiatives or interviews, weren't working any more', admitted Wegg-Prosser. At the end of January, the government tried again, with the launch of its White Paper on the provision of NHS care, described as a 'consumerist revolution'. Its aim was to bring healthcare provision closer to the community.[13] Again, the impact was less than had been hoped.

Fresh leadership at the top of the Conservative Party provided one reason why the January launches failed to re-establish Blair's authority. On 6 December, David Cameron succeeded Howard as leader, defeating rival David Davis by a margin of more than two to one. In Blair's first eleven years as Labour leader, the only serious opposition he faced had come from within his own party. This changed overnight. 'I am the heir to Blair,' Cameron had commented on the eve of the October 2005 Conservative party conference, a line defended to Tory grandees by his shadow Chancellor, George Osborne: 'We have nothing to be ashamed of by saying it.'[14] Aged thirty-nine, Cameron was notably younger than Blair, and seemed to promise a fresher and less tainted version of the Prime Minister. With his close coterie of friends in the 'Notting Hill set', Cameron presented a more appealing Tory image than Hague, Duncan Smith or Howard. 'We faced an opposition that was at last functioning, which meant that we had to refresh ourselves,' said one Cabinet minister.[15] Cameron's emergence led to heated debate in Labour circles. Brownites argued that Cameron should be portrayed negatively and that the alleged differences between him and his party should be highlighted, or indeed ridiculed, because behind the façade he was merely the 'same old Tory'. The Blairites felt that they needed to be more circumspect, and that the contradictions within Cameron's Tory party would come to the surface before long.[16] Cameron's efforts to present a more centre-leaning Conservative party were also considered helpful to Blair as ammunition to use against those in the party arguing for a lurch to the left. 'He's come onto our ground,' Blair would tell Brown repeatedly, hoping to forestall any attempt by the Chancellor to move away from the centre and put clear dividing lines between Labour and Cameron's Tories. But Cameron's newer and fresher image continued to pose a problem for the government. At his first PMQs the new Tory leader delivered his most effective lunge when he commented that Blair had been 'the future once'.[17]

On 31 January Blair suffered two Parliamentary defeats in one day. Following swiftly after his reverse on the ninety-days bill, it led to a growing impression of a Prime Minister no longer in control. The first defeat came on a House of Lords amendment to the religious hatred bill. It had been in the government's mind since 9/11 but, when the bill was eventually introduced after the 2005 election, the limits it imposed on freedom of speech aroused widespread opposition, including from Rowan Atkinson and a group of fellow performers who claimed the bill would inhibit their ability to satirise legitimate targets. Errors in the Whips' office and overconfidence amongst ministers resulted in the government losing the vote 278–288: they knew that it would be tight and blamed the defeat on backbenchers either avoiding their whip, or brazenly lying to them. 'He was really angry with me, the party, with everything. For him it didn't matter what the issue was: we didn't lose votes,' said Hilary Armstrong.[18] Worse was to follow. He said to her, 'There's no point in me staying for the next vote, is there?', believing that a rebellion of comparable size was in the offing. 'It doesn't look like it, does it?' she replied. 'Right, I'm off,' he said. The second vote, called just after 8 P.M. that evening, was lost 283–282. Had he stayed, the vote on the second House of Lords amendment would have been won. His voice was calm and steady when he next spoke to her about it, but his deep frustration was very clear.[19] The second vote was comparatively minor, and related only to one clause of the bill. After it was lost, no one suggested there should be a vote of confidence. The double defeat was made worse, however, when Cameron asked the following day at PMQs whether the country could still have confidence that the Prime Minister would be able to carry out his agenda. 'Is it not becoming increasingly clear that when the government do the right thing . . . they can do it only with Conservative support, but when they do the wrong thing, they cannot carry either their own backbenchers or the country?'[20]

A reason for the loss, the *Guardian* suggested, was because a number of Labour MPs were absent that evening campaigning in the critical Dunfermline and West Fife by-election, the first test of Labour's popularity at the polls since Cameron's election.[21] Brown was one of many high-profile politicians to canvass in the constituency, which, when created after the 2005 boundary charges, had taken in parts of Brown's former constituency, Dunfermline East. At the May 2005 election, the Labour candidate had won over 47 per cent of the vote, while the Liberal and SNP candidates could muster only 20 and 19 per cent respectively. It was considered a very safe Labour seat. Yet at the by-election on 9 February, Liberal Democrat candidate William Rennie overturned an 11,500 majority and won an 1,800 majority of his own. 'There's been too much spin and not enough delivery,' said the winning candidate, while his former boss, Charles Kennedy, hailed the result 'a seismic event in Scottish and UK politics'. However much Number 10 tried to pass it off as mid-term blues, it was clear that, with the vultures circling ever closer over Number 10, all was not well.[22]

Education Dog-fight: March 2006

As the Education and Inspections Bill was to be the major item of third-term policy to be taken through Parliament, it was inevitable that Blair would meet considerable opposition from those who disliked the direction of his marketising reforms, and from those who wanted to see him wounded, or worse. To pre-empt the clash, Number 10 had explored proceeding without legislation, but concluded that it was technically unavoidable.[23] The bill was thus going to be a major test of his own strength and that of his opponents, which included the DfES. The policy ideas had originated in the 2004 five-year plans and before. He wanted to use this last chance to reform education, to give a major push to schools gaining more autonomy from local authorities. His preferred model remained academies, where the school was able to run itself largely autonomously. The academy champion, Adonis, was now at the Education Department as a junior minister: 'Blair and Adonis wanted autonomous schools everywhere. Neither wanted local authorities to have any real control. Tony Blair really wanted each school to be an academy,' complained a senior DfES official.[24] Ruth Kelly and her special adviser, Dan Corry, were less sure. 'Blair and Adonis had an innate belief that local authorities were at the root of all problems, and that somehow if you could only make schools more entrepreneurial and business-like, they would succeed,' said Corry.[25] The divergence was hard to disguise. Only appointed Education Secretary in December 2004, Kelly was plunged into a department where the former Number 10 policy chief was her junior minister and where the Prime Minister was hell-bent on forging ahead with his controversial policies.

Blair initially favoured taking the policy forward through Cabinet committees but ran into opposition from the Treasury and the Deputy Prime Minister.[26] 'We had two of these and then they stopped . . . It was all a bit of a disaster,' recalled one DfES aide.[27] The key discussions then took place between Kelly and Corry for the DfES and new education supremo at Number 10, Conor Ryan. It was clear from early on that few DfES officials or education thinkers were committed to Adonis's agenda: said one, 'it was very much him driving it with the force of his own arguments and position. Even if academies were the answer to a problem, they were not an answer to every problem. Yet they became some kind of panacea.'[28] From Kelly's opposition to outright independence emerged the idea of 'trust schools' whereby a substantial degree of independence would be granted to schools but under the auspices of the local authority. The suggestion was greeted coolly. 'Ruth had to persuade the Prime Minister that if all state schools became independent it would be anarchy, and that local authorities would to some extent have to hold the ring,' said one official.[29] Number 10 became suspicious that Kelly was going native and absorbing the DfES's mindset, as they thought her predecessors Morris and even to some extent Clarke had done. The department had itself felt 'blamed' by Number 10 for many years: 'There was a sense of constant victimisation from Number 10 for our work on schools,' said a senior official.[30]

Relations for a time became very bad. Adonis was virtually the only 'true believer' in the department, but his role in the passage of the policy was played down as he was such a controversial figure in the party. To find a way forward, Blair convened a meeting at Chequers in July 2005. Kelly, Corry and Normington came from the DfES, Ryan from Number 10 as well as the increasingly radical John Hutton, who was to provide the grit in the oyster. They agreed that trust schools should be the model to go forward in the White Paper, though Blair and Ryan tried to whittle down the safeguards restricting independence that the department wanted.[31] Hutton argued that the model was far too tame. 'Why do trust schools have to be charities? Why can't they run schools for profit?' he asked.[32] This was too far even for Blair, who interjected, 'I don't think so,' believing trusts did not have to make money for the schools to be good. 'Intellectually, Tony Blair saw that we were artificially limiting the supply of schools by not letting private companies into education to make a profit,' he said. 'But politically he realised it was going too far,' said a Number 10 aide.[33]

What did Brown and the Treasury think? They were almost 'eerily quiet' in the run-up to the White Paper. 'We never knew where Gordon stood: it was disconcerting. There was no overt hostility, but neither was there the habitual messing around,' said one aide, though 'Blair was not as distrustful of Brown as some in Number 10 were'.[34] All autumn, conflicting signals flowed into Number 10 about what Brown thought. They suspected that he disliked academies, and they believed the hostility emanated from his aides. They were wrong. It was the Treasury officials who were more hostile: 'They thought academics were a waste of money and divisive,' said one aide.[35] Brown's lack of engagement was deliberate. He had made the decision that he was not ready to engage on schools and education policy: under the Granita division of spoils, this was Blair's territory, though Brown knew he could not avoid engaging for ever.

To minimise turbulence at the 2005 party conference, the White Paper 'Higher Standards, Better Schools for All: More Choice for Parents and Pupils' was delayed until it was over, and was published on 25 October: 'It was too controversial to publish it before.'[36] Already watered-down from the initial aspirations of Blair and Adonis, the paper still ran into the staunch opposition of the PLP, with some fifty implacable enemies. What grated most was the increased ability of trust schools to select pupils, albeit within the remit of the National Admissions Code, and the downgrading of the role of LEAs in favour of alternative providers.[37] An already fragile position was exacerbated when, on 24 October, the day before the paper's launch, a frustrated Blair deliberately exaggerated the radical nature of the proposals, describing them as 'a pivotal moment in the life of this Parliament and this government'.[38] 'He saw academies as one of the defining issues of his premiership . . . He saw this as a test case for New Labour,' said one aide.[39] The speech and the White Paper were immediately seized upon by the media and disaffected MPs as an attack upon local government: 'The communication got off on a disastrous footing and in the end you have got to lay that at Tony's door,' said one aide.[40]

Former Education Secretary Estelle Morris, now in the Lords and an increasingly vociferous critic of education policy, thought that the 'pre-publicity was mad and ill-advised, especially by exaggerating the extent by which schools would be able to select their own pupils'. Her suspicions were that 'Number 10 wanted to create an impression that radical changes were being proposed and they weren't, in part because they wished they'd gone further'.[41] One Number 10 aide felt she had become a 'very bitter person'.[42] But her successor Charles Clarke believed the same: that the negative reaction had been compounded by Blair's provocative launch.[43] Morris complained to a senior minister about the spin. 'I don't control Number 10's press machine,' came the nonchalant reply.[44] The DfES too had been caught off-guard by the way the White Paper was spun. The paper's foreword, written by Blair himself, who had rejected the 'limp' introduction the DfES had drafted, further stoked fires. It declared: 'Our reforms must build on the freedoms that schools have increasingly received, but extend them radically . . . The local authority must move from being a provider of education to being its local commissioner and the champion of parent choice.'[45] The DfES insisted that people should read the White Paper itself, but the damage had been done. 'We had hundreds of meetings with MPs, local authorities and others, but the spinning in the introduction gave them a fixed idea and it was hard to look at what was actually in the paper,' said a DfES aide.[46] Why had Blair struck out so hard? 'He was getting the feeling that the Labour Party was moving away from being on the side of the ordinary citizen and parent,' said one aide. 'He knew it was his last chance.'[47] The proposals would always have caused problems within the PLP, but, as Taylor recalled, 'A quite modest set of reforms got us into terrible trouble because of the cack-handed way they were initially briefed.'[48]

Number 10 took time to admit the mistake it had made. *The Times* summed up the position: 'Tony Blair faces a period of maximum danger as Prime Minister, as serious for him as the Iraq war . . . The battle over the schools bill . . . will be a crucial test not just of his political authority, and even his future at Downing Street, but also the whole direction of New Labour.'[49] It dominated Number 10's attention in the autumn of 2005, and it produced the first resignation from the government since the General Election when Martin Salter, Parliamentary Private Secretary to Jacqui Smith, Minister of State at the DfES, quit in protest on 30 November.[50]

Blair's position was made considerably more vulnerable when he lost the support of the already wavering Prescott. At Cabinet on 15 December 2005, he warned that the proposals would lead to a division between a first- and second-class system, as he had himself experienced when he had failed the 11-plus. In an interview on 18 December in the *Sunday Telegraph* with Susan Crosland, wife of the former Labour Education Secretary, Tony Crosland, he shocked Number 10 by breaking cover. 'I'm not totally convinced major reform is necessary,' he declared, fearing that city academies could become grammar schools by another name.[51] Blair saw him after the interview had been published and, according to aides, Prescott agreed that it had been a mistake to grant the interview. He went on to say in public that he had no 'fundamental opposition' to the proposals, but added that his litmus test was whether the proposals helped children from the most disadvantaged backgrounds.[52] His words did little to quell the rising dissent. His distaste for the reforms reflected a wider disaffection in the PLP: 'John's attitude seemed to be "you're pushing us too far, you're not as strong as you used to be, so you can't keep doing this to us",' recalled one Blair aide.[53] In Number 10 some aides also suspected that he was 'being mightily wound up by Gordon'.[54] But even in the third term, they knew that there were limits to Prescott's truculence. 'John, in the end, would never be disloyal to Tony, but that is not to say that he wouldn't be difficult.'[55]

Two weeks after the Prescott interview an 'alternative White Paper', insisting that a code of practice to cover school admissions be made legally binding on all schools, was signed by more than ninety rebel MPs including former Home Office minister John Denham.[56] Some of Number 10's growing frustration was directed at Kelly, whose presentational skills and lobbying of backbenchers were found wanting, despite her loyalty and intellect. Increasingly, they relied on Jacqui Smith to work the PLP.[57] In the New Year the rebellion nevertheless spread across the Labour movement. Teachers form one of the largest single groups of members in the Labour Party, and the NUT was viscerally opposed to the proposals. Number 10 began to worry whether

Blair would be able to carry even watered-down proposals. Many government ministers let it be known that they too were unhappy, even though they were bound to refrain from criticism in public. In January, Neil Kinnock, who hitherto had kept his mounting concerns about Blair and the direction of New Labour to private discussions, also broke cover. He condemned the proposals as 'at best a distraction and at worst dangerous', and called for the government to change the White Paper radically.[58] On 19 January, he chaired a meeting launching a pamphlet published by the left-leaning pressure group, Compass, written by Melissa Benn, daughter of Tony (who was also present in the audience), and Fiona Millar, partner of Alastair Campbell and long-time champion of comprehensive education. Campbell was present and sitting in the front row: no fan of the proposals, he was first and foremost a Blair loyalist, and was 'uncomfortable' at his conflict of loyalties.[59] The meeting was addressed by Morris, who said that it had been intended as a small meeting and she had not expected it to become such a cause célèbre. She recalled Number 10's John McTernan walking into the meeting and thinking, 'God, this is much bigger than we thought.'[60] Number 10 realised that opposition was spiralling out of control and that further compromises would have to be made.

In late January and early February there was a flurry of meetings and intense lobbying. Jacqui Smith chaired a meeting in the DfES almost every day to discuss tactics. So many came from Number 10 that one DfES aide commented: 'Sometimes it felt as if there couldn't have been anyone left in Downing Street.'[61] Blair himself held all the meetings with individual MPs and groups he could fit into his diary. Kelly tried to win round local authorities after it became apparent that they were lobbying their local MPs: 'She worked very hard and in the end, local authorities started to see that their fears were misplaced and that the legislation could help them,' said Corry.[62] It seemed as if a corner was being turned. On 3 February, Prescott made a speech to his Hull constituency coming out in support of the bill. He was now satisfied that local authorities were to remain fully involved in education and that trust schools would have to operate under a strict admissions regime, with a greater role for social organisations in the sponsorship and running of academies.[63] The White Paper had said that there would be no more community schools, but in another volte-face concession, Kelly announced that education authorities would be able to build them. Restrictions on the ability of schools to select pupils also pacified those many MPs who were worried that Blair was trying to re-create selective schools by the back door.

By early February, some of the leading rebels, including Nick Raynsford, Angela Eagle and Alan Whitehead, were coming back on side. So too was Morris, who became increasingly worried that the bill was being usurped by extremes within the party as a Trojan Horse to oust Blair, which she did not want to see. Brown, however, remained enigmatic. He had given support to the proposals in an interview in the *Sun*, but it fell far short of the ringing endorsement that Number 10 would have found helpful.[64] The continuing rebellion, was focused around the twenty-four-strong Campaign Group of left-wing MPs with John McDonnell as their chair. 'There was no Gordon Brown-organised operation, and no Nick Brown figure, as there had been on tuition fees,' stressed a Number 10 source.[65] But Blair's aides were disconcerted that the Chancellor was apparently content to see a significant section of the PLP using opposition to the bill as a way of prising out the Prime Minister. As Chief Whip Armstrong said, 'Opposition came from pragmatic opponents who were brought on side, and from those who wanted to see the Prime Minister out at any cost.'[66] They had no doubt that Brown himself wanted to get Blair out, ideally that spring or summer. Brown was the play-maker, and to Number 10's intense frustration, he knew it.

The bill was published on 28 February. Morris thought that the protestors 'had got ninety-nine per cent of what we wanted'.[67] 'Nonsense,' said Number 10, who claimed 'the concessions were of no real substance'. Which side was right? The answer is both. Despite what the opponents had wanted, there was no concession on the central concept of trust schools, which were still allowed to appoint the majority of their governors.[68] The bill allowed greater freedom to schools, including the possibility of owning their own assets, employing their own staff and, within limits, setting their own admission arrangements. But Blair and Adonis did not get as much freedom for schools to run themselves independently of local education authorities as they originally wanted, as the concessions to appease Prescott and the PLP were greater than they acknowledged. The flagship of the Blair/Adonis reformist deal remained academies, and it was to this, not trust schools, that Blair was subsequently to devote his remaining energies.

With the publication of the bill came shadow Education Secretary David Willetts' confirmation that the Tories would be supporting it, though he criticised Blair for watering down his proposals over the preceding months.[69] 'There was much in the White Paper that we agreed with: the bill was something of a disappointment to us.'[70] Cameron had indicated Tory backing in his first PMQs with Blair on 7

December: 'With our support the Prime Minister knows there is no danger of losing his reforms in a parliamentary vote, so he can afford to be as bold as he wants to be,' Cameron taunted.[71] In private, assurances were given to the government that Cameron would not renege on his public pledge.[72] But Tory support was double-edged: it further alienated the left of the PLP, and knowing the Tories would support the government encouraged more MPs to vote against. Heated discussions took place between Number 10 and the DfES about whether Tory support was a boon. Blair said, 'Look, at the end of the day, I'll do it if I have to on Tory votes,' leaving his audience unsure exactly whether he meant it.[73] So concerned was he to keep Tory support that he became increasingly agitated that the concessions he was granting might undermine opposition support: 'Tony would say, "I don't want to make too many concessions. If we make too many concessions the Tories will have an excuse not to vote with us."'[74] Others in Number 10 were more wary of Tory backing, but understood that Blair was caught in a Catch 22: 'We all believed that to get it through only because of Tory votes would be disastrous . . . but we understood that if he looked like he caved in to his own backbenchers, this would be an even more powerful thing for the Tories.'[75]

The Education and Inspection Bill went to the Commons for its key second reading on 15 March at 6:43 P.M. As expected, the Tories sided with the government and the bill was passed by 458–115 votes: 52 Labour MPs had rebelled and 25 abstained. The bill had indeed only passed with Conservative support. The more testing vote came at 6:59 P.M. when a 'timetable vote' had to be called to allow for further debate and scrutiny, which, if lost, could have led to a prolonged period of parliamentary guerrilla warfare. The Tories had only said they would vote for the bill, not for subsidiary measures including the timetable motion. Blair was on his own now: to have lost would have been as serious for Blair as losing the second reading vote itself. Unlike ninety days and the religious hatred votes, this was on his mainstream policy. Defeat, as on foundation hospitals or tuition fees, would have made his position acutely difficult. 'The mood resembled the final half an hour before the tuition fees vote. Votes on a knife-edge, no one quite sure which way it was going to go, an extremely tense atmosphere and no one having thought through what on earth we'd do if we'd lost,' said one aide.[76] To another, 'Close calls are a very deep psychological thing for him: with Tony Blair there's no Plan B, Plan C or Plan D: Plan A is the only show in town.'[77]

After last-minute lobbying, Blair managed to carry the vote, but with his majority cut to just ten. Thirty Labour MPs, the hardcore who wanted him out now, still rebelled. Blair's team think that Cameron made a tactical mistake by voting against, because it forced many Labour MPs back on side, knowing that their votes would now make the difference. They thought him opportunistic and unable to resist the chance of bringing Blair down, even if it meant compromising on his principles.[78] Willetts defended their action: 'We opposed the timetable motion because we always oppose such timetabling: it was never our intention to wreck the bill, but it allowed them to claim, however unfairly, that we were against the proposals all the time.'[79] Victory, nevertheless, had come at a price. Blair lost standing with backbenchers, who saw their party leader having to weave and duck to get his policy through, and to implore them for their support. Many thought he had been put into an almost degrading position of needing Tory support to avoid defeat.[80] It encouraged disobedience throughout the party: Blair had been wounded and kicked when he was down, and this further desensitised MPs considering rebelling again in the future. It was to prove the last battle in Parliament over public service reform, but the struggle to deliver was far from over. Number 10 immediately prodded the DfES to establish the first fifty trust schools. They were reluctant, believing the haste with which the academy programme had been pushed was responsible for some of the poor early publicity and performance. They wanted to play a longer game.[81] The fact was that Blair could no longer rely upon his backbenchers, Whitehall officials, nor even his own ministers. Nor could he produce the untrammelled policy proposals he wanted. His authority was draining away.

Cash for Honours: March–April 2006

An hour before the first of the two votes on the education bill, Jack Dromey, Labour Party treasurer and deputy general secretary of the T&G union, released a statement. For some time, he had been concerned about Labour's funding, and its possible links to the granting of honours, which had come increasingly into the public spotlight. On 15 March he announced that given that Labour had campaigned in 1997 on the need for transparency in cleaning up politics, he had thus 'commenced an inquiry into the securing of loans in secret by the Labour Party in 2005 . . . The Labour Party needs to put its house in order to restore public and party members' confidence.'[82] News of his statement was received in Blair's office only mid-afternoon, when all hands were being deployed to coax MPs into the 'yes' lobby.[83] As the second vote was taking place, Dromey appeared on *Channel 4 News* at seven o'clock and said, 'I do not think it's right that loans should be secured from wealthy individuals behind the backs of the elected officers of the Labour Party . . . Number 10 must have known about the loans.'[84] He criticised Number 10 for insufficiently respecting the Labour Party and its democratic integrity.[85] Blair was told about his claims after the vote. 'He's an incredibly calm person usually, but he was absolutely furious. He was clinically angry,' said one close confidant.[86] Blair was clear that 'it was a deliberate attempt to destabilise his position at the very moment that he'd won the education vote, in the full knowledge that the PLP did not like the bill', said one.[87] 'Jack Dromey chose the very day the Prime Minister was at his most vulnerable, with large numbers voting against the government,' said one close colleague.[88] Instead of Blair earning a 'great press' the next day, he faced a barrage of new criticisms and accusations. 'Absolute nonsense,' says Dromey. 'The timing was entirely coincidental.'[89]

Was Brown involved? Dromey denies this completely. The partisans in Number 10, however, convinced themselves otherwise. The lynchpin in their mind was Dromey's wife, Harriet Harman, who was '110 per cent behind Gordon'.[90] Despite re-entering government as Solicitor-General in 2001, they believed she still smarted from her dismissal from the Department of Social Security in 1998. One Number 10 aide detected a real hostility between Harman and Blair: 'She felt he had given Brown insufficient credit, she thought the government insufficiently left-wing, the war in Iraq was illegal, and much else besides.'[91] Reports came in to Number 10 about how she had been at the Treasury that very afternoon, as had Dromey. 'Everyone thought it was being planned by the Treasury,' said one close Blair confidant.[92] 'It couldn't have been anything other than co-ordinated,' said one source. 'You just need to look at the facts: Jack, Harriet, Gordon. You would have to be naïve to the point of being a simpleton not to be able to put certain basic facts together to do with the timing, the personnel and the tone in which it was done. It was all part of their joint plan to get the Prime Minister out early.'[93] Some in Number 10 blamed Harman for encouraging Brown to block proposals at the beginning of January to review party funding, while others thought that Dromey had struck a pre-emptive blow, believing Number 10 was about to disown him.[94]

Nothing in the third term so aroused anger in Number 10 as the 'cash for honours' issue, as it came to be known. No one thinks that Dromey deliberately set out to cause what became many months of personal anguish for Blair and others, but they do blame him for 'turning a drama' – a story that peerages were being given to those who donated money – 'into a crisis'; a full-scale scandal which highlighted the most negative angles on Blair that had been portrayed over the years: 'His alleged obsession with money, his secrecy, his weakness before powerful businessmen, his lack of sympathy for the Labour Party and trade unions, his shiftiness . . . it ticked nearly every box.'[95] A story came into Number 10 a few days later of a plan to remove Blair from office by effectively bankrupting the party and encouraging donors to say they would only be prepared to give money to get it back into the black if Brown was leader.[96] Blair himself never accused Brown of complicity, but he did tell him how outrageous he thought the timing of Dromey's comments was. Brown's reply reportedly was, 'Well, nothing to do with me.' 'But then again,' sighed one Number 10 aide, 'it's never anything to do with him, is it?'[97] Relations at this point were described as 'very, very bad'. Blair emerged from one meeting with Brown during this period saying, 'We didn't get down to any substance: all he would say is, "When are you going to F off out of here?"'[98]

Dromey's intervention, which became known in Number 10 as the 'first coup', could have been fatal. Had the second vote on the education bill been lost, it is unlikely that Blair would have survived beyond the May local elections. He would not only have been forced out of office, but forced out under a cloud. Angus MacNeil of the Scottish National Party (SNP) wrote to the Metropolitan Police asking them to investigate whether any breach of the 1925 Honours (Prevention of Abuses) Act, set up in the wake of Lloyd George's 'sale of honours', had occurred. Plaid Cymru petitioned similarly. Shortly afterwards, the Metropolitan Police launched an inquiry into the affair. Thus was launched the third major destabilising force in Blair's third term, alongside Iraq and the succession question.

Other events at this time were souring the Blair–Brown relationship. At the end of 2005, Alastair Campbell and Philip Gould had taken it upon themselves to bring Blair and Brown together to plan for an orderly transfer of power; it was the same impulse which had earlier led them to induce the *rapprochement* during the 2005 General Election campaign.[99] This time, the love-in consisted of both principals: the partisan Eds, Balls and Miliband, and Campbell and Gould themselves, meeting in great secrecy in Number 10 or 11. Sometimes the group would be widened to incude Liz Lloyd and Sue Nye. 'Alastair and Philip were very keen on securing a smooth handover: the others went along with it. We'd have a little lunch and then talk about getting both of them working better together,' said one present.[100] The balance at this meeting was against Blair: Powell absented himself because he could not bear to be in the same room as Brown or Balls, and 'hoped something would turn up to sabotage Brown',[101] while Campbell and still more Gould were perceived to be leaning over to the Brown side. 'Philip was driving quite fast towards the Gordon camp, to the general hilarity of Number 10.'[102] Some in Number 10, including Powell, took bets that the formula would not last a day. Initially, such pessimism seemed misplaced: 'For a period of weeks there was genuine optimism that there was a new willingness to make it work. Brown was personally engaging in the discussions, and Balls was behaving himself,' recalled one present.[103] The meetings started to go wrong when Ed Balls and (to Number 10's surprise) even Ed Miliband 'began to be astonishingly rude to the Prime Minister.'[104] Miliband's repeated question, which caused great resentment, was 'What is to be gained by you staying on for a further six to nine months?'[105] Ed Miliband, for a long time a white hope in Number 10, began to be written off as 'irretrievably lost to the forces of darkness and anti-reform.'[106] 'Their body language, their tone, their questions, were insulting: it was not the way you would expect a Prime Minister to be treated.'[107] One present thought Brown himself was responsible: 'Gordon was aggressive and bullying towards Tony Blair. It was a mystery why he was behaving so unpleasantly when Tony had made it clear that he was going to be going.'[108] Blair would confide in private, 'I feel like an abused and bullied wife.'[109] Soon he was attacking Gould and Campbell for getting him into the talks in the first place.[110]

In the end, it was Campbell who pulled the plug. Following a lunch thought to be with Balls, Peter Dobbie of the *Mail on Sunday* wrote a provocative article on 5 March under the title 'Blair's away with the fairies . . . and the men in white coats are coming'. It spoke about how individuals, thought to be Campbell and Gould, had been saying that Blair had a 'psychological problem' and could not come to terms with the prospect of walking away from Downing Street.[111] On reading it, according to a close friend, Campbell 'went berserk' that a report of what had been said in private had been leaked, and to the 'despised' *Mail on Sunday*.[112] Campbell felt betrayed: 'We were genuinely trying to make things better,' he was reported as saying, 'but if they're not serious about the transition, if it's just a game, that's it.' Campbell refused to attend again. Attempts were made to keep the meetings going, but 'Gordon's manner turned all Blair's people off . . . and Tony no longer wanted to come to them.'[113] There was a further attempt to revive the dialogue over strategic, political issues before the summer when Liz Lloyd, an increasingly commanding deputy chief of staff, and Wegg-Prosser held meetings with Brown's Spencer Livermore and Sue Nye. But the meetings proved fruitless. Only in the autumn was dialogue resumed, but this time it was to discuss policy, in the run-up to the policy review, and so the meetings were very different in nature.[114]

Against such a precarious backdrop, the last thing Blair wanted was to be out of the country for any time. But that is exactly what he had to do on 23 March when he went to the Brussels Council and then on Australia, New Zealand and Indonesia. The prime purpose of the trip was the Commonwealth Games in Australia; he had also promised to visit Prime Minister Helen Clark in New Zealand and he wanted to visit the country with the biggest Muslim population in the world, Indonesia.[115] He flew non-stop from Brussels on 24 March to Melbourne on a nineteen-hour flight, the longest non-stop commercial flight in aviation history (the travellers were presented with certificates). He slept for six hours, worked on his foreign policy speech for six hours and spent the rest planning meetings and working on Number 10 business.[116] At least he hoped for a few days' respite from the madness of Westminster in a particularly mad March. But on the long leg out he went to the back of the plane to talk to the journalists and was asked whether he had a date in mind for his departure, to which he replied, yes, he did. Although he spoke off the record, the press widely reported that he had set a provisional date, but wanted first to push through NHS reforms.[117] It was picked up by the Australian Broadcasting Corporation who asked him whether he thought it had been a 'strategic mistake' to have pre-announced his departure in September 2004. His response was, 'It was an unusual thing for me to say, but people kept asking me the question so I decided to answer it. Maybe it was a mistake.'[118] Number 10 immediately tried to insist that he had been cut off mid-sentence and that he had intended to say that 'it had been a mistake to have believed that the announcement would have killed off speculation as to when he would resign'. There is every reason to believe that is what he meant.[119] Nevertheless, it gave just the excuse the media needed to return to the story of his departure. Coverage of his foreign policy speech in Canberra, his climate change address in Auckland and his Indonesia visit were all but wiped out. What had been intended as a trip with no domestic political consequence turned into a 'frenzy of speculation about the prospect of an early handover to Gordon Brown'.[120] It was Blair's first taste of an overseas trip being dominated by destabilising domestic stories; a common feature of a premiership that has reached its twilight hours.

Black Wednesday: April 2006

When premierships lose the initiative and begin to unravel, they seem to break apart suddenly and violently. Although Blair's government continued to press ahead with reform, on the surface 2006 was beginning to resemble the difficult years of John Major's premiership, following Black Wednesday in September 1992. As if in uncanny echo, Blair now endured his own 'Black Wednesday' on 25 April, when three separate bad stories coincided on the same day.

Ever since he had been shadow Home Secretary from 1992 to 1994, Blair had made being 'tough on crime' a distinctive trademark of his leadership. When in 1999 asylum applications had reached a crisis point, he personally made reducing illegal immigration one of his primary domestic priorities. In 2005, he insisted that the Home Office drive even harder to tackle the problem, and in the first half of 2006, for the first time, Britain began deporting more failed asylum-seekers than were entering the country. What he did not do, however, was to give the same attention to the issue of foreign prisoners. According to one senior mandarin, 'Everyone knew that the intense focus on asylum meant that the Home Office had to back-pedal on some other aspects of the immigration system.'[121] When local elections loomed in early May Blair played one of his known strengths, his toughness on law and order, but one episode emerged out of the blue to undermine his whole approach. On Tuesday 25 April, Clarke called a press conference in which he admitted for the first time that the Home Office had failed to consider more than 1,000 foreign criminals for deportation upon their release. The press conference irritated Number 10 by fanning the flames of a problem issue in the middle of a delicate local election campaign.[122] But, in fact, Clarke had no choice. The statistics had just come to light following a request from the Commons Public Accounts Committee back in October 2005. Clarke was obliged to release them immediately. On BBC television's *Newsnight* that evening, Clarke, trying to smooth things over, said that 'very, very few' criminals had been released without being considered for deportation from the moment he had first been alerted to the crisis in July 2005. But on the very same evening the BBC revealed that 288 such criminals had been released between August 2005 and March 2006. It was a very bad night in Number 10.

The next morning, Wednesday 26 April, Clarke was on the radio saying that he had discussed the issue with Blair, who did not deem it a resigning issue. In the House of Commons that afternoon, to his acute embarrassment, Blair was forced to admit to the House that he had turned down Clarke's offer to resign before he knew about the 288 prisoners. Cameron took him apart at PMQs: 'Let us be absolutely clear about what we all just heard. The Prime Minister backs incompetent ministers, even when he does not know the facts ... When a Prime Minister cannot even deport dangerous criminals in our jails, are the public entitled to say "enough is enough"?'[123] Blair left the House before Clarke rose to make his statement amid Opposition cries of 'Resign!' Shadow Home Secretary David Davis rammed the point home: 'Two hundred and eighty-eight criminals were released after the government knew about the problem ... The Home Secretary's position is now untenable.'[124] Clarke was in combative mood in Cabinet on 27 April, and gave a brief run-down of the scale of the problem and his plans to remedy it. In a statement to the House on 28 April, he said that most of the serious offenders released had now been located and the majority were facing deportation. It then came to light, however, that five had committed offences involving drugs or violence and two more were being investigated for alleged sexual attacks.[125]

The episode was a double blow for Blair. On 30 April, he wrote in the *Observer* that he would 'hassle, harry and hound' foreign criminals out of Britain, even if they had not been convicted of a criminal offence.[126] But it was too late for rhetoric. The episode undermined his credibility in one of his strongest suits, and overnight threatened to torpedo the years of grind he had put into bringing the asylum system under control. His instinct had always been to stick by a minister in trouble, rather than rush to dump them, until all the facts were known.[127] Protecting Clarke brought him only woe. Logically, Blair should either have sacked Clarke immediately or agreed that he should stay on to sort out the mess and then backed him to the hilt. But he did neither. He now appeared vacillating and weak in shielding a minister whose position many dismissed as indefensible. Clarke's own defence, that he must stay on 'to put right what went wrong', earned more ridicule. As one Blairite said, 'It was a bit like Profumo saying he couldn't resign because he had to stick around and head the Profumo inquiry.'[128]

Patricia Hewitt at Health was another of Blair's Cabinet allies who came unstuck on Black Wednesday. For a few months after the 2005 General Election, Number 10 viewed her as one of the several ministers hedging her bets and tacking close to Brown. But at some point in the autumn of 2005, she tacked back. Number 10 admired the way that, like Hutton, she decided to press on with her work regardless of whether the Treasury high command approved. She was felt to have received a difficult inheritance from Reid in May 2005; although strong on presentation, he was not thought to have been good on policy and administration within the department. Furthermore, she had to manage the prolonged budget crisis in the NHS. Hewitt's strengths, however, did not extend to presentation or to winning over stakeholders to her cause. Health was another area of perceived Blairite strength, and on Monday 24 April, he devoted a monthly press conference to a presentation of the government's record. He acknowledged that there were still problems, but said there had nevertheless been 'major, fundamental and lasting improvements in patient care over these past few years'. He hoped to earn headlines such as 'Blair defends his record on the NHS'. But on the day of the press conference, Hewitt was heckled and jeered while giving a speech at a UNISON conference. Two days later, on Wednesday 26 April, she addressed the annual conference of the Royal College of Nurses (RCN) in Bournemouth. An RCN report had just been published suggesting that up to 13,000 posts might have to be cut. It helped create a sour mood and explains the public humiliation and booing that she received during her speech from the 2,000 nurses. The impression gained from the media was of a minister not in control of their department and running a policy derided by 'the admired and saintly nurses'. Number 10 were indignant, and thought that the RCN 'should hang their heads in shame for the way it behaved'.[129] There were calls for apologies, but the damage had been done. Blair's record had been called into question on a second area of strength.

The third component to Black Wednesday was the most ludicrous, but damaged Blair the least. For two years, John Prescott had been having an affair with his diary secretary, Tracey Temple. Number 10 had received intimations, but its imminent illumination in the press was revealed to Blair only on 25 April as part of a shock double-briefing along with news of the foreign prisoners. On Wednesday 26 April, the *Daily Mirror*'s front page carried the headline 'My Affair: by Prezza' above a picture of Prescott embracing his diary secretary at the departmental Christmas party. His defence was that the affair was long over and he said that his wife of forty-four years, Pauline, had been 'devastated' by it.[130] The continuation of the story was entirely predictable: Temple retreated to a secret location where she was receiving 'media advice' from publicist Max Clifford, who told Radio 4's *Today* programme that she was a 'wronged woman who merely wanted to set the record straight'.[131] Her record-straightening was served up in the *Mail on Sunday*, avid for the story, and willing to pay a high price for it. Prescott had long been a figure of derision in British media for his verbal infelicities and for enjoying the trappings of office. His nickname now changed from 'two Jags' to 'two shags'. The damage to Blair came from being seen to retain as Deputy Prime Minister a man who appeared not only poor at his departmental work but also unseemly in his conduct: 'The ugly aroma of the arrogance of power is rapidly attaching itself to him,' said *The Times*. The benefit to Blair was that it made an increasingly independent-minded Prescott beholden to him for the job he enjoyed so much. There were fears in Number 10 before the affair became public that if Prescott were to come out in public and endorse a Brownite takeover, the game would be up: 'It was in the power of Prescott to pull the trigger on the Prime Minister by making a public declaration demanding an early date for Mr Blair for his departure,' wrote Andrew Rawnsley.[132] Instead of Prescott holding the gun to Blair, Blair now held the gun to him. His very continuation in office depended on Blair's good will, and he knew it. As one of Brown's colleagues in the PLP noted, 'The Prescott affair was much more damaging for us [than for Blair].'[133]

Where was Brown during Black Wednesday? Campaigning for part of the day, where he was photographed with Hollywood actress Angelina Jolie during a 'local election stunt'.[134] By the end of the week he was off to Africa. His supporters were said to be unable to conceal their glee at the problems piling up on Blair. A gallows humour developed in Number 10. 'God, is there anything else that can go wrong today?'[135] Black Wednesday took its toll on Blair's popularity. A *Sunday Times*/YouGov poll at the end of the week reported 57 per cent of respondents thinking the government was 'sleazy and incompetent', and a further 58 per cent believing it was 'on its last legs'.[136] Blair's personal rating slumped badly: only 33 per cent of people thought he was doing a good job against 64 per cent who thought he was doing badly: in contrast, 51 per cent thought Cameron was doing well. Seasoned commentators like Andrew Grice noted that Blair's 'Black Wednesday' was nothing like as serious as Major's fourteen years before, when a major plank of government economic policy had shattered, leading the government to lose billions of pounds together with its reputation for economic competence.[137] Blair's own day of woe was not pivotal. Nevertheless, the cumulative effect on his standing was damaging. 'It was a steady drip, drip, drip of realising that these things together meant it was going to be very, very difficult to get ahead,' recalled one official. 'He kept saying, "Am I ever going to be free of all this stuff?"'[138]

Blair Loses Authority Abroad: January–May

With increasing frequency Blair wondered too if he would ever be free
of the problems in Iraq. The long-delayed elections in the country were
over: he hoped to see an Iraqi government speedily emerge capable of
bringing order and purpose. But when, on 12 February, Ibrahim al-Jaafari
became Prime Minister of the transitional Shia government, to Blair's
immense frustration, the Sunnis and Kurds refused to accept him, and
the Shias refused to share power. As before in Iraq, the elections proved
a false dawn: 'There was a certain amount of serial delusion in all this,'
said a senior British military figure. 'We constantly invested too much
hope in the drafting of a constitution, in the conduct of elections, in the
arrival of new faces on the scene.'[139] As violence now increased on the
ground, optimism faded. The hundredth British death in Iraq occurred
on 31 January, when Corporal Gordon Pritchard's convoy was struck by
a remote-controlled bomb. 'Nearly three years after the fall of Saddam,
our authority had progressively declined,' said John Sawers.[140] Sectarian
conflict reached a climax with the bombing on 22 February of the
Golden Mosque in Samara: the ninth-century shrine was one of Iraq's
four holiest Shi'ite sites, and was sacred to millions across the world.
'That was the point when we realised that the sectarian problems were
really taking off,' recalled one senior aide.[141] Revenge attacks began
immediately: within a day, Sunni authorities reported that 128 of their
mosques had been attacked.[142] With Iraq on the brink of civil war,
sectarian violence undermined al-Jaafari's attempts to forge a national
government. 'With weeks and weeks passing after the election and no
Iraqi government emerging, Blair turned to despair,' noted one
official.[143] From his perch at the Foreign Office, Jay recalled that Blair
'showed anger and frustration that it wasn't going as he thought it
should. He wasn't convinced that we were all doing all that we
should.'[144] With domestic policy not going well, Iraq contributed further
to a bad spring. Cabinet ministers, apart from Straw, Reid and Brown
who had departmental responsibilities, now seemed deliberately shtum
on Iraq.

Out of his disappointment was born a revised and less ambitious
objective. 'It was increasingly evident that our capacity to shape the
outcome was very limited, and it would be up to the Iraqis to sort it out
themselves,' recalled Sawers. 'In effect we now reduced our
expectations to being able to leave with a reasonably stable situation in
place.'[145] Blair's worry was that the continuing political vacuum was
exactly the seedbed that insurgents, al-Qaeda, Iran and Syria most

wanted for their efforts to thrive. The country urgently needed a strong government to assert control. He despaired of al-Jaafari's ability to provide this, and to share power with Sunnis and Kurds. He became convinced that al-Jaafari should, in the interests of Iraq's future, step down. But how? Al-Jaafari did not want to relinquish office, and so the full weight of the Bush administration would be required to shift his view. When Blair raised the issue at a VTC in late March he found Bush shared his frustration at the delay in forming a government. 'He and the President were very much of one mind,' explained Condi Rice. 'It was taking forever.'[146] Blair told Bush that he had asked Straw to go to Baghdad to 'bang heads together' and suggested that Rice join him. On 2 April, immediately after Rice had visited Straw's Blackburn constituency, a testament to their close personal friendship, the two flew to Baghdad. The British saw the trip as an opportunity to bind in the new Secretary of State: 'Condi had been in office for eighteen months, but we were concerned by the hands-off approach from Washington. Neither the State Department nor the White House was giving clear directions: it certainly wasn't coming from the President,' said an FCO official.[147] Straw and Rice were unable to dislodge al-Jaafari during their visit, but, in making it clear that they spoke with the full authority of their bosses, they made their point. Sawers and the NSC's Megan O'Sullivan remained behind to maintain the pressure. Blair kept in close contact with them, and on 20 April, al-Jaafari eventually stood down, but it took yet another month for an outsider, Nouri al-Maliki, to emerge as Prime Minister.

Blair travelled to Baghdad on 22 May to see the situation for himself, spending several hours with al-Maliki and President Talabani in the heavily fortified 'Green Zone'. He had long planned to visit once the new government was formed: their first meeting should have been a triumphant occasion after three years of war and struggle. But it was not the climax Blair had hoped for: too much had gone awry for there to be any fanfare. Troop withdrawals now became the primary focus of discussion. 'The view from Number 10 had always been "draw down as quick as you can",' said Fry.[148] Troop withdrawal had first been discussed back in 2003, the day after Basra fell: 'We had fond ideas that we would go in, Basra would fall, and other nations would come in and assist with peace-keeping. But as Iraq became more difficult, only a small number of allies showed up and we began to get an increasing sense of an enduring commitment.'[149] Escalation of British action in Afghanistan became a further reason, on top of domestic pressure, to seek an early withdrawal of troops from Iraq. The Bush administration had resisted this line of thought, arguing that continued British presence in the south was important not least in limiting Iranian penetration and preserving the oil infrastructure. Al-Maliki, however, was sympathetic to a staged withdrawal, and at their concluding press conference said that two of the four British-run provinces in the south would be handed over to Iraqi forces the following month.[150]

Blair went to Washington on 25 May to see Bush. The trip had initially been scheduled for 6–7 April, but it had been postponed because of fears that it would have a negative impact on the May local election results. It was not their most optimistic meeting. Blair shared with Bush his concerns about the deterioration in Iraq in the five months since the December 2005 election, and they discussed how to build international support for al-Maliki's government. They agreed that coalition forces should remain until Iraqi security forces were ready to take over. In a new mood of '*glasnost*', they decided that their concluding press conference should last an hour, twice the usual length and more. It proved one of the most candid. Bush admitted that he could have expressed himself in 'a more sophisticated manner' at certain moments in the war on terror, while Blair came clean: 'We could have done de-Ba'athification in a more differentiated way than we did.'[151] But on the central issue, Blair refused to apologise: 'For all the hardships and challenges in the past few years, I shall always think that it was a cause worth fighting for.'[152] He would not deviate from that position for his remaining thirteen months in power.

The situation in Iran was the other principal topic that Blair and Bush addressed. Britain and America had become increasingly concerned by covert actions masterminded by Iran and Syria that fed the disorder and violence in Iraq.[153] They were also alarmed by Iran's developing nuclear programme. Since October 2003, the 'EU-3' (Britain, France and Germany) had led diplomatic efforts to persuade Iran to abandon its nuclear ambitions. Initially the process appeared to be working, but in January 2006 Iran had announced its intention to resume efforts to enrich uranium, in clear violation of an agreement reached with the EU-3 in November 2004. The hawks in the Bush administration had long been sceptical over the EU-3 process, which had been largely handled at the foreign minister level. John Bolton, who moved from the State Department to become UN Ambassador in August 2005, recalled frequent US appeals for Blair to take a firmer grip on the situation, but to no avail: 'The President talked to Blair about it on several occasions, and frequently the response was "Well, I don't know. I'll check and get back to you."' The hawks believed that Number 10 was obfuscating.

'Whether that was due to internal Labour Party politics, or whether that was EU politics, I don't know,' said Bolton.[154] In April 2006 the situation deteriorated significantly. President Ahmadinejad announced that his country had successfully enriched uranium. Two weeks later, he escalated tension by violently denouncing Israel: 'This fake regime cannot logically continue to live,' he declared on 24 April.[155] Four days later, the International Atomic Energy Agency confirmed that Iran had made significant breakthroughs in its efforts to enrich uranium. The same day, the issue was referred to the UN Security Council, where attempts to achieve a resolution were blocked by Russia and China, who feared that a resolution could be used to justify military action against Iran. At their White House meeting on 25 May, Blair was more cautious than Bush about what they should say on the use of military action against Iran. Blair's need for circumspection was obvious. Having seen one Bush adventure in the Middle East go disastrously wrong, domestic opinion in Britain was firmly against any more American adventurism, and it was in no mood, after the errors on WMD, to accept anything that was said about a nuclear threat from Iran.

The next day, Blair gave a keynote foreign policy speech in the Georgetown district of Washington. On Iran, he declared: 'I am not saying that we should impose change,' but he left the door open for the possibility of military attack. Press reports suggested that he had altered his remarks at the last minute to reflect a more belligerent posture on Iran at the instigation of the White House.[156] This was denied outright: 'The idea that the administration would have suggested changes to his speech is preposterous,' said the Embassy's P. J. Johnson. 'That just doesn't happen.'[157] The issue overshadowed what was his last speech in a series offering a comprehensive overview of his foreign policy thinking. The first, in London on 21 March, had emphasised his belief that victory in Iraq and Afghanistan was vital in the struggle to defeat global terrorism. In Australia on 26 March he broadened his focus to call for a global alliance to tackle not just terrorism, but poverty and climate change. He covered the importance of multilateralism and addressed the theory of 'hard' and 'soft' power. To the disgust of Number 10, the speech was largely ignored by the British media. In Oxford on 2 February, at a speech at St Anthony's College mediated by the academic Timothy Garton Ash, he had delivered an upbeat message that there had never been a better time for Britain to be optimistic about its place in the EU.

The Georgetown speech was to him the most important. He had taken three hours to write it from scratch on the plane to Washington the

day before. 'It's ridiculous that a Prime Minister ends up writing all his
speeches word for word, but that is the way he preferred to do it,' said
an official in his party.[158] The speech called for a radical reform of global
institutions to meet the challenges of the twenty-first century. The time
had come, he said, to move on from the rifts over Iraq to thinking about
a new structure of global institutions underpinned by a common
understanding of moral principles, to minimise the risk of such conflicts
in the future. A Security Council which excluded Germany, Japan and
India, and which had no proper representation from Latin America or
Africa, 'cannot be legitimate in the modern world', he said.[159] The G8
+5 model, should, he said, become the norm for their meetings.
'Increasingly there is a hopeless mismatch between the global challenges
we face and the global institutions to confront them.'[160] In an echo of his
seminal Chicago speech of 1999, he returned to the theme of
humanitarian intervention: 'Liberating oppressed people in distant
lands . . . [is] not just an abstract moral duty but essential for our security.'
He had hoped for his four foreign policy speeches to make a serious
contribution to international debate, and to bring about change. They
made some impact abroad, particularly in the US, but at home they
earned far fewer column inches. 'It depressed him a bit,' admitted one
close aide, 'he put a lot into those speeches.'[161] But Blair's star was
waning. As Lawrence Freedman, who submitted drafts for his speeches,
said: 'There was a kind of earnestness in them, willing people to listen,
but he was having to try harder and harder each time because, as he
sensed, his audience was drifting away from him.'[162]

Number 10 Re-groups: April–May

Since the beginning of the year, Number 10's 'senior management team'
(a title formalised that summer) consisting of Powell, Taylor, Turner,
Hill, Wegg-Prosser, Lloyd and Bennett, had been debating how to bring
a clearer focus to Blair's remaining months in office. 'The first part of the
year had been dominated by accusations that Number 10 wasn't making
enough progress and questions about why was Blair still around. In
reality a lot was happening in many areas, despite resistance from the
Treasury,' said Bennett.[163] Their wide-ranging thoughts about policy,
internal organisation, narrative, political management, communications
and the timing of Blair's departure suggested the need to raise these
matters with Blair himself to try to reach a more strategic approach.
Their ideas were collated by Taylor and written up in a document called

'Aiming High, Right to the End' which they debated at Chequers on Thursday 13 April, just before the Easter weekend.[164] 'It was obvious that as he wasn't going to be there for the full term it would be better for Tony to control his own destiny, rather than be salami-sliced out of office,' said Ruth Turner.[165] Ever since Bennett had taken on responsibility for policy after the election, he had been trying to encourage Blair to prioritise his objectives, a heroic task. His core questions to him were: 'What is the last period to be about?', 'What concretely do we want to have achieved?' and 'How do you demonstrate to the party and the outside world that real work is being done?'[166] Throughout February and March, he wrote a series of papers on priorities for Blair's weekend box which he would return to him on Monday with scribbled comments. Bennett worked the ideas up into a document which eventually appeared as a paper on 'policy priorities'. In fact, the ordering had barely shifted, with education, health and crime at the top followed by pensions, incapacity benefit and energy. Blair's remaining aspirations for Northern Ireland, the EU, climate change, Africa, Iraq, Afghanistan and the Middle East also had to be factored into the document. The list illustrated very vividly how much work needed to be done before he departed.

Wegg-Prosser, as head of strategic communications, had to ensure that the media reflected the positive work being done in these policy areas. Intensely frustrated by the predominance of stories about a Prime Minister and government out of control, an impression he thought was being enhanced by the Brownites, he decided a fresh approach was required. Given the unlikelihood of turning round the media, the ambition emerged to turn Blair 'from being a public figure into a publisher', where he himself could communicate directly with the electorate. It was thus planned for him to give a series of farewell lectures around the country, preceded by seminars at Number 10 with a range of experts drawn from across the political spectrum. When giving the speeches, he was to engage with regional media rather than the familiar national outlets. Wegg-Prosser worked closely with Jimmy Leach, head of digital communications in Downing Street, to achieve a mini revolution in the way the Prime Minister communicated with the public. Online petitions, podcasts and Blair's own YouTube postings were all part of the new thinking. They had not expected the computer-phobic Blair to respond enthusiastically, but he 'signed up to almost everything, including mad ideas which many in the office thought were crazy'.[167] Wegg-Prosser's contribution to the 13 April seminar included a paper on planning the final exit strategy, which was deliberately leaked in early September to portray Blair in an embarrassing light. Much of the communication strategy enacted was imaginative and successful. The thinking on 'politics' was less so. The key in the short term was to plan a very effective election reshuffle in early May. In the longer term, it was decided more firepower was needed to enhance Number 10's communication with the PLP and the wider party; thus was the savvy Pat McFadden, Political Secretary in the second term, brought back into the fray.

The most fraught part of the Chequers meeting concerned discussions about Blair's own future. In the vanguard of those pushing Blair to say broadly when he was going to go was Matthew Taylor. 'If people know you are going to go, it takes the wind out of the sails of your enemies, because it will not be worth them destroying the party for the sake of getting you out one year early,' he argued.[168] He told Blair directly, 'The only way for you to ensure you have a good final year is to indicate your intention of going around next summer. You should not do a further party conference.'[169] Taylor, however, was not unmindful of the risks of setting a date in public. He would speak of the 'Robson/Keegan' dilemma, referring to Bobby Robson of Newcastle United, and Kevin Keegan of Manchester City: 'They both pre-announced their departures and were blown away within a couple of months.'[170] But so far as Blair was concerned, Taylor remained convinced that naming a date was the only way to neutralise the issue and move on. Powell disagreed fundamentally. 'Jonathan was always arguing for the PM to stay on until hell froze over. He took the most anti-Gordon, pro-TB position possible.'[171] 'I think Jonathan was advising him to stay on till 2015!' said another close aide.[172] How serious Powell was is a matter of dispute. 'Jonathan was very tongue-in-cheek about it all,' said one.[173] He certainly did not want Brown to take over, and wanted them to come up with an alternative. But in his heart Powell realised that it was untenable for Blair to stay on for very much longer, and saw the risks of naming a precise date.[174] Hill also argued strongly against naming a date, on the grounds that 'it ran contrary to the way the media worked. As soon as a date was given, they would set to work to make certain he left earlier.'[175] Midway between these two extremes sat Lloyd, Turner, Benett and Wegg Prosser: 'We recognised that Matthew was more realistic,' said one, 'but basically we were sitting on the fence.'[176] Blair agreed that they had to have a plan to get them to the summer of 2007: 'He was very clear, very happy to do that.' But, and this was the core point, he wanted to keep his options open: he categorically did not accept the summer of 2007 as the time that he would definitely be leaving office. 'That decision was not taken at Chequers.'[177] Blair was always averse to naming a precise date: 'If we were in rational world, dealing with rational people, the plan would work.'[178] But 'if you say July, they will try to get you back to April, then to January,' he told them. The Chequers discussion concluded with agreement that Blair should not give a precise date on the grounds that it would not ease tensions and would limit his freedom of action.[179] 'We agreed that the end-point of our planning was to be the summer of 2007. There was a consensus that we were in the final phase of office, and by acknowledging that, it at last gave us the space to do things differently.'[180] Blair also raised openly with the group the taboo subject of his conversations with Brown, which he only very rarely shared with the team, and told them he had 'agreed a date with him which was the summer of 2007'.[181] But clearly, Blair was not going to be held to this date if he deemed he could keep going productively for longer. The ambiguity would continue.

17

Stirrings of Dissent

May–September 2006

In Number 10 they now had their secret plan for the next twelve months. What would happen after that, in May/June 2007, no one really knew. But if Blair was to be successful before then, he would have to avoid further pitfalls at home and abroad, and drive relentlessly forward on his chosen areas. Managing the party would be easier, with no more controversial votes in Parliament planned. Brown was the wild card. The 'transition group' had ridden into the sand, and Number 10 now had no hold over him. Blair had told him in private that he would go in the summer of 2007, but did Brown believe it? Crucial to Blair's success would be limiting the damage from the three third-term 'dragons': Iraq, 'cash for honours' and the succession. But in May his immediate priority was delivering a convincing performance in the local elections, and a good reshuffle.

Local Difficulties: May 2006

'We had long been aware of how dangerous the May elections were going to be,' said Matthew Taylor.[1] In the campaign run-up, Number 10 examined possible scenarios: what would they do if Labour achieved 24 per cent, 26 per cent, 28 per cent? How might Brown react if Labour achieved these results?[2] For several weeks, Gould had been predicting that the elections would be 'disastrous' and that Blair would need to demonstrate real leadership in their wake. One Blairite minister detected signs of 'panic' within Number 10 as they 'braced themselves for results much worse than occurred'.[3] Downing Street insiders insist that 'it just wasn't like that' and recall a sense of calm in the run-up to the poll.[4] But no one could deny that optimism was short on the ground as polling day approached. Claims emerged from a second woman of a further two-year affair with Prescott, alleged to have occurred twenty years before.[5] Concerns about NHS funding rumbled on in the wake of Hewitt's jeering at the RCN conference. The foreign prisoner scandal refused to subside and raised issues about the government's competence in its primary duty, protecting British citizens. On 2 May, in a speech to the shop workers' union, USDAW, Blair tried to redress the balance: 'Nine days' headlines should not obscure nine years of achievement.'[6] Election day, Thursday 4 May, saw Labour achieve 26 per cent of the projected national share of the vote, behind the Liberal Democrats on 27 per cent and the Conservatives on 40 per cent. It was Labour's worst electoral performance since Michael Foot's leadership of 1980–83, while Cameron's Conservatives achieved their best showing since 1992. But the results were not uniformly bad for Labour: the party did well in parts of the Midlands and the north, where local organisers were angry at the attempts to describe the outcome as catastrophic for Labour.[7] The overall loss of seats was lower than some had feared. An unrepentant and defiant mood took hold in Number 10 soon after the results emerged: 'So bloody what?' became a common refrain.[8]

For some months, Number 10 had seen an early 2006 reshuffle as one of Blair's last gambits. It had been postponed from January because it was too soon after the changes necessitated by Blunkett's departure in November 2005. Blair subsequently had become embroiled in negotiations over the education bill, and distracted internationally with the incapacity of Ariel Sharon and the fresh Palestinian elections, which delayed it beyond February and March. So it was penned in for early May. He yearned for it to achieve the *coup de grâce* he had been too weak to pull off just after the General Election: promotion of his own people and stamping his authority on the government at the expense of the Brownites. 'Though he'd been in office for nine years he was keen to show he still had good young and ambitious people coming through the ranks.'[9] One Number 10 aide characterised Blair's aspiration: 'I'm the PM, don't you forget it. Here is my team for the last couple of laps.'[10] Many hours were spent in Number 10 in April and early May meticulously planning it. Blair's team knew that the Prime Minister had a poor reputation as a shuffler of his pack, and so they were determined to make his final one his best. 'The planning that went into the reshuffle was quite extraordinary. All the civil servants and the Cabinet Secretary said that they'd never been involved in anything quite like it,' one aide said.[11]

So anxious was Blair to begin the reshuffle that 'people were getting phone calls on that Thursday afternoon, telling them that he wanted to see them on the Friday, even before the polls for the local elections had closed'.[12] Charles Clarke's dismissal was the most dramatic feature. Blair had been intending to replace Straw with Clarke at the Foreign Office at the 2005 General Election: but Blunkett's departure from the Home Office in December 2004 and Clarke's promotion to fill his place shattered the carefully laid plan. To move Clarke after just six months at the politically sensitive Home Office was not a realistic option.[13] Instead Blair reassured Straw that he would 'keep him on' after the General Election.[14] By the time of the May 2006 reshuffle, Clarke seemed the obvious candidate for the Foreign Office; the department had been expecting either him or John Reid to become Foreign Secretary. On 2 May, Blair reiterated in a speech at Blackpool that he had confidence in Clarke. And even as the foreign prisoner scandal began to unfold, he still favoured promoting Clarke to the Foreign Office. But the senior staff in Number 10 took a very different view and now set about changing the Prime Minister's mind: 'No one had it in for Charles, but we said that it would look very awkward politically to promote someone who was thought to have made such a mess of something.'[15] Another aide said more bluntly: 'If things are ballsed up that badly, the public expects someone to take responsibility for it. We had to overcome Blair's sense of personal loyalty.'[16] Clarke had lost the confidence of Blair's lieutenants who had now won over their boss. His position as Home Secretary had become untenable.

Blair was not, in fact, an unqualified fan of Clarke. Although he admired him personally, and needed such a loyal 'big hitter' in a senior Cabinet post, Blair had reservations about his conduct at the Home Office. 'I don't think he ever completely trusted Charles. He was too much his own man,' said a senior civil servant.[17] Clarke was not a populist in the Blunkett mould, and was instinctively more liberal than Blair, as on the Muslim question, where Blair thought him too soft.[18] Clarke assumed nevertheless that he was over the worst and had received what he thought were reliable reassurances that he would remain at the Home Office. He felt very let down by Blair's late decision to ask him to go.[19] Blair later confided to a senior Whitehall official, 'You've got to understand why I had to move Charles. If you let out a foreign national who later committed a vicious crime, it would have been very difficult.'[20] Blair also came to believe that Clarke had made a grave error in calling his first press conference on the issue without having charted a way out of the crisis.[21] As Blair felt unable to offer him the Foreign Office, a promotion, he said: 'I'm going to give you another job so you can rehabilitate yourself. I'll give you Defence.'[22] But Clarke did not like the idea of MoD, and did not consider himself in need of rehabilitation.[23] To him, the offer was a demotion. 'We said, look, if there's anything you really want to do, Tony can organise that, but he really does feel that you can't stay at the Home Office,' recalled one involved.[24] But Clarke decided to walk. He told the media that 'the Prime Minister not only has the right' to remove him, but that he also 'has the duty to make those kinds of judgements'. He did not agree, however, that he would have stood in the way of reforming the Home Office.[25]

Blair needed someone very safe, very competent and very loyal to sort out the Home Office and put the lid on a crisis that had the potential to derail Blair's remaining domestic goals. There was only one choice: John Reid. He had held seven ministerial posts since 1997. He was a resolute anti-Brownite, and not at all popular in their camp. 'It's fair to say Tony Blair thinks more highly of John Reid than Gordon Brown does,' said Nick Brown.[26] That, of course, was a recommendation. The Brownites were deeply suspicious of Reid's appointment and with some justification: if there was to be a credible challenge to Brown in 2007 it would most likely be Reid, and this promotion increased his prominence.

In contrast to Clarke's demise, Blair's decision to move Straw from the Foreign Office had been taken some months before. The main issue was that Straw had been in the post for too long. He had been granted a stay of execution in May 2005, but his conduct in the year that followed did little to endear him to Number 10. To Blair loyalists, Straw's grip on the Foreign Office weakened in the spring of 2006 when, despite being warned by his own staff that his position was precarious, he ended up on the wrong side of Blair on three arguments. Over Iran, he repeatedly insisted that military action would be inconceivable, which put him at odds with Blair's position of leaving this option on the table to exercise maximum leverage with Ahmadinejad. The hawks in the Bush administration were infuriated by Straw's dove-ish outlook. To John Bolton it appeared that Blair had turned the entire Iran portfolio over to Straw. It seemed that 'because Blair exercised so much direction and control over British foreign policy Straw was looking around for something that he could do on his own. We thought Straw being moved to a different portfolio was a clear indication of Blair finally saying, "I'm going to assert myself".'[27]

Iraq was a second source of difference, over the identity of the successor to al-Jaafari as Prime Minister. As one official wryly observed, 'Neither of them really knew what they were talking about because they knew next to nothing about the individuals concerned.'[28] Straw unwisely had a row over the telephone with Blair about it, which marked his card. A further blow to Straw's position came after the Hamas victory in the Palestinian elections in January 2006, when he was far keener than Blair to talk to the victors, which led to a further argument.[29] Despite these difficulties Straw still thought that he was secure: 'He only realised the skids were under him a few days before it happened.'[30] Unlike Clarke, Straw did not jump, and on the Friday morning accepted the post of Leader of the House of Commons (an idea Blair had first flagged up to him in May 2005), which gave him the lead on reform of the House of Lords and party funding. 'It was still a seat at the table and an important one at that,' Straw said. 'But I was cross, especially leaving behind unfinished business and losing momentum in the Middle East, Iraq and Turkey.'[31] Blair memorably told him: 'I don't think you'll miss much: I don't think there'll be much happening in the international theatre until 2007.'[32]

Many in Number 10 wanted David Miliband to be the new Foreign Secretary. Blair had already ducked out of giving the elder Miliband a bigger job in May 2005. Morgan (from the wings) and Taylor were Miliband's chief cheerleaders: Blair saw the attraction and told colleagues it was the appointment 'to renew the party'.[33] He said he needed to go away on the Wednesday night and sleep on it. To the disappointment of many in Number 10, he decided by the morning that it was too risky. 'It's odd,' said Wegg-Prosser, 'he's always been very bold in appointing members of his staff, but remarkably cautious in appointing his Cabinet.'[34] 'In the end he got cold feet. He felt he couldn't take too many risks and lacked the political capital to be bolder,' said one figure who worked on the reshuffle.[35] Miliband had only been in Cabinet for a year, and still had not run his own department. Blair thought it too big a jump.[36] Miliband did not have to wait long: Brown appointed him to the post in June 2007.

Blair's surprise choice for Foreign Secretary was the long-serving stalwart, Margaret Beckett. He thought she had performed consistently and with considerable skill on the international stage at DEFRA. He valued her loyalty, and rather liked the idea of appointing the first ever female Foreign Secretary: 'At least that's a headline, that's a statement,' said one in Number 10.[37] 'I'm perfectly happy to stay where I am, at DEFRA,' Beckett said to him when summoned to Number 10 on the Friday. Blair demurred: 'I want you to continue working on climate change but I want you do it in the Foreign Office. I want it to be one of the major strategic priorities of foreign policy,' Blair told an astonished Beckett.[38] The appointment angered some of those around him. 'To what problem that Jack Straw suffered from did Margaret Beckett provide the answer?' demanded one.[39] Straw's detractors within the Bush administration were pleased: 'I think Blair thought that she would do what he wanted, as opposed to Jack, who I think was doing a lot of what he wanted to do.'[40] Miliband was promoted to succeed her at DEFRA: initially, he was 'bristling with rage' because he had put in so much work as Communities minister and he did not want to be pulled away after just a year. Taylor, who advocated the appointment, thought Miliband would shine looking after the environment where he could take on Cameron, who had made a big play of making the Tory party more 'green'. Within two weeks, Miliband's anger and disappointment had dissipated and he was throwing himself enthusiastically into the new challenge.

Ruth Kelly needed to be moved from Education because of her lack of rapport with the PLP and the education world, and because Blair wanted someone more sympathetic in a department of such central importance to his remaining time. But she was a loyalist and highly regarded, so she was moved sideways to the Cabinet post of Communities and Local Government, a new department created out of the empire relinquished by Prescott, who continued just as Deputy Prime Minister. In her place at the DfES came the ex-union leader and media-savvy Alan Johnson, who Number 10 trusted to advance Blair's education agenda, including academies, and who was deemed to have the requisite persuasive skills.[41] Some Brownites were elevated, Douglas Alexander into the Cabinet to handle Transport and Scotland and Alistair Darling to the DTI, while Ed Balls and Ed Miliband were promoted to junior posts in the Treasury and Cabinet Office respectively after only one year as MPs. 'He never wanted to shut Gordon's people out,' insisted one loyalist.[42] Pat McFadden was promoted to Minister for Social Exclusion: 'Pat was one of Tony's people and so that was the deal,' said one colleague. 'You were getting Balls, but also McFadden.'[43] Blair warded off pressure from elements within Number 10 who wanted him to clear out some of the dead wood and Brownites from Cabinet, including Hain and McCartney. Doing so would create more disruption than leaving them in post, he felt. To the end, he was never a happy wielder of the knife.

Cameron criticised the reshuffle for the oscillation over Clarke, while Liberal Democrat leader Menzies Campbell said 'no amount of cosmetic surgery can disguise the fact that this government has suffered a permanent loss of credibility'.[44] These comments were predictable. More damaging was the turbulence from the Brown camp and the Labour Party. More puzzling was the criticism from within Blair's own court. There was grumbling that he had not promoted enough Blairites and had been insufficiently bold: 'Geoff Hoon and Ian McCartney both talked themselves back into better positions,' complained one aide.[45] 'The reshuffle was disastrous. Even our own people couldn't understand what on earth he was doing,' said one close supporter.[46] Antagonism focused on the sacking of Clarke but not Prescott, promoting Beckett but not Miliband, promoting some Brownites and not sacking others. 'It looked like a desperate act' admitted one Blair aide, 'and seemed to legitimise the view that the May local elections were very bad indeed.' Some thought Blair should have delayed the reshuffle until he was in a stronger position. 'The reshuffle was his last bolt: once he shot it, he had nothing left,' said one.[47] The disaffected knew that his powers of patronage were now spent: he had no hold left over them. 'If he had held the reshuffle after the party conference, he would have retained that authority,' said one Blairite.[48] As for Cabinet, they 'would have as much of an eye on Gordon as they would on Tony', making for a tumultuous final year.[49] It was ironic that Number 10 and Blair were now at their wisest, and had learned much from their early mistakes. He may have been a powerful figure on the world stage, yet he lacked the authority to manage a successful reshuffle. The Brownites noted the critical undercurrents in the Blair camp. They seized their opportunity.

The Second Coup: May 2006

'Gordon could have killed Tony on Friday. But he didn't,' said a Number 10 aide.[50] They knew that Blair would suffer an assault: 'We'd had a lot of indications that there was an operation being put in place,' said Hilary Armstrong.[51] Only its ferocity and manner were unknown. Number 10 also knew of divisions within the Brown camp. The cautious wing, which included Sue Nye and Ed Miliband, emphasised the need for a stable transition and no spilling of blood. The other camp – driven, they believed, by Ed Balls and Nick Brown – was more aggressive, and no longer believed anything Blair said. This wing thought that, without pressure, Blair would merely go on and on. Brown moved between both camps, buffeted by events, powerful voices and his bipolar swings between caution and the desire to strike out.

Number 10 believed that Andrew Smith, the deposed Work and Pensions Secretary, had now emerged as another driving force.[52] 'The Prime Minister has promised an orderly transition and I believe we need to see the timetable for that sooner rather than later . . . We cannot get on with that process of rebuilding while the leadership issue is in the air,' he told the *Guardian* the day after the local elections.[53] News filtered into Number 10 of a grid of Brownite sympathisers lined up to go on the media and declare that, at the very least, the bad results indicated that Blair needed to set a precise date for the handover. They believed Ed Balls was pulling the strings, assisted by fellow MPs Nick Brown and Doug Henderson, as well as Brown's staff including Spencer Livermore and Damian McBride.[54] 'No doubt about it. It was a co-ordinated coup,' said one Blair aide.[55] But was Brown directly involved? Patricia Hewitt is one of several who thought not. 'The coup the day after the local elections was not orchestrated by Gordon, but by people around him.'[56] Other Blairites thought differently. What a coup did need, if it was to be successful, was for Brown to give a clear lead to his followers that the hour had come. That hour, his backers planned, was to be 8 A.M. on Friday 5 May, when Brown was scheduled to give an interview on the Radio 4's *Today* programme. Blair had wrongfully plucked the crown from him after John Smith's death; here was his opportunity finally to pull the trigger and claim what was rightfully his. In front of the *Today* microphone, at 8:10 A.M., he said, 'We have got to renew ourselves . . . it must start now,' and he described the events of the last two weeks as a 'warning shot for the government'.[57] In these critical minutes, he had the power to fire the shot that would have finished off a wounded Prime Minister, albeit messily. He pulled back. He could not find the words. Just over forty years before, another challenger for the premiership following the resignation of Harold Macmillan, the Conservative Rab Butler, had made a similar decision after being goaded by his own ultra, Enoch Powell: 'We said, "You see, Rab, look at this. This is a revolver. We've loaded it for you . . . Here is the trigger." Rab said, "But will it hurt him, will he bleed? Will it go off with a bang?" We said, "Yes." Then he said, "Well, thank you very much, I don't think I will. Do you mind?"'[58]

Number 10 learned of Brown's inner circle going 'completely mad' with him for pulling back from the *coup de grâce*, and for not sticking to the script which they thought they had agreed with him to call in the strongest terms for an urgent transition.[59] 'You bottled it!' Ed Balls reportedly screamed at Brown.[60] Balls' increasingly assertive role struck some as echoing the 1964 film *The Servant*, directed by Joseph Losey and scripted by Harold Pinter, in which the butler, played by Dirk Bogarde, progressively takes over as the dominant force from the owner of the house, James Fox.[61] Number 10 agreed that Brown had indeed missed his opportunity. 'Had Gordon talked about Margaret Thatcher staying on too long on the *Today* programme, it could have been fatal.'[62] They felt that their initial suspicions of a plot were confirmed when a string of pro-Brown supporters went on the airwaves and discussed how bad the local election results were and the need for a transition. Neither Number 10 nor Party HQ had been notified about their plans. 'No minister would have done that without telling the Downing Street press office,' said one Number 10 source rather missing the point that the individuals concerned were backbench MPs, not ministers, and thus not accustomed to working through the press office.[63] Brown denied utterly any involvement with the machinations, if such they were, and still does.[64]

The pressure did not let up on that Friday. A damning statement was released by the think-tank Compass run by Neal Lawson (a former special adviser to Gordon Brown), which had earlier published the Benn/Millar attack on the Education Bill. The statement said: 'Paralysis and confusion at the top of the party are the direct consequence of the announcement by Tony Blair that he would be standing down . . . [He] must tell the party exactly when he intends to stand down within a timetable that enables his successor to take on the task of rebuilding the party.'[65] Lawson went further: 'What we need is a change of direction, and if a new leader is elected at the last minute like Tony Blair wants, there won't be time to change the party's direction.'[66] Number 10 was not surprised by his comments, given his track record. But Lawson categorically denies that Compass ever circulated a letter for Labour MPs to sign calling for Blair to resign, a far more serious step.[67] There was, however, clear evidence of a letter going around collecting signatures and just seventy could have triggered a direct leadership challenge.[68] 'I hadn't seen this letter going round, and would not have encouraged it,' said Nick Brown. 'It was written by over-eager youngsters.'[69] The militant wing in Brown's camp now saw their next opportunity coming that Sunday, when their bashful champion was to record a television interview with Andrew Marr on the BBC's *Sunday A.M.* Brown was now in more pugilistic mood, and called repeatedly for a 'stable and orderly transition' and the avoidance of 'the mistake of previous parties' who failed to achieve this objective.[70] But the moment had passed. 'He tried to kill Tony on Sunday. He had lost his chance,' said one Number 10 source.[71]

The party was seething with speculation when, on Monday 8 May, Blair went before a meeting of the PLP. That morning, Blair had met his team in the den and decided that the pressure dictated he would have to make a concession to his critics. Something would have to give. The mood in the party meeting was febrile, with pockets of poison. Speaker after speaker stated that the party was losing support in the country because of the lack of a clear timetable for the transition, and that the uncertainty was damaging the party. Some of Blair's closest supporters in the PLP had no forewarning about what he would say, which was that he would leave his successor 'ample time' before the next election. It was the tensest moment in the meeting. 'You could have heard a pin drop,' recalled Nick Brown.[72] But Blair went no further on his departure plans. One Blair supporter turned to John McTernan and said quietly, 'Does that mean next year?' to which he replied, 'Yes.'[73] Number 10 believed Blair had said enough to carry the party's middle ground, which Ruth Turner estimated constituted some 70–80 per cent who were neither solidly pro-Blair nor pro-Brown. 'He came out of the meeting stronger than he went in, but it was still a very difficult period,' said Hilary Armstrong.[74] Nick Brown wasn't alone in thinking Blair's words 'ample time' were insufficient. 'He didn't carry the audience with him.'[75] John Reid, on the other side, thought Blair had said too much.[76]

Gordon Brown was to have one last foray on to the airwaves, with even less impact. Speaking on GMTV on Tuesday 9 May, he said, 'Tony said he was going to be doing it in a stable and orderly way. That means that he is going to be talking not just to me but to senior colleagues about it.' He then deployed the historical analogy his associates had wanted him to make earlier: 'Remember when Mrs Thatcher left. It was unstable. It was disorderly and it was undignified.'[77] Brown's comments went down badly in Number 10. Blair was reported to have seen them as 'a naked threat to remove him from office'.[78] The time had come to fight back in public. The press was briefed that Brown's camp had been told that 'if Tony was deposed, he and his supporters would not support Gordon as the next leader'.[79] Reports began to circulate that the newly promoted Reid would be Number 10's favoured candidate. Without Blair's blessing, one insider told the press, 'it would make it harder for Mr Brown to win votes in middle Britain'.[80] Number 10 deliberately played on Brown's fears of losing the premiership, or inheriting a bloody crown. The Brown camp chose to conserve its ammunition. Number 10's warning shot had made the point. The second attempted coup petered out. Anger within the PLP subsided. But it would not be many months before the large 'middle ground' was again to be inflamed, despite the ardent hopes of many in Number 10 to avoid this eventuality. 'There was a lot of uncertainty and insecurity,' admitted one Blair aide.[81] The next coup, which they were sure would come, might well prove deadly for Blair. At Number 10, the order of the day was to forge ahead on policy expeditiously while time remained.

Forging Ahead – Home Office, Energy, Climate Change: May–August 2006

Blair needed to reassert his authority. Within a week of the May furore, he had sent a letter to every Cabinet minister laying out what he wanted from them. To Hewitt, for example, he wrote: 'We must continue the pace of reform by improving the choices that patients have within the NHS . . . We must continue to expand the effect of choice and payment by results.'[82] On 15 May, along with Hazel Blears, McCartney's successor as party chairman, he launched 'Let's Talk: A Policy Discussion Forum', akin to the 'Big Conversation' prior to the 2005 General Election. There was no time to lose. Education reform was well on its way by now, with policy fixed by the passage of the Education and Inspections Bill, and with a headlong rush to reach the tipping point on academies before Blair left office. Health was being driven hard by Hewitt, though she struggled against financial deficits and resistance from staff within the NHS. Blair took a very close interest, holding monthly stock-takes and talking to her frequently. The second-term health reforms were slowly yielding results, and again it was a battle against time to embed change so a future government would be unlikely to shift direction. These months saw important progress on energy, climate change and pensions. The quality of Blair's new team in Number 10, which he himself considered the strongest of his tenure, and its focus on strategic goals within the limited timetable, began to yield dividends. In policy terms, the months after May 2006 were to be the most fruitful of his premiership.

To one topic, Blair gave more attention than any other: law and order. Both Reid and Blair's special adviser, Kieran Brett, were at one with him in their political instincts. This combination of believers in key positions provided the same opportunity to drive significant change as it had at education and health in the second term. In his letter to Reid, Blair made his priorities abundantly clear, stressing that he wanted to see the criminal justice system rebalanced in favour of the law-abiding majority. Inheriting a Home Office in the midst of a crisis of public confidence, Reid vowed: 'I'll fucking well work eighteen hours a day to sort this out.'[83] Time was short, and he knew it, to complete as much of Blair's agenda as was possible and to fulfil his own ambitions. He was seen as a potential Prime Minister and yet had been unable to establish much of a personal record in his previous departments. So he was bursting with adrenalin when he arrived at the Home Office on 5 May. During his first fortnight Reid, together with Brett, dived into writing reviews of key Home Office activities (especially the criminal and immigration Systems) that would guide Reid's efforts at reform. 'The negotiations were at times long and gruelling' recalled Brett. 'We spent a very long weekend hammering out the detail.'[84] Blair had been deeply involved in this process, with drafts of the reviews placed in his Friday boxes. He was delighted with the final package, saying that at last he had the framework he had been seeking. Reid's next move proved particularly controversial. On 23 May he went before the Home Affairs Select Committee of the Commons and declared famously that the Home Office's Immigration and Nationality Directorate (IND) was 'not fit for purpose' and suffering from 'inadequate' management structures.[85] He was arguing that the IND needed to adapt rapidly to cope with its new pressures: but what he was taken to be saying was that the Home Office as a whole was 'not fit for purpose'. Reid's predecessors were infuriated at his remark, as were current and retired officials in the Home Office. It caused widespread unfavourable comment and was seen in some quarters as Reid 'protecting his own back', or worse.[86] Clarke's retort was swift: 'It was wrong to describe the Home Office as not fit for purpose. It's not true. Many aspects of it are good and getting better.'[87] Reid forged ahead regardless, leading to an incredibly intense period of activity. During the first three months of his tenure he pushed through the IND transformation plan, the criminal justice system review, which sought to 'rebalance' the criminal justice system as Blair wanted, and the Home Office transformation plan. Before long, even sceptics were applauding Reid's sense of purpose. Blair seemed to have found his ideal Home Secretary, combining the loyalty of (first-term) Straw, the authoritarian zeal of Blunkett and the proficiency of Clarke.

Organised crime, the drugs trade, money laundering and 'people smuggling' had all proved difficult to tackle, and were unfinished business left over from the second term. On 1 April 2006 the government pushed ahead with the establishment of the Serious

Organised Crime Agency (SOCA). Seen as a 'British FBI', it was formed by the merger of the National Crime Squad, the National Criminal Intelligence Service and the National High-Tech Criminal Unit, and was the fruit of Birt, Heywood and Turnbull.[88] 'We had to keep pace with the rapid way organised crime was developing,' said crime special adviser Justin Russell. 'SOCA was our response.'[89] Stephen Lander, formerly Director-General of MI5 and deeply versed in the sophisticated way organised crime operated, was brought in to head it up. Blair was intensely interested in the subject, almost boyishly so. 'Let's deal with the most important hardened criminals,' he said, imagining that they totalled some 500 in Britain. He was surprised when Lander told him the number of serious criminals in Britain was closer to 10,000.[90] He valued Blair's backing, but he did not appreciate the 'back-room boys' from Number 10 who he felt were trying to interfere to no good end. In the summer of 2005, two members of the strategy unit visited him saying they were disappointed that nothing was yet happening. Lander told them to get out of the room.[91] Sensing the difficult relationship Number 10's Kieran Brett subsequently worked with Lander to repair relations and persuade the strategy unit to step back and give SOCA more space to develop.[92]

Plans to reform the police at large, however, stalled. After 1997, Straw had not wanted to move in this area, while Blunkett arrived in 2001 in macho style, wanting to bring in 'an American cop' to 'sort out' the British police. He wanted pay reformed and local accountability enhanced. He held a jaundiced view of police chiefs, falling out with Met Commissioner John Stevens over street crime. But Blair had considerable respect for the police, admired Stevens personally, and wanted at all costs to avoid a row. Blunkett's plans were vetoed.[93] Clarke's interest was in reducing the number of police forces from forty-three down to twenty-four and was deep in negotiations about mergers when his tenure ended. Blair showed some interest in whether the ideas driving public sector reform could be imported into the police reform agenda. He was clear that the practices of the highest performing forces needed to be replicated across all other forces. For a while he was persuaded that mergers might provide the vehicle for further improvement, but the level of opposition changed his mind.[94] Two months after Clarke's departure, he announced in the House of Commons on 12 July that merger plans were in effect being shelved.[95] For all his effort on crime, Blair was not to be a reforming Prime Minister when it came to the police.

Blair and Reid had more success on immigration. The issue had moved up the agenda towards the end of the second term, especially after the ten accession countries joined the EU in 2004. In a personal decision, celebrated by some, condemned by others, Blair decreed that Britain would be the only other EU country, along with Ireland, to allow citizens from all the new countries to enter and work.[96] While eager for Britain to be an open society, Blair realised that high levels of immigration would need to be handled delicately with the public, particularly in the wake of the foreign prisoners furore and concerns over asylum abuses. To allay fears he unveiled his plan at the party conference in 2004: 'We will introduce identity cards and electronic registration to all who cross our borders. We have cut radically the number of failed asylum-seekers. By the end of 2005, and for the first time in Britain, we will remove more each month than apply, and so restore faith in a system that we know has been abused.'[97] The tipping point on asylum-seekers, heralded in early 2006, was finally reached in May.[98] Identity cards endured a rocky parliamentary passage and divided opinion inside Cabinet, but eventually received Royal Assent in March 2006, paving the way for their introduction in 2009.

Public fears about immigration were heightened when, on 9 August, twenty-four British citizens were arrested for involvement in the biggest alleged terror plot ever planned in the United Kingdom. Of the suspects seized in Walthamstow, High Wycombe and Birmingham many were middle-class and three were enlisted at London universities. After 7/7 and 21/7, surveillance operations had begun to look for 'concentric' individuals affiliated to those involved in these operations. By September 2005, warrants had been obtained to install bugging devices in the homes of suspects.[99] By early 2006, MI5 believed that terrorists in east London and Birmingham were planning to smuggle explosive charges onto aircraft concealed in clothing or in passenger items including shampoo and medicine bottles. On the morning of 9 August, Reid delivered a speech in London saying that Britain now faced its most sustained threat from terrorism, warning that security forces would be unable to guarantee the public 100 per cent protection, especially as a new breed of 'unconstrained' terrorists had access to chemical and biological weapons.[100] While he was giving his speech, police were making final plans for major arrests that evening. They had their sights set on several individuals they suspected were planning to smuggle home-made bombs on board as many as nine airliners, to be detonated either over the Atlantic or above American cities, potentially killing 3,000 or more people.[101] Although large numbers had their holiday flights disrupted, a potentially catastrophic plot had been foiled and Reid maintained public confidence in the government's efforts to keep one step ahead of the terrorists. Some twenty plots were indeed pre-empted by the intelligence services and Special Branch during Blair's premiership: 7/7 was the only occasion when al-Qaeda-inspired terrorists penetrated the protective framework of the British state. In the face of Armageddon fears, especially in the wake of 9/11, Blair had played a significant role not only in reassuring the public but in protecting them against the terrorists. Had any other of those attempts succeeded, many of Blair's decisions – particularly over going to war in Iraq – would have come even more closely under the spotlight, with hugely destabilising consequences for him.

Energy was not an issue that had brought Blair into politics, nor one that he had engaged with until the second term, with the exception of the fuel protest in 2000. When sitting on the terrace at Number 10 in late August 2002, contemplating his speech for the Johannesburg summit, he threw out, 'Why can't we just come out and say we're in favour of nuclear energy?' 'Please don't say that,' his aides said.[102] In Cabinet, Beckett above all, but also Prescott and Hewitt, were highly sceptical of retaining nuclear power, and discussions leading up to the 2003 energy White Paper saw his nascent enthusiasm dampened. 'Our Energy Future', published during the Iraq war, found nuclear power an unattractive option and did not include proposals for building new nuclear power stations. Blair's mind was elsewhere and he had neither time nor inclination to campaign on a cause about which he had yet to be fully convinced.[103] But over the following two years, the need to replace Britain's ageing nuclear power stations, and concerns about the supply of energy from the Middle East and Russia caused him to rethink. He began to see nuclear power as a 'green' way to produce energy: 'When the Tories started picking up on environment, climate change became even higher-profile and we linked it more explicitly into the energy stuff,' recalled one close aide.[104] Blair had already formed a high opinion of chief scientific adviser David King, a long-term enthusiast for nuclear energy: 'He was influential in shaping all our thinking,' said one minister.[105] He provided Blair with reading on the subject before and after the 2005 General Election, which further helped to sway his thinking.[106] King found Blair one of those 'non-specialists who were intrigued by science'. In an earlier meeting in early February 2002, Blair asked him: 'What is fusion?' He was given a forty-minute seminar on the science of the fusion process. 'He was like a barrister, soaking it up, giving 100 per cent attention to it. At the end, he spun back the entire story of fusion for fifteen minutes and had it spot-on.'[107]

By the time he appointed David Bennett as his head of policy following the May 2005 General Election, Blair was already converted to nuclear energy. 'When offering me the job, he was talking about how we should replace our nuclear power stations, recognising that there may be no realistic alternative to building a new generation of nuclear stations.'[108] Blair went public with his enthusiasm for nuclear power at his party conference speech at the end of September, and again when he addressed the CBI that November. Greenpeace protesters responded by climbing up on to the roof of the Business Design Centre in Islington where he was speaking and unfurled anti-nuclear banners. When he was able to proceed, he announced the establishment of a review on the 2003 White Paper's goals and was open about his own enthusiasm. He promised a decision by early summer 2006 on whether Britain would build a new generation of nuclear power plants.[109] During the autumn of 2005, he became motivated by the debate on energy sources internationally. 'This debate is happening in France and Spain, why not here?' he would demand.[110] Despite the opposition of Greenpeace, he became convinced that he was in step with both public and Labour Party opinion. He thought the protest lobby were frankly out of date.

In May 2005, Brown had also come out in support of a new generation of nuclear power stations, though in private he said that the public still had to be convinced about the costs and benefits of the nuclear option.[111] Blair gave a second speech to the CBI on 16 May 2006. The importance of meeting carbon emission targets weighed heavily with him, and he was convinced that without a new generation of nuclear power plants, albeit combined with significant investment in renewables and energy efficiency, this would not happen. After the speech was written, he made a late insert advocating the need for a new generation of power stations: 'It was deliberate. If you look at the speech, the passage doesn't fit into the rest of it, but it became the headline, as he knew it would,' said Philip Collins.[112] 'Blair presses the nuclear button. New generation of atomic stations endorsed by Prime Minister,' said the *Guardian*.[113] 'I'll be totally honest with you. I've changed my mind,' Blair admitted to the Commons on 4 July, describing how his thinking had evolved since the 2003 White Paper.[114] These comments came only the week before the review was due to be published and his zealous advocacy was arousing widespread concern. 'As with most reviews, the Prime Minister knew what outcome he wanted from it,' observed an official.[115] The result was that the relevant department, the DTI, was not in the lead. 'Number 10 were running it because I think bluntly they didn't trust the DTI to come up with what they wanted.'[116] When Darling took over at the DTI in the May reshuffle, he recognised this reality and intervened to ensure DTI ministers retained leadership of the review. But the perception of Number 10's dominance endured.[117]

No one was therefore surprised when the energy report, published on 11 July, declared enthusiastically that 'new nuclear power stations would make a significant contribution to meeting our energy policy goals'.[118] Blair had secured the outcome he wanted, and had even brought round sceptics in Cabinet, above all Beckett.

Blair's commitment to tackling climate change received a double boost from the May 2006 reshuffle: Miliband proved a capable and tenacious champion of the climate change agenda domestically, while in Margaret Beckett at the Foreign Office, Blair had an experienced champion on the environment willing to do battle on the issue abroad. 'I gave it as much time as I could. To me it was a top strategic priority,' she said.[119] According to Justin Forsyth, 'This period became one of the most radical periods on climate change under Labour.'[120] At home, the Climate Bill was developed and Blair intensified efforts to galvanise business to lead the fight against climate change, such as the 'Together' campaign, involving Tesco, Marks & Spencer and other big companies. In Europe the government championed a tougher European Emission Trading scheme, and ambitious new EU targets to reduce emissions.

Blair redoubled his efforts at the global level in his final year to ensure that climate change was kept firmly on the agenda. He had included Australia in the G8 +5 conference at Lancaster House in November 2005 deliberately: their involvement was an important step in Prime Minister Howard's announcement that he would establish a carbon trading scheme to cut pollution.[121] It was a dramatic U-turn for a country which, like the US, had refused to ratify Kyoto on grounds of economic interest. Blair saw the G8 +5 as the ideal vehicle for taking forward his commitment on climate change, not least because, as Michael Jay observed, 'He knew he would be far more likely to get traction with Bush in a G8 forum than in the UN.'[122] So it had proved at the UN climate change conference in Montréal in December 2005. When the American delegation threatened to walk out in the midst of negotiations on the post-Kyoto framework, Blair called Bush in the White House. The following morning, the Americans were back negotiating again. Blair had convinced Bush that the agreement they were being asked to sign was exactly the same wording as they had agreed at Gleneagles. The Americans were forced to see the logic and they duly signed.[123] Blair's lobbying of Bush proved a significant factor in the administration softening its opposition to accepting the reality of climate change, though it was only one factor among several. Growing awareness in the US of the melting of the polar icecaps, publicity about the damage to coastal areas from rising sea-levels, hurricane Katrina, and reluctance to rely on Putin and Ahmadinejad for energy, all made their impact on Washington. As one British official pointed out, 'These hard realities had more influence than tree-hugging. Tree-hugging doesn't go down well with Republicans.'[124] Pressure from a growing number of governors, above all Arnold Schwarzenegger in California, and increasingly from a business community way ahead of Bush on climate change, further pressured the administration.[125]

The G8's commitment to tackling climate change lost some impetus during the Russian presidency in July 2006: it was an issue Putin showed little enthusiasm for. Progress came, however, at the Monterrey summit in Mexico in early October, a meeting spawned at Lancaster House eleven months before. Brown's deep interest in climate change became clear during the course of 2006, as his premiership loomed. King was invited in to see him several times: 'He was very different from Blair. It was more like talking to an academic. He was fully engaged; he challenged, disagreed and was not just trying to absorb a brief.'[126] The Stern Review, published in October, was unequivocal. 'The scientific evidence is now overwhelming: climate change is a serious global threat, and it demands an urgent global response . . . The benefits of strong and early action far outweigh the economic costs of not acting.'[127] Blair had chosen the right issue to champion.

Punch-up on Pensions: March–May

Blair's push on law and order, energy and climate change, occurred more or less with Brown's support. The story on pension reform was very different, and had already provoked the worst domestic policy clash of Blair's third term. Since the publication of the Turner Commission in November 2005, Brown had begun to question the wisdom of his critical position. At a brief chance encounter with Turner in the New Year; it became clear to Turner that Brown wanted to find a way out of the cul-de-sac in which he had placed himself.[128] Brown seemed increasingly isolated, even among his supporters. Turner, for instance, received letters from a number of Brown's camp saying 'this is a great report'.[129] Brown had to adopt a different stance or face the inevitable. The question was, would Blair meet him halfway on a compromise or would he opt for a purist Turner approach, above all over the latter's call for the restoration of the earnings link to pensions?

Frantic work took place in December 2005 and the first two months of 2006 in a working group, comprising officials from the Treasury, DWP and Number 10, exploring how the government might respond to Turner.[130] DWP Secretary Hutton had been planning to present the conclusions of the trilateral commission to Blair and Brown on 15 March. But out of the blue came a new twist to the long-running saga. On 13 March, Brown produced an alternative state pensions plan whistled up by the Treasury, which he wanted to announce in the Budget on 22 March. 'Gordon was very determined indeed to settle the state pension parts of the pension reform in his Budget,' said one aide.[131] Number 10 aides examined the Treasury's proposal, which included a guaranteed increase above inflation in the basic state pension between 2010 and 2020, and a limitation in the growth of pensions subject to means testing, but concluded it did not go nearly far enough to meet Turner's proposals. Above all it omitted the restoration of the earnings link to the basic state pension. Nor was the Treasury plan seen as acceptable to Turner and his colleagues on the pension commission. The atmosphere at the meeting on 15 March in Blair's study was thus tense and unpleasant, and concluded with Blair telling Brown, 'Go away and try and sort this out and come back to me.'[132] As a final gambit, Brown invited Turner and the members of his commission to the Treasury to allow Brown to explain why his own proposals were superior. Having studied them, Turner wrote back to Brown begging to differ.

With the Budget almost upon them, Hutton worked desperately to find a way forward that would be acceptable to Brown. Ever since his appointment as Pensions Secretary, Hutton had found himself under considerable pressure to ally with the Treasury view, so they could work together and isolate Blair in a pincer operation. Hutton declined the overtures even if it meant damaging his further career prospects in a Brown government (Brown in fact anointed him Business minister in his first Cabinet). 'I'm afraid, Gordon, that I support Turner's view,' he told him from early on after he succeeded Blunkett.[133] In a series of private meetings, Brown tried telling him that Turner had produced a 'mad policy' that the country could not afford, and that it was plainly irresponsible of him to be recommending to the Prime Minister that he should accept Turner. At one of their meetings in Brown's room in the Treasury, Hutton produced figures, which his private office at the DWP had cleared with the Treasury, showing that Turner's policy could be affordable. According to one witness, Brown responded, 'No, these figures aren't right. I don't accept any of these figures.' 'But Gordon, they've been agreed by your officials.' 'No, they haven't!' he shouted, before turning his back on Hutton and marching off into the private office where he screamed, 'What the hell's all this about? Who's agreed these figures? I haven't seen these figures. I didn't know anything about this.'[134] They met again soon after. Hutton kept saying, 'Gordon, it's affordable, it's affordable,' recalled one official. 'Brown's metronome response was "No, it isn't, no it isn't, no it isn't. I do the money. I'm the Treasury minister. If I say it's not affordable, it is not affordable".'[135]

On Friday 17 March, with five days to the Budget, a crisis meeting was held in Blair's office to resolve the impasse. Blair and Brown had an unminuted pre-meeting alone for an hour, described as 'pretty fruity', before they were joined by McPherson and Livermore from the Treasury, Hutton, and Number 10's Gareth Davies. With none of the newcomers certain exactly what Blair and Brown had agreed, compounded by the lack of clarity of both principals themselves, the meeting was less than satisfactory. Blair was adamant that both Turner's and the DWP's analysis showed that the Treasury proposals 'didn't stack up in terms of the analytical'.[136] He was becoming increasingly assertive, and told Brown straight that he could not use the Budget to present the government's reaction to Turner. His preference all along had been for a cross-party consensus, and he insisted the government's response appear in a White Paper.[137] Over the weekend there were 'strongly worded' phone calls between Blair and Brown, with the former insisting repeatedly, 'We do this as a package, not as part of the Budget.' By the end of the weekend, Brown had conceded on the Budget.[138] When he delivered it on Wednesday 22 March, he merely said the government welcomed the broad framework of the Turner report, that affordability would be central, and that a consultation was in train leading up to the White Paper in the spring.

On Tuesday 4 April the final version of Turner's report was published. The day began with provocative media reports that Blair was ready to over-rule Brown on pensions should he prove intransigent. With no warning to Number 10, Brown appeared on television to give his response to Turner's efforts. He told Sky News that the report was 'very much in the spirit of New Labour, in encouraging people to save as much as they can', and to the BBC he said, 'The issue which is still to be resolved – affordability – is one on which Tony Blair and I are absolutely at one.' He went on, 'I think we are actually 90–95 per cent of the way there with Turner,' and that he saw 'no issue of principle about the pension being linked to earnings'.[139] Aides in Number 10 clustered dumbfounded around the television. 'What does he mean?' they asked. 'Is this just positioning?' 'What on earth is going on?' No one was certain. 'It was all completely out of left-field for us,' said one.[140] Some speculated that this was a gallant effort to 'paper over the cracks at the top of the government' before the launch of Labour's local election campaign the following day.[141] They knew Brown agreed with much in Turner's report. He liked the extension of credit for women so more received the full pension, and he was strongly in favour of the new private pension plan, with incentives to save and shifting responsibility between the state and individual.[142] Turner was at a party on the evening of 4 April and was in 'joyful mood', thinking that his commission's view had triumphed. 'We've won,' he was saying. 'Nothing's done until it's done. Let's just wait and see how things end up,' one present warned him.[143] But the press read Brown's television comments in the same way as Turner. The *Guardian* spoke of him making 'a climb-down . . . despite previously calling [Turner] unaffordable',[144] while the *Daily Telegraph* spoke about Brown 'abandoning his insistence on means testing extra financial help for pensioners'.[145]

The problem now became the remaining 5–10 per cent of disagreements between Blair and Brown which, contrary to what Brown tole the BBC, included the vital issue in contention with Number 10 all the way through, restoring the earnings link to pensions. During conversations between Blair and Brown throughout the rest of April, often conducted by phone on Sundays, the dispute dragged on.[146] Officials continued with discussions, but as one complained: 'We were not ourselves able really to resolve anything. It all came down to the two key players and what they were going to do.'[147] Concerns were expressed in Number 10 about letting Blair, famous for his lack of grasp on detail, alone for so much with the wily Brown, whose command of minutiae was renowned.[148] Before long, however, they would be joking that Blair 'had a career as a pensions analyst in the offing after he left Number 10'.[149] Blair as policy wonk was certainly Blair under new guise, but he relished the part, regularly going head to head with Brown on technical details.

The White Paper was scheduled for publication in May. On 22 April, a meeting between Number 10, the Treasury and DWP was arranged to thrash out a final agreement. Brown said instead that he wanted to talk to Blair alone. Their meeting was not a success: 'Absolutely no progress: nowhere closer to reaching agreement.'[150] The earnings link remained the sticking point. In early May, in a meeting in the garden at Number 10, Cabinet Secretary O'Donnell weighed in on the Treasury's side against Blair and Hutton, arguing that the link should not be restored now, but be phased in over fifteen years. Hutton said to Blair: 'Tony, the politics of that are disastrous for all of us. All the other parties are going to accept the earnings link, and with Labour saying that we can only do it in fifteen years' time, it would put us in a laughable position,' said one present.[151] Blair and Hutton still could not sway the Treasury. A further attempt at a trilateral meeting was scheduled for 4 May. Yet again, John Hutton and his DWP found themselves excluded, with Blair and Brown again talking on their own for two hours. Blair yielded on one sticking point, his opposition to having a compulsory pension contribution from employers, on which Hutton had worked hard to convince him.[152] But still no agreement on the earnings link was forthcoming.

On Thursday 11 May, matters finally came to a head. With the White Paper already overdue at the printers, Blair and Brown met for two hours before Cabinet to go over the proposals line by line. After Cabinet, they met again while advisers and officials met simultaneously in Number 10. The Prime Minister and Chancellor met for a third time that afternoon for a further hour. Only on the phone at 7:30 P.M., when Blair was up in the flat, and with both men exhausted, did they agree the final text.[153] The key page was immediately sent electronically to the DWP, the Treasury and around Number 10, which included the operative sentence, 'Our objectives subject to affordability of the fiscal position will restore the earnings link by 2012 or by the end of the Parliament at the very latest.' The date '2012' was a compromise put forward by Hutton. The text at last was signed off at the printers. All was harmony on 25 May for the paper's launch, at a breakfast meeting in the pillared room at Number 10, presented jointly by Blair, Brown and Hutton. 'That's the extraordinary thing,' said one official, 'even when they plumbed the worst depths, at some level Blair and Brown still retained this capacity to do business and come up with a reasonably sane conclusion.'[154]

It was Blair's biggest victory over Brown in the ten years, which explains why he fought so tenaciously during the discussions. The Treasury did win important concessions, not least making the package more affordable than Turner had suggested. But Blair prevailed on the main argument. In the last analysis Brown yielded because he did not want to be seen to be blocking reform, even though he remained unhappy with the economics. Blair's doggedness against Brown made an impression: 'If this is the right thing to do, we're going to do it,' he repeatedly said.[155] It made Blair wish that he had stood up more often against Brown on other issues earlier. It made Brown wish he had done more earlier to see Blair finished.

War in Lebanon – Blair's Fatal Misjudgement: July–August

In January 2006, two events occurred which shook Blair's thinking on the Middle East as well as his delicately poised premiership. On 4 January, Israeli Prime Minister Ariel Sharon suffered a devastating stroke. Just over two weeks before, on 18 December, he had suffered a minor stroke, but within the same news cycle he had recovered consciousness and was rapidly working the phones to Israeli journalists to convince them he was still in command. But 4 January was different. While the world's press corps staked themselves outside his hospital in Jerusalem waiting for news, Dov Weissglass phoned the British Ambassador to Israel, Simon McDonald. He had stark news: 'It's over. His heart beats like an eighteen-year-old boy, but he has no brain.'[156] While Israel mourned the man they considered their father and protector, Blair sensed an opportunity. Sharon, aged seventy-seven, had led Israel into disengagement from the Gaza Strip and parts of the West Bank but he would go no further on the road to peace. As with the death of Arafat a year and a half before, Sharon's incapacity offered the opportunity for new thinking.[157] His likely successor was deemed to be his colleague in the Kadima party, Ehud Olmert, who Blair and other senior British figures had been cultivating for some time. Learning from the experience of his dabbling in the Israeli election of December 2002, the decision was taken to stay completely clear and offer no comment.[158] When Olmert's subsequent election victory was declared on 28 March, Blair, from New Zealand, made a feature of being the first international leader to congratulate him. The new Israeli Prime Minister took the call just before giving his acceptance speech at Jerusalem's Western Wall, and referred to it in his words.[159] After a quiet year on the Middle East in 2005, when his focus was on Africa and climate change, Blair had high hopes now of making real progress. As in Northern Ireland, he hoped that as long as 'he worked hard enough, thought broadly enough, talked long enough and was sufficiently inclusive', he could in his last few months help advance that decisive change in the Middle East which had eluded him so far.

On 25 January came the long-awaited Palestinian elections, the second event that month to change Blair's thinking. Since Arafat's death, the Bush administration had courted Mahmoud Abbas of the Fatah party, including inviting him to the White House in May 2005. The British warned the administration that they were 'hugging Abbas too tightly' and that it would not help him nor his electoral popularity in the January 2006 elections. 'But they wouldn't listen to us.'[160] In a shock result, Fatah was now beaten by the more radical Palestinian party Hamas, which claimed 76 of the 132 parliamentary seats. A core tenet of Hamas party thinking was a refusal to accept Israel's right to exist, so the election spelled greater instability for the region. The British reaction was one of 'huge dismay'. Blair himself was very surprised. 'No one had expected the result,' recalled one official. 'The election had been intended as a way of neutralising Hamas and for it to suddenly turn round and bite us in that way was astonishing.'[161] The Bush administration refused flatly to engage with Hamas. 'There was a sense that the peace process was all going to rat-shit,' said one FCO source.[162] 'Blair also took a hard line on Hamas,' recalled a senior diplomat. 'Straw argued and there was heated debate. The FCO line was that Hamas was capable of changing and that Britain anyway had a duty to help the Palestinian people, whatever the difficulties with their elected leaders.'[163] But Blair's view prevailed. Those who had worked closely with him on the Middle East thought his line had hardened since 2003. Influenced by American thinking, but also by his own evolving beliefs, 'he expected the Palestinians to jump through ever smaller hoops'.[164]

In July, the region erupted into the worst conflict of his premiership. On 12 July, the radical Islamic Hezbollah group kidnapped two Israeli soldiers close to the Lebanese–Israeli border. On 13 July, Israel launched raids into Lebanon to recover them and threatened to bomb Lebanon 'back twenty years'. The FCO made it plain it was not sympathetic to Olmert's line.[165] While the crisis had been triggered by Hezbollah, the major Israeli retaliation struck some in the FCO as 'the action of a nervous, inexperienced, anxious-to-prove-itself new Israeli government with little grounding in military realities', recalled Sawers.[166] On 14 July, the UN Security Council met to debate the crisis, where Chirac condemned the Israeli retaliation as 'completely disproportionate'. Lebanon insisted on Security Council backing for an immediate ceasefire, which received widespread international support, but not from the US or the UK. Blair 'was very clear that this was the position that had to be taken, because you couldn't let Hezbollah benefit from what they had done', recalled Condi Rice. He agreed that 'eventually the international environment was going to shift and you were going to have to find a way to get to a ceasefire',[167] but for the moment, a ceasefire *on both sides* (crucial to both Blair and Washington) was not considered a realistic proposition. 'I do think that the Prime Minister was anxious to have us get there as fast as he could, but he wasn't prepared to sacrifice the quality of the ceasefire for speed,' said Rice.[168]

The next day, Saturday 15 July, Blair travelled to St Petersburg for the G8. The preparations had been acrimonious. Putin wanted to invite a selection of Russian-friendly countries: when it proved too difficult, he backtracked and consented to the + 5 attending.[169] But he resisted Blair's wish for St Petersburg to carry on with the Gleneagles agenda; Britain concluded that Russia was less interested in substantive issues than in using the G8 as a platform to portray Putin as a world leader.[170] Despite Blair's frustration, continuity between the G8 agendas of different host countries had been rare historically and so it would have been most unusual had Putin decided to continue with the issues discussed at Gleneagles. Instead, the Russians chose energy security, education and the battle against infectious diseases as their substantive G8 issues, and significant agreements were concluded in all three areas. But at the political level, the St Petersburg Summit swiftly came to be dominated by Lebanon. The leaders said they wanted to communicate a common viewpoint, but it proved difficult to find one. Blair and Bush argued their line staunchly, that it was Hezbollah, not Israel, that had started the clash by kidnapping the Israeli soldiers and repeatedly refusing to comply with UNSCR 1559, which required militias in Lebanon to be disarmed. In private, even the French were taking a strong anti-Hezbollah and anti-Syria position. 'Chirac had a very strong view on Lebanon which was very coincident with our own,' confirmed Rice. 'In some ways our closest partner on Lebanon was France.'[171] The counter argument was that Olmert's response had been disproportionate, and not calling for an immediate ceasefire was giving the Israelis a green light to continue.

At this delicate stage, a conversation between Bush and Blair was picked up at St Petersburg by a microphone they thought was switched off, in which the President repeated his hostility to the UN's call for an immediate ceasefire.[172] Bush famously greeted Blair with 'Yo, Blair!' and proceeded to chew on a bread roll while Blair tried to engage him in the niceties of policy. 'When we told the Prime Minister about the microphone,' recalled Tom Kelly, 'he was genuinely speechless, not quite knowing whether to laugh or cry.'[173] The British press wrote it up as conclusive evidence of 'Blair the poodle'. But the words do not justify such a conclusion, and nor would it be correct to read subservience into the initial salutation. Throughout Bush's career in Texan politics, he had used surnames in an affectionate manner. When greeting Blair at the White House he would typically welcome him with arms outstretched, yelling, 'Hey Blair. How y' doin'?' Earlier in their relationship he had given Blair the nickname 'Landslide'.[174] To Karl Rove, the 'Yo, Blair' salutation was a sign of 'the enormous respect the President has for Blair, for his mind, his vision, moral clarity and political skills'.[175] That might be taking things a little bit far for just one salutation, but at the very least it seemed to illustrate the closeness of the two leaders.

G8 leaders were content to devolve drafting the summit's communiqué on Lebanon to the Americans and the French, though Britain was also to play a prominent part. Chirac was enthusiastic about reaching an agreed text, though the looming French elections threatened to limit what he could commit to.[176] On the first evening, a Saturday, Condi Rice bashed out a draft statement on her own computer: she had been travelling with Bush and had not initially planned to stay for the whole G8 (foreign ministers generally didn't), but after it became clear that the Lebanon crisis would dominate it, she changed her mind.[177] At 7 A.M. the following morning, she discussed her draft with Sheinwald, Sawers and their French colleagues.[178] They delegated Sawers and Nick Burns, his American counterpart, the task of turning her overnight paper into a document to which they all could sign up. Between 8 and 9:30 A.M. they recast and shortened it, but left in the call for both parties to end the violence coupled with the need for an international force to step in to the region to ensure peace. To Blair, here was the only viable way to ensure both sides stopped the violence: such a force would guarantee that Hezbollah stopped firing rockets into Israel, and that Israeli counter-attacks could then cease completely. The French and Americans had not previously considered it and had to be won over.[179]

Sawers reported on their progress towards the end of the Blair–Bush bilateral from 9 to 10 A.M. Three hours of debate at official level followed, during which the Russians made clear their unhappiness; as the holders of the chair, they thought they should produce the draft. Sawers volunteered to try to forge a compromise, which he did on his own between 2 and 4 P.M. sitting in the British delegation office. 'We held the pen throughout: even though it was their conference, we didn't allow the Russians to play the role of chair and let them run with their own draft. This was the key to ensuring we got the right answer,' said one British official.[180] By 7:30 P.M. the officials had the draft statement ready to show the G8 leaders, many of whom consulted with officials back in their home capitals. This only succeeded in drawing in further objections. It was back to the drawing board.

On Monday 17 July, the leaders were due to release the communiqué and hold an early afternoon press conference before flying back home. Starting early, officials were given one final chance to produce an agreed text. They whittled the differences down from twenty to eight, and then to two or three, focused particularly on the proposal that an international force would go into Lebanon. As the morning drew on the G8 leaders became increasingly unhappy. 'Where's the text?' they berated their officials. Jay, who as sherpa stayed by the Prime Minister's side, was sent the latest text electronically by the British team. 'I think we've got as far as we can,' he was told. 'The Russians and Americans will not compromise further without input from their leaders.' Jay briefed Blair on the text which included square brackets indicating the differences with Russia and the US, relating mainly to Iran and Syria.[181] Chirac was similarly informed by his own sherpa of a 'great danger' that agreement would not be reached before the scheduled press conference. On hearing this news, according to one witness, he 'essentially panicked, which set in motion a panic among the other leaders as well'.[182] Putin seemed less concerned than most, but Chirac was now becoming frantic and aired the almost unheard of notion that the leaders should negotiate the text themselves. At 12:30 P.M. Bush, Putin, Blair, Chirac and Merkel got into a huddle to see if they could find a way forward but making progress on the 'wretched text' proved 'completely impossible'.[183] Time was running out and hopes of producing the statement were fast evaporating.

With failure staring them in the face, Bush and Chirac decided that Blair should make one final effort to thrash out a final statement alone with Putin. They went off into a side room while both leaders sat down and went through it one last time, with only Sheinwald and a senior Russian official present, apart from the interpreters. They talked for forty minutes. Blair and Sheinwald quickly discovered that a distracted Putin had not been as well briefed as he might have been by his staff, and they used this to their advantage.[184] It soon emerged that Putin's political director had been a more intractable obstacle to reaching agreement than the Russian President himself: 'He was a tough cookie,' said one of his peers, 'if something could be done easily or more difficultly, he would always take the more difficult path.'[185] As time wore on the other G8 leaders were becoming increasingly agitated. Bush was no exception: 'find out what's going on, find out what's going on' he was heard saying impatiently to his sherpa.[186] Changes eventually began to appear in the text and Blair, his diplomatic skills to the fore, convinced Putin that Russia had nothing to fear: 'He won him round by force of personality, force of argument and by being very, very persuasive,' said one official.[187] Blair felt personal distaste for Putin, but had worked hard at overcoming the differences in their relationship. This now yielded dividends. By 1:15

P.M., an agreed text emerged which was readily adopted by the impatient G8 leaders, including Chirac, who was strongly supportive.[188]

The final statement avoided a call for an immediate ceasefire, but said the attacks by Hamas and Hezbollah on Israel should end 'immediately'. An indirect swipe was also taken at Syria and Iran when it declared that 'extremist elements' and those that support them could not be allowed to plunge the Middle East into chaos and provoke a wider conflict.[189] 'I know many wanted the G8 to call for an immediate ceasefire on the part of Israel. Of course we all want all violence to stop and stop immediately. But we recognise that the only realistic way to achieve such a ceasefire is to address the underlying reasons why this violence has broken out,' Blair told a sceptical House of Commons after his return on Tuesday 18 July.[190]

The consensus among the G8 unravelled with frightening speed in the days that followed. Blair found himself as isolated internationally as he had been on Iraq, and more isolated at home than on any other issue of his premiership. Fatalities in Lebanon rose apace with the apparent green light Israel had received from St Petersburg. The mantra of those disturbed by Israeli action rapidly became the demand for an 'immediate ceasefire' as the solution to all problems. With Blair becoming increasingly agitated, Sheinwald held a number of hard-hitting conversations with Olmert, making clear Blair's concerns about the scale of the Israeli violence.[191] Yet Blair still doggedly refused to call for an immediate ceasefire, believing a UN resolution and international force were the necessary prerequisites. Why did he hold his position so strongly, even as Israeli actions escalated? He believed that 'Hezbollah had been the *agent provocateur*, and that Israel had an absolute right of self-defence'. When Hezbollah started firing rockets, he increasingly saw Israel as the wronged country. The media photographs focused on Lebanese suffering, but he knew that it was 'only because one million Israelis were sleeping in bunkers that Israel's own casualties were not far higher'. The more the media criticised Israel, because of the suffering among innocent Lebanese civilians, the more stubborn he seemed to become.[192]

Blair was also desperate to see progress in the MEPP before he stood down, and keeping a good relationship with Olmert and the Israelis was fundamental. 'Robin [Cook] and Jack [Straw] lost the confidence of the Israelis very early on in their tenures and never got it back. If we are to have any real influence it's fundamental that you acquire their confidence and retain it,' he told Beckett about her two predecessors.[193] Israel would never agree to a ceasefire, he told her, and if he pressed for one, Olmert's government would conclude that Britain had joined the long list of nations who Israel felt had no understanding of the reality of its strategic and military isolation.[194] 'Sounding off is nothing: it's what Chirac does. It was just posturing, and if we'd done it, the Israelis would have stopped taking our calls and we'd have had no influence,' Blair said.[195] Throughout this period, Blair kept speaking 'very regularly' to Olmert as well as to Bush and Rice, to try to persuade Israel to stop retaliating.[196]

Blair was very clear that he would not respond in any way over the crisis 'which would put him at odds with the Americans', said one senior aide.[197] 'You have to understand that you have no influence and no leverage with the administration once you criticise them or take a line that goes against their thinking,' he told a protesting Sally Morgan.[198] But while Blair may have been hoping for a ceasefire, British officials felt that Washington had given Israel 'a pretty strong signal that it would be welcome for Israel to continue to hit Hezbollah'.[199] 'What we saw on the television was people just in despair. It looked like the Americans had said to the Israelis, "Right, we'll give you three weeks",' recalled a Blair supporter in Cabinet.[200] Increasingly, people in Whitehall and Westminster asked themselves whether Blair's over-riding aim, like many in Washington, was to see Hezbollah crippled.[201]

International criticism quickly reached a crescendo. Chirac, despite his support at St Petersburg, joined the throng. On 19 July, France requested that the UN Security Council call for an immediate ceasefire. The next day Kofi Annan spoke out against Israel's 'excessive use of force', saying that Israeli attacks constituted a 'collective punishment' in violation of the Geneva Convention.[202] The Tories condemned Israel's attacks as disproportionate.[203] Beckett herself had private doubts but loyally did not speak out and worked with Blair frantically behind the scenes. Over the weekend of 22/23 July, she phoned some ten foreign ministers in 'one of the busiest weekends of diplomacy the FCO could remember'.[204] On 22 July, one of her ministers, Kim Howells, spoke out about Israel's seemingly indiscriminate attacks, including the 'death of so many children' and hoped that the Americans 'understood what was happening to the Lebanon'.[205] On Monday 24 July, in a joint press conference with Iraqi Prime Minister al-Maliki, Blair tried again to defend his policy. He stressed that he wanted to see a cessation of hostilities on both sides as soon as possible, but he would not call for an immediate Israeli ceasefire until the necessary conditions were put in place to address the underlying causes of instability.[206] On 26 July, Beckett, under direction from Blair, blocked attempts to call for an immediate ceasefire at the Foreign Ministers' conference in Rome, where she had 'a very torrid time' at the hands of her European and Arab colleagues.

On Thursday 27 July, there was unease at the last Cabinet meeting before the recess. Miliband spoke, albeit tentatively, of the widespread concern about the damage that his line on the Lebanon was doing to the party and its standing in the country.[207] Straw had earlier told Blair in private that he thought he was making a fundamental error, but had found him unyielding.[208] The next day, Straw was outspoken publicly in his indictment of Israel. Olmert was aggrieved that Straw, a former Foreign Secretary, should have spoken as he did, and had private words with British Ambassador McDonald: 'Ask my friend Jack to put himself in my position. If in the UK tonight people in Liverpool, Manchester and Birmingham – and Blackburn and Newcastle, I choose those deliberately – were sleeping underground in a bunker because a terrorist force in Ireland was firing scores of rockets at those cities with the intention of killing as many British citizens as possible, how would my friend Jack feel?'[209]

During the final week Parliament sat, the PLP reached boiling point. This was just the kind of crisis that the political operatives in Number 10 had hoped to steer clear of. Blair's office received many passionate phone calls and strongly worded letters from MPs not normally critical of Blair. 'The feeling was that we were always too pro-Israeli and we were not distancing ourselves sufficiently,' recalled one normally loyal MP.[210] There were growing worries as to the longer-term repercussions of the ongoing conflict, and the impact of Iraq on Britain's standing in the Arab world. 'Anyone thinking about it for more than thirty seconds would think you're breeding the next generation of militants who'll point to this and say, "That's what America did to you",' commented one Cabinet minister.[211] It was Ruth Turner's unwelcome job to convey the breadth and depth of the criticism to Blair, who took it calmly. 'He was completely aware of the extent and depth of their anger,' she recalled. 'He just chose to do things they didn't like because he had different priorities.'[212] The danger for Blair was that anger over the conflict was becoming inextricably linked with the debate over the succession. 'It felt as bad as Iraq in terms of the passions it was stirring,' said one Downing Street aide.[213]

On Friday 28 July, still convinced of the rightness of his stance, Blair flew to the US. One FCO official present recalled how he 'was in a very dangerous position. Apart from the US he was completely out there by himself.'[214] He met Bush alone in the White House that afternoon over sandwiches and soft drinks. They saw no reason to change their minds, believing that 'a knee-jerk ceasefire would simply reward Hezbollah aggression, embolden Iran and Syria, and leave the conflict unresolved'.[215] They reiterated their commitment to work for a UN resolution which alone they thought would make an enduring cessation of hostilities on both sides viable. Blair didn't want the Lebanon crisis to dominate their whole discussions: his clock was ticking fast, and he was desperate to push the White House on the MEPP. In particular, he wanted Bush's agreement to take the lead in reviving negotiations for a 'land-for-peace' deal between Israel and the Palestinians. Number 10 confirmed that Bush said he was 'agreeable', but as ever, what exactly did Bush's agreement on the MEPP mean?[216] At their press conference, Blair spoke about his 'three essential steps', which included an imminent visit by Rice to the region, the deployment of an international force and the UN resolution. Despite these efforts, it was the failure to call for an 'immediate ceasefire' that again made the headlines.

While Sheinwald flew straight back to London that evening to lobby foreign governments on the UN resolution, Blair flew on to the west coast. The British Embassy in Washington and Consul-Generals in California had long been arguing the merit of Blair becoming the first serving British Prime Minister to visit California, to highlight the climate change, biotechnology, trade and innovation agendas.[217] A new element was that Governor Schwarzenegger, with his re-election looming in November, and needing to find a popular issue, had become a late advocate of tackling climate change. 'Schwarzenegger knew that Blair was the leading world statesman concerned about climate change and was very keen for him to come,' said an Embassy official.[218] Blair was something of a Schwarzenegger fan himself, having seen many of his movies with his children, and admiring his 'personal style'.[219] At the FCO, concerns were expressed about the unconventional visit to a mere state government, and whether the visit would be sensitive in the state capital of Sacramento. Blair was not troubled. Nor apparently was Washington, despite efforts in the press to portray a schism: 'It's not unusual that states do all kinds of things, and California is known to be active in foreign policy,' explained Rice. 'There wasn't any problem with it at all.'[220]

In Sheinwald's absence, David Manning, his immediate predecessor in Number 10, seized an opportunity during the six-hour plane journey westwards to argue robustly with Blair. Several who overheard their conversation were surprised at the direct way in which Manning spoke to him, telling him starkly what would be the consequences, not least on the MEPP, of carrying on as he was. 'You're the one who's been elected and so it's your decision. But you must understand that this is an issue on which we can legitimately differ with the United States.'[221] Like the barrister he once was, Blair argued back powerfully against Manning's propositions. Some listening thought that, though Blair had already been forced to iterate his position on Lebanon repeatedly in discussions with his advisers in London, 'David helped him to iterate just that bit more.'[222] Here was not only the foreign policy adviser he respected as much as anyone criticising his line: he was also challenging Blair's instinctive desire to avoid breaking with the Americans, at least in public. Manning's arguments gave him pause for thought.

Arriving in San Francisco on the evening of 28 July Blair appeared 'tired and pensive': it was indeed early morning in Britain, he'd had a long day and no sleep for twenty hours. Lebanon overshadowed his whole six-day visit, though he carefully ensured it did not undermine his discussions with the Californians on his new agenda. 'Every time he was in the car between meetings, it was Lebanon, Lebanon, Lebanon. He wanted to talk to this person, talk to that person. "Get me Merkel, I'll phone Bush, get me Chirac." He was determined to find a way through,' recalled one of those travelling with him.[223] Officials travelling with him were impressed by his ability to shift gears so abruptly: 'His mind would be on Lebanon and then suddenly we'd get our thirty seconds to brief him on who he was going to be seeing next.'[224]

On Saturday 29 July, Blair's visit began with a reception at the sumptuous residence of George Shultz, Ronald Reagan's second Secretary of State, where he chatted with many of the *glitterati* of San Francisco society, including Schwarzenegger. His popularity, at least on the west coast, seemed undiminished: he even received an impromptu standing ovation when entering a restaurant.[225] Very early on Sunday morning Blair crossed the road from his hotel to Grace Cathedral and sneaked in to join the congregation: he was eager as ever to go to church on Sunday wherever he was in the world.[226] At lunch that day with CEOs of major corporations, including Apple and HP, Blair raised the business flag for Britain. Blair was then flown down by private jet to Pebble Beach for Murdoch's annual News Corps conference, providing a bookend to his conference on Hayman Island eleven years before in July 1995, near the start of his leadership of the Labour Party, when he was still wooing the media tycoon whose support had done so much to underpin his premiership. Murdoch's opinion still mattered to Blair: 'Although we had been told that the California visit would happen in 2006, the precise timing was fixed around Rupert Murdoch's event,' said an official.[227]

On Sunday 30 July, news broke of the Israeli bombing in Qana, which at the time was thought to have killed up to fifty-six civilians, many of them children. 'Qana was the turning point,' admitted an FCO official. 'From then on, even the most loyalist of Blair's foreign policy advisers were saying to him, "Adjust our line – the Israeli attacks were becoming counterproductive." Resisting calls for an immediate ceasefire was damaging us in the region.'[228] 'It was becoming more and more of a crisis situation,' said one aide.[229] Reports began to leak out that 'foreign affairs specialists' in both Number 10 and the FCO believed that the Israeli response was 'counter-productive and further alienated the Arab world'.[230] That Sunday, Beckett, Sheinwald and others weighed in with Blair urging him that the time was right to call openly for a ceasefire, thus making plain his discomfort at Israeli actions. This he refused to do, to the anger of many. But his public statements did begin to show some subtle evolution. In his speech to News Corp, he called for 'an urgent cessation of hostilities',[231] adding later to reporters: 'We have to speed this entire process up and get a resolution now . . . then the hostilities have got to stop, stop on all sides.' The following day he called for all those involved in the conflict to exercise 'maximum restraint'.[232] But the shift was too elliptical for most. 'His language had changed in terms of some of the emotional content,' noted one close aide, 'but he never got over the "ceasefire" barrier.'[233]

On 31 July, after a visit to Genetech Inc., a leading biotech firm, during which he made it clear that Californian companies would find a more hospitable business environment for embryonic stem cell science in the UK than in the US, he headed south to Los Angeles. Joined by Schwarzenegger, Blair met leading British and American CEOs at Long Beach to discuss climate change, concluded by signing a statement of intent with the governor as part of a wider plan to involve US states in the EU's carbon trading scheme.[234] On 1 August he delivered one of the more important of his wind-up foreign policy speeches: 'Unless we revitalise the broader global agenda on poverty, climate change, trade and in respect of the Middle East, bend every sinew of our will to making peace between Israel and Palestine, we will not win.'[235] He intended it as a final powerful message to America that, alongside the wars in Iraq and Afghanistan, the West had to be seen to be taking a principled stand on global issues.[236] He returned to find many in Britain seething at his unwillingness to take a 'principled stand' on an Israeli ceasefire. A significant majority in his own party had been unimpressed by his cavorting with figures like Murdoch and Schwarzenegger, while in Lebanon, the civilian death toll crept towards the 1,000 mark.

Behind the scenes, Blair continued his efforts to resolve the conflict on his own terms and delayed his family holiday to Barbados to work on the UN resolution, spending several hours each day on the telephone: 'He stayed until we could see our way clear in getting a resolution, talking constantly on the phone to people: the number he spoke to every day was incredible,' said one senior aide.[237] With violence in Lebanon continuing into early August, negotiations proved extremely fraught. At the UN, France and the US, not the UK, took the lead. 'I know that drove the British mission in New York crazy,' recalled US Ambassador Bolton. 'It drove the FCO crazy, but that's what the French wanted and that's what we did.'[238] Ultimately, the French were going to lead the international force in the region, not the British or the Americans. So, as Rice recalled, 'We had this difficult situation of trying to negotiate a document about somebody else's forces.'[239] Beckett reached boiling point waiting in London. In desperation, she phoned Rice and told her that she was getting on a plane to New York on Thursday, 10 August. The Secretary of State replied, 'Maybe nothing will happen: you could end up looking silly,' to which she said, 'I'm coming to the strong conclusion that my boss would sooner I look silly in New York than silly in a caravan site in France.'[240] After a last-minute row over when exactly the ceasefire would begin, when all parties became highly irritated with Kofi Annan, UNSCR 1701 was passed on Friday 11 August, demanding an imminent cessation of hostilities from both Hezbollah and Israel.[241]

The immediate crisis was over, and had been concluded on the same terms as the G8 statement, echoing Blair's line of argument. He may well have been right on the policy, and his stance won him some supporters after the crisis was over, but he badly misjudged the politics and the presentation. 'Our line sounded wrong; it sounded much more callous than the reality, which was that we were beavering away massively behind the scenes,' said a very senior aide. 'His political and presentational nous deserted him at a critical moment.'[242] Greater focus on the suffering of innocent Lebanese civilians would have improved his case enormously.

When Blair was left kicking his heels in Downing Street after the family had gone, he had a 'girls' night' in the flat at Number 10 including Tessa Jowell and Margaret McDonagh, when he was chided for pretending he did not know how to use the dishwasher.[243] 'Why do men think women fall for that kind of helplessness?' said one.[244] More seriously, they chided him over Lebanon. His response was that if the choice was between saying 'the populist thing' or being effective, he would choose to be effective by working behind the scenes to bring about the ceasefire.[245] Not all those in the Labour movement expressed themselves as pleasantly as Blair's female dinner companions. Many instead agreed with Neal Lawson that 'the Lebanon crisis was a mini-rerun of Iraq. We were the poodles of America and Blair's failure to come out and condemn anyone or anything or to put any daylight between Bush and himself, or Bush and Israel, upset wide sections of the party.'[246] Jon Trickett, the chair of Compass's parliamentary group, organised a ring-round of Labour MPs in early August. On 11 August, on the day of the UN resolution, he sent a letter signed by 100 Labour MPs to John Prescott, acting Prime Minister as Blair had by then left on holiday. The letter was discounted in Number 10, and no one took seriously the request for a recall of Parliament. Ruth Turner read the runes, 'For quite a few in the PLP, Lebanon was either genuinely for them the last straw, or it was used by them as a legitimate excuse for their last straw with the Prime Minister.'[247] Within just three weeks, the consequences of his firm stand on the Lebanon would rock to the core Blair's increasingly precarious grip on power.

18

The September Coup

September 2006

Blair had long wrestled with the date of his retirement. At the 2005 party conference, he had implied he wanted to serve a full term. But his eroding political position prompted his closest aides to convince him at Chequers in April 2006 to prepare the ground for departure in summer 2007 – though he won the argument that he should not give a precise date. His vulnerable position after the May local elections and reshuffle then forced him at the PLP meeting on 8 May to concede that he would give his successor 'ample time' before the next General Election. Still he refused to give a precise date in public. In private, however, he told Brown he would leave in the summer of 2007, and he revealed to *The Politics Show* on 16 July that he was looking forward to leading the country at Merkel's G8 at Heiligendamm in June 2007.[1] With his domestic policy agenda at last bearing fruit, he became more anxious than ever to make his keynote policies irreversible before his successor took over. Abroad, his focus on Africa and climate change, and his passion to see progress on the MEPP, again suggested he had too much to achieve to quit early. At times, he blanked his departure date from his mind. Why should he go in mid-2007? He had announced in September 2004 that he would fight a full term, and had won the election in May 2005 – why shouldn't he continue until 2008? Those close to him were exasperated that 'he simply didn't seem to get it'. For a long time he did not, but the events of early September 2006 were to force him to come to terms with some home truths.

Olympian Chequers: August 2006

For several months, following the turbulence in May, rumours had been circulating that rebel left-wing MPs were planning to send a letter or mount a delegation to Downing Street to press Blair to set a timetable for an imminent departure. On 20 August, Stephen Byers wrote a policy-based article in the *Sunday Telegraph* in which he discussed inheritance tax and its abolition. 'The fact that we've had a tax on death since the 1690s is not the strongest case for its retention in the twenty-first century.'[2] The first sense the Blairites had that something was 'slightly awry'[3] was when normally loyalist MPs Sion Simon and Chris Bryant came out and attacked Byers 'savagely', in a move Number 10 suspected had been organised by Brownite MP Ian Austin.[4] The brunt of what they particularly disliked was the article's suggestion that Brown should 'nail his colours to the Blairite mast'.[5] Byers himself had no doubt that they were put up to it by the Treasury.[6]

Blair's summer holiday had not proved his most relaxing. Constantly plagued by paparazzi, the family holiday in Cliff Richards' villa in Barbados was the subject of widespread unfavourable comment at home. Journalists lurked around the holiday home hoovering up gossip: 'He gave particular attention to improving his tennis,' said one holiday-maker. 'On many days, he started as early as 7 A.M. and sometimes played twice a day, doubles and singles.' He would then work out in the gym.[7] Blair bitterly resented the press intrusion into the time he had alone with his family.[8] Before he left for the West Indies on 8 August, he had been lobbied intensively by political allies and Number 10 aides to come back with a date fixed in his mind for his departure. Matthew Taylor remained the chief advocate for a precise timetable, arguing for a Clinton-style 'final chapter' with a full programme of action to kill off the endless speculation. This was the only way to still the 'date-obsessed people' whose stirring, he argued, was making the 'succession instability' a self-fulfilling prophecy.[9] Ruth Turner told Blair very directly that the party conference would be the time for him to make a statement: 'A number of us were of the opinion that doing nothing then was no longer an option.'[10] His close parliamentary aides told him similarly, 'You must say whether it will be your last conference, or whether you intend to go on until 2008. You can't let it fester.'[11] Blair promised he would ponder the question over the summer holidays and come back with his mind made up.[12] But when he returned on 25 August, his mind continued to wander. 'Once he went away, he seemed to think to himself, "I simply don't want to think about this", and parked it. He was almost in a state of denial. He seemed to come back wanting to go on until 2008,' said one ally.[13] Others, however, including Jonathan Powell and Turner, who worked with him every day, contest this, and say that he was clear that he would leave before the 2007 party conference, and announce his decision at a Political Cabinet beforehand.[14] 'He intended to begin the Political Cabinet by saying he was going to go before the next party conference,' said one confidant.[15]

Blair was steely on his return. 'He always returns from holiday at 150 miles an hour. This was no exception,' said a close aide.[16] When David Bennett spoke to him, he found him 'very determined to stand his ground and not to be harried out early. He had work to do. He wanted to get down to it.'[17] A speech in early September on social inclusion dominated his thoughts in the last week of August. In the run-up to party conferences, he had always looked to make a speech on a subject that the party would find congenial: work, employment conditions and poverty were standard fare. This year he was particularly passionate about showing the positive impact that ten years of New Labour had made in reducing social exclusion.[18]

Concerned by the anger over Lebanon, Turner had organised for angst-ridden backbenchers to come to Chequers in the final week of August to talk to him about Lebanon and other concerns. 'We put on a huge operation to try to get MPs back on side,' said Wegg-Prosser. 'But for many of them, Lebanon was the straw that broke the camel's back.'[19] On Thursday 31 August, Blair also invited three of his closest confidants, Campbell, Morgan and Gould, up to Chequers to sound out their views. They all believed that he should name a date for his departure at the party conference. But by the time they sat out in the sun together that afternoon, Blair had already made a mistake that would bring the issue to crisis point.[20] Earlier that day, Peter Riddell and Philip Webster from *The Times* had been invited to Chequers for an audience with the Prime Minister. Blair's aim was to draw a line under the Lebanon crisis, end speculation about his future and kick-start the new political year. *The Times* was Hill's choice for the keynote interview because he regarded it as a 'serious newspaper' and trustworthy: the fear in the Blair camp was that, whatever he said, his words would be twisted and distorted.[21] So, on top of selecting a newspaper they trusted, extra care was put into preparation for the interview. That morning, Blair sat with his close team to thrash out the angle he would take: he decided on a '"let's be realistic" line. "I'm not going to do anything to damage the party. There's more I want to do in office, but I'm not going to do anything against the party's interest, so can you please all calm down?"'[22] But they had taken insufficient stock of where the only real interest in the article lay: would he give a date for his departure, and if so, what was it? Riddell and Webster who received the invitation to Chequers the day before the interview had indeed concluded that Blair would have something definite to say about timing. Upon being repeatedly pressed, Blair came up with, 'I have said I will leave ample time for my successor. Now at some point, I think people have got to accept that as a reasonable proposition and let me get on with the job.'[23] Turner drove up to Chequers just after Riddell and Webster had left. 'How did it go?' she asked Blair. 'Oh, yes, it was great,' he replied. But when she learned what he had said she became tense: 'Oh, God,' she said, 'it's just going to go down so badly.'[24] Blair rapidly realised that the interview had not worked from his point of view and told Mandelson as much that afternoon.[25] Others in his close team were not surprised: Blair had told Wegg-Prosser that he was 'just not in the market for setting a date. He was never, ever going to be convinced of that.'[26] That evening, Blair threw a party at Chequers for his staff, welcoming them back from holiday and thanking them for staying on with him 'till the end'. During the festivities, Blair became increasingly anxious about his earlier encounter with *The Times* and how the paper might portray his comments.[27] It rapidly became obvious that Blair had misjudged the mood in the party and in the country at large.

The Times made a big splash of the interview on Friday 1 September, reporting it as a defiant stand from Blair, and a snub to his detractors. The carefully crafted message that he had wanted to convey, that the party could trust him to finish his job and then leave, was drowned out. When they saw the headlines, Campbell, Morgan and Gould threw up their hands in despair.[28] In a vain attempt to limit the damage, Number 10's media operatives began frantically phoning newspaper editors, stressing that although he had not expressly said so in the interview, he would in fact be leaving Downing Street in 2007.[29] They tried saying that it was obvious he would be going within the year or he would not have held a 'thank you' party for staff the evening before. But it was too late for corrections. The article now brought the growing sense of deep dissatisfaction within the PLP to a head. 'In the last two weeks of August, there were heightened rumours that there was going to be an attempt at a letter: these rumours hardened towards the end of August,' said Peter Watt, the party's general secretary. 'There was a very definite sense of something brewing, conversations happening.' Coming against this backdrop, the interview was widely seen as a defiant and deliberate attempt by Blair to refuse to give a date. Given the Lebanon crisis, and his fuzziness on dates, there would have been some explosion even without the interview. What the interview did was pour fuel on the fire.

On the day the *Times* article was published, the Blairs left Chequers after a final meeting with four discontented MPs that afternoon and went to Balmoral for their annual weekend with the Queen. Khalid Mahmood, one of the four backbenchers, left Chequers with other plans. Before Blair had left for Barbados, Mahmood had said that he would consider whether he could remain as a Parliamentary Private Secretary if Blair's Lebanon policy did not change, a story which led *Channel 4 News* on 4 August. Later that evening, Blair phoned him and asked Mahmood not to do anything until he came back from a trip to Lebanon, where he hoped for better news. During that month, Turner and others kept in regular touch with Mahmood, nursing him along. He remained unconvinced about Blair's thinking on Lebanon at their meeting, and later that evening on the phone, spoke with fellow Birmingham MP Siôn Simon who was equally disturbed: 'The local elections had shown we were on a downward spiral and our local base was eroding. Our concern was aggravated by the fact that he was saying he'd carry on for as long as he saw fit,' said Mahmood.[30] That evening, Simon reportedly spoke with Tom Watson, junior defence minister and Brown ally, to discuss Blair's future. They discussed how to put pressure on Blair to quit early, or at least to give an early date for his departure. 'The Brown camp had been saying that he should not go on. We said they should do something. That's when Siôn got Tom involved,' said a friend of Simon.[31] 'We [the 2001 intake] had all been loyal Blair supporters and supported the government. We just felt the party needed to move on, and Tony should step aside because that was becoming more of the story than anything else,' said another disgruntled MP.[32] Siôn Simon began to phone around the 2001 intake soliciting support for a letter to Blair, asking him to step down. Earlier that day, Wegg-Prosser spoke to Simon, having got wind of what he was doing. He was liked in Number 10 and regarded as one of 'Blair's most eloquent supporters in the press'. Wegg-Prosser said to him: 'Would you be willing to do anything to support Blair?' The stark response was 'no'. 'He thought the time had come for Blair to go, and sooner rather than later.'[33] Wegg-Prosser took a sharp intake of breath. 'Do you think that Gordon would be prepared to stick the knife in this time?' he asked Simon. 'In the past I've always assumed he wouldn't; now I think he might,' was Simon's chilling reply.[34] Wegg-Prosser put the phone down and reported back to his colleagues. On Friday night and Saturday morning Simon finalised the draft of a letter to be circulated around a pre-selected and sympathetic section of the 2001 intake over the weekend.[35]

On Saturday 2 September, a conference call was held between Powell, Lloyd, Turner, Hill, Wegg-Prosser and Blair in Balmoral, during which the Prime Minister was briefed about the negative reaction to the article, and reports of rumblings in the party.[36] They concluded there was little they could do except wait and see how events unfolded. On Sunday 3 September, Alan Milburn wrote an article in the *Sunday Times* which was seen by the Brownites as a coded call for a leadership election when the time came to choose Blair's successor. He wrote that Blair had already announced that he was going to 'give ample time for his successor ahead of the next General Election. He was right to resist pressure to go any further.' Airing talk of a leadership election and a contested succession was one of the Blair camp's weapons of choice when it felt under attack. But when precisely Blair left, Milburn argued, was far less important than an internal party debate over renewal: 'Forget the date. It's the debate that matters.'[37] The prospect of 'a debate' was the very last thing the Brownites wanted. They were confident that their man would win any election, but they did not want to win after a bloody contest against a Blairite. Sunday also saw a volley from the Brown camp, with an Ed Balls article in the *Observer* calling for a 'stable and orderly transition' in order to ensure that 'history could be confounded and a fourth General Election victory won by Labour'.[38] On Monday, Tom Watson visited Brown's home in North Queensferry – an event that swiftly became public knowledge, to their intense embarrassment. Suspicion circulated that he had been talking to Brown about the emerging plot. Watson protested strongly that it was a 'wholly social visit' to deliver a present, a *Postman Pat* video, to the Browns for their new baby, Fraser, and that politics was not discussed at all.[39] None in Number 10 found Watson's story credible: 'It was just hilarious, the idea that Tom Watson would trail all the way up to Scotland just to give a baby a present,' said one incredulous aide.[40]

The Descent: 4–5 September

Four hundred miles to the south, there was hope in Number 10 by Monday that the worst might be over. Blair travelled on from Balmoral to York in preparation for the keynote speech he was to deliver the following day to the Rowntree Trust. But at 3 P.M. Blair's Parliamentary Private Secretary, Keith Hill, arrived at Number 10 with a bombshell: he had been tipped off by a Labour MP that the Simon letter was now in circulation among the 2001 intake of MPs, and that it called on Blair to resign immediately. Similar letters were apparently in circulation among the 1997 and 2005 intakes.[41] They were due to be delivered to Blair over the next couple of days and on Wednesday, Hill continued, there was to be a delegation of ministers calling on him to resign.[42] Number 10 procured a copy of the 2001 letter. The name of Watson, the only government minister among the seventeen signatories, leapt out. Number 10 assumed that Watson, who had cut his teeth as political officer at the AEEU engineering union, was the chief plotter. The message in the letter was stark. 'Sadly it is clear to us – as it is to almost the entire party and the entire country – that without an urgent change in the leadership of the party it becomes less likely that we will win the next election. This is not a plot against you by people who want to reverse or slow down the progress you've made . . . but we believe it isn't possible for the party and government to renew itself without renewing its leadership as a matter of urgency. This is the brutal truth. It gives us no pleasure to say it. But it has to be said. And understood. We therefore ask you to stand aside.'[43]

In a state of some shock, senior Number 10 staff, including Powell, Taylor, Wegg-Prosser, Turner and Lloyd, filed into the office Turner shared with Taylor, to debate how to respond. Should they go public with the 2001 letter now? Should they sit on it? Try to smother it? They telephoned Blair in York to alert him, putting him on speakerphone. They decided that Jacqui Smith, the ultra-loyal Chief Whip who had succeeded Armstrong that June, should speak to all the signatories of the letter and 'ask them what they were playing at'.[44] Taylor and Turner were delegated to call round the Cabinet and gauge reactions, as well as speaking with backbenchers and party staff to get a feel for how widespread the desire for action was. Hilary Armstrong managed to make contact with Watson directly. He told her that he had 'a responsibility to the 2001 group'. 'I thought you were a member of the government and on that basis you have not just a moral but an actual responsibility to the government,' she replied.[45] It was clear she would get nowhere with him. Powell also tried to speak directly to Watson, but initially the MP avoided his calls. When Powell eventually got through to him that evening, he asked Watson directly, 'Is it true you've signed a letter?' When he replied in the affirmative, Powell said: 'Are you going to resign from the government?' Watson replied that he wasn't intending to. 'The conversation was as curt, short and as weird as that,' said one aide.[46]

Number 10's hope of sitting tight and hoping the letter would be withdrawn exploded when the BBC carried reports that evening not only of the 2001 letter, but of a similar letter from the 2005 intake, and possibly others.[47] Turner kept phoning Blair to break the bad news: 'It's getting worse,' she told him. 'It was very difficult,' she later recalled. 'It had an almost nightmarish tone to it.'[48] 'We basically didn't know what on earth was going on,' said Wegg-Prosser.[49]

The crucial question in the corridors of Number 10 that Monday evening was: who was behind it? The Brownites tried to make out that the involvement of Simon and fellow 2001 MP Chris Bryant showed that even loyal Blairites were in revolt. 'They were the sacrificial lambs for Gordon to demonstrate that he had support from people who had been until that moment seen as Blairites,' said one minister.[51] The MPs themselves insisted they were 'acting independently'.[51] 'It wasn't co-ordinated at all from the Brown camp,' said Khalid Mahmood emphatically. 'They might have been in agreement with what we were doing, but I don't think there was huge involvement,' he added, more ambiguously.[52] The Blairites were not remotely convinced. 'These are the type of guys that don't get out of bed in the morning and break wind without first checking with Gordon whether it's okay,' said one Cabinet minister who knew the MPs well.[53] Number 10's suspicions fell on Watson and Ian Austin (known to be close to Brown) for fomenting discontent among those backbenchers who had given up any hope of being the beneficiaries of Blair's patronage, and whose advantage now lay in pleasing Brown.[54] 'It is obvious why they were used. They were bitter about not getting jobs, and after years of getting nowhere under Blair, saw their only hope of advancing was under Brown.'[55] This was unduly cynical: many of the signatories had genuine reasons for despairing of Blair, for his stance over the Lebanon, and for electoral and party reasons.

In Number 10 that Monday evening, speculation remained rife over the extent of Brown's knowledge and involvement. Even those in the building who normally gave Brown the benefit of the doubt – and there were some – thought he was behind it.[56] But Brown protested his innocence, telling a mutual friend, 'I had nothing to do with it. You've got to believe it.' Brown went on to admit, however, that he should have done more to stop the unfolding plot.[57] After Watson's visit to his home became public knowledge, Brown had no choice but to admit that Watson had indeed been to see him. Given that Watson had spoken to Simon about the 2001 letter, it is fanciful to believe the conversation was confined to toys and babies. Number 10, as ever, homed in on the

'Machiavellian' Balls, who they suspected of orchestrating the whole affair. They had learned that Balls had been in the House of Commons the whole of Monday, which, considering it was the recess, they saw as 'mighty odd'.[58] They visualised him holding meetings and being on the phone all day, pulling the strings of his latest puppets.[59] Those who knew the PLP a little better considered Ian Austin a more likely orchestrator: 'Ian's been one of those people who has just quietly but assiduously worked upon his own generation of MPs,' said one contemporary.[60]

Turner and Taylor were mildly encouraged by their phone calls to Cabinet ministers that Monday evening. They did not speak to the entire Cabinet, but concluded that the great majority were solidly behind Blair: Reid, Jowell, Falconer, Blears, Hutton, Amos and Armstrong. A second group – David Miliband, Johnson, Kelly, McCartney, Hewitt and Des Browne – were thought to be dependable though not ultra-loyalist. None of them supported an attempt to kick Blair out, even those who felt he should at least clarify his intentions and give a date.[61] Straw did not approve of what was happening, but told Blair in private that he thought his support was dwindling away.[62] Number 10 already regarded Hoon and Straw as moving towards Brown, and were not surprised by his comments. Hain they saw as already in the Brown camp, while Alexander and Darling had always been 'Gordon's people'.[63] While their calls were in progress, Blair was having a difficult evening in his hotel in York, accompanied by David Hill, speechwriter Phil Collins and a small travelling staff from Number 10. 'He was gloomy for about ten minutes, as were we all. Typically, he then bucked himself up, reassessed everything and said: "Right, we're here now, let's take stock of the position." He moved from despondency to laughing about irrelevant things to calmly deciding what he was going to do next,' said one witness.[64] Breaking off from dinner in a private room, and radiating an 'icy calm', he spoke to his closest friends including Morgan and Mandelson: 'Peter loves him, and during a crisis one naturally turns to someone who loves you,' said one aide.[65] 'If they want me to go, that's it,' Blair said to all to whom he spoke. The advice he received was unanimous: 'Do nothing, fight on.'[66] Rather than being shocked or disturbed, he became increasingly phlegmatic over the evening: 'I found him confident, consciously using his experience as PM, and focused on "getting on with things",' recalled one witness.[67]

Later on that evening, Number 10 phoned Blair in York with some news: Blair's advisers felt they needed a respected Cabinet minister to go on air, defend Blair's position and stress that he was expected to leave in around a year's time. David Miliband was willing to do it if they wanted him to. Did Blair agree with the strategy? His reply was positive: it was a big concession for him, the first time he agreed to a public statement about his departure date. He knew he had no choice.[68] Having ascertained that the *Today* programme would welcome an interview, Wegg-Prosser was deputed to wake up Miliband at quarter to midnight to confirm the line that he would take the next morning – that Blair would not fight on after the next party conference.[69] Of all Cabinet ministers, Miliband was the favoured choice to execute the mission exactly because he was not a firm Blairite. Since leaving Number 10 in 2001, he had carved out a distinct niche for himself in the party, with good links to the Brown and Prescott camps and strong support within the PLP. His well-known differences with Blair over Lebanon added further to his credibility: 'He was seen as the next generation,' explained Armstrong. 'He would have much more credibility with people because he was on the way up.'[70] Miliband's unequivocal words on *Today* should have steadied the ship: 'The conventional wisdom is that the Prime Minister sees himself carrying on for about another twelve months. It seems to me that that conventional wisdom is reasonable,' he said.[71] But by Tuesday morning, the issue had become so septic that even these words failed to hold the dam.

Tuesday morning's press brought still more bad news, with the *Guardian* carrying reports of the letter from the 2001 intake.[72] Even worse – because it was totally new – the *Daily Mirror* published details of a document that had been leaked from Number 10, 'Reconnecting With the Public – A New Relationship With the Media', authored by Wegg-Prosser for the Chequers meeting in April. No one in Number 10 knew how they had obtained it, as it had been e-mailed to just four people: they speculated that someone had left it on the Underground or elsewhere.[73] They had no doubt, though, that the leak had been timed to inflict maximum damage. 'As TB enters his final phase', the document said, 'he needs to be focusing way beyond the finishing line, not looking at it. He needs to go with the crowds wanting more. He should be the star. He won't even play that last encore.' Television appearances on *Songs of Praise* and *Blue Peter*, and guest appearances on Chris Evans' Radio 2 show were mooted. Other elements of the grand departure included visits to half a dozen cities and to twenty of the most striking buildings opened or developed since 1997. The story aroused amusement and anger, while the Brown camp alighted on a passage which said 'the more successful we are, the more it will agitate and possibly de-stabilise [Brown]'.[74] Blair was every bit as exercised about the leaked document as about the coup: it reeked of triumphalism and hubris, and he hated appearing boastful.[75] Before the leak Number 10 said he had never even set eyes on the document, yet the staged manner of his departure bore striking similarities to the leaked paper. The response to the leak helps explain the jaundiced response to his 'long goodbye'.

Blair decided to press ahead with his social exclusion visit, which included doing local and regional media, and trying to focus on 'real problems and achievements'.[76] That morning at 8 A.M., two hundred miles to the south, Blair's senior staff sat in Taylor and Turner's office and mused over where they now were. If there were indeed three letters in circulation, including one from the 1997 intake which they had heard least about, they estimated that it could involve over half the backbenchers. That would be fatal. 'It was looking as though he wasn't in a position to have any control over his destiny,' said one close aide.[77] The media speculated about failure in Iraq overshadowing an abrupt end to his premiership. The outlook appeared bleak. The pressure they faced bound the team closer together, and Blair realised how much he depended on them. The very continuation of his premiership rested upon their good judgement.

Fight-back: 5–7 September

'The worst moment was before we worked out exactly how we were going to fight back,' said Turner.[78] Blair's camp alighted on their recovery plan during the day on Tuesday 5 September. It had two prongs. 'It's no good just sitting here and waiting for this to explode on us. We've got to fight back,' Taylor said.[79] He suggested phoning the Labour MP Karen Buck, who had recently left the government and who represented the solid middle ground in the PLP, and ask her to organise a letter in support of the Miliband position as announced on air that morning. Because she was seen as an independent operator, it was hoped she would carry a particular authority.[80] Buck accepted their call, and told them she thought that most of the MPs were happy with what Miliband had said. Together with Taylor, she drafted a letter to that effect. Number 10 went into telephone blitz mode, phoning MPs after they had been sent the text of Buck's letter, and telling them that the Prime Minister fully accepted what Miliband had said on *Today*.[81] Before long they were able to come up with sixty signatories.[82] Number 10 aides said that they could easily have recruited more signatures, but chose to exclude those closely allied to Blair to emphasise that he still retained support from a wider constituency in the PLP.[83] MPs were mostly back from their holidays and in their constituencies: many found it 'a relief' after all the furore to be contacted by Number 10. Loyalist MPs were also brought in to phone their peers and say 'look, if you think this is completely nuts, you're not the only one'.[84] The Buck letter was duly published in the press on Wednesday morning, helping to show that Blair still commanded much of the centre ground. The other prong of the fight-back was covert, and took place in the shadows of Westminster. The plan originated with Wegg-Prosser, who took a unilateral decision to go on the offensive and spend two or three days 'telling journalists that this was Gordon's coup'. A colleague in Number 10 said 'it was an incredibly brave thing for him to do, well outside the normal parameters of what's expected'.[85] Wegg-Prosser operated underground and unofficially, and deliberately did not tell others in the building what he was saying or to whom.[86]

By the Tuesday evening, Blair was back in Number 10 and the tide appeared to be turning in their direction. Blair had been in regular contact with Brown throughout, but the time had come to tackle him head-on. At 7:45 the next morning, the two men met on their own for almost two hours in Downing Street. Both were defiant. Although Brown had received the assurance from Blair earlier in the year that the Prime Minister would go in the summer of 2007, he did not believe it. He now thought he had Blair on the run and, according to reports of the meeting, demanded 'bankable' public pledges on both Blair's departure date and that he would have a 'clear run at the leadership'. Blair replied, 'I can't do that. I can't stop people standing.' Further demands by Brown were that Blair rein in his 'outriders' Byers and Milburn; Brown was fed up having his policies rubbished by the duo. 'I can't stop them speaking,' said Blair. This was a common Brown complaint. 'Gordon was endlessly walking in and accusing us of briefing against him. We would just laugh. "Gordon, it doesn't matter, I can't call them off because I don't know what they're doing," Blair would say.'[87] Brown also pushed for a period of 'joint premiership' in the run-up to the succession.[88] To the media, Wegg-Prosser described Brown's stance, strictly off the record, as 'blackmail'.[89] It was 'like one of those rows between boyfriend and girlfriend' one insider told the *Sunday Times*. 'Gordon was in a sulk; he sat down and basically refused to say anything or explain what was up.'[90] Patrick Wintour, the recipient of some of the briefing, described Wednesday as 'probably the most astonishing day in the annals of New Labour'.[91] According to one Blair ally, the meeting broke up with Brown saying, 'If you don't do what I ask, then there'll be big trouble.'[92] A dazed Blair went off to the Parliamentary Committee on anti-Semitism. On entering the room, he saw his former sparring partner, Iain Duncan Smith. 'I suppose you're laughing your head off about all of this, aren't you?' he said. The former Conservative leader's response touched and surprised him. 'I know only too well what can go on,' he said.[93]

One reason for Brown's confidence that morning with Blair, Number 10 soon surmised, was that he had advance knowledge of further assaults on Blair's leadership. Around mid-morning, news reached Number 10 that Watson was resigning from the government. Blair's response came two minutes before noon. 'I've heard from the media that Tom Watson has resigned. I had been intending to dismiss him . . . To sign a round-robin letter which was then leaked to the press was disloyal, discourteous and wrong.' Watson's resignation letter arrived at Number 10 soon after. 'It is with the greatest sadness that I have to say that your remaining in office is no longer in the interests of either the party or the country,' it said.[94] At 12:35 P.M. came the long-anticipated resignation of Khalid Mahmood as a Parliamentary Private Secretary; before the day was over – in a sequence carefully choreographed, the Blairites believed, by Simon and Watson – a further six PPSs resigned.[95] Although they were the lowest echelon of ministerial life, the orchestrated resignation of seven PPSs sent out powerful shockwaves. Blair's inner circle feared that what Brown had been saying to Blair that morning was 'there'll be more resignations if you don't actually give a date'.[96] At the lowest point that day, Taylor spoke to Blair in the garden at Number 10. Blair said, 'If they've gone against me, I don't want to fight. I don't want to survive at any cost, but if you think this can be stopped then please do anything you can.'[97] He was 'incredibly calm', recalled one confidant; 'it wasn't anger, it was realism'.[98] Blair saw Brown again at 2 P.M. The meeting was steadier than earlier. Blair repeated that he would be gone next summer, and they began to explore ways of pulling back from the brink. A party in meltdown would have served neither, and that was the prospect they faced. They agreed to work more closely together, which proved the genesis of what, after many twists, became known as the 'policy review'.[99] As Brown departed from Number 10 in his car, his grin was snapped by photographers. It was widely criticised at the time as a smirk. 'I was actually smiling,' he protested, 'talking to one of my colleagues about my new baby . . . it was nothing to do with politics.'[100] His reply appeared disingenuous to many. Having waited twelve and a half years for Blair to agree to come out in public with a departure date, he could have been forgiven a smile.

During the course of Wednesday, boosted by the publication of the Buck letter, the middle ground of the PLP, including those who had been critical of the war in Lebanon and those who had campaigned against the education bill, began to swing back to Blair. To many Labour MPs, it was madness to risk tearing the party apart for the sake of getting Blair out a few months earlier than planned. The media, coaxed by Wegg-Prosser, were also beginning to question whether the plot was the spontaneous event that its perpetrators maintained, or whether it had been orchestrated either by Brown or by his allies.[101] Peter Watt talked to Blair later that afternoon while walking in the garden at Number 10. 'I'm not getting the sense now that the party doesn't want me to be their leader,' he told the general secretary.[102] Senior Labour figures were firing both barrels in defence of Blair. Hutton had spoken on the *Today* programme that morning, while Hewitt said it was 'madness' to suggest that Blair should submit to conditions for his remaining as Prime Minister.[103] Others made clear under cover that 'if there's going to be a fight, it will be a bloody one. We're not just going to roll over and let this happen.'[104] Brown had only minority support at the top level, and he knew it. 'If it came to the crunch in Cabinet, Gordon would have been the loser for sure,' said one. Now the balance of momentum began to shift. Brown and his camp realised that the mood was changing and became increasingly willing to find a way out of the impasse. Most crucial was Prescott's resolute support for Blair from the very beginning of the coup, despite a year of wavering allegiance. 'This is not right,' he told Blair. 'It's not fair and it's not what the party wants.' Had he instead told Blair that 'the party has had enough', it would probably have proved fatal.[105] The third-term Prescott was not the powerful prop for Blair that he had been in 2003–04, but on this occasion, uniquely in the third term, he held Blair's premiership in his hand.

Blair and Brown agreed at their second meeting on Wednesday that they should make statements the following day confirming their agreed positions: Brown's loyalty and Blair's departure within the year. Brown delivered his just after 2 P.M. at a Glasgow sports centre. The text was opaque, but everybody understood him to be saying that he would be supporting Blair until his departure. Blair made his an hour later, deliberately choosing a school ('a resonant venue') which had to be in London because of timing. He chose the Quinton Kynaston School in St John's Wood, in Karen Buck's constituency (as a 'thank you').[106] Not everything could be choreographed: he arrived to be greeted by demonstrators chanting 'Tony, Tony, Tony, out, out, out!' He opened his comments with some impromptu words.[107] 'The first thing I would like to do is to apologise on behalf of the Labour Party for the last week. [It] has not been our finest hour, to be frank.' He would have preferred to have made the announcement in his own time, he continued, but he wished to confirm what had been said earlier in the week by David Miliband, that the coming party conference would be his last. Significantly, and deliberately, he said nothing about endorsing Brown when it came to the leadership election. On one point he was emphatic: 'I'm not going to set a precise date now. I don't think that is right. I will do it at a future date and I'll do it in the interests of the country and depending on the circumstances at the time.'[108] 'Before the party conference' effectively only left him the option of May, June or July: hardly a wide range. But he wanted to avoid any impression of capitulation, and to show he still had some cards left in his hand: he was to play them for all they were worth over the coming months.

Pendulum Swings Against Brown: 7–10 September

During the week of the coup, Peter Hain was in his constituency of Neath, where activists had been highly critical of Blair over the last couple of years. 'But they turned like that [he clicked his fingers] and the anger towards Gordon was palpable. I rang him that night: "You must be very careful because it's turned completely against you,"' Hain told him, and they then discussed how to turn this around. Brown assured Hain that the coup was not at his instigation, an assurance Hain accepted.[109] Once the immediate crisis was over, Blair's calm and self-possession turned to anger, and it was directed principally against Brown. His covert licensing of the anti-Brown briefing operation was one manifestation. 'That's the only time briefing against Gordon was allowed,' said one aide who joined Number 10 in 2005.[110] The operation was deemed effective in shifting the heat from Blair to Brown. Criticism focused on Brown's character and his suitability for the top office. 'He risks being seen as selfish, obsessive – and dangerous', Martin Kettle wrote in Saturday's *Guardian*. 'Gordon Brown's failed coup threatens to be as much of a disaster for him as for his party.'[111] On the BBC's lunchtime news that same day, it was reported that 'the question today is not now "How long can Tony Blair hang on?" but "Is Gordon Brown fit to be Prime Minister?"' One anonymous source said, 'Brown has never had the bollocks to stand up and say what he actually thinks. He won't take the risk of putting himself on the line . . . Which says a lot about what sort of leader he would make.' The relationship between

Blair and Brown was described as 'absolutely diabolical'.[112] The Brown camp, in turn, were livid that Blair was sanctioning the backlash. 'He should have done more to end the Downing Street culture of attacks on Gordon,' said Jack Dromey. 'The briefing against ministers has gone on for ten years. Number 10 is more to blame than Gordon's camp.'[113] The Brownites counter-attacked. One MP said of Blair: 'There's no need to finish him completely. He can't control events any more. The necessary damage is done.'[114]

Into this volatile position stepped Charles Clarke, acting, Number 10 insists – and credibly so – without invitation or endorsement. 'We had no idea he was going to do it. I think he was merely appalled by the behaviour of the people who had organised the coup,' said a Number 10 aide.[115] On Friday, Clarke accused Brown of 'absolutely stupid' behaviour during the crisis and of 'eroding confidence by failing to work with his Cabinet colleagues'. He lavished praise on arch-rival Milburn who was applauded for his 'leadership potential', a statement absolutely guaranteed to inflame the Brownites.[116] A string of ministers, including Harriet Harman and (less predictably) Ruth Kelly lined up to attack Clarke for his ill-advised intervention. The closest Number 10 came to criticising Clarke was to say that they were 'comfortable with Kelly' saying that such comments were damaging to the party and unrepresentative of it.[117] But worse was to come. In an interview with Saturday's *Daily Telegraph* Clarke was reported as saying that Brown had 'psychological' issues, that he was a 'control freak' and 'totally uncollegiate'. Brown was also 'deluded' to think that Blair should anoint him as his successor now.[118] 'NOW THE CRUSADE TO STOP GORDON' roared the *Daily Mail* on Monday, 11 September.[119] In a frantic effort to calm the issue down, Brown phoned a number of ministers later that day to assure them that he had not been involved in the coup.[120]

A relieved Blair left London for Jerusalem on Saturday, secure that the corner had been turned. Blair had wanted to visit the Middle East since July, but had been talked out of it by his advisers. He saw the visit as an opportunity to repair damage with the PLP and with public opinion in the UK, to heal wounds in the region and to reinvigorate the peace process.[121] The visit was difficult: 'I feared it would be a complete disaster and it would come apart at the seams,' said one senior official.[122] Before his arrival, hundreds of Palestinians signed a newspaper advertisement in the *Al-Ayyam* newspaper criticising his visit and his stance during the Lebanon conflict. 'He is coming here in order to wash hands [that] are dripping with Lebanese blood ... Tony Blair is *persona non grata* in our country.'[123] By meeting the families of the two Israeli troops whose kidnapping had sparked the thirty-four-day conflict, he aroused more controversy. A small breakthrough was achieved when Ehud Olmert announced in the joint press conference on 9 September that he planned to meet Palestinian President Abbas and push forward the peace process. But these were small crumbs considering the damage Blair had done to himself through his support of Olmert. His visit to Beirut on 11 September proved even tougher, with Blair facing a boycott from the political leaders of the powerful Shia community. Lebanese Prime Minister Fouad Siniora had wanted to meet him, and asked him to press Olmert on being positive about the peace process. Their meeting took place protected by a tight security cordon of 'armoured cars, razor wire and troops', keeping at bay 2,000 angry protestors.[124] Number 10 insisted that it had been a 'good trip', but it was a very long way from where he wanted to be with only months of his premiership remaining.[125]

Farewell Conference

On returning from the Middle East, Blair was immediately confronted by a hostile TUC conference at Brighton on 12 September. In his speech at the St John's Wood school he had quipped that it would probably be a relief 'to both sides' that this was to be his last TUC conference. He faced unprecedented heckling with respect to Iraq and at one point lost his temper, reminding delegates that British and American troops were fighting at the request of their respective democratic governments. Demanding that the hecklers listen 'for once', he said, 'We should be proud of what we are doing to support democrats in Iraq, and are proud of it.' They should be supporting their colleagues in Iraq and Afghanistan, 'who've got trade union rights for the first time'.[126] A chastened Brown leapt to his defence at Brighton. He had ground to make up, and was acutely aware that Blair retained the power not only to choose the precise timing of his departure but also to promote a challenger.

Brown was on his best behaviour at a private TUC dinner, when he praised Blair's speech, condemned the hecklers, and insisted that the reform programme, including in the health service, would continue if he was elected leader.[127] Brown spoke in similar vein at the party conference in Manchester on 25 September, delivering what was 'deliberately designed to be a healing speech'.[128] In carefully modulated words, he set out his stall as Prime Minister-in-waiting. The speech's impact was somewhat blunted when, in response to his claim that it had been a 'privilege to work with the most successful Labour Prime Minister', Cherie was overheard by a journalist murmuring, 'Well, that's a lie.' She denied it, as did Number 10, but everyone knew that she meant it. For a few hours the issue threatened to throw a delicate conference out of balance. There were some tense exchanges behind closed doors in the inner Blair court. Brown decided not to react in a wounded or angry fashion, which helped plaster over the cracks.[129]

The Manchester conference was dominated by Blair, and it rapidly came to be seen as his swansong. For all the hype, he had not greatly enjoyed his nine previous annual party conferences as Prime Minister. Peppered with politics, composite motions and receptions, he did not find party politicising, or indeed smooth talking, congenial, though he did the latter very skilfully. But he enjoyed this conference, and not having to battle any longer against the party. His first public appearance, a reception to welcome delegates on the Saturday evening, set the tone. The exuberant response that greeted him meant he found it difficult to begin his short speech. When he walked on to the platform on the Sunday, he received a standing ovation, and when Hazel Blears praised his leadership, she herself received a standing ovation. The fuss made Blair even more determined to pitch his speech perfectly. He developed some 70 per cent of it himself, 20 per cent came from Campbell, a key figure throughout his last eighteen months, and the rest from others, including Gould, Taylor and Collins.[130] Blair rigorously checked and rewrote every sentence of the speech himself. He had praise for Brown: 'I know New Labour would never have happened, and three election victories would never have been secured, without Gordon Brown. He is a remarkable man. A remarkable servant to this country. And that is the truth.' He covered the waterfront of issues from climate change, terrorism, crime and Africa, to public services. His core message was that he had been leader of the party for twelve years and Prime Minister for nine, and that if the party stuck with the direction that he had laid out, it would be a winning formula for the future.

Responding to the frequent criticism that he was selfishly remaining in office only to secure his legacy, he said that he wanted to help build a unified party 'for the only legacy that has ever mattered to me – a fourth-term election victory'. He went on: 'The first rule in politics: there are no rules. You make your own luck. There is no rule that says the Tories have got to come back. David Cameron's Tories? My advice: get after them.' He wanted to air his views on how the world had changed during his premiership: 'In 1997, the challenges we faced were essentially British. Today they are essentially global,' thinking of climate change, organised crime and terrorism. His peroration contained his finest oratory. 'They say I hate the party, and its traditions. I don't. I love this party. There's only one tradition I hated: losing . . . It's up to you. You take my advice. You don't take it. Your choice. Whatever you do, I'm always with you. Head and heart. You've given me all I've ever achieved, and all that we've achieved, together, for the country. Next year I won't be making this speech. But in the years to come, wherever I am, whatever I do, I'm with you. Wishing you well. Wanting you to win. You're the future now. Make the most of it.'

The speech received a rapturous response, but the greatest single applause came for the way he dealt with Cherie's comment from the day before. His team knew that they could not gloss over it and would have to address it. But how? 'Trying to lock it up in a joke seemed a good way forward.' Chatting around the issue, Collins relayed an old Les Dawson joke: 'My wife ran off with the bloke next door. I'm really going to miss him.'[131] That seemed a bit much for the speech, and barely relevant. Campbell overheard the joke and now sought to adapt it. In the end it was Blair who came up with the formulation, which Liz Lloyd briefed to the Brown camp in advance. In his speech Blair thanked his family and particularly Cherie for their support during his premiership: 'At least I don't have to worry about her running off with the bloke next door,' he deadpanned. 'The joke was a theatrical triumph, an absolute clincher in getting the mood right for the conference,' said Hill.[132] By the Tuesday evening, even his critics were asking why he was going, and were saying he was the best leader the party had ever had. On the Wednesday afternoon, before he departed for London, he attended a small party for the conference organisers. When he walked into the room, they all burst out clapping and cheering and suddenly he became quite tearful. 'It's not until this moment that I realise what it's all about,' he said. 'This whole week is like an act. I have to do this as part of the process, but this is the first time that I've suddenly thought it is very real,' Watt recalled him saying.[133]

So what was the long-term impact of the September coup? Did it affect the timing of his departure? The Brown camp says 'yes', and the Blair camp 'no'. The coup forced him into a public admission that he would not address a further party conference, which meant going in the summer of 2007: 'I think it brought home to them that you just couldn't slow this process down,' said a senior member of the Cabinet. 'It was gathering its own momentum.'[134] Apart from the ultras in Number 10, the vast majority of his advisers knew that the summer of 2007 was all he could hope for, and in his heart of hearts, Blair knew himself that it was unrealistic to remain longer. Did it affect his relationship with Brown? It showed yet again, for all their vituperative comments and the goading of their camps, and whether for *Realpolitik* or love, most likely a mixture of both, neither man was prepared to pull the trigger on the other. 'Love was at the bottom of everything that went on between them. That's why they could never pull the trigger. They fight and scrap like hell, but in the last analysis they never want to eradicate each other,' said one Blair aide.[135] At the height of the coup, one associate phoned Blair to express his frustration with Brown. Blair replied, 'We all have our good moments and our bad moments with Gordon. In the end, we always end up where we started. So get back in your Brown box.'[136] As ever, Blair had a remarkable capacity to separate the personal from the political.

The September coup invites a whole range of other questions. Did it change Blair's policy? The limited time he had left focused him even more on driving through reform, and inclined him to disregard what his opponents thought. In a real sense, he had never been freer in his premiership. Did it damage the party? Despite the fears raised at the time, there is no evidence of long-term damage. The polls quickly recovered. At the end of July, MORI put the Conservatives on 36 per cent and Labour on 32 per cent: by the very end of September, just after the conference, a YouGov poll had them at level pegging, on 36 per cent.[137] The recovery helped steady the party. Divisions within the PLP became no worse and in some respects healed. The diehard left-wing MPs in the Campaign Group were never going to come round to him, and were equally hostile to Brown. The independent left-wing MPs associated with Compass saw no advantage in any further pressure on Blair, while Brownite MPs were keen to toe the line. And the line was to keep your head down. The PLP became quieter than it had been for months. In Cabinet, ministers became more united. 'There was a sense of something building up before the summer; there was a lot of surliness and it wasn't a nice place to be,' said one minister. 'Cabinet became a much better place after September.'[138] In his remaining months in power, Blair was more in command of Cabinet than at any point since before Iraq: only three or four ministers did not respect him.

Was Brown involved? Despite his protestations to the contrary, as in the March and May coups, one longstanding Brownite, speaking strictly off the record, admitted the extent of Brown's complicity: 'It was always going to happen from the moment Tony Blair came back to power in

2005 and carried on exactly as before,' he said. 'They only waited for the ideal moment. "I've put up with this for a year," Gordon said, "but no longer." We all said, "Give him his ten years," but Gordon was getting so upset that Tony wasn't consulting him and that he wasn't giving him a date. Gordon's great fear was that he would go on until 2008.' Brown's camp, said the source, were deeply involved: 'They'd been planning something like the coup from day one after the General Election. They knew that if they got into year two with no move from Gordon, they would have to promote it – provoke it would be a better word. His position on the coup would have been "I won't stand in your way, but you can't, you mustn't implicate me or show I instigated anything". But he knew of it.'[139]

Finally, what about the effect on Blair? His anger mostly burned itself out after a day or two, as he realised that he had come out of it with time still to achieve his goals. He was utterly determined to see 'Blairism' extended and he wanted a smooth and constructive transition of power. The one thing he never wanted was – like Thatcher – to be forced out of office. After the coup, Blair found a new voice, rediscovering his ability to communicate with the public with a surety of touch that he had partially lost for several years. He would need all of these skills if he was to ensure that his final nine months were to be the climax he hoped.

19

On a Knife Edge

September–December 2006

Prime Ministers often face challenges to their authority towards the end of their premierships: Churchill did in 1954, Macmillan did in 1962 and Callaghan in 1978. Thatcher achieved little in her final year after Anthony Meyer stood as a stalking-horse candidate against her in the autumn of 1989, and Major found little new impetus after he won the 'back me or sack me' leadership election in 1995. Blair was determined to carve out a new path as the only Prime Minister in modern history with a publicly declared finishing point whose premiership ended with a bang, not a whimper. By the autumn of 2006 some third-term objectives, on pensions, the Education Act, nuclear energy and Africa, were already in the bag. But an alarmingly high number – the entrenchment of academies and trust schools, completion on crime, health and welfare reform, nuclear weapons, Northern Ireland, Europe, climate and the MEPP – hung in the balance, while in Afghanistan and Iraq, he desperately craved finishing with some vindication. If that wasn't enough, he also sought to ensure his brand of Labourism, not any other variant, continued to dominate the future. The wish-list was absurdly ambitious, and his resources were severely depleted. Many thought that now he had said he would be off within the year, that he would become a lame duck, and the real power would pass to Brown. Blair was attempting to achieve something unique; playing Brown cleverly would be crucial to his success. But he had only two trumps left in his hand: deciding whether to back Brown for the leadership or to support an alternative candidate, and the precise timing and manner of his departure.

Policy Review — Cat and Mouse: October–December

Within just days of the post-coup love-in, a new battle emerged between Brown and Blair, and it went right to the heart of control of domestic policy and the future of New Labour. The Brownites ideally would have liked Blair to spend his final nine months 'talking about the past and his "legacy", while we got on with the serious work of planning for the future'.[1] Although Blair knew that he could not 'do anything to tie the hands of his successor', he was determined the party was going to continue on the path he had set since 1994.[2] Any other course, which might involve a return to the 'old days' before New Labour, was out of the question. But Brown resented bitterly the idea that Blair should have any say at all over his premiership: for over twelve years he had had to play second fiddle to a man who he thought had an infinitely inferior strategic sense, and he did not want that person now telling him what to do on his own watch. This epic drama played itself out in what became known as the 'policy review'. Its genesis lay in the second meeting that Blair and Brown had on Wednesday 6 September, when they agreed to work more closely on policy in Blair's remaining months.[3]

Just before Blair flew off to the Middle East, two days after that encounter, Matthew Taylor said to him: 'We've got to exact a price from all this. Gordon's under huge pressure now.' Friday was the day when the party's anger against Brown burst. Taylor's concern was that Blair should capitalise on it fully before the storm subsided. 'I know what you're going to do. You're going to end up backing him because that's what you always do, and you want to prevent it reaching a crisis,' he told him brutally. He agreed that it was right to avoid a bloody end to the premiership, but persisted: 'If you don't extract something concrete, it's just going to happen again.'[4] What exactly did Taylor have in mind? Blair asked. Taylor told him about his thoughts on Number 10 collaborating with Brown on future policy. 'Put it on paper,' Blair asked him. From Friday to Sunday, while Blair was seeing Olmert and Siniora, Taylor spoke to the team in Number 10. 'Matthew was being a complete pain in the arse that weekend. He kept going on about needing a "forward process" while we were just thinking "For God's sake, leave us alone. We'd just survived a coup and no one had much energy left. What are you on about?"' said one.[5] The only way it would work, they told the ebullient Taylor, was if Blair had a real appetite for it. Taylor duly rang Blair to discuss the idea. 'He saw the sense of it right away,' he told them.[6] By the end of the weekend, it had become clear that this was the only way he could make headway over the next few months.

On Blair's return from the Middle East, he sent Brown the memo with an appended message saying 'This is what I want to do'. After a bit of jockeying and thinking that it would be easier to palm off than it proved, Brown agreed. Blair had clear reasons for favouring the policy review. The approach was similar to the five-year plans of 2003–04: he wanted to show that Labour could renew itself as a party in government, and that he himself was driving that process forwards.[7] He wanted to flesh out a programme for the next ten years, taking stock of the changes in the world that he had described in his party conference speech. He told insiders that he did not feel Brown was yet thinking broadly enough for a future Prime Minister: 'In his mind, Gordon had yet to work out such a programme.'[8] The Brownites thought this was all patronising twaddle. But warding off temptations for Brown to drift leftwards was Blair's key objective. In the wake of the coup, he saw the policy review as a way of 'rehabilitating Gordon, with obvious implications if that didn't happen'.[9] Brown would either 'participate in a collective process of discussing policy, or be seen to be avoiding such a discussion. That was the purpose of it all,' said a senior Number 10 figure.[10] It was Blair at his most Machiavellian. If Brown collaborated with him, and agreed to the collective policy in public, he would substantially be adopting the Blairite policy agenda for the next five or more years. If he did not support the policy, then Blair would promote a serious alternative candidate, at least until such time as Brown saw sense.[11] Blair saw very clearly that the next few months with Brown would be a game of cat and mouse. Some of Blair's loyalists in Cabinet, apprehensive about what a Brown government might mean for them, egged Blair on to ensure that, after he left, Brown would run a government which was as congenial to them as possible: others were tacking Brown-wards, and were very carefully ensuring they did nothing that could be seen to be unfriendly to the likely new regime.

After the post-coup reaction against him began to calm down, Brown became more suspicious of Blair's true intentions in the policy review. There was no shortage of people sympathetic to him 'keen to point out that this was the big Blairite plot to tie his hands'.[12] A difficult period ensued. The first reaction of the Treasury was 'to completely rubbish it'. The ultras on Brown's side were deeply hostile, and urged Brown to be wary. Among Cabinet ministers, Douglas Alexander was the most critical, arguing in private that the review was an unnecessary distraction and that it was not Blair's business to worry about the next ten years. It was what the Brownites all thought. Blairites, including Hutton, Jowell and the increasingly loyal Hewitt, argued that the review was an excellent initiative, and wanted it to be conducted as publicly as possible, in part to ensure that Brown was fully bound in. A middle group including Straw argued that the policy review should take place, but be conducted in private.[13]

When the Brownites' confidence returned, they began to suggest a price for their playing along. Before assenting to their participation, they believed Blair should both name a firm date, and endorse Brown. Blair was not prepared to trade. To do either would render him totally dead in the water: maintaining uncertainty about the future was vital. A main Treasury concern was that the process would pre-empt elements of the comprehensive spending review (CSR) which set the Whitehall budget for the following three years. Could this be the device to tame Blair's review? Over the following weeks, Brown worked hard to ensure that any recommendations that emerged from the policy review would be locked into the CSR and his March 2007 budget, rather than allowing it to be a free-standing government process in its own right.[14] The Treasury need not have worried: the review's timeframe projected well into the next decade and beyond. Very few of its recommendations had any relevance to the CSR's three-year spending commitments. Battles raged between Number 10 and the Treasury on all fronts: how many review groups should there be? What topics should they cover? Who should sit on and chair the groups? What role should Brown play? Mutual suspicion was high, but a way forward was found. 'Typically in this period Tony would say, "This is what I want us to do", and we would say, "We're not certain Gordon'll agree", and he responded, "Well, I'll talk to him."'[15] In this way, some of the differences were ironed out by Blair and Brown in lengthy bilateral discussions.

The arrival in September of Olly Robbins, the long-delayed successor to Ivan Rogers as Principal Private Secretary, brought some stability. Robbins, a Treasury man, had good working relations with many of Brown's key officials, notably with James Bowler, his Principal Private Secretary. Robbins speedily established himself as a significant player in Number 10, effortlessly demonstrating that he carried more clout with the Treasury than anyone else in the building. Relations between the two offices improved, as Robbins and Bowler tidied up after the conversations between their two masters. Hitherto, Liz Lloyd had emerged as the figure in Number 10 who, on a political and strategic level, could talk most effectively with the Treasury, but she would regularly report back 'No, he doesn't agree with this at all', and found it hard to get much further. During the autumn, this gradually began to change. Bit by bit, remaining obstacles to the policy review were mostly removed. Both the Prime Minister and the Chancellor were to appoint a minister to oversee the work of the policy groups. Blair's choice of Pat McFadden was accepted by the Brown camp. But when Brown nominated Balls, Number 10 hit the roof. 'Everyone at Downing Street, from Blair downwards, said that there was absolutely no way that they were going to work with Ed Balls.'[16] Was this suggestion a joke? Surely Brown's camp must have known how much he was mistrusted in Number 10? For a while, it was agreed that McFadden would work on his own, but subsequently, Ed Miliband, who had initially been reluctant, was encouraged to take on the role. A steering group comprising Lloyd, Bennett, Taylor and Dan Corry (who was to become Brown's first Head of Policy in Number 10) also worked on resolving disagreements in the review.[17] Both McFadden and Ed Miliband joined the group subsequently.[18] Despite their efforts, disputes remained. One involved a proposal, which ironically became one of Brown's early initiatives as Prime Minister. Both Taylor and Wegg-Prosser advocated a series of 'citizen's juries' to re-engage the public with politics. During September and early October, they met with strong resistance from the Treasury. 'Tony liked the idea, but never believed in it so strongly that he wanted to fight hard,' said one aide, 'but Gordon's people killed citizen's juries because they didn't want Tony to do anything which they wanted to do themselves.'[19]

By the middle of October, agreement was reached on who would chair the six working groups.[20] Brown would chair only one, on economic dynamism, and Blair the other five; on public services, crime and justice, the role of the state, environment and energy, and Britain and the world. On Thursday 19 October, Blair gave a keynote presentation to Cabinet about the nature, extent and purpose of the review. One present described it as 'the best performance I ever saw him give at Cabinet: dynamic, passionate, incredibly interesting and full of command of facts and figures'.[21] The previous few days had seen a final ritual spat of briefing and counter-briefing, with Number 10 saying that Blair was going to 'lay out the next ten years' and Brown's camp saying 'it's a pointless exercise', before the review was launched on 20 October under the title 'Pathways to the Future'. The six policy groups, the announcement said, would be including the relevant ministers as well as outside experts; they would announce their findings in the spring; and their conclusions would 'inform' the March budget as well as the CSR. Blair said in public that the review would absorb much of his remaining time as Prime Minister, and that he wanted to use his experience to help Britain face up to the challenges of the following ten years. Brown was reported officially as being 'enthusiastic' about the review, and sharing Blair's belief that 'it would help both the government and the country address the unprecedented challenges facing the world in the coming years'.[22]

The first round of policy review meetings began apace, with the idea that initial reports would be produced at Christmas. In the process, each of the six groups was to make an initial presentation, then commission papers and background research before identifying key areas for further work and only then agreeing on provisional conclusions. The Policy Directorate and Strategy Unit provided much of the back-up. One official described it as 'the most traditional Cabinet committee process I've seen in Whitehall'.[23] This had been something that successive Cabinet Secretaries had been urging him to make use of for nine years. It was ironic that having spent nine years driving a coach and horses through traditional norms of government, in his twilight months Blair presided over an operation which even the most starchy of Whitehall mandarins was reluctantly compelled to approve.

Two Wicker-Chair Patio Conversations: September–December

Tony Blair loved to sit out in the sun on wicker chairs on the patio outside the Cabinet Room. Within the space of a few days in September, Blair held conversations with his two most thrusting third-term ministers: Andrew Adonis and John Hutton. These conversations were to set the timbre of policy over his final nine months. Thursday 7 September had been a trying and emotional day, when Blair had announced that the coming party conference would be his last. He was nevertheless 'calm, collected and focused on the challenges ahead' when he chatted on a balmy summer evening to an eager Adonis about education plans.[24] Blair told him how important the next few months were going to be, and how he wanted to see further bold policy announced to consolidate all he had set in train to date. That was the cue Adonis needed. He launched into three urgent school reforms he wanted Blair to introduce to round off and complete his reform programme.[25]

Academies have been Blair's most distinctive contribution to schools, and it was to these that Adonis wanted to give a final push. The summer had been a good one for academies. In July, a series of legal judgements, including a decisive High Court verdict, ruled that they were an acceptable form of state school. Hitherto, the DfES had been jittery: the judgements removed any concerns they still had about their legal basis. An independent PricewaterhouseCoopers evaluation published in July 2006 was highly positive,[26] and figures were released that showed that academies were three times over-subscribed. The summer 2005 GCSE results showed that academies, albeit starting often from a very low base, achieved three times the rate of national improvement for all GCSEs.[27] Adonis had a stream of new sponsors lined up, but they were holding back because of uncertainty about whether academies would continue into the future. Would Brown jettison them? Adonis urged Blair to be bold and to increase the existing target for academies from two hundred to five or six hundred, to show beyond all doubt that they were here to stay. Secondly, trust schools had been introduced by the 2006 Education and Inspections Act, but Adonis was worried that without a further impetus before Blair departed the tipping point on trust schools would also not be met. Finally, he argued the case for Blair to extend opportunities for sixth-form students to study the International Baccalaureate (IB) as a key way of extending the 'choice and diversity' agenda into the curriculum of state schools. Existing provision of the IB was limited to fifty state schools and colleges, insufficient to allow most students the chance to take an IB course, with the result that significant numbers of pupils were leaving state schools to go into the sixth forms of private schools because they offered the IB. Adonis pressed Blair to let every local education authority have at least one state IB provider. 'Yes, you're completely right, I'll do all three,' was Blair's ready response.[28]

Pushing the policies through the system did not prove straightforward. The DfES was not happy with the target of 100 new trusts to be planned by the spring of 2007, and had to be persuaded. On the IB, Adonis ran up against not the DfES, but the education establishment, especially the Qualifications and Curriculum Authority (QCA), who 'fought very strongly against it because they didn't want any alternative to A-level'.[29] The QCA was deemed to be fighting not in the interests of sixth-form students, but to protect its own patch and the status quo, and their objections were over-ruled. Most difficulties, however, arose in the decision to expand academies. Behind the scenes, Sally Morgan, a long-term advocate of giving state schools more independence, helped embolden Blair when the obstacles seemed too great.[30] Alan Johnson, Kelly's successor, was an enthusiast in principle on academies, but remained non-committal. 'Alan was very anxious not to be caught in the crossfire between TB and GB,' said a Number 10 source.[31] Although the DfES had been won over to academies after a period of friction in 2005, some of its officials were wary about setting a target.[32] The real opposition came from Brown and the Treasury. 'This cuts fundamentally across the CSR: we shouldn't be taking any big decisions like this,' he told Number 10.[33] Brown was described as being 'extremely negative' about the expansion, while the Treasury was said to have fought an announcement 'tooth and nail'.[34] Number 10's defence was that the money was available for academies, not from the CSR, but from the extensive 'Building Schools for the Future' programme and the money was thus already allocated.

Blair would announce all three initiatives in a speech at the Specialist Schools and Academies Trust (SSAT) conference on 30 November in Birmingham, which was planned to mark the tenth anniversary of his 'Education, education, education' speech. 'There will be 400 academies, double the present target, by the year 2010.' In the few days leading up to the announcement, the 500–600 target had been whittled down to 400, but Blair was adamant, against official advice, that he would announce a 400 target in his speech. Johnson did not challenge it: he 'neither supported nor opposed it', while the Treasury up to the very last minute tried to get the figure either removed, or further watered down. 'You realise there will be very serious consequences if Blair says this,' a Treasury official phoned to say to Number 10 on the day of the announcement. Blair brushed it aside and defied Brown to attack the figure. Instead it was teacher unions who initially condemned it: the Association of Teachers and Lecturers (ATL) response was 'the government should stop its obsession with academies before it does any further damage. ATL fails to see how academies and trust schools will address the twin evils of pupil under-achievement and inequality of opportunity . . . They are a solution in search of a problem.'[35] Brown was left simmering. He held trump cards too, and it remained to be seen whether he could play one to send out a negative signal that could yet scupper Blair's announcement and make him appear guilty of hubris. Academies were going to go to the wire.

A few weeks later, Blair had another meeting on the wicker chairs outside the Cabinet Room. This time it was with Hutton and Number 10's welfare guru, Gareth Davies, under 'an unseasonably hot sun'. Blair had been thinking hard about the welfare components of the policy review. Welfare had become one of his growth interests in the third term. He agreed with Hutton that they needed to look more deeply at the expectations the state had of benefit claimants, the role of the private and voluntary sectors in looking after them and how to manage policy given the tight CSR settlement the Treasury had imposed on the DWP in the March Budget. In June 2006, Hutton and Davies had travelled to Washington to learn more about the impact of Clinton's welfare reforms on their tenth anniversary, which had been so successful in getting lone parents back to work and improving employment.[36] Over the summer, Hutton read further about Clinton's reforms: his imagination was fired about the possibilities for similarly innovative thinking in Britain. From their discussions on the patio emerged a plan to set up a probing review into welfare provision in Britain. What interested Hutton about Clinton's reforms was the way that he had stood back and asked radical questions about the welfare framework, and did not approach it with an 'insider' mind. Why not appoint a non-welfare specialist to conduct the review in Britain? They agreed they needed someone with a brilliant and wide-ranging mind, financially literate and who could produce the report within the very tight timeframe of the policy review. David Freud's name came up early on. The great-grandson of Sigmund Freud, he had had a distinguished career as a journalist, at the *Financial Times*, and as a banker at Warburgs (UBS). He was just the man who, in Hutton's words, 'would ask the fundamental, stupid questions, about why we were where we were as part of a "ground-zero" review'.[37] He was available and willing to conduct the work. Hutton discussed it with Brown, who was reasonably relaxed: 'The Treasury's attitude was if you want to do it, fine, but it's over to you.'[38] The one concern was over the timing: Blair wanted it done very quickly, for obvious reasons, whereas the Treasury wanted it spread out, for equally obvious reasons.[39] Freud commenced his work in November, and Hutton officially announced the setting-up of the inquiry on 18 December in a provocative speech in which he talked about reducing dependency and attacking the 'can work, won't work' culture.[40] The inquiry, along with academies, created resentment between Brown and Blair in the first quarter of 2007. Ironically, Brown was to make decisive public appearances in support of both, signalling his acceptance of the broad direction of Blair's reform agenda.

The trio of Hutton, Davies and Blair would prove as fruitful on welfare in the third term as the first-term combination of Blunkett, Adonis and Blair on education, or Milburn, Stevens and Blair in the second term on health. His recent success on pensions had given Blair a taste for welfare, and for moving decisively into an area that Brown had regarded exclusively as his territory. It struck Blair and Hutton as anomalous that, with the economy doing so well, and with employment growth going strong, Britain still had 5 million people of working age claiming benefits, including 2.7 million receiving incapacity benefit, at an overall bill of £12.5 billion per annum.[41] Benefits had been a fraught issue earlier for Blair: in 1999, sixty-five backbenchers had rebelled over proposed changes to incapacity benefit. But the economics alone, he felt, dictated that action should no longer be delayed. The billions of pounds spent each year was having the effect of trapping very large numbers in poverty and excluding them from the labour market. Strong financial savings and improvements in economic vitality beckoned. Blair was also attracted by the politics. He saw the 'old sixties attitude about welfare-ism in the Labour party – that the only way a Labour government should touch benefits is by increasing them' as completely outdated.[42] It was the failure of the welfare state that so many were on benefits, not an indicator of success, he believed.[43] According to one minister, his view was 'we need to reform all this rapidly, not because we want to be punitive, but because the current system is locking people out of the labour market for long periods, during which they decline financially, physically and mentally'.[44] Early on in the third term, Blair had met resistance from Blunkett. After what Number 10 considered years of torpor with a risk-averse department, he had brought a new zeal to the department in a short time. But it was still not radical enough for Blair. A short while before Blunkett's departure in November 2005, documents were leaked to the *Mail on Sunday* about Blair's demands for a much tougher regime, including even means-testing benefits for the long-term sick.[45] Blunkett wrote an 'intemperate' letter in reply, protesting that Blair's ideas for overhauling incapacity benefit were unacceptable.[46]

Before he departed, Blunkett had worked up a draft Green Paper, which was scheduled for publication at the end of November.[47] When offering Hutton the job, Blair told him, 'You've really got to push incapacity benefit. I'll be behind you. We've got to move on it.'[48] With his response to Turner's imminent report on pensions at the top of his in-tray, Hutton asked Blair if he could delay the paper until after Christmas, allowing him time to become familiar with the many lobby groups and all the sensitivities surrounding benefits before pouncing.[49] Hutton rapidly concluded he was of the same mind as Blair, and was equally determined to tackle head-on the old Labour shibboleths about protecting the weak. Two months were devoted to his reworking of Blunkett's Green Paper from the bottom up. When published on 24 January 2006, it emerged as a tougher policy than anything Labour had produced in power since 1997. A week before publication, Hutton made a presentation to Cabinet. Blair resorted to his 'usual trick' when he wanted to get something through, of saying before any discussion, 'I think this is really important. I'm very much behind this.' In consequence, there was no real debate or dissent. 'I think ministers just wanted it dealt with in a way that didn't cause any problems, but was seen to be pushing forward the reform agenda,' explained one.[50] The Treasury expressed concerns over the politics, and whether the disability lobby would support the reforms. They did not put up any money, but nor did they try to block it.[51] The Green Paper was wide-ranging and tough: it advocated 'back to work' schemes and, for those who did not participate, the loss of part of their benefits, and it sought to encourage the 300,000 single parents and 1 million elderly people on benefit to return to work, at an overall expected saving of some £7 billion per annum. The proposals proved uncontroversial, and were speedily turned into legislation. Three months of consultation followed the appearance of the Green Paper, after which the Welfare Reform Bill was published. It went through the Commons for the rest of the session, going to the Lords at the beginning of the 2006 session and became an Act a month before Blair stood down as Prime Minister.

The autumn of 2006 saw changes also to the Child Support Agency (CSA). Created by the Major government to ensure that separated parents carried out their obligations to their children, it was widely regarded as having run into problems. When Hutton first took stock of the CSA he thought, 'God, this is a mess. We're going to have to sort this out.'[52] Blunkett had latterly signed off a commitment to £500 million to improve the CSA's administration. Hutton told DWP officials that he was going to cancel the money because he regarded the whole organisation as fundamentally flawed. The traditional view was that the CSA was let down by its IT infrastructure, but when Hutton looked into it, he realised that an even more significant factor in its poor performance was the policy framework. The CSA's model was based on married couples or partners splitting up, whereas in reality 25 per cent or more claimants had 'chaotic' relationships, where there were either multiple relationships, or no details of the father's identity. Over half the mothers entitled to support were already on benefit, and had no interest in getting their child's father to pay because they would lose maintenance from the benefit. To try to make sense of it all, Hutton brought in Liverpool City Council boss, David Henshaw, to conduct a thorough review. 'Tony, I'm going to scrub the CSA and start all over again,' Hutton said. 'I agree. Get on with it,' Blair told him.[53] The Queen's

Speech on 15 November duly announced that the CSA was to be scrapped and to be replaced by an entirely new body. It was an example of Blair having total confidence in a minister to make the right decisions. But Blair's interventions in his final months in welfare served only to further inflame his already volatile relationship with Brown.

Back to the TB/GBs: October–December 2006

The 'TB/GBs' was the name that emerged to describe the utterly unpredictable and tempestuous relationship between Blair and Brown. Two weeks after the party conference, just after Parliament began sitting again, Cameron pressed Blair at Prime Minister's Questions. Was he still happy for Brown to be his successor? Blair twice tried to parry the question and force Cameron back on to policy. But the Conservative leader struck home: 'Everyone sees that the government are divided and paralysed. We have a Prime Minister who does not trust his Chancellor, a Chancellor who's been accused of blackmail, the latest Home Secretary wants the Prime Minister's job, the Deputy Prime Minister doesn't have a job but is still being paid . . . How many more months of this paralysis have we got to put up with?'[54] Within six weeks of the coup, relations between the Blair and Brown camps were as poisonous as they had been in the months leading up to it. At the end of October, Gould handed Blair a three-page strategy document which warned about the consequences of continuing divisions at the top of the party. A 'genuine reconciliation' between the two men was needed before it became too late.[55] It fuelled Blair's concern that Labour would lose power under Brown if he did not wholeheartedly support the direction of New Labour. Brown had a clear chance to prove that he could work with Number 10 on the policy review process. If he did, Blair would endorse him as the candidate. If he did not, he would talk more about his wish to see a leadership election for the good of Brown and the party. Blair still did not fully trust him make to the right choices, still less those around him. He would use Cabinet, where his supporters were in the majority, 'to manage the transition and get Gordon in the right place in six months' time'.[56]

The Queen's Speech on 15 November was Blair's last. In his speech, Blair offered a pugilistic analogy when discussing the challenge Cameron would soon face: 'He will come within the reach of a big clunking fist . . . The fifth Tory leader to be carried out.'[57] As Blair sat down, Brown gratefully congratulated him. Here at last was the acknowledgement as the successor of choice that he craved. Or was it? The PLP saw it as a clear reference to Brown, as did most of the press the following day: 'Tony Blair anointed Gordon Brown as his chosen successor in unveiling his final packet of legislation,' wrote Andy Grice in the *Independent*.[58] Others saw it differently. 'I think that it was an off-the-cuff remark . . . He just meant, whoever succeeds will smash you into the ground,' remarked one Cabinet minister close to Blair.[59] Blair had been toying with the phrase in his mind beforehand: 'He had thought about it, but he wasn't ready explicitly to endorse Gordon,' said a Number 10 source emphatically.[60] 'If he had done so, he would have had to balance it with some reference to John Reid.' Reid, when asked, refused to specify which 'heavyweight' Blair had been referring to, repeatedly refusing to answer questions about the matter.[61] When it became clear it might not have been the endorsement they were looking for, the Brownites continued to agitate for a precise date for his departure.

By the end of November, Number 10 was concerned. Reports came through that there was 'no improvement on Brown. He's still roughing up colleagues. He competes with Reid on terror. Balls and Yvette Cooper rubbish Ruth Kelly's plans. Brown embarrasses Jowell over VAT on the Olympics.'[62] A new concern emerged: Brown's press secretary Damian McBride was considered 'more vicious than Charlie Whelan', Brown's freewheeling press secretary at the start of the first term.[63] On 6 December, Brown tried to assert his authority in his pre-Budget report, setting out the themes for what he expected to be his final budget.[64] He used it to reel off a list of statistics to mark his tenth year as Chancellor of the Exchequer, and, to cut out the ground from under Cameron, announced fuel and air duty increases to show his green credentials, while placing another Cameron priority – schools – at the heart of his future spending plans.[65] Shadow Chancellor George Osborne hit back hard, saying that Brown's much vaunted 'golden rule' was discredited, productivity had slumped, business investment collapsed, and 'Britain has some of the weakest economic growth in the developed world'. He touched a raw nerve when he said that Brown's 'greatest mistake' was to spend without reform. 'Aren't people up and down the country entitled to ask the Chancellor – as they struggle to find a decent school place or campaign to keep their hospital open, or sit in traffic on congested roads – where has all the money gone?'[66] Gould's polling remained pessimistic about Labour's ability to win the next General Election under Brown, and at the very start of December, he concluded that 'Gordon should be worried'.[67]

Talk of rival candidates came and went during the autumn but climaxed in the run-up to Christmas. If there had to be one, Brown wanted to be challenged from the left. Before the summer, Alan Johnson had emerged as a potential candidate for leader, but his star waned. Reid's name emerged strongly during the autumn in particular after his handling of the transatlantic terrorist plot in the summer. Much though he disliked Brown, he was unsure about whether to go for the leadership.[68] David Miliband's name, never far from the lips of the key figures in Downing Street, began to be heard increasingly as a credible candidate.[69] Several Number 10 aides were involved in conversations with him.[70] But in early December, Miliband was reported as saying that though he thought he could get forty MPs to support him, he was wary of standing for three reasons: he would lose, he would have to attack Brown, and his forty supporters would get 'mangled by Brown subsequently'. Milburn, an earlier 'white hope', would have acquired 'forty anti-Gordon Brown votes very easily', but was clear that he was not running. Blair said he favoured a contest, not least so Brown could be tested: 'He thought it would be one of the ways for Gordon to grow to understand the full importance of the coalition behind the New Labour reform project and declare that it would continue under his leadership.'[71] Gould went round saying voters won't like a fix, 'particularly for an unelected Prime Minister!'[72] In his darker moments in the run-up to Christmas, Brown brooded that the prize for which he had waited so long really might be snatched from him at the last moment.

Breakthrough in Northern Ireland

Wednesday 11 October was an utterly miserable day at St Andrews on the east coast of Scotland, cloaked in fog. Driving rain and biting winds greeted Ian Paisley, Gerry Adams and Martin McGuinness, who were to meet Blair for two days of talks on the future of Northern Ireland. 'I hope the wind is at your backs,' Adams joshed to the media on his arrival, while Paisley quipped, 'This is Ballymena weather.'[73] 'The Prime Minister saw this as the last chance in his premiership to resolve the future of Northern Ireland. He knew that if he didn't manage to move both parties, then it wasn't going to happen,' said Tom Kelly.[74] In early 2005, no one would have imagined him having this last chance of achieving the final breakthrough. In the aftermath of the Northern Bank robbery in December 2004 and the Robert McCartney murder at the end of January 2005, many thought that the 'fork in the road' had been taken by Sinn Féin, and they had taken the wrong turning. 'A shiver went down our spines. We were wondering what it would ever take to get the process moving again,' said an NIO official.[75] The best hope was that the shock and revulsion against both events might produce a new awareness among the Republican community that this time they needed to make unequivocal change. The story of 2005 was one of recovery: Number 10 and the NIO had no doubt that 'it would take well over a year, even if we had positive statements from the IRA on decommissioning, to get fully over both episodes'.[76] Acute pressure from both London and Dublin was brought to bear on Sinn Féin and the IRA to show them that they had absolutely no 'wriggle room' left. 'It was all or nothing this time.'[77] Blair worked hard on the problem in the first three months of 2005. 'The Republicans would give him bullshit about how something was impossible and he pushed them past it. They'd endlessly tell him where their red lines were, but he always judged whether they could go further,' said one close aide.[78]

The reaction in the United States was to shake Sinn Féin to their very core. The White House said that the President no longer regarded Adams as 'a reliable partner for peace' and 'does not want to meet him' because he had 'betrayed' efforts to restart the peace process. The Republicans learned that Bush now viewed Adams in the same light as he did Yasser Arafat.[79] A visa application for Adams to visit America for a planned week-long trip to raise money was blocked. While Robert McCartney's sisters were being welcomed by Bush for St Patrick's Day in the White House, Adams and McGuinness were frozen out. The great and good of Washington shared the revulsion and spoke supportively of the McCartney sisters' campaign to bring their brother's killers to justice. Very significantly in Republican eyes, Senator Edward Kennedy, a life-long Nationalist sympathiser, cancelled a meeting with Adams. Funds had been drying up from their supporters in the US since 9/11, but these snubs bit very deeply. 'It played a crucial part in shifting the mood,' said one NIO source.[80]

For the six weeks before the May General Election, Blair disengaged from Northern Ireland, but returned to it with vigour in tandem with new Secretary of State Hain.[81] Momentum was given a boost by Paisley's personal experience during the 2005 General Election: 'He had a sort of revelation on the doorstep. The people of Ulster had spoken to him and they wanted to see the Unionists go into government.'[82] The British thought that Paisley's serious illness before the Leeds Castle talks in 2004 also had had an effect. 'He thought he would sooner die as "Dr Yes" than as "Dr No",' said one senior aide.[83] Paisley's relationship with Blair had soured after the robbery and the McCartney murder. Blair now focused on Paisley, carving out quality time to talk to him one-on-one. He steered their conversations on to almost any subject other than Northern Ireland, and slowly Paisley grew to like and trust him, a development helped by the 'very respectful view he held of the Prime Minister of the United Kingdom'. An idea lodged in his mind that he 'did not want to disappoint the Prime Minister and to do a deal if he possibly could'.[84]

On the morning of 28 July 2005, a former Republican prisoner, filmed against a backdrop of greenery and the Irish flag, delivered a statement that all IRA units were to lay down their weapons, that existing arms would be decommissioned, and that the IRA would in future pursue its objectives through 'peaceful means'. Behind the scenes, Powell had definitely guided Sinn Féin and the IRA in their words and actions, telling them what would work and what would not.[85] 'It was a huge moment for Blair. For those of us on the inside, few things had been as significant,' said an NIO source.[86] Blair had sight of the statement two days before, when Adams had presented an advance copy to Hain at Hillsborough,[87] giving him time to craft the words he delivered from Downing Street: 'This may be the day when finally . . . politics replaces terror on the island of Ireland . . . This is a step of unparalleled magnitude and the recent history of Northern Ireland . . . It creates the circumstances in which the institutions can be revived.'[88] But would the Unionists accept the statement in good faith? The months of patient work on Paisley seemed to pay off: in contrast to the usual DUP demand of wanting to see photographic evidence of IRA arms decommissioning, Paisley adopted a more open 'wait-and-see' stance.

But they were still a long way off from both sides agreeing to form a government together. Number 10 and the NIO spent the autumn debating the next step. In January 2006, Blair hosted a key meeting at Chequers with Peter Hain, joined by Phillips, now NIO Permanent Secretary, and Robert Hannigan, its Director-General, and Powell and Kelly from Number 10. Their question was, how best could they clear the final obstacles towards the restoration of devolution and power-sharing? Should they set a deadline? The debate ebbed back and forth. 'If you don't set a deadline, you risk getting nowhere and good will dissipating: if you do set one, there's a likelihood it could be missed.'[89] Their clear conclusion was that the process needed a decisive push, and that meant a timetable, with all the risks. They settled eventually on a conference at St Andrews from 11 to 13 October, timed to come after the marching season and a key decommissioning report. As the conference neared, nerves grew in both camps, as well as in London. Hain raised the temperature in a speech in Oxford on 10 September, warning of the dangers of economic decline and stagnation 'if power-sharing is not restored this autumn'.[90] Number 10 encountered significant negativity from Unionists and Republicans in the final weeks: 'They knew perfectly well it was a forcing mechanism,' said a Number 10 source.[91] Unionists began to ask, 'Was the timetable being forced for Blair's personal reasons, and might the interests of the DUP be better served by waiting until Brown?' To head it off, Number 10 discreetly had a word with Brown's office, who were only too willing to produce a statement to say that there would be no change of policy on Northern Ireland under a Brown premiership.[92] Some in the DUP whispered that Paisley had become too identified with Blair: was his agenda still their agenda?[93]

An opposite pressure was at work on the Republican side. After ten years, and despite their cynicism and doubts, Adams and McGuinness had grown comfortable with the Blair/Powell team: 'The Republican fear was of losing them, and facing a new Prime Minister who would be unlikely to devote anything like the kind of time [Blair] did to Northern Ireland or be as understanding,' said a senior official.[94] The September coup had initially worried the Republicans, when they feared they might lose him.[95] Was this the last chance? On 4 October, the Independent Monitoring Commission (IMC) produced its report confirming that the IRA had indeed stayed true to the word of their 28 July 2005 statement. 'The IRA has done what it was asked to do . . . The IRA campaign is over . . . The door is now open to a final settlement, which is why the talks next week in Scotland are going to be so important,' said Blair.[96] British intelligence had been telling Number 10 for some time that IRA activity was ceasing and a positive report was likely.[97] 'It gave momentum: the whole process was about management and momentum,' said Kelly.[98] But pre-conference nerves were heightened again by the murder of IRA member turned British informer, Dennis Donaldson, described by Paisley as 'the ticking time-bomb in this process'.[99] It was not going to be an easy meeting.

The most difficult issue for the DUP at St Andrews was their acceptance of power-sharing, as they had hitherto been unwilling to go into government with Sinn Féin. Policing was Sinn Féin's sticking point; an unequivocal commitment to support the Police Service of Northern Ireland (PSNI) was essential to the process. The DUP and Sinn Féin were to have until 10 November provisionally to accept any agreement that emerged from the talks: both sides would then need to meet together to discuss who should be nominated as First Minister and

Deputy First Minister. A date of 24 November was fixed for all sides finally to accept the St Andrews agreement. Blair's biggest challenge was to reconcile the different aspirations of both groups. Sinn Féin arrived saying 'why can't we share power now?' and wanting devolution before Christmas. 'We have made enormous strides and now need to show our supporters tangible and immediate results.' Another person keen for speed, for his own political reasons, was Taoiseach Bertie Ahern. The DUP in contrast had no such appetite for a hasty resolution. Their mood was jaded and they resented as usual having to travel outside Northern Ireland to a high-profile event where they knew they would be placed under intense pressure.[100]

Standing next to Ahern, Blair opened the conference in front of the world's media saying: 'We've been here almost ten years working on this, myself and the Taoiseach . . . The question is whether there is the will to . . . give people in Northern Ireland the future they want . . . The discussions in the coming hours will decide.'[101] That evening Blair met Paisley alone. Afterwards, he told Powell and Hannigan that the meeting was remarkable: Paisley wanted to do the deal and quickly – by Christmas – if it could be done. But it rapidly became clear that Paisley's enthusiasm for a short timescale was rattling the rest of his delegation, who ensured that there would be no more one-to-one meetings between their leader and Blair.[102] The first full day, Thursday 12 October, was not encouraging. The DUP delegation at large showed little sign of wanting to move, and seemed, to Number 10, 'to be governed by their back-markers within the party'.[103] As the day drew on, both Sinn Féin and the Irish government delegation became frustrated and angry by what they saw as Unionist obstructionism and bad faith. It seemed to them that the DUP were playing on the fact that Blair was 'so desperate for a deal that he would be bound to move heaven and earth to get the Republicans to move', therefore 'all the unionists needed to do was hang on'.[104] Blair had indeed been trying too hard. Powell, Kelly and the NIO spoke in private to him: 'If necessary, you have to be prepared to lose – it's only if the Unionists see that you're prepared to lose the deal, and leave St Andrews with nothing, that you'll actually persuade them.'[105] The last session on the Thursday evening was particularly bad, with the DUP becoming entrenched about the timetable. Rather than becoming despondent or angry, Blair remained 'relentlessly optimistic' and spoke to delegates about previous negotiations and difficulties they faced. 'He prevented the whole thing spiralling downwards at that point,' said one present.[106] Once the talks broke for the day, Blair came back up to his suite looking out over the golf course and the town; talking with his team they realised that something had to give to break the deadlock. But they knew not what.

Two developments that evening injected some optimism. On the ten-minute walk along the coast to the St Andrews clubhouse for dinner, Blair and Ahern strode ahead and agreed that the timetable had to be extended to March, to provide time for the DUP to display serious commitment to power-sharing and for the Sinn Féin's Ard Fheis (their annual conference) to agree to support the police. During dinner, Ahern received news of an *Irish Times* poll which revealed that, despite being embroiled in a series of financial allegations in Dublin, he was more popular than ever. 'It cheered up the Taoiseach enormously, and played its part in making him more amenable.'[107] Blair was left to wonder why it was that 'when stuff was poured on Bertie's head, he becomes more popular than ever, whereas when it's poured on my head, I receive only woe'.[108] Over dinner, Ahern told Blair about the imaginative present the Irish had prepared for the Paisleys, who were celebrating their Golden Wedding anniversary: a beautiful hand-carved bowl hewn from a tree which had fallen on the site of the Battle of the Boyne. 'What have we got, Jonathan?' asked Blair. 'Er, a photo album,' said Powell. 'You're kidding!' said Blair. 'What's in it?' 'It's empty,' replied Powell.[109] He added after a moment's silence: 'But apparently it's a very posh photo-album.' It was a rare moment of levity. Blair stayed up late after the dinner, working in his room. Even with an extension, he was far from convinced he could pull it off. 'He went to bed on Thursday night convinced that unless there was movement from the DUP in the morning, it wasn't going to work.'[110] They had sanctioned a move, however, that he hoped might work. That evening, at Blair's request, Hain and Hannigan met with the DUP and Michael McDowell, the deputy Prime Minister of Ireland. They were informed starkly that the Prime Minister was preparing a 'failure' announcement, and that the British and the Irish were ready to lay the blame for the failure squarely at the feet of the DUP.[111]

The Friday still proved difficult. At one point, 'It looked as if it would all crash: the Unionists were blocking, everyone was getting tetchy because Sinn Féin were grandstanding, the Taoiseach was getting fed up.'[112] Gradually, however, it became apparent the DUP had decided to be more constructive. After their blocking of the day before, it was initially a battle to convince Sinn Féin and the Irish government that this was not 'just another negotiating ploy, but actually a serious move'.[113] The talks broke up later that day with an air of optimism, though it was far from clear what precisely, if anything, had been agreed. To move things on, at the last minute, Number 10 and the NIO produced a banner saying 'St Andrews Agreement' and ensured that the press conference took place underneath it. 'There hadn't in fact been an agreement between the DUP and Sinn Féin, but having the world's media filming them under the banner made it harder for both sides to say there hadn't.'[114] At the closing plenary, an emotional Paisley was presented with gifts from the Prime Minister and the Taoiseach in celebration of his wedding anniversary. The presentations led to an extraordinary scene with Adams and McGuinness sitting next to the two Paisleys, clearly moved by the occasion: 'For anyone with a sense of Irish history, this moment carried the promise of an entirely new dispensation,' said an official.[115] But as Blair left Scotland, he knew there was still a mountain to climb.

What there had been was an agreement to extend the timeframe. But the complex steps of the post-St Andrews timetable quickly caused problems, and Blair, Powell and Hain were regularly involved in micro-managing Paisley, the DUP and Sinn Féin through a series of mini-crises.[116] By the end of 2006, nevertheless, Northern Ireland was looking more promising than it had at any point since the Good Friday Agreement nine and a half years before. The Sinn Féin conference still had to agree to support the police. And the Unionists still had to agree, when it came to the crunch, to share power with Sinn Féin. The prize of a lasting settlement still hovered before Blair, just beyond his grasp.

Payback at Last from Bush?: August–December 2006

Over his troubled summer holiday, Blair reflected on his foreign policy achievements. Iraq remained mired in violence and the Middle East very far from the state Blair had hoped for by this late stage in his premiership. Was there any way he could use his few remaining months to persuade President Bush to push harder in the region? Positive interventions by the President would prove invaluable to him in achieving his remaining foreign policy ambitions. He spoke with Bush several times in August and September ahead of the President's speech to the UN General Assembly on 23 September. Blair saw the speech as a tremendous opportunity for the President to redefine his own remaining period in power, in his case just over two years, and he put great energy into encouraging Bush to strike a positive tone, in particular about the Middle East. After all, under Blair's pressure, Bush had said in 2004 that he would work hard to achieve a two-state solution for his remaining time as President. Having stood so closely to America over the Lebanon war, placing his own premiership at great risk, he had realistic hopes that Bush would take his ideas on board. It was not to be. Was he guilty of hubris? To Blair's 'disappointment' Bush didn't go into detail about the Middle East, nor did he set out a vision about the future role the US could play.[117] Beyond saying that 'Israel must work to create the conditions that will allow a peaceful Palestinian state to emerge', Bush fell some way short of his earlier advocacy of a 'two-state' solution.[118] Bush had his own definite views on the Middle East and would allow Blair to push him only so far. For all his admiration for the British Prime Minister, the President had his own endgame and legacy to manage.

Their VTC tempo fell away in October while Bush was absorbed with the mid-term Congressional elections on 7 November. The British Embassy in Washington predicted along with most analysts that the Republicans would lose control of the House of Representatives but just hold the Senate.[119] On polling day, they felt that the Senate could end up 50–50; given that the Vice-President serves also as President of the Senate, and holds the casting vote in the event of a tie, some mused that such a vote would have the 'not inconsiderable advantage of tying up Cheney in the Senate most of the time'.[120] The Embassy's predictions underestimated the widespread discontent with the Republicans. In the House of Representatives, the Democrats took control with 233 seats to 202; they managed a similar feat in the Senate, where their 51–49 victory was at the top end of expectations. Rumsfeld's position, after the failure of reconstruction in Iraq, was an obvious casualty: the Embassy indeed told London it was surprised that Bush had retained him as long as he had.[121] His place was taken by Robert Gates, former director of the CIA. John Bolton, Bush's hard-line Ambassador at the UN, seemed likely to prove another casualty of the Democrats' victory in Congress. Bolton had regularly infuriated Straw, but when he protested to Rice about him, she would always say that Bolton was 'still just within the realms of US policy'. The British thought that it suited her to play the good cop/bad cop routine with him, setting herself up as the reasonable voice of the administration.[122] This ended with Bolton's resignation on December 4. Some in London saw the new Democrat majority in the House as the opportunity for a renewed push in the Middle East. The Embassy had to remind them that this was wishful thinking. The House has never been as important in foreign policy as the Senate and, in any case, Congressional Democrats usually proved just as pro-Israel as the Republicans. There might be greater emphasis on climate change, but even there the Embassy advised 'they were on firmer ground, but not too firm'.[123]

Blair believed he needed to adopt a new approach. In October and early November, he worked closely with his foreign policy advisers to refine his strategy for his remaining months. Decisive progress on the MEPP was a core objective alongside climate change. Working with moderate Arab and Muslim states throughout the whole Middle East region, and a more open but robust attitude to even Syria and Iran, was part of the new thinking, which echoed his stance immediately after 9/11: 'It was an agreed Number 10 and FCO stance that we needed to start again with them,' said one senior official. 'The question then was, when and on what level?'[124] Blair's choice was direct and dramatic. In October he dispatched Nigel Sheinwald to Syria in an attempt to restart European relations with the pariah state: 'Blair has always been uneasy about not having direct contact with people who are causing trouble and who are affecting your national interest.' He wanted to test nations like Iran and Syria, to give them an opportunity, and if they didn't respond positively then we would be in a stronger position in propaganda terms having made the effort.'[125] The visit met with moderate success after Syria made efforts to normalise relations with Iraq, one of Sheinwald's conditions for warmer relations.[126] Blair laid out his vision publicly in his final Lord Mayor's Banquet speech at London's Guildhall on 13 November. 'We should unite all moderate Arab and Muslim voices behind a push for peace' in Israel/Palestine and Lebanon, he said. He reiterated the choice he was offering Iran and Syria: to give up their nuclear ambitions and support for terrorism in return for being brought in from the cold, a message he had earlier laid out in July in Los Angeles.[127] It was his 'fork in the road' message, but drawn in the sands of the Middle East.

An opportunity now presented itself for Blair to press home his new message to Washington. In March 2006 the White House had commissioned James Baker, Secretary of State during the presidency of Bush senior, and former Democrat Representative Lee Hamilton, to conduct an independent and bipartisan assessment of 'the current and prospective situation on the ground in Iraq, its impact on the surrounding region, and the consequences for US interests'. The Iraq Study Group, or Baker–Hamilton Commission, as it became known, was billed as the last chance for the Bush administration to re-assess its approach, with the real potential for a change of course. It gathered testimony from a wide range of sources, including the British, who co-operated fully. Manning spoke to the Commission at length. He stressed two points in particular, first, that military action alone would not suffice in Iraq: you had to work on political reconciliation as well, and second that Iraq could not be treated in isolation: the US would have to see Iraq in terms of its neighbours and in the context of the MEPP if there was to be any hope of stabilising the country.[128] Blair himself was eager to meet with Baker face to face and urged him to come to London. This was declined. Baker wanted to take evidence only with other Commission members present, while Blair's timetable ruled out a trip to Washington. The solution was for him to offer his evidence from Downing Street via VTC.[129] To prepare the ground for his submission on 10 November, Blair talked over with Bush what he would say. 'He wanted to help the President redirect his efforts,' said Sawers.[130] Ever-confident of his own powers of persuasion, Blair worked hard to convince Bush that, disappointing though the mid-term elections may have been, he should come out on the front foot and embrace a broad new agenda including climate change.[131] Bush listened politely, but was less than convinced. Blair's enthusiasm was undimmed for his ninety-minute VTC with the Commission, in which he stressed that Iraq's best hope in acquiring the support of Muslim countries was visible progress on the MEPP: 'The way to stop the radicalisation of moderate Muslim opinion is to have a positive strategy on resolving that issue,' he told the Commission members.[132] 'The Prime Minister was very helpful to us,' Baker later recalled. 'He and I happen to share the same view on the need for a more aggressive and hands-on approach to solving the Arab–Israeli dispute. And in the end his views largely coincided with the report we produced.'[133]

On 6 December, the Baker–Hamilton Commission published 'The Iraq Study Group Report'. The tone was serious and sober. The situation 'was grave and deteriorating', it declared, and 'there is no path that can guarantee success'.[134] It offered, however, a detailed set of proposals that it believed would offer the best chance of stability and allow a gradual withdrawal of US troops from the region. Diplomatic relations, it suggested, would need to be extended to all Iraq's neighbours, including Syria and Iran; there should be a big push on the MEPP and a major effort should be made in Iraq to consolidate the Iraqi government's position. The reception in London was understandably enthusiastic. 'We thought it wasn't perfect,' said one senior official, 'but it represented a sensible way forward.'[135] Blair himself was pleased.[136] He was in the air, flying to Washington to see Bush, when the report was published. But even before he boarded the plane, he knew that the findings would not go down well in the White House. Indeed, the report had been subject to fierce criticism from the US right for months prior to its publication: 'A fancy way of justifying surrender,' said the neoconservative journal, *The Weekly Standard*.[137] Stephen Hadley had already forewarned Sheinwald that the administration was unlikely to take many of the recommendations on board.[138] 'The problem with Baker-Hamilton was that it was seen in Iraq, and by many Republicans in Washington, as simply a cover for a withdrawal strategy, as almost an admission of failure,' explained a senior administration official, 'and that made it very hard for the President to embrace the report.'[139] 'The thing that really irked them was a denial of the Bush democracy agenda,' insisted one British official. 'To them the report was *über*-realist,' and thus a rejection of an important principle of Bush's foreign policy.[140]

To neutralise its impact, the White House made it clear that Baker-Hamilton was just one of several reports being prepared: the Pentagon, State Department and CIA were all, it was said, reviewing different options for Iraq.[141] London was disappointed by the administration's response: 'Bush had created a life-line for himself,' sighed one Number 10 official, 'but then he rebelled against it.'[142] In direct opposition to Blair's thinking, the administration appeared initially to reject out of hand the proposal for broader diplomacy. To some British officials it seemed almost a knee-jerk response: in contrast to the standard British view that it is 'more important to talk to our enemies than our friends', the administration reverted to the standard American view that you need to isolate your enemies. 'They consider it a great prize for a foreign country to be able to talk to the world's most advanced democracy, and it should be held out as a reward once they have met certain conditions.'[143]

Blair arrived in Washington late on 6 December without high hopes. He spoke privately to Bush in the White House, while the British team, Powell, Manning and Sheinwald, talked separately with Rice and Hadley. Eating together at a big table in the White House mess, they were surprised to discover just how critical of Baker–Hamilton their American counterparts were away from the public gaze – much more so than they had anticipated. 'The most critical of all at that stage was Condi,' said one present. 'She felt it was a throwback to the days of Kissinger' – a reference to Kissinger's uncompromising *Realpolitik* during the Nixon years.[144] For all the prior warnings, Blair had not expected to find Bush so inflexible on Iran and Syria in their private conversations.[145] 'He told the President that although he accepted the report was not perfect he felt it was something that Bush should respond positively to' recalled one official. 'Blair was very clear on this.'[146] At the joint press conference on 7 December the President was emphatic that there would be no engagement with Iran until the regime had altered its uranium enrichment programme, despite the report's recommendation that the nuclear issue be kept separate. This unequivocal response on behalf of the White House did ease somewhat with time: during 2007 the US made some effort to engage with Syria and Iran.[147] But this fell far short of what Blair had envisaged: 'you could hardly say that by 2007 there was a serious effort underway to communicate with senior Iranians about Iraq,' said one senior British official.[148] Blair was also disappointed that Bush seemed unwilling to engage in the MEPP with more vigour: 'Progress had been spotty,' the President admitted, but 'he blamed it on extremists rather than on any lack of impetus from Washington'.[149] Although he would have preferred Bush to take a higher profile personally, Blair did recognise that behind the scenes Condi Rice had been working patiently to edge the peace process forward. He considered this a positive development and was eager to support her efforts. 'He now felt he had a readier voice from Condi than he had from the President,' said one British official.[150] 'He thought Condi expressed Bush's more active side,' said another, 'and he wanted to reinforce it'.[151]

Instead of giving the nod to Baker–Hamilton, which suggested that, under certain conditions, all US combat brigades could be out of Iraq by mid 2008, Bush's advisers were already pushing the idea of a final 'surge' in US troops to give them the upper hand over the insurgents in Iraq. Bush had first put the idea to Blair at the Riga NATO meeting on Afghanistan on 28 November. Sheinwald told Hadley unequivocally that he thought it was 'very unlikely to work'.[152] But within the White House it was gaining in popularity: 'Bush grabbed hold of it, perhaps because it was advocated by people who believed the war could still be won,' speculated an FCO official.[153] British opposition made no impact. Some in the Foreign Office feared the surge was merely delaying recognition that the military strategy in Iraq had been a failure. Blair's arguments to the Baker–Hamilton Commission had been based on the premise that the existing strategy was not working. There was thus little optimism in London that the surge alone would succeed.[154] 'Blair wasn't wholly unsympathetic to the idea of the surge per se,' explained one senior adviser, 'he just thought that there needed to be a political surge as well as a military one.'[155] Bush's stress on the latter at the expense of the former left Blair dispirited.

But as ever, Blair refrained from coming out and expressing his frustration in public. 'We had been in there with him since the start,' explained one official, 'and at this very late stage the Prime Minister did not want to be seen to fall out with President Bush'.[156] The verdict on the December visit from the British press was unsurprisingly critical: the *Independent* railed against a 'cool' and 'unequal' special relationship in which Blair 'steals in and out of Washington by night.'[157] The *Mirror* declared that both Bush and Blair had their 'heads in the sand.'[158] 'He increasingly expected the media to be relentlessly negative,' said one aide. 'By this time, the press on these trips was basically awful. There was almost nothing he could do to cut through it.'[159] Before leaving Washington, Blair met a number of Congressional allies from both parties. On the evening of 6 December he had meetings with key Senators on climate change, including John McCain and John Warner. Hillary Clinton phoned to say she could not make it and 'could she come and meet him first thing for breakfast instead?' Without discussing it with Blair, Manning said, 'Yes, he'll do it.'[160] Blair knew that after the midterm elections, allies in Congress would be more important than ever.

In December 2006, Blair faced an unwelcome distraction from the Middle East with the investigation by the Serious Fraud Office (SFO) into the links between the British arms company BAE, and Saudi Arabia. It concerned Al-Yamamah (meaning 'the dove' in Arabic), Britain's biggest ever arms deal, dating back to 1985 and which had kept BAE afloat for the last twenty years. Relations with the Saudi royal family had been strained since the G8 Evian summit in June 2003, when the Saudis released six British detainees on the understanding that Blair would 'act' against the Saudi opposition in London.[161] In practice, the police reported that no crime had been committed by the Saudi dissidents, and they were unable to do anything. One of Blair's weaknesses as leader was to charm people into thinking he would do something, when he either could not or would not. This grievance, felt in particular by the King, underlay the episode. Blair was nevertheless persuaded to call in at Riyadh in early July 2005 on his way to the Olympic meeting in Singapore, to promote the third phase of the Al-Yamamah deal, the purchase by the Saudis of seventy-two Eurofighter Typhoons costing up to £10 billion. As part of an ongoing investigation into arms sales to Saudi Arabia going back to the days of Margaret Thatcher's premiership, in September 2006, the SFO obtained a warrant to open up the accounts of the Saudi royal family in Switzerland, following allegations of bribes. The Saudi response at the end of November was to give Britain ten days to halt the fraud investigation, or lose the Eurofighter contract. Chirac was said to be waiting in the wings, delighted, with a counter-offer. On 14 December, following advice from Attorney-General Goldsmith, Blair decided to recommend to the head of the SFO that they call off the inquiry. Fears for up to 50,000 British jobs weighed heavily in the decision, but less so than the damage that he thought would be inflicted on Britain's relationship with Saudi Arabia, with its powerful influence on the broad Middle East region and above all counter-terrorism. As leaked documents later disclosed, British Ambassador Sherard Cowper-Coles told SFO director Robert Wardle that threats of such losses to national intelligence security were 'very grave indeed', and that lives on British streets would be 'put at risk'.[162] Blair also based his judgement in part on Goldsmith's advice that the SFO would need a further eighteen months to complete its investigation and with no certainty of being able to make a case: 'We would have had months, potentially years, of ill feeling between us and a key partner and ally . . . In the end my role as Prime Minister is to advise on what is in the best national, strategic interests of our country,' said Blair on 15 December, when explaining his decision to call off the investigation.[163] The right-wing press, including the *Daily Mail* and *Daily Telegraph*, were reasonably receptive, but other newspapers protested vehemently at a decision that was seen as lacking in principle or morality. Among the public at large, Blair was no longer given the benefit of the doubt, and the broad consensus was that he had behaved shoddily.

On the day of his announcement, Blair flew to the Middle East. Reports were emerging that Bush was to recommend that America send up to 50,000 additional troops, in the 'surge', while continuing to reject Baker–Hamilton's proposals for broadening diplomatic efforts. Coupled with the SFO furore, it was a disheartening backdrop for the trip. Exactly one year before, Blair had spoken about his hope of sending many of Britain's troops home during the course of 2006. But during the autumn, Blair's faith in Prime Minister al-Maliki and President Talabani began to fade as it became clear that they were unable even to hold together a coherent national government, let alone control the insurgency. Britain would not 'cut and run', he promised them in Baghdad on 17 December. 'Don't be under any doubts at all. British troops remain until the job is done.'[164] He spoke privately with al-Maliki and tried to impress upon him the importance of political reconciliation and national unity, but the conversation left him discouraged.[165] There was little hope he could offer British troops when he addressed them in Basra, beyond recognising the difficulty of their task in fighting 'an ideology, a group of extremists that share the same perspective that is a hatred of our way of life and what we believe in'. He spoke with deep feeling: 'You are not just brave, what you're you doing is good, and right, and important, and from the bottom of my heart I thank you for it.'[166]

The prospects for Blair's visits to Israel and the Palestine territory seemed no more promising when, on 18 December, Hamas leader Ismail Haniyeh said, 'We will never recognise the usurper Zionist government and will continue our Jihad-like movement until the liberation of Jerusalem.' The fact he delivered his comments in Tehran, which Israel regarded as its biggest threat, further cast a pall over the visit. On the day Blair left for the Middle East, Hamas and Fatah factions fought on the streets of Gaza and in the West Bank, as the territories slipped further into violence.[167] Blair's visit to Abbas in his presidential compound in Ramallah on 18 December was given added focus by the Palestinian President's call for fresh elections in the territories to dislodge Hamas from political power and restore the territories to normality. When criticised for supporting Abbas's strategy of circumventing the democratically elected Hamas government, Blair responded that Abbas was the elected president of the Palestinian people. In truth, Abbas, in later 2006 and 2007, was trying to ride two horses at once: arming Fatah while pursuing an anti-Hamas strategy, and secondly conciliating Hamas in a national unity government strategy. 'Backwards and forwards, backwards and forwards, all the way through the back end of 2006 into 2007,' said a Number 10 official. 'It was not conducive to the Prime Minister making much headway.'[168] Blair saw Olmert in Jerusalem on the evening of 18 December and pressed for funds withheld from the Palestinians territories to be released as well as pushing him on the release of Palestinian prisoners. Olmert made no commitment on either.

It was a dispirited Blair who made his way back to Britain before his final Christmas in power. The Middle East seemed as far from a peaceful solution as it had been in 1997, despite the best part of ten years of effort. 'I sigh when you ask for positive impacts, because they're not thick on the ground,' said a senior FCO official when asked about Blair's contribution to the MEPP.[169] He gained the trust of the Israelis, and played a role in helping them realise that territorial concessions might be necessary, and for a time he was uniquely respected by both sides in the dispute. But ultimately his attachment to Bush damaged his standing in the Middle East. Blair as a character is not much given to resentment and blame, but when pushed he would express disappointment that the Americans had not done more. 'We certainly didn't stint on pushing it,' said one close aide. 'We really used to get on Bush's nerves going on about it.'[170] Blair's final few months in office were spent encouraging Rice, with apparent success, to take a higher profile: 'Condi is really pushing away at this now,' said one British official in June 2007, 'she's got religious on it.'[171] There was even 'a sense in

Washington that maybe a certain T Blair was right all along' noted another.[172] But Blair's role in shifting US policy in his final months should not be overstated. The growing assertiveness of Iran, and the increasing isolation of Israel in the aftermath of the Lebanon war set alarm bells ringing throughout the Middle East. 'The Moderate Arabs were screaming at the Americans,' recalled one diplomat, 'they were saying, "Are you really ready to hand over the whole of the Middle East to the Iranians?" It became clear to Washington that a hands-off approach to the peace process was no longer adequate.'[173] Blair, of course, had been pushing this line ad infinitum for most of his premiership. In 2003 and again in late 2004, he manoeuvred Bush into making positive pronouncements: but after Blair flew home, the progress fell apart. Throughout his time at Number 10, Blair was unable to make a lasting impact against the pressures within America propelling any president to adopt a pro-Israeli policy, exacerbated in Bush's case by a coterie of hardliners in the Vice-President's office. On the other hand Blair appreciated how much the unstable position in the Middle East, above all among the Palestinians, had undermined his efforts. To have made progress Blair would have needed a resolute figure like Paisley on the Israeli side committed to sharing power, and an Adams/McGuinness figure on the Palestinian side, equally committed to compromise and able to command their followers.

In early 2007, Britain's twenty leading ambassadors gathered in the Permanent Under-Secretary's large room in the FCO for their annual policy overview. One senior official said, 'Tony Blair is now in "la-la land": he wants to sort out Israel, Iraq, Afghanistan, Northern Ireland, global warming, poverty . . .'[174] Even one of the most supportive diplomats said, 'In his last year, he's become almost a bit desperate to make a difference. He has not understood how he has exaggerated the difference that he can personally make.'[175] Blair's frantic efforts were beginning to take their toll. In the run-up to Christmas he had made it clear to senior staff that he needed a break. 'Leave me alone please', he instructed. 'No books this year.'[176]

20

To the Wire

Never had Britain seen a premiership where so much hinged on what happened in the final six months. Would Blair be able to last to the summer, and in what shape? Would 'cash for honours', or Gordon Brown, force him out early, and under a cloud? The very continuity of New Labour, the nature of the transition, the completion of his domestic agenda; the fates of Northern Ireland, the EU constitution, climate change, a global trade deal, and much else, all hung in the balance. Despite the disappointing end to 2006, he yearned to see demonstrable progress on Iraq, and on the MEPP as well as on Afghanistan, before leaving office. The price of making such a slow start in his first term, and of being such a late developer as a Prime Minister, was that he left himself so much to do. His political capital at home and abroad was all but spent. He returned from his holiday in Florida in early January 'on fire', with orders flying in all directions. This was a premiership that was going to go to the wire.

Domestic Troubles: January–March

In his final twelve months, the thing that drained Blair's political capital away more than anything else was the 'cash for honours' police investigation. It was a deliberate attempt to shred his moral authority. 'It took a huge amount from him,' said one aide.[1] SNP MP Angus MacNeil had sparked the Scotland Yard inquiry into alleged financial malpractice, led by Deputy Assistant Commissioner John Yates, in the spring of 2006. Lord Levy was arrested amid much media speculation on 12 July; he was questioned a second time on 20 September. On 14 December, Blair himself was questioned in Number 10 for two hours as part of the criminal investigation. 'It was a pretty bad moment,' remarked one senior official.[2] Blair was determined to set the record straight: 'He just wanted them [the police] to interview him. He was absolutely clear right at the beginning that nobody had done anything wrong. He questioned people very closely and was confident of his and his staff's position,' said a close aide.[3] Number 10 said that he told the police that he had nominated certain individuals for peerages, as party leaders do, for those who have supported the party. The honours were not, therefore, for public service, but were expressly party peerages given for service to the Labour Party. The fact that they had supported the party financially could thus not conceivably be a barrier to their nomination for peerages. Number 10 always maintained that the police had failed to understand the way politics and the giving of honours works: 'Labour has acted no differently from the other parties, or any other government for that matter. There is no need to start arresting people or prosecuting them. These people are not criminals.'[4] At the end of the interview on 14 December, officials converged on the 'den'. 'Well, there it is', Blair said calmly, 'what's next?'[5] A senior official recalled that when Blair was being briefed on the saga, his response was: '"Why's this man talking to me about this? I'm not interested in it."'[6] But he was incensed by the intrusion, and by the way that the media (with the *Mail* and *Sunday Times* in the lead) assumed guilt on his part downwards, insinuating that the system he ran was deeply corrupt. 'The only effect it had was indirect in terms of both time and, I suspect, emotional energy,' said one aide.[7] Blair decided from day one that Number 10 was 'not going to fight the police, we were not going to accuse them of doing anything wrong, and we were not going to turn this into a big shouting match between Downing Street and the police'.[8] Downing Street, however, became progressively disenchanted the more the inquiry dragged on beyond its planned conclusion in September 2006.

Blair's and Number 10's anger turned to fury at 6:30 A.M. on 19 January 2007, when Ruth Turner was arrested at her flat by four police officers. The indignity of being forced to dress in front of a female police officer and then marched out of her flat where the waiting press had been 'tipped off' was too much for many of them. While Blair himself gave Turner his full backing – 'Ruth is a person of the highest integrity for whom I have great regard, and I continue to have complete confidence in her'[9] – Lord Puttnam, Labour peer and film-maker, sprang angrily to her defence: 'She's one of those half-dozen people who I would stake my life on. She is a woman of total, total probity.'[10] When it emerged that she was arrested not only in connection with an alleged offence under the Honours (Prevention of Abuses) Act 1925, but was also being questioned on suspicion of perverting the course of justice, the stakes became higher still. 'That is a toxic accusation,' wrote Andrew Rawnsley. 'A ghastly echo of the worst sleaze of the Tory years that has to be extremely discomforting to Number 10.'[11]

Turner's arrest was the closest Number 10 came to going public on what it thought of the investigation. 'We had a couple of discussions about whether we should fight back. But we knew in the end we couldn't. A group of apparatchiks in Number 10 versus the boys in blue? Forget it!' said one.[12] 'There are certain groups you can kick with impunity . . . [and] there are certain institutions in society – GPs, the police, nurses – who you just have to avoid arguing with.'[13] As the weeks dragged on anger in Number 10 did not fade: 'We would have a good couple of days, then some other dreadful leak would come out.'[14] Number 10 believed the leaks had come from the police: 'They used the media to bounce people, to intimidate them and to pursue their case.'[15] Some insiders felt the police came to the investigation with preconceptions: 'It was fundamentally wrong that the police seemed to have decided, without a victim, that wrong had been done and were turning over every stone to prove it,' said one.[16] When the police started conducting interviews and looking at e-mails, it seemed inevitable to some in Number 10 that the charge of obstructionism would come up. Blair's aides received little sympathy for their predicament. 'Leaks occurred on both sides and for Downing Street to criticise others for using spin will strike many as the ultimate hypocrisy,' said the *Sunday Times*.[17] For many, the issue was payback for years of accumulated resentment.

The image of Number 10 as the victim was not how the country saw the episode, and Blair himself knew it. At the height of the crisis in early February, on Radio 4's *Today* programme, he said, 'I am not going to beg for my character in front of anyone . . . I am not going to get into a situation where I am pleading for my integrity.'[18] He stressed that he would not allow the investigations to distract him from his important work as Prime Minister, and indeed he succeeded pretty well in maintaining his focus.[19] The investigation eventually ended when the Metropolitan Police submitted their report to the Crown Prosecution

Service (CPS) on 20 April. On 19 July, three weeks after Blair left office, the CPS finally reported. It found insufficient credible evidence to bring formal charges against anybody: Levy, Turner and others all emerged unscathed. Blair's statement released on 20 July was measured: 'This investigation has ended as I always expected it would. Those involved have been through a terrible, even traumatic time . . . I want to make it clear that I level no criticism at the police. They were put in an invidious position by the SNP complaint and had a very difficult task to perform . . . The government and the Labour party co-operated fully with it. All issues have now been resolved.'[20]

There was no evidence that Blair had acted improperly in any way. He behaved with dignity and restraint throughout the investigation. The episodes nevertheless highlighted three of Blair's traits. He retained a view to the end that the world shared his own evaluation of himself, of being 'a pretty straight kind of guy' as he said during the Ecclestone affair in 1997. Even at the end, he did not appreciate that was not how many saw him, after years of increasingly hostile press. He was too eager to trust friends, and to take them at their word. To the end, Blair had little time for conventions that had evolved in British government to ensure that the manipulative and powerful did not obtain undue influence. When Callaghan took over as Prime Minister from Wilson in April 1976, he was insistent that his actions would always be above board. This included trusting the traditional civil service to play its proper role as custodian of the British state and guardian over the propriety of the Prime Minister. Yet Blair in particular marginalised the Cabinet Secretary, who might have prevented such episodes blowing up, and thought he could operate the system with his own rules. 'Cash for honours' was a harsh reminder that he couldn't.

The improbable 'Catholic gay adoption row' lurched on to Blair's horizon early in the year to provide further instability, if he needed any more. Having successfully battled in October 2006 with Alan Johnson over the admissions policy of faith schools, Blair found himself again at odds with his Education Secretary over the right of Catholic adoption agencies to decline applications for adoption from homosexual couples. Same-sex adoption had been legal in England and Wales since 2002, but Catholic agencies, who find homes for some of the most difficult to place children, had been able to secure an opt-out from the equalities legislation. Blair, together with Ruth Kelly, a devout Catholic, were keen to retain the opt-out for Catholic agencies under the forthcoming Equalities Act.[21] His hope was to settle the matter with Johnson after Cabinet on Thursday 18 January. But Johnson did not want to discuss it.[22] On 22 January, Cardinal Cormac Murphy O'Connor, the head of the Catholic Church in England and Wales, weighed in, urging that steps be taken to 'enable our agencies to continue with their work with local authorities for the common good'.[23] The following day, Rowan Williams, the Archbishop of Canterbury, supported the Catholic position, commenting that the 'rights of conscience cannot be made subject to legislation, however well meaning'.[24] Suddenly, a seemingly innocuous debate flared up into a full-blown battle between church and state, and was leading the news bulletins. Some saw it as a dry run for the deputy leadership contest with ministers positioning themselves: Harriet Harman weighed in with the line 'you can't be a little bit against discrimination'.

When on 25 January, Johnson declared on BBC Radio 4's *Today* programme that he would resist calls for an exemption, Blair released a statement saying that he was personally committed to the rights of gay couples to adopt, and that he was committed to finding a solution to this 'sensitive and difficult decision'.[25] He took time to listen to the foster and adoption agencies, the churches and charitable bodies: five days later, it was announced that there would be no exemption for Catholic adoption agencies from the impending equalities legislation. Blair was portrayed poorly in the media over it: for such an open Cabinet spat to arise over such a personal issue led to questions about his continuing grip on power. Brown, Number 10 noted wryly, had resolutely refused to take a position on it.[26]

In his final months, Blair was tangibly reminded that for all his commitment to improving law and order, he had failed to alter many of its underlying problems. The Home Office had rarely been out of the news during his premiership and in January 2007 it was back in a row that went straight to the heart of Britain's criminal justice policy – overcrowding in prisons. As a direct consequence of his tougher stance on crime, the prison population had risen in the ten years from 1997 from 61,000 to over 80,000, with juvenile custodial sentences increasing by 25 per cent to almost 3,000 since 2004. The rise in inmates was not matched by an increase in prison guards, who increased only 7 per cent from the 1997 figure of 23,000.[27] When, in January, Reid – in association with the Lord Chancellor and Attorney-General – advised judges to take into account prison overcrowding when considering custodial sentences, uproar broke out, particularly when it was revealed that two judges, acting on the advice, had not given custodial sentences to sex offenders.[28] Blair was forced to concede that UK prisons were indeed 'full to bursting point', though he said that a further 8,000 places would soon be added to the total.[29]

Faced by the succession of Home Office crises of asylum, ID cards, foreign prisoners and most recently prison crowding, Reid looked again at the 2003 plan for creating a separate Ministry of Justice. Blunkett, instrumental in blocking it then, warned strongly against the move. Straw, however, warmed to the proposals. Plans were dusted off to split the Home Office, creating a department responsible for security, counter-terrorism and civil emergencies, while responsibility for prisons, the courts and sentencing would be moved to the newly formed Ministry of Justice, formed out of the Department of Constitutional Affairs (DCA) created in 2003. The change duly came into effect on 9 May, in the final weeks before Blair stood down, and was consolidated when Brown took over in late June, when Straw, as Lord Chancellor and Secretary of State for Justice, headed the new ministry, while Jacqui Smith became Britain's first female Home Secretary in charge of a more tightly focused and, it was hoped, effective Home Office.

Before Easter, Blair had to oversee the passage of another controversial piece of policy, which he was keen to do on his own watch, almost as a favour to his successor. This was the decision to renew Trident, the UK's nuclear weapons system, to last until the 2040s. To the surprise and disappointment of some in the PLP, Brown announced in his Lord Mayor's Banquet speech in June 2006 that he believed that Britain should retain the nuclear deterrent. The tradition of unilateral nuclear disarmament ran very deep in Labour, and Brown's statement sent a powerful message that he would not be swayed by those arguing against renewal. Four options for the future were on the table: extending the life of Trident missiles and Vanguard submarines beyond 2024; not replacing Trident at all (in effect unilateral disarmament); procuring a new submarine or air-based capability or buying a direct replacement for the Trident system in line with the existing US–UK agreement. The armed forces were clear that the last was their favoured option.[30] Despite signs of early flirtations with CND, Blair was never a convinced nuclear disarmer. 'There was no sense that Blair was trimming in the internal debates: he is a man who sees right and wrong very strongly and was convinced of the moral case for the new deterrent,' said Chief of Defence Staff Jock Stirrup.[31]

In latter 2006, debates took place deep in Whitehall between the MoD, FCO and Treasury. By the time the White Paper advocating a new system was produced on 4 December, it thus meant all the key Whitehall departments, above all the Treasury, were signed up to it. The one issue on which the service chiefs insisted, was that a clear decision was reached by the end of 2006: 'Because the uncertainty was proving very unhelpful.'[32] On Thursday 23 November, Defence Secretary Browne presented the case to Cabinet. Only three voiced concerns, Beckett, Hain and Benn; the majority of Cabinet were either quiet or spoke in favour. With Blair and Brown in agreement, there was never a realistic chance that Cabinet would not give its backing. Ten days later, on 4 December, Blair said 'the government's judgement, on balance, is that, although the Cold War is over, we cannot be certain in the decades ahead that a major nuclear threat to our strategic interests will not emerge . . . [And thus] it would be unwise and dangerous for Britain, alone of any of the nuclear powers, to give up its independent nuclear deterrent.'[33]

In the run-up to the parliamentary vote on 14 March, four junior figures resigned from the government, including Chris Ruane, PPS to Peter Hain. In the debate, Blair spoke about the threats from states such as North Korea, which claimed to have already developed nuclear weapons, or Iran, which was in breach of its non-proliferation duties. But he failed to sway many backbenchers. A rebellion of eighty-eight MPs was significant, but with Conservative backing, the vote was never in doubt. Menzies Campbell described it as 'a humiliation for the Prime Minister that on a policy to which he has attached his own personal reputation he is unable to carry the House of Commons without the votes of the Conservative Party . . . It's a bit like the Iraq vote once again.'[34] Blair was remarkably untroubled by the rebellion: he was convinced of his case, and almost rejoiced in standing up against the party.

Northern Ireland Breakthrough: January–May

The King David Hotel in Jerusalem has enviable views eastwards over the Mount of Olives and the hills leading down to the Dead Sea. On the evening of 17 December, from his suite on the top floor, Blair, frustrated at the disappointing progress on the MEPP, spoke to Ian Paisley. Blair rarely spoke to anyone about religion, and least of all a fellow leader, but Paisley was different and that night the two leaders chatted together over the religious significance of the Mount of Olives.[35] Progress towards a resolution in Northern Ireland seemed to Blair as precarious as it was in the Middle East: yet he sensed a settlement might be in sight. Their conversation marked the beginning of a frenetic period over Christmas and the New Year when he was to concentrate intensely on Northern Ireland. The Northern Ireland Office estimated that he spoke twenty times to Paisley, and even more often to Adams: Christmas Day and Boxing Day were the only times when the phones were silent.[36] After Christmas at Chequers, the Blairs went for a week to the Florida home of Robin Gibb, where he speedily recovered his zest: 'He likes America, he likes the sun.'[37] But his mind was on work. Time was short. Powell and the NIO's Hannigan listened in to the Paisley and Adams calls. Blair made a dozen calls on New Year's day alone, mostly to Paisley about the content of the latter's New Year message.[38] So immersed was he that when Ruth Turner asked him on his return to London, 'Did Jonathan get away as well?' he replied, 'I've no idea': he hadn't realised that he hadn't spoken to Powell on holiday in Yorkshire.[39]

Republicans and Unionists both began to have cold feet following the St Andrews conference. Paisley's doubts were about the sincerity of the Republicans' commitment to support the police: 'They're deliberately hanging back,' he protested.[40] Blair repeatedly assured him they were serious, and offered him confidential advice on how he might keep faith among reluctant followers. Adams' main worry was whether Paisley, when it came to the crunch, would really be able to bring fellow Unionists into power-sharing. 'We've done everything we can and the DUP still refuse to commit to go ahead on 26 March,' he protested.[41] Blair in turn reassured Adams that Paisley would carry his troops, and offered him council on how to bring his own constituency on board behind policing.[42] 'It was one of those classic cases where both sides were looking at the other and saying, "We don't quite believe the other side's serious,"' said one Number 10 source.[43] 'Tony and Jonathan barely stopped all over Christmas and the New Year,' said Turner.[44] With negotiations so delicately poised, he wanted to return from Florida early to be on the spot, but Tom Kelly and Hannigan warned him of the stir an early return would provoke in the press. 'Not as much of a stir as my imminent divorce from Cherie will cause if I spend any more time on Northern Ireland here!' he replied.[45] Throughout, he was obsessed about doing everything in his power to achieve the breakthrough.

January proved a good month for the peace process. At its end, Sinn Féin's membership voted in favour of supporting the police: less than 5 per cent of the party's membership were thought to have voted against.[46] Adams labelled the decision 'one of the most important . . . in the recent history of our country'.[47] Kelly, in his capacity as the Prime Minister's official spokesman, said he recognised 'the leadership it has taken to get to this point'.[48] The end of the month saw the Independent Monitoring Commission (IMC) report that the Republicans' commitment to 'pursuing the political path is clear', though it raised concerns about some IRA members continuing to engage in crime.[49] Together on the steps of Downing Street on 31 January, Blair and Ahern released a statement welcoming both the Sinn Féin commitment to the police and the IMC report. The next step in the process, they said, would be the elections to be held on 7 March to endorse the St Andrews agreement and to elect the Assembly. Absolutely vital was the agreement of politicians on both sides to form a functioning power-sharing executive on, or before, 26 March. The elections on 7 March proved comparatively uneventful. Of the Stormont's 108 seats, Paisley's DUP secured 36, reaffirming its position as Northern Ireland's biggest party; Sinn Féin took 28; the UUP 18; the SDLP 16 and the Alliance party 7. As soon as the results were announced Northern Ireland Secretary Hain reiterated that the parties absolutely had to agree to power-sharing, or devolution would not be restored.[50]

Number 10 had long been nervous of this very moment. 'We knew that as soon as the election was over, elements in the DUP would attempt to make out that Sinn Féin hadn't really delivered, and that still more time was needed,' said one Number 10 source.[51] They divided the DUP into three segments: those who definitely wanted power-sharing; those who did so but were nervous about a hurried timetable; and those who resisted it under all circumstances. To circumvent the second and third groups employing the delaying tactic of saying 'we will do much better if we wait for Brown to take over', Number 10 asked the NIO in secret to conduct an exit poll to show what the ordinary voters in the province most cared about. They discovered that water rates ranked highest with them – including with 82 per cent of DUP voters[52] (a clear signal that they wanted the political parties to get on with the business of conventional politics) – and a clear majority wanted restoration of the Assembly on 26 March. The latter was especially important for the government, which wanted to show the DUP that the people who voted for them had an early date in mind, not at some point of the DUP's choosing.[53] The results were then leaked to the *Belfast Telegraph* to show that the Northern Ireland public yearned above all for power-sharing, and above all they wanted their politicians to improve public life.[54] The message had resonance because the politicians had been hearing it themselves on the doorstep. But there was much further still to travel before they were convinced.

As 26 March drew nearer, five days of crucial talks began on Wednesday 21 March. Paisley met Blair in the House of Commons and repeated the familiar message: 'I want to go ahead, but I'm not sure I can bring my party with me.' It became clear by the Thursday that the problem was not Paisley, it was his lieutenants, particularly those who had told their constituency associations that under no circumstances would they share power with Sinn Féin in the foreseeable future.'[55] On Friday 23 March, Blair met the DUP leadership in his study and later, after a break where he dealt with events in the Iran hostage crisis, in the Cabinet Room. Point-blank they told him that they could not manage the 26 March deadline: if he pushed them further it would split the party.[56] Paisley handed Blair the party's revised timetable that they would present to its party meeting the next day. After weeks of talking to try to head off this eventuality, Blair's frustration was palpable; he couldn't bring himself to look at the document.[57] His gesture was partly tactical. He wanted Paisley to know not only that his time for them was limited, but also that there were other pressing matters like Iran requiring his attention.[58] 'I accept that you've got problems in managing your party,' Blair impressed on him, 'but I can't give you more time.'

Blair, however, pulled back from the brink and offered him a way out. 'If you can persuade Sinn Féin that your extension is credible, and that you are indeed serious about power-sharing, then a deal might still be possible.'[59] He stressed that Sinn Féin would require from them 'building blocks of confidence' (as he called it) to reassure them the DUP would stay true to their word. As soon as the DUP delegation left the Cabinet Room, plans were drawn up for a staged photograph on Monday 26 between the DUP and Sinn Féin leadership. By the time the DUP delegation arrived back in Belfast on Friday evening, they had agreed to Number 10's plans for the photograph.[60] But would Sinn Féin buy it? This was one of the most critical moments in the entire negotiations. A lot was being asked of the elderly DUP leader. 'Paisley had to go to the Republicans and hold private discussions with them and ask them their intentions,' said one witness.[61] At this perilous point, Blair had to fly off to Berlin for the fiftieth anniversary of the birth of the European Union.

The weekend 24/25 March saw crucial conversations between Powell in London, Hannigan in Belfast, Ahern in Dublin and Blair with Kelly in Germany.[62] Blair called Ahern at 9 A.M. on Saturday morning to keep him abreast. Ahern was 'pissed off': the Taoiseach told Blair that he thought the DUP would never honour the 26 March deadline and would save his congratulations 'for when they did'.[63] Ahern was nevertheless willing to support Blair's suggestion to Paisley if Sinn Féin agreed to give the DUP more time.[64] Blair also called Adams that morning, telling him, 'This could crash if you don't agree. But if you get the DUP united behind firmly wanting to engage with you on power-sharing, then it would be much better than entering a reluctant power-sharing deal with nobody properly talking to each other.'[65] To Blair's relief, Adams was ready to see the bigger picture. Tensing himself, Blair said, 'One of the ways you can show you're serious about engaging would be to meet them on Monday, in front of cameras.'[66]

While they were speaking, the DUP's party meeting had been in session, and confirmed that power-sharing would definitely not resume on 26 March. Later in the evening, while a nervous Blair listened to Simon Rattle conduct the Berlin Philharmonic, an experience that would have passed over him at the best of times, the DUP and Sinn Féin held their first ever formal talks in a private room at Stormont Castle.[67] Hannigan chaired the meeting, acting as his master's voice. 'This is the Prime Minister's position. If both your parties can agree a delayed date, he is prepared to put through the legislation necessary, on an emergency basis . . . but only if there's agreement,' he said. Sinn Féin were willing to play ball, but wanted the earliest possible date, advocating 1 May for the restoration of power-sharing. The DUP pushed for 24 May.[68] Both camps broke up into separate rooms to debate further their response, when, late that evening, the DUP's Nigel Dodds fell ill with food poisoning. He decided to go into Sinn Féin's room and tell them that his departure was 'not a political statement, but a genuine illness', a gesture seen as a huge moment for Dodds personally and for the DUP. In 1996, the IRA had attempted to kill him on his way to visit his terminally ill son in hospital, resulting in his police bodyguard being shot.[69] 'The moment we knew it was going to happen was when Dodds went in to tell Sinn Féin why he was leaving early. We knew then it was serious, that it was game on,' said one of the Number 10 team.[70]

With the talks still in the balance, Blair was invited down on the Sunday, by the President of the European Parliament to a restaurant in Osnabrück. As they were sped westwards by police escort, the shape of the table for the meeting at Stormont improbably became Blair's focal issue. On conference call, Hannigan relayed to Blair, Powell and Kelly the overnight news that the DUP were insisting on a rectangular table for the talks the next day, so they could sit on the opposite side to Sinn Féin to show their supporters they were not going soft. Sinn Féin insisted they sit on the same side as an emblem that things had changed. Hannigan came up with an idea of making the table a diamond shape – a palatable compromise.[71] There was more: the issue of *where* Adams and Paisley would be sitting. Both men had originally intended to sit in the middle of their delegations, thus putting considerable distance between them. This haggling blended into disagreements over the date of

restoration. A deal was eventually reached which saw the DUP and Sinn
Féin agree to 8 May, on the proviso that Paisley and Adams sat next to
each other at the tip of the diamond table.[72]

On Monday 26 March, all parties readied themselves for what would
be, after so many false dawns, a key date in Northern Irish history. Blair
called Paisley at 9:25 A.M. He found him holding up well, and buoyed by
the support he had received from his congregation when he preached
the evening before.[73] He then called Adams one final time. Ever the
opportunist, Adams asked for assurances about the Irish Language Act.
'Classic Sinn Féin! They would always come back and chisel away for
more,' said an official.[74] Paisley and Adams duly took part in the historic
photograph of them sitting side by side, pledging their commitment to
begin power-sharing on 8 May. The image amazed all parties. Even the
NIO had not expected the warmth of the agreed public statements
which they delivered as they sat together.[75] That night, their faces led
the news bulletins, as they did for the headlines the following day. To
have had the arch hardliner of Ulster unionism photographed with the
former IRA leader, and agreeing to share power, was indeed the decisive
moment, eclipsing utterly the Good Friday Agreement. It was one of
Blair's most fulfilling moments of his premiership.

The lead-up to 8 May was to prove 'remarkably easy'. Once the DUP
and Sinn Féin had made their public decision that they were going to
work together there could be no further procrastinating and they knew
they had to make a success of it. Within two weeks of 26 March, they
had agreed upon which government departments each side were going
to take, and by Easter they effectively had a shadow executive. Blair's
main fear now was that dissident Republicans might commit a spoiling
move like killing a police officer, which his intelligence suggested was
a distinct possibility.[76] Steps were taken to minimise this risk, but no
measure could be foolproof. 'This is going to happen, isn't it?' he asked
when his plane took off for Belfast on the night of 7 May. 'We had all
been burned so many times that we didn't really believe this was for real
until we saw it happen,' said one.[77] One aide rated Blair's emotion as
'nine out of ten' on his personal scale, though added, 'If you're going to
be working on Northern Ireland, you can't allow yourself to be
emotional.'[78] As was often the case, Blair wrote his speech on the plane
to Belfast.

The ceremony was conspicuous for its lack of incident. It was
'reassuringly dull', said one official.[79] Present were Blair and Ahern and
a host of political signatories, including Senator Edward Kennedy and
former Taoiseach Albert Reynolds. As oaths were taken by Paisley and

McGuinness, which included promises to support the PSNI and the courts, as well as commitments to 'non-violence and exclusively peaceful means', Blair watched from the gallery above. Unbeknown to him, seated a few positions down the row, were at least two very senior members of the IRA's seven-member army council. For one NIO official, this curious sight of a British Prime Minister sitting so near such hardliners was a sure sign of success.[80] After the party moved into Stormont's marbled hall, Blair said, 'Look back and we see centuries marked by conflict, hardship, even hatred among the people of these islands: look forward and we see the chance to shake off those heavy chains of history.' Ahern lavished praise on Blair, in words that were not hyperbolic: 'This was not a process that promised quick or easy rewards. But he has been a true friend of peace and a true friend of Ireland. And for that we express our heartfelt thanks. I thank him for the true determination that he had, for just sticking with it for ten tough years. He has spent more time dealing with the issues of Northern Ireland, far more time than anybody could have asked any other person to do.'

After the event, Blair went straight to open the new offices of the Unionist newspaper, the *News Letter*, Europe's oldest periodical now in its fourth century of continuous publication, before returning to London. It had been a satisfying end to a historic day. As Blair's final weeks in office played out, he would meet again with the leaders of Republicanism and Unionism for a final farewell. When Adams and McGuinness visited Blair at the Commons after his penultimate Prime Minister's Questions, they thanked him for all his efforts, and presented him with a sculpture made from ancient Irish bog oak; its symbolism was not lost on the departing Prime Minister. Paisley's farewell was less formal, but perhaps for that reason, all the more poignant. The elderly Reverend greeted Blair in the Commons while he was busy signing presents of bottles of whiskey. Blair asked Paisley to sit with him while he continued signing. Paisley, referring to the liquor as 'the devil's buttermilk', took up the offer. They reminisced affectionately about their time together and Paisley requested that he never lose touch. He meant it, and Blair responded in kind. Many people, and many events, conspired to bring about the successful restoration of power-sharing, wherever it may lead. Here was one of Blair's greatest personal and political triumphs, which may well prove to have changed the course of history. Sadly, his energies, gifts for reconciling conflicting parties and vision were not to find the same expression in the Middle East, during his decade in office.

Iraq and Iran: February–April 2007

By early 2007, Blair knew that he would leave office amidst continued instability in Iraq and with his decision to go to war in 2003 the most criticised of all in his premiership. Iraq had not achieved the stability that he longed for. Blair considered the al-Maliki government ineffective, and had real doubts about the new approach being developed by the US. On 10 January, instead of the coherent political strategy involving a progressive draw down of forces that Blair longed for, Bush announced the details of its long awaited 'surge', bringing an extra 21,000 troops to Iraq. 'If we increase our support at this crucial moment, and help the Iraqis break the current cycle of violence, we can hasten the day our troops can come home,' the President insisted.[81] The aim was to assist al-Maliki by curtailing sectarian violence in Baghdad and targeting Sunni and al-Qaeda insurgents outside. The battle was only just beginning.

Blair at least hoped for a better finish in the Basra region. Since the end of the initial campaign, British policy had been to withdraw troops gradually. The British presence had been cut from 46,000 in the spring of 2003, to 8,500 in May 2005, and the trend had continued since. On 21 February, Blair told the Commons that British forces in the Basra region would be cut from 7,100 to 5,500: 'Increasingly our role will be support and training, and our numbers will be able to reduce accordingly.'[82] Blair took some comfort that 'Operation Sinbad', launched on 27 September 2006 to rid Basra of criminal elements, had been a modest success. The aim was for British troops to withdraw into a single base on the outskirts of Basra, from which they would be able to support Iraqi security forces rather than lead them. Some in the US military felt the British action amounted to a defeat. General Keane, who advised the Pentagon after his retirement from active service, believed that by August 2007 Basra was rife with 'almost gang warfare'. He warned that with further British withdrawals the situation would 'continue to deteriorate'.[83] The administration was more circumspect: 'I think the jury's still out on British success,' said one senior US official in September 2007.[84] Blair knew that the endgame was now largely out of his hands: finishing his premiership with a flourish was not an option in Iraq. Instead, an incident that took place just a few miles off Iraqi shores now threatened to plunge his remaining time at Number 10 into crisis.

On 23 March, at 10:30 A.M. local time, seven British sailors and eight marines were seized at gunpoint by Iranian warships, just outside the disputed Shatt al-Arab waterway dividing Iraq and Iran. According to the MoD, all fifteen were securely in Iraqi territorial waters, conducting a routine inspection of a cargo ship. The Iranians disputed this hotly, insisting that British forces had strayed into their waters. 'The situation was a complete nightmare,' admitted a Number 10 source.[85] The private fear was that the hostages would be held as long as the American hostages had been in 1979 to 1980, and that 'the hostage crisis would overshadow the whole of Blair's final three months', as they did the final period of Jimmy Carter's presidency. The American experience was a deeply sobering thought in London. On 28 March, British hostage Faye Turney was paraded on Iranian television and 'admitted' to trespassing in Iranian waters.[86] That day Blair told MPs that it was time to increase international pressure on Iran 'in order to make sure the Iranian government understands their total isolation on this issue'. The British government, he said, was holding talks with all its key allies and partners, and Britain suspended bilateral contacts with Iran.[87]

The British government thought that they could rely on US support, but knew it had to be handled carefully. The conservative fringes, the British Embassy reported, wanted pressure on Blair to adopt a 'more robust' approach.[88] Footage of Carter's hostage crisis was regularly re-run on the US television networks, particularly the conservative-leaning Fox news channel. Bolton, now retired as US Ambassador to the UN, made use of his freedom to speak out, describing Britain's cautious, incremental approach to the hostage crisis as 'pathetic', and said that Blair should be threatening 'real pain, real economic sanctions'.[89] The position of the administration, by contrast, was largely helpful: 'I simply told Margaret Beckett that if there was anything we could do she should call us,' said Condi Rice. 'Our view was that we were best to stay very far out of this . . . Given our relationship with Iran, there wasn't much we could do to be helpful.'[90] The British largely agreed: 'We made it clear to the administration,' said one Foreign Office official, 'that we did not want to raise the temperature.'[91] US support was thus limited to a strong public statement of support – Bush condemned Iran's 'inexcusable behaviour' – which was just what the Blair government wanted.

Elsewhere, Britain's policy of 'internationalising' the response was at best partly successful. On 29 March, the UK took the issue to the UN Security Council, but the furthest the Council would go was to express 'grave concern', rather than agreeing to 'deplore' the Iranian actions as the British had wanted. 'That will really show the Iranians we mean business,' responded an irritated British official.[92] On 30 March, EU foreign ministers offered their 'unconditional support' for Britain in the dispute, but refused to place any restraints on the EU's lucrative exports to Iran.[93] Blair also reached out to friends in the Middle East, leading many Arab governments to press the Iranians on the issue at the Arab summit in Riyadh on March 28–29. But Britain had to tread carefully. While many Arab rulers were sympathetic in private, they were reluctant to speak out.[94] Meanwhile, a second sailor was showcased in front of the Iranian media 'apologising' for trespassing in Iranian waters.

With the situation apparently deteriorating, the Supreme National Security Council in Tehran took over the hostage dossier. This development struck Number 10 as 'mildly good news'.[95] Next, Ari Larijani, its secretary, said on *Channel 4 News* that 'our priority is to solve this through proper diplomatic channels'. Sheinwald had been trying to make contact with Larijani since the weekend the crisis unfolded, but he had refused to return his calls.[96] Following the television interview, Sheinwald spoke to Larijani twice. He told Sheinwald that Tehran wanted to be positive, which Number 10 took to mean that they were willing at least to talk. Tehran was hoping Blair would say 'something conciliatory and helpful'. Sheinwald consulted widely. What exactly was going on inside Iran? British analysts concluded that the hostages had become part of a power struggle inside the government, and that the more extreme players like President Mahmoud Ahmadinejad were exploiting the hostile comments about Iran to prolong the crisis.[97] Number 10 resolved that it should keep talking to Larijani, soften the language from London, and stress how eager they were for discussions.

On 3 April, Blair authorised the 'conciliatory and helpful' gesture that Tehran had been seeking. This came with a statement from Number 10 insisting that 'the Prime Minister remains committed to solving this [issue] by diplomatic means', and that 'both sides share a desire for an early resolution' of the crisis. That same day, Larijani told Iranian state radio that talks with Britain had begun, but 'they were only at the beginning. If they continue this path, they can change the situation logically . . .'[98] Blair himself said, 'If they want to resolve this the diplomatic way, the door is open.' Number 10 was much relieved, but no one in the government expected the crisis to end so speedily. On 4 April, the British hostages were suddenly released as a gesture Ahmadinejad branded an 'Easter gift to the British people'.[99] Quiet diplomacy appeared to have won the day. Number 10 realised the importance of having a confidential channel to Iran and worked to maintain it. Sheinwald subsequently met Larijani in May 2007 and had a tough exploratory discussion focussing on Iraq and Afghanistan. The UK kept the US and European allies closely informed of the dialogue.[100]

The release of the hostages, in ill-fitting suits, was initially a matter of national relief in Britain. It all turned very sour, however, when on

8 April the MoD allowed the former hostages to sell their stories to the media. The following day, following national furore, the MoD backtracked and banned the practice. The story, nevertheless, dominated the week leading up to Easter. It reflected badly on the government as a whole, even though Blair had not been involved in this decision, and was critical of it.[101] The Embassy reported that after this 'ridiculous decision' by the MoD, the reputation of the Royal Navy lay in tatters. While hawks in the US considered Blair's attitude to the crisis to be nothing less than appeasement, Blair himself believed that the outcome demonstrated more clearly than ever the need for dialogue with all parties in the Middle East.[102]

Labour's Future is Resolved: January–May

Over Christmas, an exasperated Blair finally decided he wanted to see an alternative candidate put up against Brown.[103] 'It lasted from the beginning of the year until the point he realised no serious candidate was going to stand,' said one well-placed insider.'[104] To Blair, the key was ensuring that New Labour would be left in safe hands. When Brown, and those around him, began talking about the 'clean break' strategy, he became very agitated. Prescott thought that Clinton's experience after 2000, when he saw his 'legacy unpicked', weighed heavily in Blair's mind (albeit by a new administration): 'He wanted to see his legacy anchored down.'[105] How was he to achieve this? The only candidate with a serious prospect of beating Brown was still David Miliband. 'There was a period when several of us thought it was possible for David to win,' said a Blair ally.[106] Miliband did not rule out standing. He and Blair had several conversations together when they were working on the Energy White Paper, published on 23 May, but managed to avoid arousing suspicion. Opinions among the inner circle differed strongly about Blair's true intentions in finding an alternative candidate. Some believe that he was stringing Miliband along to put pressure on Brown to come into the centre ground; some think that he wanted a leadership election, thinking it would be good for the party as well as for Brown; still others believe that he wanted Miliband to be his successor, having finally despaired of Brown.

So which is right? The answer is that all three were, but at different points. Blair was ambivalent to the end, but in his heart of hearts, he knew that it had to be Brown, because his hold on every part of the party made his victory the only likely outcome.[107] He also felt he owed it to him: 'Underpinning all the noise about Gordon is Tony's highly complicated love for him.'[108] One close to both principals drew an analogy: 'How many times do couples say they are going to leave each other? Often, but they don't. That was their relationship.' He added: 'Tony's ultimate loyalty was to Gordon: he wanted Gordon to be Prime Minister, but in a way that was consistent with the project.'[109] One of Blair's closest aides agreed: 'I don't think he ever wanted a candidate to stand and *beat* Brown. He did think it would be a good thing for the Labour Party and did think it would make it easier for GB to be very New Labour.' Had Blair believed deeply in Miliband, he would have promoted him to Education Secretary or to another senior post in 2005, or to the Foreign Office in 2006. He did neither, despite being strongly urged. In the last six to nine months, many in Number 10 hitherto neutral came to share Powell's deep dislike of Brown, for his rudeness, and the way he behaved to their boss. They saw a deeply unpleasant side of him. Newcomers to Number 10 were astonished at Brown's manner. Brown's camp say he had suffered worse from Number 10. But at times, he pushed Blair to the brink. Had there been a candidate capable of dislodging Brown, and who could have held the party together, it is possible at these times that Blair might have supported him. The first few weeks of 2007 were highly volatile at the heart of Whitehall.

Blair's main weapon was the policy review process. Six working groups had been established in October 2006: for Blair they were the key test of whether or not Brown would engage and accept the thrust of their policy. Brown and his allies were deeply resentful of what they saw. 'The policy reviews were an affront to Gordon. They were an attempt to see if he would sulk and provide an excuse for Blair to dilly dally even longer,' said a leading Brownite in early 2007.[110] Prescott made it clear that he thought it impertinent for Blair to tie the hands of any successor. 'Tony wanted to secure future policy in concrete. My view was that you couldn't do it in a policy review; it had to go to conference and then be put in the manifesto.'[111] To some in Number 10, the deputy leader was a diminished figure in Blair's final months. He resented not playing the role in the endgame of supervising the transition, they surmised. An offside Prescott created further instability in the system. The policy review continued to cause difficulties within Cabinet in early 2007: for those who knew they were to be leaving, like Falconer and Armstrong, there were no ambiguities, but many felt differently. 'Lots of ministers wondered how far they should be co-operating with the policy reviews when Gordon so obviously was not,' said one Cabinet minister.[112] They felt loyalty to Blair, but questioned whether this was merely an attempt to embed his personal legacy and tie the hands of his successor, and 'was he right to be attempting it so close to his departure?' Some ministers felt intimidated by Brown personally or by his acolytes: 'Gordon can be very, very unpleasant when he wants to be,' said one.[113] 'It was an unnerving period,' said another.[114]

The Brown camp put great pressure on Blair to depart in March, to give their man a run in before the local, Scottish and Welsh elections in May, which they were saying would be disastrous if Blair was still in office. Failing that, they wanted him to go immediately afterwards.[115] Blair held on even more tightly to deciding his departure date. No hint was given about when precisely he would go: May, June or July were all debated in political and media circles. Most definitely he was not in a mood to nominate Brown. All the while he was talking to Miliband, but never put pressure on him to stand.[116] 'Tony was adamant that he wasn't going to make someone run: if someone was going to do it, they had to want to do it.'[117] Deep in Number 10, they watched the ebb and flow of gossip and briefings in the press: 'We all followed it and toyed with other options to David, but not seriously.'[118]

It made for a very difficult time on the policy review. 'Tony became completely "hyper-manic", and Gordon made it clear he wasn't going to pay it any regard,' said one Cabinet minister.[119] To get more traction into the process, Blair set up a seminar in Downing Street on 19 February to learn from ministers about their progress to date. He was less than impressed by what he heard: 'The next stage, to be absolutely blunt, is to get a slightly harder edge on the outcomes,'[120] he told them, saying, to the irritation of several ministers, that he expected to see polished and wide-ranging proposals ahead of the final Cabinet discussion on the reviews on 8 March. The stage was set for a major clash. But, to the surprise of many, Brown blinked first. Out of the blue he began to move towards Blair. What exactly produced his volte-face? Number 10 were convinced it was due to his anxiety about being portrayed in the press as anti-reform. To one insider, 'He was saying to the New Labour wing of the party, "Look, I really do believe this stuff: you don't need to put anyone up against me."'[121] The deputy leadership campaign agitated him also, they believed: 'He watched the deputy leadership candidates trying to drag at least the perception of the government to the left . . . That alarmed him and required him to firmly plant his flag in the centre territory that Tony's been occupying.'[122] Academies were widely seen as the litmus test of Blairite reform. Number 10 pointed to a leader in *The Times* which argued in favour of academies as being particularly influential with Brown. He certainly wanted Murdoch's support badly. 'Brown is absolutely obsessed with the Murdoch press, in particular the *Sun* and *The Times*,' said a Blairite.[123] *The Times* leader had said: 'The strongest political signal that the next prime minister (aka Gordon Brown) could and should send in their support [for academies] is to leave Lord Adonis and his ministerial team to promote them.'[124] Brown had never shown any public enthusiasm for Blair's flagship institution before. Had the time come for him to change?

The first sign of a thaw from Brown came with the publication of the Freud Report. Although not technically one of the six policy review subjects, it was in effect part of the whole process.[125] The banker David Freud had been appointed in late 2006 to make recommendations to improve the benefits system. An interim report appeared before Christmas, and he worked hard in January and February to complete it against a background of the Treasury saying: 'It will be a dull review and we're not interested.'[126] One explanation for the Treasury's *froideur* was its fear that Freud would be critical of the 'New Deal', one of Brown's early first-term initiatives, to which he was personally attached.[127] When the Treasury learned that Freud was likely to propose a 'public–private partnership' scheme to fund employment services, it became alarmed. One actor at the heart of the debate remembered a 'very familiar "Turner-style" rumble' about it.[128] Freud, in a very short period, produced four main proposals, all of a distinctly New Labour hue. The Treasury argued that the report should remain internal and not published. Blair disagreed and confronted Brown head-on: 'You have to work out whether you want to be seen as the person who is blocking the next stage of welfare reform, including benefiting those who are excluded, or whether you want to come on board.'[129] Put that way there was only one possible answer. Brown decided that he was not going to fight. At the end of February, he spent two hours with Freud before seeing Blair to talk through the details of his package. 'We are going to publish it on 5 March and I am going to be there to launch it,' Blair told him.[130] 'Very well,' said Brown, who wanted to join him at the official unveiling.

The launch took place in the State Rooms at Downing Street, with Brown alongside Blair, Hutton and Freud. Brown endorsed the report wholeheartedly, saying, 'This starts a new phase of welfare reform which I will champion.'[131] 'Having Gordon by his side, making out it was almost his review, was nauseating,' was the reaction of one official.[132] It was just six months to the day the coup had blown up, and Brown was coming in from the cold. Across the PLP and the Cabinet, many were delighted that he and Blair were reaching an accommodation. Brown did indeed go on to champion Freud. Many of his key recommendations found their way into the Green Paper, 'In Work, Better Off: Next Steps to Full Employment,' released under his premiership on 18 July 2007.

Two weeks later, on 19 March, Brown went still further. He told Blair he wanted to launch the first of the policy reviews with him on the hitherto contentious subject of public service reform – a subject which had seen Brown at his most intransigent in the second and earlier in the third terms. Number 10 was flabbergasted, particularly because the launch was to take place at Mossbourne City Academy in Hackney, east London.[133] The Treasury had thus far been 'very reluctant for Gordon to even go to an academy: we were told that "the Chancellor didn't go to academies".'[134] Previously, Number 10 heard that the only aspect Brown liked in the review was for GP services to be run from pharmacies.[135] Now he appeared to be embracing the whole agenda. Numbers 10 and 11 quickly co-ordinated the launch, agreeing on which sections either man would speak about.[136] Blair hailed the public services review, very pointedly, as 'The most complete and convincing account of how any government that wants to be progressive and successful can stay ahead of the curve.' The review called for 'truly personalised public services that give people the information and the power they need to choose a school or hospital . . . and a greater diversity of providers'.[137] Brown now said he looked forward to 'exciting new innovative ideas, whether it is greater choice, greater competition, greater contestability and greater local accountability'.[138] Was this the same person, Blairites asked? 'I have been astonished, as I think all my colleagues in Number 10 were, at the rapidity with which Gordon suddenly started publicly supporting things which his people have been blocking for months and in some cases years,' remarked one senior aide.[139] This was the very essence of Blairism, and here was Brown endorsing it. Brown even lavished praise on the academy. 'He was very impressed with the school and Michael Wilshaw [the Headmaster]: it was his first visit to an academy,' said an aide.[140] Brown's endorsement of the Freud and public service reviews in March was a major turning point. It still did not, however, to the Brownites' disappointment, result in a Blair endorsement, nor in Miliband declaring that he was no longer a candidate.

At the end of Blair's premiership, Blairites regarded it as highly significant that, with the possible exception of choice in health, Brown embraced almost the whole of Blair's public service reform agenda. It suggested to them that Brown had been so obstructive less for policy or political reasons, and more for purely personal ones: 'it was simply a constant campaign against Blair developing a forward programme of his own' remarked one Blairite.[141] There were some things that Gordon quite frankly would like to do, but he would much rather that Tony had left', countered one of Brown's close aides.[142] With Brown coming down in favour of reform, the other five policy reviews faded in significance! Brown delivered his last Budget on Wednesday 21 March before the next review was published. His '*pièce de résistance*' was the unheralded announcement at the end of the speech that he would be cutting tuppence off the basic rate of income tax. Although the net tax take turned out to be slightly higher, he succeeded in wrong-footing Cameron, and partially succeeded in his primary objective which was to appeal to the heartlands of Middle Britain who he still had to win over.

On 20 April, another opinion poll showed that if Brown was to take over as leader, the Conservative lead over Labour would grow. The pressure on him, even though he had 'come out' as a reformer, appeared to be growing[143] when, on 22 April, Miliband ended four months and more of speculation. He announced that he would not be running for the leadership, but would be supporting Brown. Writing in the *Observer*, he said, 'I will vote for Gordon Brown to lead Labour's drive . . . I have watched him and worked with him for nearly twenty years . . . No one is better qualified to lead across a wider canvas.'[144] Miliband's reasons had altered little from those he had before Christmas for being reluctant to stand, that it was not in the party's nor his own interest. Miliband's thinking was accurately reflected by Rawnsley: 'He thought the fight would be nastily personal'; he was not ready for the job – decisions on Iraq brought him out in 'night sweats'; he worried it would irretrievably split Labour; his cheerleaders would be the anti-Brownites, including Clarke, Reid and Mandelson.[145] To that can be added the lack of a case, now that Brown had declared himself as a reformer; a dislike of fighting against those to whom he was close, including his brother, Ed; and the knowledge he could not only lose, but possibly do so by a wide margin. Brown, moreover indicated preferment would be his, and so it proved, with the foreign secretaryship finally his. Miliband's supporters hoped, also, that his time would come. As for Blair, he achieved what he needed out of the prolonged exercise. Brown was now on the 'right side of the debate.' 'The moment David said he wasn't standing, that's when he knew it would have to be Gordon,' said one Number 10 aide.[146] But before he was to endorse Brown in public, he wanted the May elections out of the way.

In the run-up to the elections, both camps frantically briefed the press that the expected mauling was the responsibility of the other side. Blair had been making regular trips to Scotland to help with Labour's campaign. Amid predictions of dire results, he travelled north on 13 April to Glasgow, in the hope of boosting the party's flagging support in the city. He included a trip to Govan where he made his first visit to Golspie Street, where his father, Leo, had been brought up by foster parents. 'My dad was actually brought up in Govan in the 1920s and '30s and his foster father was a casual labourer down here on the yards. So it's quite interesting for me to come back,' he related to an unenamoured crowd at Govan shipyard.[147] The campaign was marked by unpleasantness between both camps, with Douglas Alexander, who combined the posts of Secretary of State for Transport and Scotland, deemed by Blairites to be among ministers 'the most rude and critical of all'. They recoiled at his 'sheer offensiveness' about Blair. Ed Balls, one Number 10 source said, was ruder still, but 'we only read his words second-hand in the newspapers: we had no direct contact with him'.[148] But it was to be Alexander, in league with Philip Gould, in almost a re-run of the 2005 General Election, who persuaded Blair that Labour's prospects in Scotland would be much improved if he delayed no further his endorsement during the campaign of Brown's candidature.[149] 'Tony did it, because he would have done anything to get more people to vote Labour,' said one Number 10 source.[150] Blair had been planning to announce his endorsement the following week, but on Monday 1 May, two days before polling day, and on the tenth anniversary of the General Election that swept him into power, he told Labour Party supporters in Edinburgh that 'within the next few weeks, I won't be Prime Minister of this country. In all probability, a Scot will become Prime Minister . . . someone who has built one of the strongest economies in the world and, who, as I've always said, will make a great Prime Minister for Britain.'[151] The previous day, Brown had lavished praise on Blair, referring to him in an article in the *Sun* as 'his oldest friend in politics' and thanking him for his 'social and economic achievements, and his leadership in the world'.[152]

Labour ended up losing 505 council seats (against the Tories' gain of 911) and lost 8 local authorities in England, losing seats in Wales and losing 4 seats in Scotland compared to the SNP's gain of 20. Twelve days later, Alex Salmond made political history by becoming the first nationalist to be elected the First Minister of Scotland. The results could have been much worse for Labour. The next day Blair insisted that they provided 'a perfectly good springboard to go on and win the next General Election'.[153] The election campaign had presided over a peaceful transition, culminating in Blair's endorsement for Brown. Despite the bouts of tension since the coup, a process of reconciliation had occurred between the two men. 'It could have been absolutely bloody,' said one insider, close to both, 'but they came together at the crucial moment.'[154] Not that it was easy: 'it was exhausting and draining.'[155]

On 6 May, John Reid announced on the BBC's *Politics Show* that he would leave Cabinet as soon as Blair had left office.[156] Some Blair ultras had seen Reid as a potential challenger to Brown. Others considered him too close to Blair and insufficiently popular compared to Brown. His decision effectively ensured that Brown would have an uncontested leadership election. The atmosphere between Blair and Brown had changed noticeably: 'Blair then simply worked very hard with Brown and saw much more of him. Brown wanted to talk to him, wanted to take his advice.'[157] 'In the build-up to the handover, in fact Gordon and he were probably working more closely together than at virtually any point in the history of the government.'[158] The clear run-in was good news for the Brownites, but immediately it raised in their minds the question of why there would be such a long period before their man could take over.

Number 10 had, like the rest of the country, been debating Blair's optimum date to retire. Many were kept in the dark, although Powell, Lloyd and a few others were working on a grid using possible dates.[159] During Easter, Jowell teased him. 'Now you promise me you're not going to take all your nearest and dearest by surprise.'[160] For most of 2007, Number 10 had been clear that it would be June, which would leave his successor four clear weeks before the holiday to make his mark and then to prepare for the autumn conference season. Blair was clear that he wanted to stay for the G8 in Heiligendamm and for the EU Council, which finished on Friday 23 June. He said he wanted to go out after PMQs, which gave two possible departure dates: 27 June or 4 July. Working backwards, they realised that, given the selection period needed for his successor, if there was to be a contest, the former date would be workable.[161] Where to make the announcement? Number 10 considered whether to deliver it on the street outside Downing Street, but Blair himself was clear that he was resigning as party leader, and the most natural place for him to do that was in Trimdon in his Sedgefield constituency, where he had always said he would first announce he was leaving.[162] 'He wanted to do it as speedily and unflamboyantly as possible. He had already started to feel quite philosophical about leaving. He felt pretty satisfied on a whole range of fronts and that the last two years had been an era of positive change,' said an ally.[163] Others close to him felt he chose Sedgefield because of his 'feeling that he didn't want to ever look as if he was judging GB from the sidelines/backbenches, as Mrs T. had done'.[164] The announcement was to be on Thursday 10 May. During Wednesday afternoon he asked his aides, 'Is this a big deal tomorrow? Do you think I should make a big speech?'[165] To some, he was still 'in a mindset that it was still a long way off, rather than being imminent'.[166] Officials reminded him that he was due to speak to the Queen by phone, having missed an audience following her State visit to the United States. Suddenly removed from worrying about the next day, Blair picked up the phone. He always enjoyed talking with the Queen, and once the call was over, settled down happily to write a speech.[167] Before ministers arrived for a special Cabinet on the Thursday morning at 9 A.M. Blair had been up early finishing his speech. He was particularly keen to inform his Cabinet first about his departure date though in reality by then it was common knowledge. A short agenda concluded with Brown offering Blair a 'fulsome tribute', thanking him for 'the unique leadership he had given his party, Britain and the world' over the past ten years.[168] Blair then flew to Trimdon where he was greeted with applause from his local supporters, many of whom had worked with him since he was adopted in 1983. In front of an audience of 200, and countless television cameras, he announced that on 27 June, 'I will tender my resignation from the office of Prime Minister to the Queen.' He encapsulated the achievements of his government in one sentence, 'There is only one government since 1945 that can say all of the following: more jobs, fewer unemployed, better health and education results, lower crime and economic growth in every quarter.' His tone was elegiac, reflecting on the difficulties of leadership and the challenges he had faced since 9/11. He was also deliberately downbeat: 'I ask you to accept one thing. Hand on heart, I did what I thought was right.' He concluded, 'I give my thanks to you, the British people, for the times I have succeeded and for the times I have fallen short. Good luck.'

Conclusion:

The Long Farewell (May–June)

Blair had long seen his participation of the G8 at Heiligendamm and EU Council in Brussels in June as his ideal curtain closers, allowing him to conclude his Gleneagles exports and his European policies. He had much more to do than just concentrate on these two conferences. He wanted his final six weeks to be the climax of a premiership which more than most had seen a repeated focus on foreign affairs. There were other victories still to be won, achievements to be celebrated, and thanks to be given. 'He was incredibly busy in the last few weeks. He wasn't just there to enjoy the last perks of power. Up till the end there were genuine negotiations to be done,' said a top foreign policy adviser.[1]

Farewell World: May–June

First up was a visit to the White House on 17–18 May. After six and a half years of intense loyalty, Bush was determined to reward his old friend on his last visit as Prime Minister. National security advisor Stephen Hadley held several conversations with Sheinwald about how to mark it. The message came back to us in the White House that 'The Prime Minister wants to work until the day he leaves office, so no grand tour, nothing out of the ordinary please.' That said, Bush personally was keen that Blair have the honour of sleeping in the historic 'Lincoln's Bedroom' at the White House, as opposed to staying at the Embassy, or at nearby Blair House, the official quarters for visiting foreign leaders, where even the Queen stayed during her state visit earlier that month.[2] This was thus a unique honour, but Blair wanted more than a historic bed for the night. How would Bush's warmth translate into policy objectives? Would Blair receive something tangible in return for his longstanding loyalty and support? By the end of 2006, and after the disappointing visit in December, Blair hoped for tangible benefits from Bush over climate change and Palestine in particular. 'He didn't understand why Bush couldn't show leadership on climate change,' said one Number 10 aide, 'given that Bush faced the same pressures on energy security. In the Prime Minister's heart, he felt let down by Bush not stepping up to the mark.'[3] During the May 2007 visit, veteran officials noticed a change in Blair: 'The visit had a very different tone in comparison with previous trips,' explained one aide. 'This was "Blair Unbound". He was more relaxed and he seemed free to speak without weighing everything he said.'[4] The Americans appeared to respond. On a range of issues, including climate change, trade, the MEPP and a defence trade agreement improving technology transfer, the British felt that Bush was leaning over backwards to help: 'They saw that he was going and made a special effort,' said one present.[5]

On Iraq, they discussed progress on the surge and Blair again stressed to Bush the need for reconciliation, and his hopes for the new inter-denominational council, representing Kurds, Shias and Sunnis to create a genuine government of national unity.[6] Neither had any illusions, though, about al-Maliki's ability to weld all the elements in Iraq together. They lamented that a more inspirational leader had not emerged in Baghdad over four years after fighting officially ceased.

The issue that occupied most of their time was climate change: 'He had been pushing Bush hard on this in their VTCs ever since January.'[7] Here was a real objective on which Blair wanted to see a success, especially as the G8 was now only three weeks away. Blair detected signs that Bush had shifted since the beginning of the year, partly in response to the 'bottom-up pressure' from within the US. Blair had played his part in fomenting this pressure, such as when he met faith leaders in America during 2005, and in his California trip the following year, when, with Schwarzenegger, he helped galvanise America's business community and state governors to take the issue more seriously.[8] If Bush felt the heat from his fellow Americans, Blair lost no sleep over it. He was absolutely clear: he was going to push the President harder on this than he had ever done. He was not prepared to lose on an issue so vital to him and to his legacy. Jonathan Powell and Justin Forsyth paid an important softening-up visit to the White House in the spring, which had pushed them hard, but they had constantly been frustrated by the lack of an effective interlocutor on the subject. Stephen Hadley was close to Sheinwald and a friend of the British, but his major focus was Iraq and foreign policy. Cheney was negative: 'He didn't want to do anything other than block us.'[9] To the end, the Vice President fought against much of what Blair had tried to achieve: there was no love lost between them. Cheney attended the final meeting at the White House: 'as usual, he said nothing at the meeting, he never did. They shook hands at the end, perfectly friendly. We knew he was a key figure resisting us, but what could Blair do? He couldn't deal with the Vice President directly.' Number 10 were pleased when Josh Bolten, Chief of Staff since April 2006 in succession to Andy Card, emerged as a supportive figure on climate change. Formidable work still had to be put in, however, to persuade the administration to agree a common approach to the post-Kyoto system after 2012 and the setting of a global CO_2 goal.[10]

Using every ounce of his persuasive skill, the new 'unbound' Blair pressed Bush to accept some of the post-Kyoto framework. In private, the President consented and even hinted that he might agree to a long-term goal to reduce emissions. The battle focused on what Bush was prepared to say at the final press conference. Blair was determined to get him to commit publicly that the US considered as a long-term goal becoming part of a post-Kyoto framework – not the most daring of statements. As the talks concluded in the Oval Office, he broke a golden rule of not lobbying Bush in front of aides. 'No, no, no, I would like us to be able to say this, this, and this,' he insisted. Forsyth handed over a text he had worked up with his opposite numbers. Standing at the President's desk, Blair wrote in longhand the words he wanted Bush to speak. It marked an extraordinary ending to Blair's time in the Oval Office where so much had passed over the previous ten years. 'We spent a lot of time on climate change,' declared Bush in front of reporters. 'I agree with the Prime Minister . . . This is a serious issue, and the United States takes it seriously . . . [At Heiligendamm] we want to be a part of a solution.'[11] Blair had got what he wanted. He was delighted. 'It was the first time that the President had said he wanted to be part of a post-2012 settlement,' said Forsyth.[12] But could Blair move him sufficiently to get the outcome he wanted at the G8? 'We needed him to move two or three more steps more. We had got him out of the corner and on to the front foot, but we needed to get them out in the street and shouting,' said one Number 10 source.[13]

Their final press conference also afforded the opportunity for both men to shower each other with praise. 'Tony Blair is somebody who actually follows through with his convictions ... This good man is a courageous man,' said Bush. 'You have been a strong leader at a time when the world needed strong leadership. You have been unyielding, and unflinching and determined in the fight we face together, and I thank you for that,' Blair replied.[14] Officials described their final parting as 'emotional' and 'wistful'. Blair, four years on, still had not felt able to pick up his US Congressional Gold Medal awarded to him in July 2003, because of concern that the ceremony would reinforce the prejudices of those convinced that he was, in Manning's words, 'some sort of poodle to Bush'.[15] Blair to the end was never sarcastic about Bush; frustrated at times, certainly, sometimes intensely, but over his obduracy, not his character. 'I'm not going to apologise for having a relationship with someone I've found to be straight and true to his word,' Blair later said.[16] 'I never heard him raise his voice to Bush on Iraq, or on anything else,' said one veteran Number 10 aide.[17] Blair never doubted for one minute that Britain's best interest was to remain side by side with the US. 'You can't be half with the President. You're either with him, or you're not. Tony took the decision to be with him,' was the view one aide heard from Jonathan Powell, an equal enthusiast for the approach.[18] The White House had been contemptuous of Chirac's attempt to turn France into a world power to counter the influence of the USA; to them, Blair's determination to act in consort with the US greatly enhanced Britain's standing and leverage on the world stage.[19]

In the eyes of many, including those in his own party, however, Blair's biggest weakness as Prime Minister was his apparently supine attitude to Bush. In the 2003 film *Love Actually*, Hugh Grant, playing a British Prime Minister, stands up at a press conference beside the US President and says: 'I fear this has become a bad relationship. A relationship based on the President taking exactly what he wants, and casually ignoring all those things that matter to Britain ... And since bullies only respond to strength, from now onward, I will be prepared to be much stronger.' It struck a chord with Blair's critics and it stung Blair personally. He referred to it in his keynote speech to the Labour Party's 2005 conference in Brighton, when, to the obvious satisfaction of his ministers, he said: 'I know there's a bit of us that would like me to do a Hugh Grant in *Love Actually* and tell America where to get off. But the difference between a good film and real life is that in real life there's the next day, the next year, the next lifetime to contemplate the ruinous consequences of easy applause.'[20] With the Lebanon crisis in the summer of 2006, when Blair may, arguably, have had the strategy right, the tactics and presentation were badly wrong, and all the worst accusations of 'poodle-ism' spilled out into the open.

So what did Blair achieve with Bush? For a country at the top of the second division of nations, and one which he wanted to play an activist role in world affairs, he deemed it essential to have a very strong alliance with the United States as well as a powerful position in Europe. The strength of his US relationship was not in doubt. After two wars together, and very regular contact through memos, phone calls and from the autumn of 2003, VTCs every two weeks and often weekly, the two men came to know each other well. They substantially agreed on the goals for Western policy in the post-9/11 world. Pursuing al-Qaeda remorselessly across borders, forcing the Taliban from power, and removing the threat from Saddam Hussein, were crucial aims for both Bush and Blair. Yet often they differed on tactics, sometimes with major consequences: how far they should involve the UN in tackling Iraq, for instance, or over engaging with Syria and Iran in the Middle East, and the phasing of troop withdrawals from Iraq. Too often Blair proved unable to shift the President when key tactical differences came to the fore. Occasionally they differed over the goals themselves. Blair's biggest achievement was to move Bush on climate change. His constant pressure helped propel Bush further than domestic forces alone would have taken him. Michael Jay for one was staggered by Blair's standing on this issue in Capitol Hill: 'A number of senators said to me, "Thank God Blair has really focused on this because it has affected opinions here in the United States; the fact that he's been tenacious in keeping on about it and hasn't let go."'[21] Schwarzenegger believes no one has done more to wake up the world to the problems of climate change. Blair's achievement was to open up the dialogue between the US and Europe on climate change, to make the administration admit there is a problem, and that it can only be tackled by bringing China and India on board. But he never persuaded the administration that mandatory measures such as carbon trading were required. Blair was least successful on the MEPP, on which he had the best of the argument and on which domestic pressures on Bush were far heavier still. Bush's periodic positive words saw little follow-through. The more open attitude to the MEPP from the White House in Blair's final months was less due to Blair's constant pressure than the shock of the Lebanon débâcle, which woke the administration up to Israel's military vulnerability and its isolation, and thus the case for some form of accommodation with the Palestinians. To Blair, this was the great 'unfinished business' of his premiership. The question that will always remain is whether the concessions Blair won from Bush were enough to justify his unstinting support for American policy. Would he have achieved more if he adopted the harder tone of their final White House meeting earlier? Possibly. Would he have achieved more in policy terms if he had adopted the Chirac line? Doubtful.

A weary Blair boarded the plane on 18 May to return overnight to London, sleeping most of the way. The next morning he went straight on to Iraq, again, unusually for him, sleeping that part of the leg, but also talking about his discussions with Bush, particularly over climate change.[22] Blair arrived in Baghdad on Saturday morning and held talks with Prime Minister al-Maliki and President Talabani, reassuring them that when he left as Prime Minister the following month, it would not bring an end to Britain's support. He expressed pleasure with the appointment of the new police chief, and some other developments, but in private he felt deeply frustrated with the inability of al-Maliki to run a more effective government. 'Their system was deeply chaotic,' admitted one in the Prime Minister's party.[23] Blair left with little confidence of a stable government in the near future. He flew on to Basra for his final visit to the troops. As he was speaking, two mortars exploded, rocking the building, rattling the windows. As he brushed it off, he told troops that 'this will be my last chance to say thank you for the work that you have done here ... You have done it absolutely brilliantly.' As he chatted to groups of servicemen and women over cups of tea, he joked with them, 'I'm under strict instructions to wind everything up before the Cup Final begins.'[24]

Iraq was the biggest disappointment, and failure, of his premiership, when contrasting the record against his high-minded aspirations of a speedy transition to a democratic Iraqi government, with an exemplary model of soldiering by the British troops in the south. By the time he left office, 153 British troops had died in Iraq since the start of the 2003 invasion.[25] Every death still affected him and he still wrote his personal letters: 'To the end, he never stopped hoping. Even in the middle of other business, he'd break off and ask "What is going on in Iraq? How are things in Basra?", it was the first thing he'd always come back to. He would receive a weekly update which he would digest avidly. 'He was deep into the detail. He pored over it all very closely,' said one official.

In early May Blair invited the family of a soldier killed in Basra the year before to see him in Number 10. The widow was worried that the occasion would be overtly political and was uncertain whether to attend. She was glad she overcame her qualms. On sitting down with her children, a solemn Blair told her: 'Look ... I'm responsible for deploying British soldiers to conflict zones for war, and thereby I'm responsible for what happens when they are there, and I'm deeply sorry for what happened to your husband and father of your children.'[26] There was no political statement. 'He literally just wanted to sit down and touch and meet the families of those who've lost people as a result of his decision in a personal, straight way.'[27] The mother of the family eloquently described her pride and love for her lost husband. 'It was a very poignant moment.'[28] Blair himself was profoundly affected by the visit and spoke privately with her for another ten minutes after the children and others present had left the room.

On the positive side, he would point out, on his departure, Iraq had its own government, that Iraqis had voted in far higher proportions than anyone had expected. He never doubted, even in private, that he had done the right thing. 'I believe you would have had to have dealt with Saddam at some point,' he said in his final month in power.[29] He never stopped believing in the doctrine of liberal interventionism, and that the world 'could not afford to have people like Saddam knocking around the Middle East indefinitely'.[30] He regretted that the post-war position had been handled so badly, and the damage done to British national interests in the Middle East, to his own standing, and the loss of life, British, coalition and Iraqi.[31] He wished he had foreseen more clearly the need to govern post-conflict Iraq better, and how neighbouring countries, principally Iran, would seek to destabilise the country (and how quickly al-Qaeda would exploit the vacuum to foment discontent). Given his experience of post-war governance, it is all the more surprising that he did not press his case on post-war planning, and instead he let Washington take the brief. But even in his memoirs, he will not apologise for going to war to remove Saddam.

Blair's next trip was to Africa, from 29 May to 1 June. The subject of heated debate in Number 10, there were fears that it would attract exactly the kind of negative headlines it did for being a 'legacy tour' or a 'vanity trip', as Conservative MP Chris Grayling described it.[32] Blair himself wobbled about the trip shortly before he left, less because of the press reaction, whose cynicism he took for granted, than concern at the time it would take out of his dwindling remaining days. Liz Lloyd argued powerfully for it. Deep down, he wanted to go, as Africa had been so meaningful to him during his premiership, and President Mbeki of South Africa had personally invited him to visit.[33] As important he wanted the G8 at Heiligendamm to build on Gleneagles and he thought the trip would offer important preparation. 'This was a trip with purpose,' insisted one aide.

First stop was Libya. Here was a country which he had helped move from being an outcast in the international community to one which was rejoining the mainstream, and had given up WMD. He was proud of his role. It proved that, in contrast to US traditional thinking, engaging with hostile countries could work. Gaddafi had to be tracked down in the depths of the Libyan desert at Sirte, 150 miles south-east of Tripoli. The trip had practical benefits, helping seal a $25 billion BP deal with the Libyan government, three decades after the company had been ejected when Gaddafi nationalised the company's assets. Blair had also been working behind the scenes to secure the release of the five Bulgarian nurses and one Palestinian doctor who had been sentenced to death by firing squad for allegedly infecting 438 children with HIV at the city hospital in Benghazi. The belief was that Gaddafi was using the medics as scapegoats to abate the outrage that erupted across the country at the time.[34] Blair's mediation had a decisive role in their being freed in July 2007 after eight years of captivity.

Next up was Sierra Leone. Blair had been very keen to go to Sierra Leone, where his father had taught, and where he had played a pivotal role in helping rescue the country from chaos when British troops intervened in 2000. Sierra Leone was an example of his values-driven, interventionist foreign policy 'where British military involvement had been positive and successful.'[35] The trip proved extremely emotional for him and his party. He was greeted as a hero in Sierra Leone, as he had been in 2000. He spoke at a military barracks, and congratulated Sierra Leone's politicians, army and police for bringing the country back towards peace and democracy.[36] He then visited a local village and health and education projects. 'Despite being tired, you could see him enjoying himself,' recalled one witness. 'As he walked through the mud in the torrential rain and entered a classroom full of young African children, his face lit up. This, for him, was what it was all about.'[37]

Emotionally, South Africa touched Blair deeply, and this final visit meant much to him. With Mbeki in Pretoria on 31 May he spoke about climate change and Africa in preparation for the G8, and in public he stressed the importance of South Africa's status as one of the 'plus 5'. The two most moving moments were personal. At the Chris Hani Baragwanath hospital in the Soweto township, he met with doctors, nurses, community workers and patients. As they sat around a table a woman said, 'I'm alive because I am now on anti-retrovirals', which over a million people in Africa had received as a result of the Gleneagles commitment.[38] This experience lived in Blair's mind. As he moved into the last few weeks before the G8, he urged his aides to fight very hard for concrete commitments on HIV/AIDS in the final Africa communiqué.[39]

Mandela had had an iconic status throughout his entire premiership, and Blair was visibly moved when he visited the now frail figure with Cherie, and to spend an hour alone with him. Of all the world leaders he had met as Prime Minister, Mandela he admired most. The visit was full of nostalgia. In his last major foreign policy speech, delivered at the University of South Africa outside Johannesburg, he echoed the ideas of two men who first inspired him into political action, priest Peter Thomson and philosopher John Macmurray: 'I believe in the power of political action to make the world better, and the moral obligation to use it,'[40] he said. He could have uttered the same words thirty-five years before as an Oxford undergraduate.

But he found these words harder to apply to other challenges, notably to Zimbabwe and Darfur. He was always frustrated about Zimbabwe, and abhorred the tyrannical and ruinous leadership of Mugabe, but he had decided, rightly or wrongly, given Britain's colonial past, that any lead on Zimbabwe had to be taken by the Africans. That lead was not forthcoming despite endless private conversations with Mbeki and others. On Darfur he expended considerable political effort, but yet again, to his intense disappointment, support was lacking. He said in public that it was 'crazy for us to allow a situation like Darfur to carry on and on without acting'.[41] He had been worrying away for several months, but found that the Sudanese government 'blocked every turn and were utterly cynical'.[42] Apart from Bush, he had been unable to find fellow leaders to share his belief that action was required, while from China and Russia, he met positive resistance to intervention. The UN also disappointed him: Kofi Annan had offered some leadership in his last few months in office, but his successor, Secretary General Ban Ki-Moon, took a long time to get up to speed. The painfully slow UN bureaucracy drove him to despair. Though his detractors doubted it, he would have loved to have done more, but believed politically that, with Afghanistan and Iraq in the background, and with international opinion as it was, his hands were tied.[43]

A farewell trip to Afghanistan was aired but, with time running out, he decided against it. In his final weeks, he was encouraged by the reports he was receiving from the service chiefs, but was worried by the casualties, and depressed by the lack of success of counter-narcotic programmes to stem the export of drugs. The Americans saw this as a particularly British failure, given that London insisted British troops work with locals on the ground to eradicate poppy crops, rather than resorting to aerial spraying, Washington's favoured tactic. Overall, though, he gauged Afghanistan a success, and he was proud that he had seen as early as late 2001 the need to have a large international presence in the country.

Blair hoped the G8 at Heiligendamm would prove more promising, and provide the climax of his campaigns on climate change, Africa and trade. The fact that Angela Merkel had chosen these as her themes for her first G8, said one Downing Street aide, 'showed how well Blair chose his agenda for Gleneagles'.[44] Without Blair's impetus the FCO understood that Merkel would have chosen 'growth and responsibility' as her lead topic for the summit.[45] Africa and climate change had become something of an obsession for Blair: 'In almost every conversation he had with a world leader in the two years between the two G8s he managed to bring them up.'[46] Heiligendamm was to see the flowering of the Blair/Merkel relationship, which was seeded two years before. Blair was good with women: 'He'd sooner talk to women than to men.'[47] He was consummately skilful at handling her. 'He has a very good sense of humour, knows when to back off and how to make his points without bullying or over-pressing people,' said one official who observed Blair closely through many summits.[48] Merkel found him more interesting and fun to talk to than other European leaders: 'There was a twinkle in her eyes when she was with him,' said one observer.[49] 'I think there was a bit of personal chemistry, bordering on a degree of mutual flirtation,' said another official.[50] Their characters complemented each other: hers focused, detailed and logical, his more feminine and intuitive. Her good English too, facilitated their conversation, unlike his experiences with Schröder. From late 2006, he and Merkel started 'conspiring together' during VTCs over how to achieve their objectives at both the EU Council and the G8. 'They cooked up elaborate strategies not only to manoeuvre Bush where they wanted him to go,' revealed one aide, 'but also to bring India, China and Brazil on board.'[51]

On 3 November, Merkel visited Blair at Downing Street in further preparation for the coming Councils. After the meeting, Blair, Cherie, Merkel and her husband, went for dinner at the elegant Criterion restaurant in Piccadilly. So engrossed were they that the dinner pushed on into the night: 'They stayed on and on until the officials had to admit that they needed to catch trains back home,' recalled one aide. 'It was clear that all four of them were enjoying it hugely.'[52] At last Blair had found a fellow leader respectful of Bush but willing to join in lobbying him: 'They conspired in a clever pincer movement to put maximum pressure on the president,' said one Number 10 official.[53] Blair met Merkel on 24 April to discuss Africa with Kofi Annan and Bob Geldof, and launch the Africa Progress Panel. Blair and Merkel dined together on Sunday 3 June immediately after his return from Africa, and worked up a final strategy to get Bush where they wanted him.[54] On Africa, they agreed to press for 'seven dollar numbers' to be inserted in the text giving specific commitments on AIDS and education. Number 10's Olly Robbins and Justin Forsyth worked with their opposite numbers to make this happen in the coming days. On climate change, they also discussed how to bring Bush onside. While Blair was busy forging an alliance with Merkel to drive the Heiligendamm agenda, UK sherpa Robbins was working furiously to build a coalition among the other G8 countries as well as with the plus 5. To heighten pressure on the US, Blair sent him to Delhi, and he spoke himself by phone to Singh in India, Lula in Brazil, Stephen Harper in Canada and Shinzo Abe, the new Prime Minister of Japan. The aim was to lever up pressure on Bush. Hitherto, the administration would make out that climate change was almost a 'European plot' against the rest of the world, with a sceptical US, Japan, Canada and Russia being pressurised by unreasonable European leaders. 'Peeling Japan and Canada very gently away isolated Bush,' said an official. 'I don't want to be the skunk at the picnic,' Bush confessed to Blair at one of their final meetings.

Three days before the summit, on 31 May, Bush reiterated his commitment to making the US a part of the solution on climate change, but also suggested a multinational action plan to operate outside the UN framework. It was a big step forward for Bush but there were real concerns that it could undermine the UN process if it went ahead. Merkel and Blair both agreed that what he said was useful and could be built on but they had to ensure it was within the UN. Not everybody shared their view. 'Coming just a week before the G8, some suspected that it was just a US spoiler,' said one diplomat.[55] The day before the G8 opened, Blair abandoned another of his principles, not differing from Bush in public, and declared that he would be able to convince Bush to agree a specified cut in greenhouse gases by 2050, and within a UN framework.[56]

Merkel had lunch with Bush on the first day of the summit, Wednesday 6 June, and told him she was not prepared to compromise her ambitions for the US. She would keep pushing him to agree a global target for after 2012, and any new agreement would be part of the UN process, whether he liked it or not.[57] That evening she asked Blair to work with Nicolas Sarkozy at dinner, to keep pressing Bush. The next morning, Blair had a private one-to-one working breakfast with Bush to which he brought a paragraph of text, penned by Robbins. Blair had never been more forceful with Bush as he coaxed and urged to him to agree the statement to halve global emissions by 2050.[58] Blair's skill at producing language and stances that Bush would find appealing, including binding the high polluters China and India into an agreement, helped the President win round his staff, for whom 'Kyoto was a dirty word'.[59] By the end of the meeting, Blair had Bush where he wanted him. 'That was the real turning point, when the deal suddenly looked possible,' said Forsyth.[60] The final communiqué agreed that there would be a post-2012 framework in place by 2009, that the starting point for the negotiations would be halving global emissions by 2050, and that this would be inside the UN process. It went on to make important commitments on energy efficiency and renewables and supported carbon markets – a previous red line for the US though its opposition to mandatory controls remained. The NGOs immediately condemned the deal for being neither mandatory nor specific enough. But for Merkel and Blair, Heiligendamm was never about agreeing the detail, but rather the principles of a future framework for the G8 plus 5 to allow subsequent negotiations to move ahead more quickly. Blair himself would have liked to go even further in the direction of binding commitments, but was still pleased: 'If you'd said six months before that we got as far as we did on climate change, we'd have said "no way",' said one Number 10 aide.[61]

Blair was less happy with progress on trade, which had been overlooked at St Petersburg, and on Africa. The NGOs had built up a big campaign in Germany in the run-up to Heiligendamm. Geldof was asked to edit *Bild*, a popular German newspaper, which he gave over wholly to Africa, and with Bono he organised a huge concert which whipped up a pre-Gleneagles-style pressure, castigating leaders for failing to abide by their Gleneagles promises. In the days before the summit the US made new commitments to increase spending on HIV/AIDS from $15 to $30 billion over five years. The Germans increased their aid budget by €750 million a year over four years. Resistance came principally from the Italians and Japanese: 'They complained it was all very costly and it was all being done to please the NGOs who would slam us anyway, so why bother?' After huge pressure late in the day from Merkel who said 'I want an Africa story out of this', the leaders finally agreed to include specific commitments in the communiqué on HIV and education. None of these got the G8 back on track to achieving all the promises made in Gleneagles, but it was still progress. As Blair pointed out, since Gleneagles, three million more people in Africa were in school and nearly twenty countries had had their debt cancelled.[62] The continued focus ensured that the hosts for 2008, Japan, kept Africa on the agenda.

Blair, increasingly free of the trappings of diplomatic etiquette, saw Heiligendamm as his final opportunity to confront Putin. On 3 June, in an unnerving backdrop to the G8, the Russian leader had threatened to resume routine targeting of Russia's missiles on Europe in response to the US decision to deploy its new missile defence system in Poland and the Czech Republic. Britain's relationship with Russia had deteriorated markedly since 2002/03. Putin placed much of the blame on Britain harbouring the Russian tycoon Boris Berezovsky.[63] Blair deplored Putin's crackdown on democratic freedoms and the press, the increased influence of the FSB, the successor body to the KGB, the treatment of British citizens in Russia and the poisoning of Alexander Litvinenko, whom the British government believed had been murdered under direct instructions 'from very high up indeed in the Kremlin'.[64] Blair saw him at 1:30 P.M. on the final day, 8 June. Putin had been imagining it would be a perfunctory meeting, an opportunity for some photo calls, but Blair felt differently. As soon as he walked into the room Blair ordered all the photographers to leave, despite Russian protest. The moment had come to give Putin 'a very private, very pointed message'. If Russia continued to behave the way it was, he said, its influence and ability to form working relationships would be severely reduced. 'He wanted to leave Putin with a clear message about how he should be conducting himself on the world stage. There was nothing in it for Blair. Putin knew that. There was no need for him to say anything to the Russian leader other than how he saw it,' said a Number 10 source.[65]

Blair left the G8 in good spirits, pleased in particular that the climate change agreement unlocked the potential for a much bolder and more radical framework after 2012, to include the US, India and China. Heiligendamm had indeed underlined his achievement at Gleneagles, as he hoped it would, which he regarded as his most successful conference. It also highlighted his significant achievement in boosting Britain's global links, bringing in the + 5 at the G8, raising the profile of education and pushing ahead with trade. In championing climate change and Africa in his final two years, Blair had managed to re-engage with the idealism of the British public, which he thought had been cemented with the idealism of his liberal interventionism, but which had been damaged so badly over Iraq. He had again found how to touch the popular nerve. Over Iraq he had been made to feel a pariah: on these issues, even if he had not gone far enough for many, he had reconnected morally with many. And that mattered deeply to him.

Farewell Europe

The year 2006 had been one of consolidation in the EU. With the French and Dutch elections pending, there was a consensus that debate over the constitution should be kept on the backburner until the German presidency in the first half of 2007. Blair would happily have kicked the constitution into touch for ever, believing there were more important questions for the EU than navel-gazing on its inner workings, though he accepted that, given enlargement, new arrangements had to be made. The Lahti Summit, during the Finnish presidency in October, had seen Merkel stand up to Putin, making clear that the Schröder line of appeasing Moscow, and the Chirac–Schröder–Putin triumvirate, had gone for ever.[66] But even neutral observers believed Blair was dominant at Lahti: 'The striking point about the council was about how Blair-centric it was.'[67] He worked hard to keep Turkey's prospects of joining the EU alive, and his personal relationship with Prime Minister Erdoğan proved decisive in persuading fellow EU leaders to keep faith with Turkey's accession.

As his premiership drew to a close, Blair seemed more focused on Europe than ever. 'He devoted more time to the EU in his final six months than to any other single subject,' said one aide.[68] Chief topics at the March Brussels council were the Hampton Court agenda items of climate change, energy market liberalisation and energy security. Blair flew to see Merkel on 13 February, and 'effectively decided' on the flight over that he could commit Britain to the target of 20 per cent of energy coming from renewable sources by 2020 and a 30 per cent emission reduction target.[69] Merkel was of a like mind, and they announced the targets at their joint press conference in Berlin after their meeting.[70] It proved a pivotal moment, with the French announcing their support for the same levels shortly afterwards. At the Council on 8 March, negotiations continued through the night, with the Czechs and Poles chief among those insisting the figures were too high. Blair and Merkel ultimately achieved many of their targets, with agreement on a 20 per cent emissions cut by 2020, and a pledge to go to 30 per cent if agreement could be struck with the US and other key countries.[71] On energy, an agreement was reached to establish a genuine single market. Blair had worries that Chirac would use his last Council either to wreck negotiations or to deliver a diatribe against the direction the EU was moving in, but his fears did not transpire. One senior British official called it 'the most successful EU spring council for Britain for ten years in terms of positive agenda success'.[72] At the parliamentary debate on the following Monday, 12 March, David Cameron said, 'May I thank the Prime Minister for his statement, and may I also do something that he is perhaps not always used to from the Leader of the Opposition after European statements, and congratulate him on helping to negotiate a successful outcome to the European Council?'[73] For the Prime Minister to be congratulated by the Leader of the Opposition on his work at an EU Council was rare indeed.[74]

The March Council cleared the decks for Merkel to focus on the EU treaty in June. For all his distaste for the subject, Blair remained determined to achieve a resolution before he left. He had one great asset: with Chirac on his way out he possessed a deeper grasp of the detail than any other EU leader, with the possible exception of the fast-learning Merkel.[75] But nothing would happen before the French presidential election, which began in April. If the Socialist Party's Ségolène Royal beat the right-wing UMP's Nicolas Sarkozy, a very different constitution might emerge. Blair got on much better with leaders on the right in Europe, like Berlusconi, Barroso, Schüssel and Merkel, than on the left – he would claim they were more realistic about globalisation and were willing to engage with Bush. He hoped for a Sarkozy victory. He was flattered, if mildly embarrassed that Sarkozy pushed for a personal meeting in advance of the election. Blair first learnt of his eagerness during the British presidency in December 2005. So did Chirac. 'That man is an enemy of mine,' he told Blair sternly. 'I would like it if you did not see him.'[76] Sarkozy persisted and Blair had to tell him: 'Your president doesn't want me to see you', to which he replied: 'But you must. I am your friend. You must see me.'[77] To resolve this diplomatic impasse, Blair agreed to meet Sarkozy not at Number 10 but in the Millennium Hotel across the River Thames from Parliament. Sarkozy introduced himself in French, 'I'm not Chirac, and I want to change everything.' Blair listened to the voluble Frenchman, and when finally given an opening, asked in French, 'And how are you going to be elected?' Sarkozy, both Anglophile and 'Blair-ophile', was intrigued by Blair's three election victories and said that he would campaign, like Blair, on a manifesto for change.[78] If he was not elected on that platform, he was not interested in serving. Chirac, he said, had tried to pretend that the French did not want change, which is why the French lost faith with him.[79] He and Blair subsequently met on some six occasions before Sarkozy won his narrow second-round election victory on 6 May. By then, a significant bond had been forged.

On 11 May, Blair came to Paris, stopping off to see Chirac at the Elysée Palace in his final days as President. He was pleased that his old foe had taken the trouble to see him. Chirac was in a reflective mood as they mulled over the previous ten years. It is rare for two EU leaders to span a decade and he waxed about their achievements together on European defence, and praised Blair on Hampton Court and climate change. The meeting over, Chirac broke with the normal convention of shaking hands with his departing guest at the top of the Elysée steps, and very deliberately descended them and walked across the courtyard, pausing three or four times while doing so to talk, placing his hand on Blair's shoulder, clearly wanting to be photographed in the sunlit courtyard, sending out a message that they were parting on the best possible terms. 'To the last, he had a developed sense of theatre,' said one Number 10 official of Chirac.[80] Blair was enchanted, but not taken in. By the end, and especially after the meeting, he warmed to the French President, but he did not trust him and could never forget their disagreements over Iraq. All told, he felt that Chirac had frittered away his opportunities as President of France and had held up the evolution of the EU.[81] Blair was then driven to see Sarkozy, who was staying in a relatively modest house in the centre of Paris. They sat outside at the garden table, and talked mainly about the June Council: 'You and I want the same thing, Tony; we want a quick deal, an amending treaty, not a constitution,' he said. 'I'm completely in your hands, whatever you want I will support.' For Blair and his aides this was utterly alien ground in Anglo-French relations, and all the more welcome for that, with promising prospects for Blair's final six weeks. In the evening they went to Thiou, a Thai restaurant on the banks of the Seine, along with Sarkozy's Anglophile wife, Cécilia, who when travelling to London to see her daughter would call in to see Cherie at Number 10.[82] Blair had hugely enjoyed the evening, and left it reflecting what might have been if Sarkozy, not Chirac, had been president for the ten years of his premiership, not its dying weeks.

Blair's resignation plans, overseas travel and the G8 distracted him over the four weeks following the dinner, but he kept his focus on the June Council. It involved him in two parallel negotiations: one with Britain's twenty-six EU partners, the other with his successor. Blair was clear he thought a referendum unnecessary if all the British red lines were met and if he avoided it becoming a full constitutional treaty. But, ultimately, it would be Brown who would have to win the argument against having one, as well as dealing with the follow-up from the Council. Blair clearly would not have credibility at Brussels unless he could say his position had been agreed with his successor, and as the Council approached he spoke to Brown almost every day about it. Blair's core position was that they should not be proposing a 'constitution', as Giscard d'Estaing had advocated and which had been rejected in 2005, but an 'amending' treaty, which revised rather than replaced earlier treaties. He sensed that the mainstream of opinion among EU leaders wanted to finish off the constitution at the June Council, and were fed up with the issue. He saw his chance.

By Easter, Blair had clarified his thinking on the four British 'red lines', areas on which he would not under any circumstances accept EU control: on the charter of fundamental rights, common law, social security legislation and foreign policy.[83] His aim was to disclose these red lines late in the day, but a leak from the German Chancellery on 20 April forced a rethink. The press reported that Merkel was in effect proposing to reintroduce the European constitution but under a different name, a move the British would have found completely unacceptable.[84] Blair was at Chequers when the story broke. A conference call at 9 A.M. was booked with David Hill and Kim Darroch at Number 10; Blair's concern was that unless he responded quickly, the British media would take delight in allowing the story to snowball. With the eleven o'clock lobby briefing fast approaching, they agreed to disclose their four red lines, hurriedly agreeing them with the Treasury and FCO, which showed that Britain was not about to succumb to a federalist constitution. Blair travelled to Germany to see Merkel for dinner on 3 June. They spent a third of the evening speaking about Heiligendamm and two-thirds on the treaty. Discussions ran on; Blair was due to leave at 9:20, but ended up leaving at 11 P.M. Towards the end, Blair took Merkel aside for a forty-five-minute tête-à-tête, when he handed her his own handwritten list penned on the plane of all the points Britain wanted on the treaty.[85] On 18 June, Blair formally set out the British red lines and made clear that these positions were non-negotiable.[86] The next day, he and Brown held a two-hour conference call with Sarkozy, when they secured his support for opposing any return to a constitutional treaty.

The last of Blair's forty-two EU Councils started on Thursday 21 June. It began innocuously, with a meeting with Merkel in the morning, and again at 7 P.M. where he insisted that the four British red lines were to be guaranteed by opt-outs. This was the crunch meeting. The opt-out on the charter was the one that the British delegation thought was most at risk. Merkel protested. 'You are pushing too far.' Officials noted how 'Blair moved from his traditional affable style of negotiating into uncompromising mode.'[87] He told her, 'This text has been drafted by the Attorney-General, it has been agreed by Cabinet and with my successor. I know your officials are unhappy with it, but I can't change a word.' Merkel was urged by her officials, but when he pleaded that he had no room domestically for manoeuvre, she relented and said she would try to be helpful. And so she proved.[88]

Brown was kept updated throughout the day. A mini-crisis occurred when Sarkozy proposed an apparent watering-down of the EU's commitment to competition, but a compromise formula was produced with help from Barroso. Brown kept his own counsel on the treaty: 'All the way through Blair had an element of doubt and a sense that he was being pushed to go further by Brown,' said one official.[89] As the evening wore on, it appeared Britain would achieve most of what it sought, and the EU was close to agreement. But Poland threw a spanner in the works over the status of their voting rights. Everyone was getting tired and Merkel announced that Poland was isolated 1 to 26: she was prepared to press ahead with the treaty, with or without Poland. Blair and Sarkozy persuaded her to allow them a final attempt at persuading the Poles. They went off at 10:30 P.M. and waged battle with the Polish President Lech Kaczyński in a small room heavy with smoke from the Polish delegation. At one point, Blair had to speak to the Prime Minister's twin brother, Jaroslaw Kaczyński, who was conducting a Cabinet meeting in Warsaw. An hour and a half later they had brought the Poles back on side. At 1 A.M. on the Saturday morning, the plenary meeting was reconvened but now Belgian PM Verhofstadt delayed its conclusion. He despised Blair's attitude to Europe and tried to reopen the concessions the British and the Dutch had achieved. 'It almost came to blows,' said one witness. 'Verhofstadt and the Dutch prime minister, Balkenende, started shouting at each other across the conference room and it became extremely ugly.'[90] Merkel called a cooling off period at 4 A.M. before they met again. 'Verhofstadt was very angry and started shouting at Blair, who explained calmly why he would not change anything.' By 5 A.M. Merkel managed to bring everyone back on side, and an agreement emerged. Merkel spoke a few valedictory words about Blair as form dictates at a leader's final summit, but given the time it was fairly perfunctory 'which suited Blair very well'. Blair immediately went into the press conference and said that Britain had achieved much of what it needed to achieve with its opt-outs, and made it clear that no referendum would be required. He had managed to avoid almost all further transfers of authority from Britain to the EU, and achieve a treaty less substantive and radical than the highly contentious Maastricht in 1992, and arguably less so than Amsterdam (1997) and Nice (2001): he was said to be '90 per cent pleased' with the outcome.

In the debate in the House of Commons on Monday 25 June,

Cameron tried to argue that this had indeed been a major treaty and that it demanded a referendum. Blair had thought hard over the weekend about his response. He was convinced that the fresh changes were in fact so trivial that they could not possibly justify the time and expense of a nationwide poll. He knew that the Tory press would have 'a huge go at him' but felt reassured that he had emerged with his four red lines intact, which made the core of his defence. One particular change involved merging the separate EU Commission and EU Council offices around the world. His speech was mainly drafted by his officials, but he himself came up with a put-down for Cameron: 'Are we to have a referendum on an open-plan office? It is absurd,' he said.[91] He carried the day.

Blair's final six months on Europe were among his most successful. In his ten years, he had made a decisive contribution to the EU, if not the one he had originally intended. Brown had defeated him over joining the Euro in 1997 and 2003, but with hindsight it was economically the right outcome: although it annoyed him when anyone said, 'obviously the Euro would have been a disaster', he almost lost all interest in it, and barely mentioned it in his final few years.[92] Blair's main achievements in Europe came mostly after 2003, in his 'Unbound' phase. Principal among them was blocking Verhofstadt as Commission President in 2004 and securing the appointment of the free-market Barroso in his place. He had the vision to press for enlargement, devised the Hampton Court agenda in 2005 and spent two years embedding it. As a result, even though he failed to convince the British voters of the case for the EU, he helped change Britain's place in the EU from being the 'awkward partner' of 1997 to becoming as influential as France and Germany ten years later. It was commonplace to say that he would have achieved much more had Merkel and Sarkozy replaced Schröder and Chirac earlier: that may well be true, but it was still not a bad European legacy for a British Prime Minister.

Farewell Britain

On 21 June, just before flying off to Brussels for the EU Council, Blair attended his last Cabinet meeting. Blair wanted to keep it businesslike and to stick to the agenda, which featured the constitution prominently. It fell to Brown to lead the tributes: 'Whatever we achieve in the future will be because we are standing on your shoulders', a generous tribute. He listed Blair's achievements, which would be recognised still in a hundred years' time as peace in Northern Ireland, his response to the 7/7 bombings and threat of terrorism, the Olympic Games, the minimum wage, civil partnerships, the transformation of public services and 'the Prime Minister's leadership on the world stage'. Blair was given by his colleagues a painting of Chequers, presented to him by Tessa Jowell while the departing Prescott was presented by Hilary Armstrong with one of Admiralty House. The gifts were paid for by a Cabinet whip-round, said to have raised £1,600.[93] Jack Straw and David Miliband gave additional speeches of eulogy to both departing figures. Prescott's response was described as 'tear-jerking'. He spoke with 'very deep and genuine warmth' about Blair, who had been meticulous in ensuring that his deputy was included prominently in all facets of the choreography of his own departure. 'I am very proud of all I have achieved, and walk out with my head held high,' Prescott said. Blair himself spoke briefly 'and was less emotional than the rest of the Cabinet: he'd always adjusted himself psychologically,' said one official. His words were followed immediately by a standing ovation, which continued until Blair left the room and after. Blair had pulled off one of his greatest achievements, a smooth and harmonious transition to Brown, avoiding the party imploding as it had threatened to do during the wars of 2003–06, while also leaving at more or less the moment of his choosing. In his Blair 'unbound' years, he had become his own man, reached levels of inner calm and strength almost unique amongst modern leaders, and had developed his own distinctive agenda. For all Brown's kind words, and his own elaborate speech-making on his final leg, it lacked the coherence of Thatcherism. Blairism remained only partially worked out, and partially enacted. But it made some real achievements, as these final pages have outlined, and it influenced heavily both Cameron and Brown. Within Downing Street, the Treasury-bred officials Robbins and O'Donnell helped to ensure a smooth transition to Brown's team: for some in Blair's team it was 'pretty ghastly', while others were 'thrilled' to see Brown's team taking over where they had left off.[94] To the end, the transition was complicated by a reluctance of some key figures in both camps to speak to each other: after ten years, the bitterness had gone too deep. Said one Blair friend, 'Tony found periods of the transition incredibly hard, but he was, throughout, utterly dignified and generous.'[95]

Relations between the two principals had been good in Blair's final three or four weeks. 'Gordon has become much more mellow. He realises how ghastly he was: he's determined to be different from now on,' said one of his close friends in late May.[96] In private, Blair helped Brown prepare for the premiership, including handling PMQs and processing intelligence, but on a much deeper level, how to handle himself in the top job. 'They also spoke a lot about people, all those who Blair had found good who might prove helpful to Brown.'[97] Mutual friends talked about a warmth returning such as had not been seen since before 2001: 'There's a deep umbilical cord between them: you can see how happy Tony was when things were patched up. It makes him very happy when they get on well.'[98] Brown stopped fighting him from the moment in early May when Blair gave him the precise date. It was what he had been waiting for for thirteen years since Granita on 31 May 1994. Since the 'betrayal', frustration, contempt and finally hatred had overlain the love, in Brown's mind, but at the end, some of the love, if not excessively, returned to the surface. 'If only they could have worked together for the previous ten years as they did in the last four weeks, so much more would have been achieved,' lamented one Labour sympathising official.[99]

The 'quartet' retained their strong links to Blair personally to the end. Campbell remained the closest, despite Blair's irritation in the last few months over his diaries and what should be omitted. Blair would have preferred him to delay publication beyond the 9 July date chosen by Campbell, and 'long conversations' ensued about what should be left out, including material that would reflect badly on Brown, and on the relationship with Bush. Campbell's strategic advice on Brown had been crucial in the 2005 election as it was in the 2007 transfer of power, and he continued to be a key contributor to conference speeches. But Blair had learned to live without Campbell by his side, and he became a stronger and better Prime Minister for it, though his deep gut feeling for him remained until the end: 'When Alastair walks into the room, you can see Tony's eyes light up. There's a completely different feeling about Tony when Alastair's around,' said a mutual friend.[100] His relationship with Mandelson, in contrast, became more distant. They still spoke regularly on the phone, and Mandelson would visit Blair at Number 10 'about once a month'.[101] Blair would still value his strategic advice, but he had moved away from him. As with Campbell, he needed Mandelson to get him so far on his journey. Without them, there would have been no New Labour, and Blair would not have become Prime Minister. But he kept in with both men for too long, and their obsession with image in the media delayed Blair thinking deeply about policy. From both, his separation came about, not at his own wish, but only when circumstances dictated it. Again, Blair was a better man and Prime Minister without Mandelson. They continued to talk about trade in particular, because of Mandelson's job as EU Commissioner, but Mandelson was on the wrong side of the argument on the big issues in Blair's final years, above all the

Euro, on Brown, and on the whole culture of spin with which he was inextricably linked. Blair was naive in seeing how much his relationship with Mandelson damaged his standing in the public eye as a man of integrity. Anji Hunter was the least complicated of the four relationships, and remains one of his closest.[102] She loved him throughout and he always knew she would give him totally disinterested advice. She wanted nothing for herself and her skill was to help him connect with his truest beliefs. He also knew, uniquely in his court, that she would never write a book or speak in public about her experiences.[103]

When the quartet began to break down after 2001, Sally Morgan emerged as the key figure, holding Number 10 together after Campbell had left and taking over much of the emotional support role for Blair that Hunter had performed when she had been based in the building. Powell too emerged as a much more central figure to Blair, calmer and more considered than either Campbell or Mandelson. David Hill, Campbell's successor, epitomised the difference in style between pre- and post-2001 Blairs. Hill did not indulge in the strong-arm tactics or the input of his predecessors. His calm, reliable advice on handling the media suited the mature Blair perfectly. After Morgan left in 2005, the inner circle in Number 10 were Powell, Hill and Liz Lloyd, with Taylor, Turner and Wegg-Prosser the next circle out.

Almost alone among British Prime Ministers, Blair had time to think through what he wanted to do and say before he left Downing Street. A speech about the media was high on his list. He had initially intended to make no comment about it, believing he would be castigated for it, but the media's reporting of 'cash for honours' had been the final straw.[104] He had mused on it over Christmas, and when interviewed by John Humphrys on Radio 4 on 2 February, he gave his first indication that he would say something about his views on the media before he left office.[105] Differing opinions were expressed in Number 10 about the wisdom of this, but it was clear he wanted to do it. They concluded it would be better to make the speech while he was still in office, though it should be slotted in near the very end. The Black Rod affair, 'Cheriegate' and the Gilligan affair had been some of the episodes that turned the initially pro-media Blair, and he had become very cynical about the media for the last few years, and increasingly detached from it. Number 10 insist that he had not listened to the *Today* programme since 1998.[106] 'To the Blair camp, *Newsnight* and *Today*, and most of the BBC, are the enemy,' wrote Robert Crampton, who followed Blair for a long article in *The Times* on his last two months.[107] Unlike some Prime Ministers, he did not see the first editions before he went to bed. In the morning, he would be most likely to see *The Times*, *Financial Times*, *Daily Telegraph* and *Guardian*. Unlike Bernard Ingham, press secretary to Thatcher, Hill did not prepare a daily digest for him, though he and others would point his attention to particular pieces they thought he needed to see.[108] Preparing for PMQs was the one time when he did look particularly carefully at the media and developed 'an intuitive sense of knowing' about what could become important: '"this was worrying" or "there'll be nothing in this"' he would say.[109] He would prepare particularly carefully for his monthly press conference, an innovation which began in 2001 to try to improve his relations with journalists. Hill noted on his return to politics in September 2003, 'Number 10 and the media were already into a "guerrilla war", trust had broken down irrevocably.'[110] 'It was fairly toxic. There was a grievance on both sides, there was never a chance of having an armistice,' said his colleague.[111]

Blair delivered his 'blistering attack' on the media on 12 June. He claimed that newspapers, caught up in bitter sales wars, indulged in 'impact journalism' in which truth and balance became secondary to the desire for stories to boost sales. In his most memorable passage, he said, 'In these modes it is like a feral beast, just tearing people and reputations to bits ... [It] saps the country's confidence and self belief ... It undermines ... its institutions and above all, it reduces our capacity to take the right decisions.'[112] To the surprise of many, he singled out, not the *Mail*, which had been so consistently unpleasant to both Cherie and himself, but the *Independent*, which, he said, 'started as an antidote to the idea of journalism as views not news ... today it is avowedly a viewspaper, not merely a newspaper'.[113] He wanted to avoid attacking a paper that had been hostile to him, and singled out instead a paper which he thought personified the shift from reporting to commentary. The speech was widely and predictably attacked across the press – 'hypocriticial' was a regular criticism – though not in fact for what Number 10 had feared, that he was accusing the media for his 'failed premiership'.[114] He was pleased he had got his comments off his chest, though disappointed that the speech fell short of sparking the national debate that he sought. This was a pity. The speech contained many fair points. His premiership had indeed seen a decline in the moral and intellectual quality of the British press.

His announcement in Sedgefield in May that he would be leaving Number 10 made him think seriously about his future. He would be aged only fifty-four when leaving office, and his health was excellent, with his heart problems of 2003–04 apparently in the past. He had many years of active work ahead of him. Towards the end of 2006, he began contemplating a role in the Middle East and started talking casually to Bush about it. Over the months, his thoughts crystallised. He realised that the gap in the MEPP was the lack of an individual able to give the subject the intense interest he had given to Northern Ireland. He believed he uniquely could play such a role, and he discussed it with Bush at their meeting on 17 May.[115] 'It was a mind-meld idea,' recalled Condi Rice. 'I think we were as much the generators of it as the PM.'[116] 'It is recognised in the US far more than in Britain that Tony Blair can talk to a wider swathe of people in the Middle East than probably anyone,' said one senior British official. Many strands wove themselves together in Blair's mind on the job: his sense of incomplete business; his experiences in Northern Ireland; his love of the region and deep existing relationships with Palestinians and Israelis; his desire to bring harmony between Muslim and Jew. With Bush supportive, Blair had to seek the approval of key EU figures, and Putin. 'We thought Putin might be a problem because of Litvinenko, but in the end he was happy to go along with it,' said one aide.[117] On 27 June, just hours after he stepped down as PM and before he resigned as an MP, it was formally announced that Blair would be acting as envoy to the Middle East for the Quartet (US, EU, UN and Russia) and Brown gave him a fulsome public endorsement. 'He made it very clear to everyone that there is much more he wants to do,' said a close aide. 'He hasn't reached the end of his political career yet.'[118]

Blair liked the idea of an action role. 'When I put the idea of writing books to him it went down like a lead balloon. He looked at me and grimaced at the thought,' said John Burton.[119] That said, in his final days, he corresponded with Martin Gilbert, Churchill's biographer and historical aide to a succession of Prime Ministers, about ideas on his memoirs, and he invited one of his staff to begin looking for material.[120] His team had put much thought since the previous autumn into how his premiership would be portrayed in history. They were approached by the BBC, who were producing a television series with veteran film-maker Michael Cockerell, and by Channel 4, with a documentary series proposal with Andrew Rawnsley. They were both told directly, 'You're not going to get the Prime Minister to take part in an "obituary" while he's still in office.'[121] Subsequently, they had two approaches from teams who wanted to screen programmes after he stood down: *Observer* journalist Will Hutton, who they co-operated with on *The Last Days of Tony Blair*, screened on 2 July on Channel 4, and *The Times* journalist David Aaronovitch, for whom Blair agreed to be interviewed for a series shown in the late autumn. Cherie, 'off her own back', decided she wanted to make a programme with BBC television presenter Fiona Bruce, to put her own case across, featuring the children and her work for charity, as a response to what she considered as ten years of intrusive and often 'vile' treatment at the hands of certain sectors of the media.[122] It portrayed a side to her the public had rarely seen. Will Hutton's was the most thoughtful of the television bonanza that summer, but the most scintillating by far was the series narrated by Campbell himself, based on his diaries.

'Only quite late on did he start talking to staff about who was going to stay on with him and who would be leaving: it was difficult to get him to focus on everything he needed to do,' said one close friend.[123] 'Once he eventually reconciled himself to the fact he was going, his mood changed, but not in the way you'd expect,' said one official. 'He became irrepressibly charmingly cheerful, joking with everyone that he was looking forward to his release.' He was adamant that he did not want to go and make a lot of money on lecture tours: 'I know there's always been this idea about me that I'm fascinated by people who are wealthy. I'm not at all. If I was desperate to make money, I would have done something else,' he said.[124] Money nevertheless would be important, not least to pay for his large office (the British state is not generous in its support to former premiers) and to service the mortgage on the Connaught Square house he and Cherie bought in 2004. Figures of the memoirs selling for £8 million were soon in circulation, dismissed by his office as 'OTT', and the book would be 'some way off'. Apart from the envoy role, he said his continuing interests would be climate change, Africa and inter-faith dialogue. Another late decision was stepping down from Sedgefield. He finalised it in his mind only in May, and only told Brown just before he made the public announcement in Sedgefield on 27 June, to confirm his agreement.[125] His Middle East role meant he needed to be away a lot, but, deeper down, he felt the need to move on, and for the constituency to have an MP who could give it their full attention. He knew it would be a lot to ask the party to have to fight a by-election before the summer. He worried too that the constituency might turn against Labour, as Hartlepool did when Mandelson announced he was going off to the EU in September 2004. A poor result would have reflected badly on Brown, and it was going to cost the party money to fight it when money was in short supply. He helped flood the constituency with friends and high-profile figures to maximise the chances of his successor, long-time constituency friend and ally Phil Wilson, to achieve a strong result. Wilson won by a majority of 6,956 in the by-election on 19 July.[126] Although much reduced from his own 2005 majority, Blair was relieved.

Twenty-four years before, when his adoption as the Sedgefield candidate had been in the balance, he had gone off to nearby Durham Cathedral and prayed. Before he left, he had long wanted to pay another particular religious visit to an even more historic place. On 23 June, while his staff grabbed a couple of hours' sleep after the EU Council finished with the press conference at 5.30 A.M. on Saturday morning, Blair went back to the hotel to freshen up before catching a plane at 7.30 A.M. to Rome Campino Airport arriving at 9.30 A.M. without sleep. The Council had been scheduled to finish on Friday evening and Cherie had arrived in Rome the night before in anticipation of his arrival. All night frantic phone calls took place between Brussels and the British Embassy at the Vatican updating on progress and contemplating the dreaded scenario that the audience with Pope Benedict XVI, scheduled for 11 A.M., might be missed. Blair was driven at speed to the Palazzo Pallavicini, the residence of Francis Campbell, the British Ambassador to the Vatican. There he was reunited with Cherie and just had time to change. In his private audience, he spoke with the Pope about the Middle East, Iraq and Africa as well as inter-faith issues. Speaking of the EU Council, the Pope said, 'I heard it was very successful.' 'Yes, but it was a long night. We finished up at 5.30 in the morning,' Blair replied.[127] He presented the Pope with three original prints of Cardinal John Henry Newman, the famous British convert to Catholicism who had died in 1890, one of which was signed by Newman himself. In return, the Pope gave Blair a gold medallion recording his pontificate.[128] After meeting the press, he left the Vatican just after midday and went to the English College, where he had a meeting on inter-faith issues with some Vatican experts before lunch hosted by Cardinal Cormac Murphy-O'Connor, Archbishop of Westminster. At lunch, he told a story from the EU Council: 'The Polish President said to me, "Look Tony, there are these stories about you, you know, becoming a Catholic. Are they true?" I said, "Look, you're not having that in the Constitution as well."' He left the lunch at 2.30 P.M. in time to catch the flight just after 3 P.M. back to London.

It was a far more reassuring visit, and at a much happier time, than his visit to Pope John Paul II in February 2003 in the run-up to the war in Iraq. Number 10 were nervous that the earlier trip would awaken talk of 'is he going to convert to Catholicism?'. The media indeed speculated that the purpose of the trip was his long-anticipated conversion. Aides and officials on the way to Brussels two days before picked up on it and ribbed him about it: 'He didn't seem remotely

offended and joined in with it. "If I was going to convert, I wouldn't
be going to the Pope to do it," he said.' Blair for many years had been
a Catholic in all but name: but his 'conversion' would be some way off.
Blair flew back to London and on to Chequers, where he hosted a
dinner party. Approximately every six weeks he gave a 'Chequers
Dinner', where he invited a Cabinet minister and an eclectic mix of
people to join him and Cherie: even though he was very tired, one
guest found him 'extraordinarily relaxed and utterly charming'.[129] It
was an impressive feat of physical endurance, as well as evidence of his
good manners, that he made his guests feel so welcome. At 10.45 P.M.,
his head began to loll from side to side. Protective to the end, Cherie
put her arm around him and announced to the assembled company it
was 'time for his bed'.

At Chequers on Sunday 24 June, Blair mulled over his comments for
the following day about the EU Council, and made final preparations for
his departure. He tuned into the news about the deputy leadership
contest. All six candidates – Hilary Benn, Hazel Blears, Jon Cruddas,
Peter Hain, Harriet Harman and Alan Johnson – in their different ways
had promised renewal. Some openly advocated a break with the last ten
years. The contest was 'completely insignificant' to him, said an aide,
because he had 'little or no time for the position they were indulging
themselves in', though he did worry that the body of opinion in the party
was moving to the left. He was not delighted when Harriet Harman just
emerged as the victor over Alan Johnson by 50.4 per cent to 49.6 per cent
(exactly the same margin as Denis Healey's victory over Tony Benn in
1981), but was relieved when Brown made it clear that he had no time
for her 'old' Labour message.[130]

Blair's final Monday and Tuesday were full of farewell meetings and
parties. The highest profile visitor was Arnold Schwarzenegger on the
Tuesday. He had been keen to come for several months and this was the
date that worked best in Blair's diary. They had worked closely on
climate change since Blair's visit to California the previous summer: 'It
was quite a convenient way of rounding off . . . It was a chance to see a
foreign leader, on a big Blair subject . . . It was a fairly gentle landing.'[131]
Blair invited Brown into the meeting 'to lay the ground for the next
phase of climate change work'.[132] At lunch on Tuesday Blair hosted a
farewell for departing officials, Darroch, Davies, Kelly, Morris and
Sheinwald, and in the evening he gave a smaller party for his political
colleagues who had served him so well in the third term and before,
including Hill, Lloyd, Powell and Turner. He reminisced with them
about what he would miss and not miss, in the latter category he firmly

included 'living his life in a constant state of nervous anticipation about what would happen next'.[133]

His final morning, 27 June, saw him prepare intently for PMQs, working one final time with his team in the den in preparation: they said he worked as hard on them as ever. On the floor of the House, his mood was sombre. He went straight into offering condolences for three soldiers killed over the previous seven days, and paid elaborate tribute, very deliberately, to the bravery of the armed forces, whose company and achievement he had come to admire so greatly over his years as Prime Minister. Conscious of the occasion, Cameron asked serious questions about the floods, which were to dominate Brown's first month as Prime Minister, and about the Middle East, but also paid elaborate compliments: Cherie, watching with the children from the side gallery, facing Cameron, mouthed 'Thank you'.[134] At the conclusion of his final response to Cameron, Blair seemed almost overwhelmed: 'That is it. The end.' After a moment of hesitation, MPs from all parties rose to their feet, cheered, and gave Blair a standing ovation. It was the first time in living memory that anyone could remember the whole House giving any member a full round of applause. Watching it all on specially erected flat screens in the State Dining Room at Number 10 were the staff. When he walked back into the room from the Commons, one commented: 'It was a weird transition from us being citizens and parts of the process to suddenly seeing him there before us.'[135] The 200 or so staff assembled in the three interconnected State Drawing Rooms, where Blair bought them all a glass of champagne. Olly Robbins called for attention, and Blair gave an impromptu five-minute speech. Midway through, Cherie and the children arrived. He told his audience how much the family had enjoyed living in the building, and how strange it had been to see them grow up there. He spoke about how wonderful the staff were, from the switchboard and the café to the senior advisers, and how he could not have done it all without them. While he was speaking 'between half and two-thirds' began to cry. To lighten the mood, he told them how touched he had been by the warmth of his welcome on 2 May 1997 when he arrived, and how touched he had been, except when he realised: 'They were not tears of joy at my arrival.'[136] The tears in the eyes of the staff lining the corridor clapping him in had been for the departing John Major.

'Tony's been so open and personal with them all that they all love him, from the custodian at the door to the gardener,' said Cherie.[137] He went back into the den for a few final moments while the staff came down the staircase and lined the corridor from the Cabinet Room to the front door. As he walked along it with his family for his final time as Prime Minister, he shook hands and spoke a few personal words to many of them. Out on the street, he declined to say anything himself, but as the car drove off for the final visit to the Queen, Cherie said to the waiting journalists: 'Bye. I don't think we'll miss you.' It was what she felt. She was her own person to the end, and she did not regret saying it. As soon as their car had disappeared down Downing Street, the building leapt into a new life. Blair's advisers had been given a tight timetable to clear their desks and leave the building before Brown's team arrived. Only a few like Justin Forsyth and Geoffrey Norris would survive the transition. Blair's team were not allowed to leave through the front door and were shown speedily out through a back door, handing their passes back to the Garden Room Secretaries as they did so. 'It was like leaving a fantasy world and entering reality,' said one.[138] Several of them went off to Soho and drank till late. Like Blair himself they had become just ordinary citizens.

Driven to King's Cross Station, the Blairs, carrying their own bags, boarded a GNER train bound for the North East. 'That's it. I'm no longer in charge. I'm going to get on with the rest of my life and let Gordon and the government get on with it,' Blair said as the train sped northwards.[139] On one point he was adamant: 'I'm not going to talk to people about what Gordon is doing or not doing. I don't want anyone to say I'm carping from the sidelines.' In Darlington, the mini cab to take them to their home, Myrobella, was delayed. For the first time in many years, the Blairs were kept waiting. Careful thought had been put into where he was to spend his first night outside Downing Street. They chose their home in Sedgefield, 'The roots are very strong emotionally and personally. It has had a big impact on the development of my politics,' he said of the constituency.[140]

On arrival at Myrobella, Blair was keen to break out of uniform: '"Can I get out of this suit?" We said no, no, keep it on for the last speech . . . Normally he gets his jeans on and a sweatshirt and goes for a pint of beer.'[141] That evening Burton introduced Blair for the last time to the Trimdon Labour Party club: 'I said, "This morning I was agent to the Prime Minister, this afternoon, after he left the Palace, I was agent to the Member of Parliament; tonight, I'm nothing at all . . . A rapid demotion in one day!"'[142] Blair likewise was cheery and upbeat, but 'there was a slight glaze in his eyes'. The club was packed with party and non-party members, as Blair delivered his farewell words, and went round meeting and talking to everyone in the room: 'It wasn't miserable, [but] it was emotional.'[143] The local party remained fiercely passionate and possessive of their MP for the last twenty-four years as he looked forward to his role as Middle East envoy: 'We were lending him out to the rest of the world,' said one.[144] Blair and Cherie left by bus with a handful of their oldest constituency friends for the Dun Cow for a pint of his favourite Black Sheep bitter.[145] At last, he was able to relax. He had not achieved all he wanted as Prime Minister. His main regrets? He had not gone further earlier on with public sector reform and all his efforts at reducing crime had not had the impact he hoped for. He was disappointed at the slow progress by al-Maliki in Iraq, and worried about Pakistan. But he was pleased with his last two years, with the peaceful transfer of power to Brown, and to be leaving when he wanted. Even though he knew he had found his stride far too late in his premiership, he was a man at peace.

The house, which they had bought in late 1983, was a home in transition, with removal in the air: a dresser had a label 'maybe'; a mirror was labelled 'yes'.[146] Myrobella would soon become part of the nation's history, as his life would soon become part of the nation's history. The next morning, waking up for the first time in ten years not having to worry about what the day would bring, he walked downstairs. The television was on in the front room, relaying reports about the latest developments from Downing Street, and who was joining Brown's team. Blair's staff and friends gathered round, eager to find out who was going up and who down. He had made up his mind he would not be interfering with, or commenting on Brown's leadership. Not for him the backward glances of Thatcher, or even Kinnock. He had a new life, and was anxious for it to begin. He paused for a moment in front of the television and then calmly announced before turning away, 'I don't want to know.'[147]

Acknowledgements

My principal thanks go to my two co-authors Peter Snowdon, who worked in London throughout, and Daniel Collings, who was based in Washington, DC. Peter concentrated primarily on domestic politics and policy, while Daniel handled US relations and foreign policy more generally, especially Iraq and Afghanistan. The success of the book was down to them. They shared the interviews, designed the chapter structure, wrote the drafts and briefs, inserted many of the final comments and polished the text. They both could have written a much better book than I have done. The full-time team consisted also of Susanna Sharpe, who worked for the full duration of the project's life of eight months and who, with unyielding determination, tirelessly and cheerfully held the team and the office together. Leading on the research, the amazingly hardworking Rob McNamara also worked for the full eight months and concentrated on domestic policy and Northern Ireland, while the superbly intelligent Kunal Khatri joined for the last six months and specialised across domestic, European and foreign policy. I was enormously fortunate to have such a highly intelligent, hard-working, friendly and supportive team with whom to work. They worked six (or seven) days a week often for twelve or fourteen hours a day. I deserved neither their patience nor their loyalty. Julia Harris, the final member of the regular team, transcribed most of the interviews and typed the entire first draft with quite extraordinary skill. I am very grateful to occasional members of the team who helped for shorter periods, including Felix Cook, Tiff Forster, Ed James, Tom Lowe, Matthew Neal, Jessica Seldon and Susannah Seldon.

I owe the deepest gratitude to three extraordinarily wise, knowledgeable and benevolent individuals who read the entire book and gave invaluable comments: Vernon Bogdanor, Dennis Kavanagh and

Peter Riddell. Thank you also to David Aaronovitch for valuable comments on sections of the text. A special thank-you also goes to my brother, Michael Perrott, for kindly reading through the final proofs for the eleventh-hour copy-editing check. Many others read over sections of the book. Some even reread the drafts once they had been updated, while others took time out of their summer holidays to accommodate the book's tight schedule. I am deeply grateful to all of them for their valuable insights.

Almost all of those to whom I wrote agreed to talk for the book. I am deeply indebted to all those I interviewed. As most are still serving in government, I have decided not to mention the vast number of them by name. Among those who have consented to have their names mentioned, I would especially like to express my appreciation to Michael Barber, David Bennett, John Birt, Kieran Brett, Kim Darroch, Huw Evans, Justin Forsyth, Rob Fry, Michael Jay, Tessa Jowell, Tom Kelly, Christopher Meyer and John Sawers for all their help and support during times of constant queries and correspondence. A special mention should similarly be made of all their personal assistants who have been particularly helpful with all the arranging and re-arranging of interviews.

At Wellington College, I would like to thank the chairman, Sir Anthony Goodenough, and his fellow governors for being so supportive of the project, especially to John Yeldham for providing a 'safe house' for my writing the conclusion, and to my senior colleagues Robin Dyer, Lucy Pearson, Paul Hucklesby, Justin Garrick, Roger Auger, Liz Worthington, Jamie Walker, Martin Sherwin and Susan Meikle for their support and understanding throughout. They will be glad the book is over, I think – though will be apprehensive about the increase in e-mails the ending portends. My personal assistant Nadine Bocher and the housekeeper at the Master's Lodge, Sandra Hughes-Coppin, could not possibly have been kinder, and nor could the teaching and support staff, including ITS and porters. The book was conceived at the quite remarkable Brighton College, where I was able to write several books. My thanks in particular there to my chairmen Robert Skidelsky, Robert Seabrook and Ian White, and to colleagues Simon Smith, Tony Whitestone, Anna Parish, Joe Carr-Hill and Mary-Anne Brightwell, with whom I worked closely on many of those books.

At Simon & Schuster, I would like to thank the gifted Andrew Gordon, Jane Pizzey and Rory Scarfe. The eight-month writing schedule has proved to be extremely challenging and a great test of character for all. I am especially grateful to the production team who put the finishing touches to the book with great pace and precision, accommodating my last-minute amendments. I am also grateful to Patricia Hymans for her work on the index and for taking up this task at such short notice.

At research institutes, archives and libraries I would like to thank Helen Langley and Colin Harris at the Bodleian Library for helping my team to access my archived files from the first volume of this biography, and the staff at the Library of Congress who were my guides to a wealth of factual information. My thanks also go to Andrew McKerlie of Brook Lapping, producers of *The Rise and Fall of Tony Blair*, written and presented by Andrew Rawnsley; Katie Churcher of Blakeway Productions 3BM, producers of *The Last Days of Tony Blair*, documented by Will Hutton; and especially to Diana Martin, producer of *Blair: The Inside Story*, the BBC TV documentary presented by Michael Cockerell, for all their help in sending visual and transcript material which served to be invaluable to my research team.

On behalf of Peter Snowdon, I would like to expressly thank his family, as well as David Farley and Andrew Trinick, for their kindness and encouragement. Julia McCullough deserves special thanks for her constant support, patience and understanding. I would also like to show appreciation to Peter's colleagues at the BBC *Politics Show*, including former editor James Stephenson as well as Jon Sopel, Sue Brewer, Gareth Butler, Paul Cannon, Joanna Carr and Giles Edwards for their patience and support.

On behalf of Daniel Collings, I would like to thank Laurence Norman, for unfailingly shrewd advice; Sonja Danburg, for unstinting support and a much-needed hinterland; and his mother and father, without whose kindness none of this would have been possible.

I would like to thank my own mother and brother, Peter, my mother-in-law Jean Pappworth, and our close friends John and Louise James in whose house in Canford, Dorset I began the book in April and finished it in August. My thanks to the students and staff at Marlborough College, where I aired my first draft, and to the Reform Club and Royal Society of Arts for allowing me to address groups where I developed my arguments. The Centre for Contemporary British History, my intellectual home, continues to inspire me from afar, as does my co-founder, the incomparable Peter Hennessy. I learned much as ever from the twenty-six contributors to *Blair's Britain*, which I edited concurrently with writing this book. Although he did not help with this book, the influence of Lewis Baston, my co-author on *Major*, lived on in his example of inspirational insights and his meticulous attention to detail. Lil Jones, the irrepressible team manager on the first volume, was supportive throughout. My thanks also go to Charlotte Style, a brilliant coach over the last six months. Finally, I would like to thank my son, Adam Seldon, for checking facts and being my delightful companion along Offa's Dyke for five blissful days in August when I was contemplating the ending of the book.

In common with all my writing, any profits of this second volume go to charity. A particular beneficiary for *Blair Unbound* is the Maclyn P. Burg Graduate Scholarship Fund, set up in honour of Dr Maclyn Burg and abandoned by the History Department at the University of Washington. When, in 1978, I was writing my Ph.D. at LSE, and researching in the Eisenhower Library in the small town of Abilene, Kansas, a perceptive Dr Burg spotted my isolation and took me under his wing. A real *mensch*, and never to be forgotten.

Finally, I would like to thank my wonderful wife, Joanna, who read the whole book and improved it greatly, supported me throughout, and held family and home together. I have promised her I will never write another book on a Prime Minister, and especially not one that means eighteen- or nineteen-hour days for six months straight seven days a week. She is right (she always is): it was crazy.

ANTHONY SELDON
September 2007
Wellington College

Dramatis Personae

Norris, Geoffrey	Policy Adviser on Trade and Industry, to 2007
Powell, Jonathan	Chief of Staff to the Prime Minister, to 2007
Rogers, Ivan	Principal Private Secretary to the Prime Minister, 2003–06
Rowley, Nicholas	Policy Adviser on the Environment, 2004–05
Rycroft, Matthew	Private Secretary for Foreign Affairs to the Prime Minister, 2002–04
Sheinwald, Nigel	Foreign Policy Adviser to the Prime Minister, 2003–07
Smith, Godric	Head of Strategic Communications, 2004–07
	Prime Minister's Official Spokesman, 2001–03
Taylor, Matthew	Head of Policy, 2003-05
Turnbull, Andrew	Cabinet Secretary and Head of the Home Civil Service, 2002–05
Wilson, Richard	Cabinet Secretary and Head of the Home Civil Service, 1998–2002

Number 10 Third Term, 2005–07

Bennett, David	Head of Policy, to 2007
Brett, Kieran	Policy Adviser on Law and Order, to 2007
Coffman, Hilary	Adviser, Strategic Communications Unit, to 2007
Collins, Phil	Tony Blair's Chief Speechwriter, to 2007
Darroch, Kim	Adviser to the Prime Minister and Head of the Cabinet Office European Secretariat, 2004–07
Davies, Gareth	Welfare Policy adviser, Policy Directorate, 2002–07
	Strategy Unit, 2001–07
Doyle, Matthew	Deputy Director of Communications, 2006–07
Hill, David	Director of Communications, to 2007
Kelly, Tom	Prime Minister's Official Spokesman, to 2007
Lee, Laurie	Private Secretary to the Prime Minister, 2004–06
Lloyd, Liz	Deputy Chief of Staff to the Prime Minister, to 2007
McTernan, John	Director of Political Relations, to 2007
Norris, Geoffrey	Policy Adviser on Trade and Industry, to 2007
O'Donnell, Gus	Cabinet Secretary and Head of the Home Civil Service, 2005 onwards
Powell, Jonathan	Chief of Staff to the Prime Minister, to 2007
Robbins, Oliver	Principal Private Secretary to the Prime Minister, 2006–07

Rogers, Ivan	Principal Private Secretary to the Prime Minister, to 2006
Sheinwald, Nigel	Foreign Policy Adviser to the Prime Minister, to 2007
Smith, Godric	Head of Strategic Communications, 2004–07
Taylor, Matthew	Chief Adviser on Political Strategy, to 2006
Turner, Ruth	Head of Government Relations, 2005–07

Cabinet Second Term, 2001–05

Alexander, Douglas	Minister of State for Trade and Industry and Foreign and Commonwealth Office, to 2005
	Minister of the Cabinet Office and Chancellor of the Duchy of Lancaster, 2003–04
	Cabinet Office, 2002–03
	Minister of State for Trade and Industry, 2001–02
Armstrong, Hilary	Government Chief Whip, to 2006
Beckett, Margaret	Secretary of State for Environment, Food and Rural Affairs, to 2006
Benn, Hilary	Secretary of State for International Development, to 2007
Blears, Hazel	Minister of State, Home Office, 2003–06
Blunkett, David	Secretary of State at the Home Office, 2001–04
Brown, Gordon	Chancellor of the Exchequer, to 2007
Byers, Stephen	Secretary of State for Transport, Local Government and the Regions, 2001–02
Clarke, Charles	Secretary of State at the Home Office, 2004–05
	Secretary of State for Education and Skills, 2002–04
	Minister Without Portfolio and Chairman of the Labour Party, 2001–02
Cook, Robin	Leader of the House of Commons, Lord President of the Council, 2001–03
Denham, John	Minister of State at the Home Office, 2001–03
Falconer, Charles	Secretary of State for Constitutional Affairs and Lord Chancellor, to 2007
Goldsmith, Peter	Attorney-General for England and Wales, to 2007 (permitted to attend Cabinet meetings)
Hain, Peter	Leader of the House of Commons, 2003–05
	Secretary of State for Wales, 2002–07
Hewitt, Patricia	Secretary of State for Trade and Industry and Minister for Women, to 2005
Hoon, Geoff	Secretary of State for Defence, to 2005

Johnson, Alan	Secretary of State for Work and Pensions, 2004–05
Jowell, Tessa	Secretary of State for Culture, Media and Sport, to 2007
McCartney, Ian	Party Chairman and Minister Without Portfolio, to 2006
Milburn, Alan	Chancellor of the Duchy of Lancaster, 2004–05
	Secretary of State for Health, 1999–03
Miliband, David	Minister for the Cabinet Office, 2004–05
	Minister of State for Schools, 2002–04
Morris, Estelle	Minister of State for Culture, Media and Sports, 2003–05
	Secretary of State for Education, 2001–02
Prescott, John	Deputy Prime Minister and First Secretary of State, to 2007
	Deputy Leader of the Labour Party, to 2007
Reid, John	Secretary of State for Health, 2003–05
	Leader of the House of Commons and President of the Council, 2003
	Minister Without Portfolio and Chairman of the Labour Party, 2002–03
	Secretary of State for Northern Ireland, 2001–02
Short, Clare	Secretary of State for International Development, 1997–03
Straw, Jack	Secretary of State for Foreign and Commonwealth Affairs, to 2006

Cabinet Third Term, 2005–07

Alexander, Douglas	Secretary of State for Transport and Scotland, 2006–07
	Minister of Trade, Investment and Foreign Affairs, to 2006
Armstrong, Hilary	Chancellor of the Duchy of Lancaster, 2006–07
	Government Chief Whip, to 2006
Beckett, Margaret	Foreign Secretary, 2006–07
	Secretary of State for Environment, Food and Rural Affairs, to 2006
Benn, Hilary	Secretary of State for International Development, to 2007
Blears, Hazel	Minister Without Portfolio, and Chair of the Labour Party, to 2007
	Minister of State, Home Office, to 2006
Blunkett, David	Secretary of State for Work and Pensions, 2005

Brown, Gordon	Chancellor of the Exchequer, to 2007
Browne, Des	Secretary of State for Defence, 2006–07
	Chief Secretary to the Treasury, to 2006
Clarke, Charles	Secretary of State at the Home Office, to 2006
Falconer, Charles	Secretary of State for Constitutional Affairs, Lord High Chancellor of Great Britain, to 2007
Goldsmith, Peter	Attorney-General for England and Wales, to 2007
Hain, Peter	Secretary for Northern Ireland, to 2007
	Secretary of State for Wales, to 2007
Harman, Harriet	Deputy Leader of the Labour Party, 2007 onwards
	Minister of State at the Department for Constitutional Affairs, 2005–07
Hewitt, Patricia	Secretary of State for Health, to 2007
Hoon, Geoff	Minister for Europe, 2006–07
	Leader of the House of Commons, to 2006
Hutton, John	Secretary of State for Work and Pensions, to 2007
	Chancellor of the Duchy of Lancaster and Minister for the Cabinet Office, 2005
Johnson, Alan	Secretary of State for Education and Skills, 2006–07
	Secretary of State for the Department of Trade and Industry, 2005–06
Jowell, Tessa	Secretary of State for Culture, Media and Sport, to 2007
McCartney, Ian	Minister for Trade and Industry and Foreign and Commonwealth Office, 2006–07
	Party Chairman and Minister Without Portfolio, to 2006
Miliband, David	Secretary of State for Environment, Food and Rural Affairs, to 2007
	Minister of State, Office of the Deputy Prime Minister, to 2006
Prescott, John	Deputy Prime Minister and First Secretary of State, to 2007
	Deputy Leader of the Labour Party, to 2007
Reid, John	Home Secretary, 2007
	Secretary of State for Defence, 2005–06
Straw, Jack	Lord Privy Seal and Leader of the House of Commons, to 2007
	Secretary of State for Foreign and Commonwealth Affairs, to 2006

Whitehall

Barber, Michael	Chief Adviser on School Standards to the Secretary of State for Education, 1997–01
Casey, Louise	Director of the Respect Task Force from 2005
	Head of Anti-Social Behaviour Unit in the Home Office, 2003–05
	Director of Government's Rough Sleepers Unit, 1999–03
Corry, Dan	Chair of the Council of Economic Advisers, 2006–07
	Special Adviser to Department for Education and Skills, and Department for Local Communities and Government, 2005–06
Darroch, Kim	Director-General for European Union Affairs, FCO, 2003–04
	Director for European Union Affairs, 2000–03
Dearlove, Richard	Chief of Secret Intelligence Service (MI6), 1999–04
Gieve, John	Permanent Under Secretary of State, Home Office, 2001–05
Jay, Michael	Permanent Under Secretary of State, Foreign and Commonwealth Office and Head of Diplomatic Service, 2002–06
Lander, Stephen	Chairman of the Serious Organised Crime Agency, 2004 onwards
	Director-General of British Security Service (MI5), 1996–02
Manning, David	British Ambassador to the United States, 2003 onwards
Manningham-Buller, Eliza	Director General of British Security Service (MI5), 2002–07
Meyer, Christopher	British Ambassador to the United States, 1997–03
Ricketts, Peter	Permanent Under Secretary of State, Foreign and Commonwealth Office, and Head of Diplomatic Service, 2006 onwards
	UK Permanent Representative to NATO, to 2003
	Political Director, Foreign and Commonwealth Office, 2001
Sawers, John	Political Director, Foreign and Commonwealth Office, 2003 onwards
	Ambassador to Cairo, 2001–03
Scarlett, John	Head of British Secret Intelligence Service (MI6), 2004 onwards

	Chair of Cabinet Office Joint Intelligence Committee, 2001–04
Turnbull, Andrew	Permanent Secretary to the Treasury, 1998–02
Wall, Stephen	Prime Minister's Europe Advisor and Head of the European Secretariat in the Cabinet Office, 2000–04

Other UK

Burton, John	Sedgefield Labour Party agent and chairman, 1997–07

United States

Armitage, Richard	Deputy Secretary of State, 2001–05
Bolten, Josh	White House Chief of Staff, 2006 onwards
Bolton, John	Ambassador to the United Nations, 2005–06
	Under Secretary for Arms Control and International Security, 2001–05
Bush, George W.	President of the United States of America, 2001 onwards
Card, Andrew	White House Chief of Staff, 2001–06
Cheney, Richard	Vice-President of the United States of America, 2001 onwards
Gates, Robert	Secretary of Defense, 2006 onwards
Hadley, Stephen	National Security Advisor, 2005 onwards
	Deputy National Security Advisor, 2001–05
Jones, Elizabeth	Assistant Secretary of State for European and Eurasian Affairs, Department of State, 2001–05
Libby, I. Lewis	Vice-President's Chief of Staff, 2001–07
Powell, Colin	Secretary of State, 2001–05
Rice, Condoleezza	Secretary of State, 2005 onwards
	National Security Advisor, 2001–05
Rove, Karl	Deputy Chief of Staff at the White House, 2005–07
	Senior Political Adviser to the President, 2001 onwards
Rumsfeld, Donald	Secretary of Defense, 2001–06
Schwarzenegger, Arnold	Governor of California, 2003 onwards

Europe

Aznar, José Maria	Prime Minister of Spain, 1996–04
Balkenende, Jan Peter	Prime Minister of the Netherlands, 2002 onwards

Barroso, José Manuel	President of European Commission, 2004 onwards
	Prime Minister of Portugal, 2002–04
Berlusconi, Silvio	Prime Minister of Italy, 2001–06
Chirac, Jacques	President of France, 1995–07
Juncker, Jean-Claude	Prime Minister of Luxembourg, 1995 onwards
Merkel, Angela	Chancellor of Germany, 2005 onwards
Prodi, Romano	Prime Minister of Italy, 2006 onwards
	President of the European Commission, 1999–04
Sarkozy, Nicolas	President of France, 2007 onwards
Schröder, Gerhard	Chancellor of Germany, 1998–05
Schüssel, Wolfgang	Chancellor of Austria, 2000–07
Verhofstadt, Guy	Prime Minister of Belgium, 1999 onwards
Zapatero, José Luis Rodríguez	Prime Minister of Spain, 2004 onwards

Key G8/G8 + 5

Abe, Shinzo	Prime Minister of Japan, 2006 onwards
Calderón, Felipe	President of Mexico, 2006 onwards
Fox, Vicente	President of Mexico, 2000–06
Harper, Stephen	Prime Minister of Canada, 2006 onwards
Jintao, Hu	President of China, 2003 onwards
Koizumi, Junichiro	Prime Minister of Japan, 2001–06
Martin, Paul	Prime Minister of Canada, 2003–06
Mbeki, Thabo	President of South Africa, 1999 onwards
Putin, Vladimir	President of the Russian Federation, 2000 onwards (acting President, December 1999–May 2000)
da Silva, Luiz Inácio Lula	President of Brazil, 2003 onwards
Singh, Manmohan	Prime Minister of India, 2004 onwards

Ireland and Northern Ireland

Adams, Gerry	President of Sinn Féin, 1983 onwards
Ahern, Bertie	Taoiseach of Ireland, 1997 onwards
Hannigan, Robert	Director-General of the Northern Ireland Office, 2002–07
McGuinness, Martin	Deputy First Minister of Northern Ireland, 2007 onwards
	Minister for Education Northern Ireland Assembly, 1998–07

Paisley, Ian	First Minister of Northern Ireland, 2007 onwards
	Leader of the Democratic Unionist Party, 1971 onwards
Phillips, Jonathan	Permanent Secretary, Northern Ireland Office, 2005 onwards
	Political Director, Northern Ireland Office, 2002–05
Trimble, David	First Minister of Northern Ireland, 1998–01

Iraq and Afghanistan

Allawi, Iyad	Prime Minister of the Iraqi Interim Government, 2004–05
Boyce, Admiral Michael	Chief of the Defence Staff (UK), 2001–03
Bremer, Paul	US Presidential Envoy and Administrator in Iraq, 2003–04
Franks, General Tommy	Commander in Chief, United States Central Command, 2000–03
Fry, Lt-General Robert	Deputy Commander, Multi-National Force Iraq, 2006
Garner, Jay	Director of Office for Reconstruction and Humanitarian Assistance for Iraq, Chief Executive of the Coalition Provisional Authority, 2003–03
Greenstock, Jeremy	UK Special Envoy to Iraq, 2003–04
	Ambassador to the UN, 1998–03
Guthrie, General Charles	Chief of the Defence Staff (UK), 1997–01
al-Jaafari, Ibrahim	State Prime Minister of Iraq, 2005–06
	Vice-President of Iraq, 2004–05
Jackson, General Michael	Chief of the General Staff (UK), 2003–06
al-Maliki, Nouri	State Prime Minister of Iraq, 2006 onwards
McDonald, Simon	Director, Iraq, Foreign and Commonwealth Office, 2006 onwards
Myers, General Richard	Chairman of the Joint Chiefs of Staff (US), 2001–05
Richards, General David	Head of NATO International Security Assistance Force (ISAF), 2006–07
Sawers, John	UK Special Representative in Baghdad, 2003
al-Sistani, Ali al-Husseini	Grand Ayatollah in Iraq
Stirrup, Air Chief Marshal Jock	Chief of the Defence Staff (UK), 2006 onwards
	Chief of Air Staff, 2003–06
	Deputy Chief of the Defence Staff, 2002–03

| Talabani, Jalal | State President of Iraq, 2005 onwards |
| Walker, General Michael | Chief of the Defence Staff (UK), 2003–06 |

Middle East Peace Process

Abbas, Mahmoud	President of Palestinian Authority, January 2005 onwards
	Chairman of the Palestine Liberation Organisation, 2004 onwards
	Prime Minister of the Palestinian Authority, 2003
Arafat, Yasser	President of the Palestinian Authority, 1996–04
Cowper-Coles, Sherard	Ambassador to Israel, 2001–03
McDonald, Simon	Ambassador to Israel, 2003–06
Olmert, Ehud	Prime Minister of Israel, 2006 onwards (acting PM from January to April 2006)
Phillips, Tom	Ambassador to Israel, 2006 onwards
Sharon, Ariel	Prime Minister of Israel, 2001–06 (incapacitated from January 2006)
Siniora, Fouad	Prime Minister of Lebanon, 2005 onwards

The Brown Camp

Austin, Ian	MP for Dudley North, 2005 onwards
	Political Adviser to Gordon Brown, 1999–04
Balls, Ed	Economic Secretary to the Treasury, 2006–07
	MP for Normanton, 2005 onwards
	Chief Economic Adviser to the Treasury, 1999–04
Bowler, James	Principal Private Secretary at the Treasury, 2001–07
Brown, Nick	Minister of State, Work and Pensions, 2001–03
Cunliffe, Jon	Permanent Secretary, Macroeconomic Policy and International Finance, Treasury, 2005–07
Livermore, Spencer	Chief Political and Strategy Adviser to Brown, 2005–07
McBride, Damian	Political Adviser to Gordon Brown, 2005–07
	Head of Communications and Strategy, Treasury, 2003–05
MacPherson, Nicholas	Permanent Secretary to the Treasury, 2005 onwards
Miliband, Ed	Parliamentary Secretary, Cabinet Office, 2006–07
	MP for Doncaster North, 2005 onwards
	Special Adviser to Gordon Brown, 1997–03

Nye, Sue	Gordon Brown's Political Secretary, 1992–07
O'Donnell, Gus	Permanent Secretary to the Treasury, 2002–05
	Managing Director, Macroeconomic Policy and International Finance, 1999–02
Primarolo, Dawn	Paymaster-General, 1999–07
Robinson, Geoffrey	MP for Coventry North West, 1976 onwards
Scholar, Tom	UK Executive Director of the International Monetary Fund and World Bank and Economic Minister at the British Embassy in Washington, 2001–07
	Principal Private Secretary to Gordon Brown, 1997–01
Vadera, Shriti	Special Adviser to Gordon Brown and member of the Treasury's Council of Economic Advisers, 1999–2007

Note on Sources and Methodology

The principal source material for the book lies in over 300 original interviews conducted both in Britain and in the United States. Those who worked at Number 10 were interviewed extensively and this bank of contemporary reflections forms the biggest single source of research. Nearly all interviews were taped (with the balance recorded by hand) and the transcripts come to well over a million words. I have also re-consulted the million-plus words of interview transcripts accumulated during the research for *Blair* in 2003–04. Where possible, endnotes refer to interviewees by name; serving officials and others, however, often insisted on anonymity in return for speaking candidly, hence the ubiquity of the phrase 'Private interview' in the Notes. Sometimes, for stylistic reasons, I have used quotations without indicating their origin in the text. In each case these quotations have come from one of the Number 10 sources interviewed. I also conducted numerous interviews within the Brown camp, with Treasury officials, parliamentary colleagues and others who have worked closely with Gordon Brown. The periodic paranoia from both camps was as unattractive as it was unhelpful in trying to understand what happened during these six years. As one Number 10 official said, 'When anything went wrong, the immediate reaction in Number 10 was "Gordon's behind it".' The same syndrome was at play in the Brown camp. The book aims to transcend the passions of the partisan participants. Access to officials on the other side of the Atlantic also proved excellent and revealing. This is the first book on Blair to be based on substantial interviews with both President Bush's Secretaries of State, Secretary of Defence Donald Rumsfeld, National Security Advisor Stephen Hadley and many, many others.

This is the third book I have written with more or less the same team, with the difference that this volume has two co-authors, Peter Snowdon and Daniel Collings, who share whatever credit (but not criticism) the book inspires. With the exception of diaries, published sources proved neither as accurate nor as insightful as they had been in earlier years. Robert Peston's *Brown's Britain* was an honourable exception. Once processed, this material was collated with relevant interviews and private papers from a variety of quarters, allowing the team to prepare drafts and briefs. Working jointly in both London and Washington DC, Peter Snowdon oversaw the production of the domestic briefs and Daniel Collings supervised foreign policy. From this very detailed work, which included a full text from Daniel for Chapter 1, I wrote the first draft, then revised it before it went back to the team for their comments. It was then sent out to readers who were closely involved in events for their comments. Gaining such feedback, although frowned on by some authors, invariably added enlightening material and helped weed out inaccuracies. Every fact in the book was checked by the team at least twice in an exhaustive process. The remaining errors are entirely my own, and will be corrected in the second edition.

I wrote 300,000 words of *Blair Unbound* between April and August 2007, during a very busy summer term and unusually busy holidays at school. Advances in technology greatly facilitated the task. When I wrote *Major* ten years ago, little had changed in book-writing from a hundred years before. Most of the research took place in libraries. I wrote drafts in long-hand which were then posted to my secretaries. Interviews were recorded either by hand or on audiotape which were transcribed laboriously, and had to be delivered to typists by hand or post. With this book, I was able to write the first draft using a digital tape recorder and have it e-mailed to the typists who then produced the text and e-mailed it back. Interviews were similarly recorded on digital recorder and e-mailed to typists. Much of the non-interview research took place online, as did much of the checking. BlackBerrys meant that messages and text could be sent instantaneously around the team, which made the work enormously easier and speedier. The use of Skype also meant we could conduct regular team conferences over the internet without having to meet physically. Without this new technology, the book could not have been written.

The two million-plus words of interview records, and the extensive reader comments, are joining my papers in the Bodleian Library, where they will be locked away for many years.

Notes

1: 9/11

1 *The 9/11 Commission Report*, p.1.
2 Campbell (2007), p.559.
3 *Daily Telegraph*, 11.09.01.
4 Interview, Robert Hill, 24.01.07.
5 *Observer*, 16.09.01.
6 Private interview.
7 Private interview.
8 Correspondence with author, Robert Hill, 13.03.07.
9 *The 9/11 Commission Report*, p.35.
10 *Washington Post*, 27.01.02.
11 *The 9/11 Commission Report*, p.35.
12 Interview, Godric Smith, 13.03.07.
13 Correspondence with author, Robert Hill, 30.01.07.
14 Interview, Robert Hill, 24.01.07.
15 Interview, Godric Smith, 13.03.07.
16 Correspondence with author, Robert Hill, 30.01.07.
17 Interview, Jeremy Heywood, 09.02.07.
18 Private interview.
19 Private interview.
20 Campbell (2007), p.560.
21 *The 9/11 Commission Report*, p.38.
22 Ibid.
23 Ibid., p.39.
24 *Washington Post*, 27.01.02.
25 Ibid.
26 Interview, Lord Wilson, 23.02.07.
27 Interview, Jonathan Powell, 13.02.07.
28 Interview, Lord Wilson, 23.02.07.
29 Correspondence with author, Robert Hill, 31.01.07.
30 *Independent on Sunday*, 16.09.01.
31 Private interview.
32 Campbell (2007), p.560.
33 Private interview.
34 *Scotsman*, 16.09.01; *Observer*, 16.09.01.
35 *The 9/11 Commission Report*, p.39.
36 *Washington Post*, 27.01.02.
37 Ibid.; *The 9/11 Commission Report*, p.40.
38 Clarke (2004), p.18.
39 *The 9/11 Commission Report*, p.40.
40 Clarke (2004), p.12.
41 Meyer (2005), p.187.
42 Private interview.
43 Meyer (2005), p.187.
44 Private interview.
45 Meyer (2005), pp.188–9.
46 Meyer (2005), p.190.
47 Private correspondence with author.
48 Private interview.
49 Interview, Peter Hyman, 22.02.07.
50 Private interview.
51 Interview, Lord Wilson, 23.02.07.
52 Private correspondence with author.
53 Private interview.
54 *New Statesman*, 23.09.02.
55 Interview, Lord Wilson, 23.02.07.
56 Ibid.
57 Kampfner (2003), p.112.
58 Interview, Lord Wilson, 23.02.07.
59 Interview, Robert Hill, 24.01.07.
60 *Scotsman*, 16.09.01.
61 Private interview.
62 Interview, Jack Straw, 26.03.07.
63 Correspondence with author, Robert Hill, 31.01.07.
64 Private interview.
65 Correspondence with author, Robert Hill, 31.01.07.
66 Private interview.
67 Kampfner (2004), p.111.
68 Interview, Godric Smith, 13.03.07.
69 Interview, Robert Hill, 24.01.07.
70 Campbell (2007), p.560.
71 Private interview.

72 *Washington Post*, 27.01.02.
73 Ibid.
74 *Observer*, 16.09.01.
75 Private interview.
76 Interview, Tom Kelly, 14.02.07.
77 Kampfner (2004), p.112.
78 Interview, Sir Stephen Lander, 12.02.07.
79 Riddell, p.150; Campbell (2007), p.561.
80 Campbell (2007), p.561.
81 Interview, Sir Stephen Lander, 12.02.07.
82 Riddell (2003), p.150.
83 *The Times*, 14.06.02; Kampfner (2004), p.113.
84 Interview, Sir Peter Ricketts, 24.01.07.
85 Ibid.
86 Private interview.
87 *Guardian*, 12.09.01.
88 Interview, Sir Stephen Lander, 08.02.07.
89 Interview, John Sawers, 12.01.07.
90 Ibid.
91 Interview, Sir Stephen Lander, 08.02.07.
92 Interview, John Sawers, 12.01.07.
93 Private interview.
94 *BBC News*, 13.08.06; 'List of AQ-Related Attacks and Planned Attacks Prior to 911', unpublished British government paper.
95 Interview, Lord Wilson, 23.02.07.
96 Campbell (2007), p.561.
97 Ibid.
98 Private interview.
99 Interview, Lord Wilson, 23.02.07.
100 Interview, Geoff Hoon, 15.03.07.
101 Campbell (2007), p.561.
102 Ibid., p.562.
103 Kampfner (2004), p.114; *The Times*, 29.09.01.
104 Private interview.
105 Interview, Lord Stevens, 13.03.07.
106 Blunkett (2006), p.290.
107 Interview, Simon MacDonald, 10.02.07.
108 Interview, Lord Stevens, 13.03.07.
109 Interview, John Sawers, 12.01.07.
110 Interview, Simon MacDonald, 10.02.07.
111 Interview, Tom Kelly, 14.02.07.
112 Tony Blair, 'Statement in response to terrorist attacks in the United States', 11.09.01.
113 Interview, Tom Kelly, 14.02.07.
114 *Washington Post*, 27.01.02.
115 Ibid.
116 Private interview.
117 Campbell (2007), p.562.
118 Private interview.
119 Private interview.
120 Campbell (2007), p.561.
121 Interview, Jonathan Powell, 08.03.07.
122 Tony Blair, 'Campaign against Terror', *Frontline* (WGBH Boston), 2002.
123 Interview, Lord Wilson, 23.02.07.
124 Private interview.
125 Interview, John Sawers, 12.01.07.
126 Ibid.
127 Private interview.
128 Interview, John Sawers, 12.01.07.
129 Interview, Elizabeth Jones, 06.03.07.
130 Clarke (2004), p.21.
131 *Washington Post*, 27.01.02.
132 Ibid.
133 Private interview.
134 Correspondence with author, John Sawers, 28.03.07.
135 Correspondence with author, John Sawers, 28.03.07.

2: Finding His Theme

1 Private information.
2 Private information.
3 Private papers.
4 Private interview.
5 Interview, Tom Bentley, 13.09.06.
6 Private interview.
7 Private information.
8 Interview, Jeremy Heywood, 12.03.07.
9 Private interview.
10 Private interview.
11 Campbell (2007), p.501.
12 Interview, Baroness Morgan, 08.11.06.
13 Private interview.
14 Interview, Lord Birt, 26.03.07.
15 Interview, Jeremy Heywood, 12.03.07.
16 Private information.
17 Interview, Geoff Mulgan, 21.07.03.
18 Interview, Patrick Diamond, 19.02.04.
19 Private correspondence with author.
20 See Seldon (2005), pp.47–59.
21 Private information.
22 *Independent on Sunday*, 01.04.01.
23 Ibid., 04.01.01.
24 Private interview.
25 Private correspondence with author.
26 Interview, Lord Wilson, 23.02.07.
27 Ibid.
28 Private interview.
29 Private interview.
30 Campbell (2007), p.517.
31 Ibid.

32   Private interview.
33   Price (2005), p.325.
34   Blunkett (2006), p.257; private information.
35   Private information.
36   Private correspondence with author.
37   Price (2006), p.315.
38   *Independent*, 24.03.01.
39   Interview, John Sawers, 01.09.03; private correspondence with author.
40   Blunkett (2006), p.257.
41   Price (2005), p.317.
42   Campbell (2007), p.515–16.
43   Private interview.
44   Interview, John Sawers, 01.09.03.
45   Private interview.
46   Price (2005), p.318.
47   Private interview.
48   Interview, Sir David King, 07.02.07.
49   Blunkett (2006), p.259.
50   *Guardian*, 26.04.01.
51   Interview, James Purnell, 08.09.03.
52   See Seldon and Snowdon (2004), pp.131, 248.
53   Private interview.
54   Private interview.
55   Campbell (2007), p.526.
56   Private interview.
57   Price (2005), p.349.
58   Private information.
59   Campbell (2007), p.528.
60   Private information.
61   Private information.
62   Private interview.
63   *Sunday Times*, 10.06.01.
64   Private interview.
65   *Daily Telegraph*, 14.05.01.
66   *Independent*, 17.05.01.
67   Interview, Simon Stevens, 18.11.06.
68   Private interview.
69   Price (2005), p.351.
70   Private interview.
71   *Guardian*, 26.05.01.
72   Private interview.
73   *Sunday Times*, 10.06.01.
74   Campbell (2007), p.537.
75   Private interview.
76   Private interview.
77   Private information.
78   *Observer*, 10.06.01.
79   Private information.
80   Private information.
81   *Observer*, 10.06.01.
82   *Sunday Times*, 10.06.01.
83   Private information.
84   *Guardian*, 09.06.01.
85   Interview, Lord Wilson, 23.02.07.
86   Private interview.
87   Private information.
88   Private information.
89   Private information.
90   Private interview.
91   Private interview.
92   Private interview.
93   Peston (2006), p.329.
94   Private information.
95   Private interview.
96   Private information.
97   Private interview.
98   Private interview.
99   Private interview.
100   Private interview.
101   Private information.
102   Private information.
103   Private interview.
104   Cook (2004) p.7.
105   Private interview.
106   Private interview.
107   Private interview.
108   Interview, Jack Straw, 02.04.07.
109   Private interview.
110   Private interview.
111   Private interview.
112   Private interview.
113   Interview, David Blunkett, 08.11.06.
114   Private interview.
115   Interview, Lord Turnbull, 05.07.06.
116   Ibid.
117   Private information.
118   Private information.
119   Private information.
120   Private information.
121   Private information.
122   Private information
123   Interview, Sir Stephen Wall, 12.12.06.
124   Private interview.
125   Interview, Robert Hill, 24.01.07.
126   Private interview.
127   Private interview.
128   Private interview.
129   Private interview.
130   Private interview.
131   Private interview.
132   Private information.
133   Private information.
134   Interview, Lord Adonis, 29.08.06.
135   Private interview.
136   Barber (2007), pp.75–9.
137   Ibid, p. 49.
138   Interview, Sir Michael Barber, 06.12.06.
139   Private papers.
140   Barber (2007), pp.56–8.
141   Private interview.
142   Private interviews.
143   Interview, Baroness Jay, 15.10.03.
144   Private interview.
145   Private papers, 25.06.01.
146   Ibid.
147   Hyman (2005), p.175.
148   Private interview.

149 Interview, Peter Hyman, 22.02.07.
150 Ibid., Hyman (2005), pp.175–7.
151 *Guardian*, 21.06.01.
152 Ibid.
153 Private interview.
154 Private interview.
155 Interview, Stephen Byers, 19.03.07.
156 Campbell (2007), p.558.
157 Ibid.
158 Ibid.
159 Private papers, 25.06.01.
160 Interview, Robert Hill, 24.01.07;
    Robert Hill, 'Pick the right clubs to
    drive service reform', SOLACE
    Foundation (September 2006),
    pp.8–20.
161 Barber (2007), p.41.
162 Ibid.
163 Private papers, notes of meetings,
    June and July 2001.
164 Private interview.
165 Private papers, 01.08.01.
166 Private interview.
167 Interview, Baroness Morgan,
    12.12.06.
168 Private interview.
169 Private interview.
170 Private interview.
171 Interview, Baroness Morgan,
    04.04.07.
172 Private papers, 06.09.01.
173 Interview, Sir Michael Barber,
    06.12.06.

3: Riding Two Horses

1 Private interview.
2 Interview, Sir Christopher Meyer,
    02.06.03.
3 Interview, Karl Rove, 19.03.07.
4 Private interview, Condoleezza
    Rice, 11.06.07.
5 Campbell (2007), p.506.
6 Private interview.
7 Interview, Lord Wilson, 27.05.03.
8 Interview, John Sawers, 13.01.07.
9 Interview, Lord Wilson, 27.05.03.
10 Private interview.
11 Private interview.
12 Private interview.
13 Campbell (2007), p.564.
14 Private interview.
15 Campbell (2007), p.564.
16 Kampfner (2004), pp.115–16;
    Riddell (2003), pp.151–2; *Washington
    Post*, 28.01.02.
17 Private interview.
18 Interview, Dan Fried, 14.07.07.
19 Tony Blair, 'Campaign against
    Terror', *Frontline* (WGBH Boston),
    2002.
20 Private interview.
21 *Sunday Times*, 09.08.02; Riddell
    (2003), pp.150–1.
22 Interview, John Sawers, 13.01.07.
23 Interview, Dan Fried, 14.07.07.
24 Woodward (2002), p.44.
25 Meyer (2006), p.188.
26 Campbell (2007), p.565.
27 *Guardian*, 15.09.01.
28 Campbell (2007), p.564.
29 *Washington Post*, 01.03.02.
30 Campbell (2007), p.566.
31 Ibid.
32 Woodward (2004), pp.25–6.
33 Interview, Sir Jock Stirrup, 02.04.07.
34 Private interview.
35 Interview, Richard Armitage,
    04.04.03.
36 Woodward (2002), p.48.
37 Private interview.
38 Interview, Richard Armitage,
    04.04.03.
39 Meyer (2006), p.196.
40 Campbell (2007), p.569.
41 Meyer (2006), p.198.
42 Campbell (2007), p.569.
43 Interview, Lord Jay, 10.06.07.
44 Tony Blair, 'Campaign against
    Terror', *Frontline* (WGBH Boston),
    2002.
45 *Observer*, 23.09.01.
46 Campbell (2007), pp.571–2.
47 Meyer (2006), p.201.
48 *Guardian*, 21.09.01.
49 Meyer (2006), p.201.
50 Meyer (2006), p.204.
51 Sir Christopher Meyer, 'Blair's War',
    Frontline (WGBH Boston), 2003.
52 Campbell (2007), p.573.
53 Ibid.
54 *Observer*, 23.09.01.
55 Riddell (2003), p.160.
56 Campbell (2007), p.574.
57 Meyer (2006), p.204.
58 Tony Blair, 'Campaign against
    Terror', *Frontline* (WGBH Boston),
    2002.
59 Interview, Karl Rove, 19.03.07.
60 Interview, Sir David Manning,
    09.04.07.
61 Riddell (2003), p.161.
62 Private interview.
63 Private interview.
64 Interview, Lord Wilson, 27.05.03.
65 Interview, Baroness Morgan,
    04.04.07.
66 Interview, Stephen Lander,
    12.02.07.
67 Private interview.
68 Campbell (2007), p.565.
69 Private interview.

70 Interview, Sir Lawrence Freedman, 16.03.07.
71 Interview, Andrew Neather, 23.01.07.
72 Campbell (2007), p.576.
73 Private interview.
74 *Independent*, 03.10.01.
75 *New York Post*, 03.10.01.
76 *Independent*, 03.10.01.
77 *Observer*, 07.10.01.
78 Interview, Baroness Morgan, 04.04.07.
79 Interview, Lord Boyce, 17.02.07.
80 *Independent*, 05.10.01.
81 Interview, Lord Wilson, 23.02.07.
82 Private interview.
83 Private interview.
84 Private interview.
85 Campbell (2007), p.575.
86 Ibid., p.576.
87 Interview, Sir Roderick Lyne, 15.01.04.
88 Private interview.
89 Interview, Sir Roderick Lyne, 15.01.04.
90 *Daily Telegraph*, 26.09.01.
91 Campbell (2007), p.576.
92 Private interview.
93 Private interview.
94 Private interview.
95 Interview, Lord Guthrie, 24.07.03.
96 Tony Blair, 'Campaign against Terror', *Frontline* (WGBH Boston), 2002.
97 DeYoung (2006), p.350.
98 *Sunday Times*, 07.10.01.
99 *The Times*, 08.10.01.
100 *Observer*, 14.10.01.
101 Interview, Sir Rob Fry, 16.01.07.
102 Interview, Geoff Hoon, 15.03.07.
103 Interview, Stephen Lander, 08.02.07.
104 Private interviews.
105 *Guardian*, 31.10.01.
106 Campbell (2007), p.580.
107 Private interview.
108 Interview, Sir John Kerr, 15.09.03.
109 Tony Blair, 'Campaign against Terror', *Frontline* (WGBH Boston), 2002.
110 Private interview.
111 *Daily Telegraph*, 11.10.01.
112 *Guardian*, 11.10.01.
113 'Joint Press conference: Prime Minister Tony Blair and President Mubarak', 11.10.01.
114 *Observer*, 14.01.01.
115 Interview, Sir David Manning, 09.04.07.
116 Private interview.
117 Interview, John Sawers, 13.01.07.
118 Private interview.
119 Correspondence with author, Sir Christopher Meyer, 08.06.07.
120 Interview, Lawrence Wilkerson, 10.07.07.
121 Private interview.
122 Private interview.
123 Interview, Ken Adelman, 16.01.07.
124 Campbell (2007), p.585.
125 Ibid., p.586.
126 *Sunday Telegraph*, 04.11.01.
127 *The Times*, 02.11.01.
128 Interview, John Sawers, 21.10.06.
129 Private correspondence with author.
130 Ibid.
131 Riddell (2003) p.167.
132 Kampfner (2004), p.138.
133 Private interview.
134 Interview, Lord Boyce, 17.02.07.
135 Private interview.
136 Interview, Robert Cooper, 04.09.04.
137 Woodward (2002), pp.296–7.
138 Meyer (2006), p.232.
139 *The Times*, 08.11.01.
140 Interview, Sir Jock Stirrup, 02.04.07.
141 Private interview.
142 Interview, Sir David Manning, 09.04.07.
143 Private interview.
144 Woodward (2002), p.310.
145 Sir Christopher Meyer, 'Blair's War', *Frontline* (WGBH Boston), 2003.
146 Interview, Lord Boyce, 14.04.04.
147 Interview, Geoff Hoon, 15.03.07.
148 Interview, Ronald Rumsfeld, 15.08.07.
149 *The Times*, 20.12.01.
150 Campbell (2007), p.600.
151 Private interview.
152 Private papers.
153 Private papers.
154 Private interview.
155 Peter Hyman, 'Strategy 2002' Memo, 02.12.01.
156 Private interview.
157 Private interview.
158 *Guardian*, 02.10.01.
159 Private papers.
160 Campbell (2007), p.586.
161 Private papers.
162 Private interview.
163 Campbell (2007), p.589.
164 Private papers.
165 Private correspondence with author, 06.06.07.
166 Interview, Simon Stevens, 05.10.06.
167 Interview, Paul Corrigan, 06.02.07.
168 Interview, Alan Milburn, 13.12.06.
169 Interview, Paul Corrigan, 06.02.07.
170 Howard Glennister, Seldon and Kavanagh (2005), p.287.

171 The story of the Treasury's subsequent bare-knuckle resistance to foundation hospitals is related in Chapter 9.
172 Private papers.
173 Private information.
174 Private papers.
175 Peston (2006), p.296.
176 Interview, Simon Stevens, 18.11.06.
177 Campbell (2007), p.617.
178 Interview, Paul Corrigan, 06.02.07.
179 Campbell (2007), p.618.
180 Private correspondence with author.
181 Private interview.
182 Private interview.
183 *Guardian*, 09.06.01.
184 Interview, Huw Evans, 02.03.07.
185 Barber (2007), p.148.
186 Ibid.
187 Interview, Jeremy Heywood, 09.02.07.
188 Barber (2007), p.155.
189 Interview, Lord Stevens, 13.03.07.
190 Ibid.
191 Barber (2007), p.157.
192 Ibid., pp.157–8.
193 *Hansard*, 24.04.02, Col.326.
194 BBC News Online, 12.09.02.
195 Private interview.
196 Interviews, Louise Casey, 24.01.07, 07.02.07.
197 Ibid.
198 Private interview.
199 Private papers.
200 Private interview.
201 Interview, David Blunkett, 20.02.07.
202 Private interview.
203 Private interview.
204 Interview, Jeremy Heywood, 12.03.07.
205 Private interview.
206 Private interview.
207 Interview, Huw Evans, 02.03.07.
208 *Observer*, 31.03.02.
209 Campbell (2007), p.610–11.
210 *The Times*, 04.04.02.
211 *Spectator*, 11.04.02.
212 Private interview.
213 Private interview.
214 Private interview.
215 Private interview.
216 Interview, Baroness Morgan, 04.04.07.
217 Private papers.
218 Private papers.
219 Campbell (2007), pp.609–10.
220 Private interview.
221 Campbell (2007), p.620.
222 Private interview.
223 Private interview.
224 Private interview.

4: The Road to Baghdad

1 George W. Bush, 'The President's State of the Union Address'.
2 Interview, Elizabeth Jones, 06.03.07.
3 Private information.
4 *New York Times*, 09.12.98.
5 Clinton, 'Remarks on the Situation in Iraq', 15.11.98, Public Papers of the Presidents.
6 See Mann (2004)
7 Mann (2004), p.xvi.
8 Daalder and Lindsay (2003), pp.13–16.
9 Interview, John Sawers, 13.01.07.
10 Interview, Condoleezza Rice, 11.06.07.
11 Private interview.
12 Woodward (2004), pp.1–3.
13 Interview, Elizabeth Jones, 06.03.07.
14 Private interview.
15 Interview, Sir David Manning, 09.04.07.
16 Private interview.
17 Private interview.
18 Private interview.
19 Private interview.
20 Private interview.
21 Private interview.
22 Correspondence with author, Sir Christopher Meyer, 08.06.07.
23 Private interview.
24 Private interview.
25 Private interview.
26 Interview, Sir Rob Fry, 16.01.07.
27 Interview, Robert Cooper, 04.09.03; Cooper (2003).
28 Private interview.
29 Ashdown (2002), p.127.
30 Private interview.
31 Interview, Sir David Manning, 17.02.04.
32 Interview, Jack Straw, 11.11.03.
33 Private interview.
34 Correspondence, Tony Blair to George Carey, 30.03.02.
35 *Sunday Times*, 01.02.98.
36 *Independent*, 24.02.01.
37 Stephens (2004), p.211.
38 Interview, Sir Christopher Meyer, 07.08.06.
39 Stothard (2003), p.42.
40 Private interview.
41 Stephens (2004), p.210.
42 Interview, Paul 'PJ' Johnson, 05.02.07.
43 Tony Blair, 'Doctrine of International Community at the Economic Club, Chicago', 24.04.99.
44 Tony Blair, 'Speech at the George Bush Senior Presidential Library', 07.04.02.

45 Private interview.
46 Interview, Lord Jay, 02.08.06.
47 Private interview.
48 Correspondence, Tony Blair to George Carey, 30.03.02.
49 Private interview.
50 *The Times*, 01.03.02.
51 *Daily Express*, 06.03.02
52 Private interview.
53 Correspondence with author, Sir Christopher Meyer, 26.07.07.
54 Campbell (2007), p.609.
55 Press Conference, 'Tony Blair and Vice-President Dick Cheney', 11.03.02.
56 *Financial Times*, 12.03.02.
57 Cook (2003), p.115.
58 Ibid., p.116.
59 Campbell (2007), p.612.
60 Private interview.
61 Private interview.
62 Memo, Manning to Blair, 14.03.02. This is one of a series of six memos leaked to Michael Smith, then defence correspondent at the *Daily Telegraph* in September 2004. See www.michaelsmithwriter.com.
63 Memo, Meyer to Manning, 18.03.02 – see Note 62.
64 Interview, Sir Christopher Meyer, 25.01.07.
65 Interview, Karl Rove, 19.03.07.
66 Memo, Straw to Blair, 25.03.02 – see Note 62.
67 Memo, Manning to Blair, 14.03.02 – see Note 62.
68 Campbell (2007), p.612.
69 Ibid.
70 Private interview.
71 Campbell (2007), p.612.
72 Interview, Lawrence Wilkerson, 29.06.07.
73 Daalder and Lindsay (2003), pp.132–6.
74 Interview, Colin Powell, 01.02.07.
75 *Sunday Telegraph*, 07.04.02; Correspondence with author, Sir
76 Campbell (2007), p.613.
77 Interview, Sir David Manning, 09.04.07.
78 Private interview.
79 Private interview.
80 Cabinet Office Paper, 'Iraq: Conditions for Military Action', 21.07.02. See *Sunday Times*, 12.06.05.
81 Tony Blair, 'Speech at the George Bush Senior Presidential Library', 07.04.02.
82 Private interview.
83 Tony Blair, 'September 11: Prime Minister's Statement', 11.09.01.

84 Interview, Sir Christopher Meyer, 11.03.04.
85 Private interview.
86 Interview, Sir Christopher Meyer, 29.03.04.
87 Interview, Colin Powell, 11.07.07.
88 Interview, Karl Rove, 19.03.07.
89 Kampfner (2004), p.168.
90 Ibid., p.169.
91 *Time*, 09.03.98.
92 Interview, Lord Boyce, 14.04.04.
93 Cook (2003), p.135.
94 Kampfner (2004), pp.167–9.
95 Memo, Straw to Blair, 25.03.02 – see Note 62.
96 Campbell (2007), p.613.
97 Meyer (2005), pp.243–4.
98 Private interview.
99 Meyer (2005), pp.264.
100 Private interview.
101 Private information.
102 Interview, Lawrence Wilkerson, 10.07.07.
103 Interview, Sir Christopher Meyer, 16.03.07.
104 Interview, Lawrence Wilkerson, 10.07.07.
105 Meyer (2005), p.245.
106 Interview, Condoleezza Rice, 11.06.07.
107 Meyer (2005), p.246.
108 Private interview.
109 Campbell (2007), p.626.
110 Interview, Condoleezza Rice, 11.06.07.
111 Private interview.
112 Kampfner (2004), p.183.
113 Private interview.
114 Correspondence with author, Sir Christopher Meyer, 08.06.07.
115 Private information.
116 Private interview.
117 Memo, Rycroft to Manning, 23.07.02 – see Note 62.
118 Campbell (2007), p.630.
119 Private information.
120 Interview, Lord Jay, 22.03.07.
121 Campbell (2007), p.630.
122 Memo, Rycroft to Manning 23.07.02 – see Note 62.
123 Private interview.
124 Interview, Lord Boyce, 17.02.07.
125 Campbell (2007), p.630.
126 Private correspondence.
127 Interview, Sir Christopher Meyer, 25.01.07.
128 Private interview.
129 Private interview.
130 Interview, Sir David Manning, 09.04.07.
131 Interview, John Bolton, 10.07.07.

132 Daalder and Lindsay (2003), p.135.
133 Woodward (2003), p.161.
134 Interview, Colin Powell, 01.02.07.
135 Interview, Jack Straw, 26.03.07.
136 Interview, Simon McDonald, 10.02.07.
137 Private interview.
138 Private interview.
139 Private interview; Correspondence with author, Sir Christopher Meyer, 08.06.07.
140 Private interview.
141 Interview, Colin Powell, 01.02.07.
142 Private correspondence with author, 09.06.07.
143 Private interview.
144 Private interview.
145 Interview, Colin Powell, 01.02.07.
146 Interview, Lawrence Wilkerson, 29.06.07.
147 Private interview.
148 Interview, Lawrence Wilkerson, 29.06.07.
149 Dick Cheney, 'Speech to the Veterans of Foreign Wars', 26.08.02.
150 Campbell (2007), p.631.
151 Ibid., p.634.
152 Interview, Baroness Morgan, 04.04.07.
153 Interview, Lord Boyce, 17.02.07.
154 Kampfner (2004), p.196.
155 Private information.
156 Woodward (2003), pp.175–6.
157 Interview, Sir Christopher Meyer, 16.03.07.
158 Campbell (2007), p.634.
159 Private interview.
160 Woodward (2003), p.178.
161 Campbell (2007), p.635.
162 Interview, Condoleezza Rice, 11.06.07.
163 Campbell (2007), p.635.
164 Ibid.
165 Interview, Baroness Morgan, 04.04.07.
166 Interview, Sir Jeremy Greenstock, 26.02.04.
167 Ibid.
168 Kampfner (2004), p.200.
169 Cook (2003), p.205.
170 Private interview.
171 Interview, Marc Grossman, 27.10.06.
172 Private interview.
173 Interview, Sir David Manning, 27.10.06.
174 Correspondence with author, Sir Christopher Meyer, 08.06.07.
175 Stephens (2004), p.217.

5: 'Make or Break' at Home

1 Private interview.
2 See Barber (2007), pp.240–2 and Chapter 2 for a brief account of Barber's impact at the DfEE from 1997 to 2001.
3 Interview, Ivan Rogers, 23.10.06.
4 Interview, Sir Michael Barber, 06.12.06.
5 Private interview.
6 Interview, Ivan Rogers, 23.10.06.
7 Private interview.
8 Private interview.
9 Private interview.
10 Private interview.
11 Private interview.
12 Private papers, 07.01.02.
13 Private interview.
14 Private interview.
15 Campbell (2007), p.501.
16 Private interview.
17 Private interview.
18 In particular, there was evidence of improvement in Key Stage 3 results. See 'Schools extending excellence: Excellence in Cities annual report 2000-2001' (Department for Education and Skills, April 2002).
19 Private correspondence with author, 30.04.07.
20 Michael Barber points to primary school test results reaching a plateau in 2001, followed by results for eleven-year-olds in English (Level 4) and Maths falling short in 2002. See Barber (2007), pp.184–5.
21 Private interview.
22 Private interview.
23 Campbell (2007), pp.645–6.
24 Private interview.
25 Private interview.
26 Campbell (2007), p.623.
27 Ibid.
28 Ibid.
29 Ibid.
30 Private interview.
31 Campbell (2007), p.268.
32 Ibid.
33 Ibid.
34 Ibid.
35 Ibid.
36 Ibid.
37 Private interview.
38 Ibid.
39 Ibid.
40 Private interview.
41 Campbell (2007), p.629.
42 Ibid.
43 Private interview.
44 *Guardian*, 06.08.02.
45 Blair to Policy Unit, 01.04.02.

46 Private interview..
47 Private interview.
48 Cook (2003), p.223.
49 Private interview.
50 Private interview.
51 Interview, Baroness Morgan, 20.04.07.
52 *Guardian*, 03.10.02.
53 Private interview.
54 Private interview.
55 Private correspondence with author.
56 Interview, Tom Kelly, 06.03.07.
57 Ibid.
58 Private interview.
59 Godson (2005), p.679.
60 Private interview.
61 Private correspondence with author.
62 Private interview.
63 Private interview.
64 Private interview.
65 Goodson (2005), p.728.
66 Private interview.
67 Godson (2005), p.730; *Guardian*, 08.10.02.
68 Interview, Tom Kelly, 13.04.07.
69 Interview, Tom Kelly, 15.04.07.
70 Private interview.
71 Private interview.
72 Interview, Tom Kelly, 06.02.07.
73 Private interview.
74 Private interview.
75 Interview, Andrew Neather, 25.10.03.
76 *Guardian*, 24.11.01.
77 Ibid.
78 Private interview.
79 Private interview.
80 Interview, Sir Stephen Wall, 06.03.07.
81 Private interview.
82 See Chapter 8.
83 Interview, Sir Stephen Wall, 06.03.07.
84 Private interview.
85 Private interview.
86 Private interview.
87 Private interview.
88 Private interview.
89 Private interview.
90 Private interview.
91 *Guardian*, 05.04.04.
92 BBC News Online, 30.10.02
93 Private interview.
94 Interview, Sir Stephen Wall, 06.03.07.
95 Interview, John Stevens, 13.03.07.
96 Private interview, 226.
97 *Daily Telegraph*, 27.02.07.
98 Interview, Lord Stevens, 13.03.07.
99 Private interview, 226.
100 *Daily Telegraph*, 27.02.07.

101 Private interview.
102 Private correspondence with author.
103 Private interview.
104 Private interview.
105 Scott (2004), p.27.
106 Private interview.
107 Private interview.
108 Private interview.
109 Interview, Lord Turner, 21.05.07.
110 *Guardian*, 13.11.02.
111 Interview, Jeremy Heywood, 12.03.07.
112 Private interview.
113 Private interview.
114 Private interview.
115 Private interview.
116 Private interview.
117 Private interview.
118 Private interview.
119 Campbell (2007), p.647.
120 Ibid., p.648.
121 Ibid.
122 Ibid.
123 Ibid.
124 Private interview.
125 *The Times*, 11.12.03.
126 Private interview.
127 Private interview.
128 Private interview.
129 Cherie Blair's statement to the Partners in Excellence awards, 10.12.02, cited in the *Daily Telegraph*, 10.12.02.
130 The Real Cherie Blair', BBC One, 04.07.07.
131 Campbell (2007), p.651.
132 Stothard (2003) p.73.
133 Ibid.
134 Campbell (2007), pp. 652.
135 Private interview.
136 Private interview.

6: Confronting Saddam

1 Interview, Jeremy Heywood, 12.03.07.
2 Private interview.
3 Kampfner (2004), p.198.
4 Correspondence with author, Sir Christopher Meyer, 30.06.07.
5 Kampfner (2004), pp.165–7.
6 Campbell (2007), p.633.
7 Private interview.
8 Meyer (2005), pp.251–2; Private interview.
9 *The Times*, 11.09.02.
10 Cook (2003), p.203.
11 Campbell (2007), p.636.
12 Interview, Lord Butler, 07.02.07.
13 Powell and Scarlett, 17.09.02, 19.14, CAB/11/0069.

14 Powell, Campbell and Manning, 17.09.02, 13.36, CAB/11/0053.
15 Campbell and Scarlett, 17.09.02, CAB/11/0066.
16 'Iraq's Weapons of Mass Destruction', 24.09.02, p.4.
17 Stephens (2004), pp.220–1.
18 *Hansard*, 24.09.02, Col.2.
19 *Jerusalem Post*, 26.09.02.
20 *Financial Times*, 25.09.02.
21 Private interview.
22 Private correspondence with author.
23 Campbell (2007), pp.639–40.
24 Cook (2003), pp.212–13.
25 Campbell (2007), p.639.
26 Ibid.
27 Interview, Sir Christopher Meyer, 01.10.03.
28 Cook (2003), p.203.
29 Interview, Baroness Morgan, 19.04.07.
30 Interview, Lord Butler, 07.02.07.
31 Interview, Lord Boyce, 14.04.04.
32 Interview, Lord Boyce, 17.02.07.
33 Interview, Lord Jay, 02.08.06.
34 Testimony to the Armed Services Committee, David Kay, 28.01.04.
35 Butler Report, p.152.
36 Isikoff and Corn (2006), p.308.
37 Robin Cook, 'Iraq, Tony and the Truth', BBC *Panorama*, 04.04.05.
38 Interview, Sir Ivor Roberts, 15.02.07.
39 Private interview.
40 Private interview.
41 *Hansard*, 24.09.02, Col.2.
42 Private interview.
43 Interview, Lord Butler, 07.02.02.
44 Interview, Iain Duncan Smith, 28.06.07.
45 Interview, Sir David Manning, 17.02.04.
46 Correspondence, Sir Jeremy Greenstock, 27.06.07.
47 Interview, Sir Jeremy Greenstock, 26.02.04.
48 *Vanity Fair*, May 2004.
49 Private interview.
50 Private interview.
51 Riddell (2003), p.220.
52 Private interview.
53 Interview, Sir David Manning, 09.04.07.
54 Private interview.
55 Interview, John Bolton, 03.12.03.
56 Private correspondence with author.
57 Private interview.
58 Correspondence, Sir Christopher Meyer, 24.06.07.
59 Private interview.
60 Interview, Sir Rob Fry, 16.01.07.
61 Ibid.
62 Interview, Lord Boyce, 17.02.07.
63 Private interview.
64 *Sunday Telegraph*, 10.11.02.
65 Rubin, J., 'Stumbling into War', *Foreign Affairs*, September/October 2003.
66 Private interview.
67 Quoted in Kampfner (2004), p.230.
68 Meyer (2005), p.257.
69 Interview, Donald Rumsfeld, 15.08.07.
70 Woodward (2004), pp.234–5.
71 Ibid., p.240.
72 Meyer (2005), pp.258–9.
73 Woodward (2006), p.106.
74 Interview, Sir Rob Fry, 16.01.07.
75 Campbell (2007), p.655.
76 Ibid., p.656.
77 Private interview.
78 Private interview.
79 Interview, Sir Peter Ricketts, 24.01.07.
80 Private interview.
81 Private interview.
82 Interview, Lord Jay, 22.03.07.
83 Private interview.
84 Private interview.
85 Interview, Lord Jay, 02.08.06.
86 Private interview.
87 Interview, Lord Jay, 22.03.07.
88 Private correspondence.
89 Private interview.
90 Private correspondence.
91 Private interview.
92 Private interview.
93 George W. Bush, State of Union Speech, 29.01.03.
94 Private papers.
95 Campbell (2007), p.659.
96 Private interview.
97 Interview, Sir Christopher Meyer, 25.01.07.
98 Campbell (2007), p.660.
99 Correspondence, Sir Christopher Meyer, 24.06.07.
100 Interview, Baroness Morgan, 08.11.06.
101 Interview, Colin Powell, 01.02.07.
102 Woodward (2004), pp.296–7.
103 David Manning's record of a meeting between George W. Bush and Tony Blair, 31.01.03, cited in *New York Times*, 27.03.03.
104 Interview, Marc Grossman, 27.10.06.
105 Private interview.
106 Meyer (2005), p.261.
107 Private interview.
108 David Manning's record, 31.01.03, cited in *New York Times*, 27.03.06.
109 Meyer (2005), p.262.
110 David Manning's record, 31.01.03, cited in *New York Times*, 27.03.06.

111　Interview, Sir David Manning, 09.04.07.
112　Interview, Lord Jay, 22.03.07.
113　Private interview.
114　Interview, Jack Straw, 26.02.07.
115　Interview, Sir Rob Fry, 16.01.07.
116　Interview, Lord Turnbull, 04.04.07.
117　Short (2004), pp.165–6, 210.
118　*Guardian*, 02.05.07.
119　Private interview.
120　Private interview.
121　Interview, Jack Straw, 26.02.07.
122　Interview, Elizabeth Jones, 26.10.06.
123　Private interview.
124　Interview, Lawrence Wilkerson, 29.06.07.
125　Private interview.
126　Gordon and Trainor (2006), pp.141–2.
127　Interview, Sir Rob Fry, 16.01.07.
128　*Daily Telegraph*, 01.09.07.
129　Campbell (2007), p.657.
130　Private interview.
131　*Associated Press*, 06.02.03.
132　Ibid.
133　Private interview.
134　Private interview.
135　Interview, Lord Turnbull, 24.04.07.
136　Interview, Godric Smith, 13.03.07.
137　Campbell (2007), p.664.
138　Interview, Lord Jay, 22.03.07.
139　Interview, John Sawers, 26.01.07.
140　Campbell (2007), p.667.
141　Ibid.
142　Private interview.
143　Interview, Glyn Davies, 29.01.07.
144　Private interview.
145　Interview, Godric Smith, 13.03.07.
146　Private interview.
147　Campbell (2007), p.667.
148　*Observer*, 16.02.03.
149　Private interview.
150　Private interview.
151　Private interview.
152　Private interview.
153　Interview, Sir Stephen Wall, 06.03.07.
154　Private interview.
155　Private interview.
156　Private interview.
157　Private interview.
158　Private interview.
159　Private interview.
160　Private interview.
161　Woodward (2004), pp.319–20.
162　Private interview.
163　Private interview.
164　Private interview.
165　Private interview.
166　Private interview.
167　*BBC News Online*, 19.02.03.
168　Private interview.
169　Private interview.
170　Private interview.
171　Private interview.
172　Campbell (2007), p.666.
173　Ibid., p.669.
174　Ibid., p.671.
175　Private interview.
176　Private correspondence.
177　Campbell (2007), p.672.
178　Ibid.
179　*Guardian*, 10.03.03.
180　Campbell (2007), p.675.
181　Private interview.
182　Private interview.
183　Private interview.
184　Interview, Huw Evans, 02.03.07.
185　Private interview.
186　Interview, Jack Straw, 26.03.07.
187　Private interview.
188　Ibid.
189　Interview, Hilary Armstrong, 22.03.07.
190　Campbell (2007), p.669.
191　Interview, Lord Jay, 22.03.07.
192　Ibid.
193　*Daily Telegraph*, 11.03.03.
194　Private interview.
195　Sir Stephen Wall, cited in 'Blair: The Inside Story', BBC TV, 27.02.07.
196　Correspondence, Sir Christopher Meyer, 24.06.07.
197　*Sun*, 12.03.03.
198　*Independent*, 19.07.07.
199　Interview, Sir Stephen Wall, 19.12.06.
200　Private interview.
201　Stothard (2003), p.14.
202　Interview, Lord Jay, 22.03.07.
203　Interview, Sir David Manning, 17.02.04.
204　Private interview.
205　Interview, Glyn Davies, 29.01.07.
206　Interview, Condoleezza Rice, 11.06.07.
207　Woodward (2004), p.338.
208　Interview, Condoleezza Rice, 11.06.07.
209　Woodward (2004), p.338; Private interview.
210　Private interview.
211　Interview, Geoff Hoon, 15.03.07.
212　Interview, Jack Straw, 26.03.07.
213　Interview, Elizabeth Jones, 29.06.07.
214　Interview, Lord Boyce, 17.02.07.
215　Private interview.
216　Interview, Lord Boyce, 14.04.04.
217　Interview, Sir Michael Jackson, 08.03.07.
218　Interview, Lawrence Wilkerson, 29.06.07.

219 Interview, Elizabeth Jones, 29.06.07.
220 Private interview.
221 Interview, Donald Rumsfeld, 15.08.07.
222 Campbell (2007), p.676.
223 Interview, Godric Smith, 13.03.07.
224 Stothard (2003), pp.20–1.
225 Private interview.
226 Campbell (2007), p.671.
227 Private interview.
228 Interview, Lord Jay, 22.03.07.
229 Private interview.
230 Interview, Lord Turnbull, 24.04.07.
231 Woodward (2004), pp.343–5.
232 Campbell (2007), p.677.
233 Interview, Elizabeth Jones, 26.10.06.
234 Interview Jeremy Greenstock, 26.02.04.
235 Cook (2003), p.320.
236 Private interview.
237 Campbell (2007), p.681.
238 Interview, Sir Stephen Wall, 12.12.06.
239 Short (2004), p.179.
240 Kampfner (2004), p.212.
241 Private interview.
242 Private interview.
243 Cook (2003) pp.320–1.
244 Interview, Lord Turnbull, 17.01.07.
245 Private interview.
246 Interview, Lord Boyce, 17.02.07.
247 Interview, Alan Milburn, 08.11.06.
248 Interview, Robin Cook, 22.03.04.
249 Interview, Baroness Morgan, 08.11.06.
250 Interview, Alan Milburn, 08.11.06.
251 Butler Report, p.95.
252 Interview, Lord Boyce, 17.02.07.
253 Interview, Lord Jay, 02.08.06.
254 Correspondence, Lord Turnbull, 16.07.07.
255 See Philippe Sands's *Lawless World* (2006) for a tightly argued critique of the evolution of the legal advice.
256 Lord Goldsmith, BBC Radio 4, 27.06.07.
257 Interview Baroness Morgan, 19.04.07.
258 Interview, Lord Turnbull, 24.04.07.
259 Sir Stephen Wall, 'Iraq, Tony and the Truth', BBC *Panorama*, 04.04.05.
260 Private interview.
261 Interview, Elizabeth Wilmshurst, 06.03.07.
262 Private interview.
263 Private interview.
264 Interview, John Sawers, 13.01.07.
265 Interview, Nigel Sheinwald, 24.11.03.
266 Correspondence, Sir Jeremy Greenstock, 27.06.07.
267 Interview, Sir David Manning, 17.02.04.
268 Interview, Baroness Morgan, 05.02.04.
269 Interview, Hilary Armstrong, 22.03.07.
270 Interview, Condoleezza Rice, 11.06.07.
271 *Independent on Sunday*, 29.02.04.
272 Private interview.
273 Campbell (2007), p.679.
274 Interview, Condoleezza Rice, 11.06.07.
275 Kampfner (2004), p.303.
276 Private interview.
277 Private interview.
278 Private interview.
279 Interview, Geoff Hoon, 15.03.07.
280 Private interview.
281 Campbell (2007), p.678.
282 Cook (2003), p.324.
283 Private papers.
284 Short (2004), p.186.
285 Interview, Patricia Hewitt, 30.10.06.
286 Interview, Jack Straw, 26.03.07.
287 Interview, Geoff Hoon, 15.03.07.
288 Interview, Lord Turnbull, 24.04.07.
289 Campbell (2007), p.680.
290 Short (2004), p.188.
291 Private interview.
292 Interview, Baroness Morgan, 19.04.07.
293 Woodward (2004), p.342; Private interview.
294 Interview, Hilary Armstrong, 22.03.07.
295 Interview, Iain Duncan Smith, 28.06.07.
296 Woodward (2004), p.365.
297 *Guardian*, 26.04.03.
298 Sir Jeremy Greenstock, cited in 'Blair: The Inside Story', BBC TV, 27.02.07.
299 Interview, Lord Turnbull, 24.04.07.
300 Interview, Alan Milburn, 08.11.06.
301 Interview, Godric Smith, 13.03.07.
302 Interview, Hilary Armstrong, 22.03.07.
303 Interview, Jack Straw, 11.11.03.
304 Interview, John Burton, 07.07.03.
305 Interview, Lord Boyce, 17.02.07.
306 Stothard (2003), p.96.

7: *Iraq: From Agonising to Vindication*

1 Woodward (2004), p.387.
2 Ibid., pp.386–97.
3 Private interview.
4 Kampfner (2004), pp.310–11.
5 Private interview.
6 Woodward, (2004), p.399.

7   Stothard (2003), pp.106–7.
8   Seldon (1997), p.157.
9   Tony Blair, 'Address to the Nation', 20.03.03.
10 *Observer*, 23.03.03.
11 *Guardian*, 21.03.03.
12 Private interview.
13 Private interview.
14 Private interview.
15 Interview, Baroness Morgan, 19.04.07.
16 Ibid.
17 Private interview.
18 Stothard (2003), p.189.
19 Private interview.
20 Campbell (2007), p.683.
21 Ibid.
22 Private interview.
23 Private interview.
24 Interview, Lord Boyce, 17.02.07.
25 Interview, Baroness Morgan, 19.04.07.
26 Stothard (2003), p.186.
27 Private interview.
28 Interview, Lord Turnbull, 04.04.07.
29 Interview, Mike Jackson, 08.03.07.
30 Campbell (2007), pp.683–4.
31 Ibid.
32 Interview, Sir Rob Fry, 16.01.07.
33 Interview, Lord Turnbull, 04.04.07.
34 Interview, Lord Boyce, 14.04.04.
35 Interview, Godric Smith, 13.03.07.
36 Cook (2003), p.270.
37 Interview, Lord Boyce, 17.02.07.
38 Stothard (2003), pp.134–5.
39 Ibid., p.145.
40 Interview, Sir Rob Fry, 21.01.07.
41 Interview, Sir Roy Fry, 16.01.07.
42 *Guardian*, 28.03.03.
43 Stothard (2003), p.182.
44 Campbell (2007), p.687.
45 Stothard (2003), p.197.
46 BBC News Online, 01.10.02.
47 Kampfner (2004), p.213.
48 Short (2004), p.153.
49 Interview, Karl Rove, 19.03.07.
50 Private interview.
51 Kampfner (2004), p.263.
52 Short (2004), p.182.
53 Kampfner (2004), p.297.
54 Interview, Colin Powell, 01.02.07.
55 Stothard (2003), p.49.
56 Private interview.
57 Private interview.
58 Stothard (2003), p.139.
59 Ibid., p.140.
60 Hansard, 26.03.03, Col.284.
61 Campbell (2007), p.684.
62 Stothard (2003), pp.150–1.
63 Campbell (2007), p.684.
64 Ibid., p.685.
65 Ibid.
66 George W. Bush, press conference with Tony Blair, 27.03.03.
67 Interview, Elizabeth Jones, 29.06.07.
68 Interview, Ken Adelman, 16.01.07.
69 Interview, Lawrence Wilkerson, 29.06.07.
70 Private interview.
71 Interview, Baroness Morgan, 19.04.07.
72 Private interview.
73 'Joint press conference with President Bush at Camp David', 27.03.03.
74 Interview, Lawrence Wilkerson, 29.06.07.
75 *Independent*, 28.03.03.
76 *Financial Times*, 28.03.03.
77 Woodward(2006), p.136
78 Private interview.
79 Stothard (2003), p.216.
80 Campbell (2007), p.688.
81 Private interview.
82 Private interview.
83 Stothard (2003), p.227.
84 Interview, Tom Kelly, 06.02.07.
85 Interview, Lawrence Wilkerson, 29.06.07.
86 Interview, Elizabeth Jones, 29.06.07.
87 Kampfner (2004), p.336.
88 'Press Conference: PM Tony Blair, and President George Bush', 08.04.03.
89 Interview, Elizabeth Jones, 26.10.06.
90 Interview, Lawrence Wilkerson, 10.07.07.
91 *Guardian*, 09.04.03.
92 Campbell (2007), p.688.
93 Stothard (2003), p.233.
94 Private interview.
95 Interview, Simon MacDonald, 10.02.07.
96 Woodward (2006), p.161.
97 Hansard, 14.04.03, Col.617.
98 Sir Jeremy Greenstock, cited in 'Blair: The Inside Story', BBC TV, 27.02.07.
99 Donald Rumsfeld, DoD Statement, 11.04.03.
100 *Daily Telegraph*, 12.04.03.
101 Private interview.
102 Hansard, 14.04.03, Col. 615.
103 Hansard, 14.04.03, Col. 616.
104 Private interview.
105 Interview, Sir Rob Fry, 16.01.07.
106 Woodward, (2006), pp.108, 113.
107 Interview, Simon MacDonald, 08.03.07.
108 Interview, Jack Straw, 26.03.07.
109 Interview, Lord Boyce, 17.02.07.
110 Gordon and Trainor (2006), p.463.

111 Interview, John Sawers, 21.10.06.
112 Interview, Donald Rumsfeld, 15.08.07.
113 Private interview.
114 Interview, Condoleezza Rice, 11.06.07.
115 Woodward (2006), pp.186–7.
116 Interview, Sir Rob Fry, 24.10.06.
117 Interview, John Sawers, 21.10.06.
118 Sawers telegram, 11.05.03 cited in Gordon and Trainor (2006), p.574.
119 Ibid.
120 Private interview.
121 Interview, John Sawers, 21.10.06.
122 Private interview.
123 Sawers telegram, 11.05.03 cited in Gordon and Trainor (2006), p.575.
124 Campbell (2007), p.690.
125 Private interview.
126 Sawers telegram, 11.05.03 cited in Gordon and Trainor (2006), p.575.
127 Private interview.
128 Private interview.
129 Interview, John Sawers, 26.01.07.
130 *Guardian*, 27.05.06.
131 Woodward (2006), p.194.
132 Interview, John Sawers, 26.01.07.
133 Interview, John Sawers, 21.10.06.
134 Interview, Sir Rob Fry.
135 Bremer (2006), p.40.
136 Private interview.
137 Interview, Lawrence Wilkerson, 10.07.07.
138 Interview, John Sawers, 26.01.07.
139 Interview, Lord Boyce, 17.02.07.
140 Interview, John Sawers, 21.10.06.
141 Private interview.
142 Private interview.
143 Private interview.
144 Peter Mandelson, cited in 'The Rise and Fall of Tony Blair', Channel 4 Television, 20.06.07.
145 Private interview.
146 Private interview.
147 *Guardian*, 30.04.03.
148 Campbell (2007), pp.693–5.
149 Short (2004), p.209.
150 Private interview.
151 Campbell (2007), p.689.
152 Private interview.
153 Private interview.
154 Bremer (2006), pp.78–9.
155 Private interview.
156 Private interview.
157 Private interview.
158 Campbell (2007), p.701.
159 Private interview.
160 Interview, John Sawers, 21.10.06.
161 Ibid.
162 Private interview.
163 *Independent*, 30.05.03.
164 Interview, John Sawers, 26.01.07.
165 Ibid.
166 Andrew Gilligan, *Today*, BBC Radio 4, 29.05.03.
167 *Mail on Sunday*, 01.06.03.
168 Private interview.
169 Private interview.
170 Interview, Godric Smith, 13.03.07.
171 'Joint press conference in Poland: PM and Polish PM Leszek Miller', 30.05.03.
172 Interview, Jeremy Heywood, 12.03.07.
173 Private interview.
174 Private interview.
175 'PM says he is "100 per cent" behind Iraq evidence – G8 summit', 02.06.03.
176 Interview, Lawrence Wilkerson, 10.07.07.
177 *Financial Times*, 27.06.03.
178 *Guardian*, 30.06.03.
179 *Jerusalem Post*, 16.07.03.
180 Ibid.
181 Press conference with President Bush at the White House, 17.07.03.
182 Private interview.
183 Private interview.
184 Campbell (2007), p.713.
185 Interview, Godric Smith, 13.03.07.
186 Private interview.
187 Private interview.
188 Tony Blair, Address to Joint Session of Congress, 17.07.03.
189 Ibid.
190 Ibid.
191 Ibid.
192 Interview, Godric Smith, 13.03.07.
193 *Daily Mirror*, 18.07.03.
194 *Daily Mail*, 18.07.03.
195 *The Times*, 18.07.03.
196 *Washington Post*, 18.07.03.
197 Private interview.
198 Interview, Godric Smith, 13.03.07.

8: Losing My Agenda

1 Private interview.
2 Private interview.
3 Private interview.
4 Private interview.
5 Private interview.
6 Private interview.
7 *Guardian Unlimited*, 07.01.03.
8 *The Times*, 30.01.03.
9 Private interview.
10 Private interview.
11 Interview, Ken Livingstone, 21.05.07.
12 Private correspondence.
13 Interview, Peter Hyman, 22.02.07.

14 Private interview.
15 Interview, Sir John Kerr, 26.09.03.
16 Interview, Sir Stephen Wall, 12.12.06; Private Interview.
17 Private interview.
18 Scott (2004), p.223.
19 Campbell (2007), pp.552–3.
20 Private interview.
21 Private papers.
22 Interview, Baroness Morgan, 19.04.07.
23 Peston (2006), p.228.
24 Campbell (2007), p.592.
25 Private information.
26 Private interview.
27 Short (2004), pp.124–5; 'Blair: The Inside Story', BBC TV, 06.03.07.
28 Private interviews.
29 Blunkett (2006), pp.379–80.
30 Private interview.
31 Interview, Peter Hyman, 22.02.07.
32 Private interview.
33 Private information.
34 Stephens (2004), pp.182–6.
35 Private interview.
36 Scott (2004), p.223.
37 Peston (2006), p.233.
38 Ibid., p.234.
39 *Guardian*, 10.06.03.
40 Private interview.
41 Interview, Lord Turnbull, 17.01.07.
42 Interview, Jeremy Heywood, 09.02.07.
43 Private interview.
44 Private interview.
45 Private interview.
46 Private interview.
47 Private interview.
48 Interview, Sir Stephen Wall, 12.12.06.
49 Private interview.
50 Private interview.
51 Private information.
52 Peston (2006), p.233–7.
53 Private interview.
54 Private interview.
55 Private interview.
56 Private interview.
57 Private interview.
58 Private interview.
59 Private information.
60 Peston (2006), p.238; Private interviews.
61 Ibid.
62 Private interview.
63 Interview, Peter Hyman, 22.02.07.
64 Interview, Sir Stephen Wall, 12.12.06.
65 Private interview.
66 Private information.
67 Peston (2006), p.239.
68 Blunkett (2006), p.480.
69 Scott (2004), p.224.
70 Interview, Sir Stephen Wall, 12.12.06.
71 Private interview.
72 Blunkett (2006), p.501.
73 Interview, Sir Stephen Wall, 12.12.06.
74 Interview, Peter Hyman, 22.02.07.
75 Interview, Sir Stephen Wall, 12.12.06.
76 Scott (2004), p.226.
77 Interview, Sir Stephen Wall, 12.12.06.
78 Keegan (2003), p.328.
79 Blunkett (2006), p.511.
80 Private interview.
81 Private interview.
82 'The Rise and Fall of Tony Blair', Channel 4, 23.06.07.
83 Interview, Sir Stephen Wall, 12.12.06.
84 Ibid.
85 Private interview.
86 Interview, Lord Turnbull, 24.04.07.
87 Private interview.
88 Private information.
89 Private interview.
90 Private interview.
91 Interview, Lord Falconer, 19.04.07.
92 *Guardian*, 14.06.03.
93 Private interview.
94 Campbell (2007), p.704.
95 Ibid.
96 Private interview.
97 Private interview.
98 Blunkett (2006), p.512.
99 Interview, Paul Corrigan, 06.02.07.
100 Interview, Lord Falconer, 19.04.07.
101 Private interview.
102 Private interview.
103 Campbell (2007), p.705; Private interview.
104 Private interview.
105 Interview, Godric Smith, 13.03.07.
106 Private interview.
107 Interview, Lord Turnbull, 04.04.07.
108 Interview, Jeremy Heywood, 19.04.07.
109 Interview, Godric Smith, 13.03.07.
110 Interview, Lord Falconer, 19.04.07.
111 Campbell (2007), pp.724–5.
112 *Independent*, 20.07.03.
113 *Scotland on Sunday*, 20.07.03.
114 Campbell (2007), pp.722–3.
115 Ibid.
116 Private interview.
117 Private interview.
118 Private interview.
119 Interview, Alan Milburn, 08.11.06.
120 Private information.

121 Interview, Sir Michael Barber, 06.12.06.
122 Ibid.
123 'Blair: The Inside Story', BBC TV, 06.03.07.
124 Private interview.
125 Private interview.
126 Private interview.
127 Private interview.
128 Interview, Sir Michael Barber, 06.12.06.
129 Private interview.
130 Interview, David Hill, 13.03.07.
131 Private information.
132 Private interview.
133 Private interview.
134 Interview, Matthew Taylor, 02.01.07.
135 Interview, Geoff Mulgan, 23.03.07.
136 Private interview.
137 Private interview.
138 Private interview.
139 Private interview.
140 Hyman (2005), pp.10–11.
141 Private interview.
142 Private interview.
143 Private interview.
144 Hyman (2005), p.14.
145 Private interview.
146 Private interview.
147 Private interview.
148 Hyman (2005), pp.16–17.
149 *Sunday Times*, 09.11.03.
150 Private interview.
151 Private interview.
152 Private interview.
153 Private interview.
154 Private interview.
155 *Sunday Telegraph*, 09.11.03.
156 Private interview.
157 *Sunday Times*, 09.11.03.
158 Peston (2006), p.335.
159 *Sunday Telegraph*, 09.11.03.
160 Private interview.
161 Letter, John Prescott to author, 11.01.07.
162 Interview, John Prescott, 03.01.07.
163 *Observer*, 09.11.03.
164 Private interview.
165 Private interview.
166 Private interview.
167 Private interview.
168 Peston, (2006), p.335.
169 Private interview.
170 Campbell (2007), p.592.
171 Private interview.
172 Interview, David Blunkett, 08.11.06.
173 Interview, Baroness Morgan, 08.11.06.
174 Tom Bower (2004), p.434–5.
175 Private interview.

9: The Descent

1 Bremer (2006), p.142.
2 Private interview.
3 Interview, Edward Chaplin, 02.05.07.
4 Interview, Sir Nigel Sheinwald, 24.11.06.
5 Interview, Sir Jeremy Greenstock, 09.08.06.
6 Private interview.
7 Sir Jeremy Greenstock, cited in 'Blair: The Inside Story', BBC TV, 27.02.07.
8 Private interview.
9 Interview, Sir Rob Fry, 24.01.07.
10 Ibid.
11 Private interview.
12 Private interview.
13 Private interview.
14 Interview, Steve Hadley, 16.04.07
15 Interview, Elizabeth Jones, 06.03.07
16 Private interview.
17 Interview, Steve Hadley, 16.04.07
18 Interview, Donald Rumsfeld, 15.08.07
19 Private interview.
20 Interview, Sir Nigel Sheinwald, 22.03.07
21 Private interview.
22 Private interview.
23 Interview, Lord Jay, 31.05.07
24 *Guardian*, 25.10.03
25 Private interview.
26 Private interview.
27 Private interview.
28 *Independent*, 11.11.03.
29 Private interview.
30 Private interview.
31 'President Bush discusses Iraq policy at Whitehall Palace in London', 19.11.03.
32 Private interview.
33 Interview, Elizabeth Jones, 29.06.07
34 *Sunday Telegraph*, 23.11.03.
35 Interview, Karl Rove, 06.06.07.
36 *Scotsman*, 21.11.03.
37 Interview, Elizabeth Jones, 29.06.07.
38 Private interview.
39 Private interview.
40 Private interview.
41 Private interview.
42 Private interview.
43 Interview, Lawrence Wilkerson, 29.06.07.
44 Interview, John Burton, 02.10.06.
45 Ibid.
46 Justin Webb, 'Reporters' log: Bush in Britain', 21.11.03.
47 Interview, John Sawers, 13.02.07.
48 Private interview.
49 Private interview.

50 For the full twists and turns of Gaddafi's disarmament striptease see Gordon Corera's excellent *Shopping for Bombs* (2006).
51 Peston (2006), p.297; Private correspondence.
52 Interview, Paul Corrigan, 06.02.07.
53 Private papers.
54 Private correspondence.
55 Private correspondence.
56 Private correspondence.
57 Private correspondence.
58 *The Times*, 07.08.02.
59 Peston (2006), p.298.
60 Private correspondence.
61 *Guardian*, 09.09.02.
62 Interview, Paul Corrigan, 06.02.07.
63 Peston (2006), pp.300–1.
64 Private interview.
65 Peston (2006), pp.301–2; Private correspondence.
66 Private interview.
67 *The Times*, 02.10.02.
68 Ibid.
69 Peston (2006), pp.301–2.
70 *Independent*, 02.10.02.
71 Interview, Alan Milburn, 13.12.06.
72 Private interview.
73 Private interview.
74 Private interview.
75 Private papers.
76 Private interview.
77 Private interview.
78 Private interview.
79 Private correspondence.
80 *Guardian*, 17.10.02.
81 Bower (2005), p.417.
82 *Observer*, 03.11.02.
83 Peston (2006), p.303.
84 Interview, Michael Howard, 04.07.07.
85 Campbell (2007), p.695.
86 Private interview.
87 Private interview.
88 Private interview.
89 *Guardian*, 01.10.03.
90 Campbell (2007), p.706.
91 Ibid.
92 Ibid.
93 Private interview.
94 Private interview.
95 Private information.
96 Interview, Baroness Morgan, 16.05.07.
97 Interview, Godric Smith, 13.03.07.
98 Private interview.
99 Interview, Robert Hill, 24.01.07.
100 Interview, Geoff Mulgan, 21.07.03.
101 Private papers; Private interview.
102 Private interview.
103 Private interview.
104 Peston (2006), p.313.
105 Private interview.
106 Private papers.
107 Private interview.
108 Interview, Charles Clarke, 02.03.04.
109 Interview, Robert Hill, 24.01.07.
110 Ibid.
111 Private papers.
112 Peston (2006), p.314.
113 Private interview.
114 Interview, John Prescott, 03.01.07.
115 Private interview.
116 Private papers.
117 Private papers.
118 Private interview.
119 Private interview.
120 Private papers.
121 *Guardian*, 05.12.03.
122 Private interview.
123 Private interview.
124 Private interview.
125 Private interview.
126 Alan Johnson, cited in 'Blair: The Inside Story', BBC TV, 06.03.07.
127 'Blair: The Inside Story', BBC TV, 06.03.07.
128 Peston (2006), pp.316–18.
129 Private interview.
130 Private interview.
131 Blunkett (2006), pp.581–3.
132 Bower (2005), pp.437–8.
133 Interview, Baroness Morgan, 14.03.07.
134 Interview, Geoff Mulgan, 22.03.07.
135 Private interview.
136 Private interview.
137 Peston (2006), pp.316–18.
138 *Independent on Sunday*, 01.02.04.
139 Interview, Hilary Armstrong, 22.03.07.
140 Private interview.
141 Blunkett (2006), p.583.
142 'Blair: The Inside Story', BBC TV, 06.03.07.
143 Private interview.
144 Private interview.
145 *The Times*, 29.01.04.
146 Campbell (2007), p.753.
147 Interview, David Hill, 13.03.07.
148 Interview, Godric Smith, 13.03.07.
149 Ibid.
150 Interview, David Hill, 13.03.07.
151 Ibid.
152 Private interview.
153 Private correspondence.
154 *Independent on Sunday*, 01.02.04.
155 *Guardian*, 29.01.04.
156 Private interview.
157 Private interview.
158 Private interview.
159 Private interview.

160 Prime Minister's Monthly Downing Street Press Conference, 02.12.03.
161 Bremer (2006), pp.253–4.
162 *Guardian*, 14.12.03.
163 Interview, Baroness Morgan, 16.05.07.
164 Private interview.
165 Interview, Sir Nigel Sheinwald, 08.12.06.
166 Interview, Sir Rob Fry, 24.01.07.
167 Interview, John Sawers, 21.10.06.
168 Prime Minister's Monthly Downing Street Press Conference, 26.02.04.
169 Interview, Sir Rob Fry, 21.07.07.
170 Interview, Sir Rob Fry, 24.01.07.
171 Private interview.
172 Interview, Sir Jeremy Greenstock, 09.08.06.
173 Ibid.
174 Interview, Lawrence Wilkerson, 29.06.07.
175 Interview, Sir Jeremy Greenstock, 09.08.06.
176 Ibid.
177 Ibid.
178 Bremer (2006), pp.267–70.
179 *Guardian*, 05.01.04.
180 'PM thanks armed forces in Basra visit', 04.01.04.
181 Private interview.
182 Interview, Lord Jay, 31.05.07.
183 Private interview.
184 *Reuters*, 19.03.04.
185 Bremer (2006), pp.316–17.
186 Woodward (2006), p.297.
187 Bremer (2006), p.335.
188 Ibid., p.337.
189 Private interview.
190 Private interview.
191 Bremer (2006), p.339.
192 Private interview.
193 *Independent*, 17.04.04.
194 Press Conference with President Bush in Washington, 16.04.04.
195 Bremer (2006), p.342.
196 Statement to Parliament on PM's visit to America, 19.04.04.
197 Interview, Lord Turnbull, 24.04.07.
198 Interview, John Sawers, 21.10.06.

10: The Recovery

1 Interview, Jack Straw, 02.04.07.
2 Private interview.
3 Private interview.
4 Interview, Sir Stephen Wall, 06.03.07.
5 Interview, Jack Straw, 02.04.07.
6 Private interview.
7 Private interview.
8 Private interview.
9 Private interview.
10 Private interview.
11 *Observer*, 14.12.03.
12 Interview, John Prescott, 30.04.04.
13 *News of the World*, 28.03.04.
14 *Independent on Sunday*, 25.04.04.
15 Private interview.
16 Private interview.
17 Interview, Baroness Morgan, 16.05.07.
18 Interview, John Prescott, 30.04.04.
19 Private interview.
20 Peston (2006), p.350; Private interview.
21 Private interview.
22 Interview, Sir Stephen Wall, 06.03.07.
23 Private interview.
24 *Guardian*, 16.04.04.
25 Private information.
26 *Sun*, 15.04.04.
27 *The Times*, 16.04.04.
28 Private interview.
29 Interview, Jack Straw, 02.04.07.
30 Private interview.
31 *Sunday Times*, 25.04.04.
32 Private interview.
33 *Hansard*, 20.04.04, Col.157.
34 Interview, Kim Darroch, 30.10.06.
35 Private interview.
36 Private interview.
37 Interview, Tessa Jowell, 06.05.07.
38 Private interview.
39 Private interview.
40 Private interview.
41 Interview, Baroness Morgan, 16.05.07.
42 Ibid.
43 Peston (2006), p.338.
44 Private interview.
45 Interview, Lord Gould, 12.02.07.
46 Interview, Tessa Jowell, 26.03.07.
47 Private interview.
48 Private interview.
49 Private interview.
50 Private interview.
51 Private interview.
52 Private interviews.
53 Private interview.
54 Blunkett (2006), p.637.
55 Private interview.
56 Private interview.
57 Private interview.
58 Private interview.
59 Interview, Tessa Jowell, 26.03.07.
60 Private interview.
61 Private interview.
62 Interview, Patricia Hewitt, 30.10.06.
63 Interview, Peter Hain, 07.12.06.
64 Private interview.
65 Interview, John Burton, 02.10.06.

66 Private interview.
67 Interview, Lord Falconer, 19.04.07.
68 Private interview.
69 Private interview; Peston (2005), p.337.
70 Interview, David Blunkett, 28.03.07.
71 Private correspondence.
72 Private interview.
73 Peston (2006), p.338.
74 Private interview.
75 Interview, Lord Turnbull, 05.07.06.
76 Interview, John Burton, 02.10.06.
77 Interview, David Hill, 13.03.07.
78 Blunkett (2006), p.638.
79 Interview, Geoff Mulgan, 23.03.07.
80 *Sunday Times*, 16.05.04.
81 Private interview.
82 *Sunday Times*, 16.05.04.
83 *The Times*, 15.05.04.
84 Private interview.
85 *Guardian*, 18.05.04.
86 Interview, Tom Kelly, 21.05.07.
87 Interview, Ivan Rogers, 20.07.06.
88 Private interview.
89 Interview, Tom Kelly, 21.05.07.
90 Blunkett (2006), p.648; *Observer*, 13.06.04.
91 Private interview.
92 Private interview.
93 Peston (2006), p.340.
94 Private interview.
95 Private interview.
96 Private interview.
97 Private interview.

11: Back in Charge

1 Interview, Sir Stephen Wall, 06.03.07.
2 Private interview.
3 Private interview.
4 Interview, Kim Darroch, 24.11.06.
5 Private interview.
6 Private interview.
7 Interview, Sir Stephen Wall, 06.03.07.
8 Private interview.
9 Interview, Tom Kelly, 27.02.07.
10 Private interview.
11 Private interview.
12 Interview, Kim Darroch, 30.10.07.
13 Interview, Sir Stephen Wall, 06.03.07.
14 Private interview.
15 Private interview.
16 Private interview.
17 Private interview.
18 Private interview.
19 Interview, Tom Kelly, 27.02.07.
20 *Sunday Telegraph*, 20.06.04.
21 Private interview.
22 *Sunday Telegraph*, 20.06.04.
23 Private interview.
24 *Le Monde*, 26.06.04.
25 *Der Spiegel*, 25.06.04.
26 *El Mundo*, 20.06.04.
27 Private interview.
28 Private interview.
29 Interview, Sir John Grant, 23.03.07.
30 'PM's UN Speech on Iraq in Georgia', 08.06.04.
31 Interview, Lord Jay, 31.05.07
32 Interview, Sir Jeremy Greenstock, 09.08.06.
33 Private interview.
34 Interview, John Bolton, 10.07.07.
35 Bremer (2006), pp.384–5.
36 Private correspondence.
37 Private interview.
38 Bremer (2006), p.391.
39 *Guardian*, 29.06.04.
40 Bremer (2006), p.394.
41 *Independent*, 29.06.04.
42 Interview, David Hill, 13.03.07.
43 Interview, Lord Turnbull, 04.04.07.
44 Interview, Lord Butler, 07.02.07.
45 Interview, Lord Turnbull, 04.04.07.
46 Private interview.
47 Kampfner (2004), p.373.
48 Interview, Lord Butler, 07.02.07.
49 Private interview.
50 Private correspondence.
51 Correspondence with author, Lord Butler.
52 Private interview.
53 Private interview.
54 Private interview.
55 Interview, Lord Butler, 07.02.07.
56 Interview, David Hill, 13.03.07.
57 *Sunday Times*, 18.07.04.
58 Butler Report (2004), p.110.
59 Ibid., p.114.
60 Interview, Lord Butler, 07.02.07.
61 Ibid.
62 Private interview.
63 Private interview.
64 Private interview.
65 Interview, Tom Kelly, 27.02.07.
66 *Guardian*, 14.07.04.
67 *Sunday Telegraph*, 18.07.04.
68 *Sunday Times*, 18.07.04.
69 Private interview.
70 Interview, Lord Birt, 06.06.07.
71 Private interview.
72 *Guardian*, 25.02.04.
73 Private interview.
74 Interview, Sir Michael Barber, 06.12.06.
75 Ibid.
76 Interview, Lord Birt, 06.06.07.
77 Correspondence with author, Ivan Rogers, 07.09.07.
78 Interview, Lord Birt, 06.08.07.

79 Private interview.
80 Private interview.
81 Interview, Ivan Rogers, 15.02.07.
82 *Guardian*, 07.07.04.
83 Private interview.
84 Private interview.
85 *Guardian*, 25.06.04.
86 Interview, Sir Michael Barber, 06.12.06.
87 Ibid.
88 Ibid.
89 Private papers.
90 Private correspondence with author.
91 Private interview.
92 Interview, Ivan Rogers, 15.02.07.
93 Private interview; private correspondence with author.
94 Interview, Sir Michael Barber, 06.12.06.
95 Private interview.
96 Private interview
97 Private interview.
98 Private interview.
99 Private interview.
100 Private correspondence with author.
101 Private information.
102 Private interview.
103 *Independent*, 13.07.04.
104 Bower (2005), p.448.
105 Private interview.
106 Private interview.
107 Private interview.
108 Interview, John Burton, 02.10.06.
109 Private interview.
110 Private interview.
111 Private interview.
112 Interview, Stephen Byers, 04.06.07.
113 *Sunday Telegraph*, 25.07.04.
114 *Independent on Sunday*, 25.07.04.
115 Interview, Geoff Mulgan, 23.03.07.
116 Interview, Alan Milburn, 08.11.06.
117 Private interview.
118 Private interview.
119 Interview, Alan Milburn, 08.11.06.
120 Private interview.
121 Peston (2006), p.343.
122 Private interview.
123 Interview, Ivan Rogers, 15.02.07.
124 *Independent*, 10.08.04.
125 Interview, John Burton, 02.10.06.
126 Interview, David Hill, 13.03.07.
127 Private interview.
128 Private interview.
129 Interview, Lord Turnbull, 05.07.06.
130 Interview, Ivan Rogers, 20.07.06
131 Private interview.
132 Interview, Alan Milburn, 08.11.06.
133 Interview, David Blunkett, 08.11.06.
134 Private interview.
135 *Sunday Times*, 05.09.04.
135 Blunkett (2006), p.686.
137 Interview, Alan Milburn, 08.11.06.
138 Private correspondence.
139 Private interview.
140 Private interview.
141 *Sunday Times*, 12.09.04.
142 Private interview.
143 *Sunday Times*, 12.09.04.
144 Interview, Alan Milburn, 08.11.06.
145 *Observer*, 12.09.04.
146 Private interview.
147 Private interview.
148 Peston (2006), pp.344–5.
149 Private interview.
150 Private interview.
151 Private interview.
152 *Observer*, 03.10.04.
153 Peston (2006), pp.345–6.
154 *Guardian*, 28.09.04.
155 Ibid.
156 *The Times*, 29.09.04.
157 *Guardian*, 29.09.04.
158 *The Times*, 29.09.04.
159 Peston (2006), p.346.
160 Ibid., p.347.
161 Ibid.
162 Private interview.
163 Private interview.
164 Private interview.
165 Interview, Ivan Rogers, 20.07.06
166 Private interview.
167 Private interview.
168 Private interview.
169 Private interview.
170 Interview, David Hill, 06.03.07.
171 Interview, David Hill, 12.06.07
172 Private interview.
173 Interview, Lord Turnbull, 05.07.06.
174 Private interview.
175 Interview, Peter Hain, 07.12.06.
176 Private interview.
177 Private interview.
178 Private interview.
179 Private interview; *Observer*, 03.10.04
180 *Observer*, 03.10.04.
181 Interview, Peter Hain, 07.12.06.
182 Interview, Alan Milburn, 08.11.06.
183 Alan Milburn, cited in 'The Rise and Fall of Tony Blair', Channel 4, 20.06.07.
184 Interview, Lord Turnbull, 05.07.06.
185 Private interview.

12: Crafting a Bold Future

1 Peston (2006), p.348.
2 Ibid., pp.348–9.
3 Peston (2006), p.349; Private interview.
4 Private interview.
5 Private interview.
6 Private interview.

7 *Sunday Telegraph*, 28.11.04.
8 Private interview.
9 *Guardian*, 24.11.04.
10 Ibid., 23.11.04.
11 *The Times*, 24.11.04.
12 *Independent*, 24.11.04.
13 Barber (2007), pp.232–3.
14 Ibid., pp.236–7.
15 *Sunday Telegraph*, 28.11.04.
16 Private interview.
17 *Daily Mail*, 06.12.04; *Daily Telegraph*, 07.12.04.
18 Interview, David Blunkett, 28.03.07.
19 Private interviews.
20 Blunkett (2006), p.736.
21 Interview, Huw Evans, 02.03.07.
22 Private interview.
23 Interview, Huw Evans, 02.03.07.
24 Blunkett (2006), p.736.
25 Private interviews.
26 Private interview.
27 Private interview.
28 Private interview.
29 Private interview.
30 Private interview.
31 Private interview.
32 Private interview.
33 Private interview.
34 Private interview.
35 Private interview.
36 *Sunday Telegraph*, 16.01.05.
37 *Observer*, 16.01.05.
38 Interview, Nick Brown, 13.07.06.
39 *Sunday Telegraph*, 16.01.05.
40 *Independent*, 17.09.04.
41 Private interview.
42 Private interview.
43 Private interview.
44 Private interview.
45 Interview, Tom Kelly, 21.05.07.
46 Private interview.
47 Private interview.
48 Interview, Tom Kelly, 21.05.07.
49 Ibid.
50 *Independent*, 17.09.04.
51 Private interview
52 Private interview
53 Private interview
54 Interview, Tom Kelly, 06.02.07.
55 Private interview.
56 Private interview.
57 Private interview.
58 Private interview.
59 Ibid.
60 Private interview.
61 Private interview.
62 Interview, Tom Kelly, 06.02.07.
63 Private interview.
64 Private interview.
65 Private interview.
66 Private interview.
67 Private interview.
68 Interview, Tom Kelly, 06.02.07.
69 Private interview.
70 Private interview.
71 Private interview.
72 Interview, Condoleezza Rice, 11.06.07.
73 Interview, Dan Fried, 14.07.07.
74 Private interview.
75 Interview, Colin Powell, 01.02.07.
76 Interview, Condoleezza Rice, 11.06.07.
77 Private interview.
78 *Guardian*, 27.04.04.
79 Ibid., 21.07.04.
80 Private interview.
81 Private interview.
82 Private interview.
83 Woodward (2006), pp.346–7.
84 Private interview.
85 Private interview.
86 Interview, Sir David Manning, 27.10.06.
87 Interview, Condoleezza Rice, 14.08.07.
88 Private interview.
89 Private interview.
90 Interview, Dan Fried, 14.07.07.
91 Interview, Sir David Manning, 27.10.06.
92 Private interview.
93 'US and UK Joint Statement Concerning the Middle East Peace Process', 12.11.04.
94 *Independent*, 13.11.04.
95 Interview, Paul 'PJ' Johnston, 19.10.06.
96 Private interview.
97 Interview, John Sawers, 26.01.07
98 Private interview.
99 Woodward (2006), p.371.
100 *Guardian*, 31.01.05.
101 Private interview.
102 Interview, Sir David Manning, 27.10.06.
103 Interview, John Bolton, 10.07.07.
104 Private interview.
105 Private interview.
106 Private interview.
107 Private interview.
108 Private interview.
109 Private interviews.
110 Private interview.
111 Private correspondence.
112 Private interview.
113 Interview, John Sawers, 13.01.07.
114 Private interview.
115 Interview, Lord Jay, 02.08.06.
116 Private interview.
117 Private interview.
118 Interview, Lord Jay, 02.08.06.

119 Interview, Liz Lloyd, 27.02.07.
120 Private interview.
121 Interview, Lord Jay, 02.08.06.
122 Interview, Laurie Lee, 02.02.07.
123 Private interview.
124 Private interview.
125 Interview, Lawrence Wilkerson, 10.07.07.
126 Private interview.
127 Interview, Dan Fried, 14.07.07.
128 Interview, Elizabeth Jones, 06.03.07.
129 Interview, Condoleezza Rice, 14.08.07.
130 Interview, Karl Rove, 19.03.07.
131 Private interview.
132 Interview, Faryar Shirzad, 01.08.07.
133 *Independent*, 02.01.05.
134 'Joint findings on lessons from handling of the response to the Indian Ocean tsunami', National Audit Office/FCO, October 2005.
135 Interview, Laurie Lee, 05.02.07.
136 Interview, Lord Jay, 02.08.06.
137 *Independent*, 31.12.04.
138 *The Times*, 07.01.05.
139 Private interview.
140 Interview, Laurie Lee, 05.02.07.
141 Interview, John Sawers, 13.01.07.
142 BBC News Online, 06.09.00.
143 Private interview.
144 Private interview; *Independent*, 11.03.05.
145 Interview, Justin Forsyth, 19.09.06.
146 Ibid.
147 Interview, Laurie Lee, 02.02.07.
148 Interview, John Simon, 16.02.07.
149 Interview, Nick Brown, 13.07.06.
150 Interview, Justin Forsyth, 19.09.06.
151 Ibid; Interview, Laurie Lee, 02.02.07.
152 Interview, Laurie Lee, 02.02.07.
153 Private interview.
154 Private interview.
155 Interview, Sir David King, 23.02.07.
156 Private interview.
157 Interview, Nick Rowley, 14.02.07.
158 Ibid.
159 Interview, Lord Jay, 02.08.06.
160 Interview, Nick Rowley, 23.02.07.
161 Interview, Nick Rowley, 14.02.07.
162 Ibid.
163 Private interview.
164 Private interview.
165 *Daily Telegraph*, 15.09.04.
166 Interview, Sir David King, 23.02.07.
167 *The Economist*, 29.12.04.
168 Private interview.
169 Interview, Lord Jay, 31.05.07.
170 Private interview.
171 Private interview.
172 *The Times*, 20.01.05.

173 Private interview.
174 Private interview.
176 Interview, Lord Birt, 06.06.07.
176 Interview, Lord Birt, 19.07.07.
177 Private interview.
178 Interview, Lord Birt, 19.07.07.
179 Private interview.
180 Private interview.
181 *The Times*, 25.07.07.
182 Interview, Ivan Rogers, 16.07.07.
183 Private interview.
184 Private interview.
185 Private interview.
186 Private interview.
187 Private correspondence.
188 *Sunday Times*, 16.01.05.
189 Private interview.
190 *Independent*, 12.07.07.
191 Private interview.
192 Private information.
193 Private interviews.
194 Private interview.
195 Private interview.
196 Private interview.
197 Interview, Matthew Taylor, 02.01.07.
198 *The Times*, 16.01.05.
199 *Guardian*, 18.03.05; *Sunday Telegraph*, 20.03.05.
200 Private interview.

13: General Election, 2005

1 Private interview.
2 Interview, Alan Milburn, 08.11.06.
3 Interview, Ivan Rogers, 15.02.07.
4 Private information.
5 Private interview.
6 Private interview.
7 Private interview.
8 Interview, Alan Milburn, 08.11.06.
9 Private interview.
10 Private interview.
11 Private interview.
12 *The Times*, 20.01.05.
13 Private interview.
14 Private interview.
15 Private interview.
16 Private interview.
17 Interview, Stephen Byers, 04.07.06.
18 Interview, Alan Milburn, 08.11.06.
19 Private interview.
20 Interview, David Bennett, 10.05.07; *Britain: Forward Not Back*, p.25.
21 Interview, Matthew Taylor, 02.01.07.
22 Blunkett (2006), p.767.
23 Private interview.
24 Interview, Matthew Taylor, 02.01.07.
25 Private correspondence.
26 Kavanagh and Butler (2005), p.68.
27 *Sunday Times*, 27.02.05.
28 Private interview.

29 Private interview.
30 Private interview.
31 Private interview.
32 *Sunday Times*, 27.02.05.
33 Private interview.
34 Interview, Nick Brown, 13.07.06.
35 Private correspondence.
36 Private interview.
37 Private correspondence.
38 *The Times*, 19.03.05.
39 *Sunday Telegraph*, 20.03.05.
40 Interview, John Prescott, 03.01.07.
41 Interview, Matthew Taylor, 02.01.07.
42 Correspondence with author, Alastair Campbell, 04.06.07; Private interview.
43 Private interview.
44 Private interview.
45 *Observer*, 24.04.05.
46 Private interview.
47 Interview, Matthew Taylor, 02.01.07.
48 Private interview.
49 Interview, David Blunkett, 08.11.06; Kavanagh and Butler (2005), p.58.
50 Private interview.
51 Wring *et al.* (2007), pp.23–4.
52 Private information.
53 Private correspondence.
54 Kavanagh and Butler (2005), p.75.
55 Interview, Huw Evans, 02.03.07.
56 Kavanagh and Butler (2005), p.111.
57 Interview, David Hill, 12.06.07.
58 Private interview.
59 Private interview.
60 Private interview.
61 See 'Labour's Political Strategy' in Wring *et al.* (2007) for Gould's account of Labour's election strategy.
62 Private correspondence.
63 Private interview.
64 *The Times*, 07.05.05.
65 Private interview.
66 Interview, Huw Evans, 02.03.07.
67 Private interview.
68 *Guardian*, 27.04.05.
69 Interview, David Hill, 13.03.07.
70 Interview, Nick Rowley, 23.02.07.
71 Ibid.
72 Interview, Huw Evans, 02.03.07.
73 *The Times*, 25.04.05.
74 Private correspondence.
75 Kavanagh and Butler (2005), p.57.
76 Private interview.
77 Kavanagh and Butler (2005), p.72.
78 Ibid., p.96.
79 Private correspondence.
80 Private interview.
81 Interview, Alan Milburn, 08.11.06.
82 Interview, Peter Hain, 07.12.06.
83 Private interview.
84 Private interview
85 Interview, Baroness Morgan, 15.02.07.
86 Interview, Huw Evans, 02.03.07.
87 *Sunday Times*, 01.05.05.
88 Interview, Baroness Morgan, 14.03.07.
89 *Sunday Times*, 01.05.05.
90 Interview, Huw Evans, 02.03.07.
91 Interview, Nick Rowley, 23.02.07.
92 Interview, David Blunkett, 08.11.06.
93 Private interview.
94 Wring *et al.* (2007), p.22.
95 Interview, John Burton, 02.10.06.
96 *Independent*, 05.05.05.
97 Private interview.
98 Private interview.
99 Private interview.
100 Private interviews.
101 Private interview.
102 Private interview.
103 Interview, Baroness Morgan, 14.03.07.
104 Private interview.
105 Private interview.
106 Interview, John Burton, 02.10.06.
107 Private interview.
108 Sally Morgan, cited in *The Rise and Fall of Tony Blair*, Channel 4, 25.06.07.
109 Private interview.
110 Private interview.
111 *Guardian*, 06.05.05.
112 Private interview.
113 Private interviews.
114 Private interview.
115 *The Times*, 07.05.05.
116 Private interview.
117 Interview, Peter Watt, 22.03.07.
118 *The Times*, 07.05.05.
119 Private interview.
120 Interview, Lord Birt, 06.06.07.
121 Interview, David Hill, 13.03.07.
122 Private interview.
123 Private interview.
124 Private interview.
125 Private interview.
126 Private interview.
127 Private interview.
128 Private interview.
129 Interview, Matthew Taylor, 13.03.07
130 Private correspondence with author.
131 Private interview.
132 Private interview.
133 Private interview.
134 Private interview.
135 Private interview.
136 Private interview.
137 Private interview.
138 Private interview.
139 Private interview.

140 Private interview.
141 Private interview.
142 Interview, Nick Brown, 13.07.06.
143 Private interview.
144 Private interview.
145 Private interview.
146 Private interview.
147 Private interview.
148 *Observer*, 08.05.05.
140 Private interview.
150 Private interview; *Guardian*, 13.05.05.
151 Private interview.
152 Andrew Rawnsley, *Observer*, 08.05.05.
153 *Independent on Sunday*, 08.05.05.
154 *Scotsman*, 12.05.05.
155 Private interview.
156 Private interview; *Scotsman*, 12.05.05.
157 Private interview.
158 Private interview.
159 Private interview.
160 Interview, Matthew Taylor, 02.01.07.

14: Second Honeymoon

1 Private interview.
2 Private interview.
3 Interview, Stephen Byers, 04.07.06.
4 Private correspondence.
5 Private interview.
6 Private interview.
7 Private interview.
8 Private interview
9 *Daily Telegraph*, 31.05.05.
10 Interview, Kim Darroch, 24.11.06.
11 Private interview.
12 Private interview.
13 *Evening Standard*, 06.06.05.
14 Private interview.
15 Private interview.
16 Private interview.
17 Private interview.
18 Private interview.
19 Private interview.
20 *Financial Times*, 15.06.05.
21 Private interview.
22 Private correspondence.
23 Private interview.
24 Private interview.
25 Private interview.
26 Private interview.
27 Private interview.
28 Private interview.
29 Private interview.
30 'Press Conference following Brussels EU Summit', 18.06.05.
31 *Daily Telegraph*, 19.06.05.
32 HC Debs, 20.10.05, Col.540.
33 *Independent*, 21.06.05.
34 Private interview.
35 Private interview.
36 Interview, Philip Collins, 29.11.06.
37 Private interview.
38 Reuters, 22.06.05.
39 Private interview.
40 Private interview.
41 Private interview.
42 Private interview.
43 Interview, Phil Collins, 29.11.06.
44 Interview, Kim Darroch, 24.11.06.
45 *Guardian*, 24.06.05.
46 Ibid.
47 Private interview.
48 Interview, Ken Livingstone, 21.05.07.
49 Interview, Lord Coe, 13.09.06.
50 Ibid.
51 *Daily Telegraph*, 05.07.05.
52 Ibid.
53 Interview, Tom Kelly, 27.02.07.
54 Interview, Ken Livingstone, 21.05.07.
55 Private interview.
56 Interview, Lord Coe, 13.09.06.
57 Ibid.
58 Private interview.
59 Interview, Lord Coe, 13.09.06.
60 Interview, Tom Kelly, 27.02.07
61 Private interview.
62 Interview, Tessa Jowell, 06.05.07.
63 Interview, Lord Coe, 13.09.06.
64 Interview, Ken Livingstone, 21.05.07.
65 Private interview.
66 Interview, Tessa Jowell, 06.05.07.
67 Private interview.
68 Private interview.
69 Interview, Tom Kelly, 27.02.07.
70 'Olympic Speech to the IOC', 06.07.05.
71 Interview, Tom Kelly, 27.02.07.
72 Interview, Lord Jay, 31.05.07.
73 Interview, Tom Kelly, 27.02.07.
74 Interview, Lord Coe, 13.09.06.
75 Interview, Tom Kelly, 27.02.07; *Independent*, 07.07.05.
76 *Independent*, 07.07.05.
77 Private interview.
78 Interview, Nick Rowley, 14.02.07.
79 Interview, Ken Livingstone, 21.05.07.
80 Interview, Justin Forsyth, 19.09.06.
81 Interview, Sir Michael Jay, 02.08.06.
82 Ibid.
83 Private interview.
84 Private interview.
85 Interview, Justin Forsyth, 19.09.06.
86 Interview, John Simon, 16.02.07.
87 Correspondence with author, Justin Forsyth, 08.08.07.
88 Private interview.

89 Correspondence with author, John Simon, 12.08.07.
90 Private interview.
91 Private interview.
92 Interview, Stephen Hadley, 16.04.07.
93 Private interview.
94 Private interview.
95 Interview, Stephen Hadley, 16.04.07.
96 Interview, Faryar Shirzad, 01.08.07.
97 Private correspondence.
98 *Guardian*, 08.06.05.
99 Private interview.
100 Private interview.
101 Interview, Lord Jay, 02.08.07.
102 Interview, Sir David King, 23.02.07.
103 Interview, Justin Forsyth, 19.09.06.
104 Interview, Nick Rowley, 14.02.07.
105 Interview, Sir David Manning, 27.10.06.
106 Interview, Laurie Lee, 02.02.07.
107 Interview, Justin Forsyth, 19.09.06.
108 *Independent*, 25.05.05.
109 *The Times*, 14.06.05.
110 Private interview.
111 Interview, Justin Forsyth, 19.09.06.
112 Ibid.
113 Interview, Lord Jay, 02.08.07.
114 Interview, John Simon, 16.02.07.
115 Private interview.
116 Interview, John Simon, 16.02.07.
117 Interview, Lord Jay, 31.05.07.
118 Ibid.
119 Interview, Justin Forsyth, 19.09.06.
120 Private interview.
121 Private interview.
122 Private interview.
123 Ibid.
124 *Financial Times*, 07.07.05.
125 Interview, John Simon, 16.02.07.
126 Private interview.
127 Private correspondence with author; Lee comments.
128 Private interview.
129 Private interview.
130 Interview, Baroness Morgan, 16.06.07.
131 *Sunday Times*, 10.07.05.
132 BBC News Online, 12.07.05.
133 Interview, Tom Kelly, 27.02.07; *Independent on Sunday*, 10.07.05.
134 *Sunday Times*, 10.07.05.
135 Interview, Tom Kelly, 27.02.07.
136 Private interview.
137 Private interview.
138 Private interview.
139 Private interview.
140 Private interview.
141 Private interview.
142 Private interview.
143 Private interview.
144 Interview, Ivan Rogers, 20.07.06.
145 Private interview.
146 Interview, Tom Kelly, 27.02.07.
147 *Sunday Telegraph*, 10.07.05.
148 *Financial Times*, 08.07.05.
149 Private interview.
150 Private interview.
151 Interview, Ken Livingstone, 21.05.07.
152 Interview, John Burton, 02.10.06.
153 Private interview.
154 Interview, Lord Stevens, 13.03.06.
155 Private information.
156 Interview, Lord Stevens, 13.03.06.
157 Ibid.
158 BBC News Online, 30.04.07.
159 *Hansard*, 07.07.05, Col.465
160 Interview, Sir Ian Blair, 30.05.07.
161 Private interview.
162 *Financial Times*, 08.07.05.
163 Interview, Tom Kelly, 27.02.07.
164 *Sunday Telegraph*, 10.07.05.
165 Interview, Justin Forsyth, 19.09.06.
166 Private interview.
167 Private interview.
168 *Financial Times*, 09.07.05.
169 Interview, Lord Turnbull, 05.07.06.
170 Interview, Lord Jay, 02.08.06.
171 *Guardian*, 12.09.05.
172 Interview, John Simon, 16.02.07.
173 Interview, Steven Hadley, 16.04.07.
174 Interview, Paul 'PJ' Johnson, 29.10.06.

15: Promise Fades

1 Private interview.
2 Private interview.
3 *Observer*, 11.09.05.
4 Private interview.
5 Interview, David Bennett, 10.05.07.
6 Private interview.
7 Private interview.
8 Private interview.
9 *Sunday Telegraph*, 02.10.05.
10 Ibid.
11 Private interview.
12 Interview, Sir Ian Blair, 03.05.07.
13 Ibid.
14 Interview, Tom Bentley, 14.09.06.
15 Private interview.
16 Private interview.
17 *Independent*, 26.09.05.
18 Private interview.
19 *Sunday Times*, 25.09.05.
20 *New Statesman*, 25.09.05.
21 *Daily Telegraph*, 29.09.05.
22 Private interview.
23 Private interview.
24 Private interview.

25 Private interview.
26 Private interview.
27 Interview, Benjamin Wegg-Prosser, 02.07.07.
28 Private interview.
29 *Daily Telegraph*, 29.09.05.
30 *Sunday Times*, 28.08.05.
31 *Guardian*, 27.09.05.
32 Ibid., 28.09.05.
33 *Daily Telegraph*, 28.09.05.
34 Ibid.
35 *Guardian*, 28.09.05.
36 Interview, Philip Collins, 06.02.07.
37 Interview, Ruth Turner, 16.03.07.
38 Interview, Philip Collins, 06.02.07.
39 *The Times*, 26.10.05.
40 *Guardian*, 16.12.05.
41 Private interview.
42 Private interview.
43 Interview, Lord Jay, 04.07.07.
44 Private interview.
45 Private interview.
46 Interview, Sir Rob Fry, 21.07.07..
47 Private interview.
48 Interview, Sir Rob Fry, 21.07.07.
49 Private interview.
50 Private interview.
51 Interview, Rob Fry, 21.07.07.
52 Interview, Sir Jock Stirrup, 02.04.07.
53 Private interview.
54 Private interview.
55 Private interview.
56 Private interview.
57 Interview, Sir Rob Fry, 21.07.02.
58 Interview, Sir Rob Fry, 21.07.02.
59 Private interview.
60 Interview, Jack Straw, 12.07.07.
61 Private interview.
62 *Daily Telegraph*, 27.01.06.
63 Private interview.
64 Interview, Donald Rumsfeld, 15.08.07.
65 Interview, Matthew Taylor, 13.03.07.
66 *Observer*, 09.10.05.
67 Private interview.
68 Private interview.
69 Interview, Baroness Morgan, 15.06.07.
70 Interview, Matthew Taylor, 13.03.07.
71 Ibid.
72 Private interview.
73 Interview, Benjamin Wegg-Prosser, 02.07.07.
74 *Daily Telegraph*, 27.10.05.
75 *Sunday Telegraph*, 30.10.05.
76 Private interview.
77 *Observer*, 30.10.05.
78 Private interview.
79 Blunkett (2006), pp.850–1.
80 Private interview.
81 Private interview.
82 Blunkett (2006), p.851.
83 Ibid., p.852.
84 *Hansard*, 02.11.05: Col.818–19.
85 Private interview.
86 *Hansard*, 02.11.05: Col.820.
87 Private interview.
88 Private interview.
89 *Guardian*, 16.12.04.
90 Private interview.
91 Private interview.
92 Private interview.
93 Private interview.
94 Private interview.
95 Interview, Hazel Blears, 24.04.07.
96 Interview, Matthew Taylor, 02.03.07.
97 Interview, Sir Ian Blair, 30.05.07.
98 Private interview.
99 BBC News Online, 12.10.05.
100 Private interview.
101 Private interview.
102 *Observer*, 13.11.05.
103 Private interview.
104 Private interview.
105 Private interview.
106 *Observer*, 13.11.05.
107 Private interview.
108 Interview, Matthew Taylor, 02.03.07.
109 Interview, Sir Ian Blair, 03.05.07.
110 *Observer*, 13.11.05.
111 Private interview.
112 Interview, Nick Brown, 13.07.06.
113 Private interview.
114 Interview, Nick Brown, 13.07.06.
115 *Observer*, 13.11.05.
116 Interview, Hilary Armstrong, 22.03.07.
117 Ibid.
118 *Observer*, 13.11.05.
119 Ibid.
120 See www.publicwhip.org.uk.
121 Interview, David Bennett, 06.02.07.
122 Interview, Matthew Taylor, 13.03.07.
123 Private interview.
124 Interview, Hazel Blears, 24.04.07.
125 Interview, Matthew Taylor, 13.03.07.
126 Private interview.
127 Private interview.
128 Interview, Nick Brown, 13.07.06.
129 Private interview.
130 Private interview.
131 Interview, Michael Howard, 04.07.07.
132 Private interview.
133 Private interview.
134 Private interview.
135 *Sunday Telegraph*, 04.12.05.
136 Private interview.
137 Private interview.
138 Private correspondence.
139 Private interview.
140 Private interview.

141 Private interview.
142 *Guardian*, 11.04.05.
143 Interview, Matthew Taylor, 13.03.07.
144 Interview, David Blunkett, 28.03.07.
145 Ibid.
146 Private interview.
147 Private interview.
148 Private interview.
149 Interview, Matthew Taylor, 13.03.07.
150 Private interview.
151 *Financial Times*, 23.11.05.
152 Ibid., 24.11.05.
153 *Observer*, 27.11.05.
154 Interview, Matthew Taylor, 13.03.07.
155 Interview, Lord Turner, 21.05.07.
156 Private correspondence.
157 Private correspondence.
158 Private interview.
159 Private interview.
160 Private interview.
161 Private interview.
162 Private interview.
163 Private interview.
164 Private correspondence.
165 Private interview.
166 Private interview.
167 Private interview.
168 Interview, Sir John Grant, 23.03.07.
169 Private interview.
170 Interview, Sir John Grant, 23.03.07.
171 Interview, Kim Darroch, 03.02.07.
172 Private interview.
173 Private interview.
174 Private interview.
175 Private interview.
176 Interview, Sir John Grant, 23.03.07.
177 Interview, John Sawers, 21.10.06.
178 Interview, Sir Stephen Wall,
    06.03.07.
179 Private interview.
180 Interview, Sir Stephen Wall,
    06.03.07.
181 Private interview.
182 Private correspondence.
183 Private interview.
184 Private interview.
185 Private interview.
186 Private interview.
187 Private interview.
188 Private interview.
189 Private interview.
190 Private interview.
191 Private interview.
192 Private correspondence.
193 Private interview.
194 Private interview.
195 Private interview.
196 Private interview.
197 Private interview.
198 Private correspondence.
199 Private interview.
200 Private interview.
201 Private interview.
202 Private interview.
203 Private interview.
204 Private interview.
205 Private interview.
206 Private interview.
207 Private interview.
208 Interview, Kim Darroch, 03.02.07.
209 Private interview.
210 Private interview.
211 Interview, Kim Darroch, 03.02.07.
212 Private interview.
213 Private interview.
214 Private interview.
215 Interview, Kim Darroch, 03.02.07.
216 Private interview.
217 Private interview.
218 Private interview.
219 Interview, Sir John Grant, 22.03.07
220 *Daily Telegraph*, 17.12.05
221 Interview, Kim Darroch, 03.02.07.
222 Private interview.
223 Private interview.

16: Losing His Authority

 1 *Guardian*, 08.05.06; Private
   interview.
 2 Private interview.
 3 *Guardian*, 07.05.05.
 4 Interview, Louise Casey, 07.02.07.
 5 Private interview.
 6 Interview, Louise Casey, 23.03.07.
 7 Private interview.
 8 Private interview.
 9 'Respect Action Plan Launch',
   10.01.06.
10 Interview, Benjamin Wegg-Prosser,
   02.07.07.
11 *Guardian*, 11.01.06.
12 Private correspondence.
13 *Guardian*, 31.01.06.
14 *The Times*, 05.10.05.
15 Private interview.
16 Private correspondence.
17 *Hansard*, 07.12.05, Col.861.
18 Interview, Hilary Armstrong,
   22.03.07.
19 Ibid.
20 *Hansard*, 01.02.06, Col.309.
21 *Guardian*, 02.02.06.
22 Ibid., 10.02.06.
23 Private interview.
24 Private interview.
25 Private interview.
26 Private interview.
27 Private interview.
28 Private interview.
29 Private interview.
30 Private interview.

31 Private interview.
32 Private interview.
33 Interview, Phil Collins, 29.11.06.
34 Private interviews.
35 Private interview.
36 Private interview.
37 Interview, Conor Ryan, 13.02.07.
38 Speech on Education, 24.10.05.
39 Private interview.
40 Private interview.
41 Interview, Estelle Morris, 12.09.06.
42 Private interview.
43 Private interview.
44 Interview, Estelle Morris, 12.09.06.
45 'Higher Standards, Better Schools for All: More Choice for Parents and Pupils', DfES, 25.10.05.
46 Private interview.
47 Private interview.
48 Interview, Matthew Taylor.
49 The *Times*, 24.01.06.
50 *Independent*, 01.12.05
51 *Sunday Telegraph*, 18.12.05.
52 *Guardian*, 19.12.05.
53 Private interview.
54 Private interview.
55 Private interview.
56 *Independent*, 20.01.06.
57 Private interview.
58 *Guardian*, 12.01.06.
59 Private interview.
60 Interview, Estelle Morris, 12.09.06.
61 Private interview.
62 Private interview.
63 *The Times*, 04.02.06; Private interview.
64 *Sun*, 24.01.06.
65 Private interview.
66 Interview, Hilary Armstrong, 14.06.07.
67 Interview, Estelle Morris, 12.09.06.
68 Private interviews.
69 *The Times*, 01.03.06.
70 Interview, David Willetts, 19.03.07.
71 *The Times*, 08.12.05.
72 Private interview.
73 Private interview.
74 Private interview.
75 Private interview.
76 Private interview.
77 Private interview.
78 Private interview.
79 Interview, David Willetts, 19.03.07.
80 Private interview.
81 Private interview.
82 *Guardian*, 16.03.06.
83 Private interview.
84 Jack Dromey, *Channel 4 News*, 15.03.06.
85 *Guardian*, 16.03.06.
86 Private interview.
87 Private interview.
88 Private interview.
89 Interview, Jack Dromey, 16.07.07.
90 Private interview.
91 Private interview.
92 Private interview.
93 Private interview.
94 Private interviews.
95 Private interview.
96 Private interview.
97 Private interview.
98 Private interview.
99 Private interview
100 Private interview.
101 Private interview.
102 Private interview.
103 Private interview.
104 Private interview.
105 Private interview.
106 Private correspondence.
107 Private interview.
108 Private interview.
109 Private interview.
110 Private interview.
111 *Mail on Sunday*, 05.03.06.
112 Private interview.
113 Private interview.
114 Private interview.
115 Interview, Tom Kelly, 02.02.07.
116 Interview, Justin Forsyth, 09.11.06.
117 *Guardian*, 26.05.06.
118 BBC Online, 27.05.06.
119 Ibid.
120 *The Times*, 29.04.06.
121 Private interview.
122 Private interview.
123 *Hansard*, 26.04.06, Col.564.
124 Ibid., Col.575.
125 *Observer*, 30.04.06.
126 Ibid.
127 Private correspondence.
128 *Sunday Telegraph*, 30.04.06.
129 Private interview.
130 *Daily Mirror*, 26.04.06.
131 *Observer*, 30.04.06.
132 Ibid.
133 Private interview.
134 *Sunday Telegraph*, 30.04.06.
135 Private interview.
136 *Sunday Times*, 30.04.06.
137 *Independent*, 29.04.06.
138 Private interview.
139 Private interview.
140 Interview, John Sawers, 29.08.06.
141 Private interview.
142 *Guardian*, 24.02.06.
143 Private interview.
144 Interview, Lord Jay, 02.08.06.
145 Interview, John Sawers, 21.10.06.
146 Interview, Condoleezza Rice, 14.08.07.

147 Private interview.
148 Interview, Sir Robert Fry, 24.01.07.
149 Ibid.
150 *The Times*, 23.05.06.
151 *Financial Times*, 26.05.06.
152 *The Times*, 26.05.06.
153 Private interview.
154 Interview, John Bolton, 10.07.07.
155 *Independent*, 25.04.06.
156 *Sunday Telegraph*, 28.05.06.
157 Interview, Paul 'PJ' Johnston, 03.01.07.
158 Private interview.
159 *Independent*, 27.05.06.
160 Ibid.
161 Private interview.
162 Interview, Sir Lawrence Freedman, 16.03.07.
163 Interview, David Bennett, 03.07.07.
164 Private information.
165 Interview, Ruth Turner, 20.06.07.
166 Interview, David Bennett, 03.07.07.
167 Private interview.
168 Private interview.
169 Interview, Mathew Taylor, 03.07.07.
170 Private interview.
171 Private interview.
172 Private interview.
173 Private interview.
174 Private interview.
175 Private interview.
176 Private interview.
177 Interview, Benjamin Wegg-Prosser, 02.07.07.
178 Interview, Matthew Taylor, 03.07.07.
179 Interview, David Bennett, 06.02.07.
180 Private interview.
181 Private interview.

17: *Stirrings of Dissent*

1 Interview, Matthew Taylor, 13.03.07.
2 Interview, Philip Collins, 29.11.06.
3 Private interview.
4 Private correspondence.
5 *Guardian*, 02.05.06.
6 Ibid.
7 Private correspondence.
8 Private interview.
9 Interview, Ruth Turner, 16.03.07.
10 Private interview.
11 Private interview.
12 Private interview.
13 Private interview.
14 Interview, Jack Straw, 12.07.07.
15 Private interview.
16 Private interview.
17 Private interview.
18 Private information.
19 Private interview.
20 Private interview.
21 Private interview.
22 Private interview.
23 Private interview.
24 Private interview.
25 BBC News Online, 05.05.06.
26 Interview, Nick Brown, 13.07.06.
27 Interview, John Bolton, 10.07.07.
28 Private information.
29 Private interview.
30 Private interview.
31 Interview, Jack Straw, 12.07.07.
32 Ibid.
33 Private interview.
34 Interview, Benjamin Wegg-Prosser, 05.07.07.
35 Private interview.
36 Private interview.
37 Private interviews.
38 Interview, Margaret Beckett, 28.03.07.
39 Private interview.
40 Interview, John Bolton, 10.07.07.
41 Private interview.
42 Private interview.
43 Private interview.
44 *Guardian*, 05.05.06.
45 Private interview.
46 Private interview.
47 Private interview.
48 Private interview.
49 Private interview.
50 Private interview.
51 Interview, Hilary Armstrong, 28.07.07.
52 Private interview.
53 *Guardian*, 06.05.06.
54 Private interview.
55 Private interview.
56 Interview, Patricia Hewitt, 30.10.07.
57 *Today*, 05.05.06.
58 Thompson and Barnes (1971), p.152.
59 Private interview.
60 Private interview.
61 Private interview.
62 Private interview.
63 Private interview.
64 Private interview.
65 *Guardian*, 06.05.06.
66 BBC News Online, 07.05.07.
67 Interview, Neal Lawson, 11.07.07.
68 *Daily Telegraph*, 06.05.07.
69 Interview, Nick Brown, 13.07.06.
70 BBC TV, *Sunday A.M.*, 07.05.06.
71 Private interview.
72 Interview, Nick Brown, 13.07.06.
73 Private interview.
74 Interview, Hilary Armstrong, 28.07.07.
75 Interview, Nick Brown, 13.07.06.
76 Private interview.
77 *Guardian*, 10.05.2006.

78 *Independent*, 15.05.06.
79 Ibid.
80 Ibid.
81 Private interview.
82 *Independent*, 15.05.06.
83 *Daily Telegraph*, 27.05.06.
84 Correspondence, Kieran Brett, 26.07.07.
85 BBC News Online, 23.05.06.
86 Private interview.
87 *Guardian*, 27.06.06.
88 Interview, Justin Russell, 09.02.07.
89 Ibid.
90 Private interview.
91 Private interview.
92 Private correspondence.
93 Interview, Justin Russell, 09.02.07.
94 Interview, Kieran Brett, 21.03.07.
95 *Hansard*, 12.07.06, Col.1383.
96 Interview, Justin Russell, 09.02.07.
97 *Guardian*, 28.09.04.
98 PMOS Morning Press Briefing, 23.05.06.
99 *Sunday Times*, 13.08.06.
100 *The Times*, 09.08.06.
101 *Sunday Times*, 13.08.06.
102 Interview, Andy Neather, 23.01.07.
103 Private interview.
104 Private interview.
105 Private interview.
106 Private interview.
107 Interview, Sir David King, 16.02.07.
108 Interview, David Bennett, 06.02.07.
109 *Guardian*, 30.11.05.
110 Interview, Philip Collins, 06.02.07.
111 *Independent*, 18.05.06.
112 Interview, Philip Collins, 09.03.07.
113 *Guardian*, 17.05.06.
114 Ibid., 06.07.06.
115 Private interview.
116 Private interview.
117 *Guardian*, 10.07.06.
118 'The Energy Challenge', 11.07.06, p.17.
119 Interview, Margaret Beckett, 28.03.07.
120 Correspondence, Justin Forsyth, 08.08.07.
121 BBC News Online, 03.06.07.
122 Interview, Lord Jay, 10.06.07.
123 Interview, Justin Forsyth, 19.09.06.
124 Private interview.
125 Private interview.
126 Interview, Sir David King, 16.02.07.
127 Stern Review, p.vi.
128 Interview, Lord Turner, 21.05.07.
129 Private interview.
130 Private interview.
131 Private interview.
132 Private interview.
133 Private interview.
134 Private interview.
135 Private interview.
136 Private interview.
137 Private interview.
138 Private interview.
139 *Daily Telegraph*, 05.04.06.
140 Private interview.
141 *The Times*, 05.04.06.
142 Private interview.
143 Private interview.
144 *Guardian*, 04.04.06.
145 *Daily Telegraph*, 05.04.06.
146 Private interview.
147 Private interview.
148 Private interview.
149 Private interview.
150 Private interview.
151 Private interview.
152 Private interview.
153 Private interview.
154 Private interview.
155 Interview, Ruth Turner, 16.03.07.
156 Interview, Simon McDonald, 08.03.07.
157 Private interview.
158 Private interview.
159 Private interview.
160 Private interview.
161 Private interview.
162 Private interview.
163 Private interview.
164 Private interview.
165 *Guardian*, 13.07.06.
166 Private interview.
167 Interview, Condoleezza Rice, 14.08.07.
168 Ibid.
169 Interview, Lord Jay, 10.06.07.
170 Private interview.
171 Interview, Condoleezza Rice, 14.08.07.
172 BBC News Online, 18.07.06.
173 Interview, Tom Kelly, 13.07.07.
174 Private interview.
175 Interview, Karl Rove, 19.03.06.
176 Private interview.
177 Private interview.
178 Interview, John Sawers, 21.10.06.
179 Private interview.
180 Private interview.
181 Interview, Lord Jay, 02.08.06.
182 Private interview.
183 Private interview.
184 Private interview.
185 Private interview.
186 Private interview.
187 Private interview.
188 Private interview.
189 G8 Communiqué, http://en.g8russia.ru/docs/21.html.
190 *Guardian*, 19.07.06.

191 Private correspondence.
192 Private interview.
193 Interview, Margaret Beckett, 28.03.07.
194 Ibid.
195 Private interview.
196 Private interview.
197 Private interview.
198 Interview, Baroness Morgan, 04.07.07.
199 Private interview.
200 Private interview.
201 Private interview.
202 *Washington Post*, 20.07.06.
203 *Guardian*, 20.07.06.
204 Interview, Margaret Beckett, 28.03.07.
205 *Guardian*, 23.07.06.
206 Joint press conference with Nouri al-Maliki, 24.07.06.
207 Private interview.
208 Interview, Jack Straw, 12.07.07.
209 Private interview.
210 Private interview.
211 Private interview.
212 Interview, Ruth Turner, 16.03.07.
213 Private interview.
214 Private interview.
215 *Observer*, 06.08.06.
216 Ibid.
217 Private interview.
218 Private interview.
219 Private interview.
220 Interview, Condoleezza Rice, 14.08.07.
221 Private interview.
222 Private interview.
223 Private interview.
224 Private interview.
225 Private interview.
226 Private interview.
227 Private interview.
228 Private correspondence.
229 Private interview.
230 *Guardian*, 03.08.06.
231 'Speech to News Corps on the impact of the modern world on leadership', 30.07.06.
232 BBC Online, 31.07.06.
233 Private interview.
234 *Guardian*, 01.08.06.
235 Ibid., 02.08.06; 'Foreign policy speech to the Los Angeles World Affairs Council', 01.08.06.
236 Interview, Justin Forsyth, 09.11.06.
237 Private interview.
238 Interview, John Bolton, 10.07.07.
239 Interview, Condoleezza Rice, 14.08.07.
240 Interview, Margaret Beckett, 28.03.07.
241 Private interview; Interview, John Bolton, 10.07.07.
242 Private interview.
243 Interview, Tessa Jowell, 26.03.07.
244 Private interview.
245 Private interview.
246 Interview, Neal Lawson, 11.06.07.
247 Interview, Ruth Turner, 28.03.07.

18: The September Coup

1 *The Times*, 17.07.06.
2 *Sunday Telegraph*, 20.08.06.
3 Interview, Benjamin Wegg-Prosser, 28.06.07.
4 Private interview.
5 *Independent*, 21.08.06.
6 Private interview.
7 *Sunday Times*, 10.09.06.
8 Private interview.
9 Interview, Matthew Taylor, 02.03.07.
10 Interview, Ruth Turner, 16.03.07.
11 Private interview.
12 Private interview.
13 Private interview.
14 Interview, Ruth Turner, 16.03.07.
15 Private interview.
16 Private interview.
17 Interview, David Bennett, 22.05.07.
18 Private interview.
19 Interview, Benjamin Wegg-Prosser, 28.06.07.
20 Private interview.
21 Private interview.
22 Private interview.
23 *The Times*, 01.09.06.
24 Private interview.
25 Private interview.
26 Private interview.
27 Private interview.
28 Private interview.
29 *Independent*, 03.09.06.
30 Interview, Khalid Mahmood, 27.07.07.
31 Private interview.
32 Private interview.
33 Private interview.
34 Private interview.
35 Private interview.
36 Interview, Benjamin Wegg-Prosser, 28.06.07.
37 *Sunday Times*, 03.09.06.
38 *Observer*, 03.09.06.
39 *Sunday Times*, 10.09.06.
40 Private interview.
41 Private interview.
42 Private interview.
43 *Sunday Times*, 10.09.06.
44 Private interview.
45 Interview, Hilary Armstrong, 28.07.07.

46 Private interview.
47 *Guardian*, 05.09.06.
48 Interview, Ruth Turner, 28.03.07.
49 Interview, Benjamin Wegg-Prosser, 26.06.07.
50 Private interviews.
51 *Sunday Times*, 10.09.06.
52 Interview, Khalid Mahmood, 27.07.07.
53 Private interview.
54 Private interview.
55 *Sunday Times*, 10.09.06.
56 Private interview.
57 Private interview.
58 Private interview.
59 Private interview.
60 Private interview.
61 Private correspondence.
62 *Guardian*, 07.09.06.
63 Private correspondence.
64 Interview, Phil Collins, 29.11.06.
65 Private interview.
66 Private interview.
67 Private correspondence with author.
68 Private interview.
69 Private interview.
70 Interview, Hilary Armstrong, 28.07.07.
71 BBC Radio 4, *Today*, 05.09.06.
72 *Guardian*, 06.09.06.
73 Private interview.
74 *Daily Mirror*, 05.09.06.
75 Private interview.
76 Private interview.
77 Private interview.
78 Interview, Ruth Turner, 28.03.07.
79 Private interview.
80 Private interview.
81 Private correspondence.
82 *New Statesman*, 11.09.06.
83 Private interview.
84 Private interview.
85 Private interview.
86 Private interview.
87 Private interview.
88 *Sunday Times*, 10.09.06.
89 Private interview.
90 *Sunday Times*, 10.09.06.
91 *Guardian*, 07.09.06.
92 Private interview.
93 Interview, Iain Duncan-Smith, 28.06.07.
94 *Guardian*, 07.09.06.
95 *Independent*, 07.09.06; Private interview.
96 Private interview.
97 Interview, Matthew Taylor, 16.08.07.
98 Private interview.
99 Private interview.
100 BBC TV, *Sunday A.M.*, 10.09.06.
101 Private interview.

102 Interview, Peter Watt, 22.03.07.
103 *Guardian*, 07.09.06.
104 Private interview.
105 Private interview.
106 Private interview.
107 Interview, David Hill, 12.06.07.
108 *Financial Times*, 08.09.06.
109 Interview, Peter Hain, 07.12.06.
110 Private interview.
111 *Guardian*, 09.09.06.
112 *Sunday Times*, 10.09.06.
113 Interview, Jack Dromey, 23.10.06.
114 *Sunday Times*, 10.09.06.
115 Private interview.
116 *Evening Standard*, 08.09.06.
117 Ibid.
118 *Daily Telegraph*, 09.09.06.
119 *Daily Mail*, 11.09.06.
120 *Guardian*, 12.09.06.
121 Private interview.
122 Private interview.
123 *Guardian*, 08.09.06.
124 *Daily Telegraph*, 12.09.06.
125 Private interview.
126 *Guardian*, 13.09.06.
127 Ibid.
128 Private interview.
129 Private interview.
130 Private interview.
131 Private correspondence.
132 Interview, David Hill, 25.07.07.
133 Interview, Peter Watt, 25.07.07.
134 Private interview.
135 Private interview.
136 Private interview.
137 YouGov poll, 10.02.07.
138 Private interview.
139 Private interview.

19: On a Knife Edge

1 Private interview.
2 Private interview.
3 Private interview.
4 Interview, Matthew Taylor, 10.06.07.
5 Private interview.
6 Interview, Ruth Turner, 30.05.07.
7 Private interview.
8 Private interview.
9 Interview, David Bennett, 03.07.07.
10 Private interview.
11 Private interview.
12 Private interview, *Guardian*, 24.11.06.
13 Private interview.
14 Private interview.
15 Interview, David Bennett, 03.07.07.
16 Private interview.
17 Private information.
18 Private information.
19 Private interview.

20 Private interview.
21 Private interview.
22 *Guardian*, 20.10.06.
23 Private interview.
24 Private interview.
25 Private interview.
26 PricewaterhouseCoopers, Academies Evaluation, 2nd Report, 15 June 2005.
27 Of the fourteen academies taking GCSEs in 2005, ten saw rises on what they had achieved in 2004 and twelve had achieved results greater than that of the schools they replaced. The average increase in results per academy from 2004 to 2005 was 7.7 percentage points up to 36.4 per cent, three times the national average increase of 2.6 percentage points. See DfES, Academies, Sponsors Prospectus 2006.
28 Private interview.
29 Private interview.
30 Private interview.
31 Private interview.
32 Private interview.
33 Private interview.
34 Private interview.
35 BBC News Online, 30.11.06.
36 Private interview.
37 Private interview.
38 Private interview.
39 Private interview.
40 *Guardian*, 19.12.06.
41 BBC News Online, 24.01.06.
42 Private interview.
43 Private interview.
44 Private interview.
45 Private interview.
46 *Financial Times*, 30.10.05.
47 Private interview.
48 Private interview.
49 Private interview.
50 Private interview.
51 Private interview.
52 Private interview.
53 Private interview.
54 *Guardian*, 12.10.06.
55 Private information.
56 Private interview.
57 *Financial Times*, 15.11.06.
58 *Independent*, 16.11.06.
59 Private interview.
60 Private interview.
61 *Daily Telegraph*, 17.11.06.
62 Private information.
63 Private interview.
64 *Daily Telegraph*, 07.12.06.
65 *Financial Times*, 05.12.06.
66 Ibid., 06.12.06.
67 Private information.
68 Private interview.
69 Private interview.
70 Private interview.
71 Private interview.
72 Private interview.
73 BBC Northern Ireland, 11.10.06.
74 Interview, Tom Kelly, 02.07.07.
75 Private interview.
76 Private interview.
77 Private interview.
78 Private interview.
79 *Daily Telegraph*, 13.03.05.
80 Private interview.
81 Private interview.
82 Private interview.
83 Private interview.
84 Private interview.
85 Private interview.
86 Private interview.
87 Private interview.
88 *Financial Times*, 29.06.05.
89 Private interview.
90 *Guardian*, 11.09.06.
91 Interview, Tom Kelly, 02.07.07.
92 Private interview.
93 Private interview.
94 Private interview.
95 Private interview.
96 *Independent*, 05.10.06.
97 Private interview.
98 Interview, Tom Kelly, 06.02.07.
99 *The Times*, 04.10.06.
100 Private interview.
101 *The Times*, 12.10.06.
102 Private correspondence.
103 Private interview.
104 Private interview.
105 Private interview.
106 Private interview.
107 Private interview.
108 Private interview.
109 Private correspondence.
110 Private interview.
111 Private correspondence.
112 Private interview.
113 Private interview.
114 Private interview.
115 Private correspondence.
116 Private correspondence.
117 Private interview.
118 *Financial Times*, 24.07.07.
119 Private interview.
120 Private interview.
121 Private interview.
122 Private interview.
123 Private interview.
124 Private interview.
125 Private interview.
126 Private interview.
127 *Independent*, 14.11.06.
128 Private interview.

129 Private interview.
130 Private interview.
131 Private interview.
132 *Guardian*, 15.11.06.
133 Interview, James Baker, 12.07.07.
134 'The Iraq Study Group Report',
    16.12.06.
135 Private interview.
136 Private interview.
137 *Weekly Standard*, 12.04.06.
138 Private interview.
139 Private interview.
140 Private interview.
141 Private interview.
142 Private interview.
143 Private interview.
144 Private interview.
145 Private interview.
146 Private interview.
147 Private interview.
148 Private interview.
149 Private interview.
150 Private interview.
151 Private interview.
152 Private interview.
153 Private interview.
154 Private interview.
155 Private interview.
156 Private interview.
157 *Independent*, 08.12.06.
158 *Mirror*, 08.12.06.
159 Private interview.
160 Private interview.
161 Private interview.
162 *Associated Press*,12.07.07.
163 *Daily Telegraph*, 16.12.06.
164 *Guardian*, 18.12.06.
165 Private interview.
166 *Daily Telegraph*, 18.12.06.
167 *Guardian*, 16.12.06.
168 Private interview.
169 Private interview.
170 Private interview.
171 Private interview.
172 Private interview
173 Private interview.
174 Private interview.
175 Private interview.
176 Private interview.

20: *To the Wire*

1 Private interview.
2 Private interview.
3 Private interview.
4 *Sunday Telegraph*, 04.02.07
5 Private interview.
6 Private interview.
7 Private interview.
8 Private interview.
9 BBC News Online, 19.01.07

10 Ibid.
11 *Observer*, 21.01.07.
12 Private interview.
13 Private interview.
14 Private interview.
15 Private interview.
16 Private interview.
17 *Sunday Times*, 22.07.07.
18 BBC Radio 4, *Today*, 02.02.07.
19 *Independent on Sunday*, 24.02.07.
20 BBC News Online, 20.07.07.
21 *Tablet*, 03.02.07.
22 Ibid.
23 Ibid.
24 Ibid.
25 *Guardian*, 25.01.07.
26 Private interview.
27 *Sunday Telegraph*, 29.01.07.
28 BBC News Online, 26.01.07.
29 Ibid., 28.01.07.
30 Private interview.
31 Private interview.
32 Private interview.
33 BBC News Online, 04.12.06.
34 Ibid., 15.03.07.
35 Private interview.
36 Private interview.
37 Private interview.
38 Private correspondence.
39 Private interview.
40 Private interview.
41 Private interview.
42 Private interview.
43 Private interview.
44 Interview, Ruth Turner, 28.03.07.
45 Private interview.
46 *Guardian*, 29.01.07.
47 Ibid.
48 *Daily Telegraph*, 29.01.07.
49 *The Times*, 31.01.07.
50 BBC News Online, 12.03.07.
51 Private interview.
52 Private interview.
53 Private correspondence.
54 Private interview.
55 Private interview.
56 Private interview.
57 Private interview.
58 Private correspondence.
59 Private interview.
60 Private interview.
61 Private interview.
62 Private interview.
63 Private interview.
64 Private correspondence.
65 Private interview.
66 Private interview.
67 Private correspondence.
68 Private interview.
69 Private interview.
70 Private interview.

71   Interview, Tom Kelly, 02.07.07.
72   Private interview.
73   Private interview.
74   Private interview.
75   Private correspondence.
76   Private interview.
77   Private interview.
78   Private interview.
79   Private interview.
80   Private interview.
81   CNN, 10.01.07.
82   *Guardian*, 22.02.07.
83   *Daily Telegraph*, 23.08.07.
84   Private interview.
85   Private interview.
86   *Independent*, 29.03.07.
87   BBC News Online, 28.03.07.
88   Private interview.
89   *The Times*, 31.03.07.
90   Interview, Condoleezza Rice,
      14.08.07.
91   Private interview.
92   *Sunday Times*, 01.04.07.
93   *The Times*, 31.03.07; BBC News
      Online, 30.03.07.
94   Private interview.
95   Private interview.
96   Private interview.
97   Private interview.
98   *Independent*, 04.04.07.
99   Ibid., 05.04.07.
100 Private interview.
101 Private interview.
102 Private interview.
103 Private interview.
104 Private interview.
105 Private interview.
106 Interview, Hilary Armstrong,
      25.07.07.
107 Interview, Tessa Jowell, 06.05.07.
108 Ibid.
109 Private interview.
110 Private interview.
111 Private interview.
112 Private interview.
113 Private interview.
114 Private interview.
115 Private interview.
116 Private interview.
117 Private interview.
118 Private interview.
119 Interview, Hilary Armstrong,
      25.07.07.
120 *Financial Times*, 20.02.07.
121 Private interview.
122 Private interview.
123 Private interview.
124 *The Times*, 01.12.06.
125 Private interview.
126 Private interview.
127 Private interview.
128 Private interview.
129 Private interview.
130 Private interview.
131 *Guardian*, 06.05.07.
132 Private interview.
133 Private interview.
134 Private interview.
135 Private interview.
136 Private interview.
137 *The Times*, 20.03.07.
138 *Guardian*, 20.03.07.
139 Private interview.
140 Private interview.
141 Private interview.
142 Private interview.
143 *Financial Times*, 20.04.07.
144 *Observer*, 22.04.07.
145 Ibid.
146 Private interview.
147 Channel 4, *The Last Days of Tony
      Blair*, 02.07.07.
148 Private interview.
149 Private interview.
150 Private interview.
151 *Guardian*, 01.05.07.
152 *Sun*, 30.04.07.
153 *Independent*, 04.05.07.
154 Private information.
155 Private information.
156 BBC News Online, 06.05.07.
157 Private interview.
158 Private interview.
159 Private information.
160 Correspondence with author, Tessa
      Jowell.
161 Private interview.
162 Interview, John Burton, 02.07.07.
163 Private interview.
164 Private correspondence.
165 Private interview.
166 Private interview.
167 Private interview.
168 *Evening Standard*, 10.05.07.

Conclusion: The Long Farewell

1   Private interview.
2   *Daily Telegraph*, 18.05.07.
3   Private interview.
4   Private interview.
5   Private interview.
6   Private interview.
7   Private interview.
8   Private interview.
9   Private interview.
10   Private interview.
11   *Financial Times*, 18.05.07.
12   Interview, Justin Forsyth, 03.07.07.
13   Private interview.
14   *Daily Telegraph*, 19.05.07.
15   *The Times*, 26.04.07

16 Ibid., 23.06.07
17 Private interview.
18 Private interview.
19 Private interview.
20 BBC News Online, 27.09.05.
21 Interview, Lord Jay, 10.06.07.
22 Private interview.
23 Private interview.
24 BBC News Online, 19.05.07.
25 Ibid., 01.08.07.
26 Private interview.
27 Private interview.
28 Private interview.
29 *The Times*, 23.06.07.
30 Private interview.
31 Private interview.
32 Private interview.
33 Private interview.
34 *Guardian*, 11.07.07.
35 Private interview.
36 Private interview.
37 Private correspondence.
38 Interview, Justin Forsyth, 03.07.07.
39 Private correspondence.
40 *Independent*, 01.06.07.
41 *Daily Telegraph*, 01.06.07.
42 Private interview.
43 Private interview.
44 Private interview.
45 Private interview.
46 Private interview.
47 Private interview.
48 Private interview.
49 Private interview.
50 Private interview.
51 Private interview.
52 Private interview.
53 Private interview.
54 Private interview.
55 Private interview.
56 *Guardian*, 06.06.07.
57 Private interview.
58 Private interview.
59 Private interview.
60 Interview, Justin Forsyth, 03.07 07.
61 Private interview.
62 Private correspondence.
63 Private interview.
64 Private interview.
65 Private interview.
66 Private interview.
67 Private interview.
68 Private interview.
69 Private interview.
70 *Financial Times*, 14.02.07.
71 *Guardian*, 10.03.07.
72 Private interview.
73 *Hansard*, Col.25, 12.03.07.
74 Private interview.
75 Private interview.
76 Private interview.

77 Private interview.
78 Private interview.
79 Private interview.
80 Private interview.
81 Private interview.
82 Private interview.
83 Private interview.
84 *The Times*, 21.04.07.
85 Private interview.
86 *Guardian*, 18.06.07.
87 Private interview.
88 Private interview.
89 Private interview.
90 Private interview.
91 *Financial Times*, 26.06.07.
92 Private interview.
93 *The Times*, 22.06.07.
94 Private interview.
95 Private interview.
96 Private interview.
97 Private interview.
98 Private interview.
99 Private interview.
100 Private interview.
101 Private interview.
102 Private interview.
103 Private interview.
104 Private interview.
105 *Guardian*, 03.02.07.
106 Private interview.
107 *The Times*, 23.06.07.
108 Private interview.
109 Private interview.
110 Private interview.
111 Interview, Godric Smith, 13.03.07.
112 *Guardian*, 12.06.07.
113 *The Times*, 13.06.07
114 Private interview.
115 Private interview.
116 Interview, Condoleezza Rice,
    14.08.07.
117 Private interview.
118 Private interview.
119 Interview, John Burton, 02.10.06.
120 Private interview.
121 Private interview.
122 Private interview.
123 Private interview.
124 *The Times*, 23.06.07.
125 Private interview.
126 *Independent*, 20.07.07.
127 BBC News Online, 23.06.07.
128 *Independent*, 24.06.07.
129 Private interview.
130 *Guardian*, 24.07.07.
131 Private interview.
132 Private interview.
133 Private interview.
134 *Independent*, 01.07.07.
135 Interview, Kieran Brett, 25.07.07.
136 Private interview.

137 Private interview.
138 Private interview.
139 Private interview.
140 Channel 4, *The Last Days of Tony Blair*, 02.07.07.
141 Interview, John Burton, 02.07.07.
142 Ibid.
143 Ibid.
144 Ibid.
145 Ibid.
146 *The Times*, 23.06.07.
147 Private interview.

Bibliography

Biographies and Memoirs

Ashdown, Paddy, *The Ashdown Diaries, Volume 2: 1997–1999* (London: Penguin, 2002)

Benn, Tony, *Free at Last: Diaries, 1991–2001* (London: Arrow, 2002)

Blix, Hans, *Disarming Iraq: The Search for Weapons of Mass Destruction* (London: Bloomsbury, 2004)

Blunkett, David, *The Blunkett Tapes* (London: Bloomsbury, 2006)

Bower, Tom, *Gordon Brown* (London: HarperCollins, 2005)

Bremer, L. Paul, *My Year in Iraq: The Struggle to Build a Future of Hope* (New York: Simon & Schuster, 2006)

Campbell, Alastair, *The Blair Years: Extracts from the Alastair Campbell Diaries* (London: Hutchinson, 2007)

Clinton, Bill, *My Life* (New York: Alfred A. Knopf, 2004)

Clinton, Hillary Rodham, *Living History* (New York: Simon & Schuster, 2003)

Cook, Robin, *The Point of Departure* (London: Simon & Schuster, 2003)

DeYoung, Karen, *Soldier: The Life of Colin Powell* (New York: Alfred A. Knopf, 2006)

Dyke, Greg, *Greg Dyke: Inside Story* (London: HarperCollins, 2004)

Godson, Dean, *Himself Alone* (London: HarperCollins, 2005)

Hamilton, Nigel, *Clinton: An American Journey* (London: Century, 2003)

Keegan, William, *The Prudence of Mr Gordon Brown* (Chichester: Wiley, 2003)

Lacey, Robert, *Monarch: The Life and Reign of Elizabeth II* (New York: The Free Press, 2002)

Langdon, Julia, *Mo Mowlam: The Biography* (London: Warner Brooks, 2001)

McDougall, Linda, *Cherie: The Perfect Life of Mrs Blair* (London: Politico's, 2001)

Meyer, Christopher, *DC Confidential: The Controversial Memoirs of Britain's Ambassador at the Time of 9/11 and the Iraq War* (London: Weidenfeld & Nicolson, 2005)

Mowlam, Mo, *Momentum* (London: Hodder & Stoughton, 2002)

Oborne, Peter, and Walters, Simon, *Alastair Campbell* (London: Aurum, 2004)

Peston, Robert, *Brown's Britain* (London: Short Books, 2005)

Pollard, Stephen, *David Blunkett* (London: Hodder & Stoughton, 2004)

Price, Lance, *The Spin Doctor's Diary: Inside Number 10 with New Labour* (London: Hodder & Stoughton, 2006)

Proud, Keith, *The Grit in the Oyster: The Biography of John Burton of Trimdon* (Newcastle: Northern Echo, 2003)

Rentoul, John, *Tony Blair: Prime Minister* (London: Warner Books, 2001)

Scott, Derek, *Off Whitehall: A View from Downing Street by Tony Blair's Advisor* (London: I. B. Tauris, 2004)

Seldon, Anthony, *Blair* (London: The Free Press, 2004)

Short, Clare, *An Honourable Deception?: New Labour, Iraq, and the Misuse of Power* (London: The Free Press, 2004)

Stephens, Philip, *Tony Blair: The Making of a World Leader* (New York: Viking, 2004)

Monographs

Atkinson, Simon; Green, Jane; Mortimore, Roger, and Wring, Dominic, *Political Communication: The General Election Campaign of 2005* (London: Palgrave Macmillan, 2007)

Barnes, John, and Thompson, Alan, *Day Before Yesterday* (London: Panther, 1971)

Beckett, Francis, and Hencke, David, *The Blairs and the Court* (London: Aurum, 2004)

Butler, David, and Kavanagh, Dennis, *The British General Election of 2005* (London: Palgrave Macmillan, 2005)

Clarke, Richard, *Against All Enemies: Inside America's War on Terror* (New York: The Free Press, 2004)

Cooper, Robert, *The Breaking of Nations: Order and Chaos in the Twenty-first Century* (New York: Atlantic, 2003)

Corera, Gordon, *Shopping for Bombs* (Oxford: OUP, 2006)

Coughlin, Con, *American Ally* (London: Politico's, 2006)

Craig, David, and Brooks, Richard, *Plundering the Public Sector* (London: Constable, 2006)

Daalder, Ivo, and Lindsay, James, *America Unbound: The Bush Revolution in Foreign Policy* (Washington DC: Brookings Institution Press, 2003)

Fielding, Stephen, *The Labour Party: Continuity and Change in 'New' Labour* (London: Palgrave Macmillan, 2003)

Foley, Michael, *John Major, Tony Blair, and a Conflict of Leadership* (Manchester: MUP, 2002)

Gordon, Michael, and Trainor, Bernard, *COBRA II* (New York: Pantheon Books, 2006)

Gould, Philip, *The Unfinished Revolution: How the Modernisers Saved the Labour Party* (London: Little, Brown, 1998)

Hennessy, Peter, *The Prime Minister* (London: Penguin, 2001)

Hyman, Peter, *1 Out of 10* (London: Vintage, 2005)

Isikoff, Michael and Corn, David, *Hubris: The Inside Story of Spin, Scandal, and the Selling of the Iraq War* (New York: Crown, 2006)

Jeffreys, Kevin, *Labour Forces: From Ernest Bevin to Gordon Brown* (London: I. B. Tauris, 2002)

Jenkins, Simon, *Thatcher and Sons* (London: Allen Lane, 2006)

Jones, Nicholas, *The Control Freaks* (London: Politico's, 2001)

Kampfner, John, *Blair's Wars* (London: The Free Press, 2003)

Kavanagh, Dennis, and Seldon, Anthony, *The Blair Effect, 2000–05* (Cambridge: CUP, 2005)

Ludlam, Steve, and Smith, Martin, *New Labour in Government* (London: Macmillan, 2002)

Mandelson, Peter, *The Blair Revolution Revisited* (London: Politico's, 2002)

Mann, James, *Rise of the Vulcans: The History of Bush's War Cabinet* (New York: Viking, 2004)

Micklethwait, John, and Wooldridge, Adrian, *The Right Nation: Why America is Different* (London: Penguin, 2004)

Naughtie, James, *The Rivals* (London: Fourth Estate, 2001)

——, *The Accidental American: Tony Blair and the Presidency* (London: Macmillan, 2004)

Oborne, Peter, *The Rise of Political Lying* (London: The Free Press, 2005)

Ramsey, Robin, *The Rise of New Labour* (Harpenden: The Pocket Essential, 2002)

Rawnsley, Andrew, *Servants of the People: The Inside Story of New Labour* (London: Penguin, 2001)

Riddell, Peter, *Hug Them Close: Blair, Clinton, Bush and the 'Special Relationship'* (London: Politico's, 2003)

——, *The Unfulfilled Prime Minister* (London: Politico's, 2006)

Rogers, Simon (ed.), *Sexed Up: The Hutton Inquiry and its Impact* (London: Politico's, 2003)

Rosen, Greg (ed.), *Dictionary of Labour Biography* (London: Politico's, 2001)

Sampson, Anthony, *Who Runs This Place? An Anatomy of Britain in the 21st Century* (London: John Murray, 2005)

Sands, Philippe, *Lawless World* (London: Penguin, 2006)

Seldon, Anthony (ed.), *Blair's Britain, 1997–2007* (Cambridge: CUP, 2007)

——, *The Blair Effect: The Blair Government, 1997–2001* (London: Little, Brown, 2001)

Seldon, Anthony, and Snowdon, Peter, *The Conservative Party: An Illustrated History* (Stroud: Sutton, 2004)

Stelzer, Irwin, *Neo-Conservatism* (London: Atlantic Books, 2004)

Stothard, Peter, *Thirty Days: A Month at the Heart of Blair's War* (London: HarperCollins, 2003)

Suskind, Ron, *The Price of Loyalty* (New York: Simon & Schuster, 2004)

Toynbee, Polly, and Walker, David, *Did Things Get Better?* (London: Penguin, 2001)

——, *Better or Worse?: Has Labour Delivered?* (London: Bloomsbury, 2005)

Woodward, Bob, *Bush at War* (New York: Simon & Schuster, 2002)

——, *Plan of Attack* (New York: Simon & Schuster, 2004)

——, *State of Denial* (New York: Simon & Schuster, 2006)

Journal Articles

Akgül, Deniz Altinbas, 'The European Union Response to September 11' (*Review of International Affairs*, Vol. 1, No. 4, 2002)

Burrough, Bryan; Peretz, Evgenia; Rose, David, and Wise, David, 'The Path to War' (*Vanity Fair*, May 2004)

Campbell, Colin, and Rockman, Bert, 'Third Way Leadership, Old Way Government: Blair, Clinton, and the Power to Govern' (*British Journal of Politics and International Relations*, Vol. 3, No. 1, 2001)

Finlayson, Alan, 'Elements of the Blairite Image of Leadership' (*Parliamentary Affairs*, Vol. 55, 2002)

Hill, Robert, 'Pick the Right Clubs to Drive Service Reform' (*SOLACE Foundation*, September 2006, pp.8–20)

McConnell, Alan, and Stark, Alastair, 'Foot and Mouth 2001: The Politics of Crisis Management' (*Parliamentary Affairs*, No. 55, 2002)

Rubin, James, 'Stumbling into War' (*Foreign Affairs*, Vol. 82, No. 5, 2003)

Stephens, Philip, 'The Blair Government and Europe' (*Political Quarterly*, Vol. 70, No. 1, 2001)

Published Papers and Unpublished Documents

Correspondence between Tony Blair and Archbishop George Carey (2001–02)

'Iraq's Weapons of Mass Destruction' (Number 10 International Newsroom, 24 September 2002)

'The Hutton Report' (HMSO, January 2004)

'The Butler Report: Review of Intelligence on Weapons of Mass Destruction' (HMSO, July 2004)

'The 9/11 Commission Report' (National Commission on Terrorist Attacks Upon the United States, 22 July 2004)

'Economic Survey of the United Kingdom' (OECD, 2004)

PricewaterhouseCoopers, 'Academies Evaluation, 2nd Report' (DfES, 15 June 2005)

'Joint findings on lessons from handling of the response to the Indian Ocean Tsunami' (National Audit Office/FCO, October 2005)

'Higher Standards, Better Schools for All, More Choice for Parents and Pupils' (DfES, 25 October 2005)

'The Iraq Study Group Report' (ISG, 16 December 2006)

Documentaries

Blair: The Inside Story (BBC TV, 20, 26 February & 6 March 2007)
Iraq, Tony and the Truth (BBC TV, *Panorama*, 4 April 2005)
Shape Up, Sir Humphrey (BBC Radio 4, 8, 15 & 22 March 2007)
The Alastair Campbell Diaries (BBC TV, 11, 18 & 25 July 2007)
The Last Days of Tony Blair (Channel 4, 2 July 2007)
The Real Cherie (BBC TV, 4 July 2007)
The Rise and Fall of Tony Blair (Channel 4, 23 & 25 June 2007)

Tony Blair's speeches and press conferences are referred to in the Notes by their official title and date. This material can be accessed in the 'Tony Blair archive' section of the 10 Downing Street website, www.number-10.gov.uk/output/Page12009.asp. Public statements from President George W. Bush can be found via the White House website, www.whitehouse.gov.

Index

Page references in **bold** denote chapter/major section devoted to subject.